continued inside back cover

HANDBOOK OF
BEHAVIORAL INTERVENTIONS

HANDBOOK OF BEHAVIORAL INTERVENTIONS

A Clinical Guide

Edited by

ALAN GOLDSTEIN
EDNA B. FOA
Temple University

A WILEY-INTERSCIENCE PUBLICATION
JOHN WILEY & SONS, New York • Chichester • Brisbane • Toronto

Library of Congress Cataloging in Publication Data:

Main entry under title:

Handbook of behavioral interventions.

   (Wiley series on personality processes)
   "A Wiley-Interscience publication."
   Includes index.
   1. Behavior therapy.   I.   Goldstein, Alan,
1933- II. Foa, Edna B.   [DNLM:1. Behavior
therapy—Handbooks. WM425 H236]
RC489.B4H35   616.8 '914   79-16950
ISBN 0-471-01789-2

Printed in the United States of America

10   9 8 7 6 5 4 3 2

Contributors

L. MICHAEL ASCHER, Behavior Therapy Unit, Temple University Medical School, Philadelphia.

DAVID H. BARLOW, Department of Psychology, State University of New York at Albany.

JOHN P. BRADY, Department of Psychiatry, University of Pennsylvania School of Medicine, Philadelphia.

KELLY D. BROWNELL, Department of Psychiatry, University of Pennsylvania School of Medicine, Philadelphia.

THOMAS H. BUDZYNSKI, University of Colorado School of Medicine, Denver.

DAVID BURNS, Department of Psychiatry, University of Pennsylvania School of Medicine, Philadelphia.

JOSEPH R. CAUTELA, Department of Psychology, Boston College, Chestnut Hill, Mass.

DIANNE L. CHAMBLESS, Department of Psychology, University of Georgia, Athens.

EDNA B. FOA, Behavior Therapy Unit, Temple University Medical School, Philadelphia.

IRIS GOLDSTEIN FODOR, School of Psychology Program, New York University, New York City.

ALAN GOLDSTEIN, Agoraphobia Program, Temple University Medical School, Philadelphia.

DONALD J. LEVIS, Department of Psychology, State University of New York at Binghamton.

KIRK E. PEFFER, Private Practice, Denver.

GAIL S. STEKETEE, Behavior Therapy Unit, Temple University Medical School, Philadelphia.

JOHANN M. STOYVA, Department of Psychiatry, University of Colorado School of Medicine, Denver.

ARND TILLMANNS, Rehabilitationsklinik Windach, Federal Republic of Germany.

CAROL CARRBERY WALL, Department of Psychology, Boston College, Chestnut Hill, Mass.

JOSEPH WOLPE, Behavior Therapy Unit, Temple University Medical School, Philadelphia.

Series Preface

This series of books is addressed to behavioral scientists interested in the nature of human personality. Its scope should prove pertinent to personality theorists and researchers as well as to clinicians concerned with applying an understanding of personality processes to the amelioration of emotional difficulties in living. To this end, the series provides a scholarly integration of theoretical formulations, empirical data, and practical recommendations.

Six major aspects of studying and learning about human personality can be designated: personality theory, personality structure and dynamics, personality development, personality assessment, personality change, and personality adjustment. In exploring these aspects of personality, the books in the series discuss a number of distinct but related subject areas: the nature and implications of various theories of personality; personality characteristics that account for consistencies and variations in human behavior; the emergence of personality processes in children and adolescents; the use of interviewing and testing procedures to evaluate individual differences in personality; efforts to modify personality styles through psychotherapy, counseling, behavior therapy, and other methods of influence; and patterns of abnormal personality functioning that impair individual competence.

IRVING B. WEINER

University of Denver
Denver, Colorado

Contents

HANDBOOK OF
BEHAVIORAL INTERVENTIONS

Introduction

EDNA B. FOA AND ALAN GOLDSTEIN

Temple University
Department of Psychiatry

During the last decade, behavior therapy has gradually ceased to be the "black sheep" of clinical psychology and psychiatry. Since then numerous volumes have been published in which behavioral techniques are outlined, research findings are summarized, and theoretical issues relevant to the mechanisms of behavioral change are discussed. However, most existing books are descriptive in nature in that they talk about behavior therapy rather than illustrate its use. Practitioners reading through these texts may well become interested in employing behavior therapy but are often left ignorant of how they might actually do so.

The present volume is intended to provide such practical knowledge. The various techniques are illustrated through the presentation of cases that exemplify the variety of transactions between client and therapist as behavioral programs are applied. Although addressed to mental health providers, this step-by-step description of the therapeutic process will assist graduate students in their practicum and internship programs.

Clearly a psychotherapeutic situation involves more variables than can be accounted for by any one theory. Variables such as the expressed attitudes, flow of feelings, communication styles, and defenses of the client and the therapist and their interaction cannot be best understood or studied by drawing on the learning models (stimulus-response and stimulus-stimulus) that provide the basis for behavioral therapy and theorizing. Since these and other variables are extremely important in the process and outcome of therapy, a truly comprehensive therapeutic system must attend to them.

In response to these generally acknowledged inadequacies of early behavioral models, two trends have developed. A few behaviorists have at-

1

tempted to expand behavior therapy so that additional laboratory analog models are brought to bear in order to systematize some of these variables. For example, drawing heavily from social learning models, Goldfried and Davison (1976) have looked at the important factor of relationship variables, while Kazdin and Wilcoxen (1976) have reviewed the role of client expectations. A second trend is one that utilizes a blend of behavioral and other models. Stampfl and Levis (1967) have from the beginning acknowledged the unconscience and emphasized the importance of dealing with the dynamics of cognitive associations in utilizing implosive therapy. Lazarus (1973) has vigorously defended the use of techniques originating with other theoretical models, primarily from humanistic psychology. And Wachtel (1977) has demonstrated the possibility of integrating behavioral and psychoanalytic theory in deciding on intervention strategies. It is an open question as to which of these approaches will prove most productive; however, practicing behavioral clinicians require immediate methods of dealing with the intrapersonal and interpersonal factors encountered in their day-to-day therapy practice.

With these thoughts in mind, we presented an outline to the authors in this volume that probes for overt statements about the intrapersonal and interpersonal variables that they view as influential in outcome. What is the interactional flow, the blending of technique, and relationship; what is the totality of the process in which behavior therapists find themselves when doing therapy?

In accordance with this predetermined outline, each chapter begins with a short theoretical discussion and description of research findings; we have purposely limited this part since such information may be found elsewhere (e.g., Agras, 1978; Garfield and Bergin, 1978; Hersen, Eisler, and Miller, Vols. I–VII). The indications and contraindications for the use of a given technique are specified in the second section of each chapter, and the therapeutic process is described and illustrated with extensive verbatim material in the third. In the final section we have asked the authors to emphasize problems likely to arise during the therapeutic process and ways in which they might be prevented or handled.

The handbook is organized into two main parts. A chapter on behavioral analysis is followed by a section in which the application of various behavioral techniques and procedures is illustrated. Treatments for specific disorders are detailed in the second section. The content of the book, the choice of topics, and their order of presentation has been dictated largely by the history of behavior therapy and its current status.

The appearance of Wolpe's book (1958) describing the theoretical and practical aspects of systematic desensitization marked the beginning of an era of vigorous developments in behavior therapy and behavior modification. The use of systematic desensitization is demonstrated in Chapter 2. Other learning-theory-based techniques were developed and refined through research. Malleson (1959) described the use of prolonged imaginal exposure of the patient to stimuli evoking high levels of fear. This technique, based on experimental extinction, is called implosion or flooding. Its theoretical basis and usage form the topic of the third chapter, and its use in the treatment of obsessive-compulsive symptoms is illustrated in Chapter 8.

One of the most controversial issues in behavior therapy is the use of aversive stimuli such as electrical shock or unpleasant imagery. Although the popular press often over-emphasizes the use of punishment in the practice of behavior therapy, such interventions are used infrequently. Yet we think that therapists should be familiar with techniques used to suppress persistent, undesirable behaviors. One such technique, covert sensitization, is described by its innovator, Joseph Cautela, in Chapter 4; other aversive techniques utilizing imagery are also included. The cautious and responsible application of aversive procedures is further demonstrated in Chapter 10, which deals with the treatment of sexual deviations.

Behavioral medicine, the application of behavioral principles to the treatment and prevention of physical ailments, has recently become the focus of great interest. Several programs and techniques have been developed to prevent or reduce physical discomfort by behavioral means. Among the best known and most widely used is biofeedback, the subject of Chapter 5.

Behavior therapy has traditionally focused on overt behavior and autonomic responses, for example, anxiety. However, the role of private events such as thoughts, fantasies, and attitudes in changing overt behaviors has been emphasized by Ellis (1962) and Beck (1976). For the systematic study and development of cognitive techniques we are indebted to Goldfried (e.g., Goldfried, 1975) and Meichenbaum (1975). Though borrowed from logotherapy (Frankl, 1960), paradoxical intention may be incorporated into a cognitive-behavioral framework. This procedure is described in Chapter 6. Other cognitive techniques are discussed in the section on specific neurotic patterns, especially in Chapter 7 on agoraphobia and Chapter 9, which deals with communication problems.

As a way of defining behavior therapy, Agras (1978, p. 6) listed the following therapeutic procedures: systematic desensitization, shaping by positive reinforcement, aversion therapy, implosion/flooding, modeling, assertiveness training, relaxation therapy, and paradoxical intention.

While individual chapters are devoted to most of these procedures, others are demonstrated in the second part of the book, embedded in the description of treatments for specific neurotic complaints. Thus shaping techniques are presented in the context of treating communication problems, sexual deviations, and stuttering; relaxation training is described in Chapter 2 in relation to systematic desensitization. Finally, assertiveness training and modeling techniques are described and demonstrated in Chapter 9 as primary interventions for the treatment of communication problems.

In the preparation of this volume we have been guided by the desire to be of practical assistance to mental health providers. It has been our aim to demonstrate how relief from unadaptive and often painful symptoms can be provided within the interactional process of behavior therapy. We hope we have offered here a realistic, concrete, and clear picture of the therapeutic process, from the first time the client enters the therapist's office to the conclusion of therapy.

REFERENCES

Agras, W.S. *Behavior modification: Principles and clinical applications.* Boston: Little, Brown, 1978.

Beck, A.T. *Cognitive therapy and the emotional disorders.* New York: International U.P., 1976.

Ellis, A. *Reason and emotion in psychotherapy.* New York: Stuart, 1962.

Frankl, V.E. Paradoxical intention: A logo-therapeutic technique. *American Journal of Psychotherapy,* 1960, *14,* 520–535.

Garfield, S.L., and Bergin, A.E. *Handbook of psychotherapy and behavior change: An empirical analysis, (2nd ed.).* New York: John Wiley and Sons, 1978.

Goldfried, M.R., and Davison, G.C. *Clinical behavior therapy.* New York: Holt, Rhinehart & Winston, 1976.

Goldfried, M.R. and Goldfried, A.P. Cognitive change methods. In F.H. Kanfer and A.P. Goldstein (Eds.), *Helping people change.* New York: Pergamon, 1975.

Hersen, M., Eisler, R.M., and Miller, P.M. *Progress in behavior modification* (4 vols.). New York: Academic, 1975–1978.

Kazdin, A.E., and Wilcoxen, L.A. Systematic desensitization and non-specific treatment effects: A methodological evaluation. *Psychological Bulletin,* 1976, *83,* 729–758.

Lazarus, A.A. Multimodel behavior therapy: Treating the basic "ID." *Journal of Nervous and Mental Disease,* 1973, *156,* 404–411.

Malleson, N. *Panic and phobias. Lancet,* 1959, *591,* 225–229.

Meichenbaum, D. *Cognitive behavior modification.* New York: Plenum, 1975.

Stampfl, T.G., and Levis, D.J. Essentials of implosive therapy. *Journal of Abnormal Psychology,* 1967, *72,* 496–503.

Wachtel, P.L. *Psychoanalysis and behavior therapy: Toward an integration.* New York: Basic, 1977.

Wolpe, J. *Psychotherapy by reciprocal inhibition.* Stanford: Stanford U.P., 1958.

CHAPTER 1

Behavior Analysis and Therapeutic Strategy

JOSEPH WOLPE

Temple University School of Medicine and Eastern Pennsylvania Psychiatric Institute

The workshop whose edited transcript is the main substance of this chapter was designed to give its participants some practical exposure to the activity of behavior analysis and the planning of therapeutic strategy. For the sake of perspective, a general outline of procedure in behavior analysis is given first.

Behavior therapy makes use of experimentally established principles of learning to weaken and eliminate habits that are inappropriate and unadaptive (Wolpe, 1958, 1973). A habit is a repeatable response to a particular class of stimulus situations. Therefore, in order to set up a rational program toward elimination of a habit, it is indispensable to have precise information about the stimuli or stimulus chains that lead to the triggering of the behavior that is to be eliminated. This information gathering is what is called *behavior analysis*. Inadequate behavior analysis (Wolpe, 1977) is both the commonest cause of failure in clinical behavior therapy and the greatest source of confounding in behavior therapy research.

The gathering of information for purposes of behavior analysis usually follows the routine (Wolpe, 1973, pp. 22–52) that is summarized in the following, but this may be varied if indicated by the thrust of the case. For example, the investigation of a marital problem may lead naturally into an exploration of the general sexual history much earlier than in the routine sequence.

The first interview begins by asking the patient to state his major behavioral problems. In respect to each of these, an attempt is made to establish the circumstances of its origination. Unadaptive anxiety is often at the forefront; but even when it is not, careful probing usually shows that it underlies the presenting problem, whether that is sexual inadequacy, stuttering, an obsession, or a psychosomatic condition. The course of each problem is followed through the years, with special attention to any circumstances that may have ameliorated or exacerbated it, or that may have resulted in the second-order conditioning of anxiety to other stimuli. Finally, the stimuli currently controlling the anxiety responses are carefully examined. Historical information not only gives perspective, but often has a bearing upon the stimulus complexes relevant to the patient's present problem. The following excerpts from the early part of a first interview illustrate the foregoing.

Dr: How old are you?

Pt: 21.

Dr: What is your complaint?

Pt: I am very very nervous all the time.

Dr: How long has this been so?

Pt: Since I was about fourteen.

Dr: Are you saying that before you were fourteen you were not nervous?

Pt: Well, I was, but not to this extreme. Especially in elementary school when I would have to read something in front of the class I would get very nervous about that—giving speeches or answering in class. That would bother me.

Dr: Well, that is a special situation.

Pt: Yea, but now it's all the time. When I go out of the house.

Dr: Well, let's try to build up the story. You say that in elementary school you were only nervous when you had to get up and speak in front of the class.

Pt: Yes.

Dr: And then in high school?

Pt: It got worse. When we would go out with boys I would be very nervous.

Dr: Did you become more nervous in front of the class?

Pt: I wouldn't sleep for nights worrying about giving a speech in front of class.

Dr: And you also said that you became nervous about going out with boys.

Pt: Yes. I was afraid. Especially if I would have a blind date I would be scared to death.

Dr: And if you went out with somebody you knew?

Pt: Well, after a while I would be a little calmer, but still nervous.

Dr: And what about if you went out with girlfriends?

Pt: Not as much.

Dr: What year did you graduate from school?

Pt: 1963.

Dr: And what did you do then?

Pt: I went to school and became a technician.

Dr: What kind of technician?

Pt: X-ray.

Dr: Do you like this work?

Pt: Not really. I didn't know really what else to do. I thought it was interesting, but once I got there I was very nervous about everything. It would scare me to be with patients.

Dr: Patients would scare you?

Pt: Well, especially the sick ones. If something would happen to them.

Dr: You were scared that something might happen to them?

Pt: Yes, like they would have an attack or something.

Dr: Has this ever happened?

Pt: No, not really.

Dr: Well, it is now about four years since you became a technician.

Pt: Four years, yes.

Dr: During those four years have you become more nervous or less nervous or stayed the same?

Pt: Definitely more.

Dr: Now, are there any special things that make you nervous nowadays?

Pt: Special things?

Dr: Well, let's start off by considering your work situation.

Pt: Yes?

Dr: You said that sick patients make you more nervous.

Pt: And my boss.

Dr: Yes?

Pt: He makes me extremely nervous. I am afraid of him.

Dr: Why, is he very strict?

Pt: Um, yes, he gives that appearance.

Dr: Does he carry on? Does he scream and so on?

Pt: Never at me. But I am always afraid that will happen.

Dr: I see. And who else scares you?

Pt: Men.

Dr: Men?

Pt: If I go out with them.

Dr: Yes. What about men who come in where you are working, like medical students?

Pt: Yes, they scare me too.

Dr: They scare you, how?

Pt: I don't know. I am not afraid of them really. I am just afraid of how I'll act—that my nervousness will show through. And I think about it so much.

Dr: Well, is it correct to say that you are sort of scared of being watched?

Pt: Yes. I think everybody is always watching me.

Dr: Well now, that is at work. What circumstances scare you when you are away from work?

Pt: Just going out. I am afraid, you know, that they'll see the way I am. I am afraid to pick something up, because I am afraid that I am going to shake, and my mouth is all tightened up. I am afraid to look at people directly in the eye.

Dr: Are you only afraid of looking at the person who is with you in the eye, or afraid of anybody?

Pt: Anybody.

Dr: So looking at a person face to face increases your nervousness?

Pt: Yes.

Dr: Suppose that you are walking down the street and there is a bench across the road with some people waiting for a bus. Those people are vaguely looking across the street. Would you be aware of their presence?

Pt: Yes, definitely.

Dr: Even though they might not be particularly looking at you?

Pt: Yes.

Dr: Now, supposing we take people away together. Suppose that you were just walking all by yourself, say, in a park. There is no one else at all there. Are you then completely comfortable?

Pt: Yes.

Dr: Well, what about your mother?

Pt: No, it doesn't bother me at home.

Dr: Your mother can look at you as much as she likes?

Pt: Yes, it's really silly but . . .

Dr: It's not silly. It's just the way things have developed.

Pt: I know.

Dr: And who else can look at you without bothering you?

Pt: My whole family.

Dr: Who is in your family?

Pt: My father, my mother, my sister, my grandmother.

Dr: Besides these people, are there any others at all who can look at you without disturbing you?

Pt: No.

Dr: What about a little baby?

Pt: No, that doesn't disturb me, nor an older person who is senile or something.

Dr: What about a little boy of four?

Pt: No.

Dr: Six?

Pt: No.

Dr: Eight?

Pt: No. It's when they get older, I get nervous.

Dr: At what age do children begin to bother you?

Pt: Around in their teens.

Dr: I take it that a boy of twelve wouldn't be as bad as one of eighteen.

Pt: No.

Dr: If you go to a movie and see a very handsome film star, does that bother you?

Pt: No, not really, because I know he is not looking at me.

Dr: And if there is a very handsome actor on the stage?

Pt: Yes, that would.

Dr: Besides looking at you, what else can people do to make you nervous? You have mentioned being scared of your boss criticizing you.

Pt: Any criticism gets me upset, even if I know that I am right. I can't talk back and tell them that I am right. I just get all choked up and feel like I am going to cry.

Dr: Is there anything else that people can do to upset you?

Pt: Well, just tell me that I'm wrong—if I am wrong or if I'm right it still bothers me.

Dr: That's a kind of criticism. Supposing people praise you?

Pt: That makes me feel good.

The reader should note the care that was taken to establish with precision the stimulus factors controlling this young woman's unadaptive anxiety. The same question was sometimes put in several ways to guard against misunderstanding. It is better to be repetitious than to be misled. We now know that the patient had, since the age of twelve, been excessively anxious under the scrutiny of strangers, especially if performing before them in some way. Her sensitivity had increased over the years, so that she was now anxious when she felt herself observed in the most casual way, such as when walking down the street. She was more affected by men than by women, especially when there were erotic overtones. Anxiety was further raised by eye contact. The only people under whose gaze she was comfortable were members of her own family, very young children, and old people. She was also easily upset by criticism, whether just or unjust.

A characteristic feature of behavioristic questioning is the stress-reducing attitude of the therapist. He is not merely nonjudgmental, but positively counter-critical: as shown, for example, in the manner of rejection of the patient's view that it was "silly" that she was not disturbed by her mother looking at her.

When all the presenting problems have been as far as possible analyzed along these lines, the therapist turns his attention to the patient's background. He does this partly because it gives perspective, partly because it provides an opportunity to see how the patient has responded to a variety of key events and relationships in his life, but most of all because it may provide additional clues to the stimulus-response relations of the problems of the present. The patient is questioned about his early home life: how he perceived his parents through his childhood, whether they were kind and interested, and whether they dealt out punishment fairly or unfairly and in what manner. He is asked how the parents related to each other, how much religious training they instilled, and whether he is still influenced by it. How did he get along with his siblings? Did he have any childhood fears or nervous habits?

His educational life is the next topic: whether he liked school, how successful he was as a student, whether made friends and any especially close friends, and whether individuals among his teachers or fellow students were sources of fear or other distress. At what age did he leave school and why, did he continue his education or take a job, and how did he fare in each educational and occupational setting? His relationships with superiors, peers, and underships in each situation are examined.

The following excerpts are from the background history of the girl whose presenting complaints were explored above. As is seen, helpful perspectives did emerge, and the coverage also led naturally into an account of the school experience at 14 that was responsible for the original exacerbation of her main fear constellation.

Dr: Who is older, you or your sister?

Pt: I am.

Dr: By how much?

Pt: Three years.

Dr: What sort of person is your father?

Pt: He's on the quiet side, and both of my parents are on the nervous side. My sister too. The whole family, really.

Dr: Was your father kind to you when you were a little girl?

Pt: Yes.

Dr: And your mother?

Pt: Yes. She's the stronger one. I'm more like my father and my sister more than my mother.

Dr: In what way is your mother stronger?

Pt: Well, things don't bother her, at least outwardly. She sort of makes decisions.

Dr: What does your father do?

Pt: He sells insurance.

Dr: Did either of your parents punish you when you were young?

Pt: My mother used to hit me once in a while. My father hardly ever did—not if I did something wrong.

Dr: Did your mother do anything else to discipline you?

Pt: She would have little talks.

Dr: Did you feel when she punished you that it was unreasonable?

Pt: Sometimes I did.

Dr: Were there any other adults who played any important part in your home life—grandmothers, aunts, nurses?

Pt: Yes, my grandmother—she lives with us.

Dr: What kind of a person is she?

Pt: She is very good to me. I am her first grandchild, so she pays more attention to me than to my sister, but she doesn't understand a lot of things because she wasn't born in America and she did not have an education.

Dr: How do you get along with your sister?

Pt: We used to fight an awful lot, but lately we have been getting along better. We are not really close because she is completely different.

Dr: What is she like?

Pt: She's more talkative than I am—more outgoing. I'm on the quiet side.

Dr: Did you go to school in Philadelphia?

Pt: Yes. I did.

Dr: Did you like school?

Pt: Not really.

Dr: What did you dislike about it?

Pt: I was afraid of getting up in front of the class, as I mentioned.

Dr: Yes. Is that all?

Pt: Yes.

Dr: How well did you do?

Pt: I had a B average.

Dr: Did you take part in sports?

Pt: No.

Dr: Did you make friends?

Pt: Yes. I have a lot of friends.

Dr: Any close friends?

Pt: Yes—one in particular.

Dr: Apart from this fear of getting up and speaking, did you have any other fears when you were small?

Pt: I was afraid to take a shower because I had claustrophobia.

Dr: When was that?

Pt: It was about 10 or 11. I was afraid to be closed in. After somebody locked me in a closet, I couldn't stand it. It scared me.

Dr: After you were 12, that fear disappeared?

Pt: Well, I am still afraid if someone would lock me in a closet. I am not afraid to take showers.

Dr: Do you like going into elevators?

Pt: I used to be afraid—not anymore.

Dr: Do you remember any experience at all when you were at school that was particularly frightening in relationship to getting up and talking in class?

Pt: Yes, when I was in seventh grade.

Dr: Yes?

Pt: I had to read something in front of the class.

Dr: Yes?

Pt: I was holding the paper and I started shaking. The teacher said, "What's the matter?" and I couldn't talk. From then on, if I had to read something, I'd put it down on the desk and look at it. I would be too nervous to read it.

Dr: Before this happened were you already nervous?

Pt: Yes.

Dr: And after this incident, you were much worse?

Pt: Yes.

The final part of the history consists of a systematic inquiry into the patient's love life. This is traced from his first awareness of sexual feelings. He is asked at what age they arose and in what context, and then about later experiences, in sequence. Did he masturbate and was this associated with feelings of guilt or thoughts of dreadful consequences? At what age did he begin heterosexual (or homosexual) relationships? When and with whom was his first emotionally important relationship, and how did it work out? The course of all subsequent relationships is similarly traced. In each case one must ascertain what attracted him to his partner, how they got on, and how satisfactory the sexual side of the relationship was. The aspects of love and emotional warmth are given at least as much attention as actual sexual behavior.

Finally, one asks about the patient's present social situation and whether there are particular problems, in respect to either the handling of friends or of casual acquaintances.

After the history taking, the patient is routinely given two questionnaires (Wolpe, 1973): the Willoughby Neuroticism Schedule which contains 25 questions relevant to neurotic behavior, and a Fear Survey Schedule of 108 items that have been found clinically in neurotic patients. Both of these are answered on a 5-point scale. The total Willoughby score gives a useful index of the patient's range and severity of neurotic reactions, especially in relation to social situations. In addition, high-scoring responses to particular questions provide leads for detailed probing. For example, if the Willoughby indicates that the patient is much hurt by criticism, the therapist is prompted to elicit how the distress is related to the character of the criticism and the identity of the critic, and to surrounding circumstances. This information may significantly influence the interventions undertaken. The Fear Survey Schedule often reveals areas of neurotic sensitivity that history taking may miss, for example, anxiety at ideas of possible homosexuality, at taking responsibility, or at medical odors.

Therapeutic strategy is determined by the findings of behavior analysis. Assertive training, systematic desensitization, or both are very commonly indicated, as are various programs for deconditioning anxiety in cases of inhibited sexual responses. However, it can not be too strongly stressed that, contrary to the widespread belief of outsiders, tactics are not mechanically dictated by broad diagnoses, but carefully adjusted to the requirements of each case. The following excerpts from an interview with a 34-year-old married woman illustrate this in the context of a sexual problem. The solution indicated was not primarily sexual but the rekindling of interpersonal warmth.

Pt: I hardly enjoy sex with Bill at all now. I avoid it. I haven't had an orgasm in six months.

Dr: Do you think that your depression has anything to do with the frustration of your lovelife?

Pt: Probably, because I have been thinking about other men a lot. Bill and I went to bed very late last night, and I just wanted to go right to sleep. We haven't been kissing good-night for a year or so on a regular basis. I sort of waited for him to come over to me and kiss me good-night. He expected me to come over to him, and I was face-down on the pillow. He made no move, so I made no move. He went back to the old questions of last year—"Do you love me or don't you? I want to know right now."

Dr: What is the true answer?

Pt: I don't really know.

Dr: What did you say?

Pt: I didn't answer. He went on to say that he needs affection just like anybody else. I explained that I had my period. He said, "I'm not talking about sex." I said to him, "Remember in the old days, it was the other way around. I was the one who wanted affection and I couldn't come near you or it meant sex. I had to stop cuddling up to you because if my foot touched your foot, that meant sex. At night if I wanted affection on the sofa, you were busy reading the paper."

Dr: Don't you think we should make a real effort to try and straighten things out? Your relationship must either be put on a good basis or abandoned. You don't want to go on living like this for the rest of your life, do you?

Pt: I'm just wondering what can be done.

Dr: Well, suppose that you and he both gave each other a lot of emotional warmth, apart from sex. Would there be a chance?

Pt: But how are we going to make me want that?

Dr: Well, I'm exploring that with you now. Is it the case that you are so negative towards him that no matter what he does now, you feel that nothing could possibly change?

Pt: I don't know. Yesterday when I was reading one part of a book and it was describing a father's love for his daughter, it made me start thinking about my husband and when he comes home tonight I'm going to welcome him with open arms. He is the only one who loves me. I really felt a rush of love. Then half an hour later I'm thinking, "Why don't I commit suicide?"

Dr: I think it would be a good idea if I gave you a general outline of what I feel the sequence of events might be. First of all, a frontal attack should be made so that we can see whether by changing Bill's behavior to you, a rekindling of affection may be brought about. What is first of all needed is communication. We can try to start that at a joint meeting of the three of us. At the present moment, you're in a kind of never-never land—nothing is happening, nothing is changing.

Pt: I don't know how this would accomplish anything—I don't know what questions he is going to ask.

Dr: It's not his questions we want—it is behavior. If Bill were to come here, I would get from his point of view what is troubling him about the marriage and it would undoubtedly be certain aspects of your behavior. He will say what he wants from you and you will say what you want from him. Finally, there would be an understanding—that each would try to give the other what is desired.

Pt: I think most of the time and even now, he would be willing to give me what I would normally want.

Dr: Supposing he would come up to you in the kitchen and put his arm around you . . .

Pt: That's the key, *if* I would respond. That is one of the things he asked me, "Do you enjoy it when I come to the kitchen and kiss you?" How do you say no? There are many nights when I'm sitting in bed and I look at him, and I feel a strong desire to go and melt in his arms.

Dr: What stops you?

Pt: I don't know.

Dr: If he was sitting here and hearing this, that would be very important information to him because it would give him hope, and encouragement to encourage you. If the old strong fellow-feeling could return, its expression in sexual behavior would become increasingly automatic and increasingly satisfactory.

In many cases, the initial behavior analysis provides an accurate and sufficient basis for effective therapy. In others, new information emerges in later sessions that changes the direction of therapy. Lack of progress with particular procedures is a particularly important reason for reassessment. For example, when unduly slow progress is noted in desensitization using imaginary scenes, two possible reasons are that the patient has little or no anxiety when he imagines situations that he fears, and that the hierarchy content is off target. A fairly common happening that comes the way of inexperienced therapists is the agoraphobic who does not respond to desensitization to increasing distances from home, because it is initially not realized that the real fear is of a heart attack. The patient fears separation from home merely because that diminishes the accessibility of help. When the error is detected, the hypochondriacal fear becomes the focus of treatment.

A QUESTION AND ANSWER WORKSHOP ON
BEHAVIOR ANALYSIS

In this workshop, I first gave basic information about a case of agoraphobia, and then took the role of the patient and gave the members turns asking me questions to extend the information in relevant ways. If I thought they went wrong, I corrected them. I had the transcript of the first interview of the case before me as a guide.

This patient's fear was a direct function of distance from safe places or persons. In fact, only a minority of cases of agoraphobia have this simple basis. Very commonly encountered is the agoraphobia of the unhappily married woman who, due to low self-sufficiency, is unable to take any action towards getting out of the marriage and in whom the fear is actually the spatial equivalent of a *social* fear of aloneness. In such cases, no therapeutic action is adequate that does not include a solution of the marital problem, either by the satisfactory reconstruction of the marriage, or by its dissolution. Another requisite of treatment in these cases is the raising of self-sufficiency. Other cases of agoraphobia are based on misconceptions: for example, a woman of 30 feared going out on her own because she perceived her anxiety symptoms as indicative of impending mental breakdown and dreaded the possibility of a catastrophic worsening in the absence of someone she could depend upon. Her treatment consisted of convincing her of the unsubstantiality of her fear of insanity. Agoraphobia based on hypochondriacal fear has already been mentioned.

Mr. S. is a 52-year-old architect who has the following history. Twenty years ago his wife died of cancer. He had been very fond of her, had suffered greatly through her illness and had had the excruciation of seeing her die of suffocation. In due course he re-entered the stream of life and developed other relationships. One evening about 4 years after his wife's death, he and his girlfriend were making love in his apartment. While having her orgasm, the woman made respiratory movements as though she were choking. He became greatly upset, dressed rapidly, and hurried her into his car to take her home—a distance of 4 or 5 miles. When they were half-way home he noticed that he was having trouble breathing and was feeling very anxious. He turned the car around, drove to a hotel where there is a taxi stand, put the woman in a taxi, and went home alone. From that time he had been fearful of venturing from his apartment. In addition, especially when he did go out, he was now liable to paroxysmal anxiety attacks that would range from 20 to 50 SUDs in intensity and last from a few minutes to several hours.

Soon after the agoraphobia began, he consulted a psychoanalyst, continuing for 10 years without improvement. Then he went for 2 years to a so-called behavior therapist who accomplished nothing. I say "so-called" because he committed such elementary errors as persisting for months with standard desensitization though the patient was not anxious to imagined scenes. Mr. S. then went to another psychoanalyst for a year, who made him worse. When he stopped seeing him, Mr. S. improved somewhat. He had not had therapy for about a year when he came to see me last year.

Tell me what you would like to know next. Pretend I'm the patient. What do you want to know? *(Here the therapist takes the double role of the patient being questioned and commentator on the questioning. The comments are in parenthesis.)*

Member 1:   Give me a recent incident when you experienced anxiety.
Dr. W.:   Well, I'm anxious all the time.

Member 1:   How does it affect your life?

Dr. W.:   It affects my life terribly.

Member 1:   What part of your life is most affected? How does it affect your work situation?

Dr. W.:   It affects it enormously.

Member 1:   Give me an example of its effect on your work situation.

Dr. W.:   The architectural profession is in very bad shape these days. There is very little building going on. The economic situation, as you know, is bad.

Member 1:   Are you in private practice then?

Dr. W.:   Yes.

Member 1:   How did you get through the day—what did you do?

Dr. W.:   I went to my office and read some architectural journals. (Let me ask you, what are you getting at? What are you trying to find out?)

Member 1:   I am trying to get a concrete example of how the anxiety affects his life. That is, you have said that the person is very anxious and that it keeps him from venturing forth. I want to know what that means.

Dr. W.:   (But you are not really asking the kinds of questions that will give you that information. You are saying, does it affect your life, does it affect your work life? And I am saying yes, it does terribly. But this does not give you anything that you can use. Would someone like to suggest what is wrong with these questions?)

Member 2:   I think we need to get an idea of his anxiety in given situations. Even though a patient says, "I am anxious all the time," with questioning it may emerge that there are times when he is not anxious.

Dr. W.:   (That is absolutely correct. So she was not asking me the right questions. What was wrong with this questioning?)

Member 2:   It wasn't specific enough. How do you feel when you are having anxiety?

Dr. W.:   (No. That is a different kind of question.)

Member 3:   I want the patient to tell me that yesterday he was walking here and there.

Dr. W.:   (That is not what we want to know.)

Member 4:   What are the conditions under which you feel more anxious?

Dr. W.:   I've already told you that I am more anxious when I go out and sometimes I have anxiety attacks. You know that already. (But how do you extend this?)

Member 5:   From the way you are answering the questions, I assume the patient is being difficult.

Dr. W.:   (No, absolutely not. You are accusing me of being resistant?)

Member 5:   Yes. The question is why did you come for therapy.

Dr. W.:   I didn't just start. I have had ten years of psychoanalysis.

Member 4:   Let's assume you have a list of the symptoms. Do you want to know the frequency?

Dr. W.:   (No. It would not help us to study the frequency of the constituents of his anxiety.)

Member 4:   You might start out by asking, "On a scale of 0 to 100 how anxious did you feel when you woke up this morning?"

Dr. W.:   (No. You do seem to have the right general idea; but the way you are asking your questions is not getting us anywhere. He tells us that he has anxiety going out. So the next thing we want to know is how far out he must go to get anxiety. What does he mean by going out? Does he get anxiety when he walks out of the door of his apartment, or out of the apartment building? How far and so on. You need to establish the quantitative relations between external situations and his anxiety.)

Member 4:   When you were playing the part of the patient, you said that you had anxiety all the time.

Dr. W.:   (Yes.)

Member 4:   You didn't say, when I asked when you feel anxious, that you feel anxious when you go out.

Dr. W.:   (I had told you that already.)

Member 6:   She is asking you to specify the situations.

Dr. W.:   (No she is not. We know that he becomes more anxious when he goes out. It is too general. I want to know how the anxiety is quantitatively related to the quantity of going out.)

Member 6:   The SUD scale?

Dr. W.:   Yes. You can ask me the right question now.

Member 6:   You feel anxious when you leave your apartment?

Dr. W.:   Yes.

Member 6:   As you leave your apartment, at what point do you begin to feel anxious? As you are walking to the door, as you leave the building, or when you are some distance away?

Dr. W.:   I begin to have some anxiety when I walk out of the door of the apartment and I become very anxious when I go one block.

Member 6:   You become very anxious when you go one block? I want to know what happens. Do you keep going?

Dr. W.:   Well I can't do that. At one block I am too anxious, and I turn back.

Member 6:   Each time that you leave your apartment and go one block, you turn back?

Dr. W.:   Well, I hardly ever do such a thing, because why should I upset myself?

Member 6:   Do you leave your apartment at all?

Dr. W.:   Yes.

Member 6:   And how far do you go?

Dr. W.:   Well, I've come here to see you in your office, Doctor.

Member 6:   So there are some times when you go considerably further than one block?

Dr. W.:   Yes. It is about three miles from my apartment to here.

Member 6:   Am I on the right track?

Dr. W.:   (Yes.)

Member 6:   Well, this is one occasion when you have gone further than one block—how do you feel now?

Dr. W.:   Sitting here with you I don't feel so bad. I only have about 20 units of anxiety on our scale.

Member 6:   In the waiting room while you are waiting to see me?

Dr. W.:   Well, I didn't know what you were like. It is our first interview and I was more anxious. I think I was about 50.

Member 6:   And it has dropped to 20 now?

Dr. W.:   Yes.

Member 6:   Good. May I pass now?

Dr. W.:   (Yes, you have learned a lot.)

Member 7:   How did you manage to get here at all?

Dr. W.:   By car.

Member 7:   You drove yourself?

Dr. W.:   Yes, I drove the car.

Member 7:   And you did not have to turn back after one block?

Dr. W.:   Well, my mother came with me.

Member 7:   Did that help?

Dr. W.: Yes, I can go some distance when my mother is with me.

Member 7: What does she do to make it easier for you?

Dr. W.: Well, I just feel more comfortable. I have a feeling that if something were to happen there would be somebody there.

Member 7: What might happen that she could take care of?

Dr. W.: Well, she could take over the car and she could take me home and get medical assistance.

Member 7: Physical concerns are the chief things that you worry about when you get anxious? You worry that you will not be able to drive the car—that you will get sick?

Dr. W.: No, my heart pounds. I just have a terrible sense of panic.

Member 7: Do you live with your mother?

Dr. W.: Yes, we have been sharing an apartment since my wife died.

Member 7: You say that you don't go great distances?

Dr. W.: No, I don't go great distances.

Member 7: Well, what other effects has this problem created? What aren't you able to do now that you were able to do before?

Dr. W.: Before I had no restriction, I could go anywhere. But now— what a terrible disability it is for an architect not to be able to go places where buildings are being put up and so on.

Member 7: Then this has curtailed many of your activities?

Dr. W.: Oh yes. It has. I haven't been able to go more than about 4 or 5 miles even with my mother. And this has made life very awkward. There are certain other people, like my girlfriend, who also give me protection from anxiety. But it means that I can't go and meet contractors without somebody in the car, and I am completely unable to participate actively in the construction of any building any more than five miles from my house.

Member 7: When you think about going to a job, does this bring anxiety?

Dr. W.: You mean a job where?

Member 7: A job where you have to leave the house. Do you have anxiety when you are about to leave, or only when you are out of the door?

Dr. W.: I become anxious in anticipation of the event.

Member 7: What have you been doing to try on your own to reduce your anxiety?

Dr. W.: I have sought professional help, and none of it has done any good.

Member 7:   In talking about it now and thinking about it now, how many SUDs are you now?

Dr. W.:   Talking to you? Well, as I said, about 20.

Member 7:   It hasn't changed since we started talking about it?

Dr. W.:   Well, it goes up and down a bit when we talk about different things. I would say an average of about 20.

Member 7:   When does it seem to get worse?

Dr. W.:   When I talk about the constriction of my activity. (We don't seem to be getting very far do we?)

Member 7:   Am I right in assuming that you don't leave the house at all unless you are accompanied by your mother or your girlfriend?

Dr. W.:   Yes. Except I can go one block by myself, to my office.

Member 7:   Does anyone besides your mother or your girlfriend accompany you when you leave the house?

Dr. W.:   At present, no.

Member 7:   You said that you can ride up to five miles in a car accompanied by your mother?

Dr. W.:   Yes.

Member 7:   What happens after 5 miles?

Dr. W.:   Well, up to five miles I have a tolerable level of anxiety—it doesn't go above 50, which I can tolerate. And then beyond five miles the anxiety begins to rise rapidly.

Member 7:   When the anxiety goes up, how do you feel?

Dr. W.:   I have palpitations and a feeling of suffocation and I have some tremor. It is just a terrible feeling. I feel that I am approaching panic.

Member 7:   What do you do about it?

Dr. W.:   Well, I just want to get back.

Member 7:   What do your mother and girlfriend do, do they go back with you?

Dr. W.:   Well, I know in advance where I am going. (What are you trying to find out?)

Member 7:   The factors that modify the anxiety.

Dr. W.:   (I've told you that there is nothing that modifies the anxiety in these situations.)

Member 7:   Are you anxious at all when you are at home?

Dr. W.:   (That's an important direction.) I always have between 20 and 50 units of anxiety even when I am at home. It is usually around

20 but every now and then I get an anxiety attack. While I was seeing my last psychoanalyst, these attacks would reach an intensity of 100, and might last from anywhere from 10 minutes to two days. But since I left him they have been less frequent and have not gone above 50.

Member 7: Did the therapist do anything to cause the anxiety?

Dr. W.: Well, he used to make it seem that I was inadequate and I was responsible for my condition.

Member 7: Could you possibly give me an example of what he might say?

Dr. W.: (I'm not going to give you an example because it is not going to get us anywhere. A therapist can easily say distressful things to patients. I think you are on a good line now. It is desirable to have some idea of what the previous therapist did to help.) The first psychoanalyst made me lie on the couch and free associate and he said that if I just did what he said, within six months I would be much better, but after ten years I was no better, and that is why I left him.

Member 7: Did you feel comfortable with your first analyst?

Dr. W.: Yes, I felt quite comfortable with him.

Member 7: And then you went to another therapist?

Dr. W.: Yes, I went to a behavior therapist. I went to Dr. X.

Member 7: What did you think of him?

Dr. W.: I thought he was a rather nice guy. He was very enthusiastic.

Member 7: Did the fact that he was nice and enthusiastic produce less anxiety?

Dr. W.: (I don't think that is a good question. Maybe the patient does and maybe he doesn't feel less anxious with enthusiastic people. It is worth knowing whether or not he was comfortable with the therapist, but if he was, the reasons are a secondary matter.)

Member 7: Can you think of something that you and I can do together that would make you feel less anxious?

Dr. W.: (You mean you want the patient to prescribe the treatment?)

Member 7: I'm not too sure that you want to work with me.

Dr. W.: That is why I've come here. I want to work with you. (Now you are really going off the track, because what you are following now is the interactions with the previous therapist. In any case, that statement, imputing "resistance" to the patient, has no justification.)

Member 7: What did Dr. X do?

Dr. W.: Well he gave me assignments. He first gave me relaxation sessions, and then later on systematic desensitization. He made me imagine scenes of increasing going out, which he went on doing most of the time, but nothing changed. He also gave me assignments to force myself to go out increasing distances.

Member 7:   Were you able to complete the assignments?

Dr. W.:   Well I did them. I went to the places he told me, but I just got very upset.

Member 7:   Was it difficult to complete the assignments?

Dr. W.:   Yes, it was difficult.

Member 7:   When you went to these places, did you feel anxious?

Dr. W.:   Yes. He would tell me to force myself to a place where I became very anxious and to stay there for a long time. I would do it and stay very upset. (This was presumably supposed to be flooding, but guidance was inadequate and the details were left to the patient with predictably poor results.)

Member 7:   But you would always be anxious?

Dr. W.:   Yes.

Member 7:   What about the instructions?

Dr. W.:   He just said I was to go to a certain place for 15, 30 minutes, and so on.

Member 7:   He didn't give any specific instructions on how to let your feelings decide your actions?

Dr. W.:   No. (The foregoing has been a commendably logical sequence of questions.)

Member 8:   One of the questions I would like to ask concerns the relationship with your mother. Is there any anxiety in this relationship?

Dr. W.:   Well, just the fact that she is a person I can trust. (Now I don't approve of that question. I answered it because you asked it. It takes us away from the topic we were developing. I want to return to the matter of what Dr. X was doing. I told you something about that. Don't you want to know more? He was a "behavior therapist." You must want to know more. Dr. X did systematic desensitization for two years and nothing was happening.)

Member 8:   Were you getting better?

Dr. W.:   I told you I wasn't getting any better. (Now what do you want to know? There is something very important that you need to know.)

Member 8:   What was he desensitizing you to?

Dr. W.:   He was desensitizing me to distance. He was making me imagine going one and a half blocks, two blocks, and so on.

Member 8:   Could it be that the real problem was not with distance?

Could it be something about your girlfriend? Were you guilty? How did you perform sexually?

Dr. W.: I performed fine. (Now wait a minute. You are suggesting a lot of possibilities. I'm the patient, so you don't have to speculate; you can get information from me. But you should first finalize the information about the previous treatment.)

Member 8: When you imagined these scenes did you use the anxiety scale?

Dr. W.: No, the therapist didn't use that scale.

Member 8: Can you remember if the anxiety dropped as you went over and over these scenes? You imagined you went further and further from home?

Dr. W.: Yes. I had no anxiety when I imagined the scenes. (Now have I told you anything important?)

Member 8: I'm puzzled, because my expectation would have been that your anxiety level would have gone up or down, so I am very puzzled that you remained the same.

Dr. W.: (Think carefully. What I said was that I didn't have anxiety when I imagined the scenes. Is this an important statement?)

Member 9: So it is not distance that causes the anxiety. The scenes were scenes of distance.

Dr. W.: (The patient has already told us that distance increases anxiety.)

Member 9: Because if anxiety was not being engendered in the desensitization procedure then nothing could be deconditioned.

Dr. W.: (Exactly.)

Member 9: Well my original thought was that the client didn't get anxious because he didn't get a clear image. In any case, you can't desensitize until the client has a reaction.

Dr. W.: (Right. The important part of your statement is that if anxiety is not elicited, you can't desensitize. The patient was not getting anxiety to the imagined scenes; therefore, he could never be desensitized. Now why is that an important statement? What does it mean regarding his transactions with Dr. X?)

Member 9: The presumptive conclusion is that that is why nothing happened in this particular therapy.

Dr. W.: (Yes, exactly. And what does it tell us about Dr. X?)

Member 10: It tells us that Dr. X does not know one of the basic things about desensitization—that if the patient is not feeling anxiety from the scenes that he imagines, then you cannot use imagined scenes for desensitization.

Member 10:   When you speak of imagined scenes, does the therapist imagine the scene as he poses it to the patient, or does he ask the patient to imagine the scene?

Dr. W.:   (Let me make this clear. This patient has anxiety when he goes as far as a block away from his house and the farther he goes the greater the anxiety becomes. So the target of therapy, for Dr. X, for us, for any therapist, is to break the anxiety habit in the context of these excursions. Now, Dr. X had decided to use systematic desensitization in order to break the anxiety habit. That means that he was going to ask the patient to imagine, to begin with, that he goes for a walk one block from his house. Now, it turned out that although the patient had anxiety when he actually went one block from his house, when he imagined doing it he had no anxiety. Other patients would have anxiety. In a patient who has anxiety upon imagining a relevant scene, we would expect that the relaxation would counteract the anxiety, progressively weakening it with repetition, so that we would be able to introduce the the imagining of increasingly distant excursions. But because this particular patient did not have anxiety to imagined scenes, any attempt to use them was bound to fail.)

Member 10:   It is my impression that *in vivo* desensitization is the course when the imaginal things don't work. Is that false?

Dr. W.:   (No. It is correct.)

Member 10:   But though Dr. X wasn't creating anxiety in the imaginal scenes, he did try desensitization *in vivo*.

Dr. W.:   (Did he?)

Member 11:   He did tell him to go out.

Dr. W.:   (That is right.)

Member 10:   Wasn't that *in vivo* desensitization?

Dr. W.:   (No. I'm glad that you are raising that question. Those who are sophisticated might think this a redundant question. But it is a very important question for people who are learning. Let me ask anybody to say why that was not *in vivo* desensitization.)

Member 11:   There was no hierarchy. He always went by himself.

Dr. W.:   (There was no hierarchy. That is exactly the point. He was given exposure as though he would overcome it just by toughing it out. It didn't work and it certainly was not *in vivo* desensitization. For *in vivo* desensitization he would have been given graduated assignments under conditions that permitted counter-anxiety responses.)

Member 5:   Even if you were successfully using imagined scenes, wouldn't you still try to generalize the effect by giving him real assignments to do the same thing in various situations?

Dr. W.:   (Yes, but that is quite a different thing. To successful imaginal desensitization we would add *in vivo* trials to augment the work with imagery and to test how it transferred to reality. Okay, so now we know why Dr. X was a flop. The analyst who followed Dr. X displayed a critical intolerant attitude that made the patient a lot worse.)

Member 12:   There is some discrepancy in your information. I got the impression that we were totally excluding the efficacy of imaginary stimulation. Yet you said there were anxiety attacks that occurred in relation to some kinds of contemplation. This would seem to indicate that there are some imaginal scenes which did evoke anxiety.

Dr. W.:   (It is not a discrepancy. The situation is that this patient gets anxiety in real situations. It is a real situation when he walks one block. It is also a real situation when he knows that he has got to walk one block in an hour's time. Although he is only imagining it, it is part of his reality. Perhaps you would like to find out what might be related to these attacks.)

Member 13:   What type of feeling do you get?

Dr. W.:   Well, as I told you, I get a feeling that my heart palpitates, and I shake and sweat. Now, I've already told you that I usually get them when I'm out, but sometimes also when I'm in. (What you want to find out now is if you can relate anything to these attacks.)

Member 13:   Do you get these attacks when someone is around?

Dr. W.:   (Now why is that a bad question?)

Member 7:   It is a yes or no question.

Dr. W.:   (Yes. If you ask that kind of question, you've got to ask it about everything in the universe. Of course, I'm exaggerating a little bit.)

Member 13:   Do you feel more anxious at home?

Dr. W.:   (No, that is still not the correct question.)

Member 14:   When the anxiety attacks occur at home, are they correlated with the presence or absence of someone else?

Dr. W.:   (No. You are asking the same sort of question that he is. You aren't asking the question in an open-ended way. Now do it.)

Member 14:   What is going on at the time that you have these anxiety attacks?

Dr. W.:   (That isn't quite right either. Who has an open-ended question? In a way the question is implied in what I'm asking you to find out.)

Member 14:   Under what conditions do you have anxiety?

Dr. W.:   (Right. That is the question. Then he tells you. These are the answers he gave me: he tends to have these big anxiety attacks when he is out on social occasions, when he is in a crowd, and when he is at home and thinking that there is a business meeting that he should go to and can't. Whenever he is thinking about these things, it is reality as distinguished from what he might be asked to imagine.)

The interview practicum has ended. Those are the answers that he gave me at the first interview. Now let me tell you a little about how this case developed. Because of the multiplicity of the symptoms and because they included sweating and dizziness, I made him hyperventilate—also at the first interview. After hyperventilating for 45 seconds, he said his mouth was dry. After 165 seconds his hand was numb and he was sweating. After 270 seconds he complained of dizziness. These were all symptoms that were part of the anxiety complex. I then told him how he could control these symptoms by keeping his mouth closed. Since I also wanted to know whether to any extent his anxiety was pervasive (so-called "free floating"), I gave him a few discrete, full-capacity inhalations of carbon dioxide and oxygen. I told you that he had 20 units of anxiety just sitting in front of me, but with three inhalations the anxiety went down to 10, 5, and 2. So it was clear that probably all this anxiety was pervasive anxiety.

At the second session we did a Willoughby and a Fear Survey Schedule. You remember that when we were talking yesterday about how one proceeds to do behavior analysis, first the history is taken and then the questionnaires are administered. You do not have to stick religiously to the standard order of procedure, particularly if the case is rather severely ill as this man was. At the end of the first interview I gave him these questionnaires to do at home. The Willoughby score was 66; he had maximum scores of 4 for heights, feeling miserable, crying easily, lack of confidence, being self conscious about his appearance, and feeling inferior. He had 3s for stage fright, humiliation, hurt feelings, and avoiding the important person on social occasions. The Fear Survey Schedule had many items with maximum scores: being alone, public places, strange places, heights, trains, cars, dull weather, watching bullying, dead animals, surgical operations, rejection, planes, being disapproved of, being ignored, leaving home, and hospitals. So an enormous amount of disturbability was revealed by these questionnaires, adding to the agoraphobia we have been focusing on.

This second interview took place a week after the first. It was noteworthy that most of this week he had felt better than before; his average anxiety level having gone down to 25. The range 25 to 50 had made the average 37.5 previously. Unfortunately, the improvement had only lasted until the previous evening, when his girlfriend had not phoned him as expected. This had made him angry, then depressed, and then anxious. I'll tell you what we did to deal with this kind of reaction. Since Mr. S. had a lot of interpersonal anxiety and did not know how to handle people, I introduced assertive training. One person with whom he needed to assert himself was this girlfriend, and he did progressively well with her.

As far as the agoraphobia was concerned, since it was clear that we could not use imagination, we would have to do therapy in the real-life situation. Two possibilities were considered initially. One was a kind of *in vivo* desensitization in which the therapist or an assistant would go with the patient to progressively far places. The second possiblity was *in vivo* flooding. That would also have involved graduated exposures, but in a large step way. Both of these programs would have involved a lot of therapist time. As I mentioned, Mr. S. was earning very little because he was incapacitated, and in any case, business was bad in the architectural profession. It was important, therefore, to use an economical method if possible.

What gave me a lead was the fact that he had reported a good deal of relief from anxiety with doses of 5 mg of Valium. There is a treatment in which tranquilizing drugs are used as inhibitors of anxiety. If you can find a drug that effectively tranquilizes the patient, you can use it to diminish the anxiety aroused in a mildly anxiety-evoking situation. After a few exposures he will have no anxiety in that situation. He will be able to be exposed to increasingly strong stimuli with little or no anxiety under the influence of the tranquilizer. In time he can be exposed to the worst situation, and then one finds it possible progressively to decrease the drug dose without the patient having anxiety. Eventually, the dose comes down to zero while the patient has no anxiety in any of the relevant situations. I believe that the way it works is this. If, by means of a centrally acting drug, you can bring the anxiety of a situation down very low, then the emotional effects of other life experiences may be strong enough to inhibit the weak anxiety; and counterconditioning may take place.

I saw this patient once a week for about three weeks, every two weeks for about six months, and subsequently once a month. He has been monitoring his own responses. He has been taking increasingly long drives. I found that to bring the anxiety down to 10 or 15 during excursions, I had to give him 25 mg of Valium, and on certain occasions 30 mg. With an adequate dose of the drug inside him he soon started driving alone, and then going farther and farther. Within three weeks he was able to come on his own to my consulting room. As time went on he could go increasingly far and then slowly reduce the dose of Valium. The situation now is that he can easily take trips of twenty miles alone with 5 mg. He takes usually a total of 15 mg of Valium per day. With individual doses of 5 mg he is able to travel the 5 miles on the expressway to the center of the city. He has driven unaccompanied over the Delaware River to cities in New Jersey. And he is doing all this on 20% of the original dose of Valium. He is jubilant. His life has been transformed.

Question: Did the doses of 25 mg make him dizzy?

Dr. W.:   A little, but not significantly; he just drove carefully. He got used to the dose after a time. If it had made him seriously dizzy then we would not have been able to use it, and we would probably have turned to some other tranquilizer.

Question: Is there a systematic way of therapeutic exposure without using drugs?

Dr. W.:   Yes. One way is to use what Jacobson calls "differential relaxation," which means relaxing muscles that are not in use. It is fine lying down to relax for systematic desensitization with imagination; but if you are going to use relaxation in the life situation you can't have the patient lying down. It has been observed that relaxing the muscles not in use can also produce a calming effect. For example, while sitting here at the lecture, you are using your facial and neck muscles, but you are not using your legs and, unless you are taking notes, you are not using your arms, so you could be relaxing these limbs. If you are walking, you can't be relaxing your legs but you could be relaxing your face. And so, by differential relaxation you can keep yourself calm while active.

Question: Another alternative suggests itself to me, and I want to know why it wouldn't be appropriate? That is for the mother or girlfriend to do what the therapist would have done.

Dr. W.:   That might be possible. But then you would have to train the mother or girlfriend.

Question: Was he able to utilize the relaxation he learned with the previous behavior therapist?

Dr. W.:   Yes. The fact that he could relax was helpful now *in vivo*. When he went for increasing drives, his anxiety was not zero, but anything up to 15 units of anxiety, levels that were quite tolerable and that he would bring down further by relaxation. So the relaxation was a counterconditioning agent *in vivo*, adding to the counteranxiety effects of the Valium and to those of the competition of intercurrent emotional responses—such as his responses to beautiful scenery (of which we have a lot around here), of music, and so on.

Question: Did you analyze his relationship with the mother and the girlfriend?

Dr. W.: I don't think that had the relevance you suggest. Actually, very soon, with the help of the Valium, he didn't need the "protection" of the mother or the girlfriend. This girlfriend was really unsuitable for him, and he was able to give her up after two months. Of course, he didn't give up his mother, but he didn't need her as before. As long as he was terribly incapacitated it would have been impractical as well as cruel to take away his mother or his girlfriend. Are you suggesting that without their presence he would have been forced to go out to the supermarket and so forth?

Question: That is what the other therapist had tried unsuccessfully?

Dr. W.: Yes, in a way you are right.

Question: If you had decided on *in vivo* flooding how would you have done it?

Dr. W.: Because I knew that he was comfortable up to a certain distance when accompanied, I would have taken him somewhat beyond that distance and just stayed there until the anxiety level came down. Then I would have increased the distance. This is exactly what was done with another patient, a young woman. One of our students last year treated her by taking her out in a car increasing distances and just staying with her until the anxiety subsided. She completely overcame her agoraphobia by this method.

Question: So you go so far and wait for the anxiety to subside and then you go on a little further?

Dr. W.: That is right.

Question: What was Mr. S. afraid of? Was he afraid of suffocating?

Dr. W.: He wasn't very overtly afraid of suffocating. He was afraid of something happening to him, and he was afraid particularly of the symptoms that we found to be producible by hyperventilation.

Question: So you took care of that right away?

Dr. W.: Yes. As a matter of fact, when he went on that crucial drive with that girl, the symptoms that were so terrifying were produced by hyperventilation. His anxiety was associated with the fact that she was behaving as though she were choking.

Question: When you instruct in the office to hyperventilate, exactly what do you say?

Dr. W.: I say I want you to breath very rapidly and very deeply. I demonstrate this and say, "Just go on doing it, and don't stop at all except when you feel some new sensation; then quickly tell me what it is, and go on."

Question: For how long?

Dr. W.:   Up to 5 minutes. Usually we don't have to go on for 5 minutes because before that time their typical symptoms have appeared.

Question: What would happen if they continued? Would they pass out?

Dr. W.:   One can eventually faint. If a person felt that he were fainting then I would tell him to stop.

Question: What if they had high blood pressure or cardiovascular problems?

Dr. W.:   Well, it is not a dangerous activity.

Question: I want to ask the question about shortening the length of treatment because most patients that I see can afford 12 sessions or less.

Dr. W.:   Well this particular patient has had—in a year—about 22 sessions.

Question: Are there ways of reducing a phobia for someone who can only be with you two weeks?

Dr. W.:   There are various things that you can do to expedite therapy, though not in Mr. S's case, because the actual therapeutic events are not occurring in the consulting room, but in the life situation. His therapy is really going about as fast as it can go. He is enormously gratified. He wrote me a letter about a month ago that is full of elation. One measure to expedite therapy is to give the patient tape-recorded assignments. You put relaxation instructions and hierarchical items on a tape, and then the patient takes them home with him and relaxes himself and presents scenes to himself. This can save time and money.

Question: At the beginning of this case you mentioned the man's wife choking to death. That never came up again, nor was there anything mentioned about his fear of harming his girlfriend. Was there a fantasy about hurting the girlfriend or hurting someone else?

Dr. W.:   No. I did indicate that he was very much involved with his wife, had suffered very much during her cancer, and was enormously distressed by her final passing out by suffocation. The girlfriend exhibited a kind of choking behavior. It was because he had been conditioned to react to this with great distress, that he tried to get her home as quickly as possible. During the drive, his sense of urgency due to the fear that she might suffocate kept him anxious and caused him to hyperventilate to the extent that he could not breathe. It was that which made him return home. It was a fear of suffocation, not a guilt about killing or wanting to kill anybody.

Question: I was wondering if you had considered or would ever consider re-evoking the scene that seems to have precipitated the anxiety?

Dr. W.: I didn't consider it. In some circumstances it is helpful to re-elicit a precipitating event, but not very often. I think it can be said that to see somebody suffocate is not a thing that one should be expected to take with equanimity. It is a dreadful thing. This patient's recovery did not require subjecting him to this kind of stress.

Question: Can you make somebody calm about something dreadful they have seen?

Dr. W.: It depends on what the emotions are. If the suffering evokes feelings of pity, that is one thing; if anxiety, that is another thing. You should have pity; you shouldn't have anxiety.

Question: How do you treat people with excessive anxiety following a traumatic experience to themselves: What technique should be considered?

Dr. W.: Probably the most common example is the automobile accident. A person who has been involved in an automobile accident may be anxious just getting into a car afterwards. Usually the anxiety is not very great, so that he can drive notwithstanding it; and in the course of two or three weeks the anxiety subsides. This is an example of life itself providing emotional competition to break an anxiety-response habit. We would call this a short-lived maladaptive habit, not a neurotic habit, precisely because it is not persistent, which the definition of neurosis requires. As to the criterion for persistence—if the reaction were undiminished after a couple of months I would call it persistent. Treatment would probably entail systematic desensitization.

Question: Is this a new kind of treatment? Did he ever have this kind of anxiety about going out in his previous life?

Dr. W.: No, but he did have a lot of other anxieties. I gave you the scores from the Willoughby and the Fear Survey Schedules, which included anxiety sources such as dead animals, watching bullying, elevators. Now, it could be that when he is completely free from his agoraphobia and is getting around freely there may be some such areas that are important enough to require further treatment, and then we will deal with them. Interestingly enough, with regard to being disturbed by bullying, he has dealt with this himself through becoming more expressive. In the course of the past year there have been situations in which he has observed other people's bullying behavior and has been able to respond very strongly. He now has a feeling of control in that context.

Question: I also asked about the hierarchy.

Dr. W.:   In his case there has not been a formal hierarchy for the ago-raphobia. We knew, as I mentioned, that his anxiety went up sub-stantially when he has gone one block. That is what we started with, but since he was doing the treatment on his own, he had to feel his way and he had to find out how far he could go without the anxiety going beyond 15 SUDs.

Question: How do you generally proceed in tapering off the Valium?

Dr. W.:   Well in the case of Mr. S., he has been guided by his own reactions. He has found as time has gone on that he can do more and more things with less and less drug. He has really paced himself in the main. He comes to me with a sheaf of notes and tells me what he has done in the past month. He now makes all the decisions on the drug and the excursions. In the beginning I kept a close watch on these things.

Question: If this man's problems were presented clinically after the incident with his girlfriend, would it not have seemed to be depres-sion rather than anxiety?

Dr. W.:   This man has had a lot of depression. It is a very depressing thing to be confined by anxiety. In fact, at the second interview he said that he felt as if he wanted to break out of prison. He had a feel-ing of absolute helplessness, constriction, limitation, with a lot of frank depression mixed among these feelings. Many cases of depres-sion have this kind of history. The depression is partly an anxiety equivalent, and partly an expression of the helplessness related to be-ing confined by the anxiety. So, the fact of depression does not change the treatment at all; I might add that psychophysiologically there is no distinction between reactive depression and anxiety. The physiology of reactive depression is very much like the physiology of anxiety (see Wolpe, 1979).

Question: You would start with the anxiety?

Dr. W.:   Yes. Of course, there are certain cases in which depression is the primary emotion. There is general incapacitation, and one course of action is to give the patient certain tasks, such as have been de-scribed by Elaine Burgess (1968). But in a general way it is my policy to treat neurotic depression as if it were anxiety. It is a different mat-ter if there is reason to believe that it is an endogenous depression.

Question: If a patient is unable to experience anxiety to a scene from a hierarchy would it be safe to assume that he would be unable to ex-perience it to any imagined scenes?

Dr. W.:   You would have to try several scenes and be sure of com-munication before reaching this conclusion. Even then, there are certain things that you can do to evoke anxiety. First, you can see what happens if the patient *verbalizes* the scene instead of just imagining to your command. A few people get emotional responses to their own verbalizations, but not to passive imagining. A second thing that you can do is repeat your procedure after hypnotic induction. What that does in some people—not too many—is to increase the concentration and heighten the impact of the scene. Another line of action is to try and train them to respond better. This means putting the patient through a type of training designed to make him more sensitive to his own images (Phillips, 1971).

REFERENCES

Burgess, E. The modification of depressive behavior. In R. D. Rubin, and C.M. Franks (Eds.), *Advances in Behavior Therapy*, New York: Academic, 1968.

Phillips, L.W. Training of sensory and imagined responses in behavior therapy. In R. Rubin, H. Fensterheim, A.A. Lazarus, and C.M. Franks (Eds.), *Advances in Behavior Therapy*. New York: Academic, 1971.

Wolpe, J. *Psychotherapy by Reciprocal Inhibition*. Stanford: Stanford, 1958.

Wolpe, J. *The Practice of Behavior Therapy* (2nd ed.) New York: Pergamon, 1973.

Wolpe, J. *Theme and Variations: A Behavior Therapy Casebook*. New York: Pergamon, 1977.

Wolpe, J. The experimental model and treatment of neurotic depression. *Behav. Res. Ther.*, in press, 1979.

CHAPTER 2

Systematic Desensitization

EDNA B. FOA, GAIL S. STEKETEE, AND L. MICHAEL ASCHER

Department of Psychiatry
Temple University Medical School

INTRODUCTION

"Systematic desensitization is one of a variety of methods for breaking down neurotic anxiety-response habits" (Wolpe, 1973, p. 95). We refer to neurotic anxiety when a person reacts with intense fear to situations or objects in which objective danger is minimal or nonexistent. These situations are perceived by most people as neutral and do not elicit anxiety.

Once a link between a neutral stimulus (e.g., situation, object, etc.) and an anxiety response has been established, a neurotic habit has been learned. The treatment goal is to disassociate this particular stimulus from the anxiety response, thus "undoing" the previous maladaptive learning.

A technique developed by Wolpe (1958, 1973) for this purpose is systematic desensitization. It consists of exposing the client to anxiety-arousing stimuli while inducing a physiological state that inhibits anxiety. Such a state may be induced, for example, through muscular relaxation, anti-anxiety drugs, sexual arousal, expression of anger, or eating when hungry. The anxiety-evoking situations are presented in hierarchical order, gradually exposing the client to situations of increasing anxiety-evoking potential. Systematic desensitization, then, involves two main components: reciprocal inhibition (i.e., a state that is incompatible with an anxiety response) and a hierarchy—a series of situations of increasingly higher anxiety-evoking potential.

Informal employment of systematic desensitization is often described by parents helping their children to overcome fears. Strangers often play with their friends's babies keeping a distance from them while they play, then gradually approaching them until the babies become more comfortable with their presence and are willing to sit on their laps. The first deliberate use of systematic desensitization was described by Mary Cover Jones (1924). However, the theoretical and methodological conceptualization of this technique was developed by Wolpe (1958, 1973).

Theoretical Basis of Systematic Desensitization

Wolpe (1958, p. 71) formulated the principle of reciprocal inhibition: "If a response antagonistic to anxiety can be made to occur in the presence of anxiety-evoking stimuli the bond between these stimuli and the anxiety-responses will be weakened." This formulation was based primarily on experiments with cats in which an experimental neurosis was first induced by electric shock to the floor of the animal's cage. The animals' anxiety reaction to this cage was then alleviated by offering it food in locations progressively similar to the experimental cage. Eventually the cat could eat without anxiety inside the cage to which it had previously shown a marked anxiety reaction. Mary Cover Jones (1924) also utilized the appetitive drive as the counter-conditioning agent in her treatment of the phobic child Peter.

Wolpe subsequently adopted Jacobson's technique of progressive relaxation (1938) as the primary anxiety-inhibiting agent during systematic desensitization of phobic responses. Once mastered by the patient, this technique could be employed at almost any time in a variety of situations both in and outside of the therapist's office. Wolpe also found that the use of imaginal rather than *in vivo* exposure expanded greatly the range of situations that were amenable to treatment by systematic desensitization.

Experimental Evidence

The effectiveness of systematic desensitization with a variety of phobias in human beings has been amply demonstrated in numerous studies. As Kazdin and Wilcoxon (1976, p. 730) note, "desensitization is well established, and few individuals . . . . can question the overwhelming data in support of its efficacy." Several controlled analog studies using snake-phobic student populations showed systematic desensitization superior to "pseudotherapy" (Lang and Lazovik, 1963; Lang, Lazovik, and Reynolds, 1965) and to relaxation with an unrelated hierarchy or to a hierarchy without relaxation (Davidson, 1968). In a classic study with speech anxious subjects, Paul (1966) found systematic desensitization superior to insight therapy and no treatment controls. In this study nine subjects were assigned to each of five nonbehavioral therapists. Each therapist used one of three treatment methods for each patient, that is, three subjects to each method. The methods were (1) insight therapy consisting of psychoanalytically based interpretations of feelings and behavior, (2) attention-placebo in which therapists listened attentively and responded in a nondirective manner, and (3) systematic desensitization utilizing relaxation as the counter-conditioning agent. After five treatment sessions 100 were improved or much improved by systematic desensitization in contrast to 47 in these categories for both insight and attention-placebo.

In uncontrolled clinical findings, Wolpe (1961), Hain and coworkers (1966), Kraft (1970), Paul (1969a), and Lazarus (1961) have reported success rates ranging from 70 to 92% utilizing systematic desensitization for patients with a wide variety of neurotic disorders. Controlled clinical studies conducted by Gelder and Marks (1968) indicate that systematic desensitization with individuals and groups is significantly more effective than conventional psychotherapy in the treatment of phobic patients. While follow-up results vary widely in these studies, it appears that, in general, gains from desensitization are maintained and at times increased, and that evidence for symptom substitution is absent. For a detailed discussion of experimental evidence regarding systematic desensitization, readers are referred to Paul (1969b) and Bandura (1969).

Indications for the Use of Systematic Desensitization

The decision as to whether or not to employ desensitization in treatment depends on the nature of the presenting complaints as well as on individual characteristics of the patient.

Presenting Complaints

Desensitization is generally indicated when the complaint involves an anxiety reaction to situations or stimuli that present minimal or no objective danger and when this anxiety response is not based upon cognitive misconceptions (i.e., beliefs about the phobic stimulus that are factually incorrect). The technique is used primarily for specific phobias where the stimuli are easily identified. Additionally, other types of neurotic disturbances such as social anxiety and sexual dysfunction may require systematic desensitization as a preliminary or secondary treatment adjunct.

Desensitization is not indicated when an anxiety is nonspecific, for example, in cases of pervasive or free-floating anxiety. Unless discreet stimuli for the anxiety can be identified, another procedure should be selected. In addition, a careful behavioral analysis must be conducted when the therapist considers a treatment program for two populations, agoraphobics and obsessive compulsives, for whom desensitization is usually not the treatment of choice, except under special circumstances described subsequently.

Cognitive Misconceptions

If a patient is simply misinformed about the actual danger of the phobic object, the therapist's first task is to correct the misconception by providing convincing factual information. Should the fear remain even after the patient feels convinced that no danger will follow exposure to the feared stimulus, desensitization should then be employed. The following example of an elevator phobic serves to illustrate the correction of a cognitive misconception:

T: Well, you say you are unable to enter an elevator without feeling quite panicky.

P: I could enter one, I suppose, but not if the doors were going to be closed.

T: You mean you could step onto one without feeling panicked but if the doors closed you would then get very anxious? Why is that?

P: Well, you understand, I'd still be nervous just stepping on one because the doors always close of course. But if I knew for sure they wouldn't close, I wouldn't be very nervous.

T: Is there something about the doors closing that upsets you?

P: Yes. Other people don't seem to think about it but you know there's not much air in that little space, especially with several people in it. If it were to get stuck or something and the door wouldn't open, I'm afraid we'd suffocate before they fixed it. I've known of people who've been stuck for 2 or 3 hours like that.

T: Did they suffocate?

P: Well, no, but they were probably lucky.

T: Do you know that all elevators are required by law to have adequate ventilation systems. They are not closed boxes at all.

P: Well, a little air probably leaks in but maybe not enough.

T: No, all elevators have large vents to let air in so it is impossible for even a full elevator to become short of air.

P: Are you sure of that?

T: Suppose I get some official information about elevators for you and we can go look at several, with the doors open of course, so you can see for yourself. Would that help you?

P: Yes, I think it would.

T: Then, I will get the information. It may be that because you have been afraid and have avoided elevators for so many years, we will still need to do some additional treatment to remove all the fear, but we'll see about that after you feel convinced that you won't suffocate.

Specific Phobias

A clear indication for the use of desensitization occurs when a patient presents one or more specific phobias that concentrate around fear of a given situation or object. Examples of such phobias are claustrophobia, elevator phobia, fear of dogs, fear of hypodermic needles, and so forth. One may conceptualize phobic patients as persons who react to situations with an extremely low probability of danger, as if they were, in fact, quite dangerous. These phobic patients are characteristically aware of the fact that their fear "does not make sense" and is unrealistic. Therefore, attempts to convince them rationally that they should stop being afraid because their fear is illogical are doomed to fail.

T: What is it about needles that upsets you so much?

P: I don't really know.

T: You know, of course, that a shot in the arm cannot harm you in any way. The pain is quite minimal.

P: Yes, I know that, but I still get very upset about it. I've been putting off a visit to my doctor for the past two years. I get so nervous every time I try to call that I don't. I'd ask him to be sure I wouldn't get a shot but he'd think I was a little kid if I asked him that.

T: Have you seen a hypodermic needle? Do you know how fine the points are, they're really very small.

P: I know, but even the sight upsets me. Even my wife's sewing needles make me nervous. It's really ridiculous for a grown man to feel this way, I can laugh about it now, but when I see a needle, or even a doctor's office, I feel really uncomfortable.

In general we assume that in the patient's past history the phobic situation became associated with anxiety by being paired with a stimulus that evokes anxiety (Unconditioned Stimulus), such as fainting, physical pain, choking, and so forth. Occasionally, however, the patient is not able to report such conditioning events. Despite such lack of information, desensitization can be successfully undertaken. On rare occasions, memories of the original conditioning event may be recalled during the treatment procedure (Wolpe, 1973, p. 202).

Social Anxieties

Assertiveness training, which is actually a variant of systematic desensitization (see Chapter 9), is the technique of choice for social anxieties. Wolpe (1973) suggests that various emotions aroused by the presence of others, for example, affection, pleasure, annoyance, or anger, may produce bodily sensations incompatible with anxiety. The appropriate expression of these feelings inhibits unadaptive anxiety responses. Additionally, positive reinforcement from the environment following assertive responses, in the form of approval, affection, or fulfilling one's own needs, further increases the occurrence of these behaviors. The major component of assertive training, behavior rehearsal, is essentially a counter-conditioning procedure in which both the therapist's presence and the expression of emotion are anxiety-reducing agents. In general, rehearsals are hierarchically organized beginning with situations of least difficulty and progressing to more difficult ones.

Formal systematic desensitization in conjunction with assertiveness training becomes necessary when a patient cannot utilize assertive responses successfully rehearsed in the office in the real situation because of intense fears aroused by that particular social context.

Consider the following example: the therapist role-plays a woman in a bar, and the patient is able to say "Hello, my name is Steve M., may I invite you for a drink?" Both positive and negative responses by the woman are role-played, and Steve responds appropriately and without anxiety to both in the office, using all the suitable nonverbal gestures and intonation he has been taught. He is then instructed to actually approach a woman in a bar. He returns to the next session.

T: How did it go?

P: I went in to the bar like you said and I did see a woman sitting with another woman at a booth. They were looking around and drinking, as if they expected someone to come over. I was pretty attracted to the one and I went over in my head what to say, like we rehearsed. But every time I tried to make myself get up and go over, I felt really shaky and afraid. It seems so silly, because I know that's what's expected, and I know what to say, but I was so nervous I was sure the words would come out backward or not at all and they'd think I was some kind of idiot.

T: When did you start to feel so nervous?

P: As soon as I went inside. It went up real high when I sat down with my drink at the bar and saw them.

T: It sounds as if there is something about being in a bar and seeing an approachable woman that really triggers off a lot of anxiety even though you know what to say.

P: Yeah, I could do it and here it's no problem, but there I just couldn't do it. I'm sorry.

T: No need to apologize. We simply need to reduce your discomfort in that particular situation. I'll explain what I think is needed here.

In this case, the use of desensitization in conjunction with assertiveness training is indicated. The hierarchy will be composed of social scenes which evoke progressively more anxiety, for example, entering the bar, watching a young woman, approaching her accompanied by a friend, approaching her alone, and so forth. When anxiety evoked by these scenes diminishes, the patient will be instructed to expose himself to these situations *in vivo*.

Sexual Dysfunction

Sexual problems, especially erectile failure and orgasmic dysfunction, are usually the result of anxiety that interferes with normal sexual response. Treatment generally involves a form of *in vivo* desensitization with a partner. Systematic imaginal desensitization may be required whenever a specific stimulus, such as an upsetting sexual memory, interferes with progress *in vivo*. In such cases, increasingly longer exposures to the anxiety-evoking scene are presented until it loses its disturbing potential. Additionally, systematic desensitization may be employed when no partner is available.

As noted previously, systematic desensitization is not the technique of choice for agoraphobias and obsessive-compulsive neurosis. However, it is indicated under certain circumstances.

Agoraphobia

Although defined as a fear of open spaces, the term "agoraphobia" encompasses several subclasses of symptomatology. Some agoraphobics are not afraid of open space *per se*, but rather of the consequences of being away from a "safe" person or place. The common manifestation is fear of panic attacks, hyperventilation, fainting, losing control, and going crazy. In general, this population may be perceived as afraid of the symptoms of anxiety rather than of prescribed situations. A large percentage of agoraphobics experience difficulties in family relationships; they are unassertive and uncomfortable in the relationship but at the same time are unable to leave. This conflict is often accompanied by the physical symptoms described. In an attempt to prevent these symptoms, agoraphobics become increasingly confined to the home, unable to leave except in the company of those few whom they trust.

Although desensitization may be applied to this population, flooding (see Chapter 7), or paradoxical intention (Chapter 6) accompanied by assertiveness training (see Chapter 9) appears to be the treatment of choice. Those agoraphobics who are actually space phobics, that is, their fear increases as a function of distance from home, would benefit from systematic desensitization.

Obsessive–Compulsive Neurosis

The picture emerging from uncontrolled studies and case reports in which systematic desensitization was implemented with obsessive-compulsives is not consistent. Evidence indicates that cases of recent onset may respond favorably to systematic desensitization, while chronic cases require interventions directed at the ritualistic behavior (see Chapter 8).

In summary, the technique of choice for specific phobias is systematic desensitization. A careful behavior analysis should determine which agoraphobics and obsessive-compulsives would benefit from it.

Patient Variables

Although the type of neurotic disturbance is a major consideration in the choice of treatment, other factors related to the patient should be taken into consideration when the use of systematic desensitization is considered. The frequency of treatment sessions and the length of time available for treatment will vary from one patient to the next.

For a patient who cannot be seen more than once every two or three weeks, desensitization seems to be preferable to flooding. Additionally, longer sessions, 1½ to 2 hours, are required for maximal effectiveness of flooding, while desensitization can be conducted in shorter sessions. Occasionally, it yields dramatic changes within a very short time. If, for example, a test-phobic patient requests treatment only a few days before an examination, the necessary time is not available for teaching relaxation, constructing a hierarchy along the correct dimensions, and then conducting desensitization. In this case flooding would be employed, even though desensitization would have been chosen had more time been available.

The patient's ability to imagine scenes clearly, to experience anxiety while imagining, and to relax effectively are crucial variables in successful desensitization. Occasionally, patients are unable to picture scenes clearly—either the scene remains vague and undefined or it cannot be retained with any clarity for more than a second or two. Some aids to imagining may be employed at this point: the patient may be requested to visualize a specially constructed scene designed to include several senses in a familiar setting. An example might be slicing and tasting lemons in one's kitchen. In addition, the patient may be asked to focus on an object, then close his eyes and visualize it in his mind. Gradually larger numbers of objects and eventually entire scenes are pictured. Daily practice is suggested. Should the patient still be unable to imagine clearly, *in vivo* desensitization will be necessary. Alternatively, some patients can imagine the required scenes clearly but do not experience any anxiety even though the scenes might arouse considerable discomfort in actuality. Again, *in vivo* treatment is required.

Effective relaxation can be achieved by a variety of methods which are discussed in the section on relaxation training. Regardless of the method used, the patient's subjective level of anxiety should be between 0 and 10 before beginning the presentation of scenes. For those unable to achieve this, alternative counter-conditioning agents should be sought (e.g., anger or tranquilizers).

THERAPEUTIC SETTING

Environmental Variables

Systematic desensitization is most often conducted in an outpatient setting, since the neurotic disturbances for which it is used rarely require hospitalization. If progressive relaxation is being used as the counter-conditioning agent, a comfortable chair, preferably a recliner, and a quiet, pleasant atmosphere are required. The therapist need not be affiliated with any institution, unless relaxation agents such as carbon dioxide inhalation or tranquilizing drugs, which must be administered by a physician, are used.

Group desensitization has been shown to be effective in analog studies utilizing student populations (Paul and Shannon, 1966; Donner and Guerney, 1969). For those with similar phobias, one hierarchy may be developed and administered to all patients simultaneously. For those with differing phobias, each patient may have his or her own hierarchy written on a card and progress through it as general instructions are given to all patients. In either case a complete individual behavioral analysis is required for each patient to verify the pertinance of the hierarchy variables. The disadvantage of a group desensitization is the loss of individual control of the therapist over each patient's progress through the hierarchy.

Therapist's Attitude

In contrast to insight-oriented psychotherapy, behavioral treatment is not something an active therapist does to a passive patient. From the outset it is, rather, a joint undertaking in which both partners play an active role in working toward a designated goal. The therapist's attitude is warm and accepting, but at the same time, the information exchange in the sessions is structured to identify the stimulus-response patterns, that is, the cues that elicit anxiety. The patient possesses knowledge that the therapist requires in order to plan the course of systematic desensitization. A good working relationship between the therapist and patient is essential to successful treatment.

Most phobics tend to make negative self-statements when discussing their phobia, precisely because of the discrepancy between their cognitive assessment and their emotional reaction to the anxiety producing stimuli. Most patients are relieved to hear these statements contradicted by the therapist through an explanation of the inconsistencies between their feelings and beliefs.

P: I realize I can't be hurt by a needle and I really feel like a little kid, especially when other people joke about my attitude. And I know how dumb it is but I can't help it. I just can't make myself go to the doctor's office no matter what I tell myself.

T: Well, your fear and your behavior are quite understandable under the circumstances. Your fear is not a rational one; that's why you came for help. Most phobics experience the feeling that their behavior doesn't make sense. Other people who don't have this problem don't understand your agony when you try to go to get an injection. You have simply become conditioned to fear these particular situations and you now react automatically with anxiety. It doesn't matter what you think about it, you still react automatically with intense fear.

P: That really makes me feel better. After so many years of feeling foolish about this and being told by my wife and before her, my parents, that I should just go ahead and force myself, it's a relief to find somebody who understands my problem.

T: I'm glad you feel relieved. Let's concentrate now on getting specific details about your fear which we will use to plan your treatment.

DATA GATHERING

The information necessary to the therapist in deciding the course of treatment is gathered in the initial interview with the patient. One cannot exaggerate the importance of this beginning phase; a premature start based on inadequate information may result in failure of the treatment or in needlessly prolonging it. (See Chapter 1.)

General Information

The data obtained in the initial stage of interviewing should determine the treatment program. Accordingly, the first session is devoted to the presenting complaint, its severity, frequency, duration, history, and relationship to other problems in the patient's life. The second session focuses on a wide range of aspects, both present and past—details of childhood fears and experiences, relationship to peers and family members, academic success or failure, illnesses or injuries, hobbies, work record, sexual activity, and so forth. A life history questionnaire (See Appendix A) and a Fear Survey Schedule (Wolpe and Lang, 1964) are particularly recommended to elicit information that may be important but which was not mentioned during the interview. The patient may also be requested to record in a daily log between sessions all situations in which he experiences anxiety. From this information a coherent picture of the patient's life is assembled so that the presenting problem can be viewed in context and related variables can be assessed.

Communicating in SUDs

When the information gathered in the initial stage indicates that systematic desensitization is the appropriate treatment then the goal of the interview narrows, focusing on the data that are specifically required for the implementation of this technique: identifying the specific phobia and the dimensions along which the anxiety varies.

At this point it becomes convenient to establish effective communication with the patient regarding the degree of anxiety experienced in various situations. Wolpe (1973, p. 120) has developed a simple but effective device for recording subjective anxiety levels. The patient is introduced to an imaginal scale of Subjective Units of Discomfort, or SUDs, ranging from 0 to 100 as follows:

> T: To communicate between us in a convenient way, let's imagine
>   that we have a scale in which zero will indicate complete relaxation,

the point at which you have no tension at all. Have you ever been in a situation where you felt completely calm, even if briefly?

P: Well, I think so. Do you mean like times when I'm on vacation and I'm sunning myself on the beach? Like that?

T: Yes, can you describe a specific moment you remember when you felt very relaxed?

P: Yes, last summer. I remember when I was at Ocean City with my family. There was one morning when I got up really early and went down to the beach. Almost no one was around and I was lying on the sand listening to the waves and the gulls. It was so pleasant.

T: That sounds like you were very relaxed, let's call that zero. Now can you think of another situation where you felt really panicked, the most anxious you have ever felt?

P: Sure, that time two years ago, the last time I was in a doctor's office. I had to have a tetanus shot after I cut my foot on a tin can. Before this I hadn't had a shot for at least 10 years because of my condition, so I knew I really had to go and my foot seemed like it was getting infected. I wouldn't have gone except that my wife nagged me so much I wanted to shut her up. She was right of course. On the way there, she drove me, and I started to feel faint; the blood left my face and I felt like I was going to throw up.

T: Yes, it seems like you were extremely anxious then. Let's call the state you described 100.

Some patients are not used to describing their feelings in terms of anxiety. It may then be advisable to use equivalent terms, such as discomfort, tension, disturbance, or nervousness. In addition, patient's experiences may differ with regard to the anchoring points of the scale, 0 and 100. It is, therefore, best to use the patient's own experience to exemplify the two extremes rather than those proposed by the therapist.

The last step in familiarizing the patient with the SUD scale is to reach an understanding with her/him on the intermediate levels. Since SUDs are used very frequently during desensitization treatment, agreement between patient and therapist regarding the scale is most important. It is useful to first ask, "How much are you now on this scale?" If the patient says "70" even though she/he seems rather relaxed, further probing is needed: "Seventy, that's quite close to panic. Are you really feeling so anxious?" Patients may, in fact, feel very anxious although they do not show it. Often, however, they will say, "Oh no, I didn't understand, I'm closer to 20 or 30." The therapist then asks: "Well, why are you thirty?" The patient responds, "It is the first time I've seen you and I really feel uncomfortable about going into the therapy." Other patients may tend toward the lower end of the scale; presented with a high-anxiety situation, they may say, "Yes, that was really difficult, maybe I was 30 or 40." Again, further probing is required to assist the patient in accurately assessing her/his SUDs level. Facile use of this scale may require some practice. Certain patients who have difficulty initially may find it useful to take careful note of the physical cues with which they associate anxiety. One patient for instance, would assess her SUDs level by saying, "Well, in that situation, I would get a slightly queasy feeling in my stomach, and I would feel some shakiness, but I wouldn't be sweaty or dizzy so I guess that's about 40 or so."

Hierarchy Construction

Once communication regarding anxiety levels has been properly established, the therapist proceeds with defining the phobia and constructing the hierarchy.

A phobia can be defined as a class of stimuli belonging to the same theme and which elicit an anxiety response. Each anxiety-evoking situation contains many stimuli, both relevant and irrelevant to anxiety. Determining those stimuli that relate to anxiety, since these denote the dimensions along which anxiety varies, is of paramount importance. Thus the therapist first identifies the phobia and then the dimensions relevant to anxiety. For instance, a pure elevator phobic will not object to being locked in a small room, or being in a high place, but would experience intense anxiety in elevators. Conversely, a claustrophobic would experience anxiety in any confined place, including elevators, but may feel comfortable in high places.

Once the theme or class of feared stimuli has been delineated, an inquiry is conducted regarding the dimensions along which anxiety varies, and a hierarchy is constructed. A hierarchy is defined as a list of stimuli ordered along one or more dimensions according to the amount of anxiety they evoke. Examples of relevant dimensions include number of people, distance from a specified point, height, time, size of an object, status of a person, severity of criticism, and so forth.

It is important here to emphasize that not every list of situations varying in degree of anxiety constitutes a hierarchy. Suppose, for example, that a patient is very anxious about flying in planes, somewhat less anxious about meeting women, and only mildly afraid of rats. These are essentially different phobias rather than variations of the same phobia. It is, therefore, rather unlikely that desensitization to rats will generalize to an encounter with a woman, substantively reducing the patient's anxiety in the latter situation. Similarly, reduction of fears of meeting women would not provide a distinct advantage when boarding an airplane.

For generalization of anxiety to occur from one situation to the next higher on the hierarchy, it is necessary that the situations be linked by a common thread. More precisely, the items on a hierarchy should (1) be of a given specific phobia, (2) be ordered by increasing potential for anxiety, and (3) have a common dimension. The detailed inquiry involved in the process of identification of dimensions is well illustrated by the following example:

T: What can I do for you, Mr. S?

P: Well, I'm afraid of sitting in the back seat of small cars, like Volkswagons, Toyotas, and cars of that type.

T: Just in small cars—what happens in big cars?

P: I have a little bit of fear but not too much.

T: So, actually, the smaller the car, the greater the fear?

P: Yes, the more confined the space, the more the fear. (This answer may tentatively identify one dimension—size of the car).

T: Tell me, are cars the only place where you feel anxiety?

P: Well, no, when I fly in airplanes, when I have to sit in the rear of a plane.

T: So, the back seat—what if it's in the front?

P: No, I'm fine; no anxiety at all. I can fly in front without any problems.

T: What if you sit in the middle?

P: Well, that wouldn't bother me—it has to be the last few seats.

T: Now, suppose you were in the back of the smallest car you can think of, how much anxiety do you think you would have?

P: Oh, I would say maybe eighty to a hundred.

T: Depending on what?

P: On whether the car is moving or parked. (This answer could indicate another dimension—movement).

T: O.K. The car is very small and it is parked—would you be less anxious?

P: No, if the car is small, but yes, I would be less anxious if the car is parked, not moving. . . .

T: So parked would be lower, right? And if the car is very small, and is moving. . . .

P: If it's moving it would be 100—if it's parked it would be about 80.

So far, two dimensions that may be related to anxiety level have been identified: the size of the car and whether it is moving. The interview has also revealed that the position of the seat can be disregarded—all hierarchy scenes will be in the rear seat since no anxiety is experienced when sitting in the front or middle.

The probe continues:

T: And if it's parked closer to your home is there any difference?

P: No. It doesn't make any difference, as long as it's the back seat of a small car.

T: How about when you're approaching a small car to sit in the back seat?

P: Oh, just looking at somebody else in a car creates a lot of anxiety— at least 50. Just watching; because I would project myself into their place and imagine that I'm sitting in the back seat of a car.

T: What about being in the car 24 hours from now?

P: Probably about 20 or 30. I would feel some anxiety.

These further exchanges show that time is also a relevant dimension. It becomes possible, then to vary this dimension and keep the other two at the highest point—the rear of a small moving car—in order to construct a unidimensional hierarchy.

A SUD of ten is low enough to provide the first step of a hierarchy. Once such a scene has been identified, the procedure can be reversed; instead of asking how many SUDs this patient would feel at a given time, he is asked how many hours would produce a given anxiety level; in this way, the hierarchy scenes can be spaced at intervals of five or ten SUDs.

In this case, an alternative to the time-interval variable would be to keep time constant and change the size of car, and whether it is moving. The patient could be asked to list cars by size or by type (whichever is more convenient for him). Starting from the least anxiety-evoking car the patient is asked: "Sitting in the back of a parked station wagon, how much anxiety would you have?" If the patient answers "About 30 or 40," this scene may not be used first since the level of anxiety is rather high and may not be reduced by the counter-conditioning agent. Therefore, another question follows:

T: Can you think of a vehicle which would produce not more than ten SUDs?

P: Yes, maybe in a bus. Being the only one in a bus.

This answer indicates that the number of people constitutes a relevant variable. The interview takes a new turn following this lead:

T: Tell me, if you are in a locked room, do you feel any anxiety?

P: If there's no other person in the room, between myself and the door—very little. But if there's someone near the door. . . .

T: But, the door is locked.

P: Oh, I can't get out? Well, I'll be anxious.

T: How much?

P: I would say 50 or 60.

T: And if there are other people in the room?

P: Yes, if there are other people in the room that would upset me a bit more.

T: Now, if there are six people in a very small room?

P: A little bit more. Probably 70.

T: Eight people?

P: The same, 70. I don't think it would go higher than that.

In the room situation, anxiety never reaches 100 as it does in the car. Apparently there is some element in the car situation that is not captured by other confined spaces. Therefore, for this patient, the therapist will proceed with the car scenes.

P: Almost as bad as the car is thinking about being confined in the back of an ambulance—not being able to move.

T: How much would that be?

P: That would be about 90.

T: And being in a moving Volkswagon?

P: That would be 100.

T: How much would it be if two people were in the bus with you?

P: The driver and another person sitting in the back? Maybe 70. No, wait, the bus alone would be 10 . . . that would be maybe 40.

T: Do you have any situation in which you would be 15 in a car?

P: Yes, probably sitting alone in the back seat of a Cadillac.

The ease with which this patient was able to state his SUDs in a situation or to suggest a situation to fit a given SUDs level is characteristic of phobic patients. They have spent a lot of time thinking about and anticipating anxiety-arousing situations. However, one cannot ask them, "What are the dimensions along which your anxiety varies?" They would not know. The therapist must extract the dimensions, by comparing SUDs in various situations.

In general, it is easier to construct hierarchies along one dimension, although two and even three may be used. Quantifiable dimensions, such as size, time, space, distance, and number of objects are convenient and should be used whenever possible. However, the relevant dimensions of many phobias may not be quantifiable. Even when relevant, quantifiable dimensions do not always relate to anxiety in a linear function. Test anxiety provides an example of a nonlinear relationship between time and anxiety: discomfort is often higher a few hours before the exam than at its commencement. In such cases, the degree of anxiety rather than the time dimension determines the order of the items on the hierarchy. Thus "sitting in front of the exam" is presented earlier than "three hours before the exam."

An example of a one dimensional hierarchy, time, for test anxiety is provided by Wolpe (1973, p. 116):

1. A month before an examination.
2. Two weeks before an examination.
3. A week before an examination.
4. Five days before an examination.
5. Four days before an examination.
6. Three days before an examination.
7. Two days before an examination.
8. One day before an examination.
9. The night before an examination.
10. The examination papers lie face down before her.
11. Awaiting the distribution of examination papers.
12. Standing before the unopened doors of the examination room.
13. In the process of answering an examination paper.
14. On the way to the university on the day of an examination.

Proceeding with the previous example of the back seat phobia, the final hierarchy presented to Mr. S. was as follows (all scenes are in rear seats):

1. Being the only person in a parked bus.   10
2. Being alone in a parked Cadillac.   15
3. Being in a parked bus with another passenger and the driver.   25
4. Being in a parked van with another person and the driver.   35
5. Being in a moving bus with another passenger and driver.   40
6. Being in a moving van with another passenger and the driver.   50
7. Being in a parked Volkswagen with another passenger and the
   driver.   60
8. Being in a moving Cadillac with another passenger and the
   driver.   70
9. Being confined in a moving ambulance with driver and
   attendant.   85
10. Being in a moving Volkswagen with another passenger and the
    driver.   100

This hierarchy includes three dimensions: size of the vehicle, whether it is parked or moving, and number of passengers. The last dimension is varied only in the first two items in order to construct low anxiety-evoking situations.

Construction of a hierarchy concludes the data gathering; the stage is now set for the commencement of treatment. Nevertheless, relevant new information may emerge spontaneously or be actively sought later on during therapy, necessitating revisions in the original hierarchies. While adherence to a structured treatment program is recommended, the therapist should always be prepared to re-examine it and to deviate from it in the presence of novel information or unforeseen difficulties.

PREPARING THE PATIENT

After establishing the existence of unadaptive anxiety elicited by identifiable stimuli, the therapist proceeds to explain to the patient the nature of a neurotic habit.

T: Well, it is quite clear that being in the back seat of a moving car makes you feel highly anxious despite the fact that you recognize the senselessness of your reaction. It seems that you can't help feeling anxious in these situations.

P: That's exactly it, Doctor. But what's wrong with me?

T: In order to answer your question, let's consider how fear originates. You've probably observed children who keep away from the stove after accidentally burning their fingers. These children have associated stoves with pain in their minds. Thus a fear reaction was conditioned to a stove and generalized to other stoves as well. The same process has taken place in your case. After the accident where you were in the back seat and weren't able to get out of the two-door car, you experienced a normal fear reaction. At the same time, this accident resulted in your associating being in the rear seat of a car with an anxiety reaction even in situations where there is no danger. At that time you had learned an unadaptive habit which is also called a neurotic habit. Your fear of rear seats of small cars then generalized to rear seats of all vehicles, even when they are parked. As you can see, your reaction is a result of learning and, therefore, we are going to use procedures that will help you unlearn this habit.

P: That really makes a lot of sense, but it seems like such a strong fear. What sort of procedure are you going to use? The fear is very strong, you know.

T: Do you remember that in the last session we talked about various situations that make you feel fearful? We are going to put them in order from the least anxiety provoking to the most anxiety provoking. In addition, I am going to teach you a technique that will enable you to relax very deeply at will. Of course, a person cannot be anxious and relaxed at the same time. That means that relaxation and anxiety reactions are incompatible with one another and that relaxation inhibits anxiety. After you have learned to relax, I will ask you to imagine being in a situation that arouses only a little anxiety, like being in a parked bus. When you are deeply relaxed, you will be able to imagine the scene with very little and eventually no anxiety. In this way a new association is established between being in a bus and feeling calm. We will then proceed gradually with the various situations, associating each one of them with calmness. In this way, eventually you will be able to react again to being in the back seat of any car with the same calmness you felt before the accident. This technique is called systematic desensitization.

P: I think I see the point. But do you think that just imagining those scenes will help me?

At this point, the therapist can introduce the need for homework.

Homework

Patients are expected to carry out homework assignments and should be told about this at the outset, stressing that this will speed their progress.

For most specific phobias, it is feasible to do desensitization in imagination at the office, followed by homework *in vivo* (in actual practice). For example, while relaxing, patients may be asked to imagine the first scene from the hierarchy, and when anxiety to this scene has extinguished, they will be requested to shadow the situation *in vivo*, actually exposing themselves to it while relaxing. The same procedure is followed for each scene. The homework is explained to Mr. S. as follows:

T: You raised a very important question. Although often just imagining the scenes results in considerable reduction in the fear response, you'll be expected to do some homework in-between therapy sessions. This homework will consist of exposing yourself to those situations that you had previously imagined in the office during desensitization. For instance, after you can imagine the first scene in the parked bus without anxiety, I will ask you to do the same in reality. Can you think of a place where you would be able to do it?

P: Yes, the G Bus stops and sits on 6th and Main for about 15 minutes before it starts the run again. I could get on and sit in the back and then get off before it starts.

T: Very good. We'll have you do this for each step as we go along.

In some phobias, *in vivo* situations are not readily available and, therefore, require specific arrangements. When, for example, a patient who fears speaking in public is asked to imagine lecturing to five persons, it is not always possible to arrange for him or her to shadow this scene in reality right away. Arrangements for *in vivo* situations often call for the ingenuity of both therapist and patient.

Although patients may reach zero while imagining the scene, they often experience some anxiety *in vivo*. It is helpful to advise them in advance, "In real life we rarely go around with zero anxiety; there is always some tension. Up to now you have only imagined this scene which is not quite the same as really being there. When you try it at home this week, you may experience a small amount of anxiety, and you shouldn't worry about it. Also, the anxiety might be lower one day and somewhat higher the next; these fluctuations are quite normal and should be expected."

The probability of successful treatment should be discussed with the patient. A therapist might say, for example, "According to sources in the literature the proportion of phobic cases successfully treated by systematic desensitization is around 80%." If a client requests written information, one or two articles from among those cited in the introduction may be suggested.

The duration of treatment varies greatly from one patient to another. Desensitization is usually completed within 10 to 20 sessions, depending on the complexity of the phobia and the amount of homework accomplished by the patient. It is unwise, however, to raise the patient's expectations that treatment will be short since disappointment may follow if a larger investment in time is required. Therefore, it is advisable to state that treatment may take between 10 and 30 sessions.

In conclusion, it is suggested that patients be provided with a complete explanation of the desensitization procedure and of the rationale behind it. Prior to commencement of therapy, they should know as much as the therapist about the requirements, phases, and chances of success of the treatment. The level of explanation should be appropriate to the educational background of the patient, avoiding unnecessary technical terms. On the other hand, suitable scientific papers can be made available to well-educated clients who show an interest.

Relaxation Training

Systematic desensitization is based on the principle of reciprocal inhibition, that is, the inhibition of anxiety by the introduction of a response that is incompatible with it. The most common of these responses is deep muscle relaxation, derived from a technique developed by Jacobson (1938).

The training of a patient in deep muscle relaxation is described in detail by Wolpe (1973, pp. 104–108). Essentially, the procedure is as follows: The patient is asked to recline in a comfortable chair. The therapist begins by teaching the patient to distinguish between tensed muscles and relaxed ones. This distinction can be achieved by asking him or her to alternatively flex and release various muscle groups. Customarily the therapist begins with the muscles of the arms and continues with those of the face, the torso, and the legs. The following is a modified transcript of relaxation instructions given to a patient by Dr. Joseph Wolpe:

Dr. W: The reason why we do deep muscle relaxation training is that if you can relax your muscles really well, that is to say, beyond the point of ordinary muscle tone, then you get autonomic changes that are the opposite of anxiety. Now first, you have to be aware of what you are acting upon in becoming relaxed. You are acting on muscles, on tension in muscles. So now, in order to demonstrate this, I would like you to grip the arm of the chair quite strongly with your right hand. Now when you do that, you notice a number of sensations in the hand and probably in the forearm and the arm. With your left forefinger, point out all the places on your right side where you are getting tension or sensation. Yes, forearm. Where else? Fingers, that's right, and on the under surface of the forearm. Well, those are the main muscles that we expect. Keep on holding it, and I want you to notice one very important thing, and that is that the sensations in the hand are different than the sensations in the forearm. The sensations in the hand are due to pressure and touch; the sensations in the forearm are due to muscle tension. So I want you to register in your mind the exact quality of that sensation in your forearm, distinguishing it from other sensations. You don't need to describe it, just know it. And also remember those two places that you pointed to where you felt the tension in the forearm. Now let go. Let me draw attention to the muscle in the upper arm. I am going to hold you by the wrist and I want you to pull against me. Now pull against me. You should get tension, in your biceps. Feel it? O.K., now if you push— push—you should feel tension at the back of your arm. Do you? Good. Now I want you to think of the four muscles to which I've drawn your attention. Remember there were two muscles in the forearm and two in the arm. Think of those muscles on the right side on which we've been working, and also the same four muscles on the left side. Try to let go all of those muscles. In other words, try to insert a negative action into the four muscles on each arm. O.K., now do that. While you're doing it or as a result of doing it, you may notice some sensations such as tingling or warmth develop. Now don't try to make them happen; they will just come by themselves, and if you are aware of any sensations, let me know.

P: I feel some twitching.

Dr. W: It's quite common to get some twitching. Just keep on trying to let go even further. The more you let go, in fact, the more sensations you're likely to get. The most common sensations are tingling, feeling of warmth of the hands and right up the arms. Not everybody actually gets them, but most people do.

Now let us turn our attention to the next group of muscles, those of the head and neck. Those muscles are particularly important from an emotional point of view. It is not surprising when you consider how much of our emotions we express in that part of our body. We start with the muscles of the face. The upper face contains muscles of the forehead of which there are two groups. I want you to feel them both. First of all, raise your eyebrows. Good. The other muscles you can tense by frowning. So frown. Do you feel the tension? O.K. Now I'm going to give you a demonstration that tells you something about the step-like manner in which relaxation characteristically proceeds. I'm going to contract both my frowning muscles and my eyebrow-raising muscles simultaneously. You will see that I get a very worried expression. Then we're going to let the muscles go gradually. In fact, I'm going to let the decrements coincide with exhalation. Every time I breathe out, I'm going to let go of a little bit more of the tension. Now these steps as I said, are artificially controlled. But spontaneous relaxation does take place in steps, and these controlled steps do give you something of a feeling of what happens. So here it is—the two groups of muscles contracted simultaneously produces this worried expression, see? Now I let go a little . . . more . . . more . . . more . . . more . . . more . . . . From about this point onward, there is very little that you can see, but the relaxation goes on. And this part that you can't see is the important part that carries with it the emotional effects that we feel. Now I don't want you to imitate precisely what I've just done, but I do want you to see that you can concentrate on these forehead muscles and smooth out your forehead. Good. . . . very good. You see, it really takes quite a bit of practice. In fact, when you're first learning to relax, it can easily take 20 or 30 minutes to relax one muscle imperfectly. But later on when you have practiced, you can relax the whole body very well in a matter of maybe 2 or 3 minutes.

O.K., now the next group of muscles are those in the jaws that you can feel by biting on your teeth. If you do that, you feel tension in front of your ears, and also in the temple, although the temple muscles are not as easy to feel. Relax those muscles. The ordinary effect of relaxing the jaws is that your mouth drops open. If the mouth does not drop open, then you know that you are not relaxing those muscles. Next we have the muscles of the tongue, which you can feel by pressing the tip of your tongue up against the roof of your mouth. Now where do you feel the tension? You should feel it partly in the tongue itself, but mostly in the floor of your mouth, because most of the tongue muscles are in the area between the branches of the jaw bone. When you relax the tongue muscle, you may feel a sensation which may be a numb feeling, or quite often, a feeling that the tongue has become too large for the mouth to retain it. It seems to rest on the back teeth.

After the tongue, we have the muscles of the neck. In order to feel the muscles of the neck that we're interested in, you should sit straight up. Don't lean back at all. Now the muscles of the back of your neck are in action; just by having your attention drawn to them. If you were to let those muscles go, of course, the head would fall forward. So now let them go. Commonly, when a person is not accustomed to relaxing and the head is allowed to fall forward like this, there is a feeling of discomfort or even pain in the back of the neck, because the whole weight of the head is being imposed upon a few muscle fibers. Relaxing the neck muxcles should be practiced, partly with the head leaning forward, and partly with the head leaning back against the chair. Next come the muscles of the shoulders which you can feel, when you raise your arms horizontally. You can feel some of them at the shoulder tip, and then if you swing your arms back, you can feel muscles around the shoulder blade. If you swing your arm forward across your chest, you feel the muscles in front of your chest, and then coming back to the original position, you move your hand upwards and feel some other muscles at the back of the neck. Having recognized these muscles, you can proceed to relax them. Then we have the muscles of the back that you feel by arching your back. You can feel two parallel columns on either side of the spine. The muscles of the abdomen can be felt by tightening your abdomen as though you're expecting someone to punch you in the belly.

Let's concentrate on the lower part of your body, beginning with your feet. You can feel a little muscle inside the sole by pulling your toes inside your shoe. You can feel your calf muscle by pointing your toes away from you. Then you can feel the muscles in your shin by pointing your toe upward. All right, do you feel that? Now for the groin and thigh muscles; you can feel those in the front by straightening your leg and lifting your knee. Feel that muscle? You can feel those in the back, the hamstrings, by bending your knee. Bend your knee. That's it, feel the hamstring? Good. You can feel the muscles on the outside of the thigh by pressing your knee sideways against my hand. Do you feel the tension in those muscles? Now I will move my hand toward the inside of your knee and I want you to push against it there so that you contract the muscles on the innerside of your thigh. O.K. That covers the relaxation training of the main muscles of the body, those that are routinely practiced. Relaxation should be practiced for 10 to 15 minutes twice a day until there is good control of the relaxation.

Patients are asked to practice relaxation at home for a minimum of 15 minutes per day. The SUDs scale is generally used to assess the patient's progress in learning relaxation. Formal desensitization does not begin until the patient is able to relax to a level of zero or near-zero SUDs. This usually requires two to six sessions of training and practice at home. In addition to self-report, it is advisable to observe whether body tension is evident, particularly in the facial muscles. Most patients are quite reliable in communicating their level of anxiety; in assessing this level each patient usually focuses on the area of the body that is most often tensed during discomfort evoking situations (e.g., stomach, neck, jaw, thighs).

Deep muscle relaxation is not the sole counter-conditioning agent to anxiety used in systematic desensitization. Other agents include tranquilizing drugs (valium, brevitol, etc.), single inhalations of a carbon dioxide/oxygen mixture, yoga, transcendental meditation, and expression of anger. Relaxation is preferred over other counter-conditioning agents since it is a readily learned skill that can be used in a variety of anxiety-arousing situations.

Hierarchy construction and relaxation training can be conducted within the same session. Thus relaxation training can begin immediately after the initial interview. Even if the therapist decides later on to employ therapeutic techniques other than systematic desensitization, relaxation may still prove beneficial. Patients may utilize this acquired skill to relax themselves in life situations that evoke tension.

COURSE OF THERAPEUTIC INTERVENTION

When the patient has mastered the relaxation technique and a hierarchy has been constructed, the therapist proceeds with systematic desensitization. Essentially, the procedure involves the presentation in imagination of the scenes while the patient is relaxed. Beginning with the lowest on the hierarchy, each scene is presented and continued for 5 to 10 seconds after the patient signals (by raising a forefinger) that the scene is clear. This procedure is repeated until the scene ceases to evoke anxiety. Alternatively, the scene may be imagined continously until the patient signals that it no longer evokes anxiety. The former procedure is illustrated as follows:

T: O.K. We're ready to begin now. Push the chair back into the reclining position and relax yourself. (By now the patient is able to relax him/herself without assistance from the therapist.) Begin by relaxing your arms completely and continue as always. Signal me by raising your right forefinger about one inch when you reach a level of zero. . . .

P: I'm at zero.

T: It's better if you don't speak unless necessary since it disturbs the relaxation. Just raise your finger . . . (finger is raised). Fine. Now, I'll ask you to imagine the first scene, signal me when you have a clear image of it in your mind. Imagine that you are coming into work and you pass by John who looks at you with a scowl. Signal when it's clear. (Patient signals after 5 seconds). Continue imagining. (10 seconds pass). Now, erase the scene from your mind. Signal me if it raised your anxiety. (Patient signals). How much anxiety did you feel? Just whisper a number.

P: About 5.

T: Relax again and signal me when you reach zero.

When a scene no longer evokes anxiety, the next on the hierarchy is presented in the same manner. If the hierarchy is correctly constructed, generalization will occur so the next scene that formerly evoked 20 SUDs will now evoke only 10. In general, therefore, when anxiety is eliminated for each hierarchical step, subsequent items will evoke considerably less anxiety than at the beginning of treatment. Although a scene may require as many as six presentations before anxiety reduces to zero, often two or three suffice.

At the initial presentation of a scene, it is not unusual to find that the patient's report at the time of the hierarchy construction was inaccurate. If anxiety to a scene was underestimated, but does not exceed 20 or 25 SUDs, desensitization may proceed. When anxiety exceeds this level, it is advisable to find an intermediate scene.

In general, about 20 to 30 minutes of each session are devoted to desensitization. Occasionally, patients are able to concentrate for longer periods. In the remainder of the session, other treatment techniques may be employed. In the early stages of the treatment, part of the session may also be used for completion of the hierarchy and construction of new hierarchies for other fears. Homework instructions consist of direct in vivo confrontation of those situations that had been imagined in the office. Patients are instructed to relax while exposing themselves to the assigned homework situation. Occasionally a tranquilizing drug or the presence of a trusted person may be suggested as an aid. As treatment progresses, these facilitating conditions are gradually removed.

When starting a new session of desensitization, it is not necessary to repeat already-imagined scenes. Rather, the therapist begins with the last scene from the previous session, or at most, from one just below it.

In order to illustrate the clinical implementation of systematic desensitization, the following two cases are given in detail. The first case demonstrates the use of a unidimensional hierarchy for a specific phobia (public speaking) presented as the patient's main complaint. The second case required a two-dimensional hierarchy for a common fear (criticism) that often accompanies other neurotic habits, although it is rarely presented as the primary problem. In each case, general life history taken during the initial sessions is presented in summary form.

Public Speaking Phobia

General Life History

The patient, Shawn, was a 35-year-old white male with a Ph.D. in chemistry. He was employed by a university where his responsibilities included lecturing, research, and presentations at professional conventions. Shawn was married and divorced twice and was dating several women at the commencement of treatment. He recognized that his interactions with women were not satisfactory but did not wish treatment for this problem. The patient was an only child. He described his mother as anxious and overprotective. She had been agoraphobic until 5 years previous to Shawn's treatment and had relied on him to accompany her whenever she left the house. Widowed for the last three years, she was very dependent on Shawn's company. His father, a civil engineer, was described as a passive and withdrawn man who rarely displayed emotion toward his wife or son. The father had stuttered heavily and, therefore, had avoided social interactions throughout his life.

Although he had one or two close friends as a child, Shawn felt uncomfortable in social situations, especially parties, and avoided interactions that would draw attention to himself. At the time of treatment, he had several good friends and was active socially. Academically, his grades were mediocre until graduate school, where he became a "straight A" student. Shawn has always doubted his intellectual abilities and was uncomfortable before exams but did not have difficultly speaking in class. Sexual development was normal and presented no problems.

Session 1 (Information Gathering)

T: What can I do for you?

P: The whole problem started 2 years ago. It's very difficult for me to give a lecture or talk about my work in front of even a couple of students. Lately I've avoided lecturing, but students or other faculty come into my office to talk about a chemistry problem and that makes me very uncomfortable.

T: Do you feel anxious only at the university, or also when you're talking to friends?

P: Well; it has nothing to do with where I am but what the topic is. It's only when I talk about my work that I feel anxious. So if I'm talking to my friends about something else, I'm fine, but if it's about chemistry, immediately I start to feel my heart race and my mouth gets dry and my hands start to shake.

T: You said it started 2 years ago. Did anything special happen at that time?

P: Well, I've always been somewhat afraid. It's normal to be a bit nervous before a presentation, isn't it?

T: It depends on the degree of discomfort. Most people feel a small amount of anxiety when speaking to a group.

P: Well, I suppose I always felt more than most people, but I could handle it. Then 2 years ago, I was asked to teach a graduate course that I didn't know a lot about. I always spend a lot of time preparing. So even though I knew the material, I still felt very uptight before the class and during the lecture.

T: And what about after that?

P: After this course the fear seemed to get worse. More and more types of situations started to bother me. Now, even if a student stops by to talk about chemistry, I get uptight.

At this point the SUDs scale is introduced, since the information gathered from now on will be used toward hierarchy construction.

T: Let's be specific about the amount of anxiety you're feeling in these situations. We'll use a scale, to measure your subjective level of discomfort, and call it the SUDs scale. This scale ranges from 0 to 100. Zero indicates complete lack of discomfort or anxiety and 100 represents extreme anxiety, panicky feelings. On this scale, how would you rate your anxiety level right now?

P: Oh, about 15.

T: O.K., now what about the situation when a graduate student comes to your office for informal discussion?

P: I'd be 30.

T: And if two students come to your office?

P: That would be 35 to 40.

T: 10 people?

P: That would be 60 to 70 because that's formal already.

T: How would you feel in a lecture of 50 people?

P: You mean during or beforehand?

T: Does that make a difference?

P: Yes, I'm much more anxious before a lecture than during. If 50 people were there, I'd be 90 before and 75 during.

T: How about 100 people?

P: Oh, that would be the worst. Over 100 people doesn't make any difference. A hundred or thousand, it's all the same. I'd be at 100 before and 95 during the lecture.

T: It's clear from our conversation that the number of people in the lecture is directly related to how uptight you get. What else might affect your anxiety?

P: Oh, I've thought about all that many times because I've tried to make things as easy on myself as possible. For instance, if I'm behind a podium and only my face is visible, I feel a bit less anxious. If I show slides, that helps because the lights are off and they watch the slides and not me.

T: Anything else that's related to how anxious you get?

P: Depends on how important the lecture is. You know, if it's a national convention, that's worse, of course, than a local lecture. And informal talks are a lot easier than formal ones. The length of time I have to talk matters too; 1½ hours is much worse than 20 minutes or half an hour.

T: O.K. We know that the number of people, the importance of the lecture, how visible you are, and the length of the lecture are all relevant factors. Any other factors you are aware of?

P: Yes—the more time for discussion the more anxious I am because I can prepare a lecture, but in a discussion I don't know what questions will be asked.

T: How about time? If you have to give a lecture a month from now, are you as anxious as when you have to give one two days from now?

P: Of course I'm more anxious the closer it gets.

It is apparent that several dimensions affect the patient's level of discomfort in public speaking: time, size of audience, length of lecture, visibility, discussion time, importance of the event. In construction of the hierarchy, the therapist has two options: each dimension may constitute a separate hierarachy, or five of the six dimensions may be held constant at their highest point while the sixth is varied. The second option is clearly more efficient and was, therefore, tried first. Sometimes, however, more than one dimension should be varied to eliminate the conditioned anxiety.

P: I guess all these details are important.

T: Yes, they are. Let me explain what we will do. You have learned to associate any interaction related to your work with anxiety. Our goal in therapy is to have you unlearn this unadaptive habit so you can lecture and present with very little or no anxiety. The technique we are going to use is called systematic desensitization. You were *sensitized* to speaking in public and now we need to *desensitize* you.

P: That makes sense. How are you going to do this?

T: You will first learn a response that counteracts the anxiety response and, of course, the most obvious choice is relaxation. Obviously, one cannot be both anxious and relaxed at the same time. Once you have learned how to relax well, I will ask you to imagine those situations that make you anxious starting with the least disturbing ones and gradually moving to more anxiety provoking ones.

P: I understand, but how will that help?

T: By repeated association between lecturing and a relaxed state, rather than an anxious state, you will break the habit of being anxious in those situations.

P: But will just imagining those situations help when I'm really there?

T: That's a very good question. Usually the effects of just imagining these situations without any anxiety generalizes to real situations. But I'm going to assign homework to you so you can practice in reality what we've done in the office in imagination.

P: You mean I'll have to arrange for different types of lectures to practice?

T: Exactly.

P: I hope I can work that out.

T: That will be very helpful.

The first session terminates with the introduction of the rationale for systematic desensitization.

Second Session

The second session is usually spent on history taking as summarized previously. Relaxation training, as described on pages 58 to 62, was begun at the end of this session.

Third Session (Hierarchy Construction and Relaxation Training)

The therapist has chosen in this case to construct a single hierarchy holding constant the dimensions of importance of lecture, length of presentation, visibility, size of audience, and discussion time. This was done by selecting a maximally disturbing lecture—a major presentation of one hour's length with a ½-hour discussion in a national convention with an expected audience of 150 people where no podium or slides would be used. Shawn was actually due to deliver such a lecture four months hence.

T: Let's suppose that it's three months before your presentation at the convention in Boston. You're sitting at your desk working on your paper. On the 0 to 100 scale, how much discomfort will you feel?

P: Three months before? I won't be anxious yet. It's too far off.

T: How about 10 weeks?

P: That's still minimal if at all.

T: How about 2 months?

P: At two months I'd just start to worry, say 25.

T: How would you feel six weeks prior to presenting?

P: Same, still 25.

T: One month?

P: That's slightly higher, say 30.

T: How about 3 weeks before the lecture?

P: I guess that would be about 40.

T: Two weeks?

P: Now it starts to get really uncomfortable—45.

T: How about 10 days?

P: Still 45 I think.

T: One week?

P: Yes, that makes a difference, one week is pretty short, I'd be 55.

T: Six days?

P: Still about the same.

T: Five days before presenting in Boston?

P: Sixty. From then on I think about it constantly and I'm always upset about it. I don't sleep well and I don't concentrate at work.

T: How would you feel four days before?

P: That would be about 65.

T: And three days?

P: Pretty bad. I'd say 75.

T: Two days.

P: Still 75.

T: How about one day before the lecture?

P: I'd be close to panic, about 80 then.

T: Imagine that it's seven hours before, say it's 8:00 A.M. and you're presenting at 3:00 in the afternoon.

P: I'll be 85 then.

T: And 1 hour before?

P: At this point I'm a real wreck, 90 for sure.

T: Entering the lecture room just before your talk?

P: That's the worst, 100. It upsets me even to think about it.

On the basis of the above interview the following hierarchy was constructed:

1.	2 months prior to presentation	25
2.	1 month prior to presentation	30
3.	3 weeks prior to presentation	40
4.	2 weeks prior to presentation	45
5.	1 week prior to presentation	55
6.	5 days prior to presentation	60
7.	4 days prior to presentation	65
8.	3 days prior to presentation	75
9.	1 day prior to presentation	80
10.	7 hours prior to presentation	85
11.	1 hour prior to presentation	90
12.	Entering the lecture room	100

Not all patients are as articulate as Shawn. Some hesitate to attach numbers to items for fear they won't be accurate. Others insist on clarifying minute details of a scene before committing themselves to rating the scene. The therapist may reassure those patients that the details are unimportant and that perfect accuracy is unnecessary, as long as he can imagine the scene clearly.

Fourth Through Tenth Sessions (Systematic Desensitization)

These seven sessions were devoted to relaxation, hierarchy presentation, homework assignment, and discussion of progress. The following verbatim material exemplifies the use of systematic desensitization.

T: Did you practice your relaxation?

P: Yes, almost every day for about 15 or 20 minutes as you said. Wednesday was a bad day—I was on campus all day and went straight to dinner with friends and didn't get home until 11:30 so I just went straight to bed.

T: That's O.K. as long as you practiced almost every day. How well can you relax?

P: Not as good as here, but I got pretty close to zero the last couple of times.

T: Let's try it here. Do you need me to help?

P: I'll try it on my own and I'll ask for help if I need it.

T: O.K. Settle back then and relax yourself. Signal me by raising your right forefinger about an inch when you get to zero. (Shawn relaxes himself within five minutes and signals the therapist.)

P: How much anxiety do you feel?

T: Zero.

P: Good. I'd like you now to imagine yourself sitting in your living room at home reading the newspaper. Signal me as before when the scene is clear in your mind. (Shawn signals with his finger after 30 seconds.)

T: Good. Continue to imagine the scene (10 seconds pass). Erase the scene and open your eyes. Can you describe in detail the scene you just imagined?

P: Well, I was sitting on my couch in the evening after dinner and I was reading the front page of the paper.

T: What did you read?

P: It was about the situation in Cambodia.

T: Was the scene very clear to you?

P: Yes, quite clear.

T: Was there any discomfort with the scene or with closing your eyes and imagining it?

P: No, none at all, I was quite comfortable.

After thus ascertaining that the patient can visualize clearly and is not disturbed by complying with the requirements of the procedure, the therapist proceeds with the first scene on the hierarchy.

T: Relax again and signal me when you are zero. (30 seconds pass and patient signals.) O.K. Imagine yourself sitting by your desk examining data that you will include in your lecture in Boston exactly 2 months from now. Signal when the scene is clear. (Patient signals.) Keep the scene (10 seconds pass). Stop the scene. How much anxiety did you feel?

P: 10.

T: Relax again and signal when you're ready. (Patient signals after 30 seconds.) Now, imagine again that you are working on your lecture which will be given two months from today. Signal when it's clear. (Patient signals after 15 seconds.) Continue imagining. (10 seconds pass.) Stop imagining. How much anxiety did you feel?

P: 15.

T: Relax again and signal when you are at zero. (Patient signals after 45 seconds.) Imagine the same scene again, one month before you're giving the lecture. Signal when it's clear. (Patient signals after 10 seconds.) Continue imagining (10 seconds pass). Stop the scene. How anxious did the scene make you?

P: 10.

Two more presentations were required to eliminate the anxiety associated with this scene. The third scene (three weeks before presenting) evoked 20 SUDs in the first presentation and reached 0 SUDs after four additional presentations. The fourth scene (two weeks before) evoked no anxiety. The fifth scene (one week before) evoked 15 SUDs, which reduced to 0 SUDs after five additional presentations.

As is apparent from the above verbatim material, the amount of anxiety reported at the first presentation in imagination of each scene was lower than that reported by the patient at the time the hierarchy was constructed. This discrepancy becomes larger as the patient progresses along the hierarchy; for instance, the fifth scene which would have aroused 55 SUDs evokes 10 in imagination. This increased difference is due to generalization of habituation along items on the hierarchy.

At the sixth scene, Shawn experienced 30 SUDs, which decreased only slightly even after eight repetitions. He reported he could not imagine himself five days before lecturing without experiencing anxiety. In order to facilitate habituation it was decided to introduce intermediate steps by varying the importance of the lecture, the number of people present, and the length of the presentation. In this way, the following "subhierarchy" was constructed:

a. 5 days before giving a 1-hour lecture at a friend's class to 7 students   35

b. 5 days before giving a 2-hour lecture at a friends' class to 7 people   45

c. 5 days before giving a 1-hour lecture to 30 people in a different department   55

d. 2 days before giving a 1-hour lecture to a friend's class of 7 people   55

e. 2 days before giving a 1-hour lecture to 30 people in a different
department   60

Anxiety did not exceed 10 SUDs in the first presentation of these hierarchy items. When discomfort to the "subhierarchy" extinguished, the
therapist returned to the original hierarchy. Anxiety to the sixth scene
then extinguished rapidly.

In general, when anxiety persists despite repetitions of a scene, it may
indicate the need to introduce intermediate steps. These may vary along
the same dimension along which the original hierarchy is constructed. For
example, the hierarchy for an agoraphobic patient may skip from the 14th
floor to the 18th floor. If anxiety does not reduce to zero for the latter
item, intermediate steps of 15th, 16th, and 17th floors may be introduced.
However, in some instances of a unidimensional hierarchy, adding intermediate items on the same dimension does not facilitate extinction. In
such situations other relevant dimensions must be varied as in Shawn's
case.

The seventh scene (four days prior to lecturing) evoked 20 SUDs,
which reduced to 0 SUDs with three presentations. The remaining four
scenes followed approximately the same pattern of extinction. Four sessions were required to complete both the original and the "sub" hierarchies. After the third session, thinking about going to Boston to give the
lecture in three weeks evoked 15 SUDs in contrast to the original 45
SUDs. Minor lectures given at the university during this period evoked almost no discomfort. On finishing the hierarchy, Shawn felt that the final
item, "entering the lecture room," no longer constituted the worst scene,
and he added the following items: 5 minutes before presenting, uttering
the first sentence while several listeners look at him, his mind goes blank
midway through the lecture for 5 seconds, then 10 seconds, 15 seconds,
and 20 seconds.

When anxiety reduces to the higher items on the hierarchy, patients are
often able to differentiate among items that formerly appeared to be
equally disturbing. At this point, additional items may be added to the top
of the hierarchy for desensitization.

After the original hierarchy items were desensitized, Shawn felt no
need to over-prepare for lectures at the university and the upcoming national conference. In addition, he no longer found himself trying to avoid
lectures. Unfortunately, 2 weeks before the Boston presentation, the entire conference was canceled. However, a regional conference in which
he would be the final speaker at a symposium was scheduled for 4 weeks

hence. Since he requested additional desensitization for this presentation, the following hierarchy was constructed:

1.	2 days before the symposium	20
2.	1 day before the symposium	30
3.	The morning of the lecture	40
4.	The first speaker begins his talk	50
5.	The second speaker begins his talk	55
6.	10 minutes before second speaker finishes	65
7.	Chairman introduces Shawn	70
8.	First 2 sentences of his talk	75
9.	Standing in front of the microphone before speaking	80

All of these items were desensitized within one session since no item required more than two presentations. While the patient felt comfortable anticipating the lecture and its presentation, he still experienced anxiety when thinking about the discussion period. Further inquiry regarding the nature of the anxiety about the discussion period revealed a fear of criticism specific to his professional stature. Accordingly, still another hierarchy was constructed including two relevant dimensions, complexity of the questions and severity of the criticisms expressed by the audience:

1. "What other information did you get from the data?" 20
2. "How did you collect the data?" 30
3. "I've never encountered the problem you describe in my own work." 35
4. "Do I understand you to mean that little worthwhile research has been done in this area?" 40
5. "How do you account for reliability and validity of your results?" 50
6. "Others have reported contradictory results. Can you explain this?" 60
7. "I think there are some important factors that you have overlooked." 70
8. "Those statistics are meaningless for this research." 80
9. "You have told us nothing new or of interest in your presentation today." 90

Systematic desensitization was applied to this hierarchy in this manner. Three sessions were required to complete it.

Immediately following the last session of desensitization, Shawn gave an important 1½ hour lecture. He had 20 SUDs of anticipatory anxiety and felt calm and comfortable during the lecture. In a final summary session following this presentation, Shawn expressed some concern about the presence of anticipatory anxiety. The therapist advised him that the experience of some anxiety before an important lecture is normal and should not be of concern.

At the end of treatment Shawn discovered he was no longer afraid of job interviews and began to look for positions in other universities; he, indeed, moved to the Midwest a few months later. At a 2-year follow-up he reported being completely free of public-speaking anxiety.

Fear of Criticism

Susan, 30 years old, requested treatment for anxiety in social situations. She had been separated from her husband for 1 ½ years, and divorce was pending. After several years of secretarial work, she had recently completed a masters degree in business and found a satisfactory position with a medium-sized company. The separation and her new job had increased her discomfort because of the required exposure to new social situations. When asked about any history of these complaints, Susan reported that feelings of anxiety in social situations had begun in high school when she and her family moved from a small midwestern town to an east coast city where she felt out of place and unsophisticated in relation to her peers. She became concerned about her style of dress, make-up, hair, and speech; and this was heightened by overhearing critical remarks on several occasions. Although she made a few friends, she noticed increasing anxiety in the presence of peers and teachers. She began to avoid school parties and became uncomfortable answering questions or volunteering information in class. These fears persisted to the present time with some increase in anxiety in unfamiliar social situations.

> T: When you say that you feel uncomfortable with other people, what do you mean?
> P: Well, I just don't feel at ease.
> T: What situations make you feel ill-at-ease?
> P: I don't know, it depends. Sometimes it feels like it's coming out of the blue. I can be out with my boyfriend and one time I feel uncomfortable and another, I feel fine.

T: Can you give me a recent example of a situation where you felt uncomfortable?

P: It's hard to remember a specific time. I feel uncomfortable a lot of the time. All I know is I feel better when I'm alone, but I don't really want to be alone.

It is not uncommon for a patient to have difficulty in presenting a clear account of their fears. When the therapist is unable to define the dimensions for hierarchy construction, the information can be obtained by asking the patient to keep a daily log between sessions. The log should include a description of situations, persons involved, the nature of the interactions, and associated thoughts and feelings. This record is then examined during the following treatment session.

Susan was asked to record all events that raised her anxiety level. She was taught the SUD scale and was asked to use this in her recording.

T: I see that on Monday evening you say you were eating dinner out with Mark (boyfriend) and you were anxious when you met some friends. Is that right?

P: Mark's business acquaintance, not my friends. Yes . . . we were having a good time—my anxiety was maybe 15 or so—and then this man came to the table and said "Hello" to Mark and something else. Then Mark introduced me and I immediately felt flushed. . . .

T: What was your level then?

P: Well, maybe 35 or 40 but it went a bit higher, maybe 50 when he introduced his wife to us. They were only there for a couple of minutes, but it took me awhile to calm down again.

T: What were you concerned about that caused you to feel uncomfortable?

P: I didn't really think about it at the time . . . what they thought of me, I guess. Also, I want to make a good impression for Mark. You know what I mean. . . .

T: Sure, I understand. It seems important to you what people think of you.

P: Yes. That's right, now that I think about it.

T: O.K. Let's look at the other situations here. On Tuesday you were anxious at work because of Ellen. What happened then?

P: Ellen's a secretary—she works for the part of the office I'm in, so she's sort of my secretary and about four other people's. I needed typing done by Wednesday early and asked her if she could get it done on time. She must've been in a bad mood or something because she said to me "Look, I'm going home at 5:00, that's quitting time, and I have a family." She really took me by surprise. It was a 5-minute job, and I asked her at 4:00. She knew that this letter had to go put in the morning mail.

T: What did you say?

P: I really didn't say anything. I just left. I felt sort of hurt at first, you know, and I don't think I'd done anything before to upset her, but still, I felt pretty nervous—it's such a stupid thing to get nervous about, but this kind of thing happens all the time. Like once I was trying on shoes and the salesman said something really impatient and I just got flustered and ended up buying a pair of shoes that I didn't really like. That's really dumb, isn't it?

T: Well, it sounds as if you get easily upset whenever someone gets annoyed with you. Do you have a sort of automatic reaction—your body gets tense and you feel like leaving?

P: Yes, that's exactly right. But you know, they don't even have to get annoyed with me. If I just hear someone sounding angry at somebody else, even strangers on the street, I get uptight.

T: Anger in general, then, makes you feel anxious, right? (Nod, yes.) The next situation involved your boss. What was that about?

P: For the last two weeks I was working on a report for one of our clients and I finished it on Monday and gave it to my boss to look at. He was sort of critical.

T: What did he say?

P: He said something like "This is quite comprehensive, but it's really a bit too long."

T: That wasn't a very harsh criticism, was it?

P: No, I suppose not, but even that made me feel almost like crying. In fact, I felt like it but I controlled myself.

T: So even mild criticism will bother you a great deal.

Susan continued to record anxiety-evoking events for 2 weeks while the history was taken and details about her current concerns discussed.

History

Susan's early history was unremarkable except for some marital difficulties between her parents that engendered a 2-month separation when she was ten. She felt closest to her father, who was a quiet, unassertive man. Her mother was described as critical and controlling, less physically demonstrative than her father. Susan recalled striving to please her mother, especially in schoolwork, with little recognition or praise for her efforts.

The relationship between herself and her two older sisters had been somewhat strained but was quite comfortable at present.

Susan's academic performance was always considerably above average. However, she reported feeling uncomfortable with peers, especially girls, whom she described as catty and critical. She began dating at age 16, had sexual relations at age 18, and experienced no difficulty in this area. Susan met her husband during college and married him after graduation. She did not regret their current separation and felt it was due to divergent interests and to difficulty in working out problems.

A Fear Survey Schedule identified moderate fear to heights and to medical situations. Stronger fear was reported to public speaking, being observed, criticism, failures, looking foolish, and rejection.

Hierarchy Construction

The daily records indicated that in addition to being disturbed by all situations in which she felt she was being evaluated, Susan also had difficulty asserting herself. Further clarification was necessary, however, to construct the hierarchies.

T: It seems pretty clear from all you've said and written down that you have two types of problems to deal with. The first is your oversensitivity to criticism, especially when it's said in an angry tone. The second is your difficulty in expressing your feelings to other people. Let's concentrate on the first problem for now, since we may find it has some bearing on your difficulty in asserting yourself.

P: That makes sense, O.K.

T: About the negative evaluation situations, Susan, you seem to be more disturbed by criticism from women than men. Is that right?

P: Yes, but it's not so simple, because if Mark didn't like a new dress or something, that's worse than if Jane (a close girlfriend) didn't like it.

T: I see. What makes Mark's opinion so important? How do you explain it?

P: Well, I'm very close to Mark. I mean, if I'm not very close to the person that's criticizing me, then women are more of a problem than men, but once I know someone well, then the sex doesn't make any difference; it's how important they are. I've always had more men friends than women friends—I seem to avoid women because I don't feel very comfortable around them in the beginning, especially women my age.

T: Does it matter how old the person is?

P: With criticism? I guess maybe it is—somebody who was quite a bit younger, say 20 or 22 wouldn't upset me much. I guess that's true of older people too. On second thought, I don't think age really makes that much difference.

T: O.K., I think I have a good idea of the type of people who upset you. Let's talk now about the type of criticism that disturbs you. For instance, if Mark said he was surprised that you didn't know a certain fact, would it bother you as much as his not liking your dress?

P: No, it wouldn't. I'm pretty sure I'm fairly intelligent and I'd just think, "Well, I didn't know it because I never heard it before." But my taste in clothes, in anything really, that's upsetting.

T: I see. What about remarks like "she's too shy," "she's often late," "she's inconsiderate,"—that sort of thing.

P: Being inconsiderate is the only one that would bother me.

T: O.K. It would help if we could make a list now of the types of negative remarks that would upset you and another list of the people who might say them. We'll put these in order from least disturbing to most disturbing and see what we have. Let's start with the list of people.

P: Let me think . . . for people, the least upsetting are, of course, people I barely know.

T: Like who?

P: Names? Well, Evelyn, my hairdresser, or Mr. Stern, my landlord. Next would be people at work, like secretaries and clerks. For the others, it gets a bit confused because it sort of makes a difference what they are criticizing me for.

T: Can you give me some instances?

P: Well, Jane, Mark, my mother.

T: Your mother?

P: Yes, she has a way of saying certain things that really sets me on edge. Things like my coming to visit her more often, or my choice of apartments.

T: I see, O.K. Who else shall we list? What about at work, people other than secretaries or clerks. I think we left them out.

P: You want names? Um, my boss, Mr. Winston, would be the worst, and less than him would be Francis—she has a know-it-all way about her.

T: Anybody else that especially bothers you at work?

P: Not really. No.

T: What about other people outside work?

P: Bob, an old friend of mine—that's about it. The others I can think of aren't really that important.

T: O.K. Now, let's list types of criticisms.

P: Well, as I said, my taste in clothes, that's high.

T: O.K.

P: Oh, somebody thinking I don't look properly dressed for the occasion. Someone might say I was too thin, that would bother me, even if I'm not.

T: Any implication that you're not attractive?

P: Yes, that's right. Also, being inconsiderate, as I said before.

T: What about being called "irresponsible," or "selfish," or "unsophisticated," or "lazy"?

P: Only "unsophisticated" would really upset me.

T: What about criticisms of your professional work?

P: That would bother me a little, more so if it was about looking unsure or nervous with clients or at a conference when I have to speak.

T: O.K. We'll list these in a minute. Any others you can think of?

P: Not right now.

T: O.K. Then let's put this together. I'm going to list all the people across the top of the page in the order of how much they upset you. Down the side of the page we'll list the criticisms that bother you, again in the order that they disturb you. Then, for each person and criticism, I'll ask you to tell me how much it would bother you on the scale from zero to a hundred. Do you follow me?

P: Yes.

The items of the two-dimensional hierarchy and the corresponding SUDs levels are given in Table 1.

Items on the hierarchy are presented in the order of their anxiety-evoking potential. Hence, all the items in Table 1 marked 10 SUDs will be presented first, followed by items marked 20 SUDs, 30 SUDs, and so forth. Some cells remain blank since Susan felt that a particular person would not express a given criticism.

Systematic desensitization was conducted as described previously. Susan progressed steadily through the hierarchy without difficulty in eight sessions. Assertiveness training (see Chapter 9) was begun during the eighth session when it became apparent that although her discomfort diminished considerably, she still experienced some difficulty in responding to criticism.

After a total of 14 sessions of systematic desensitization and assertive-

Table 1: A two-dimensional hierarchy for fear of criticism.

	"too thin"	"inconsiderate"	"work could be improved"	"poor choice in apartment (furniture)"	"unsophisticated"	"looks nervous"	"improperly dressed"	"distastefully dressed"
Evelyn	10	10	—	—	20	10	30	40
Mr. Stern	—	20	30	—	30	40	35	45
Sara	20	30	—	20	35	50	40	50
Francis	30	35	—	25	40	50	40	50
Mr. Winston	—	40	50	—	35	75	50	50
Jane	35	50	—	35	50	50	60	60
Mark	50	30	—	45	55	45	70	75
Mother	40	60	—	70	75	60	80	85

ness training Susan reported that she felt comfortable with mild-to-moderate criticisms. Progress was particularly apparent in her reaction to her mother. When her mother disapproved of a newly purchased dress, Susan experienced no distress when saying "I'm sorry you don't like it; I guess we just have different tastes." At a 1-year follow-up, the gains had been maintained.

SPECIAL PROBLEMS

A myriad of factors may complicate the application of systematic desensitization. While the following is not an exhaustive list, the difficulties most likely to be encountered are included.

Inability to Relax

Generally, the vast majority of clients are able to achieve relaxation. Those who cannot, despite careful following of instructions, may be hampered by a fear of losing control, discomfort in the therapist's presence, or concern about being observed. Often fear of being observed can be overcome simply by turning the patient's chair around. With patients who are fearful of losing control, the therapist should emphasize the active role that the patient takes in relaxation, while avoiding phrases such as "Let go." Discomfort in the therapist's presence can be allieviated by teaching relaxation with the aid of taped instructions without the presence of the therapist. If necessary the patient can be desensitized *in vivo* to the therapist's presence.

If the patient experiences difficulty in relaxing, tranquilizing drugs, carbon dioxide, or biofeedback may be introduced. Of the tranquilizing drugs, valium is probably the most commonly used both to enhance relaxation and as an aid when exposure *in vivo* is implemented. The optimal dosage varies greatly across individuals. A dosage high enough to eliminate anxiety but low enough to avoid sleepiness is required and may range from 5 to 70 mg. It is administered 1 hour prior to each session. Once the patient is able, under the influence of the drug, to enter the situation without anxiety, the dosage should be rapidly reduced.

Utilization of carbon dioxide/oxygen inhalation to facilitate relaxation and reduce pervasive anxiety has been discussed previously. Biofeedback training is suggested if these procedures prove inadequate.

When methods for facilitating relaxation in patients experiencing difficulties are unavailable, ineffective, or contraindicated, an alternative counter-conditioning response, such as anger, may be introduced (Goldstein, Serber, and Piaget, 1970), since rage, like relaxation, is incompatible with anxiety. To induce anger, the patient should visualize a situation that enrages him or her, focusing on the most irritating details until the anger is experienced intensely. Hierarchy items are then paired with the induced anger response.

Difficulties in Imagining

Inability to concentrate on a scene and intrusion of extraneous material into a scene are two major problems that may impede the effectiveness of systematic desensitization. A patient who is unable to visualize scenes adequately may be treated alternatively with exposure *in vivo*. Exposure *in vivo* is also the procedure of choice when a patient can visualize clearly but does not experience the anxiety associated with the situation.

Consistent inability to imagine scenes without the intrusion of irrelevant material should lead to an inquiry into the context of the intruding thoughts. If they are of an obsessional nature, desensitization should be discontinued and treatment for obsessions introduced. When no other symptoms support the diagnosis of obsessions, yet extraneous material continues to appear, the patient may require desensitization to the figure or image that appears in his or her imagination. The original desensitization can then be resumed.

Failures in Anxiety Reduction

Occasionally a patient will progress smoothly through the items of a hierarchy but fail to habituate to a particular scene. Several strategies may be adopted to overcome this obstacle. The therapist may skip one or two items, and then return to the difficult scene. If, for instance, the difficulty occured at the fifth scene, the seventh or eighth scene may be presented under relaxation. It will evoke considerable anxiety, and by contrast, anxiety to the fifth item may then diminish. Should anxiety fail to decrease, the therapist may instruct the patient to continue imagining the scene until complete habituation occurs. Alternatively, a subhierarchy may be constructed as described in Shawn's treatment.

Lack of generalization from one hierarchy item to the next may be indicative of an inaccurately constructed hierarchy.

The patient may habituate to each item as it is presented, yet no habituation is evident across scenes. By the time the fourth item is presented, for example, it continues to evoke 40 SUDs, although previous scenes had ceased to evoke anxiety. In this case, the hierarchy should be re-examined and revised. More than one hierarchy may be necessary to accommodate the relevant dimensions.

Occasionally, progression through the hierarchy is smooth, but the patient fails to improve. In such cases, it is probable that the behavioral analysis of the phobic stimuli was incorrect and the hierarchy, therefore, was irrelevant. The therapist must re-examine the data given by the patient and redefine the phobic stimuli. For example, one patient complained of a fear of choking while eating. A hierarchy was constructed based on the solidness of the food to be eaten. She habituated to all items on the hierarchy yet continued to be fearful while eating. A reanalysis revealed a general fear of death, of which choking was only one aspect. Once desensitization to death was completed, the fear of eating disappeared.

Of the various behavioral techniques, systematic desensitization is probably the most researched and widely practiced procedure. During the last two decades since its introduction, numerous variants have been reported in the literature. In this chapter, we have attempted to describe and illustrate the classical usage of this technique.

REFERENCES

Bandura, A. *Principles of behavior modification*, New York: Holt, Rinehart & Winston, (1969).

Davison, G. C. Systematic desensitization as a counterconditioning process. *Journal of Abnormal Psychology*, (1968), *73*, 91–99.

Donner, L., and Guerney, B. G. Automatated group desensitization for test anxiety. *Behaviour Research and Therapy*, (1969), *7*, 1–13.

Gelder, M. G., and Marks, I. M. Desensitization and phobias: A cross-over study. *British Journal of Psychiatry*, (1968), *114*, 323–328.

Goldstein, A., Serber, M., and Piaget, J. Induced anger as a reciprocal inhibitor of fear. *Journal of Behavior Therapy and Experimental Psychiatry*, (1970), *1*, 67–70.

Hain, J. D., Butcler, R. H. G., and Stevenson, I. Systematic desensitization therapy: An analysis of results in twenty-seven patients. *British Journal of Psychiatry*, (1966), *112*, 295–307.

Jacobson, E. *Progressive relaxation*. Chicago: University of Chicago, (1938).

Jones, Mary C. A laboratory study of fear: The case of Peter. *Pedagogical Seminary*, (1924), *31*, 308–315.

Kazdin, A. E., and Wilcoxon, L. A. Systematic desensitization and non-specific treatment effects: A methodological evaluation. *Psychological Bulletin*, (1976), *83*, 729–758.

Kraft, T. A short note on forty patients treated by systematic desensitization. *Behaviour Research and Therapy*, (1970), *8*, 219–220.

Lang, P. J., and Lazovick, A. D. The experimental desensitization of a phobia. *Journal of Abnormal and Social Psychology*, (1963), *66*, 519–525.

Lang, P. J., Lazovick, A. D., and Reynolds, D. Desensitization, suggestibility and pseudotherapy. *Journal of Abnormal Psychology*, (1965), *70*, 395–402.

Lazarus, A. A. Group therapy of phobic disorders by systematic desensitization. *Journal of Abnormal and Social Psychology*, (1961), *63*, 505–510.

Paul, G. L. *Insight versus desensitization in psychotherapy*. Stanford: Stanford U.P., (1966).

Paul, G. L. Outcome of systematic desensitization I: Background, procedures and uncontrolled reports of individual treatment. In C. M. Franks (Ed.) *Behavior therapy: Appraisal and status*. New York: McGraw-Hill, (1969a).

Paul, G. L. Outcome of systematic desensitization II: Controlled investigations of individual treatment, technique variations and current status. In C. M. Franks (Ed.) *Behavior therapy: Appraisal and status*. New York: McGraw-Hill, (1969b).

Wolpe, J. *Psychotherapy by reciprocal inhibition*. Stanford: Stanford U.P., (1958).

Wolpe, J. The systematic desensitization treatment of the neurosis. *Journal of Neurotic and Mental Disorders*, (1961), *132*, 189–203.

Wolpe, J. *The practice of behavior therapy*. New York: Pergamon, (1973).

Wolpe, J. and Lang, P. J. A fear survey schedule for use in behavior therapy. *Behaviour Research and Therapy*, (1964), *1*, 27–30.

APPENDIX A
LIFE HISTORY QUESTIONNAIRE

Purpose of this questionnaire:

The purpose of this questionnaire is to obtain a comprehensive picture of your background. In scientific work, records are necessary, since they permit a more thorough dealing with one's problems. By completing these questions as fully and as accurately as possible, you will facilitate your therapeutic program. You are requested to answer these routine questions in your own time instead of using up your actual consulting time.

It is understandable that you might be concerned about what happens to the information about you, because much or all of this information is highly personal. *Case records are strictly confidential. No outsider is permitted to see your case record without your permission.*

Date: _____

1. General

Name: _____

Address: _____

Telephone: _____

Age: _____ Occupation: _____

Marital Status—(circle one): Single   Married   Divorced   Widowed
Remarried

By whom were you referred? _____

With whom are you now living? _____

Do you live in a—(Circle answer): house   apartment   room   hotel
other

How much education have you had—(Circle answer): Grammar school
High school   College   Graduate school

2. Personal Data

Date of birth: _____ Place of birth: _____

Mother's condition during pregnancy (as far as you know): _____

_____

Underline any of the following that applied during your childhood:

night terrors   concern about cleanliness   sleep walking
thumbsucking   bedwetting   stammering
fears   nail biting   unhappy childhood
happy childhood   concern about orderliness   repetitious behavior

Health during childhood? _____

List major illnesses: _____

Health during adolescence? _____

Height: _____Weight: _____

List surgical operations along with age at the time: _____

_____

List serious accidents: _____

List fears that disturb you:
    a. _____

    b. _____

    c. _____

d. _____

e. _____

Underline any of the following that apply to you:
Headaches, palpitations, bowel disturbances, nightmares, feeling tense, depressed, unable to relax, don't like weekends and vacations, can't make friends, can't keep a job, financial problems, dizziness, stomach trouble, fatigue, taking sedatives, feeling panicky, suicidal ideas, sexual problems, overly ambitious, feeling lonely, inferiority feelings, memory problems, fainting spells, no appetite, insomnia, alcoholism, tremors, taking drugs, unable to have a good time, shy with people, can't make decisions, bad home conditions, concentration difficulties; others: _____

Underline the words below which apply to you:
Worthless, useless, a "nobody," "life is empty."
Inadequate, stupid, incompetent, naive, "can't do anything right."
Guilty, evil, morally wrong, horrible thoughts, hostile, full of hate.
Anxious, agitated, cowardly, unassertive, panicky.
Ugly, deformed, unattractive, repulsive.
Depressed, lonely, unloved, misunderstood, bored, restless, doing senseless things.
Confused, unconfident, in conflict, full of regrets.

Any athletic participation? _____

Present interest, hobbies, and activities _____

How is most of your free time occupied? _____

What is the last grade of school that you completed? _____

Were you bullied or given a nickname? _____

Do you make friends easily? ____ Do you keep them? _____

3. Occupational Data

What sort of work are you doing now? _____

What kinds of jobs have you held in the past? _____

Does your present work satisfy you? _____. If not, in what ways are you dissatisfied? _____

What do you earn? _____

List your ambitions:

Past:

Present:

4. Sex Information

Parental attitudes toward sex (was there any sex instruction or discussion in the home?) _____

Social and religious attitudes toward sex: _____

When and how did you derive your first knowledge of sex? _____

When did you first become aware of your own sexual impulses? _____

Did you ever experience any anxieties of guilt feelings arising out of sex or masturbation? _____. If yes, please explain: _____

_____

_____

Is your present sex life satisfactory? _____. If "no," explain providing information about any significant heterosexual (and/or homosexual) reactions: _____

_____

5. Menstrual History

Age at first period_____. Were you informed or did it come as a shock? _____

Are you regular? _____

Duration: _____ Do you have pain? _____ Date of last period: _____

Do your periods affect your moods? _____ If "yes," explain: _____

_____

6. Marital History

How long did you know your marriage partner before engagement? __

Husband's/wife's age: _____.Husband/wife's occupation: _____

Describe in your own words the personality of your husband or wife:

_____

In what areas is there compatibility?   _____

In what areas is there incompatibility? _____

How do you get along with your in-laws?   _____

How many children have you? _____ Do any of your children
present special problems? _____

Give details of any previous marriage: _____

_____

7. Family Data

a. Father

Living or deceased? _____. If deceased, give your age at the
time of his death: _____.

If alive, give father's present age and occupation: _____
Describe his health: _____

Father was—(circle as appropriate): very clean   meticulous   disorganized   orderly   withdrawn   religious   guilt inducing   easy
going   affectionate   permissive   over-protective   demanding

In what ways were you punished by your father as a child? _____

_____

Give description of your father's personality and his attitudes toward you: _____

_____

b. Mother

Living or deceased? _____. If deceased, give your age at the time of her death: _____.

If alive, give mother's present age and occupation: _____
Describe her health: _____

Mother was—(circle as appropriate): very clean   meticulous disorganized   orderly   withdrawn   religious   strict   guilt inducing   easy going   affectionate   permissive   over-protective demanding

In what ways were you punished by you mother as a child? _____

_____

Give description of your mother's personality and her attitudes toward you: _____

_____

c. Siblings

List names and ages of brothers and sisters: _____

_____

Relationship with brothers and sisters
Past: _____

_____

_____

Present: _____

_____

Give your impression of the home atmosphere in which you grew up describing the state of compatibility between your parents and the children: _____

_____

Were you able to confide in your parents? _____

If you have a step-parent, give your age when parent remarried: __

Give an outline of your religious training: _____

_____

If you were not brought up by your parents, who did bring you up and between what years? _____

Has anyone (parents, friends, relatives) ever interfered with your marriage, occupation, and so forth? _____

Does any member of your family suffer from alcoholism, epilepsy, or anything that can be considered a mental "disorder"? _____

_____

Are there any members of the family about whom information regarding illness, and so forth, is relevant? _____

_____

Recount fearful or distressing experiences not previously mentioned: _____

_____

List benefits you hope to derive from therapy: _____

_____

List situations which make you feel calm or relaxed: _____

_____

Have you ever lost control—(e.g., temper, crying or aggression)?
Describe: _____

_____

CHAPTER 3

Implementing the Technique of Implosive Therapy

DONALD J. LEVIS

State University of New York at Binghamton

Imagine the suffering of a woman who becomes so panic stricken by the obsession she has cancer that psychiatric hospitalization is required. No matter the extent of medical assurance that she is in excellent physical health, the nagging doubt somehow remains that she is not. Consider a man who is forced to relinquish his professional career because he is afraid to leave his home out of fear that dog feces may exist in his yard. His day becomes preoccupied with disturbing thoughts that find relief only in repetitious washing of his hands, clothes, and body. Perhaps it is hard to comprehend how one could become so frightened of bath water that a life preserver must be worn, or that a sound of a locomotive whistle in the distance evokes such terror in an individual that he runs around in a circle screaming at the top of his voice.

The range of human fears may be extended almost indefinitely. Some individuals break out in a cold sweat at the sight of a car, airplane, or tall building. Others become so afraid of their own sexual feeling that they avoid the opposite sex, become convinced they will die and be sent to hell, or are plagued with thoughts that they may even molest their own children. Still others fear failure, loss of control, taking responsibility, being angry, or giving love and expressing compassion. There are those who become so immobile that they remain in a fetal position in the back ward of a hospital, hear voices, see visions, or simply convince themselves they are someone else.

Committed to the goal of seeking methods to ameliorate such psychological suffering, the mental health worker is confronted with the difficult task of selecting from one of over seventy different treatment techniques available in the therapeutic arsenal. Most of these techniques reportedly are designed to be applicable to a wide variety of psychopathological problems. Some are intended for individual treatment and others for groups. The duration of treatment is long-term for some and short-term for others. However, one can be assured that all claim considerable therapeutic effectiveness. Needless to say, not only is controlled research almost completely lacking on the majority of available techniques, but whatever experimentation is performed usually falls short of incorporating even a minimum degree of methodological sophistication. Even those techniques that have been subjected to research scrutiny fall short in generating sufficient controlled data with patient populations for one to draw but only the most tentative conclusions.

The existing, rather chaotic state of the field suggests the need to search for some common denominators amongst therapeutic techniques in order to delineate more precisely potentially researchable therapeutic-change agents. Four possible change agents common to most, if not all, therapeutic approaches avail themselves. The first possibility deals with the importance of the therapist's attitudes toward the client, their relationship, and the milieu in which the client is treated. The second involves the effects of therapeutic suggestion, and the third, the degree of patient's self-understanding or personal insight. The fourth factor common to most techniques stems from the observation that behavior change in therapy appears to occur following a strong emotional response to material presented during the therapeutic interaction.

This chapter describes one technique that attempts to maximize in a systematic manner the last-noted common denominator of therapeutic interaction, that of emotional responding and its resulting effects. Disillusioned with the insight-oriented emphasis of the time period, Thomas G. Stampfl in 1957 developed the technique of implosive therapy (IT) or flooding. The therapeutic system was initiated by him as the outgrowth of two general observations (Stampfl, 1966). First, he noted that his success in conducting play therapy with children seemed to depend on the degree to which the child's play patterns of behavior were accompanied by emotional responding by the child during the play session. Second, he became convinced that Maslow and Mittleman (1951) were correct in their insistence that the neurotic's symptoms, defense mechanisms, and general maladaptive behavior resulted from a state that had as one of its primary features anticipation or expectation of some catastrophe. Although it appeared that this anticipation provided the motive force for symptom development, the catastrophe anticipated usually was unspecifiable by the client. Maslow and Mittlemann concluded that what was feared involved the anticipation of abandonment, injury, and annihilation, condemnation and disapproval, humiliation, enslavement, loss of love, and utter deprivation.

THEORY

Aware of the turbulent history of psychotherapy, Stampfl was committed to developing a clinical technique that took into consideration the findings established in the basic research area of experimental psychology. One of the most reliable formulations growing out of laboratory research is the establishment of Pavlov's original principle of experimental extinction. This principle states that the repeated presentation of the conditioned stimulus (CS) in the absence of the unconditioned stimulus (US) will lead to the unlearning of the learned response. Considerable evidence exists which suggests that this principle is a valid one whether overt action or emotional states have been learned. In essence, Stampfl's implosive therapy follows the dictum expressed by such experimental psychologists as Solomon, Kamin, and Wynne (1953, p. 299):

. . . the best way to produce extinction of the emotional response would be to arrange the situation in such a way that an extremely intense emotional reaction takes place in the presence of the CS. This would be tantamount to a reinstatement of the original acquisition situation, and since the US is not presented a big decremental effect should occur.

In most cases, maladaptive behavior is viewed as a learned response that is considered to be an end product of antecedent aversive conditioning. The theoretical learning model adopted by Stampfl is primarily based upon O.H. Mowrer's two-factor theory of avoidance responding (Mowrer, 1947, 1960; Rescorla and Solomon, 1967) and upon the writing of Dollard and Miller (1950). In theory the learning of maladaptive behavior can be separated into two different response categories. The first response category learned is to become afraid. This state is achieved by learning to respond in a fearful manner to previously nonfearful stimuli. The sequence of events required for fear development simply follows from the pairing of the initially nonfearful stimulus with an inherently aversive event producing pain. For example, the stimulation involved in physical punishment to the body or generated by severe states of primary deprivation such as hunger. Following sufficient repetition of these two sets of stimuli, the nonfearful stimulus through the procedure of classical conditioning will acquire the capability of eliciting a fear response even in the absence of further pairing of the inherently aversive event.

Learned or conditioned fear is viewed as a secondary source of drive possessing motivational or energizing effects that set the stage for the learning of the second class of responses referred to as avoidance behavior. Avoidance behavior, which is believed to be governed by the laws of instrumental learning, is acquired because of the effect this response class has in the termination or reduction of the conditioned aversive state (drive reduction). Symptoms and defensive maneuvers by a given client are then seen as being equivalent to avoidance behavior (Freud, 1936; Stampfl and Levis, 1967; Wolpe, 1958). Such behavior is engaged in by the individual to avoid previously conditioned aversive stimuli that function as "dangerous," anxiety-eliciting signals.

In principle, this model of symptom formation presupposes that the human acquires anxieties or fears much like a laboratory animal that has been conditioned to respond with fear and avoidance behavior to a tone paired with electric shock. However, it is recognized that symptom formation at a human level may be motivated by drive states other than fear (e.g., sex, anger, hunger) and involves more complex learning paradigms incorporating both approach and avoidance conflicts (see Levis and Hare, 1977; Stampfl and Levis, 1967, 1969, 1973). To account for the transference of fear to a variety of external and internal stimuli, a theoretical reliance is placed upon such concepts as stimulus generalization, higher order conditioning, response-mediated generalization, and/or the principle of memory redintegration.

Although symptomatic behavior is nonfunctional in the sense that no inherently aversive stimulation follows the absence of symptom occurrence, it is funtional in that it reduces or eliminates the source of conditioned stress shortly after execution. However, the well-established laboratory principle of experimental extinction suggests that repetition of the conditioned stimulus in the absence of the unconditioned negative reinforcement will result in the unlearning of fear to this stimulus. Why then doesn't repetition of the fear stimuli lead to extinction of the emotional response and subsequent avoidance behavior? Some clients' symptoms appear to resist extinction over periods of years.

Stampfl attempts to answer this paradox by placing theoretical emphasis on the position that conditioning occurs to a complex set of stimuli involving both external and internal stimulation. Furthermore, the multiple-stimulus patterns of conditioned cues are frequently serially or sequentially organized in time. It is also possible that a given environmental stimulus that elicits fear may also release a chain of memories of similar fear-eliciting situations as well as the neural representation of the historically presented unconditioned stimuli. It is misleading to assume that a given discrete stimulus is the only cue responsible for eliciting the behavior labeled a symptom. The notion that conditioning occurs to a CS complex is central to the argument advanced by Stampfl.

The translation of conditioning events into theory may prove helpful. Assume that an individual has been conditioned to fear three sets of cue patterns ordered sequentially in terms of memory retrieval and aversiveness (S1, S2, and S3). Because of the fear-eliciting properties of S1 the subject will be motivated upon this cue's exposure to engage in symptomatic behavior in order to remove the aversive consequences of the S1 presentation. In principle, such avoidance behavior should become overlearned so that the time of exposure to the S1 cue is at a minimum. Keep in mind that a quick avoidance of the S1 stimulus prevents much of the exposure to and subsequent extinction of the remaining duration of this stimulus pattern. A response to S1 also prevents S2 and S3 from being exposed, maximizing the conservation of fear to these stimuli (Levis, 1966a). When the fear to S1 eventually extinguishes, S2 will be exposed, and since it has been infrequently experienced previously, it will elicit considerable anxiety. In theory, the exposure of S2 can secondarily recondition fear to the S1 cue resulting in the return of fast avoidance behavior. This process of intermittent secondary reinforcement will continue to occur as long as sufficient drive value remains to the S2 and S3 patterns. In essence, Stampfl has extended, via the notion of serial cue presentation, the anxiety conservation hypothesis of Solomon and Wynne (1954). A more detailed presentation of the serial stimulus hypotheses can be found in Levis (1966; in press) and in Stampfl and Levis (1969, 1973).

Clinically, one can see this process operating when observing an individual who is attempting to "fight" his symptomatic behavior by not avoiding the feared situation. What frequently happens is that the individual experiences, as a direct result of his failure to avoid, an unbearable anxiety reaction that often progresses to a panic-like intensity. In a sense, such individuals are punished for trying to "fight" their fears and quickly return to earlier avoidance behavior. In theory, what is happening is that S2 and S3 cue patterns become exposed increasing the overall level of anxiety experienced. By increasing the level of anxiety, responding to the S1 pattern can be reinstated via secondary or higher order conditioning. However, it should be noted that the overall level of fear has been reduced by forcing oneself to be exposed to the S2 or S3 cue pattern.

Support for Stampfl's learning model has mainly been obtained at the infrahuman level of analysis. (Since a review of these results are beyond the scope of the present paper, the interested reader is referred to the following articles: Boyd and Levis, 1976; Dubin and Levis, 1973; Levis, 1966, 1970, 1970a; Levis, Bouska, Eron, and McIlhon, 1970; Levis and

Boyd, 1973, 1976; Levis and Dubin, 1973; Levis and Stampfl, 1972; Shipley, 1974.

Therapeutic Extension of the Theoretical Model

According to the model, symptoms can be removed by extinguishing the conditioned stimulus complexes that provide the motivation for symptom occurrence and maintenance. To achieve this objective in therapy one must represent, reinstate, or symbolically reproduce in the absence of physical pain the cue patterns to which the symptomatology has been conditioned. Since many of the conditioned cues that will elicit anxiety are believed to include neural representation or specific past events of pain and punishment, the therapist's usual strategy is to attempt to reproduce the avoided cues in the client's imagery, rather than by simple verbal statement or a complete reliance on *in vivo* presentation. Through verbal instruction to imagine, scenes are presented to the client that include the various stimuli (visual, auditory, tactual) hypothesized to be present in the original conditioning events. The position is taken that all cues reproduced in imagery that elicit negative affect do so because of previous learning and thus are extinguishable. Images per se are not considered inherently aversive.

The therapist's task is to approximate for the client the presentation of the total avoided conditioned stimulus complex (e.g., S1, S2, S3, etc.) by presenting scenes. Such scene exposure should elicit a strong emotional reaction followed by an extinction effect since the images instructed are not followed by a primary reinforcement. By repeating the scene over and over again the emotional response elicited should become less and less until complete extinction occurs. Once sufficient drive value of the fear stimulus has been extinguished through repeated exposure and by varying cue presentation, symptomatic behavior should be markedly reduced or eliminated.

Complete accuracy in reconstructing the original conditioning events is not essential since some effect, through the principle of generalization of extinction, would be expected when an approximation is presented. The more accurately and realistically the hypothesized cues are presented, the greater the obtained extinction effect. It is critical, therefore, that the therapist has a clear understanding of what cues are being avoided. Therefore, a good diagnostic workup is needed. The therapist should remember that since the original aversive conditioning events are assumed to result from contiguity of stimuli with physical injury or pain, it would follow that the cues immediately associated with these events (e.g., sight of blood, flashing eyes of the attacker, sight of a hand approaching) will carry a greater weight in evoking the anxiety response. Furthermore, if conditioning events early in childhood are viewed as important then scene material relating to potential stress events like toilet training, infantile sexuality, expression of aggression, and withdrawal of affection may be considered for inclusion. The details of the manner in which the implosive procedure is implemented is discussed later in this chapter.

RESEARCH FINDINGS AND IMPLICATIONS FOR TREATMENT

Both Stampfl and I have found the IT technique quite useful for treatment of a wide variety of psychoneurotic problems including anxiety, phobic, obsessive, compulsive, and depressive reactions, and behavior labeled as psychotic including affective, schizophrenic, and paranoid reactions. Numerous published case reports by others tend to confirm our observations. Nevertheless, one should be careful not to use such clinical observations in the scientific defense of the position's efficacy. An extensive review of the experimental literature evaluating the IT or flooding technique has been completed recently by Levis and Hare (1977). Twenty-three studies were evaluated under the classification of analog studies with nonpsychiatric populations, and fifteen studies which used clinical populations were reviewed. Support for the efficacy of the approach was found at both levels of analysis. Although the overall quality of some of the studies were excellent, many were considered methodologically weak and poorly executed. Since this material is presented in detail by Levis and Hare (1977) only the major implications of their review if discussed here.

The clinical populations evaluated using the IT or flooding technique included psychotics (Hogan, 1966; Boudewyns and Wilson, 1973; Boudewyns, 1975), a mixed outpatient population (Levis and Carrera, 1967), phobics (Watson and Marks, 1971; Boulougouris and Marks, 1969; Boulougouris, Marks, and Marset, 1971; Hussain, 1971; Crowe, Marks, Agras, and Leitenberg, 1972; Watson, Mullett, and Pillay, 1973; Emmelkamp, 1974; Emmelkamp and Wessels, 1975), obsessive-compulsive behavior (Rachman, Hodgson, and Marks, 1971; Hodgson, Rachman, and Marks, 1972; Rachman, Marks, and Hodgson, 1973), and alcoholics (Newton and Stein, 1974). Each of these studies, with the exception of the study using alcoholics (Newton and Stein, 1974), found that the extinction approach utilized was effective. The above finding tentatively suggests that an IT or flooding procedure may be effective with a wide variety of symptoms.

The following four additional implications were extracted from the existing literature. First, the length of scene duration and total scene or *in vivo* exposure was found to be a critical variable. Extinction will not be complete unless sufficient repetition of the aversive CS sequence is administered. Second, the literature suggests that the presentation of material other than those cues correlated directly with symptom onset may not be appropriate when isolated fears of a rat or snake is the target behavior. Third, some data suggest that tape-stimulus presentation of IT material may not be effective because (a) the cues presented usually are not tailor made to a given subject's history or altered by a subject's feedback or lack of it, and (b) avoidance behavior on the part of the subject during the taped session can be blocked or extinguished. Live therapist presentation or cue material appears to be much more effective.

The fourth and final implication emphasizes the importance of determining whether the boundary conditions of the technique are met by obtaining individual measurement on each subject to determine objectively the following points: (a) do the cues introduced lead to an increase in anxiety; (b) do their continued repetition produce an extinction effect; and (c) does the extinction effect correlate positively with a corresponding reduction in symptoms. It was clear from the literature review that two further stipulations are needed. The diminution in anxiety must result from habituation or extinction effects and not from the operation of defensive or blocking mechanisms of the patient (Boudewyns and Levis, 1975), and the material presented must be "relevant" to the target behavior analyzed (McCutcheon and Adams, 1975).

THERAPEUTIC PROCESS

As noted in the preceding section, the extinction technique of IT or flooding has been applied to a wide variety of psychoneurotic and psychiatric reactions. It has been administered to both adults and children. Research has yet to determine the client variables one should consider before using this technique, nor has sufficient work been done to suggest that certain behavior problems should be eliminated from treatment consideration. The objective of this section is to outline in detail how the procedure is administered. Although the application of the technique is essentially the same when applied to neurotic or to hospitalized psychotics, some finer distinctions in procedural execution do exist. This section concentrates on the use of the technique with nonpsychotic populations carried out in the typical office setting. A separate section on the treatment of psychotics is presented later.

To summarize, the fundamental task of the implosive therapist is to re-peatedly re-present, reinstate, or symbolically reproduce those stimulus situations to which the anxiety response has been conditioned. By expos-ing the client to the stimulus situations that are being escaped or avoided, the full emotional impact of the drive state associated with these cues will be experienced. In the absence of any primary reinforcement a marked reduction in the negative emotional state generated should occur with continual repetition of the CS complex. Once the motivating source for driving the clients symptoms is sufficiently reduced the symptom itself will cease to be elicited.

The implementation of this well-established principle of experimental extinction appears straightforward at the infrahuman level of analysis where the CS are known conditions and, therefore, easily reproducable. However, in the case of the human client, the contingencies of the condi-tioning history are usually unknown. In an attempt to restructure such conditioning events the therapist usually is forced to rely mainly upon verbal reports of the client, the accuracy of which clearly can be ques-tioned. Furthermore, considerable treatment time would be required be-fore sufficient information is available to allow the reconstruction of the important contingencies. Thus the question can be raised as to the merits of using an extinction approach if the objective is to devise a short-term treatment approach (Stampfl and Levis, 1967).

Despite the fact that it is frequently difficult, if not impossible, to speci-fy the aversive conditioning events in the client's life history with exact precision, it is feasible as Stampfl noted for a trained clinician to locate "key" stimuli associated with the problem areas of the clients. Once these are located it is not difficult to formulate hypotheses as to the type of traumatic events which may have contributed to the client's problem. After conducting only a few diagnostic interviews it is not uncommon for a trained therapist to make a "good guess" about the significant personal, environmental, and interactive conflicts shaping the client's behavior. Of course, these initial hypotheses must be conceived as only first approxi-mations of the original conditioning sequences, but it is quite possible that they incorporate a number of the more significant avoided CS compo-nents. As therapy progresses it is usually possible to obtain additional in-formation as to the validity of these cues and to generate new hypotheses. By presenting these hypothesized cues to the client the extinction ap-proach of implosive therapy can be begun shortly after initial contact (within two or three sessions). It is not essential to present cues that are completely accurate since some effect through the principle of generaliza-tion of extinction would be expected. Naturally the more accurate the hypothesized cues and the more realistically they are presented, the greater will be the emotional arousal obtained and subsequent extinction effect (Stampfl and Levis, 1967, 1969).

Information Gathering

One of the most critical and perhaps least understood aspect of the implosive or flooding procedure involves the selection, classification, and ordering of cues to be presented by the therapist via instruction to imagine scenes. As Stampfl and Levis (1973) noted, the first task of the therapist is to identify as accurately as possible those conditioned aversive stimuli that are presumed to mediate the emotional responses (e.g., anxiety, anger, depression) that are determinants of the symptoms and problems of the client.

In-Depth Interviewing

In an attempt to achieve this goal, the first task of the therapist is to conduct two or three 1-hour sessions of in-depth interviewing with the client. Interviewing and treatment are carried out in an ordinary office or therapy room with the client and therapist seated facing each other. The diagnostic work-up should include not only a thorough analysis of the situational cues surrounding the onset of each symptom reported by the client but also a thorough review of individual's family, sexual, religious, cultural, and medical history. Early memories of aversive events with parents or siblings should be solicited as well as any reoccurring nightmares or other such material that may aid the therapist in an attempt to restructure the life-history-conditioning events. Careful notes are taken listing both internal stimuli (images, thoughts, and impulses) and external stimuli (stimuli associated with public events, e.g., phobic objects, social situations, parental arguments, etc.).

Experience indicates that the enhancement of rapport with the client can be facilitated by conducting a skillful interview process. Difficult areas of discussion should be attempted with the first session in order to establish with the client a communication pattern in which any subject can be discussed. The areas of sexuality, expression of anger, or thoughts of suicide should be explored early if they are assumed to be areas disturbing the client. For example, if the client is depressed, the question might be asked as to "when was the last time you had suicide thoughts" and/or "how have you planned to kill yourself." To maximize the obtainment of information it is important to raise these "base-rate" questions in such a manner that the question implies that the therapist assumes such conflicts exist within the client. If a question is phrased to allow a "yes" or "no" answer, the possibility exists that the client may deny the problem area. Such a denial makes the topic under discussion difficult for the client to reintroduce. The same strategy applies to obtaining a sexual history. Questions of masturbation, premarital sex, homosexual contact, and difficulty in achieving orgasm should all be handled in a matter-of-fact way. Even if such material turns out to be unrelated to a given symptom, such frankness upon the therapist's and hopefully the client's part will enhance further communication. For example, in reviewing one client's fear of dog feces, the therapist asked "When was the first time you had sexual contact with animals?" The client paused for a moment, looked at the therapist, and revealed that he had never told anyone before but when he was an adolescent he had frequently engaged in such activities and has been worrying about this behavior ever since. Given the nature of the client's presenting problem and given the fact he lived on a farm when he was a teenager, the probability of an affirmative answer was viewed as being reasonably high. Even if the client had not engaged in or was worried about such behavior, experience has indicated that discussion of such a sensitive topic makes it more easy for one to involve himself in areas where a problem does exist.

Thus the interview process should touch upon all the potentially significant life-history areas whether or not they appear relevant or related to the presenting problem. If additional information is desirable, significant other people, with the client's consent, may be interviewed, or a battery of psychological tests may be administered. The point of such an interview is to determine the strong and weak functioning areas of the client and to generate hypotheses about which areas of conflict may relate to a given symptom. Two or three hours should be sufficient to obtain the necessary material. As therapy progresses ample opportunity will present itself for securing more detailed information.

It is recommended that during the first session the medical history of the client be determined and if a recent physical has not been administered the client should be asked to obtain one prior to the start of therapy. Since the implosive procedure involves the subject being exposed to high degrees of anxiety, the physical health of the client is an important factor to consider before starting therapy. If any questions arise, the therapist should consult with the client's physician before starting treatment. If the client is taking tranquilizers, consideration for recommending that the client be taken off the drugs during therapy should be given if a medical reason does not present itself. This point especially should be considered if the drug in question would reduce the level of anxiety experienced during therapy.

Finally, an excellent policy to follow is to provide an objective basis for establishing the extent of the client's psychopathology prior to starting treatments. This is done in order to provide an objective yardstick for measuring whether the client improved, remained the same, or became worse following treatment. If the client's symptom is externalized as in the case of phobic reaction, an objective *in vivo* behavioral test can be administered. If the client's avoidance tendencies are internalized as is the case of the depressive or obsessive, a baseline self-report index may be constructed and/or a more global personality inventory like the MMPI (Minnesota Multiphasic Personality Inventory) may be adminstered. It has also been found useful prior to the start of treatment to ask the client to list how he or she would like to change following treatment.

To illustrate some of these points the following excerpts of an initial interview of a young married woman are reported.

T: In what way can I be of help?

P: I have severe attacks of anxiety that I cannot control.

T: When did they start?

P: A little over a year ago.

T: Would you describe how you felt the first time you experienced the attack and in what situational context you were in.

P: I was with students of mine and all of a sudden I lost my voice and started to talk backwards. I became very frightened and felt like I was going to lose control and faint.

T: How long did the attack last?

P: About 10 minutes.

T: Are the attacks you are currently experiencing like the first one?

P: I haven't lost my speech since the first one but they begin by a feeling of dizziness and pressure on my nose. I then feel faint and am afraid I am going to loose my voice or pass out.

T: How often do they occur and last?

P: Some last for 2 hours. They occur two to six times a week.

T: Have you discussed your problem with a physician?

P: Yes, several times. I have had a complete neurological work-up and each time the results have been negative.

T: May I have your physician's name and may I talk to him about your problem?

P: Yes. His name is _____

T: In the last 2 weeks what were you doing when the attacks occurred?

P: The last one occurred in a grocery store.

T: Were you talking to anyone.

P: No

T: Was the store crowded with people?

P: Yes.

T: Do crowds bother you?

P: Yes, I seem to have attacks when there are a lot of people around.

T: What kind of work do you do?

P: I am unemployed now but I used to teach. My husband's job required him to move here and I had to give my job up.

T: How long ago?

P: About a year ago.

T: Did you have your first attack right before your move?

P: Yes.

T: Was the attack during class and what were you talking about before it happened?

P: It was after class. The student gave me a surprise party because I was leaving.

T: How did you feel when the students showed their appreciation?

P: I was embarassed and somewhat surprised.

T: Is it difficult for you to accept compliments?

P: Yes.

T: At what age did you have your first period?

P: Around age 13.

T: During adolescence would you consider your physical development to be slow, average, or fast?

P: Slow.

T: Do you think this fact had an effect on your personality development?

P: Yes.

T: How?

P: I felt inferior to other girls my age and became a loner.

T: You were not one of the group.

P: Yes, they use to tease me.

T: Because you were flat-chested?

P: Yes.

T: How did you respond?

P: I avoided them. I had no friends. I used to eat my lunch in the girl's room by myself. . . .

T: As an adult, do you still feel the effects of these experiences?

P: Yes, I still feel unattractive and shy.

T: You do not appear to be unattractive; don't people compliment you on your looks?

P: Yes they do. But I still feel unattractive.

T: How would you describe your marriage?

P: Good. My husband is a wonderful and patient man.

T: How frequently do you have sexual relations?

P: Infrequently.

T: Once a week, a month?

P: Around once every two weeks. It varies.

T: Do you usually achieve orgasm?

P: Yes.

T: Do you enjoy sex?

P: Sometimes, but intromission hurts me and is painful. That is why sex is infrequent.

T: Have you consulted a physician.

P: Yes, there is nothing physically wrong.

T: How frequently did you engage in premarital sex?

P: Infrequently, only with my husband.

T: (After obtaining more detailed information about sexual history) Would you like to deal in therapy with the problems you are having in the sexual area?

P: Yes.

T: How do you feel about having to quit your job and move to this city?

P: It was best for my husband's career.

T: But how do you feel?

P: I didn't want to move.

T: Do you feel any anger about having to move?

P: (Pause) Yes, but I can't blame my husband.

T: Do you find it easy to express your negative feelings and anger?

P: Yes, I am a bitch. I am always complaining. I have always been a bitchy person.

T: Can you express anger directly?

P: No.

Following a detailed inquiry into the patient's family, religious and early upbringing, the therapist was able to generate the following hypothesis:

1. The anxiety attacks started shortly following the client's learning she was going to move.
2. Talking to people and being in the presence of crowds were stimuli correlated with the onset of the attacks.
3. The client reported being uncomfortable when she received praise or succeeded at something. She also appeared to be avoiding cues associated with rejection and failure as well as cues associated with being assertive and expressing negative feelings in a direct manner.
4. Her anxiety attacks appear to prevent her from actively seeking employment in a job like teaching and appear to create stress for her husband and some secondary gain for herself.

Classification of Avoided Stimulus Cue Categories

As these excerpts from an initial interview session suggest, tentative hypotheses and conclusions can be reached concerning the significant stimuli motivating symptom onset. The therapist must continually ask: What are the external and internal conditioned cues that the client is avoiding? The assumption is made that these cues are multiple, involve varied forms of stimulation, are possibly interdependent, historical in origin, and are ordered sequentially or serially in terms of avoidance strength and accessibility. In procedurally administrating the technique, this therapist has found it useful prior to the start of treatment to categorize conceptually those cues deduced from intake material. Stampfl and Levis in their 1967 article adapted two general categories for this purpose. These were labeled symptom-contingent cues and hypothesized sequential cues. In 1975, Levis extended the cue classification areas to the following seven separated categories: (1) Inherently nonharmful situational and environmental cues (CSs) preceding symptom onset and believed correlated with it; (2) inherently nonharmful situational environmental cues (CSs) directly avoided by symptom onset; (3) physically harmful cues (USs) hypothesized to be anticipated given the failure of symptom onset; (4) hypothesized external environmental cues deduced to be associated with the original (historical) conditioning sequences; (5) hypothesized internal thought processes deduced to be associated with the original (historical) conditioning sequences; (6) hypothesized stimulus generalization equivalent cues associated to the phobic stimulus; and (7) hypothesized avoided cues eliciting reactions other than those represented by the label of fear or anxiety (e.g., anger, feeling of pleasure, love, and hope). Examples and detailed instructions of how to classify various cues into these seven categories can be found in Levis and Hare (1977).

For clinical purposes, Stampfl's (1970) fourfold classification scheme would appear adequate for organizational purposes. It emphasizes the important point that the implosive procedure includes the specification of internal and external stimuli and response-correlated stimulation associated with overt and covert behavior. A description of these categories taken directly from Stampfl (1970, pp. 195–198) with additional illustrative examples appears below:

1. *Symptom-Contingent Cues.* These cues are defined as those situational or environmental cues which are determined to be highly correlated with the occurrence of the client's symptom or a marked increase in negative affect. Symptom-contingent cues are assumed to have less of an anxiety loading, to be more accessible and indentifiable by the client, and can be deduced usually from a purely descriptive analysis of the contingencies surrounding the occurrence of the symptom. Considering the interview material previously described, the symptom-contingent cues surrounding the client's anxiety attack would include a crowd of people or other situational cues associated with such attacks. In cases involving a phobic reaction, the cues in this category may involve the sight of a tall building, the driving of a car, or being confined to an enclosed space. The strategy for determining these cues is essentially the same whether the symptoms involve an obsessive thought, a compulsive thought, a compulsive ritual, a hysterical or conversion reaction, or a mood change. That is to say, the task at hand is to identify as much as possible the circumstances surrounding the occurrence of the symptom. As Stampfl noted, any stimulus in the external environment that correlated with an increase in negative affect or instrumental symptomatic behavior such as compulsive reaction would also fall in this category. For example, compulsive handwashing may increase when the external stimulus situation includes "dirty" objects (waste baskets, used handkerchiefs, etc.) or following certain events such as an argument with a parental figure. The failure of instrumental symptomatic behavior that leads to an increase in negative affect would also be included under this classification.

Once the symptom-contingent cues have been analyzed, scenes can be constructed for their reproduction in imagery. Typically, such scenes describe the client confronting those cues that elicit or are correlated with symptom onset. However, unlike reality the subject is also asked to imagine not engaging in any avoidance behavior. Thus the client may be asked to imagine climbing the stairs of a feared tall building until he reaches the top floor or carrying out in fantasy a particular feared obsession. In some cases it may be beneficial to present some of the symptom-contingent cues *in vivo*. The term "flooding" has sometimes been used in the literature to describe an implosive procedure when only symptom-contingent cues are utilized (see Levis and Hare, 1977).

2. *Reportable Internally Elicited Cues.* In addition to the symptom contingent cue and related to it are internal stimuli (e.g., thoughts, feelings, or images) reportable by the patient that appear to have aversive properties. From the excerpts of the initial interview cited earlier, the client reported feelings that she was going to lose her voice or faint, and her worry about how people were reacting to her symptoms would fall into this category. In the case of a claustrophobic patient, a closed space may represent a symptom-contingent cue, but the set of internal responses that refers to the patient's mentalistic description of a fear of suffocation in the closed space is interpreted in IT as a covert aversive stimulus pattern functioning as a reportable internally elicited cue. As Stampfl noted, similar reports may be obtained from patients displaying a rather wide diversity of maladaptive behavioral reactions. The compulsive handwasher may report that thoughts of dirt and vague feelings of guilt are associated with his behavior. Frequently, the patient merely reports that he senses an impending disaster or "catastrophe." However, when the patient is questioned more closely, he frequently is able to supply additional details that are classifiable under this category. The claustrophobic upon questioning may report that his fear of suffocation is associated with marginal thoughts that he is being punished for something.

A similar sequence of cues is present in nearly every patient. This appears to be true of psychotic disorders as well as neurotic ones.

3. *Unreportable Cues Hypothesized to Relate to Reportable Internally Elicited Cues.* Hypothesized unreportable cues are those cues that to the therapist appear to have a logical relationship to the symptom-contingent and reportable cues. From the interview material of a woman who experiences anxiety attacks one might suspect that her symptoms were, in part, motivated by internalized feelings of anger toward her husband for moving to a new city. Thus cues in this category also represent inferences made by the therapist based on aspects of the conditioning history of the patient and can be viewed as guesses of the therapist that depend on his or her interpretation of the critical features of the conditioning processes. Mental representation of aversive conditioning may be assumed to involve tissue injury (physical punishment, falling, being cut). Stimuli immediately associated with bodily injury (for example, the sight of blood) also may be assumed to be integral elements of the aversive stimulus complex, even though not reported by the patient. According to Stampfl, it may readily be inferred that the patient who fears falling from high places also fears the bodily consequences of the impact following the fall. Stimuli associated with his mangled body is a logical consequence of the aversive sequence related to his phobia—S^1 (high places), S^2 (falling), S^3 (impact), S^4 (stimuli associated with mangled body). If the patient is religiously inclined, then the implications of his death in an af-

terlife may be reduced to their stimulus equivalents (S^5, suffering in hell). The therapist may hypothesize that the fear of suffocation in the claustrophobic includes the fear of dying a slow agonizing death while he is completely helpless. Also, if the marginal thought is reported that suffocation in a closed space is punishment of some kind for having done something wrong, the therapist may introduce logical figures (parents, God, siblings) to apply the punishment, and also provide specific transgressive behaviors that answer the question as to why the patient is being punished. The theme of punishment for wrongdoing is very frequently related to symptomatic behavior; therefore, the therapist may routinely introduce cues of this nature on a hypothetical basis. Since punishment for transgressive behavior is a common occurrence, it represents features of the inferred aversive conditioning history, whether or not it is included in the patient's report. Other common hypothesized cues are those involving sexual and aggressive stimuli. Hypothesized cues may include the stimulus characteristics of events inferred to have existed in the conditioning history or actually reported by the patient to have occurred. In all cases, unreportable details of the events are supplied by the therapist. Aversive events of this type may involve dominating mothers, punative fathers, or teasing siblings. It is difficult to adequately describe all the ramifications of the use of hypothesized cues as these apply to different types of patients. However, the basic logic of the procedure as illustrated applies to almost all types of neurotic and functional psychotic disorders.

4. *Hypothesized Dynamic Cues.* Cues included in this category are those derived from psychoanalytically based theories of personality. For the most part they can be deduced from hypothetical events in the early conditioning history. Oedipal, anal, oral, primal scene, death wish impulses, castration, and a variety of responses of a primary process type are reduced to their stimulus equivalents. Dynamic cues appear to be especially useful in the treatment of more severely disturbed patients. The more aversive the reaction obtained from the cues introduced, the greater the probability of the cue set being closer in time to the historical event in which the original unconditioned stimulus was presented.

Many behavioral therapists have been reluctant to incorporate "dynamic"-type cues into scene material. The reluctance appears not to be based upon the nonrelevance of such material to the client's case history but rather upon the desire of some therapists to completely reject psychoanalytic theory. Although analytic theory does emphasize the importance of such areas as aggression, rejection, guilt, and sexual material upon personality development and symptom formation, so does social learning theory (Dollard and Miller, 1950). The rationale for selecting cues should not be based on preconceptions, but rather on questions of whether the material fits the available case history material or appears to be a probable area of avoidance on the client's part.

Treatment Plan

Following the interview phase and the classification of the obtained material into cue areas, a treatment plan is formulated by the therapist. Cues and their integration into scenes should be ordered along the hypothesized avoidance serial cue hierarchy from the least to most anxiety eliciting. Scenes consisting of cues low on the hierarchy should be presented first. This strategy is followed in order to reduce interfering defenses and to maximize the development of imagery content. Even though at a theoretical level the more anxiety-eliciting scenes should produce the greater extinction effect, their introduction prematurely will increase the likelihood of sensory blocking reducing the client's cooperation. Furthermore, by introducing and extinguishing cues surrounding symptom onset, the client will frequently report a number of other anxiety-eliciting situations previously forgotten completely. Such information not only provides further cues but allows a check on the merits of previous hypothesized cues. The theoretical assumption made is that by extinguishing one set of cues, the next set of cues, through the principle of generalization of extinction, will be more accessible. It is as if the extinction process results in a reactivation or redintegration of the memory process. As the new source of material is provided, the previous planned sequence of scenes is modified. This process of readjustment is continual throughout therapy. If following the extinction of the cues correlated with symptom onset the symptom disappears, the need for introducing the hypothesized sequence of cues becomes unnecessary.

"Neutral" Imagery Training

Approximately 20 minutes is set aside at the end of the last diagnostic interview in order to train the client in imagining "neutral" scenes. During this period the therapist selects scenes to be presented that do not evoke emotionality in the client. If any affect to the scenes is experienced by the client, the scene is quickly changed in the direction of emotional neutrality. The purpose of such training is to allow the therapist to establish a crude baseline for the ability of the client to imagine various stimuli and to establish the therapist as the essential director of the scenes. Such neutral scenes may include watching TV, school games, walking down a street, eating a meal, and so forth. Periodically, the therapist asks the client to focus closely on the details of the scene. Examples of such detail may be to observe closely the facial expression of a person to whom the client is speaking or to pay attention to the reflection of the chrome of an automobile toward which one is walking. An important part of the procedure is to have the client pay attention to any sensations in the various anatomical parts of the body (e.g., head, neck, shoulders, stomach) such as might be experienced when swimming or hitting a ball or tennis racket (Stampfl and Levis, 1973).

During the treatment proper it is conceivable that the client will be asked to imagine things or events that either never happened in reality or are impossible. Although such events may be hypothesized to have occurred in the client's fantasy, it is unlikely acknowledgement of this possibility will be forthcoming readily from the client. To establish that one can imagine unrealistic events, neutral imagery is also given involving such content. The following excerpt provides an example of this kind of neutral imagery:

> Now I want you to close your eyes again and get a clear image of yourself standing in a field. It is mid-afternoon and you can feel the heat of the sun as it shines over the field. The grass is a rich dark green and the flowers are in bloom. You can feel a light wind cross your face. Smell the various odors of the field. Suddenly, you have an urge to run through the field. See yourself running. You feel lighter than air. You feel you almost could fly. See your feet leaving the ground, your arms flapping like a bird. See yourself making a beautiful take-off. Look at your arms they are turning into wings and you are actually flying. Now see yourself coming in for a soft landing. Your feet gently touch the ground, the wings disappear and you come to a stop.

General Considerations in the Implementation of Implosive Therapy

First Session Preparation

The first implosive session is initiated during the third or fourth session following the data-gathering stage. After a few minutes of conversation at the start of this session, the client is asked to close his eyes and imagine while the therapist describes some of the neutral imagery practiced in the previous session. This additional practice session is usually brief, lasting between 5 and 10 minutes. At this point the rationale of the implosive process may be described. Stampfl prefers to wait until after the first scene presentation or until the client asks, while this therapist usually outlines the rationale prior to the start of the first scene. In either case both of us agree that considerable resistance on the part of the client can be removed by providing such a rationale. In providing such information, the therapist might give a simple explanation to the client in terms of the avoidance model of conditioning emphasizing the role of serial CSs and the principle of experimental extinction. It is important to communicate that consistent efforts must be made by the therapist to develop scenes that are anxiety evoking. The following rationale is sometimes used by this writer.

Before we actually start the treatment procedure, I would like to take a little time and describe to you the rationale behind the technique we are going to use. First, let me ask you a question. If you were learning to ride a horse and you fell off, what would your instructor have you do? (The usual answer given by the client is to get back on the horse.) Exactly. And if you didn't your fear would increase and generalize not only to the surrounding stimuli but even may back up to the entrance of the stable. By forcing yourself to be exposed to what you are afraid of, you can overcome your fears. Let me try another example. Have you ever been frightened by a horror movie? If you have and you stayed to see that movie over and over again, it is unlikely by the tenth showing you would have any fear to the situation. In fact, you would probably have fallen asleep. It is the same situation with the young medical intern who, upon seeing his first operation, faints from fear at the sight of the opening of a patient's chest. However, because of continual exposure to such operations the fear is overcome, and the intern may well develop into a skillful surgeon. This technique that we are going to use follows the same basic principle. You will be asked to imagine scenes in imagery that are designed to elicit anxiety. By going over these scenes many times the fear will become reduced or extinguished. These are learned fears and they can be unlearned through exposure in imagery. Images can't hurt you in reality. Do you have any questions?

At this point the client is asked to play act various scenes that will be presented by the therapist. A typical instructional set is provided in the following excerpt.

Your task is much like that of an actor (actress). You will be asked to play the part of yourself and to portray certain feelings and emotions in imagery. Like an actor (actress) you are to "live" the scenes with genuine emotion and affect. I (the (therapist) will direct the scenes. You will be asked to close your eyes and follow the scenes in imagery. Please put yourself into the scene as best you can and imagine the events described as clearly as possible. The scenes like movies do not necessarily involve real events. You only have to believe or accept the scenes as real when you are visualizing them. Do you have any questions before we start?

In order to circumvent resistance, it is important that little or no attempt be made by the therapist to secure any admission from the client that the cues or hypotheses introduced into the scene actually apply to the client. In order to achieve this objective, Stampfl and Levis (1969) outlined two levels of communication that must be maintained with the client. One mode of communication occurs when the therapist suggests scenes incorporating aversive stimuli. The other mode of communication is the conventional therapeutic role which involves the ordinary kind of conversation that occurs between therapist and client. For example, at the start of each session the therapist may inquire how the week went, did anything unusual occur, what dreams did the client have, and so forth. The posture taken by the therapist between scenes is usually nondirective and supportive. Therefore, no inference is made by the therapist that implications from the scenes presented constitute an accurate reflection of the client's behavior or mental life. The client need not accept the attributes and meaning as existing within the real world. If the client reports that perhaps some of the scene material is actually true, the therapist has an option to agree, disagree, or remain neutral. Therefore, the client is asked to believe the implications for a given behavior in one mode of communication (during scene presentation), but need not accept them in the other mode. This dual process of communication helps the client to discriminate the various roles of the therapist and seems to reduce or eliminate any negative feeling toward the therapist from exposing the client to aversive material. At no point is the client asked to suppress whatever symptoms are being experienced. No suggestion concerning real-life events are given unless an *in vivo* procedure is being used.

On the basis of analysis of the information secured concerning the client, the stimulus patterns to be presented during the first therapy session should have been worked out prior to the session by the therapist. As noted earlier, scenes are introduced in proportion to their hypothesized anxiety-eliciting value. It is usually convenient to begin by incorporating some past punishing or traumatic incident reported by the client. Or one might begin by "replaying" a frequently recurring dream. At times the therapist may use animals (wolves, bears, spiders, snakes) or objects (cars, money, telephone poles) for their symbolic (generalization) value. In cases where there are clearly defined situational cues, as in phobic reactions or compulsive behavior, the therapist may start or move quickly to scenes involving these symptom-contingent cues. By starting with events that were actually experienced by the client, the process becomes more readily understood. It should be kept in mind that the therapist is not simply attempting to arouse anxiety, but to arouse anxiety to stimulus patterns presumed to underlie the symptom picture of the client (Stampfl and Levis, 1973a).

At each stage of the process the therapist attempts to attain a maximal level of anxiety evocation to a given scene. When a high level of anxiety is experienced the client is held at this level until a diminution of the anxiety-eliciting value of the scene occurs. The scene is presented again and again until it ceases to elicit anxiety. New variations of the theme are introduced in order to maximize the process of generalization of extinction. Following a few repetitions of a particular scene, the client is given an opportunity to act out the scene without the therapist's aid. During a given scene it is not unusual to have the client verbalize the part he or she is playing. Be sure to insist that the client verbalizes his or her role in the present tense as if the scene was actually happening.

The therapist's attitude also can play an important role. The more sensitive and empathic the therapist is in understanding the client's problem, the better able the therapist is in presenting the scene material. The therapist should try to feel the role being played. By varying the inflection in one's voice at appropriate places, the therapist can produce a greater effect. The more involved and dramatic the therapist becomes in describing a given scene, the more realistic the scene becomes and the easier it is for the client to participate (Stampfl and Levis, 1967).

Cooperation on the client's part is essential for maximum effects to be obtained. The skills of the therapist are critical in this regard. Because of the nature of the material presented, resistance on the part of the client should be expected. In this regard at least two strategies can be taken. The first is to over-ride or over-power the resistance directly. As Stampfl and Levis (1973a) noted, it is common in the initial session for some clients to say: "It is not true." The therapist's response is, "Whether it's true or not, just imagine it." Client: "I wouldn't do that." Therapist: "I don't care whether you would really do that, just do it now." Client: "I can't see that." Therapist: "Yes, you can. Now see it." If, on the other hand, the direct approach doesn't work and after several minutes of pressure no progress is obtained, the therapist can employ the second strategy of circumventing the defense structure. This can be achieved by changing the content of the scene to a lesser anxiety-arousing content. After a while the therapist can then return to the more anxiety-eliciting material previously avoided. More will be said about methods of dealing with resistance later in this chapter.

Objectively Determining Merits of the Hypothesized Cues

Cue usage is constantly modified by the obtained feedback from the client. The therapist can operationally determine whether a given set of cues are related to the client's history. If the cues selected elicit anxiety or defensive behavior, the assumption is made that the client has been conditioned to them previously. The greater the degree of affect generated by a given scene, the greater the justification for continuing the presentation of this material. Although the monitoring of anxiety through behavioral observation (e.g., sweating, flushing of the face, increased motor activity) or relying on verbal report may be sufficient in many cases, the use of objective, psychophysiological techniques (e.g., GSR. heart rate, temperature) is preferred. Experience indicates clients show a wide range of emotional activity during a scene in terms of overt behavioral expression. An index like GSR permits a more systematic and objective analysis of responsivity and following repetition of a given scene. In either case, it is usually easy for a therapist to assess, following presentation of a given set of cues, whether they are relevant or not.

Issues Related to Scene and Session Spacing

The duration of the scene varies and in large part depends upon content. Research on methods of scene presentation is totally lacking. Stampfl and Levis (1973a) refer to a case involving a depressed client where the behavior manifested suggested that "death wishes" toward the client's father were close to awareness. In this case the depressive response was of insufficient strength to avoid internal anxiety-eliciting thoughts concerning hostile feelings toward the father. The first strategy suggested was to present scenes incorporating aggression that initially involved verbal expression of hostility by the client to the father or father figure (e.g., boss). The next scene escalated the expression of aggression by including scenes involving slapping, punching, and kicking, and then scenes were suggested that included "primary process" aggression such as killing and bodily mutilating. The procedure suggested in this case was one of relatively rapid scene presentation with scenes frequently changing every several minutes. As the authors noted, any scene presented is constantly changing. Changes occur within scenes and between scenes. Numerous variations within a given scene setting are possible. After completing a given scene the therapist has the option of stopping the scene and waiting for a period of time for the anxiety to subside or continuing the scene immediately with a repetition or another scene. Clinical judgement must be used. If the client is really involved in the process one should continue the material in order to maximize the extinction effect.

In other cases, this author has found it useful to develop a scene slowly, allowing the client sufficient time to formulate relatively good images of the sequence. At the beginning of the scene a reasonable amount of time is usually permitted so the client can get involved in the scene's setting. Situational or contextual cues are elaborated in detail. For example: "I want you to see yourself in your bedroom. Describe what you are wearing. . . . What is the color of the room, what does it look like, and so forth. Now see your wife lying in bed. Look at her hair, her eyes, and features. Get a clear image of the shape of her breasts as they cling to her night gown, and so forth." Whether the scenes are rapid or drawn-out will depend on the individual case, the objectives of the therapist, and most importantly whether or not the method of presentation is effective in evoking the affect desired. Feedback from the client will be helpful in determining the method deemed most appropriate for a given case. Thus scene duration may vary from a couple of minutes to 40 or 50 minutes depending on subject's responding and the material to be presented. Repetition of the important ingredient of a given scene should occur at least once within a session. However, it should be noted that within a given scene presentation of the relevant material can be repeated over and over even though other features of the scene are changing.

A given scene is usually terminated after some diminution in anxiety is noted. Never stop a scene in the middle of a given theme—always complete the sequence. Following the last scene in a session, allow at least 10 minutes to pass to insure that the client's anxiety level is back to normal. Experience indicates that no matter how much anxiety is elicited during a session, clients upon opening their eyes usually return to the presession or lower anxiety level within a 5-minute period. If for some reason the anxiety does not subside quickly, repeat the scene over and over until it ceases to evoke much responding. Repetition is the key to success with this therapy.

It should be clear from this discussion that a given therapy session cannot necessarily be held to the usual 50-minute period. The therapist must be flexible in this regard. If 50 minutes is alloted for scenes to be presented, allow 1½ hours between clients. Again data are not available concerning the most effective session or scene length. Some sessions have run 2 or 3 hours, some 20 minutes. The desired spacing between sessions is also not known. Usually, one meeting a week is scheduled, but this is a function of convention rather than data. Good effects have been obtained at the clinical level analysis when clients were seen on a more frequent basis.

Homework Assignments

Following each session, the client is instructed to re-enact in imagination scenes that were presented during the treatment session. These homeworkassignments provide additional repetition and, therefore, additional extinction trials. Such homework assignments are critical to the execution of the technique and probably are an important factor as to why treatment time is relatively short compared to other techniques. time is relatively short compared to other techniques. The client is instructed to practice the homework each day and after some training is encouraged to vary the scene content to make them more effective. From 20 to 50 minutes a day of practicing is usually recommended.

Another important purpose of the homework assignments is to bring the therapy under the control of the client. As therapy progresses, the therapist attempts to instruct the client in the use of the technique so the client can become his or her own therapist. The client is taught to analyze what is being avoided when they are anxious and immediately construct a scene involving the avoided cues or the worst possible outcome of a given situation. By repeating such a scene over and over while trying to elicit as much anxiety as possible to the self-presented material, the client is taught how to master and extinguish daily fears. With training and following some treatment, clients can become very experienced at administering the technique to themselves.

Duration of Treatment

Duration of treatment clearly varies with the individual case. Symptom removal has occurred following one session, and usually considerable reduction in symptomatology is obtained after 10 or 15 sessions (hours). However, with more difficult cases involving multiple problems or problems of long standing, more time may be needed to obtain significant gains. Longer periods of treatment are also needed when the defense structure is strong and the therapist finds it difficult to evoke much anxiety in the client.

From the point of view of a novice, one would expect, because of the nature of the material presented, that such scenes would generate considerable anxiety in every client. Experience indicates this is not the outcome in all cases. With some individuals it is surprising how hard the therapist must work before any reasonable amount of affect is experienced. This therapist has had cases where 20 or 30 sessions were needed before the client experienced any appreciable amount of anxiety. The constant repetition appears to produce an effect over time, and once anxiety is discharged to the material, progress usually is very rapid. Persistence does pay off with this technique.

At an empirical level it is not known whether the intensity of the anxiety reaction is critical. It is possible that the key variable is total amount of CS exposure independent of the anxiety level elicited at a given point in time. At the infrahuman level some data suggest that the important variable is total amount of CS exposure with the degree of autonomic responding at a particular time not being critical (Shipley, 1974; Shipley, Mock, and Levis, 1971). What is being suggested is that even if a minimal level of anxiety appears to be elicited from a scene judged relevant, the extinction effects may be cummulative and summative with additional repetitions. Nevertheless, symptom reduction appears to occur at a faster rate following a session where considerable anxiety was experienced.

Termination of treatment is usually based upon clinical judgement and/ or objective test indices. Clients also typically communicate when they think the therapeutic process is complete. At the time of termination most of the symptomatology should have been eliminated or markedly reduced. Clients will usually make statements such as: "Yes, I guess I did behave that way in the past but I seem so different now"; "All my problems are not over but I really feel I can deal with them directly and that I am over the hurdle"; or "I really feel confident now and I am not afraid to deal with my emotions or stand up for myself."

Course of Therapeutic Intervention

The key to successful implementation of the implosive procedure in part rests with the construction of scene material that captures the relevant cues motivating the client's symptomatology. As noted earlier, a good intensive interview prior to the start of treatment should provide the therapist with sufficient material to start treatment. A careful description and analysis of each of the presenting symptoms also will provide useful material. Since, in theory, the symptom is designed to reduce stress immediately upon its execution, the response topography of the symptom itself can be a valuable source of information from which hypotheses can be formed. In the case of an externalized phobic reaction like fear of driving or high places, or a conversion reaction in a combat situation, the functional role the avoidance behavior plays is quite obvious. The symptom keeps the client physically removed from the feared situation. In many such phobic cases, the avoided cues are believed to extend beyond the client's report that one fears a given stimulus situation. The implosive therapist would reason that it is not the car or high building per se that is being avoided but the anticipation or expectation of what might happen in such situations, like the car crashing and killing the client or the client falling off a tall building (i.e., fear of bodily injury cue).

Consider the case reported by Stampfl and Levis (1973) concerning a woman client who could not take a bath without wearing a life preserver. While in the bathtub the client occasionally had the feeling that the bathtub was without a bottom. Although aware of the irrationality of such a thought, the client was unable to dispell her emotional conviction that the bathtub was indeed bottomless. The therapist then asked the client if she could swim. The answer was no. Now on logical grounds, does it not make sense to put on a life preserver if one cannot swim and feels they are in a bottomless bathtub filled with water? As Levis and Hare (1977) argued, all symtoms make sense in a functional way if the source of conditioned aversive stimulation is taken into consideration.

At first glance, some symptoms seem to present a puzzle as to why they developed. Consider an individual who repeatedly has to wash his hands upon seeing a wastepaper basket or upon touching money. If in the client's history he were conditioned to fear death or disease from being exposed to dirt or germs, then washing one's hands to remove the potential contamination clearly makes sense. Or, as Dollard and Miller (1950) noted, if one is afraid of thinking sexual thoughts, counting one's heart beat may well provide a nice distraction to prevent the occurrence of such thoughts. In a case where the origin of the symptom is not easily detectable, the implosive process itself frequently leads to the development on the client's part of previously unreported material.

Reactivation of Memory

Perhaps one of the most interesting phenomena to occur with the use of implosive therapy is the apparent reactivation or redintegration of early memories following scene presentation. The emergence of this new material helps shape the course of new scenes and paves the way for obtaining a better approximation of the avoided CS complex. To illustrate this point two case reports are summarized. The first case involved a female client, 30 years of age, who came to therapy because she was reporting a tremendous fear of crowds. She did not have any close friends, and avoided people at work and in social settings. She also became panic stricken when in the midst of a crowd such as on a bus, or in a theater or auditorium. She constantly worried about people staring at her and attributed the problem to a fear that she produced a body odor that they would detect. She also was clinically depressed.

The first scene to be introduced involved a work situation in which the client was required to attend a lecture at which many people were expected. The first part of the scene centered on the client walking toward the auditorium ruminating about her fears of entering into the room. Once inside she started to sweat and she could feel and see the eyes of the audience watching her. As the scene progressed, people got up and sat far away from her. She could hear them talking about her and about how badly she smelled. The scene ended with her sitting by herself—alone and rejected. Variations of this basic scene were repeated over and over again. Good emotional responding was obtained, and with repetition the emotional response appeared to dissipate considerably. The client reported she was less afraid of such situations and that now she was able to eat lunch with a group of her colleagues.

Nevertheless, she still reported that she constantly worried that somehow people would be able to smell her body odor. The fact that she maintained good hygiene didn't help reduce her worry. At this point the therapist decided to concentrate on a scene that emphasized the client's imagining she could smell the odor. The format of the scene remained essentially the same. She was seated in a crowd of people. Sweat was pouring off her, and she could smell her own body odor. In the middle of the scene description, the client interrupted and stated she could smell the odor and it wasn't a sweaty body odor. Asked if it was like the smell of passed gas, she said "more so, but that was not quite it either." The therapist kept her concentrating on the odor and asked if any associations or thoughts passed into her awareness. The client reported that she wasn't as worried about what the people whom she could see in front of her were thinking, but more concern was expressed about what the people who were seated behind her thought about her. She was asked to continue concentrating on the scene and especially on the odor. She then blurted out a host of memories that "popped" into her consciousness. She recalled that when she was about the age of six her girlfriend started to whisper to her friends (behind her back) that they shouldn't play with her because she was a bad girl and would let the boys touch her. She next recalled how a couple of older boys she knew used to take her into an alley and put their fingers up her vagina. She then recalled on one occasion a man about 50 sat next to her and started to put his hand up her dress. While he was doing this, the elastic rubber band on her panties snapped. The client became frightened that all the people behind her knew what was going on and that they would tell her parents.

These memories provided new material for scenes. The odor was changed from one of sweating to that involved with sexual foreplay. Naturally, in the scene her parents found out and rejected her. A final scene consisted of the client confessing all her "sins" to God after death. God condemned her to hell, and when asked to describe what she visualized hell to be the client said: "I am in the middle of a circle burning and people around me are staring at me. Everyone is pointing at me. They know all the things I don't want them to know." The client's interpretation of hell was extended and she confesses to all her "sins" accepting full responsibility and guilt. To alleviate the client's guilt the scene was repeated over and over emphasizing the pain and rejection felt. This theme produced good affect and results. While in hell she could smell the sexual odor clearly. The case is illustrative of how the therapist's initial hypothesis that the body odor of concern was that of sweating was disconfirmed and redirected by her reactivated memories.

The next case involved a woman client who was clinically depressed. She had difficulty feeling any anger, especially toward her parents for whom she continually professed her love, but also reported numerous events in which they apparently had hurt and rejected her. The following excerpt starts in the middle of the scene in which the therapist was attempting to elicit feelings of rejection from her mother who was hitting the client. Previous scenes of this type produced repeated denial.

T: She's jumping up and down. She brings that up and she brings it down right on your head. Your own mother, she's hitting you. You're falling to the ground. In comes your father. Do you see your father come in? He sees this, he sees this. What are you going to do? He turns to your mother and he says I'm glad you did that. She deserves that. Your mother starts jumping up and down and she takes the pot and she hits you right across the head (client breathes heavily). Your father says good. Now we get rid of her. I never wanted her anyway and he starts to kick you. He kicks you in the side, he kicks you in the chest. See and feel him kicking you. He's angry. It's as if they both lost control. They're both wild. They're both mad. Do you see them hitting you? They're beating on you. They're hitting you. You're looking up, you are seeing your mother. See her clearly, how angry she is. She's angry. See her face, see her face. Do you see your father's angry face? They're really angry at you. They're going to hurt you. You're the one that's wrong. You're the one that has created this mess. Why did we ever have you? You've just been one big pain. You're the one that caused us to fight. I wish we had never had you.

C: (Crying) I'm the one that should be mad!

T: They're the ones that want to get rid of you because it's your fault. Your fault!

C: (Crying) No!

T: Your fault, your fault! They kick you again and they kick you again!

C: (Crying) It is not!

T: They kick you again! You keep saying it isn't but they keep saying that it is. Your fault, your fault. They smash you, they hit you, and they kick you. Kick you in the air. You're bleeding in the teeth. They kick you in the teeth. They disform and disfigure you, so you look like some kind of freak. They're kicking you and. . .

C: (Crying) Don't, don't!

T: Feel it, see it. It's your fault they say. You're the one responsible. You're the one that makes this family so disruptive. You're the one!!! It's your fault! They kick you again. You're bleeding, you're bleeding, and they're both together and they're both kicking you. Your father kicks you in the chest. He kicks you in the chest. He kicks you in the legs. Do you feel him kicking your legs? Do you feel that foot going into your stomach? He kicks you in the stomach. Do you feel the foot going in? Feel it going in! See it going in! Your own father doing this to his own daughter. That's all they care about you. You're like the scum of the earth. That's the way they treat you. That's what they think of you. They kick you again. Nobody wants you. Your brother comes in and sees it, and he says "Boy am I glad she's getting it. She's getting it, am I glad. (Client crying) She is responsible, she's guilty, she's done a lot of bad things." He hates you. (At this point the client started screaming and reported what seemed to be a hallucinatory level of experience.)

C: She was beating me with an ashtray. She was beating at me, and my brother was holding me down and she was beating me! It happened! It really happened (screaming and crying)!

T: See it! See it clearly. They're hitting you again, and again, and again! They're hitting you. Hitting you with that ashtray. See it. Visualize it clearly. (Client crying) Visualize it clearly. Your own mother hitting you. Visualize it clearly. (Client coughing) See it. Over and over again, feel it. It actually happened. She actually beat you. Your own parents. See that. See it!

C: (Crying) She does, I know she does hate me.

T: She hates you! You're dead on the floor, you're lying there and you're dead.

Another source of material that leads to the uncovering of new material is reoccurring nightmares. The next case of a middle-age woman client provides an example of how such material can be solicited . The dream, which occurred about the age of 11, centers around a pair of hands that closed around the client's neck. That's all the client could remember about the dream. There was no face or body to the pair of hands. She would wake up screaming after such a dream. Since the start of the dream the client has been unable to wear anything around her neck.

The setting of the implosive scene occurred in the client's bedroom at about the age of 11. Care was taken to describe the contextual cues of the room and the nightclothes the client was wearing. The excerpt presented picks up while the scene is in progress.

T: Your eyes are heavy. It's pitch black. Everything is so black and you look up and you see those hands. Those hands are very close to you and they're coming at you. They are big hands! They are strong hands! They are demanding hands. There is no uncertainty in those hands. Those hands are starting to wrap themselves right around your neck, pressing against your white skin, starting to close and squeeze out your life. Feel them squeezing the life out of you. They are big hands and they are starting to squeeze and you want to scream, you want to yell. You want to get it out of your system. You want to fight back but you don't. You can't fight back. You try, you try to lift your hands, stretch those arms, pull those hands off of your neck but you don't. There is part of you that won't let you fight. There is part of you that doesn't want to fight and another part that does want you to fight. You struggle for survival but you can't win. You give in and those hands start to go all over your face and in your hair and they start to go below your neck. The one hand is holding your neck down. You can hardly breathe because of the big thumb right over your windpipe and it's difficult for you to breathe. Those hands start to explore your body, start to explore your breast and you don't know what to do. You're frightened. The hand starts to rip off your clothes, your nightgown and you want to scream. Those hands have a body but you can't make out whose body it is and you just think how horrible it is. Why do you have to go through this suffering. You want to scream. See yourself screaming.

The client at this point reported a memory of a hired hand who worked on their farm. She remembered how they used to be alone a lot and how he used to frighten her. He had huge ugly hands. This memory cued off related childhood memories which were subsequently used as material for new scenes.

Case Presentations

Although the objective of the therapist is to outline the course of therapy prior to the initial implosive session, as illustrated by these excerpts, new material and hypotheses are continually being fed into treatment plans. In order to more fully acquaint the reader with actual scene descriptions, material from three different cases are given.

Case I

The first case illustrates the technique with the woman patient who reported experiencing numerous anxiety attacks following her and her husgand's move to a new job location. Excerpts of this client's initial interview were previously reported in this chapter. It should be recalled that the first attack occurred following the last class of a course she was teaching shortly before she was scheduled to move to a new city. The purpose of the move was to further her husband's career, but in making the move it disrupted the client's professional plans. The symptom-contingent cues and the internally reported cues were deduced to involve stimuli associated with being in the presence of people and internal fears that she was unable to speak and going to lose control by fainting. It was additionally hypothesized that the client was afraid of her unexpressed feeling of anger toward her husband, feeling of rejection, and fear of accepting feelings of warmth and closeness.

In the first scene the therapist presents the sympton-contingent cues and initially reportable cues. The hypothesized cue involving feelings of rejection was also introduced.

T: Now, please close your eyes and we will begin. Remember you are an actress and I am the director. Try to see as vividly as you can the scene I am about to describe. Don't block any emotions you feel during the scene. Any questions?

P: No.

T: See yourself back in the classroom, the day of your last class just before you move. Get a clear picture of the room, the people in it. Notice the clothes you are wearing and the color of them. Do you have a clear image of the scene?

P: Yes.

T: Class has just terminated, and the students start to gather around you. How do you feel?

P: I am nervous, not sure why they don't go home.

T: They want to thank you. One of them, a male, steps forward and presents you with a small package. You can hear him saying, "We all chipped in to get you this. We really like your class and want to thank you." Everyone moving closer to you, telling you how they like the class. See them. Look at them. They are waiting for you to say something. How do you feel?

P: I wish they wouldn't get so close. I feel nervous and uneasy.

T: You look at them! They really genuinely like you. You start to thank them, but when you speak the words come out backward! Hear yourself. You feel dizzy now. You're feeling faint. They press closer. You try to get them to move back. But each time you speak, the words don't make sense. They start to smile at you; then one person starts to laugh. Others join in. They are all laughing at you. They are making fun of you. They really don't understand or care about what you are going through. The anxiety is getting stronger and stronger. You try to leave the room. You start to loose control—you feel faint. See yourself fainting. Your body slumps to the floor. Now what will they think of you? You can hear one of them saying: "Boy, is she crazy. I am glad she is leaving." Pay attention to your body sensations, feel them, monitor your thoughts. O.K. open your eyes. How do you feel.

P: My stomach feels sick.

T: What was your worst feeling?

P: They laughed at me. They really don't care. I won't be able to teach again.

This scene elicited anxiety in the patient and was repeated using different situational settings until a marked reduction in responsivity was noted. To test the merits of the hypothesized cue of supressed anger, the following scene was described.

T: Now I want you to switch scenes. See yourself getting up in the morning. Your husband has gone to work. Another day faces you sitting around the apartment doing nothing but wasting time. You really feel bored, unproductive. What is going through your mind?

P: I need to find a job. I have to do something with my life.

T: That's right. You don't want to waste your time. This morning you set out to find a job. You go down to the employment bureau. See yourself there. You're filling out forms. But no jobs are available for you. Next, you look through the want ad section of the newspaper, but nothing in your area is advertised. You already tried the colleges in the area but they are not hiring. How do you feel?

P: Depressed.

T: That's right. Feel the depression. You had a good teaching job. People liked you. You had friends. But you moved and your life has become worthless, empty, and unproductive. You now think about your husband. He likes his job. He is moving up the ladder of success. How do you feel?

P: I feel angry.

T:　Try to feel the anger toward your husband.

P:　No, it is not his fault. We both agreed to the move.

T:　Whether it is his fault or not, try and imagine that all he is really concerned about is his work and his needs. Your needs and aspirations are not important. See him, get a clear image. Ask him to go back to his former job so you can return to your old job. Verbalize it.

P:　"Can we go back to _____?"

T:　Put some feeling into the request.

P:　"Can we?"

T:　He looks at you in a cold, rejecting manner. "No. You agreed to come here. I am making more money. You will find something here. Stop feeling sorry for yourself." Feel that concern. Try and communicate to him so he will understand.

P:　"Please. I can't stand it here."

T:　"Stop acting like a baby. Grow up." How do you feel?

P:　Mad.

T:　Tell him off, express your anger. Tell him you hate him.

P:　"I hate you."

T:　Say it with feeling.

P:　"I hate you, I hate you, I hate you."

Following this scene, the patient was asked to visualize herself back in high school. During this period she felt alone, isolated, and rejected. Yet, she appeared only to blame her own behavior for creating the situation. She did not recall feeling anger toward the students who rejected her. The main theme of the first set of scenes covering this period emphasized rejection cues. Following each scene, new material was solicited and incorporated in a later scene. Later on, she was able to experience considerable anger and hostility toward the people that rejected her. Sexual material was also introduced, and each cue area of concentration was repeated until little affect was experienced. As this occurred a marked drop in symptomology was reported.

Case II

The second case involves a multiphobic reaction of a 40-year-old male client. The most incapacitating symptom reported was the client's inability to leave his home for fear of being contaminated by dog feces situated in his yard. Because of the phobia the client had been out of work for six months. During the interview process it was ascertained that the client was afraid to return to work because his boss was viewed as an additional source of contamination. The boss' home was described as literally being covered with animal feces. The client's fears generalized to the point where he was afraid to open mail because his boss used the same post office and somehow may have transmitted his germs to the client's mail. The client reported that he repeatedly washed his hand, usually more than 20 times a day, as well as showering frequently. Out of fear of being contaminated, he would not touch or talk to his children when they came home from school until after they had changed into clean clothes. The client also abandoned his family car for over 3 months in a parking lot from fear it also was contaminated. The client described his wife as not being fully appreciative of his problems, especially the point about his unwillingness to retrieve the car. Intense interviewing revealed that the client's problems started approximately 3 years prior to the start of treatment. At about this time he had an affair with a work client. It was established that they repeatedly had intercourse in his car. The client also revealed that he still felt guilty and ashamed over his early adolescent sexual activities which included frequent intercourse with farm animals.

The scene to be described was presented in the first implosive session and mainly centered on describing symptom contingent cues associated with his reported fear of leaving his house. An attempt was also made to integrate into the scene the cue areas of aggression toward his wife and feelings of being rejected by her (Categories 1, 2, and 3).

T: Do you have any questions? Now what I am going to do is to describe some scenes to you just like we practiced yesterday. Some of the scenes will perhaps be relevant to events that occurred in your life and some not. Your task will be to try to project yourself into these scenes like an actor. Try to see them as clearly and vividly as you can. I want you to try to particularly pay attention to the details of what I describe. At times you might want the scenes to go one way as opposed to the way it will be described. But you try as hard as you possibly can to follow exactly what we say. O.K.? If some of these things cause uneasiness in you try to experience the uneasiness. Don't block it out. Now I want you to close your eyes and I want you to visualize as best as you can seeing yourself sitting in your living room in your house. (Pause) Now I want you to try to describe to me what you see so I can visualize along with you what the living room looks like. See yourself there sitting on a chair, perhaps your favorite chair. Look around the room and get that picture as clear as you possibly can and describe what you see in as much detail as you can.

C: On the west walls of our house I see book shelves with books on them. The walls are painted white. I see a davenport and easy chair in the living room. There are also two television sets and another book shelf.

T: Can you see them fairly clearly?

C: Yes.

T: Is the TV on?

C: Yes.

T: What are you doing now? What kind of chair are you sitting in?

C: (A description of the chair is given.)

T: Is your wife in the room?

C: No.

T: Now I want you to see your wife coming into the room. Look at her and see her clearly. Describe what she looks like and what she is wearing listing as many of the details as you possibly can just as if you are seeing it.

C: She is a tall girl about 5 foot 6½ or 5 foot 7, weighs about 130, and is large boned. She has reddish brown hair, wearing a blue sweater, black stretch slacks, and looking glasses.

T: What kind of dress does she have on?

C: She doesn't. She has stretch slacks on.

T: Slacks on?

C: Yes.

T: O.K., you're watching television now. She just entered the room and starts talking to you. See yourself turn now and look at her face. She appears to be a little upset and she is a little irritated. You can see it in her face and hear it in her voice as she mentions your name.

C: I can hear it in her voice but I can't see it in her face; she seldom changes her expression.

T: O.K., but you can hear it in her voice and she is upset and she has been upset for the last couple of weeks, upset about your problem. She asks you, "When are you going to get the car? You still haven't returned that car. It's just sitting in a vacant lot." Can you hear her say that? "That car is sitting in a vacant lot. Now when are you going to get it. Somebody might steal it." What do you think?

C: I am not going to get it until I'm ready.

T: "You're not going to get it until you're ready to?"

C: Perhaps never.

T: "Perhaps never! You are going to throw all that money away?"

C: I have to.

T: "What kind of man are you to do that?"

C: Very confused man.

T: "Very confused man, you surely are. Our life is going down the drain because you're afraid to go out of this house. Now why don't you get out of this house and go get that car. I'm sick and tired of your whining."

C: There's more to your life. I will go down the drain if I go and get that car. I'm very disturbed. Don't you know what disturbed means?

T: "I think you're just putting it on. Now you get out and get that car."

C: What if I say I'm not going to get the car?

T: Don't say what you would say. Just say it as if you were talking to her.

C: I'm not getting the car. I'm staying home.

T: All right now say it with some feeling.

C: I'm not getting the car! I'm not going to get the car! It's staying where it is.

T: Feel that now. You are a little irritated. She doesn't understand. She doesn't know what hell you've been going through and here she's asking you to go out and get the car and she knows damn well that you can't go out and get that car. You're sick. What an understanding wife!

C: I won't get the car.

T: That's right, you're not going to get that car. She looks at you and she says, "You get that car. I'm tired of this." What do you say?

C: Go to hell.

T: Say it with some feeling.

C: Go to hell!

T: That's it. Tell her again.

C: You go to hell! You go to hell!

T: All right. She just looks at you surprised. Here she has been with you through all this, taking all this behavior of yours and trying to live with it. It's getting her down. Can you feel that? Try to feel that she has been a little supportive of you, and after you think about it, why maybe you can please her. She hasn't been the best wife, but at least she tries. Do you feel that? She's been with you, she's loved you, and although she irritated you and got you a little angry a minute ago you think about her. All right? Now I know you don't want to do this but you're going to get up and you're going out to get that car. All right? You are going to try to please her. You don't want to do it but you're going to. You've made up your mind. You're tired of this not getting out of that house. You're going to get that car. See yourself slowly getting up to leave. You slowly start to walk over to the door. Now I want you to see that door. I want you to visualize that door. You're going over one step after another, you're getting closer. On the other side of that door is your yard. You see that. How do you feel?

C: I can't get the car.

T: You can't get the car but you are going to try to get the car. There is a little voice telling you that you can't get it, and another voice is saying that you are going to try and you're going to go out in that yard. O.K.? You're getting closer to the door. How do your insides feel?

C: Nervous, my stomach feels upset.

T: All right, concentrate on your stomach now. Churning. You feel nauseated, you're setting sick. You don't want to go out, every bone in your body tells you not to go out, but you're going to push yourself. You are going out! You're going to try it. You get closer to the door. Feel you hand reaching out, feel your hand reaching out, feel it touching the door knob. Do you have a hold of it now? Do you feel the sweatiness of your hand? All right. Slowly turn that door knob and the door opens. The door opens and you look out. What do you see in the yard?

C: Motorcycle on the porch.

T: O.K. Motorcycle on the porch. What color is the motorcycle?

C: Black. Black and chrome.

T: Who's motorcycle is it?

C: Mine.

T: It's your motorcycle. Now you look around the yard. You look at the yard and you don't see any feces do you? No feces in your yard. All right, so you step out. You step out on to the porch. Your wife has been watching you. How do you feel now?

C: Very upset.

T: Very upset. Now concentrate on feeling upset. You're outside in your yard and you're sick and you shouldn't be out there but you're trying. You are trying. Notice the door still open and your wife is coming out and she closes the door behind you and she locks the door. You're out there in your yard by yourself. Feel yourself becoming panicky. Feel that now. You turn around and you try to open the door but it is locked. There is no way of getting back into that house. Now I want you to see this. You look at the yard and here comes one of the neighbor's dogs. Can you see that dog?

C: Yes.

T: He comes into your yard. You look at him. You don't want to look at him but you force yourself now. You see that dog. All right? Now he starts to defecate. He starts to squat and you can see the feces coming out of him. Do you see that? How do you feel?

C: Very angry. Very angry.

T: What are you angry about?

C: My wife locked me out.

T: Your wife locked you out. Feel that anger. Concentrate on that. You're mad. There's another dog coming and it comes into your yard. You have two of them there now. They both start to defecate all over your lawn. You're angry now. I want you to feel that anger towards those dogs. Those dogs are putting all those germs and filth and dirt all over your clean yard. Do you feel that? See it. It's the dogs' fault. They're messing up all over your yard and you kept that yard so clean. You have to keep that yard clean, free of that dirt and filth. All right. Now see yourself picking up a club. You've got a club in your hand. It is a pretty good size club and you're going to show those dogs that they better get the hell out of your yard. Start to walk over to one of them. You see that? And you take that stick and you grasp it, feel it. Feel your hands around that. You swing back on that stick and you smash that dog. You hit him. Hear him squealing. Hit the dog again! He shouldn't be in your yard. You'll teach him a lesson for dirtying your yard. Hit him again! You see your hand going up and coming down on that dog. Look at the dog now it is squealing. It's on the ground. You see that? Feel that anger, you're angry. You should be angry. These dirty dogs coming up and messing up your yard. Feel that, now capture that.

C: I can't, I feel sorry for the dog.

T: No, try to feel angry at the dog. Try to feel angry even though it's difficult. I know some of this is difficult for you. Try to feel that anger as you hit the dog. You're just trying to teach him a lesson. A lesson to keep him away from your yard. Now the other dog has started to come over and is biting on your trousers. Barking at you and biting at your trousers. Can you feel that? Can you feel that? And another dog, a bigger dog, comes in. A collie, and it starts to come towards you. And you're swinging that club now at the dogs. There's three of them at you. Can you see them? And the collie, the big dog, the powerful dog, male collie, a very powerful dog, and it stands up on its back legs and pushes at you and growls at your feet. The dog knocks you on the ground. See yourself fighting the dog. The club fell out of your hand. See that? You reach for that club and your hand goes into the feces. Your hand is covered with that dog's feces. You look at your hand and it's got feces all over it. How does that feel? Now capture that feeling. It's your hand and it has feces all over it. That is your hand. Dirty. Your hand is covered with dirt. And another dog comes now, there's four of them and they start defecating. They start defecating all over you. You would like to move but you can't and some of the feces drops on your face. It hits your face. That dirty, smelly, fecal matter. See if you can smell that feces. The odor is terrible. An awful odor. The feces is now all over your face and you move your hand up to wipe it off. Your hand is dirty and it spreads all over your face. Instead of wiping it off you just push that dirty brown smelly feces right into your skin. It goes into your pores. Your face is covered with shit. Dog shit. You can't move. You're almost paralyzed. Now this cow comes into your yard and he starts defecating and he produces these big piles of feces all over your yard. You can see it, smell it. Try to capture that smell. Can you see yourself there with that brown fecal material all over your face? The cow comes up and he starts to defecate over your body. You lie paralyzed. You can't move. You just have to take it and these big globs of shit fall onto your face, on to your clothes, on to your hands, all over your hands, and you try to rip the glob of shit off your face but you can't. You just seem to push it into your nostrils. You can smell it. You have some of it in your nostrils. You are helpless now. Your wife comes out and looks at you and she can't do anything. She doesn't do anything. She just sees you there. You try to call out for help. You look at your wife now and you are paralyzed, almost so frightened you can't move, and you call out to her and you ask her, ask her to help you. You need to be helped. You need to get cleaned. This dirty material is all over you. Feel it. Feel its grittiness. It has a gritty sensation as you rub it into your hands. Oh, it's awful! It's horrible stuff! Now call out for her to help you. You need her. You don't want to call out but you have to. It's your only hope. Call out, ask her to help. Come on, you can do it. Come on you can do it. Now you try, you call out, "Please help me, please help me." Say it with some feeling. Look at her and say, "Please help me, please help me." You've got this feces all over you. As you open your mouth to say it again these animals are hovering over you and they're dropping their feces all over your body. As you open your mouth to call to her a big chunk of this fecal material is dropped into your mouth. You've got some in your mouth now. You can feel the grittiness of it around your tongue. You can smell the odor. The brownish, soft, brownish fecal material that is full of dirt and germs and it's in your mouth. It's in your mouth and you can't do anything with it. You can feel it as your tongue rolls it around the frame of your mouth. You can't do anything with it and you start to cough. A little of it gets caught in the back of your throat. You start to cough. This dirty, ugly, stinky, gritty material, slime. It has a yellowish tinge to it. You start to cough and as you start to cough some of it goes down your throat. Some of that dirty material goes down your throat. You can feel it. Almost like it is an acid, burning away at your throat and your stomach lining. The feces is all over you now. You look at yourself. Feel that feces go down your throat. Feel it in your mouth. It gets in your teeth. It is covering your white teeth, this yellow shitty color. Look at your hands. You've got it all on your hands. Take your hands and rub them together. Feel that shit, feel it. You rub it. Feel the grittiness of it. You've got it on your face. Feel it on your face, your clothes. There seems to be tons of it all round you now. You're covered in a sea of shit and nobody helps you. Your calls for help didn't move her. She just sits there and watches you. Do you feel a little anger about that?

C: I'm pretty angry..

T: You're pretty damn angry.

C: Sure.

T: I want you to feel that. I want you to feel that anger. You are mad! You try to wipe this shit away but you can't, it's just covering your body. There is about three feet of it, and these animals are coming in and she doesn't do anything about the animals. She lets them come into your yard. There's cows now, and pigs, and dogs. All of them are excreting all over you and they are burying you alive with this shit. It's hard enough for you to ask for help, and it's hard enough for you to ask her for help but you did. You are on your knees asking her for help and she didn't come. Feel that anger. You're also mad at the animals. The animals, you didn't hurt them. Why are they doing this to you? You can feel the crap mounting on your body and your body was clean before you went outside. It was clean, pure, but now the fecal material has just sort of embedded itself into the pores of your skin. You know that even if you get out of this you'll never be able to get some of this dirt off your body no matter how often you shower. It's just sort of being rubbed in there. There's so much of it and the odor of it is just so horrible. The odor is driving you crazy, and you can't move because there's more and more of this shit and you look up and there is this cow. See that cow. That cow's ass is right over your face. You can see it. It starts to defecate. Now look up at that ass. Look up at that ass and you can see the fecal material slowly coming out of it. Now look at that. It's a hard thing for you to do now. This is a hard scene but I want you to see them. Now take your time, look up at the animal's ass and get a clear picture of it. Now this is difficult but you can do it if you try. Look up. Don't blank out your feelings now. Look up and you see it! Look at his anus.

C: Yes, I can see it.

T: Did you get the anus there? Now look at the fecal material starting to come out of that anus. All right. You're right below it. It's slowly coming out. Big stuff, dirty stuff. Those cows are dirty animals. It's coming out and it starts to drop it. You see it falling, falling down, down on your face. Over your face it falls. It almost disfigures your face. It is this dirty, gritty, slimy, yellowish, brownish, shimmering shit. All over your face and you say my God how can this happen? You put your hands up to your face and you just push it. This cow feces goes in deeper in the pores of your skin, into your nose, into your mouth. You can feel the chocolaty, dirty, gritty taste of that fecal material. You're swallowing it. You're eating it. It's stuck in your ears, in your hair and it is so dirty, so slimy, you can feel your hair starting to fall off. It has an after-taste to it. It starts to eat away at your skin. See yourself there. You are in that shit. You're covered with it, you're being buried alive in it and there's nothing you can do. Nobody will help you. Your wife won't and she locked the door and that makes you angry. The animals seem to be taking a delight in doing this to you. You never really hurt the animals but they're doing this to you. They're shitting on you. Do you feel the disgust of this material all over you, the dirt? They're making you unclean. You are unclean. You are also angry, very angry. Angry at your wife. You could kill her. Angry at these animals, you could kill them. You've got this crap all over your body. Now you see that! You feel that fecal material over you! You smell it! Catch that image! Don't block on me, let your emotions go to it. I want you to feel it, feel the grittiness of it, smell the odor, feel that helplessness as more of it is poured on to you. Feel the chemicals eating into your skin, disfiguring you. You can never get it off, nobody would want to come close to you after this. It eats away at your face, your hair, your hands, and your body. It even goes through your clothes. It's almost as if the dirt just eats away at your clothes and gets to your chest. It covers your chest now and your legs. You are in sort of a bath of fecal material. You can feel the grittiness and uncleanliness, the dirt. You're covered with dirt. Now see that, capture that. It's awful, unclean. You are dirty.

Case III

The last case outlines the treatment plan for a client who manifested a severe depressive reaction. Depression involves a response that is conceptually more complex than the straightforward avoidance model previously discussed. Thus prior to describing a given case, the theory underlying the depressive reaction is elaborated. Stampfl and Levis (1969) provide two different conditioning analysis of the depressive reaction which led to the formulation of a treatment plan for clients who manifest this symptom. The attempt here is to summarize their thinking about this problem. As Stampfl and Levis noted, an analysis of the depressive reaction from an implosive therapy position introduces an additional learning component not emphasized in the discussion of other nosologies. This component involves the conditioning of stimuli that elicit positive emotional responding. Stimuli coincident with positive reinforcement function as conditioned stimuli by the same principles as those that govern conditioning in general. To describe an individual as feeling good emotionallly in learning terms is to say that environmental and internal cues conditioned to produce positive affect are functioning. If such cues are reduced or eliminated, the resulting effect will be a corresponding loss in positive affect experienced that can summate with other previously conditioned negative emotional states leading to reported feelings of sadness, guilt, and worthlessness.

The child is tempted to engage in some tabooed or forbidden behavior. He yields to temptation and engages in the forbidden behavior, which is followed by his being apprehended, "caught," or "found out." The parent (the captor) may then continue along a verbal repetitive theme which focuses on the child's worthlessness and his guilt (e.g., "How could you do a thing like that?" "What kind of child are you?" "What an awful terrible thing to do!" "You should be ashamed of yourself." "Don't you ever do a thing like that again." "You are a bad child.") Direct physical punishment then follows, such as slapping, spanking, whipping, and/or punishment consisting of painful deprivation states, such as being sent to bed without supper and/or denial of privilege. Behavior on the part of the parent, which is equivalent in conditioning terms to "withdrawal of love", may accompany the sequence. If cues representing withdrawal of love have been previously conditioned, the child is punished additionally by the strong secondary aversive properties of these cues.

These authors go on to note that the "withdrawal of love" cues frequently acquire anxiety-arousing properties because of their correlation with primary negative reinforcers such as painful physical punishment and states of physical deprivation.

If this model appears to be consistent with a given client's history, then treatment with implosive therapy might progress as follows. In order to obtain an extinction effect the avoided cues must be presented more fully. Thus the first task of the therapist is to continue the depressive response while focusing more closely on the internal cues producing the response. Scenes would be constructed in which the client is directed to imagine himself engaging in some "sinful" or taboo behavior that may be hypothesized to be tied to the client's guilt. The next part of such a scene would emphasize the client's being caught, accused, or apprehended for engaging in such behavior (e.g., family, friends, police). As a result of being found out, rejection cues are emphasized with the client being asked to concentrate on feelings of loss of love, worthlessness, and guilt. The client is then asked to imagine himself "owing up" to such behavior and taking individual responsibility for his actions. As is frequently the case when a child "confesses" his wrong-doings, this scene is followed by more rejection cues and a punishment sequence. The basic themes involved in such a scene are repeated until divested of all secondary aversiveness.

The second model proposed by Stampfl and Levis is based on a conflict multiprocess approach-avoidance paradigm. The first stage consists of the association of conditioned anxiety to those stimuli that precede punishment for involving oneself in an undesirable act as defined by the punisher. Not only does continual primary and secondary punishment for such behavior heighten anxiety and avoidance of such behavior, but if the completion of the taboo behavior involves another primary drive, as is the case if the behavior in question is sexual, an approach-avoidance conflict situation will emerge. Such a situation should lead to frustration and, in turn, the enhancement of aggressive behavior. If the aggressive tendencies on the part of the child are also punished, the overt aggressive behavior will in turn be suppressed.

In an attempt to mitigate the conflict with a partial solution, the child may channel the aggressive behavior primarily into internal cues involving aggressive fantasies toward the punishing agent. Such a solution may produce, in turn, another conflict if the punishing agent is a source of considerable positive reinforcement as is the case with a protective, nurturant mother. By fantasizing aggressive and hostile thoughts and impulses toward a source of positive reinforcement, the strength of the past positively conditioned internalized cues (e.g., image of the mother as loving and supporting) will decrease or be suppressed by the aggressive fantasies. To avoid this loss of positive reinforcement and to reduce additional secondary anxiety over expressing the internal aggressive cues (guilt), the internalized aggressive fantasies as well as an overt aggressive behavior may be inhibited (suppressed). This additional internalization of the conditioned aggressive cues are believed by Stampfl and Levis to involve responses directly antagonistic to overt aggressive responses leading to the state experienced as depression. Furthermore, as the authors noted, the self-punishing effects of the depressive reaction also help reduce secondary anxiety that may be continually positively reinforced because it usually elicits considerable secondary gain.

The recommended method for deconditioning the avoided cues believed operating in this model is to suggest scenes including strong aggressive impulses directed toward important nurturant figures emphasizing
feelings of guilt for such aggressive acts. Punishment scenes are in turn
introduced for engaging in such aggressive acts.

To illustrate the implosive procedure with a depressive client, the following case of a 45-year-old male is described. The client was diagnosed
as having a severe, "psychotic" depressive reaction. The client refused
to eat, spoke in a monotone voice, and appeared to be seriously considering commiting suicide. In fact, the suicide ruminations had started some
two years prior to the start of therapy. Recently he had been going down
into his cellar daily, where he would stare at a rafter that he was going to
use to hang himself and try to muster the "courage" to commit suicide.
He expressed having difficulty with his boss and his wife, neither of which
he felt appreciated him. The client seemed unable to assert himself appropriately or to express a direct overt anger. He knew his wife was faithful
to him, being a "good" Catholic, but he could not shake the "paranoid
thought" that she was secretly having an affair with his brother-in-law.
The client's father was described as a strict disciplinarian that nobody
would dare talk back to or contradict.

The therapist was given three days to treat the client since he was
scheduled to be hospitalized on the fourth day if the depression persisted.
The client was seen for a 2-hour period on each of the three successive
days. Because of the imposed time restriction, the therapist moved into
the hypothesized cue areas more quickly than would normally be the
case. It was hypothesized that the client had internalized considerable
hostility to his wife and boss and that he was experiencing considerable
guilt over this matter. He also was continually frustrated both at home
and in the work situation because of his inability to take a stand on issues.
The therapist treatment plan was to first extend the depression in order to
confront the client with the rejection cues he was avoiding. Once the client was fully experiencing the rejection cues in imagery, the next task
was to elicit the internalized anger by developing scenes in which the client was asked to see himself expressing aggression. The attempt was to
design a scene in which the client could feel justified in his expression of
aggression. Once the rejection cues were experienced, the anger in theory
would be closer to the surface and more easily elicited. It was decided
that if the aggressive material was introduced prematurely the client's
avoidance behavior may have been too strong to produce much involvement. After the aggression was easily expressed, an attempt would be

made to get the client to accept responsibility for his negative emotions and behavior. The plan was to follow this scene with a punishment sequence and more rejection cues.

T: Now, close your eyes. . . . Try and obtain a clear image of yourself in your living room. You are all alone and very depressed. Your wife is in the kitchen and she has been ignoring you for most of the day. Things are not going well at work. You are thinking that everything is hopeless. Feel the depression. Your thoughts turn to suicide. It would be better if you were dead! See yourself getting up and walking down the basement stairs. You walk over to the rafter in the basement you had thought of using. You can see the grain in the wood. See yourself looking around for a rope. There it is in a corner. You walk over and pick it up. Feel the rope in your hand. Now throw it over the rafter and tie a noose in the rope. Place a chair directly under the rope. Now see yourself getting up on the chair. Place the rope around your neck and pull the noose tight. Now see yourself hanging yourself and describe to me what you see.

P: I kicked the chair out from under me and I died.

T: No, you are not dead yet! Feel the rope closing tightly around your neck. Feel it burning against your skin. The breath is going out of you. You are struggling. You don't want to die but it is too late. Feel the pain, the loss of breath and see your body twitching and struggling for life. You don't want to die. The blood is leaving your face. You're white, gasping for air, twitching and turning. You want to cry out for help but can't. It is too late. You are dying and it's painful. (The visual component of this death scene was described again. The client experienced a high degree of anxiety to the details of the scene and gave the impression he wanted the scene to be over with.)

T: You are dead. See your dead body dangling from the rafter. Your soul is outside your body and you can visualize the scene. The door to the basement opens up and you can see your wife coming down the stairs. She sees your body. Get a clear image of her face. What is happening?

P: She is crying. Now she will be sorry that I am dead. Now she will miss me and realize how important I was.

T: No, you're wrong! Look at her face again. See the smile as she looks at your body hanging from the rafter. She's glad you're dead. In fact, she is so glad she ran upstairs and called all your neighbors and friends and invites them over for a party. They are all gathered in the basement now. Get a clear image of each of them. They are eating food and drinking, having a good time. They all seem happy you are dead. You can hear them making fun of you. (At this point, the patient appeared to be very anxious and very involved in the scene.

As the scene developed, the friends all left except for the patient's brother-in-law, who at this point was dancing with the patient's wife.)

P: See them dancing together. Her breasts are touching his chest. He pulls her closer. She looks into his eyes. They kiss. See their lips touching. It is a long kiss. He starts to take her clothes off. She lets him. He gently touches and caresses her bare breasts. He pulls her underpants off and lowers her to the floor. You can see him taking his clothes off. His penis is erect and it is huge. She brings him closer to her. You can see him entering her. She loves it. Their bodies move together in a rhythmic fashion. They are both enjoying each others pleasures, and they are doing this right above your dead body. (The details of the sexual act were made as explicit as possible in order to "prime" the patient for the aggressive scenes that were planned to follow.)

T: Now, I want you to imaging you really are not dead and that you used a trick noose in order to test your wife's loyalty. (The client's facial expression changed from one of anxiety to anger.) What do you see yourself doing?

P: I hate them. I'll show them.

T: See yourself taking the rope off your neck. Your wife and brother-in-law can't believe you're still alive. What's happening?

P: I start hitting both of them with my fist.

T: That's right. See yourself hitting and kicking them. (The client got so involved as his anger flooded forth he started swinging his fist in the air and kicking the desk directly in front of him as he was imagining the scene.) Both of them are hurt, but nothing is too good for them. See the knife on the table, pick it up. See yourself stabbing your brother-in-law and then your wife. Blood is pouring out of their chest. It's just like they caused your mind to snap. You are crazy with anger. Take that knife and see yourself disfiguring your brother-in-law. Cut his penis off. That will serve him right. Go ahead, you can do it. Now, your wife. Cut each of her breasts off. She will never let anyone touch them again.

The attempt here was to elicit an almost primary process level of aggression expression. The themes of rejection and aggression was repeated using different significant individuals in the patient's life (e.g., the client's father, boss, and mother) until a significant extinction effect was obtained. The patient appeared considerably relieved following the first and subsequent scenes involving his expression of aggression. The scenes appear to be very cathartic.

The next scene was an attempt to deal with the resulting guilt associated with the feeling of expressing anger. The scene involved the client being placed in jail for killing his wife, and so forth. A court room scene developed in which the client was asked to owe up and confess all his guilt and "sinful" actions to the judge and jury. The scene provided for additional replication of the aggressive scene material. The jury did not bother to go out and deliberate, he was found guilty and condemned to die in the electric chair. The electric chair was selected because of the stimulus similarity to pain and fire associated by the client to his image of hell. (Using hindsight it perhaps would have been better to have death occur by hanging.) The client's "sins" were considered so horrible that after the confession of all his life's wrong-doings (those that actually occurred and those made up by the therapist) to a priest, the priest refused absolution. The death march to the electric chair was described in detail as was the placement in the chair. The warden threw the switch and left it on until the client's body was burned to a crisp. The client's soul then went before God, and another replication of the aggression and confession scenes occurred. God condemned the client to eternal damnation in hell which really shook up the client, who thought God would even forgive him for commiting suicide. The client blurted out "God no, not hell, purgatory." In the scene God held fast and the client's soul was described as tumbling to hell. The client saw God as a brilliant light, and as he fell, the light became smaller and smaller until it faded out. Somewhat surprisingly, this latter scene also produced a very high level of anxiety in the client. The client was held in hell for about 20 minutes, visualizing all his sins of omission (e.g., not giving to his wife) and commission. He was asked to experience the pain in hell, which was designed to serve as punishment for his "evil" behavior.

The client's depression lifted after the second session. His appetite returned, as did his voice inflection. He reported no more suicide ruminations. The Depression scale T-score on his pretest MMPI was over 100. On the post-test, the depression T-score was in the normal range as was each of the other four scales (Hs, Hy, Pd, Pt) which were above 70 on the pretest. A follow-up evaluation a year later indicated that treatment effects were holding. Although case studies are not to be used in scientific support of the technique, the test data for this case are presented because they substantiated the clinical observation that the technique appears to produce fast results in reducing feelings of depression. Hopefully, these observations will stimulate more objective work on this topic.

From these case descriptions it might appear that the implosive procedure is a complex technique to utilize. It should be understood that the last case presentation involves the use of the technique with rather severe psychopathology. In many cases the approach is straight-forward with the therapist mainly developing scenes around symptom-contingent cues. Experience also indicates that many of the background cues used for one client can be used for others (e.g., court room scenes, hell scenes). Furthermore, the basic themes of rejection, punishment, loss of love, sex avoidance, expression of anger, and acceptance of responsibility are common to the problem areas of many clients. With experience, the technique becomes easy to administer. For additional case material, the reader is referred to Stampfl and Levis, 1967a, 1969, 1973, and 1973a.

Special Problems

This section is devoted to a discussion of those difficulties an implosive therapist might experience while engaged in the therapeutic process. The main issues to be considered deal with problems associated with client variables, therapist variables, and those involved in the treatment of psychotics.

Client Variables

With the use of a direct extinction approach like that of flooding or implosive therapy it is understandable why some observers might consider the technique to be dangerous for some clients. Such an important question must be resolved by experimental data, not rhetoric. To date, a review of the existing literature at both the human analog and clinical level has not revealed one study that demonstrated that the implosive procedure yielded reliably worse results than the controls on the issue of therapeutic outcome. Despite considerable pressure to the contrary, Stampfl waited 10 years (1957–1967) before publishing his technique, in part, because he wanted to insure at the personal level that the technique was effective and nonharmful. During this time he treated numerous clinical cases. It also has been my clinical experience and that of a number of other implosive therapists that I have sampled, that no client treated has been harmed through the use of the procedure. However, it is probable that in some future case a client may well appear to get worse following implosive therapy. In inspecting the individual data of the conventional treated group (CT2) of the Levis and Carrera (1967) study, some clients got better as indexed by the MMPI and some got worse. It is suspected that examples of clients getting worse following treatment can be found with any therapeutic technique existing today. Such an observation, however, does not imply causality between the behavior change and technique used. Only controlled experimental analysis can reliably answer this point.

Experience also indicates that the human organism can sustain considerable CS exposure and resulting anxiety without experiencing even short-term, ill effects. Perhaps this observation is related to the clinical finding that even though the therapist is continually attempting to maximize emotional responding, the experience of anxiety on the part of the client rests in large part upon the cooperation received. Clients can easily avoid, if they really desire to, the impact of the most dramatically presented scene. Yet, they mainly cooperate with the instructional set. Surprisingly, this therapist has found that not only do clients rarely miss sessions, but therapy is hardly ever terminated prematurely by the client. Although more objective data is needed on this point, Levis and Carrera (1967) found that the implosive treatment group had zero attrition rate, while four of ten subjects in a conventional treatment group (CT1) prematurely terminated treatment.

Of course, one can only speculate as to why implosive therapists have success in keeping clients in treatment. One factor that appears important is the finding that the rationale of the treatment procedure of confronting one's fears makes intuitive sense to most people. A second possibility stems from the observation that after experiencing a high level of anxiety to a given scene, symptoms of the clients appear to show a corresponding reduction in intensity. Such a state of affairs may well provide additional motivation for staying in therapy. It is also possible that clients are reinforced by developing mastery over their fears, which is facilitated, in part, by the assigned homework. A related point is reflected in the comment of one of my clients who described the technique "as the most Rogerian experience" she had encountered. Upon questioning, she surmised that it must take considerable empathy and energy for the therapist to crystallize so clearly the conflicts that she was avoiding. Clients, especially if they have had treatment previously with another technique, also seem to appreciate the speed at which therapy progresses and the fact that their defense tactics are not as effective in manipulating the therapist.

Complete cooperation in following the therapist's instructions is not, however, always obtained. Especially in the more difficult cases the problem usually centers on how one can elicit anxiety. Some client's defense against experiencing anxiety to the implosive material is very strong. As Stampfl and Levis (1973a) noted, certain types of clients resist the procedure more than others. In almost all cases neurotics are cooperative except in cases of scrupulosity, when almost anything can be defended against by designating the implosive procedure as sinful. Some clients with characterological disorders are especially resistant because they appear unable or unwilling to tolerate discomfort of any type. Finally, it is difficult to secure the cooperation of some psychotic patients because of their general disorientation.

In a previous section of this chapter, two strategies have been outlined for dealing with a client's resistance. One strategy involves the circumventing of the defense structure by temporarily changing the content of a resisted scene to a lesser anxiety-arousing content. Another way to achieve this objective is to encourage the clients to involve themselves in difficult content by providing a rationalization for such actions. If one desires the client to visualize scenes in which he is aggressive, it is best to precede the scene with material in which the client is rejected or frustrated. Or the therapist can say: "Now you see this, you have lost control; you are crazy and are not responsible for your actions." Later on, after some extinction effect to the preceding material, the therapist can then introduce scenes where the client is depicted as being responsible for his actions if this is viewed as therapeutically important. The main point here is to construct scenes that maximize the likelihood of the client's involvement. If resistance is anticipated to a given scene, the therapist's task is to design ways to mitigate such avoidance behavior.

The second way to deal with defenses is to overpower the resistance directly. The therapist might say: "Now you see it; don't block on me, you see it." A third way to deal with resistance, which has not been mentioned previously, is to implode the defense directly. For example, if the client says: "I can't imagine that. I will get worse or go crazy," or "This technique will make me sicker." The therapist may deal with such resistance by simply saying "That's right. Now I want you to see the following." At this point the therapist can describe a scene in which as a result of the client's cooperating with the therapist, the client gets worse, loses control, is taken out of the office in a straight jacket, and has to spend the rest of his life in the back ward of a mental hospital. A few repetitions of such a scene will usually extinguish the defense, and the therapist can return to the previous scene that elicited the resistance. Such defenses rarely occur, but when they do the best strategy is to extinguish the emotional element behind the defense.

To further illustrate the point of resistance, consider the client who manifests religious scruples. If this particular situation arises, put the client into a scene where the material introduced causes him to die and as a result of his dying he is confronted with God. The client confesses his sins to God and admits that he has had these awful horrible thoughts. As a result of these horrible thoughts, God condemns him to hell. The stimulus situation associated with the client's conception of hell are presented over and over until the event ceases to elicit anxiety. Another example of a defense that sometimes occurs is the comment by the client that even this technique can't help him. "There's no sense in trying." A scene would be constructed for such a client in which he is asked to imagine that he is told that the therapist comes to the realization that the client is beyond anyone's help. In the scene nobody can help the client. He is taken off to a mental hospital, and vivid details are described in which the client sees himself wasting away like a vegetable. Friends and loved ones stop coming to see him. The therapist as well as other professionals give up because the client is too sick, nothing will work. The client is asked to see himself beyond help. The final example deals with the fear of losing control reported by some clients. If such a fear interferes with therapy, the therapist can stop and directly implode this defense with a scene in which the client is asked to see himself losing control. Such scenes are usually followed by a scene in which the client is caught, punished by the authorities, sent to jail or to a mental hospital.

Considerable variability also exists in the ability of clients to imagine scenes presented. Research has not been conducted to determine whether the technique is less effective with individuals who express difficulty in this area. Clinically, the problem is handled by simply asking the client to do the best they can. Extra time is also taken to develop the scenes carefully by emphasizing the contextual or background cues (e.g., color of walls, dress one is wearing, furniture in room). Feedback on developing the contextual cues is routinely solicited from the client. It also seems helpful for at least the first few sessions to design the scenes around actual events the client can recall. If imagery is still reported to be unclear, proceed with the scene without worrying about the matter. By dramatically presenting the scene material and repeating the content of the scenes, imagery should become clearer over time. Some extinction can be obtained simply from the auditory input.

Some clients at the start of treatment also frequently express difficulty in imagining the scenes assigned for homework on their own. Simply instruct such a client to keep trying, and inform him that with continued repetition the homework should be easier to execute. It can take up to ten sessions before the client really has mastered the homework technique. Some practice during the therapeutic session occasionally might be given in homework execution. The therapist can make helpful suggestions by simply observing the client conducting such a session. It might also prove beneficial to tape record each therapy session and let the client play back the tapes as an aid in executing the homework assignment (Denholtz, 1970).

If a crisis in the life of a client occurs during the course of therapy, the subject matter eliciting anxiety should be imploded directly. Although it occurs rarely, the anxiety experienced between sessions might heighten for some reason. If such a situation arises, the client should be told experiencing anxiety to situational cues is good since such an experience provides an additional extinction trial. The client also should be instructed that if he should re-experience a similar situation a scene should be developed immediately around the event. Such *in vivo*, self-implosive exercises have been found by this therapist to be useful in helping the client overcome his fears.

Another problem that can sometimes interfere with therapy relates to the feelings developed toward the therapist by the client. Conventional therapists refer to such an occurrence as transference and believe it is a natural outgrowth of a therapeutic relationship. Behavior therapists, on the other hand, usually pay little attention to the positive and negative feelings developed by the client toward the therapist. Perhaps the direct approach of the behavioral therapists attenuates the possibility that such feelings will interfere with the therapy process. This therapist has had to deal with such feelings directly in only a very few cases. The standard procedure is to implode directly such feelings. If the client at some point in treatment expresses stong negative feelings, scenes should be developed in which the client sees himself expressing aggression directly toward the therapist even to the point of involving himself in primary process thinking (e.g., killing and mutilating the therapist). A few repetitions of such a scene will usually discharge the feelings. If the situation arises where positive feelings interfere with the technique, scenes can be described where the client falls in love with the therapist and is subsequently rejected. Such a scene might then be followed by introducing oedipal-type material if the client's history suggests such material might be useful in facilitating the therapeutic process.

The final point to be considered under this section relates to those clients who do not appear able to experience any emotional responding to the scene material. If the client is taking a drug that reduces anxiety, consideration should be given to taking the client off the drug. Mass or lengthy sessions may also help break down the client's resistance. If the client is cooperative in other ways, the therapist might either switch to a different technique or continue with the implosive procedure hoping for a breakthrough. This therapist has found that with a few clients where responding was minimal, continual repetition of the scenes eventually resulted in the elicitation of strong affect. If emotional responding cannot be elicited, the technique theoretically cannot benefit the client. The only research conducted on this issue was a report recently presented by Boudewyns and Levis (1975). It will be recalled that this study was reviewed earlier in the paper. The emotional responses of low and high ego-strength in-patient subjects to scenes designed to elicit anxiety were compared. Subjects defined as low in ego strength displayed little autonomic reactivity to the scenes introduced. Further work is needed to determine whether such a criterion as the Barron's ego-strength scale will help select subjects more amenable to the implosive procedure.

Therapist Variables

In administering the technique of implosive therapy a certain amount of imagination and sense for drama might be expected as a necessary prerequisite. One might also suspect that an aggressive or assertive personality would be desirable therapeutic skills. One self-proclaimed critic who has had no training or experience in the area, found the technique conceptually so distasteful he concluded that it is quite likely that very few clinicians would find implosion "palatable" and would, therefore, be unable or unwilling to use the technique (Morganstern, 1973).

It is understandable why such misconceptions might develop. Implosive therapy is a direct, confrontation-type technique that requires the therapist to have a strong foundation both in the area of learning and dynamic psychology, as well as being comfortable with the anxiety generated from scene presentations. If the reader defines the material introduced into therapy as "horrifying" and "unrealistic," as Morganstern (1973) did, then perhaps this technique is not suited for such an individual. It has been both Stampfl's and my experience that most trained therapists, independent of their orientation readily see at a theoretical level why a given set of cues are introduced for a given client when the client's case history is reviewed. The objective of therapy is not to be sadistic or scare the client, but rather to extinguish those anxiety-eliciting cues that are motivating the client's symptomatology.

The writer has been involved in training therapists in this technique for some 16 years. Experience indicates the technique can be successfully used by a wide variety of different therapeutic personalities. Individuals who are sensitive and empathetic clinicians seem to make the best implosive therapists. Experiencing an initially negative reaction to the technique is not in itself a hindrance to developing skills in this area. Boudewyns and Wilson (1973) noted that, while their study was in progress, the two trainee-therapists expressed negative attitudes toward some aspects of the implosive technique. Interestingly, once the study was completed, the attitudes of these two therapists were considerably more positive, and both are using the technique in their clinical practice.

Training and experience are clearly important factors in the successful administration of the technique. It is possible that if an inexperienced therapist panics or becomes uneasy when the client experiences a high level of anxiety, the client may receive the communication that the technique will make him worse. Such a communication may unnecessarily create an additional source of anxiety or provide a vehicle by which the client can manipulate the therapist. Training time varies considerably. Some therapists pick up the basics of technique administration after a few sessions, while others take longer. A good background in learning and psychopathology is an important prerequisite. The trainer may have to implode the trainee in areas where the trainee's own anxieties may interfere with successful administration of the technique. In fact, the administration of the technique should also provide extinction of the therapist's fears in areas where they exist. Initial training cases usually involve clients who have limited fears and are in good contact with reality or a severely impaired back-ward patient who has been labeled untreatable. In both of these cases, the trainee's fears of making the client worse will be mitigated.

If an untrained therapist stops a scene prematurely before the anxiety level of the client is reduced or if he communicates that the technique will make the client worse, it is theoretically possible that this increased source of anxiety could make the client temporarily worse. In theory, however, since the therapist is introducing only secondarily aversive cues, the ill effects generated should only have a temporary effect producing no permanent damage. Nevertheless, the therapeutic interaction is a serious and professional matter. No matter what the nature of the technique is, adequate training should be obtained before any technique is tried without back-up supervision.

Treatment of Psychotics

A number of the research findings reviewed that evaluated the implosive procedure used hospitalized patients (e.g., Boudeywns and Wilson, 1972; Hogan, 1966). Although this writer has not had extensive experience using the technique with psychotics, Stampfl has treated a number of such cases and has found the technique to be clinically useful with such a population. The psychotic population presents certain problems in that cooperation may not be fully obtained, the heavy administration of anti-anxiety drugs may also reduce the possibility of obtaining good emotional responding, and case history material may not be readily available or accessible. However, concerning the latter point, the presenting symptoms usually provide leads as to what cues are being avoided. For example, the content of the patient's hallucinations or delusions is a rich source of information. Such material usually can be classified as being either anxiety eliciting or anxiety reducing.

The classification of anxiety-eliciting symptoms is seen in a patient's delusion in which he insists with absolute conviction that he receives secret messages from TV sent by his enemies announcing his imminent annihilation or in the case of a hallucination where the patient hears voices telling him that he is dirty and evil, that he spreads disease and is doomed to hell. Such material can be elaborated and expanded upon by the therapist in order to maximize the extinction effect and to introduce cues that are still avoided (e.g., sexual thoughts). In the case where the delusions are anxiety reducing such as with the patient who believes he is God and sees himself as all powerful and omnipotent, the therapist simply asks himself what cues do the delusions prevent the patient from experiencing. In the example given, a good guess would be that the patient is avoiding cues associated with feelings of rejection, worthlessness, impotence, and sinfulness. Scenes could then be constructed incorporating these hypothesized avoided cues. By noting the feedback obtained from such scenes the therapist can increase the probability of zeroing in on the correct cues.

Although the administration of the technique with the psychotic patient remains basically the same as previously described for the neurotic, Stampfl does suggest some refinement (personal communication). First, there is an increased likelihood that the effective hypothesized cues will involve primary process type material including a sexual and aggressive component. Avoidance of rejection and guilt cues are also commonly observed with such patients. Second, to maximize cooperation and involvement in the imagery process, Stampfl spent considerable time in asking the client to visualize relatively "neutral" background cues leading up to the point where more anxiety-eliciting material will be presented. More work with this population clearly appears to be warranted.

REFERENCES

Boudewyns, P.A. Implosive therapy and desensitization therapy with inpatients: A five-year follow-up. *Journal of Abnormal Psychology*, 1975, *84*, 159–160.

Boudewyns, P. A. and Levis, D. J. Autonomic reactivity of high and low ego-strength subjects to repeated anxiety eliciting scenes. *Journal of Abnormal Psychology*, 1975, *84*, 682-692

Boudewyns, P. A., and Wilson, A. E. Implosive therapy and desensitization therapy using free association in the treatment of inpatients. *Journal of Abnormal Psychology*, 1972, *79* 259–268.

Boulougouris, J. C., and Marks, I. M. Implosion (flooding)—a new treatment for phobias. *British Medical Journal*, 1969, *2*, 721–723.

Boulougouris, J. C., Marks, I. M., and Marset, P. Superiority of flooding (implosion) to desensitization for reducing pathological fear. *Behavior Research and Therapy*, 1971, *9*, 7–16.

Boyd, T. L., and Levis, D. J. The effects of single component extinction of a three component serial CS on resistance to extinction of the conditioned avoidance response. *Learning and Motivation*, 1976, *7*, 517–531.

Crowe, M. J., Marks, I. M., Agras, W. S., and Leitenberg, H. Time-limited desensitization, implosion and shaping for phobic patients: A crossover study. *Behavior Research and Therapy*, 1972, *10*, 319–328.

Denholtz, M. The use of tape recordings between therapy sessions. *Journal of Behavior Therapy and Experimental Psychiatry*, 1970, *1*, 139–143.

Dollard, J., and Miller, N. E. *Personality and psychotherapy.* New York: McGraw-Hill, 1950.

Dubin, W. J. and Levis, D. J. Influence of similarity of components of a serial CS on conditioned fear in the rat. *Journal of Comparative and Physiological Psychology*, 1973, *85*, 304–312.

Emmelkamp, P. M. G. Self-observation vs flooding in the treatment of agoraphobia. *Behavior Research and Therapy*, 1974, *12*, 229–238.

Emmelkamp, P. M., and Wessels, H. Flooding in imagination vs flooding *in vivo:* A comparison with agoraphobics. *Behavior Research and Therapy*, 1975, *13*, 7–16.

Freud, S. *The problem of anxiety.* (H. A. Bunker, trans.). New York: 1936.

Hodgson, R., Rachman, S., and Marks, I. M. The treatment of chronic obsessivecompulsive neurosis: Follow-up and further findings. *Behavior Research and Therapy*, 1972, *10*, 181–189.

Hogan, R. A. Implosive therapy in the short-term treatment of psychotics. *Psychotherapy: Theory, Research, and Practice*, 1966, *3*, 25–31.

Hussain, M. Z. Densitization and flooding (implosion) in treatment of phobias. *American Journal of Psychiatry*, 1971, *127*, 1509–1514.

Levis, D. J. Effects of serial CS presentation and other characteristics of the CS on the conditioned avoidance response. *Psychological Reports*, 1966, *18*, 755–766.

Levis, D. J. Implosive therapy, Part II: The subhuman analogue, the strategy, and the technique. In S. G. Armitage (Ed.), *Behavioral modification techniques in the treatment of emotional disorders.* Battle Creek, Mich. U. S. Veterans Administration. 1966a.

Levis, D. J. Behavioral therapy: The fourth therapeutic revolution? In D. J. Levis (Ed.), *Learning approaches to therapeutic behavior change.* Chicago: Aldine, 1970.

Levis, D. J. Integration of behavior therapy and dynamic psychiatric technique: A marriage with a high probability of ending in divorce. *Behavior Therapy,* 1970a, *1,* 531–537.

Levis, D. J., Bouska, S., Eron, J., and McIlhon, M. Serial CS presentation and one-way avoidance conditioning: A noticeable lack of delayed responding. *Psychonomic Science,* 1970, *20,* 147–149.

Levis, D. J. and Boyd, T. L. Effects of shock intensity on avoidance responding in a shuttlebox to serial CS procedures. *Psychonomic Bulletin,* 1973, *1,* 304; 306.

Levis, D. J., and Carrera, R. N. Effects of 10 hours of implosive therapy in the treatment of outpatients: A preliminary report. *Journal of Abnormal Psychology,* 1967, *72,* 504–508.

Levis, D. J., and Dubin, W. J. Some parameters affecting shuttle-box avoidance responding with rats receiving serially presented conditioned stimuli. *Journal of Comparative and Physiological Psychology,* 1973, *82,* 328–344.

Levis, D. J., and Hare, N. A review of the theoretical and rationale and empirical support for the extinction approach of implosive (flooding) therapy. In M. Hersen, R. M. Eisler, and P. M. Miller (Eds.), *Progress in behavior modification.* New York: Academic, 1977.

Levis, D. J., and Stampfl, T. G. Effects of serial CS presentation on shuttlebox avoidance responding. *Learning and Motivation,* 1972, *3,* 73–90.

Maslow, A. H., and Mittlemann, B. *Principles of abnormal psychology: The dynamics of psychic illness.* New York: Harper and Brothers, 1951.

McCutcheon, B. A., and Adams, H. E. The physiological basis of implosive therapy. *Behavior Research and Therapy,* 1975, *13,* 93–100.

Morganstern, K. P. Implosive therapy and flooding procedures: A critical review. *Psychological Bulletin,* 1973, *79,* 328–334.

Mowrer, O. H. On the dual nature of learning—a re-interpretation of "conditioning" and "problem-solving". *Harvard Educational Review,* 1947, *17,* 102–148.

Mowrer, O. H. *Learning theory and behavior.* New York: Wiley, 1960.

Newton, J. R., and Stein, L. H. Implosive therapy in alcoholism: Comparison with brief psychotherapy. *Quarterly Journal of Studies on Alcohol,* 1974, *35,* 1256–1265.

Rachman, S. , Hodgson, R., and Marks, I. M. Treatment of chronic obsessive-compulsive neurosis. *Behavior Research and Therapy,* 1971, *9,* 237–247.

Rachman, S., Marks, I. M., and Hodgson, R. The treatment of obsessive-compulsive neurotics by modelling and flooding *in vivo. Behavior Research and Therapy,* 1973, *11,* 463–471.

Rescorla, R. A., and Solomon, R. L. Two-process learning theory: Relationships between Pavlovian conditioning and instrumental learning. *Psychological Review*, 1967, *74*, 151–182

Shipley, R. H. Extinction of conditioned fear in rats as a function of several parameters of CS exposure. *Journal of Comparative and Physiological Psychology*, 1974, *87*, 699–707.

Shipley, R. H., Mock, L. A., and Levis, D. J. Effects of several response prevention procedures on activity, avoidance responding, and conditioned fear in rats. *Journal of Comparative and Physiological Psychology*, 1971, *77*, 256–270.

Solomon, R. L., Kamin, L. J., and Wynne, L. C. Traumatic avoidance learning: The outcomes of several extinction procedures with dogs. *Journal of Abnormal and Social Psychology*, 1953, *48*, 291–302.

Solomon, R. L., and Wynne, L. C. Traumatic avoidance learning: The principle of anxiety conservation and partial irreversibility. *Psychological Review*, 1954, *61*, 353–385.

Stampfl, T. G. Implosive therapy, Part I: The theory. In S. G. Armitage (Ed.), *Behavioral modification techniques in the treatment of emotional disorders*. Battle Creek, Mich.: U. S. Veteran's Administration 1966.

Stampfl, T. G. Implosive therapy: An emphasis on covert stimulation. In D. J. Levis (Ed.), *Learning approaches to therapeutic behavior change*. Chicago: Aldine, 1970.

Stampfl, T. G., and Levis, D. J. Essentials of implosive therapy: A learning theory-based psychodynmaic behavioral therapy. *Journal of Abnormal Psychology*, 1967, *72*, 496–503.

Stampfl, T. G., and Levis, D. J. Phobic patients: Treatment with the learning theory approach of implosive therapy. *Voices: The art and sciences of psychotherapy*, 1967a, *3*, 23–27.

Stampfl, T. G., and Levis, D. J. Learning theory: An aid to dynamic therapeutic practice. In L. D. Eron and R. Callahan (Eds.), *Relationship of theory to practice in psychotherapy*. Chicago: Aldine, 1969.

Stampfl, T. G., and Levis, D. J. *Implosive therapy: Theory and technique*. New Jersey: General Learning, 1973.

Stampfl, T. G. and Levis, D. J. Implosive therapy. In R. M. Jurjevich (Ed.), *Handbook of direct and behavior psychotherapies*. North Carolina: North Carolina U. P., 1973a.

Wolpe, J. *Psychotherapy by reciprocal inhibition*. Stanford: Stanford U. P., 1958.

CHAPTER 4

Covert Conditioning in Clinical Practice

JOSEPH R. CAUTELA AND CAROL CARBERRY WALL

Boston College

"The term covert conditioning refers to a set of imagery based procedures which alter response frequency by the manipulation of consequences" (Cautela and Baron, 1977).

This chapter focuses on the use of covert conditioning procedures in the individual behavior therapy process. Covert conditioning is based on operant procedures and is used to increase or decrease the rate of a particular response. In the covert conditioning procedures, both the response to be modified and the events contingent upon it are presented in imagination. These procedures developed by Cautela (1967, 1970a, 1970b, 1971, 1976, 1977) are based on two assumptions: the homogeneity assumption and the interaction assumption.

According to the homogeneity assumption, covert events, that is, thoughts, feelings, and images, have the same parameters and obey the same laws as overt events.

This assumption is shared by the contributors to behavior therapy who manipulate covert events according to the learning theory paradigm (Wolpe, 1958; Stampfl, 1961; Homme, 1965; Bandura, 1969).

The second assumption of the covert conditioning procedures is that the manipulation of covert events may influence other covert events, physiological events, and overt behaviors. This second assumption is the basis of many types of therapeutic interventions including rational-emotive therapy (Ellis, 1962), rational restructuring (Davison, 1966; Mahoney, 1974), and multimodal therapy (Lazarus, 1976).

The advantages of the covert-conditioning procedures are that images are not limited by practical reality, no equipment is needed, more trials are available because the client is able to practice the procedure outside the therapy session, and lastly, the covert-conditioning procedures may be used by the client as self-control procedures by applying these techniques both to the problems dealt with in the therapy setting and to new problem behaviors.

This chapter describes six covert-conditioning procedures, examines the experimental and theoretical evidence relevant to these procedures and presents detailed and specific accounts of the use of these procedures with case examples. In addition, client setting, and therapist variables are explored in relation to therapeutic intervention.

COVERT CONDITIONING PROCEDURES

Covert Sensitization

Covert sensitization is analogous to the punishment procedure of the operant paradigm. It is used to decrease the occurrence of maladaptive approach behaviors. In this procedure, a highly aversive imaginal consequence is contingent upon the imagining of a maladaptive approach behavior. Through repeated trials, the cues previously associated with the noxious or aversive stimulus become discriminative stimuli for avoiding the aversive consequence by not performing the undesirable behavior.

The literature on covert sensitization parallels the results obtained by the implementation of other aversive procedures in modifying maladaptive approach behaviors. As a punishment procedure, covert sensitization is usually applied in combination with reinforcing antagonistic behavior. The advantages of using covert sensitization over overt punishment are many. One of the more obvious advantages is that the effects of strong overt punishment (i.e., high drop-out rate from treatment, overgeneralization of the avoidance response) are less apt to occur (Cautela, 1973).

Covert sensitization has been an effective treatment procedure in eliminating drug abuse (Wisocki, 1973; Cautela and Rosenstiel, 1975; Gotestam, Melin, and Dockens, 1972; O'Brien, Raynes, and Patch, 1972), alcoholism (Cautela 1970a; Ashem and Donner, 1972), obesity (Cautela, 1972; Janda and Rimm, 1972; Manno and Marston, 1972), sexual disorders (Barlow, Leitenberg, and Agras, 1969; Curtis and Presley, 1972; Segal and Sims, 1972), and smoking (Cautela, 1970b).

Covert Positive Reinforcement

Covert positive reinforcement (Cautela, 1970c) is designed to increase the probability of a particular response. It refers to a procedure in which the client is required to imagine himself performing a behavior that he is unlikely to commit followed immediately by an image that is reinforcing to him. This technique draws from the abundant information available from experimental work on positive reinforcement that indicates that when a positive reinforcer is made contingent upon a specified response, the probability of that response reoccurring will increase.

There are five parameters that seem to influence the effectiveness of overt and covert positive reinforcement. An increased number of trials, pairing the particular response with the reinforcement, will increase the strength of that response (Pavlov, 1927; Skinner, 1938; Hull, 1943). The shorter the interval between the completion of the response and the reinforcement, the greater the response strength will be (Kimble, 1961). The response strength will increase if the reinforcement is initially continuous but after acquisition maintained through an intermittent reinforcement schedule (Skinner, 1938). By manipulating the drive state of the individual, the effectiveness of an appropriate reinforcer should increase (Skinner, 1938). For instance, when using food consumption in imagery as a reinforcer, trials should be practiced when hungry.

Covert positive reinforcement has been used to successfully modify attitudes toward others (Cautela, Walsh, and Wish, 1971; Cautela and Wisocki, 1969), to enhance an individual's self-concept (Krop, Calhoon, and Verrier, 1971), and in the modification of overt behavior (Wisocki, 1970).

Covert Negative Reinforcement

Covert negative reinforcement is a technique drawn from the escape paradigm in learning theory. In this procedure, the probability of a given response is increased through imagining that an aversive event is terminated by the performance of a behavior that is to be increased.

There are several parameters of this procedure which are based on experimental work within the operant paradigm. In covert negative reinforcement, the rate of responding seems to be a function of the intensity of the aversive stimulus as it is in overt negative reinforcement (Reynolds, 1968). The less time elapsing between the termination of the aversive stimulus and the onset of the imagined response, the more effective the procedure will be (Dinsmoor, 1968). After the individual has learned the escape response through conditioning trials employing covert negative reinforcement, a stimulus of lower intensity may be presented in imagination to maintain the response strength (Reynolds, 1968).

Covert negative reinforcement may be applied in the treatment of maladaptive avoidance behaviors, such as school phobias, agoraphobia, and impotency (Cautela, 1970d). It also appears effective in the treatment of maladaptive approach behaviors, for instance, alcoholism and obesity (Cautela, 1970d).

The use of covert negative reinforcement is indicated in cases in which covert positive reinforcement cannot be employed. For example, depressed clients will often express an inability to imagine rewarding situations, but are able to imagine aversive scenes needed for covert negative reinforcement.

Covert Extinction

Covert extinction is analogous to overt extinction in the operant paradigm. In overt extinction, reinforcement is no longer presented after a response has been emitted. In covert extinction, the client imagines himself performing a problem behavior and then imagines that the reinforcing events which usually follow this behavior no longer occur.

This procedure is guided by laboratory evidence that demonstrates that if a response maintained by reinforcing consequences is consistently not reinforced, it decreases in frequency or is eliminated completely.

This therapeutic strategy, developed by Cautela (1971), has been employed in cases of "hysterical" blindness, disruptive classroom behavior, multiple phobias, sexual problems, psychosomatic complaints, obesity, and self-injurious behavior (Cautela, 1971).

Several of the parameters of overt extinction have been taken from the empirical data and related to covert extinction. (1) Response strength weakens as a function of the number of (covert) extinction trials (Skinner, 1938). (2) There is less chance of a spontaneous recovery when more extinction trials are given (Pavlov, 1927). (3) Although massed practice generally hastens extinction, distributed practice of the trials decreases the probability of spontaneous recovery (Pavlov, 1927). (4) Tasks (or imagined tasks) requiring more effort extinguish more quickly than tasks requiring less effort (Capehart, Viney, and Hulicks, 1958). It should be noted that in covert extinction as in overt extinction, there may be an increase in the undesired behavior (extinction burst) at the initiation of this procedure.

Covert Modeling

Covert modeling (Cautela, 1976) is based on Bandura's work in overt modeling. Modeling is used as a therapeutic procedure to serve several different functions. It is utilized in teaching a client a completely new response (Lovaas et al., 1966): teaching a client the conditions under which a particular response is appropriate (Chittenden, 1942), in facilitating the occurrence of a response that has been avoided because of fear or anxiety, and in promoting vicarious extinction of anxiety associated with specific approach behaviors (Bandura, Grusec, and Menlove, 1967). Overt modeling has proven effective in the elimination of phobias (Bandura, Blanchard, and Ritter, 1969), and has been used in conjunction with other techniques to teach imitation and linguistic skills (Lovaas et al., 1967) and in the treatment of withdrawal or isolation behaviors (O'Connor, 1969).

In the covert modeling procedure the client is asked to imagine that he is observing another person performing a series of behaviors in a particular situation. Usually the model in the imagined scene experiences the consequences of the modeled behavior. The covert modeling procedure may be used to either increase or decrease a specific response.

A number of studies have compared the efficacy and parameters of covert and overt modeling. Cautela, Flannery, and Hanley (1974) compared the effectiveness of both procedures in reducing a maladaptive avoidance response and found covert modeling as effective as overt modeling in reducing fear of rats in an analog study.

Kazdin (1973, 1974) found the parameters of covert modeling equivalent to overt modeling in that his work demonstrated that a coping model, rather than a mastery model, enhances imitation, and perceived that similarity enhances model effectiveness.

The advantages of covert modeling are that no live models are needed for the procedure. This allows the therapist to use a wide range of models. Further, overt modeling may be used as a self-control procedure.

Covert Response Cost

Covert response cost is an aversive procedure derived from the overt response cost technique. Response cost has been defined as the removal of a conditioned reinforcer contingent upon a response (Kazdin, 1972). In this procedure, the client imagines the loss of a reinforcer contingent upon performing an undesirable response in imagination.

The literature on overt response cost indicates that, unlike other punishment procedures, response cost does not have some of the undesirable side effects associated with punishment, such as escape (Phillips et al., 1971) or disruptive behaviors (Schmauk, 1970).

Evidence from the clinical setting and preliminary experimental evidence point to the efficacy of covert response cost in decreasing response rate. Weiner (1965) observed the effect of actual cost (point loss on a counter) and imagined cost (instruction to imagine point loss on a counter) as compared to baseline. Both conditions suppressed responding. Tondo, Lane, and Gill (1975) found covert response cost effective in suppressing excessive eating of specific target foods. Scott and Jackson (1974) found covert response cost equivalent to covert reinforcement in reducing test anxiety when compared with a control group.

Covert response cost seems to have several advantages when compared with overt response cost. First, there is added flexibility in terms of the number and quality of reinforcers which may be removed. For instance, a client may imagine the loss of a winning lottery ticket without having had to buy the ticket. Second, covert response cost is more readily used as a self-control and self-management procedure.

INDICATIONS

Behavioral Analysis

The criteria for selecting a particular therapeutic technique(s) is dependent upon the information obtained through a behavior analysis. Central to the behavioral analysis is the operational definition of the problem(s). This involves an adequate assessment of the specific behavior(s) by citing the observable and covert components of the behavior(s), determining the frequency of its occurrence, and the duration and intensity of the behavior.

In addition, the conditions under which the undesirable behavior is likely to occur are determined, and the consequences of the behavior are delineated.

The therapist and client discover the salient aspects of the problem and the components that seem to exert the most control over the problem behavior. The treatment procedures chosen depend largely upon the outcome of the behavioral analysis.

As an example, if the client were to present himself for therapy with a complaint of "depression," the therapist would first define depression in terms of the individual client's behaviors. In a particular case, perhaps depression is operationally defined as frequent crying, a decrease in activity, and constant thoughts such as, "What's the use, I wish I were dead, and so forth" with accompanying imagery of suicide attempts.

The therapist attempts to identify environmental variables that seem to exert some control over the behaviors subsumed under the term "depression." The therapist gathers information about how long the client has been "depressed," if he feels "depressed" on particular days, or certain times of the day, or all of the time. The therapist would also have to determine if the feelings labeled "depression" have the same degree of unpleasantness at all times and if the intensity of the "depression" changes across time.

In addition to collecting information about the situations or variables that consistently precede this client's "depression," the therapist needs to know what the consequences of being "depressed" are. Is the client able to avoid unpleasant duties or receive solicitous attention from family members? Or does the client's behaviors prohibit any reinforcing events from happening to him?

Choice of Procedures

We have found the covert-conditioning techniques applicable to the treatment of all types of behavior problems. The covert procedures, particularly when used in conjunction with *in vivo* homework practice, appear as effective as overt procedures. The advantages of using the covert conditioning procedures are considerable. The imagery used in the covert conditioning procedures, as with other imagery based procedures, allows for more diversity in scene presentation. The covert procedures are more efficient in terms of time and in terms of arranging situations as compared with *in vivo* performance.

One of the major advantages of the covert conditioning procedures is added flexibility and self-control given to the client. As indicated in a previous chapter (Cautela, 1969), self-control refers to a client's ability to be able to increase or decrease the probability of certain behaviors by manipulating environmental events and his own behavior. As the client is taught the covert conditioning procedures, he is informed that these procedures may be helpful to him for the rest of his life, both in working on the problems covered in therapy and on new problems.

For example, as a part of therapy, clients are told that they should apply covert conditioning daily before retiring in the evening.

All six covert-conditioning procedures may be used by the client as self-control techniques. If during the day, there were instances in which a client felt that he should have made a more appropriate response, he can apply the procedures to rehearse an appropriate response.

As an example of covert positive reinforcement applied as self-control, if the client felt that during the day he should have made a more assertive response in a particular situation, before retiring that evening, he might imagine himself being assertive, and follow his rehearsal with a pleasant scene.

Covert sensitization can be used by the client who has eaten food or had an alcoholic beverage that he feels may be harmful to him. In this situation, the client would imagine that he is about to consume that particular food or drink, he becomes suddenly ill and vomits all over the food or drink.

Covert extinction may also be used as a daily self-control procedure. For instance, the client may imagine himself making a sarcastic remark to his wife with her appearing not to notice or respond to his comment in any way.

Finally, the covert procedures may be used in combination. For example, if the client eats a sandwich during the night and hopes not to eat during the night in the future, he might imagine himself picking up the sandwich and then deciding that it would be bad for him to eat it and imagine a pleasant scene (covert positive reinforcement). He could also imagine that he is about to eat the sandwich and he becomes violently ill (covert sensitization). Finally, he can imagine that he is eating the sandwich and it has no taste, texture, or fillingness to it (covert extinction).

When introducing the concept of the covert conditioning procedures as self-control methods, the therapist gives the client a criterion to follow in his practice. In order for this practice to be effective, the client is instructed to practice the scenes to the criterion, that is, being able to experience appropriate affect several times in a row before discontinuing practice for the evening.

With the use of one or a combination of the covert-conditioning procedures most responses can be gradually altered.

The rationale for attempting to modify daily behaviors through self-practice is that eventually most undesirable responses or situations that require an appropriate response will be repeated. Therefore, clients will have the opportunity to work on a particular response on a number of occasions. It is very important that the client knows he has a repertoire of procedures to control behaviors that he targets outside of the therapeutic setting.

Choice of Covert Conditioning Procedures

Covert sensitization, covert extinction, covert response cost, and covert modeling may be used to decrease undesirable behaviors. Covert positive reinforcement, covert negative reinforcement, and covert modeling may be used to increase the frequency of particular behaviors.

When the task of therapist is to decrease or eliminate a particular behavior, there is a rationale for choosing among these four covert-conditioning procedures used to decrease behavior.

Generally, covert sensitization is the treatment of choice for eliminating undesirable behaviors for a number of reasons: (1) the rationale for this procedure appears easiest for the client to understand and accept, (2) covert sensitization is simpler in application than the other procedures, (3) clients usually have less problems in designating aversive stimuli that can be used as compared with the items needed for covert response cost, (4) covert sensitization appears to work more rapidly than covert extinction, and (5) covert sensitization requires less scene elaboration and involves the client more directly than covert modeling.

Covert extinction is the technique of choice when a behavior has to be decelerated but the environment is reinforcing the behavior at a higher rate than the use of covert sensitization alone can punish it.

Covert response cost is sometimes employed when there are a number of behaviors to be decelerated because many trials of covert sensitization may lead to boredom or satiation with the procedure. Therefore, it is helpful to vary homework assignments by including covert response cost. Further, for some clients, covert response cost scenes may be more emotionally intense than covert sensitization scenes. For example, some clients report that imagining losing their wallet, with all of their credit cards, is more aversive than imagery of vomiting or other aversive stimuli employed in covert sensitization.

Covert modeling is occasionally employed to reduce undesirable behavior if the client has difficulty in imagining *himself* in a particular situation but is easily able to imagine another person performing a particular behavior.

In increasing certain behaviors, covert positive reinforcement is generally preferred over covert negative reinforcement. Experience indicates that for the client covert positive reinforcement is easier and more enjoyable than covert negative reinforcement. Consequently, it is more difficult to involve the client in homework assignments using covert negative reinforcement.

Covert negative reinforcement is employed whenever the criteria for covert positive reinforcement are not met, for example, in cases in which the client claims that he either cannot generate or has great difficulty in imagining any pleasant experience.

Covert modeling may be used for increasing the probability of behaviors in the client who claims inability to perceive *himself* performing particular behaviors in imagery scenes.

Although, at this time, covert positive reinforcement and covert sensitization are the most commonly used of the covert procedures, it may be that the covert modeling procedures will be the treatment of choice, regardless of whether or not the client is able to imagine himself in scenes. The experimental evidence concerning the efficacy of covert modeling appears uniformly positive (Cautela, Flannery, and Hanley, 1974; Kazdin, 1973, 1974, 1975, 1976).

Client Variables

Several factors of the client's makeup are important in either facilitating or interfering with the course of therapy; and these variables are taken into consideration in choosing or modifying the covert conditioning procedures.

When working with elderly or physically debilitated individuals, special adaptions may be made. Cautela and Mansfield (1977) suggest implementing more relaxation-training trials and shorter imagery scenes when working with elderly clients because this seems more effective. Thought stopping, a procedure in which the therapist initially startles the client by shouting "Stop!" unexpectedly is not recommended for clients with a history of cardiac problems.

Although it is possible to use the covert-conditioning procedures with the very young or with persons functioning at a low level intellectually, imagery techniques must be tailored to the individuals. For instance, when developing a program for a child, the developmental level, control over motor responses, and ability to use and comprehend language should be considered. Further, covert sensitization is avoided when working with the very young except in cases where the problem behavior(s) is life-threatening and found intractible by other procedures.

Organic limitations may necessitate modification of the procedures. For example, blindness may limit the number of sense modalities usable in imagery procedures (Monroe and Ahr, 1972). Tightening and releasing certain muscles as a part of progressive relaxation training may not be appropriate in certain organic illnesses (e.g., arthritis).

Finally, clients vary in their ability to use imagery adequately, in their elaboration of scenes presented to them, and with respect to the clarity with which they are able to produce images. This is of particular concern in the use of covert-conditioning procedures. A determination is made of the client's ability to use imagery during the behavior analysis. The Imagery Survey Schedule, developed by Cautela and Tondo (1977), rates the client's ability to use imagery. Without further training in imagery, the score on this scale correlates with treatment outcome.

THERAPEUTIC PROCESS

Environmental Variables

The covert conditioning procedures may be used in private office, school settings, and institutional settings.

Generally, therapy is conducted on an individual basis in a private office. In the case of some clients, it is necessary to conduct therapy sessions in the client's home. For example, one client had been physically unable to drive himself to the therapist's office. Another client had to be seen initially in his home to treat a phobia of driving further than a 1-mile radius from his home.

Another type of case that prohibits the use of a private office is the medical or psychiatric emergency. A client who at an earlier time had been successfully treated for claustrophobia was hospitalized in a medical facility when his family contacted the therapist. He had been diagnosed as having "hysterical" paralysis and was unable to move from the waist down. Since there was expressed need for additional therapy, sessions were conducted in the hospital facility.

Although it is feasible to use behavioral procedures in an institutional setting, many times a therapeutic program must be adapted to staff procedures in the institution. Baron and Cautela (1973) found that when using overt behavioral procedures, such as positive reinforcement and time out, all three shifts of staff had to be trained in the use of the procedures and needed to cooperate with the program. In settings where the cooperation of other individuals is not forthcoming, the covert-conditioning procedures may be preferable to other behavioral techniques.

Significant Others

The term significant others refers to individuals in the client's environment who appear to have a great deal of control over the client's activities, for instance, chief nurses in an institutional setting. In addition, individuals who consistently supply consequences to the client's behaviors, such as spouses, parents, children, or close friends are "significant others."

It is our practice when evaluating any new client to interview significant others. There are a number of reasons for this practice. First, in working through a behavioral analysis, it is often helpful to obtain clarification about the behaviors to be changed, the situation in which these behaviors occur, and the manner in which these behaviors are responded to by people close to the client. For instance, in the case of an illness with a psychosomatic component, such as tension headaches, the therapist needs to know that when the client is suffering with a headache, usually his spouse reacts very sympathetically and he is excused from completing any pressing work assigned to him. Often the client himself may be unwilling or unable to tell the therapist how he is typically reinforced for being sick. The client may feel that such an admission would indicate that his behavior is manipulative or foolish; he may be simply unaware of the typical consequences of his headaches.

An additional function is achieved by interviewing significant others. These individuals are presented with the aim of the therapeutic process and instructed in the actions they can take to help the client's progress.

An area that requires the extensive work with significant others is in doing therapy with children. Since working with children should always involve seeing their parents or guardians, often a co-therapist's assistance is needed to meet with the parents several times a month. Parents exert extensive control over their children in terms of presenting reinforcing or aversive consequences.

Children are usually at a disadvantage in articulating specific problems or unable to conceptualize the consequences of their behavior. When using the covert-conditioning techniques, cooperative parents can be a good resource for information needed for the behavior analysis. They can also insure a child's home practice of imagery scenes.

Client-Therapist Relationship

In forming a contract with a client, an attempt is made to establish a client-consultant relationship. The client is seeking advice from a therapist who has been trained to be an expert in modifying maladaptive habits.

In addition to making the client aware of the therapist's expertise in modifying behavior, the therapist attempts to become reinforcing to the client by talking about shared feelings or hobbies, and taking an advocate stance for the client.

Clients may judge their therapist on the basis of age, sex, weight, use of humor, and other variables. If the client finds himself liking the therapist, therapy process will be facilitated due to increased cooperation on the client's part and the greater social reinforcing value of the therapist.

In every therapy situation an agreement is made between client and therapist that responsibility for treatment outcome is shared. It is especially important with the use of covert conditioning procedures that the client should be willing to honestly represent his covert experiences, and practice procedures on his own. Imagery practice and completion of homework are particularly critical for the successful use of the covert conditioning procedures.

If it appears that progress is not being made due to lack of cooperation in doing homework, the therapist may suggest that he and the client schedule more frequent sessions since treatment will take longer and be more expensive if the client does not do his assignments.

Finally, in terms of the client-therapist relationship, an agreement is made that the therapist's judgments of the client's behavior will not be made according to value or moral imperatives. Rather, the therapist will attempt to assess behavior in terms of social acceptability. For example, although the therapist may convey a judgment about the client's treatment of his spouse, this judgment will be made on pragmatic grounds (e.g., if the client were more affectionate to his spouse, living with that person might be easier).

Data Gathering

Data gathering is important throughout the course of therapy. Data is collected and used for initial and ongoing assessment of the client's behavior.

Primary emphasis is placed on inventory and questionnaire responses. The *Behavioral Inventory Battery*, developed by Cautela and Upper (1976), is a standardized series of self-report inventories divided into three levels: primary, secondary, and tertiary.

The primary scales are general and of wide scope. They provide a questionnaire framework for obtaining information applicable to every client. There are four primary questionnaires. The Behavior Analysis History Questionnaire (Cautela and Upper, 1976; Cautela, 1977) yields comprehensive summary data on a client's demographic, marital, educational, career, health, behavioral, and sexual history and explores previous treatment history and referral sources for the presenting problem.

A second primary scale, the Behavioral Self-Rating Checklist (Cautela and Upper, 1975), presents a list of a number of adaptive behaviors that the client may indicate that he would like to have in his repertoire. These items may be totally new behaviors for the client or they may be behaviors that the client would like to perform more frequently in lieu of maladaptive behaviors. Some examples from this checklist are: "I need to learn to stop drinking too much"; "I need to learn to stop thinking the same thoughts over and over."

A third scale, the Reinforcement Survey Schedule (Cautela and Kastenbaum, 1967), asks the client to rate the reinforcing value of a variety of potential overt and covert reinforcers (i.e., ice cream, tennis, reading). In the final section of the Reinforcement Survey Schedule, the client is asked to list activities that he frequently engages in or thinks about.

The final primary scale, the Aversive Scene Survey Schedule (Cautela, 1977), lists a number of items related to maladaptive avoidance behaviors. Derived from the Fear Survey Schedule of Wolpe and Lang (1969), this questionnaire assesses feared items (e.g., "fear of death") for possible use as aversive stimuli in covert sensitization and to record stimuli for which the client may need desensitization.

After discussing these completed inventories with the client, the therapist is able to readily summarize the behaviors that the client is interested in changing, potent reinforcers and aversive stimuli for a particular client, and topics that require further exploration.

The secondary scales provide specific information needed to assess the client's capabilities in terms of factors relevant to four interventions that are frequently used.

The Assertive Behavior Survey Schedule (Cautela and Upper, 1976; Cautela, 1977) questions the client about the degree of assertiveness he generally exhibits in a variety of situations and toward different individuals. It also questions the client's beliefs about the consequences of assertive behavior.

The Thought-Stopping Survey Schedule (Cautela and Upper, 1976; Cautela, 1977) assesses the degree to which particular undesirable thought, feeling, and image statements occur, and which have the ability to make a client feel anxious, depressed, or lead him to avoid making an adaptive response.

The Imagery Survey Schedule (Cautela, 1977) is the third secondary scale. Ratings are made of the ease, clarity, and degree of pleasantness or unpleasantness of an image that arises in response to single-word cues (i.e., ugly, crash, brown). The single word cues cover the six sense modalities. Since the covert procedures are imagery-based techniques, an assessment of the client's initial imagery helps the therapist to create scenes that will be potent for a particular client and may indicate a need to facilitate the client's imagery ability through training.

The final secondary scale, Cues for Tension and Anxiety (Cautela and Upper, 1976; Cautela, 1977), presents a list of physical responses and asks the client to report those responses that he feels are associated with being tense or anxious (e.g., your hands shake, you feel tension in the back of your neck). Information derived from this survey serves two purposes. First, the therapist and client put more emphasis on the areas indicated during relaxation training to ensure that those areas become relaxed. Second, the client will become more aware of tension by attending to physiological feedback.

The tertiary scales cover a variety of specific problem areas. They are given selectively to a client only when detailed information is needed in a particular treatment area. Some examples of scales in this category are the Eating Habits Questionnaire and the Smoking Questionnaire (Cautela, 1977).

In addition to gathering information by questionnaire and interviewing the client and significant others for further clarification, in some cases medical or psychiatric records may be helpful. Although it should be noted that often psychological records are not a good information source because the material was gathered from a different theoretical orientation.

Occasionally, it is helpful to have a client engage in behavior rehearsals to determine social interaction skills, assertiveness, or inappropriate avoidance behaviors.

Often is it necessary to observe an individual's behavior in a particular setting by accompanying and observing the client. This is a particularly good resource when working with children; and the therapist may need to observe the child in home, school, and recreational settings.

Physiologic measures are a good source of data, especially with particular problems such as psychosomatic complaints or chronic tension. Physiologic measures are also helpful as an adjunct to other forms of data gathering, for instance, to assess sexual arousal in the treatment of maladaptive sexual behavior.

Nonverbal behavior is also used as an evaluative tool. In employing covert conditioning procedures it is very important to observe the client carefully while presenting imagery instructions. For example, the therapist may watch the client's expressions when an aversive scene is being described.

Aside from the information obtained to develop a treatment plan, data is collected throughout treatment so that continual evaluation is possible.

At the beginning of each session the therapist evaluates the client's progress by raising questions relevant to the treatment. For instance:

1. How many times have you relaxed since the last session?
2. How many times have you used thought-stopping?
3. How have your appetite and sleeping been?
4. Has anything happened during the interim to increase your anxiety? What?
5. Did you practice the covert conditioning scenes assigned? How often? Were the images clear? How did the scenes make you feel?

6. Did you perform a maladaptive behavior?

7. How many situations did you encounter in which you had the opportunity to perform an adaptive response? How did you behave in that situation?

Preparing the Client

Preparing a client for a change in his behavior is considered by some therapists to be as important as teaching the procedures themselves. More and more attention and therapy time is being used to prepare the client for change.

One strategy that may be used to make a client more receptive toward a change and to enlist cooperation for therapy is to indicate that the therapist has a technique to eliminate the complaint. For example, when a client complains that he is unable to sleep at night because he continually has thoughts running through his mind, the therapist may express an understanding of the client's predicament without being overly sympathetic and indicate a solution for his problem. The therapist might say, "It is difficult for anyone to sleep when they are continually thinking, however, there is a technique, called thought-stopping, that I can teach you to use when you are unable to sleep at night."

In the therapy situation, whenever a client makes a response, the therapist's reaction to that particular statement will either reinforce, punish, or extinguish that response. So the therapist should be constantly aware of his own reactions to a client's behavior. Responses such as smiling, ignoring remarks, and verbal responses may be influential feedback in treating a client. As an example, if during every session a particular client complains about the same issues, regardless of the events in his environment, the therapist may want to consistently ignore these complaints while continuing with the session.

This awareness of the effect of verbal and nonverbal feedback on the therapist's part should occur throughout therapy.

While working on the behavioral analysis, the therapist is concurrently attempting to increase the client's understanding of what services the therapist is able to provide and preparing him to accept behavioral treatment.

Rationale Presented to Client

T: As you may be aware, I have a behavioral approach to problems. I assume that you are neither sick nor crazy but have learned some bad habits. As an expert in learning, I will help you rid yourself of behaviors you don't want, and help you acquire some new, more suitable habits. We will, for the most part, be interested in the here and now, and work on a day to day basis. This does not mean that we won't pay any attention to your past. In many instances, past events give us clues to the salient features of your present problems. However, in general we will focus on clarifying what the problem is, what situations are triggering this problem off, and what the consequences of the problem behavior are.

Our main goal is not only to rid you of specific problem behaviors; but also to teach you self-control. When you leave therapy with me, you will have acquired a series of techniques which will help you for the rest of your life. You will know how to relax whenever you feel anxious. You will have learned how to get control over your thoughts and behaviors.

Since I view you as a consumer coming to me for consultation, we will decide together what problems we want to work on. I will describe the procedures I recommend, and tell you why I advise their use. In order for treatment to be effective, I will ask you to keep records and teach you to record your own behavior. We will need this to evaluate the efficacy of our therapeutic intervention, so that we can continue modifying the technique until we are successful.

Course of Therapeutic Intervention

The following is a case presentation, which begins with the initial interview and traces the course of therapy through termination. It is illustrative of the use of the covert procedures.

T: How can I help you?

C: I have asthma and I have heard that psychological techniques can help a case like mine. I want to know how you would treat it?

T: Why don't you describe to me what your asthma is like? How long you have had it, and what medication you are taking for it. First describe a typical asthma attack to me.

C: I start to feel shortness of breath, then I have trouble breathing. I start to wheeze, and sometimes I feel like I am going to choke and then I start to worry about dying.

T: Is there anything that warns you that you are about to have an attack?

C: No, except that my nose starts to itch and I begin to breathe a little faster, and I notice a noise.

T: How long have you had asthma?

C: I've had hayfever all of my life, but the asthma has been getting steadily worse for about the last five years, and the medication doesn't seem to be helping. I use sprays and all sorts of antihistamines and other pills.

T: Why do you think psychological or behavioral techniques might help you?

C: I have noticed that when I become upset my asthma gets much worse. I am a social worker, and I have read that psychological factors can bring on an asthma attack. I've tried other kinds of therapy and they didn't seem to affect the asthma.

T: What other kinds of therapy have you tried?

C: I have seen a dynamically oriented therapist, and I saw a Gestalt therapist for a very short time.

T: You saw both of them to treat your asthma?

C: Because I thought that if my general mental health improved, my asthma would improve, but my asthma didn't get better. I've heard about some of the work on biofeedback and the treatment of asthma; and the fellow who recommended you said that you work on this type of case.

T: Tell me a little bit about your life. You said that you are a social worker?

C: Yes, I am getting my Master's degree in social work.

T: Are you married? Do you have any children?

C: I am married. My wife is getting her doctoral degree in history. We don't have any children at this time; but we may when we get through our schooling.

T: How does your wife react to your asthma attacks?

C: She is usualy very nice about it. When I start to get red in the face, she looks worried and sometimes puts her arms around me. She asks if I've taken my medication and if I've sprayed my throat.

T: You said sometimes. What does she do at other times?

C: It depends, for instance, if we are at a party and I start to feel really bad, she is apt to ask me if I want to go home.

T: How do you get along with your wife?

C: I think we are very compatible. We seem to meet each other's needs. We're both interested in our work. We've been married for 4 years; but, we're both so busy that we don't see very much of each other.

T: How do you get along sexually?

C: Quite well. We don't seem to have any problems in that area.

T: Do you think your sex life is related to your asthma in any way?

C: I don't think so, except of course, when I am having an attack or have just had one, we don't feel sexy, and she wouldn't approach me as she sometimes does. I don't think I try to avoid sex by having asthmatic attacks, if that is what you're getting at.

T: No. I'm not trying to "get at" anything in particular. I am trying to determine how your asthma interferes with your life.

C: I try not to let it interfere with my life. For instance, I usually still go to class; although sometimes I may have to leave school if it gets really bad or if I feel like it is going to be a full blown attack. Occasionally, if I know I am going to wheeze all day, I don't go. I have a few days like that.

T: Can you give me an estimate of how often you don't go to school because you think that you will be wheezing all day, how many times a semester for example?

C: Oh, not often, about three or four times a month.

T: How is your sleeping?

C: I don't usually have trouble falling asleep, although occasionally in August and several other times during the year I wake up wheezing, but in general I get a good night's sleep.

T: Can you give me an idea of how frequently you wake up wheezing?

C: It is really fairly rare. Maybe two or three times a year, I will wake up wheezing, one day a week, for several weeks in a row.

T: But other than those occasions you have no trouble sleeping?

C: No, not at all.

T: How is your appetite?

C: Good. I am a vegetarian.

T: Why did you become a vegetarian?

C: Well, I don't believe in animals being killed, and also I think it is a healthier way to live.

T: Do you have any milk or dairy products in your diet?

C: No.

T: How long have you been a vegetarian?

C: For the last six months.

T: Do you think that this diet helps your asthma?

C: Well, I thought that it would, but it hasn't seemed to help. I don't think it can hurt. I really think that it is a healthier way to live.

T: Does your diet present any problems when you are visiting people or eating out?

C: Usually I can find a way around it. The other day I was at a buffet lunch, and a friend, who is also a vegetarian, and I made up our own plates from the lettuce and the vegetables.

T: All right. Let me talk to you about my point of view on organic dysfunction such as asthma. I look at asthma as I would any other maladaptive behavior, in the sense that there are probably antecedent conditions that may trigger off an attack. Also, the attacks may be reinforced by certain consequences. Perhaps you are being positively reinforced for them or perhaps they help you avoid something unpleasant. Maybe without your realizing it, the asthma is related to certain tasks or social situations, or the way your wife or other people respond to your asthma. I am not saying that you are deliberately having asthmatic attacks to obtain rewards. I am saying that the consequences may be linked to the asthmatic event. We will be working together to uncover the antecedents (that is the things that trigger an attack). Once we find the antecedents to your asthmatic behavior, we will try to remove them. If the antecedents can't be avoided, we will try to desensitize you to these antecedents through the use of covert positive reinforcement or a similar procedure. In addition, I will teach you alternative responses for those situations. We will also work on altering the consequences; for instance, you should not avoid anything unnecessarily, but continue doing what you're scheduled to do whenever possible. I'll speak with your wife and ask her to react differently to your attacks. In addition to working on the antecedents and consequences, we will try to deal directly with the behavior itself by having you use a combination of techniques. For instance, as soon as you notice that an attack is beginning you will be able to stop yourself by thought-stopping, taking a deep breath, relaxing, and imagining a pleasant scene. I will teach you the thought-stopping, and the deep breathing will become more efficient after you have learned progressive relaxation, which is a technique in which you are taught to tense and relax sets of muscles based on Jacobsen's (1938) technique. So the asthmatic response itself will be dealt with through thought-stopping, then relaxing, and then imagining pleasant scenes. The pleasant scene serves to calm you, and it reinforces the connection between whatever the antecedents conditions are and your response of thought-stopping and relaxing. In other words, the pleasant scenes reinforces the relaxation response.

Instead of using the word attack to describe your asthmatic behavior, let's use the word "episode." From now on you are not going to be having attacks. The word "attack" implies that the behavior is something out of your control. We will both refer to your asthmatic behavior as episodes. Do you have any questions so far?

C: No.

T: Of course, we will need records. I would like you to keep track of every time you have an asthmatic episode. I will need to know where it takes place and how long it lasts. If it is different from the one you have already described to me, I will want to know about it and about what was occuring prior to the episode. For instance, I will need to know what someone else was saying and what happened directly afterwards. Especially concentrate on discovering what you did differently as a result of the episode. We really won't know what is related to your asthma until we explore many of the variables in your life. I will give you several questionnaires to fill out in order to discover some of the information. We'll want to know what you find reinforcing, and your completing the Reinforcement Survey Schedule will help with that. A general behavior analysis of your life history will be needed, so I will ask you to complete the Behavior Analysis History Questionnaire. I will also give you a Physical Complaint Survey Schedule for completion; it will help me know about your physical symptoms. These questionnaires will be a lot of work for you, and I assume that as a student you are very busy; however, it will yield very important information. Do you feel that you will have time to work on these records before I see you again?

C: I guess so.

T: Good. Incidently, one last question for today. If your asthma disappeared how would your life change?

C: I'd be less fearful of going into situations where I've had asthmatic attacks. Also, I worry that my asthma will get progressively worse and my health will be impaired.

T: But will anything change dramatically? Would you have any change of plans? Is the asthma keeping you from carrying out any plans, such as getting your doctoral degree or taking particular jobs?

C: At least not that I'm aware of. I think that my plans are set whether or not I get rid of the asthma. But maybe if the asthma goes away, I will be more likely to carry out the plans that I already have.

T: The reason I ask, is that for some people, solving their problem might mean great expectations on the part of others. Suddenly, they have no excuse not to go to a party, or visit their mother, or do heavy work. Often I wonder if I am going to meet with resistance from a client in doing the assigned work, because as the behavior changes so do the expectations of others for that person.

C: I don't think that this will happen in my case.

The session terminated with the client being given the questionnaires mentioned. During later sessions he was given the remainder of the primary and secondary scales of the Behavioral Inventory Battery.

In the following session, the therapist began by looking over the records and completed forms brought by the client. Usually, the therapist attempts to clarify any questions he has from the information on the questionnaire and goes over record-keeping with the client.

T: There is something that I would like to know. Did your father have asthma or hayfever?

C: I knew you would ask me that. The hayfever and asthma seems to come from my mother's side.

T: Did your mother have asthma?

C: Well, she has been dead since I was a child, but I think that I remember her having it. Why do you ask? Do you think that it is inherited?

T: It may be a combination of an inherited predisposition to asthma, and perhaps modeling factors. Perhaps you observed your mother's asthmatic behaviors and learned them. Whether or not that is the case, we will concentrate on looking at your behavior in the present.

After looking over the questionnaires and clarifying any issues that the answers brought to light, the therapist went over record-keeping with the client. Often additional clarification is needed to convey the antecedents and consequences, and reminding the client to write about the behavior as soon as it occurs, rather than, relying on memory. In addition to obtaining the data that the therapist needs for a complete behavior analysis, it shapes the client into viewing his behaviors in terms of antecedents and consequences.

Generally at this point in therapy, the therapist makes a double appointment with the client. One session is spent completing the behavioral analysis, and the second session is spent training the client in progressive relaxation. After the therapist has spent a full session teaching progressive relaxation, he and the client usually spend approximately one quarter of the following four or five sessions going over the relaxation technique to insure that the client knows how to relax correctly and is practicing at home. When this client was taught progressive relaxation, special emphasis was placed on relaxing the facial area, the nose, throat, and chest.

When the behavioral analysis is complete to the point where the therapist may begin applying specific procedures, it is our practice to talk with the "significant others." In this case, the client's wife was seen.

T: What do you usually do when your husband is exhibiting asthmatic behavior?

W: As he told you, I used to put my arms around him until he talked with you. Now as I understand it, I am to let him know that if he has an asthmatic attack, that I am available, but try to ignore him other than that.

T: I certainly don't mean for you to take this to the extreme. If he were to be rolling on the floor, you should certainly come to his assistance. I just hope that you won't go out of your way to soothe him, it also may be increasing the probability of the asthma. I think that as long as he knows if anything serious happens to him, you will get his medications or take him to the hospital that will be sufficient. It is also very important to show your husband affection and pay attention to him when he is not having an episode. Have you noticed any relationship between certain events in his or both of your lives which seem related to his asthmatic episodes?

W: It seems if there is dust stirring around that he is likely to have an asthmatic attack or episode as you call them. Also, sometimes it seems that when he is actually very angry, he is less likely to have an asthmatic episode. For instance, I cannot remember a time when he has expressed his anger and then had an attack. Sometimes after he has had an attack, he will tell me that he had been angry at something. But when he loses his temper or spouts off, he doesn't seem to have these episodes.

T: Do you think that your husband is assertive enough?

W: No. He is getting better, but I think he tends to let things simmer and then every once in a while he'll explode.

T: How do you react when he explodes?

W: Oh, it depends on the situation. If we are out somewhere and get into a fight I become embarassed and get very angry with him. I don't remember; usually we get along pretty well.

T: Perhaps I can teach him to be more appropriately assertive, and perhaps you can encourage him by asking him to tell you when things are bothering him. It will help if you don't criticize him for expressing himself. Perhaps when he tries to tell you what is bothering him, you punish him by criticizing him and becoming defensive.

W: Maybe I do. I am fairly sensitive myself, and when he does say something critical of me I do tend to snap back at him.

T: You may be punishing him when he speaks up. Will you make an attempt at least for the time being, not to snap back at him when he is critical?

W: I'll try.

Through the behavior analysis, it was determined that for this client, antecedent conditions such as being unable to assert himself in particular situations, anxiety in certain social situations, and dust were some of the factors related to the frequency and intensity of the asthmatic episode. Also, the client's episodes often resulted in avoidance of certain plans, such as making a class presentation. In addition, his wife's expressions of sympathy and concern appeared to inappropriately reinforce the asthmatic behavior.

Covert reinforcement for social anxiety and to dust was employed. Covert positive reinforcement was chosen over systematic desensitization because it seemed as if the hierarchy was unnecessary in this case, it had been proven effective in similar cases, and it appears easier for the client to adapt it as a self-control procedure.

Basically, the client was to imagine himself in a specific social situation, not feel anxious or asthmatic, and subsequently imagine a reinforcing scene. He was also to practice imagining himself in particularly dusty situations in which his nose did not itch, he felt comfortable, and then imagine a reinforcing scene. A typical covert positive-reinforcement training session on social anxiety follows:

T: From the inventory responses and our discussions, I feel that there are specific social situations that make you feel uncomfortable or anxious, and your anxiety in these situations seems to consistently precede an asthmatic episode. One thing we can work on to decrease these episodes is to desensitize you to the social situations in which you feel particularly uncomfortable. In addition to helping you get the asthmatic episodes under control, you can expect to benefit from this training by enjoying yourself in situations in which currently you feel uncomfortable and would prefer to avoid.

C: It would be nice if it worked.

T: I expect that if we work on this together, and you work consistently by yourself at home with the procedures I will teach you, you will likely become more comfortable in social situations.

The therapist presented a typical rationale for the covert-conditioning procedures, working through most of the skepticism on the client's part by relating similar case successes, and presenting experimental evidence for covert positive reinforcement. After the rationale had been presented, the therapist began teaching the client the procedure. Since the therapist had material from questionnaire responses, plus the client's additions, he had a good idea of which situations made the client uncomfortable and preceded asthmatic episodes. For example, this client tended to be uncomfortable at social gatherings and when speaking in groups. A training session dialogue follows:

T: Since you seem uncomfortable at social gatherings, we will build scenes around that topic. I want you to imagine that you and your wife are getting ready for a dinner party with the neighborhood group. I want you to relax, close your eyes and imagine that you and she are walking out the door. Try to imagine this scene as clearly as possible. But instead of feeling anxious as you normally would, I want you to imagine that you are feeling very comfortable and looking forward to talking with your neighbors. All right, go ahead, relax, and imagine the scene I have presented, try and experience it as if you were really there using all of your senses. Raise your finger when you feel the image is clear. How did that go?

C: Well, it was fairly clear, but I still felt a little nervous.

T: We'll do it again. However this time after you have imagined the scene, I want you to reinforce yourself. You may do this by thinking of an image which brings you pleasure. For instance, on your Reinforcement Survey Schedule, you said that you enjoy lying on the beach on a hot, dry, day. Is that right?

C: Yes.

T: Perhaps you will take some time now and imagine yourself lying on a beach. How was that?

C: That was nice.

T: Good. Now whenever I ask you to imagine performing some behavior comfortably that you normally would feel uncomfortable about doing, you should reinforce yourself by thinking about the beach scene or some other scene which you find pleasant. All right, let's practice the entire sequence again.

The therapist and client worked together to construct a number of scenes around the neighborhood party topic. They attempted to build a scene around every situation in which the client generally felt anxious. The therapist and client then practiced scenes such as arriving at the party and meeting other guests, participating in a heated conversation about community politics, and so forth. The therapist then asked the client to take the scenes practiced in each session and practice them at home. The client agreed to practice each scene several times a day for each following week.

At the beginning of the following session, the therapist asked the client how the practice went. The therapist and client usually went over any problems with the scenes and constructed new scenes around social situations which provoke anxiety.

In conjunction with covert positive reinforcement on social situations and dust, the therapist and client worked together on assertion training.

This client understood and accepted the basic rationale behind assertion training and became very proficient at asserting himself within several weeks. During the sessions, the client and therapist would discuss situations in which the client felt that he had not asserted himself appropriately, and he and the therapist would work together on a response. Occasionally, the therapist modeled assertive behavior, and the client rehearsed the behavior in the therapist's office.

The client was also taught a technique called the self-control triad, in which the client was taught thought-stopping, relaxation, and reinforcement. In this procedure, the client was taught to say "Stop" to himself whenever he began to feel the symptoms that preceded an asthmatic episode. After thought-stopping, he was then instructed to take a deep breath and exhale while relaxing his entire body. After taking a deep breath and relaxing the client was then instructed to imagine a pleasant scene.

Finally, the client was asked to make a list of tasks that he usually avoided. He and the therapist discussed the list and agreed upon which particular tasks should no longer be avoided, even if the client were just about to or had just had an asthmatic episode. For example, it was agreed that painting the house on a scaffold was something he would not have to do if he were recovering from or anticipating an asthmatic episode, but he was to attend all of his classes whether he was having an episode or not.

The therapist continued to interview the client's spouse periodically. She was instructed to differentially reinforce nonasthmatic behavior and ignore asthmatic behavior. When the client's spouse had a problem handling an incident properly, the therapist suggested an alternative response and modeled it.

As the client achieved more control over his asthmatic behavior, in terms of reduction in frequency and intensity of the episodes, the client gradually decreased his medication until, at the end of a 4 month period of treatment, he was no longer using medication of any type and no longer experiencing asthmatic episodes.

Before discharging the client, he was told to continue practicing relaxation every day, and if the asthmatic episodes occurred again, no matter how benign they appeared, he was to institute all of the procedures including recording episodes, antecedents, and consequences; the self-control triad; covert positive reinforcement practice; and so forth. He was also informed that if he had any trouble using the procedures or motivating himself to use the procedures, he could call the therapist for a booster session.

One of the important features in this case was the client's conviction that a psychological approach could help his asthmatic behavior. This conviction insured cooperation and record keeping, doing homework assignments, and good attendance at therapy sessions. His wife's cooperation was also very important and was insured by her belief in a relationship between her husband's asthmatic episodes and her behavior toward him.

It is evident from this case illustration that (1) the rationale that is presented to the client is extremely important, (2) a behavioral analysis should be thorough (this includes the assumption that we have no *a priori* knowledge of what antecedents and consequences are causing or maintaining the behavior), and (3) the treatment procedures require cooperation on the part of the client and significant others.

SPECIAL PROBLEMS

The covert conditioning procedures are subject to the same problems as other behavioral techniques. As in other behavioral therapies, the reinforcing consequences of a client's maladaptive behavior may inhibit the client's actions or "motivation" toward change. For example, the successful alleviation of an alcohol-abuse problem may simultaneously limit the reinforcing events available to the individual. Since imagery procedures such as covert conditioning rely on the cooperation of the client in terms of honest reporting, completion of assigned work, and attendance at therapy sessions, "motivation" problems may be of major concern to the therapist.

The Motivation for Behavior Change Scale questionnaire developed by Cautela and Upper (1975) is helpful in assessing the client's motivation for changing a particular behavior.

A number of specific procedures may be applied to increase a client's cooperation when using the covert conditioning procedures. Shaping an individual's performance by guiding him through successively more difficult steps of a procedure may be helpful. Providing the client with recording forms, developing a schedule for practicing homework, or teaching the client how to record the incidence of particular behaviors are all useful in obtaining greater cooperation from a client.

Often tape recordings of relaxation procedures, instructions for homework, or scenes for the client are prepared and given as an aide in homework.

The client's efforts may also be reinforced through the use of covert positive reinforcement. The client would be instructed to imagine that he is performing the assigned task, and immediately afterwards imagine a reinforcing scene.

As with other behavioral techniques, some clients feel that the rationale for the covert techniques is too simplistic, and other clients attempt to control the therapy situation. The expectations of other clients are so great that they become disillusioned when positive results are not immediately overwhelming. Another person who is difficult to successfully treat with the covert procedures is one who is involved with a series of ongoing disasters. Also, progress in therapy may be retarded if the individual is seeking therapy to satisfy others.

Occasionally, the progress in covert-conditioning therapy may be inhibited by the therapist who is unable to utilize certain procedures because of the detrimental effect the procedures produce in him. For example, some therapists avoid using vomiting imagery as the aversive stimulus in covert sensitization because they themselves feel nauseated during the therapy session.

The covert procedures are generally more adaptive than other behavioral techniques in terms of setting variables. When the cooperation of significant others can not be gained, the covert procedures may be applied as self-control procedures as has been previously mentioned. For example, in a case where a client's misbehavior in the classroom setting is being reinforced by attention from other students and the teacher, the therapist may be unable to enlist the cooperation of the pupils and teachers. The therapist then has the option of training the client in covert scenes to decrease the probability of the misbehavior.

Imagery Problems in the Application of Covert Conditioning

The problem that occasionally arises with the covert-conditioning procedures, which also arises with other imagery-based procedures, concerns the client's ability to develop appropriate imagery.

By appropriate imagery, we mean sufficient clarity to perform the scenes and adequate controllability over imagery while practicing the scenes. In addition, the attitude of the client while he is engaging in the covert procedures is important.

When any of the imagery procedures are to be employed, an inquiry is made as to the extent of clarity and pleasantness or aversiveness of the scene. If covert positive reinforcement is used, the client is asked to rate the scene on a 1 to 5 basis in terms of clarity, 1 representing not at all clear and 5 representing very clear. When an aversive stimulus is presented, the client is asked to rate stimuli in terms of clarity and aversiveness. Reinforcing or aversive stimuli are only employed if the client reports either a 4 or 5 on clarity and pleasantness or unpleasantness.

It is important to emphasize that imagery should not be equated with visual imagery. Usually the client is able to obtain adequate imagery with the use of one or more sense modalities. As previously mentioned, the Imagery Survey Schedule is helpful in discovering the vividness of imagery in the different sense modalities.

If a client has difficulty employing visual imagery, the therapist has a number of options. First, he may teach the client to use visual imagery more efficiently. The therapist may have the client practice looking at particular objects or scenes, closing his eyes, and attempting to reproduce the object or scene as accurately as possible in imagination. The client needs to continue this practice until he is able to reproduce the scene with clarity. For example, if a particular stimulus is involved, such as boats, the client may go to a marina for practice or pictures of ships may be employed in the same manner. A second method for increasing visual imagery ability is to have the client practice looking at various objects in the office, and then have him describe them to the therapist with his eyes shut. As homework, he may be asked to carefully note the visual details of any new situation encountered, such as visiting another person's home for the first time or seeing a beautiful sunset.

Another way to circumvent poor visual imagery is to emphasize the other sense modalities during the presentation of a scene. For example, when working with a fear of riding in elevators, the therapist may emphasize the auditory stimuli of the bell ringing at each floor, whir of machinery, or people talking. Kinesthetic sensations of movement of the elevator may also be emphasized. Pressure and tactile stimuli may be described concerning the floor underneath the client's feet or the feel of the buttons. Odors, such as smoke or perfume, may be presented in some detail.

We have not encountered a case in private practice with adults and children where the covert conditioning procedures could not be employed because of a case of deficient imagery. Currently, covert conditioning procedures to be used with various categories of retarded and autistic children are being developed. Imagery procedures have already been effective with schizophrenics (Cowden and Ford, 1962; Steffen, 1971).

Sometimes when instructions are given to clients to imagine a particular set of covert events, they report that the occurrence of images other than those the therapist presented intrude upon a scene. For example, a client who recently separated from his spouse chose a scene of walking along a beach on a beautiful evening as a reinforcing scene. When that scene was used as reinforcement, the client reported that he became sad because his wife and children appeared on the beach and this reminded him of his recent separation. Another example involved a woman who chose the scene of eating lobster at a wharf looking at the fishing boats in the distance. The scene was spoiled by the appearance of her husband complaining about the price of lobster. In a third example, a client who was using scenes of himself skiing as positive reinforcement reported that sometimes he would fall while skiing. One way to remedy the situation is to choose another scene that does not have negative association and does not involve the intrusion of unwanted images.

A second method to increase the controllability in imagery is to make clear to the client that the scene is his. He is the writer, director, and may construct the scene anyway he desires. The scene is then practiced until the client reports no intrusion of a hindering image. Further, clients sometimes are asked to use thought-stopping whenever an unwanted image occurs.

The third special problem that occurs in the use of covert conditioning procedures is the attitude of the client that events occuring in imagination can have no effect on observable behavior.

When a client complains that imagery scenes are not comparable to actual situations and a real situation would be different in terms of feeling anxious or giving into temptation, the therapist needs to deliver a convincing rationale, such as the following:

Experiments indicate that there is a transfer from imagery scenes to real-life situations. In my experience, I have found that when clients are able to perform the scenes adequately it does affect the targeted behavior. I am not asking you to take this on faith; but to try it for yourself.

As a last note, it is also very important to instruct the client not to use faulty imagery such as imagining that he is molesting a child, eating between meals, or panicking on an airplane. The premises of the covert-conditioning procedures make a good case for the assumption that faulty behaviors are maintained by inappropriate covert behavior. For instance, imagining that you are in an elevator and it crashes is an example of covert sensitization used inappropriately.

REFERENCES

Ashem, B., and Donner, L. Covert sensitization with alcoholics: A controlled replication. *Behavior Research and Therapy*, 1968, 6, 7–12.

Bandura, A. *Principles of Behavior Modification*. New York: Holt, 1969.

Bandura, A. Psychotherapy based on modeling principles. In A.E. Bergin and S.L. Garfield (Eds.), *Handbook of psychotherapy and behavior change*. New York: Wiley, 1971.

Bandura, A., Blanchard, E.B., and Ritter, R. The relative efficacy of desensitization and modeling approaches for inducing behavioral, affective and attitudinal changes. *Journal of Personality and Social Psychology*, 1969, *13*, 173–199.

Bandura, A., Grusec, J.E., and Menlove, F.L. Vicarious extinction of avoidance behavior. *Journal of Personality and Social Psychology*, 1967, *5*, 16–23.

Barlow, D.H., Leitenberg, H., and Agras, W.S. Experimental control of sexual deviation through manipulation of the noxious scene in covert sensitization. *Journal of Abnormal Psychology*, 1969, *74*, 596–601.

Baron, M.G., and Cautela, J.R. Multifaceted behavior therapy of self-injurious behavior. *Journal of Behavior Therapy and Experimental Psychiatry*, 1973, *4*, 125–131.

Capehart, J., Viney, W., and Hulicka, I.N. The effect of effort upon extinction. *Journal of Comparative and Physiological Psychology*, 1958, *51*, 505–507.

Cautela, J.R. Covert sensitization. *Psychological Reports*, 1967, *20*, 459–468.

Cautela, J.R. Behavior therapy and self-control: Techniques and implications. In C.M. Franks (Ed.), *Behavior Therapy: Appraisal and status*. New York: McGraw-Hill, 1969.

Cautela, J.R. The use of covert sensitization in the treatment of alcoholism. *Psychotherapy: Theory, Research and Practice*, 1970, 7, 86–90. (a)

Cautela, J.R. Treatment of smoking by covert sensitization. *Psychological Reports*, 1970, *26*, 415–420. (b)

Cautela, J.R. Covert reinforcemet. *Behavior Therapy*, 1970, *1*, 33–50. (c)

Cautela, J.R. Covert negative reinforcement. *Journal of Behavior Therapy and Experimental Psychiatry*, 1970, *1*, 273–278. (d)

Cautela, J.R. Covert extinction. *Behavior Therapy*, 1971, *2*, 192–200.

Cautela, J.R. The treatment of over-eating by covert conditioning. *Psychotherapy: Theory, Research and Practice*, 1972, *9*, 211–216.

Cautela, J.R. Covert modeling. *Journal of Behavior Therapy and Experimental Psychiatry*, 1976, *6*, 323–326. (a)

Cautela, J.R. Covert response cost. *Psychotherapy: Research and Practice*, 1976, *13(4)*, 397–403. (b)

Cautela, J.R. *Behavioral analysis forms for clinical intervention*, Champaign, Ill.: Research, 1977.

Cautela, J.R., and Baron, M.G. Recent history of covert processes in psychology. *Behavior Modification*, 1977, 1*(3)*, 351-368.

Cautela, J.R., Flannery, R.B. and Hanley, E. Covert modeling: an experimental test. *Behavior Therapy*, 1974, *5*, 494–502.

Cautela, J.R., and Kastenbaum, R. A reinforcement survey schedule for use in therapy, training, and research. *Psychological Reports*, 1967, *20*, 1115–1130.

Cautela, J.R., and Mansfield, L. A behavioral approach to geriatrics. In W.D. Gentry (Ed.), *Geropsychology: A model of training and clinical services*. Cambridge, Mass.: Ballinger, 1977.

Cautela, J.R., and Rosenstiel, A.K. The use of covert conditioning in the treatment of drug abuse. *International Journal of the Addictions*, 1975, *10*, 277–303.

Cautela, J.R., and Upper, D. The process of individual behavior therapy. In M. Hersen, R.M. Eisler, and P.M. Miller (Eds.), *Progress in Behavior Modification* (Vol. I). New York: Academic, 1975.

Cautela, J.R., and Upper, D. The behavioral inventory battery: the use of self-report measures in behavioral analysis and therapy. In M. Hersen and A. Bellack (Eds.) *Behavioral assessment: A practical handbook*. Elmsford, N.Y.: Pergamon, 1976.

Cautela, J.R., Walsh, K., and Wish, P. The use of covert reinforcement in the modification of attitudes toward the mentally retarded. *Journal of Psychology*, 1971, *77*, 257–260.

Cautela, J.R., and Wisocki, P.A. The use of imagery in the modification of attitudes toward the elderly: A preliminary report. *Journal of Psychology*, 1969, *73*, 193–199.

Cautela, J.R., and Wisocki, P.A. The thought-stopping procedure: Description, application and learning theory interpretations. *Psychological Record*, 1977, *2*, 255–264.

Chittenden, G.E. An experimental study in measuring and modifying assertive behavior in young children. *Monographs of the Society for Research in Child Development*, 1942, 7, (Whole No. 31).

Cowden, R.C., and Ford L.I. Systematic desensitization with phobic schizophrenics. *American Journal of Psychiatry*, 1962, *119*, 241–245.

Curtis, R.H., and Presley, A.S. The extinction of homosexual behavior by covert sensitization: A case study. *Behavior Research and Therapy*, 1972, *10*, 81–83.

Davison, G.C. Differential relaxation and cognitive restructuring in therapy with a "paranoid schizophrenic" or "paranoid state". *Proceedings of the 74th Annual Convention of the American Psychological Association*, 1966, 177–178.

Dinsmoor, J.A. Escape from shock as a conditioning technique. In M. Jones (Ed.), *Miami Symposium on the Prediction of Behavior, Aversive Stimulation* Miami: Miami U. P., 1967.

Ellis, A. *Reason and emotion in psychotherapy*. New York: Lyle Stuart, 1962.

Gotestam, K.G., Melin, G.L., and Dockens, W.S. Behavioral program for intravenous amphetamine addicts. Paper presented at the *International Symposium on Behavior Modification:*, Minneapolis, Minn., October 4–6, 1972.

Homme, L.E. Perspectives in psychology: XXIV. Control of coverants: the operants of the mind. *Psychological Record*, 1965, *15*, 501–511.

Hull, C.L. *Principles of behavior*. New York: Appleton, 1943.

Janda, L.H., and Rimm D.C. Covert sensitization in the treatment of obesity. *Journal of Abnormal Psychology*, 1973, *80*, 37–42.

Jacobsen, E. *Progressive relaxation*. Chicago: Chicago U.P., 1938.

Kazdin, A.E. Response cost: The removal of conditioned reinforcers for therapeutic change. *Behavior Therapy*, 1972, *3*, 533–546.

Kazdin, A.E. Covert modeling and the reduction of avoidance behavior. *Journal of Abnormal Psychology*, 1973, *81*, 78–95.

Kazdin A.E. Covert modeling, model similarity, and the reduction of avoidance behavior. *Behavior Therapy*, 1974, *5*, 325–340.

Kazdin A.E. Covert modeling, imagery assessment and assertive behavior. *Journal of Consulting and Clinical Psychology*, 1975, *43*, 716–724.

Kazdin, A.E. Assessment of imagery during covert modeling treatment of assertive behavior. *Journal of Behavior Therapy and Experimental Psychiatry*, 1976, *7*, 213–219.

Kazdin, A.E. Research issues in covert conditioning. *Cognitive Therapy and Research*, 1977, *1*, 45–58.

Kimble, G.A. *Hilgard and Marquis' conditioning and learning*. New York: Appleton, 1961.

Krop, H., Calhoon, B., and Verrier, R. Modification of the "self-concept" of emotionally disturbed children by covert reinforcement. *Behavior Therapy*, 1971, *2*, 201–204.

Lazarus, A.A. *Multimodal Behavior Therapy* (Vol. I). New York: Springer, 1976.

Lovaas, O.I., Berberich, J.F., Kassorla, I.C., Klynn, G.A., and Meisel, J. Establishment of texting and labeling vocabulary in schizophrenic children. Unpublished manuscript, University of California, Los Angeles, 1966.

Lovaas, O.I., Freitag, L., Nelson K., and Whalen, C. The establishment of imitation and its use for the development of complex behavior in schizophrenic children. *Behavior Research and Therapy*, 1967, *5*, 171–181.

Mahoney, M.J. *Cognition and behavior modification*. Cambridge, Mass.: Balinger, 1974.

Manno, B., and Marston, A.R. Weight reduction as a function of negative covert reinforcement (sensitization) versus covert positive reinforcement. *Behavior Research and Therapy*, 1972, *10*, 201–207.

Monroe, B.D., and Ahr, C.J. Auditory desensitization of a dog phobia in a blind patient. *Journal of Behavior Therapy and Experimental Psychiatry*, 1972, *3*, 315–317.

O'Brien, J.S., Raynes, A.E., and Patch, V.D. Treatment of heroin addiction with aversion therapy, relaxation training, and systematic desensitization. *Behavior Research and Therapy*, 1972, *10*, 77–80.

O'Connor, R.D. Modification of social withdrawal through symbolic modeling. *Journal of Applied Behavior Analysis*, 1969, *2*, 15–22.

Pavlov, I.P., (G.V. Anrep, trans). *Conditioned reflexes: An Investigation of the physiological activity of the cerebral cortex*. London: Oxford, 1927.

Phillips, E.L., Phillips, E.A., Fixen, D.L., and Wolf, M.M. Achievement Place: Modification of behaviors of pre-delinquent boys within a token economy. *Journal of Applied Behavior Analysis*, 1971, *4*, 45–59.

Reynolds, G.S. *A primer of operant conditioning.* Glenview, Ill.: Scott Foreman, 1968.

Schmauk F.J. Punishment, arousal and avoidance learning in sociopaths. *Journal of Abnormal Psychology,* 1970, *76,* 325–335.

Scott, D.S., and Jackson, W. Covert response cost: An experimental test. Unpublished manuscript. Boston College, 1974.

Segal, B., and Sims, J. Covert sensitization with a homosexual: A controlled replication. *Journal of Consulting and Clinical Psychology,* 1972, *39* , 259–263.

Skinner, B.F. *The behavior of organisms.* New York: Appleton, 1938.

Skinner, B.F. *Contingencies of reinforcement.* New York: Appleton, 1969.

Stampfl, T.G. Implosive therapy: A learning theory derived from psychodynamic therapeutic technique. Paper presented at the University of Illinois, Urbana, Ill., 1961.

Steffan, J.J. The effects of covert reinforcement upon hospitalized schizophrenics. Paper presented at the *Eastern Psychological Association,* New York, 1971.

Tondo, T.R., Lane, J.R., and Gill, Jr., K. Suppression of specific eating behaviors by covert response cost: An experimental analysis. *Psychological Record* , 1975, *25,* 187–196.

Weiner, H. Real and imagined cost effects upon human fixed-interval responding. *Psychological Reports,* 1965, *17,* 659–662.

Wisocki, P.A. A covert reinforcement program for the treatment of text anxiety: A brief report. *Behavior Therapy,* 1973, *4,* 264–266.

Wisocki, P.A. The successful treatment of a heroin addict by covert conditioning techniques. *Journal of Behavior Therapy and Experimental Psychiatry,* 1973, *4,* 55–61.

Wolpe, J. *Psychotherapy by reciprocal inhibition.* Stanford, Calif.: Stanford U. P., 1958.

Wolpe, J., and Lang, P.L. A fear survey schedule for use in behavior therapy. *Behavior Research and Therapy,* 1964, *2,* 27–30.

CHAPTER 5

Biofeedback Techniques In Psychosomatic Disorders

THOMAS H. BUDZYNSKI

University of Colorado Medical Center
and
Biofeedback Institute of Denver

JOHANN M. STOYVA

University of Colorado Medical Center

KIRK E. PEFFER

Biofeedback Institute of Denver

BACKGROUND AND ASSUMPTIONS

Clinical biofeedback involves the modification of a maladaptive physiological response according to learning principles. The essence of biofeedback training is to provide the client with continuous information regarding the activity of a particular physiological parameter. Generally, it is the *bioelectric* activity of the physiological response that is electronically detected and amplified, that is, electromyographic activity, (EMG) electroencephalographic rhythms (EEG), or heart rate (EKG). In clinical biofeedback the client characteristically attempts to change some physiological response in a direction thought to be beneficial to that person.

Since the *assumptions* involved in the clinical use of biofeedback have rarely been made explicit, these are first briefly outlined. Next we describe the two basic approaches to biofeedback applications. Following this is a discussion of the kinds of disorders treatable with biofeedback. Presenting problems, client variables, and other details of the therapeutic process are covered in the next sections. Since skeletal muscle relaxation is the backbone of our generalized low-arousal training, we then spend some time describing these procedures. In addition, in Appendix A, a flowchart approach to a systematic progression of training from skeletal muscle through autonomic responses is presented. Finally, in the last section of this chapter we present several case studies illustrating the application of this systems approach, augmented by behavior therapy, to a variety of disorders including migraine and tension headache, generalized anxiety, sexual dysfunction, and a temporamandibular joint problem.

A notable feature of those disorders variously called psychosomatic, stress-related, or functional, is first that there is an aberrant physiological response, and second that this response is one that began as a perfectly normal and adaptive reaction of the organism. Responses frequently implicated in psychosomatic disorders are those that are part of the defense-alarm reaction; this is a condition characterized by sympathetic activation in the autonomic nervous system, muscular activation, and a great many hormonal changes. Involved in this reaction are release of glycogen from the liver, secretion of epinephrine from the adrenal medulla, increased heart rate and blood pressure, peripheral vasoconstriction, and a decrease in blood clotting time. These events may be thought of as a cluster of integrated reactions that act to energize the organism when it is threatened— the *fight-or-flight* response. Although this response probably evolved as a reaction to physical danger, research over the past quarter century in psychophysiology and psychosomatic medicine has supplied abundant evidence that this reaction can be psychologically triggered, that is, by central nervous system (CNS) stimuli (Greenfield and Sternbach, 1972). For example, Mason (1972) has stated that in man it is most likely psychosocial stimuli that predominate in the triggering of pituitary-adrenal cortical activity and in the release of stress-linked hormones such as catecholamines and hydroxycorticosteroids. A number of investigators (Charvat, Dell, and Folkow, 1964; Selye, 1956; Wolff, 1968) have proposed that this reaction—and its triggering by CNS influences—may be at the root of man's stress-related disorders.

It is important to note that, although the various components of the defense-alarm reaction begin as perfectly natural responses, they frequently evolve into psychophysiological disorders. Thus in essential hypertension we see sustained elevations of blood pressure. In tension headache we observe elevations in skeletal muscle tension. In chronic anxiety many indicators of high physiological arousal are observed.

It may also be noted that psychosomatic disorders are typically gradual in onset. There seems to be a slow evolution of pathology and a gradual shift from the normal to the abnormal. In essential hypertension, for example, there is a gradual increase in blood pressures over many years (Pickering, 1968).

Another prominent feature of psychosomatic disorders is the presence of *response stereotypy*, that is, when the client is placed under stress, he responds powerfully in the afflicted system. For example, Malmo and Shagass (1949) noted that when clients with cardiovascular-type symptoms—palpitations, hypertension, fainting—were subjected to a stressor, they showed cardiovascular-type responses such as high heart rate variability. On the other hand, clients with head and neck pains showed high neck muscle variability under the same stress. Moos and Engel (1962) compared essential hypertensives with arthritics. Under stress, the hypertensives typically showed strong pressor responses; the arthritic clients showed strong muscle reactivity. In the case of tension-headache clients seen in our laboratory, we have observed resting frontal EMG levels about twice that of normal individuals (Budzynski, Stoyva, Adler, and Mullaney, 1973). With migraine clients, high variability of temporal pulse amplitude has been noted, even on days when clients were not suffering from an attack (Dalessio, 1972). The preceding phenomena, which are extremely common (though not invariable) in psychosomatic disorders, lead to a set of assumptions which provide a basis for biofeedback work with such disorders.

Assumption 1:

There is a learning component involved in psychosomatic disorders. This is suggested by the gradual evolution of such disturbances and the fact that they are closely related to the struggles and coping endeavors of everyday life, that is, to the interaction between the individual and his environment. Furthermore, once we assume that learning plays a part in the origin of these disorders, then it becomes reasonable to employ learning techniques in an attempt to modify the maladaptive learning which has occurred. In other words, if the individual's disorder is one that involves a continuing maladaptive response to psychological stress, and if this response is partly learned, then perhaps it may be altered through biofeedback or other learning techniques.

This conception is actually very similar to that of Wolpe concerning neurotic disorders. Wolpe (1958) views neurotic anxiety as a continuing maladaptive emotional response to environmental stimulation. This maladaptive response is mainly the result of the individual's learning history.

Assumption 2:

A second main assumption in the clinical use of biofeedback techniques is that some physiological activity is aberrant or in some way different from normal. And, it is assumed that biofeedback training may be useful in altering this aberrant physiological responding. As just discussed, a major way in which aberrant physiological responding manifests itself is through response stereotypy; when the individual is stressed he responds powerfully in the afflicted system. Perhaps it is possible to moderate this excessive responding. It is at this point that biofeedback techniques come into play.[1]

Direct and Indirect Approaches

The clinical use of biofeedback may be divided into two main approaches—*direct* and *indirect* methods. The direct approach falls squarely into the tradition of North American experimental psychology as it has developed over the past 75 years. A particular response is measured (detected), and its frequency or magnitude is altered by reinforcing it. Thus we may attempt to alter levels of EEG alpha activity, skin temperature (a function of local blood flow), electrodermal response (EDR), or the electromyographic activity generated by a particular muscle group. Some clinical examples are the following: In tension (muscle contraction) headache, clients have been taught to relax the head musculature; in migraine headache—in which the pain is closely associated with the excessive pulsating of the extracranial arteries—clients have been taught to reduce the amplitude of such pulsations (Zamani, 1974; Friar and Beatty, 1976). In cases of Raynaud's syndrome, which involves severe constriction of cutaneous circulation as a consequence of arterial spasm, clients have been taught to increase peripheral circulation by means of skin temperature feedback (Surwit, 1973). Individuals with the cardiac arrhythmia known as premature ventricular contractions have been taught to diminish the frequency of the arrhythmia (Weiss and Engel, 1973).

Another major approach to clinical biofeedback involves an *indirect approach*. The best example of this is muscle relaxation as it has been commonly employed in anxiety- and stress-related disorders. Essential to

---

[1]if the client does not show any aberrant physiological responding, especially when stressed, then the purpose of biofeedback training becomes questionable. This point is often overlooked. (The aberrant physiological responding may include the failure to habituate normally.)

the use of muscle relaxation in this context is the assumption that it has effects on other bodily systems. For example, with chronic-anxiety clients we are not generally interested in altering some specific or localized physiological response. Instead, we seek some general dampening of physiological activity, which, in turn, will act to diminish anxiety. Thus it is an everyday clinical observation that the anxious client, especially the one suffering from chronic pervasive anxiety, shows high arousal levels. There is, moreover, a good deal of experimental support for this observation, as may be seen in the work of Malmo (1975) and others. With systematic relaxation training, we attempt to lower this excessive arousal level.

There is a growing body of evidence that muscle relaxation—whether it be induced by biofeedback or other means—has physiological effects opposite in nature to those induced by psychological stress. For more details on these effects see Benson (1975), Stoyva and Budzynski (1974), and Stoyva (1977). Additional evidence that cultivated low arousal has properties of an anti-stress nature may be noted in older psychophysiologically oriented therapies such as progressive relaxation (Jacobson, 1938) and autogenic training (Luthe, 1969; see especially Volume IV, pp. 132–133). Although the profile of physiological responding is not the same for each individual, the thoroughly relaxed subject characteristically shows decreased sympathetic responding and increased parasympathetic activity. It was this property of a generalized relaxation response that led to its adoption in behavior therapy. In developing his technique of systematic desensitization, Wolpe stated (1958, p. 72):

In selecting responses to oppose the anxiety responses, I was guided by the presumption that responses that largely implicate the parasympathetic division of the autonomic nervous system would be especially likely to be incompatible with the predominately sympathetic responses of anxiety.

Explicit in Wolpe's formulation is the concept that muscle relaxation has extensive effects on the autonomic nervous system. In general, muscle relaxation is associated with parasympathetic activity, whereas muscle tension is associated with sympathetic activation. Considerable neurophysiological evidence supports this position. This has been summarized in Germana's (1969) review article on autonomic-somatic integrations. Evidence indicating that the autonomic and somatic systems act in an integrated way was provided by the experiments of W.R. Hess (1954), who discovered that when he stimulated certain diencephalic (hypothalamic) regions he observed simultaneous behavioral arousal and sympathetic activation—an "ergotropic" response. Stimulation of other diencephalic regions produced parasympathetic activity along with behavioral quiescence—a "trophotropic" response.

The essential validity of the "ergotropic-trophotropic" distinction was demonstrated by Gellhorn (1964, 1967). According to Gellhorn, the "ergotropic syndrome" consists of sympathetic-adrenal events—increased heart rate and blood pressure, adrenomedullary secretion, sweat secretion, pupil dilatation, EEG desynchronization, and increased somatomotor activity. Generally, the trophotropic responses are opposite in nature.

Gellhorn has also stated that the organism's response is graded, depending on the type and intensity of stimulation. For example, when the animal is exposed to a moderate stimulus, only the sympathetic or "neurogenic" responses may occur. The adrenomedullary component is absent. But with more intense stimulation, both the sympathetic and adrenomedullary responses typically appear.

Gellhorn (1958) has also shown, in animal preparations, that reduction of proprioception through curare-like drugs greatly reduces the ergotropic responsiveness of the hypothalamus and diminishes hypothalamic-cortical discharges. Moreover, the loss of muscle tone produced by these drugs results in behavioral sleep. Thus there is a shift towards trophotropic activity. It is this mechanism, suggested Gellhorn and Kiely (1972), that accounts for many of the similarities among progressive relaxation, autogenic training, Wolpe's systematic desensitization, and certain techniques of meditation. In all of these, muscular relaxation results in reduced proprioceptive input to the hypothalamus, a diminution of hypothalamic-cortical discharges, and in a dominance of the trophotropic system through reciprocal innervation (see Stoyva, 1977).

Before we conclude this section, it should be noted that although much is known about muscle relaxation, the picture is far from complete. A major practical question is how muscle relaxation can best be accomplished—what is the best means of relaxing a particular muscle or muscle group, what is the best way to teach a generalized (whole-body) relaxation response, and what is the best way to achieve transfer to the stress situations of everyday life? Conclusive answers to these questions are not yet available, but given the considerable activity in the field, work in the next decade should provide us with many of the answers.

In our laboratory, we began work with muscle relaxation because of evidence from various older psychophysiological therapies that this was a clinically useful response. These older therapies, however, were not without problems. A major one was that of assessing whether, in fact, the client really was relaxed. To what extent could we trust his verbal report? For example, the demand characteristics of the training situation may be such that the client reports "relaxation" even in its absence. An added difficulty is that many clients, for example, those who suffer from chronic anxiety, often have a very poor idea of what it feels like to be relaxed. Frequently, they have been anxious and tense for years.

Another problem is of some historical interest. Several older relaxation techniques have been in existence for some decades and were reported to be useful in a great many disorders. Yet they were not widely adopted. Why not? One reason is probably ideological. From the 1930s to the 1960s, psychology and psychiatry were polarized into psychoanalytic and behavioral outlooks. Psychophysiological approaches did not fit neatly into either of these camps. Second, the apparent simplicity of progressive relaxation and autogenic training as treatment modalities is deceptive. Our conjecture is that, although these techniques were effective in the hands of their originators, Schultz (1932) and Jacobson (1929), the same was not generally true for their emulators. Simply reading a book about these techniques is probably not enough to assure precise mastery of them. There is much more involved than simply giving the verbal instruction to "relax" or to repeat "relaxation-type" phrases to oneself. Moreover, how does either client or therapist know that a relaxed condition has been achieved?

In our view, it is in the latter respect that biofeedback technology will prove extremely useful. In biofeedback training the therapist takes measurements. Has the client's EMG activity decreased or has it not? Moreover, if muscle tension has remained high, EMG feedback can be used to shape the client in the desired direction. Thus the biofeedback techniques—despite their seemingly esoteric and even science-fictionish flavor—should act to standardize relaxation training and to make it more reliable. And, in point of fact, criteria for what constitutes a relaxed condition are already beginning to develop. A particular set of such criteria have evolved in this laboratory (Budzynski, 1976) and are described in Appendix A (A Systems Approach to Relaxation Training). This approach, which may be thought of as the *shaping of low arousal*, begins with an easy response and then progresses to more subtle ones. For example, in teaching clients to increase hand temperature (peripheral vasodilatation), the comparatively easy response of forearm relaxation is taught first. Next, clients are taught to lower frontal EMG activity (at the same time that low forearm EMG activity is maintained). After this, clients are given hand temperature feedback. Finally, they may be trained to decrease EDR activity if this appears to be excessive. Note that this training is consistent with a shift from sympathetic to parasympathetic responding.

Before going on to specifics of biofeedback training, however, let us briefly describe the indications for this kind of intervention.

INDICATIONS

Presenting Problems

Every month seems to bring about new applications of biofeedback; however, most biofeedback clinics handle a select number of disorders. For example, in the Biofeedback Institute of Denver we see clients for common and classic migraine, chronic tension headache, anxiety problems, insomnia, certain types of muscle rehabilitation, tinnitus, Raynaud's disease, sexual problems related to anxiety, cardiac rehabilitation, colitis, and a variety of other stress-related disorders. Because our program is one emphasizing stress-coping skills in three general systems (cognitive, physiological, and overt behavioral), we feel that we can be of help with most disorders considered to be stress-related. We also offer several levels of stress-management training (group and individual, biofeedback, and nonbiofeedback) for those individuals, such as business executives, who wish to guard against the development of such disorders and who wish to increase their work efficiency.

We feel that biofeedback may not be indicated and that other therapy may be more immediately helpful for severe emotional crises, borderline psychoses, severe marital difficulties, and hysterical conversion-reaction cases. If our initial biofeedback measurements indicate normal relaxed physiological responding we may not use biofeedback at all, but we will use behavior therapy, if appropriate. If biofeedback therapy is not appropriate, we refer such clients to other therapy settings. We do not accept clients with epilepsy, multiple sclerosis, or muscular dystrophy. If, at some later time, research studies show that biofeedback can be of help with these disorders then we may accept such clients.

In general, if the client's disorder is known to be associated with maladaptive physiological responding, or if we detect this in the initial biofeedback monitoring session, then biofeedback training can be said to be indicated. If strong secondary gain factors are present, then behavior therapy may be required in parallel with the biofeedback training.

Client Variables

Motivation is an important variable in all therapy, and especially since biofeedback is a self-regulation procedure, its success is dependent upon the client's wanting to succeed. If in the initial interview or in the referral documents we detect secondary gain complications, we are alerted to the fact that at some stage in the training motivation will be lacking. For example, if a severe migraine client reveals that she gets her headaches before or during social situations and, therefore, must retire from or avoid the scene, we must determine what aspects of these situations cause her distress. If we do not take steps to solve this problem, the client will find herself unable or unwilling to (a) learn to correct her maladaptive physiological responding in the clinic, (b) practice her home relaxation exercises, or (c) transfer her new skills to social situations. Training progress will be sabotaged at one of these points if secondary gain problems are not handled. The client may have to develop more effective behavior so that she no longer needs to avoid social situations. Assertive training, role rehearsal, and cognitive therapy are employed to build in these appropriate, alternative behaviors.

Related to motivation is the assigning by the client of a high priority to the twice-daily home practice. Type A individuals (Friedman and Rosenman, 1974), with their compulsively busy schedules, rebel at the thought of "doing nothing" for 20 minutes twice a day. If, after we have presented a rationale for the home practice and have pointed out how "irrational" it really is *not* to do the daily relaxation, and the client still indicates a reluctance to do the training, we will advise that he or she seek a different type of therapy. It is essential that the client agrees to do the twice-daily relaxation. In fact, it is useful to have them specify *when* they will do it, and if for some reason they cannot at a given time, when else they can do the practice.

If the client has not been referred by a physician, or if it seems that appropriate medical tests have not been performed in order to rule out organic problems, then we will advise the client to have these tests performed. Since we handle many headache cases at our clinic, we have on our staff a neurologist who will order such tests as he deems necessary.

THERAPEUTIC PROCESS

Therapeutic Setting

Up to the present, most clinical use of biofeedback has taken place in a traditional office setting (with portable instruments). Within recent years, however, several clinics designed primarily for biofeedback applications have been established. The Biofeedback Institute of Denver is one of these. At this clinic the therapy is directed by psychologists, although a neurologist goes over all intake reports and will see certain clients if this is deemed important. Since the clinic receives many headache cases, close association with a neurologist is a necessity.

Clients are first seen in a typical therapy office, and all subsequent non-biofeedback interactions occur in this office. At times one or more biofeedback units are brought into this setting, but primarily for demonstration purposes. The biofeedback training itself takes place in another pair of rooms. The client, with his sensors and feedback displays, sits in a reclining chair in a relatively soundproof room. The therapist or facilitator monitors from an adjacent room. An intercom system permits communication between client and therapist. This setting provides a pleasant, quiet, and unobtrusive environment in which the client can learn to relax deeply.

In addition, there is a second biofeedback room arranged so that the therapist can monitor the instruments while in the room with the client. This arrangement is more suitable for those clients who prefer to have the therapist/facilitator close by and where visual contact may be necessary. Such a setting is often required in muscle rehabilitation work with accident or stroke clients who are recovering the use of muscle function.

Although we view the biofeedback clinic as the ideal physical environment for such therapy, the instruments, because of their portability, can be used in a variety of settings, including hospital wards. There would seem to be no limitations on their use, with the possible exception of close proximity of large electrical machines whose fields may cause interference with signal detection and processing. The presence of such interference, however, can be easily ascertained during the set-up of the instrument before any training is begun.

Instruments

Since most biofeedback instruments are portable, they can be used in a variety of settings. In fact, one of the major breakthroughs—a result of the extensive demand for biofeedback devices—was the development of electronically sophisticated, easy-to-use, aesthetically pleasing instruments. Rather than having to rely on large, clumsy, "client-frightening" polygraphs to monitor physiological activity, psychologists, physicians, and psychiatrists now have available small desktop instruments that provide easy monitoring of the relevant physiological responses. This new breed of physiological recorders (and feedback devices) does *not* require electrically shielded rooms and in most instances does not involve messy ink writeouts that must still be interpreted and quantified. Consequently, many therapists in private practice have installed biofeedback instruments in their offices. Here the setting is usually warmer and less scientific-looking than in some heavily instrumented biofeedback research laboratory at a university or medical school.

Therapist Attitude

Because biofeedback often involves the training of autonomic responses—usually in the direction of lowered arousal—it is important that the presence of the therapist not drive those responses in the direction of heightened arousal. This tends to occur if the client initially feels threatened or angered by the therapist. A warm, friendly attitude on the part of the therapist helps to set the stage for successful biofeedback training.

It must be made clear to the client, however, that the responsibility for success lies with him. Some clients believe that biofeedback will *cause* them to relax, much as would a tranquilizer. They must understand that the feedback simply mirrors or tracks the physiological response, it does not force the response. The analogy of a bathroom scale or a thermometer is often useful.

Data Gathering

As in a typical behavior therapy approach, the initial interview-discussion of the history and characteristics of the maladaptive response(s) and the antecedents and consequences of the response(s) provide the raw data base. In addition, the biofeedback equipment is used to make precise measurements of relevant physiological responses in the clinic. However, cognitions, feeling states, and overt behavior can also be quantified. It should be emphasized that ours is a *multidimensional* approach to the modification of maladaptive stress responding. In addition to the physiological aspects of the problem, cognitive and behavioral components have to be considered as well. On the basis of extensive research on behavior therapy techniques in anxiety disorders, Borkovec (1976) has reached a similar conclusion.[2]

Cognitive Components

Cognitive self-statements and visual images may contribute to chronic high tension, anxiety, or depression (Meichenbaum, 1976). Hence it is

---

[2]Some behavior therapists, like many psychologists, are averse to considering physiological variables. We think this is a serious tactical error. A multidimensional approach is required, particularly with psychosomatic patients.

useful to determine as specifically as possible the nature of these events so that they can later be modified. As with subtle maladaptive physiological responses, the client must be made aware of inappropriate cognitions. Once this awareness is heightened, he can begin to substitute more positive cognitions. Thus, the therapist might ask the client, "What exactly went through your head; what were you saying to yourself as you entered the cocktail party?" Quite often an anxious client will report a series of self-defeating verbalizations such as, "Well, here I go, into the lion's den. I'll bet they're all more sophisticated and more intelligent than I. I can't seem to talk about these things. I'll bet I look funny—should have dressed differently." Often the client thinks about his physiological fear responses also. "Oh boy, there's the thumping heart and the cold, wet palms. I can't seem to breathe. This is horrible!"

In most instances the client will not realize that these thoughts can actually make him more anxious. This must be made clear to the client before attempting to develop positive self-statements reflecting more realistic appraisals of situations. To begin with, the situations may have to be analyzed one by one to discover if the client is making unrealistic appraisals of the threat potential in each. Perhaps the client is, in fact, lacking in certain social skills; e.g., "I'm not an interesting person. I don't know how to start a conversation. I couldn't take it if the person I was talking with just got bored and walked away from me." In this instance, role-playing such a situation with the therapist modeling appropriate behaviors would be helpful. Moreover, the client must be brought to the realization that having someone walk away from a conversation is not the end of the world. It happens to all of us. At times it is helpful to remind the client that a good attentive listener is highly prized at social functions. Finally, developing a knowledge about one or more unusual areas such as, for example, futuristic city planning can transform one into an "interesting" individual.

The client may also experience maladaptive and self-defeating visual images. These are often triggered by the verbal self-statements (Meichenbaum, 1976). Consequently, changing the verbal statements towards a positive valence will often do the same for the visual thinking. However, there are occasions when undesirable visual images remain to plague the client. "Thought-stopping" procedures can be taught in order to produce at least a temporary cessation of these images. A more gradual approach is the deliberate substitution of positive visual images when one becomes aware of a negative image. But, a note of caution! The new, positive image must be one that the client can successfully and easily generate. If the new image is too discrepant from his basic self-image he may be unable to form it clearly or accurately.

Just as the self-defeating verbal self-statements tell the therapist a great deal about the client, so do the negative visual images. The content of both the verbal and visual thinking are an important guide to therapeutic process and, therefore, should be tapped at frequent intervals across therapy sessions. The client should also be asked to verbalize his thoughts and images with regard to the biofeedback as he proceeds through the training, since inappropriate cognitions about the biofeedback can slow or impede progress.

Subjective pain, feeling states and physiological responses can also be quantified. An example of a general-purpose graph for recording responses that vary in degree of intensity over time, such as pain, is shown in Figure 1. The graph provides a good picture of the course of the vari-

INTENSITY RATING SCALE

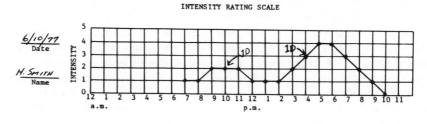

SYMPTOM INTENSITY

5 Unable to perform any work or social
   activities; confined to bed.
4 Unable to concentrate; can do simple tasks.
3 Pain moderate, can work however if
   necessary.
2 Pain irritating, can work and engage in
   social activities; pain can be ignored
   at times.
1 Pain there if attended to; otherwise ignored.
0 No pain.

MEDICATION RATING

A Aspirin, Tylenol, Datril, Excedrin.
B Darvon, Fiorinal, Midrin.
C Valium, Librium, Tranxene, Vistaril.
D Cafergot, Gynergen, Sansert.
E Alcohol (1 beer, glass of wine,
   highball, etc.).
F Codeine, Emperin w/codeine, Percodan.
G Elavil, Triavil, Etrafon, Sinequan,
   Aventyl, Trofanil, Norpramin.
H Demerol.
I Other_____.

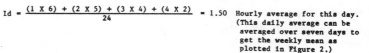

$$Id = \frac{(1 \times 6) + (2 \times 5) + (3 \times 4) + (4 \times 2)}{24} = 1.50$$

Hourly average for this day.
(This daily average can be
averaged over seven days to
get the weekly mean as
plotted in Figure 2.)

Figure 1.   Daily Intensity Rating Scale.

able during the day. Daily graphs can be averaged in various ways to get weekly scores which can be plotted as in Figure 2. The equation for this averaging technique, which was used in our tension-headache studies (Budzynski, Stoyva and Adler, 1970, Budzynski et al., 1973), is shown in Figure 1.

More discrete responses can simply be counted by means of a wrist counter. Examples of some of these responses are teeth grinding or bruxism, discrete, short-term, constant-level pains, and the occurrence of heart palpitations.

Behavioral Components

Overt behaviors relevant to the problem should be quantified if possible. Such behaviors may include the number of times an event, object, or person is avoided; relevant verbal statements; acts of aggression; behavior lacking appropriate assertiveness; behavior designed to manipulate others; and specific responses such as hair pulling, fingernail biting, eye twitches, and excessive frowning. Again, wrist counters are useful, and weekly or daily graphs can provide valuable information feedback for both client and therapist.

In order to modify behavior of the foregoing types, traditional behavior-modification techniques such as role modeling, behavior rehearsal, contingency management, assertive training, and systematic desensitiza-

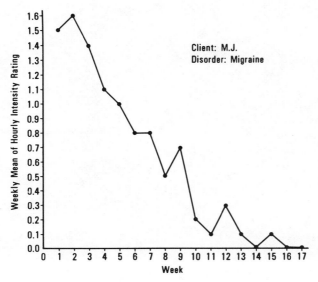

Figure 2.   Graph Derived from Daily Intensity Rating Scale.

tion are used. Awareness of the behavior in question is enhanced by the use of small brightly colored pieces of plastic tape on wristwatch faces, telephones, refrigerators, and steering wheels, in short, anywhere the client's gaze is likely to fall often during the day. The color of the "reminder" tape must be changed about every three to five days because of adaptation effects.

Physiological Components

Data from selected physiological responses are recorded with the biofeedback equipment. Electromyographic units may have a meter displaying the moment-to-moment average of EMG activity (muscle tension), or the unit may drive a digital display such as shown on the B-2 EMG unit in Figure 3. The latter type of quantification is quite accurate and registers the average amplitude of EMG activity in microvolts peak-to-peak for a given sample period. Thus, minute-to-minute readings of muscle tension can be obtained.

The *autonomic nervous system* is sampled by measuring *peripheral skin temperature* (usually from one of the fingers). Temperature devices, some of which can track accurately to one-tenth of a degree or better, record moment-to-moment changes in peripheral blood flow, which is mediated by the sympathetic branch of the autonomic nervous system. Generally

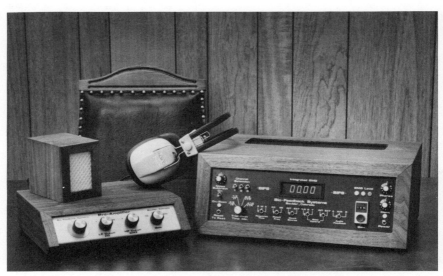

Figure 3. "BIFS" B-2 EMG Biofeedback Unit.

(but not always), when an individual becomes afraid or anxious, peripheral skin temperature will drop as peripheral vasoconstriction takes place.

Another autonomically mediated response is that of *emotional sweating*. This *electrodermal response* (EDR), more commonly known as the galvanic response (GSR), is controlled by the sympathetic branch as well. When an individual is in a fight-or-flight state there will generally (but not always) be an increase in the conductance between two sensors on adjacent fingers. A small, undetectable current passing from one sensor to the other is affected by the amount of sweating. As sweating increases, the resistance to the current decreases, thus allowing more conductance of current. The unit of conductance is the micromho. As measured with the EDR unit from Bio-Feedback Systems, Inc. (Boulder, Colorado), an average conductance level for the initial session is 3.0 micromhos (the latter is the unit of conductance). Clients with severe, generalized anxiety often show much higher EDR levels and more fluctuations per unit time than normals or those clients with less severe anxiety problems.

Strangely enough, some anxious clients may exhibit warm, wet palms or cool, dry palms instead of the expected cold, wet condition. It is, however, rare for a highly anxious client to show warm, dry palms—if he does, you may expect to find high skeletal muscle tension levels. Such dissociations are possible because the neurohumoral transmitter substances are different for sweating than for peripheral vasomotor responses. Emotional sweat glands, while activated by sympathetic neurons, respond to a *cholinergic* chemical at the synapse between neuron and sweat gland, whereas the small arterioles vasoconstrict with an *adrenergic* transmitter across the synapse. Vasoconstriction of these peripheral blood vessels, therefore, can be maintained by high levels of adrenergic substances (adrenaline) in the blood stream. This is not the case for the emotional sweating responses.

Certain *CNS functions* also can be quantified by commercially available biofeedback equipment. Typically, this includes the average level of alpha EEG (8 to 12 Hz) or theta EEG (4 to 7 Hz). Measurements may be taken in microvolts peak-to-peak or as the percentage of time a given rhythm has been present. Sometimes both are used. Typically, an anxious patient or one in pain will exhibit high cortical arousal (primarily a beta 13 to 20 Hz pattern) with little evidence of alpha or theta rhythms. Training such an individual to produce alpha EEG rhythms can result in feelings of distinct relaxation. Theta feedback may have some application to sleep onset insomnia (Budzynski, 1973; Sittenfeld, Budzynski, and Stoyva, 1976).

Procedures for recording the data obtained from biofeedback equipment vary from clinic to clinic. Clinicians interested primarily in the therapy process may not record much physiological data. On the other hand, those with a research interest may take readings of all instruments each minute. An example of such a data sheet is Figure 4.

Immediately after a session the data sheet can be shown to the client, and a discussion usually ensues. Although care must be taken to minimize performance anxiety, the debriefing can be quite illuminating. For example, if the EMG scores increased for a few minutes at a particular point in the session this might be brought to the attention of the client. He might say something like, "Oh yes, that must have been when I started thinking about that problem at work. Boy, it really sent up that tension, didn't it." This sort of "physiological insight" is quite important.

Information from these session data sheets also can be averaged and plotted along with the symptom as illustrated in Figure 5. Such graphic data can be useful in various ways. Figure 5 suggests a possible relationship between the frontal EMG decrease across sessions and a reduction in headache activity. However, if laboratory EMG levels declined but headache activity remained high, one might suspect that the client was not doing her home practice of relaxation. There may be secondary gain factors operating as well. Medication amounts can be plotted on the graphs if these amounts are changing, as they typically do. If a decrease in medication is followed by too great an increase in headache activity it may signal that the client is not yet ready to face the headaches without medication.

Preparing the Client

Most of the clients we see at the Biofeedback Institute of Denver have been referred by physicians or psychologists. Although these clients may know that they have been sent to us for biofeedback, the extent of their knowledge about this technique may be limited. If this is the case, then an explanation of biofeedback is in order. Examples, analogies, and diagrams are given until the concept is reasonably clear to the client. The relationship between stress, anxiety, tension, and biofeedback is carefully explained. Clients are often unaware that thoughts produce physiological changes. Important also is a clear understanding of maladaptive responding in the three response systems: cognitive, physiological, and overt behavioral. (We are preparing a series of "Disney-like" diagrams to facilitate this education process.)

BIOFEEDBACK INSTITUTE OF DENVER

TRAINING SESSION DATA (B)

M
PN
VOL(s)

Client:_____ Reason for Training:_____

Date:_____ Day:_____

Facilitator(s):_____ Time:_____

Total Sessions:_____ Phase:_____ Session:_____

Before Session Comments:

Room Temp:_____
Noise:_____
Null: head:_____
arm:_____
R's: head:_____
(meter) arm:_____
Types(s) of FB _____
H.R. Before:_____
After:_____
B.P. Before:_____
After:_____

(EMG)

	Trial	Gain	Head	Arm	Temp.	EDR	Alpha	Theta
No FB	1							
"	2							
"	3							
"	4							
	X̄b							
FB	1							
"	2							
"	3							
"	4							
"	5							
"	6							
"	7							
"	8							
"	9							
"	10							
"	11							
"	12							
	X̄f							
No FB								
"	1							
"	2							
"	3							
"	4							
	X̄a							

After Sessions Comments:

Homework Assignment:

Xo's: head:_____
arm:_____
temp:_____
EDR:_____
Alpha:_____
Theta:_____

Figure 4. Data Sheet - Biofeedback Institute of Denver.

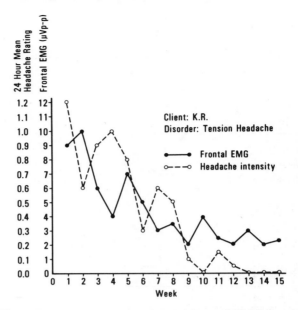

Figure 5. Headache Intensity and Frontal EMG Levels.

Attitude Toward Biofeedback

It is important also to determine the client's attitudes. How does he or she feel about biofeedback? This question—presented in an informal, friendly manner—will often elicit negative, pessimistic, or perhaps magical attitudes. In exploring such misconceptions, it is helpful if the therapist first acknowledges the client's point of view and then proceeds as tactfully as possible to present a rational, clear picture of biofeedback.

If the client asks how many sessions the training will encompass, it is best to explain that this depends on several factors such as age, duration of problem, genetic predisposition, ongoing environmental problems, and so on. We have found that if an average number is given, the client will expect to complete the training when that particular number is reached and will be disappointed if he is not finished. If the client insists on some estimate, a wide range can be given, for example, from 10 to 30 sessions.

Before any training is begun, the client must be made aware that part of the training may be provided by a facilitator rather than the therapist. Clients tend to feel cheated if this occurs without forewarning.

Necessity for Home Practice

The client should become aware that an essential part of the program is the twice-daily relaxation practice with cassette tapes. All clients receive this tape series (Catalog Number MV-3 from BioMonitoring Associates, New York), which carries them through a thorough course of home training. Busy clients must find time to fit these two practice periods into their daily schedule. It is best to get them to make this decision right in the clinic. Later the client will be asked to estimate the degree of relaxation obtained during each home practice session.

In order to keep accurate records the client must receive clear instructions about the data she will need to record outside the clinic. Figure 1 illustrates one common general-purpose form that can be used to record responses and medications.

These forms are discussed as the client brings them in each week. They constitute perhaps the most important data form and, therefore, must be done accurately.

Attitude Toward Relaxation

The client must shift to a *passive* condition rather than one of *active* striving during his training with biofeedback. Thus the client may be instructed to "let go" and to *allow* the responses to change in the desired direction. "Never try to force the change—*let* it happen." This concept is difficult to convey to individuals raised in strongly achievement-oriented technological cultures, but it is crucial to success in controlling autonomically mediated responses and to producing low levels of striate muscle tension.

If the client appears to be chronically tense it may be necessary to describe some of the body image changes he may experience as tension is released. If these are experienced without any forewarning they can be very disturbing. Some common reports include: "My right arm is eight feet long and my other one has shrunk to one foot in length!" or "My whole body is expanding!" Another is: "I'm floating about two feet off the chair!" Some of these chronically tense individuals may report pain as selected muscles relax while others remain tense. It should be explained before training commences that some of these sensations may occur, but that they are only a sign that one is relaxing and are not a cause for concern. (For further discussion, see the section on *Special Problems, Client Variables.*)

Finally, performance anxiety must be minimized at all times. Some clients can be motivated by means of data sheets; yet others become anxious or upset if too much is fed back to them. The therapist must be careful to proceed in gradual steps in the initial interactions with a client in the ' biofeedback situation. A success experience is an important goal, especially in the early stages of the training.

Course of Therapeutic Intervention

In general, the therapy follows a sequence of identifying and correcting maladaptive responses, first in the therapy setting and then in everyday life. The course of biofeedback training is shown in Appendix A. This flow chart should not be interpreted mechanically. It is only intended to provide *some* structure, especially at important decision points. Deviations from the flow chart sequence are sometimes necessary. For example, a client may be having great difficulty in reducing frontal EMG activity and, yet, when switched to temperature feedback, does quite well. In other words, the client is able to shift from one type of feedback to another without meeting the criterion for the former. At a later time the client might be more successful with frontal EMG feedback.

After the criteria for EMG, temperature, and EDR activity have been met, systematic desensitization with biofeedback can be initiated. We feel this sequence is an ideal one to promote transfer of the new biofeedback-trained skills to real life situations. Some clients, however, will terminate when their symptoms begin to diminish, rather than complete the sequence.

MAIN STEPS IN RELAXATION TRAINING

As has been apparent from our discussion, EMG feedback as a means of producing relaxation has, so far, proved to be the clinical workhorse of the biofeedback area. But before considering EMG feedback with a particular disturbance, such as tension headache or anxiety, let us examine the main steps in relaxation training, since these are fairly similar for the several disorders considered in this chapter.

A good rule with biofeedback training is first to try it on yourself. In doing this you become acquainted with the instruments, and you experience some of the difficulties encountered by the client—in addition to satisfying your own curiosity about the procedure. Of particular value in trying the training yourself is that you become more effective in imparting it to others. In your own training experience, some of its most prominent aspects will be the following:

The Volitional Component—Learning Not To Try

Let us suppose you begin with EMG leads on your forehead (the head-band containing the sensors is placed 1 inch above the eyebrows). One of the first things you notice is that if you try hard to relax, you are courting failure. The feedback tone immediately informs you that you are proceeding in precisely the wrong direction. The harder you try, the tenser you become.

What then is required? Actually, you must learn to do the opposite—to not try. Allow yourself to shift into a "drifting," "letting go" condition. Try various strategies, and let yourself be guided by what the tone tells you. At the start of a session, especially the first one, it is generally useful to have the client make the feedback tone go both ways. "What makes it go up? What makes it go down? Try tensing and relaxing, grimacing, jaw clenching, eye movement, frowning. Do the opposite."

One instructive exercise is this: The trainee allows himself to become quite relaxed, especially in the facial area. Then he thinks about some unfinished work. Tension rises with surprising rapidity! One is reminded of the Zeigarnik (1927) effect.

This volitional component is a prominent feature of relaxation training, of temperature training, of alpha and theta EEG feedback training. And the client should become aware of it. The importance of shifting to a non-striving condition is also strongly emphasized in related disciplines such as autogenic training (the use of "passive" concentration as opposed to "active" concentration), in progressive relaxation (Jacobson, 1938), and in Zen and other forms of meditation.

Bodily Sensations

Another important aspect of relaxation training is the various bodily sensations that occur with it. Although these vary with the individual, some common ones are heaviness in the arms and legs; warmth in the arms and legs—and sometimes in the epigastric region; and an increase in salivation, tearing, a need to urinate, drowsiness, tingling, and so forth. These various cues are associated with a shift from a sympathetic dominance to parasympathetic dominance in the autonomic nervous system. For example, warmth sensations are probably a result of vasodilatation arising from diminished sympathetic outflow to the peripheral vascular beds.

Shifts in Thought Processes

A neglected but important feature of profound relaxation is the alteration in cognitive activity that occurs. There is a shift—virtually a transformation—from goal-directed, reality-oriented, information-processing thinking to more of a free-flowing, nonvoluntary, drifting kind of thinking. Should the client become drowsy, hypnagogic imagery is likely to occur (see Stoyva, 1973, pp. 399–402). Generally, the possible occurrence of visual images is not emphasized since the client may become preoccupied with them. But it should be pointed out to the client that directed, reality-oriented thinking will probably keep him from reaching profound relaxation. He needs to shift away from it. "Just let this kind of thinking melt away."

Explaining Biofeedback Training

The client needs to understand why the relaxation training might help him and what is involved on his part. Often the client is someone who appears to be responding too powerfully to environmental stresses or emotional ones. Biofeedback can be helpful in producing relaxation and in moderating his reaction to stress episodes. It should be explained, too, that the benefits of relaxation training come gradually—after several weeks, and after diligent and frequent home practice. Eventually, the physiology of tranquility comes to replace the high-arousal physiology of stress and anxiety. Details about explaining a biofeedback program to the beginning client are described in the next major section.

Working with the Client

The client should be seated comfortably in a reclining chair—a sofa may also be used. Make sure that restrictive clothing, such as ties and belts, is not bothering the client. Neither should the legs be crossed, since this position interferes with circulation. After the sensors (electrodes) are properly affixed and a few *no-feedback* data points are gathered, the feedback tone is *gradually* turned on. The client is allowed to experiment with the tone for a couple of minutes after being told: "O.K., now work with the tone for a couple of minutes. See what makes it go up; what makes it go down." This allows the client to explore various strategies, it satisfies his curiosity, and it makes him realize that, in fact, he does already have some control over the tone.

Frequency of Training

In our setting, training sessions normally last 20 minutes. However, by the time the client is prepared, various aspects of his disorder are explored, sensors are removed afterwards, and his experiences for that day discussed, the time consumed is close to an hour. In most instances, we have clients come to the clinic or laboratory once a week or more. If they are only able to come in less than once a week, they have difficulty learning the relaxation response, and we recommend that they not begin bio-feedback training. (It should be noted that the laboratory sessions are supplemented by the tape cassette series on relaxation, see Appendix B).

Retaining What Has Been Learned

To retain what he has learned and to be able to use the relaxation response in other situations, it is important for the client to become aware of the various bodily sensations he experiences during profound relaxation. Many clients, especially ones who have been chronically anxious, may have difficulty in becoming aware of these bodily sensations. With these clients, it may be necessary to practice this "awareness" training on a number of occasions. The client should be encouraged to scan for these sensations once he has become proficient at relaxing in the clinic setting. Also, the client needs more than just a few seconds to become aware of the characteristic sensations of relaxation. A longer period—5 to 10 minutes—is much better. He then has more time to become aware of characteristic sensations (probably the autonomic correlates of profound relaxation take more than just a few moments in order to manifest themselves). Sensations that frequently occur are those of warmth, heaviness, floating, tingling, drowsiness, and so forth. The important thing is to find what are the characteristic bodily cues and psychological states associated with profound relaxation for *that* client. It is here that a considerable advantage of biofeedback over older relaxation techniques becomes apparent. For example, if the client is not really relaxed, then it is unwise to ask about the bodily sensations since the *wrong* cues may be present.

Actually, feedback serves kind of as a radar to the therapist. Is the client relaxed or not? And if he is, let him remain in this condition for some minutes before asking him to report any sensation.

A number of techniques may be utilized to assist the client in recapturing the relaxation response on his own. These techniques have been drawn from a variety of disciplines. One comes from the Rinzai sect of Zen: "Imagine you have a tuft of rabbit's fur under your nose. Breath so gently that you don't disturb the rabbit's fur." Also one can think of the sensations of cool air coming in—how it feels in one's nostrils upon inspiration—and of the warm air flowing out. Both are frequently useful practices for dampening out the flow of normal ideation.

It needs to be made clear to the client from the beginning of biofeedback training that much home practice is required. Generally, we recommend that the client perform the relaxation response (by listening to the cassette tape program or on his own) twice a day for 20 to 30 minutes each time. An important thing here is that the client actually makes time for such practice. The therapist should ask the client to specify particular times during the day when he will take time out for the relaxation. Otherwise, the home practice often simply does not get done. Usually the client will indicate that he is extremely busy, that it would be selfish and denying his family to take this time out, that his schedule is fully packed, and so forth. The client must be made strongly aware of how *irrational* it really is to miss the daily home-practice sessions.

Some other useful techniques to encourage home practice are drawn from the behavioral self-control area. For example, the client puts a bit of colored tape on his watch. Every time he looks at the watch he is to perform a brief relaxation response. A variant of this technique makes use of the Premack principle. If a low-probability behavior is frequently made to precede a high-probability behavior, the rate of the low-probability behavior will begin to increase on its own. Thus suppose reaching for a telephone is a high-probability behavior in the client's life. His instructions are that whenever he hears the telephone ring, to first do a brief relaxation response before picking up the telephone. This helps the relaxation response to become part of his habitual reactions in everyday settings.

Some of the behavior self-control literature is quite helpful in selecting aids to training. For example, *Self-Directed Behavior* by Watson and Tharp (1972) is quite useful in this regard. Since the issue of transferring the newly acquired response to the less protected environment of everyday life is so important in biofeedback training, and is so frequently a source of difficulty, the topic is dealt with more extensively in the section on *Special Problems.*

Recently we have begun to experiment with a very brief but systematic relaxation response. This is taught only after proficiency has been acquired in the laboratory setting. The client is instructed to make use of it every half hour during the day and to complete it in 30 to 60 seconds. The instructions are as follows (Brief Relaxation Exercise 30 to 60 seconds):

Assume a comfortable position. Close your eyes and scan your body for any muscle tension. Relax it out; let it melt away.

Then become aware of your breathing; a gentle, even breathing. Become aware of cool air flowing in, and warm air flowing out. Take 3 or 4 breaths this way—cool air in and warm air out. Allow your jaw to go limp and your shoulders to relax: cool air in, warm air out. Then let the warmth and relaxation flow into your neck, and down into your shoulders, chest, abdomen and legs, and finally into your arms and your face. Again, become aware of cool air in; warm air out.

At this point, open your eyes and continue with normal activity.

Though we do not yet have systematic data on the efficacy of this exercise, clients often report it to be useful. Worth noting, too, is that in autogenic training the recommended time for a particular exercise is about 1 minute (see Luthe, 1969, Vol. I).

Motivation

A related question concerns motivation. Many clients will find a relaxation period to be quite refreshing. Their body sensations are more pleasant: they are less tense, less anxious, and their mental focus is better. Prior to his training, the client can be told that a period of relaxation is quite refreshing. When the client begins to discover for himself that the relaxation is in fact, mildly pleasurable, this serves as an inducement to continue the training. Also helpful in motivating the client, is that he have a success experience early in the biofeedback program. Generally, this is not too difficult to achieve since, with EMG feedback, levels of muscle tension typically begin to decrease below baseline levels. Even a modest success experience can be a potent source of motivation for patients. Generally, at the time therapy commences, their life has contained many failure experiences, and even a small success makes the world look brighter.

Sometimes a self-deprecating client will say that he hasn't learned anything, even though the instruments indicate that a degree of learning actually is occurring. With such clients it is sometimes useful to show them a record of their progress—a graph is preferable (see Figure 5)—to emphasize to them that, in fact, their EMG levels have begun to decline despite their being subjectively unaware of it.

COMMON PROBLEMS IN RELAXATION TRAINING

A number of problems are commonly encountered in the course of relaxation training:

The Response is Too Difficult

In our early work, we found that many clients experienced difficulty when they begun training with frontal EMG feedback. Clients often find that thorough relaxation of the frontalis is a subtle and frustrating task.

If the response appears too difficult, a couple of things can be done. Should the feedback unit be one that has considerable shaping capability, then the criterion for successful responding (such as hearing a low-frequency tone) can be set so that it is easier for the client to reach the criterion. Later, the criterion can gradually be made more difficult as the client becomes more proficient. Another alternative is to shift the client to a muscle that is easier to relax (such as the forearm extensor). The masseter is also good. Prior to attaching the sensors to the masseter have the client tense the muscle; then palpate it to determine its location.

Generally, if the patient has difficulty in relaxing a particular muscle—which may be one closely connected with his pathology—then it is a good idea to shift to some easier muscle. Sometimes the client may have difficulty in relaxing his dominant arm, but may do quite well in relaxing his nondominant arm. The latter may be less involved in the tension pattern. With such a client, one would first work to achieve good relaxation in the nondominant arm, then in the dominant arm. Next, relaxation training would occur with the response system that seems most in need of further training (see Appendix A, A Systems Approach to Relaxation Training).

Wrong Hypothesis

Sometimes a client may persist in an incorrect hypothesis. For example, one client who was making virtually no progress turned out to be operating on an incorrect theory of what produces relaxation. Finally, the therapist noticed the sounds of heavy, labored breathing coming over the intercom. Upon being questioned, the client indicated that he knew that it was deep breathing that resulted in profound relaxation. Even though the feedback tone told him that this was not so, he persisted in his incorrect strategy. The therapist then suggested that he abandon the theory and pay attention to what the feedback tone was telling him. Subsequently he made good progress in achieving relaxation.

Sometimes, with clients who are having considerable difficulty in achieving relaxation, it is useful to tell them right during the session when they are doing well—and to continue what they were doing at that point. At first, these successful periods may be quite brief, but the client should be encouraged to pay attention to them.

"The Feedback Makes Me Tense Up"

Sometimes there are clients who begin to relax pretty well during the baseline period, but when feedback training commences they tense up. If this continues for very long—more than 5 to 10 minutes—it is often useful to turn the feedback tone off on alternative trials: one trial on, one trial off. This allows the client to continue what he has been doing during the off trials and to pay attention to what he has been doing correctly on those trials.

Sometimes, too, clients report feelings of tension or even of slight pain (e.g., in arm muscles) after they have begun to achieve relaxation. This seems to be caused by high-frequency EMG components. The pain, and presumably the high-frequency EMG, generally disappears with increasing practice of relaxation. Even brief excursions to low EMG levels may produce anxiety in some individuals who are afraid of relinquishing control or who feel body-image changes as they become deeply relaxed. Both complaints can be handled by giving the client permission to "drop down" but then to tighten up if he finds this frightening.

Home Practice

Many clients complain that during their home practice they aren't able to sense muscle tension very well. Jacobson's (1938) technique is often useful here. The client is asked to tense a muscle, then to relax it. He is asked to note the sensation that occurs when he is contracting the muscle. Also, he is to note the difference between what the muscle feels like when it is contracted and when it is relaxed. Later, the client learns to scan internally as a means of detecting muscle tension. He then relaxes the tense areas.

With some clients, phrases adopted from autogenic training are useful (e.g., "My arms and legs are heavy and warm"). A variety of these phrases and techniques have been incorporated into a series of six tape cassettes. A summary of the material on the tape cassette series is provided in Appendix B. Many clients find these cassettes a valuable supplement to the clinic biofeedback training. The series is designed to integrate the biofeedback relaxation training program.

Secondary Gain

As already mentioned under *Indications*, a common problem with many clients is the existence of secondary gain from the symptom. This is often signaled by a failure to carry out the requisite home practice. For example, the client may have learned a relaxation or a temperature response quite well in the clinic, but reports that he rarely has time to practice at home. In such instances, it is important to look for a secondary gain factor. This factor is not common in cases of tension headache, but is often observed in migraine headache, insomnia, and Raynaud's syndrome. For example, it may be that migraine headaches are useful in helping the client avoid unpleasant or embarrassing situations. In cases where a secondary-gain component appears probable, it is important for the therapist to explore the environmental and social consequences of the disorder. What happens when the client develops a migraine headache? Does he get out of unpleasant tasks, does it enable him to avoid unpleasant social situations? Frequently, an accurate answer is not immediately forthcoming. Sometimes, family members may have to be questioned. In such cases, a good deal more than "pure" biofeedback training is required. Thus if social situations are implicated, the client may have to be trained in certain coping skills—to carry on a conversation at a party, for example. Similarly, role modeling and assertive training may sometimes also be necessary.

When Muscle Relaxation is Not Enough

What if an anxiety client learns to relax quite well, seems to be practicing assiduously at home, and yet still reports no decrement in anxiety? Such clients probably react similarly during systematic desensitization; that is, even though they are quite relaxed, they still report anxiety. These clients appear frequently to be individuals who are not muscle responders but autonomic responders. A common pattern in anxious clients is that they show comparatively low peripheral temperature—usually in the range of 80 to 85 degrees rather than the normal 89 to 90 degrees F—even when they are muscularly relaxed. These individuals are started on temperature feedback after their training in muscle relaxation has been completed.

Another important feature that we are beginning to incorporate into our training is to develop a physiological *stress profile* of the individual. During the baseline sessions, the individual is subjected to some mild stressors such as performing mental arithmetic (subtracting serial 7s), imagining some fearful scene, or becoming upset over something. We then observe which system it is that responds strongly under the extra load. Typically, for tension headaches, there is a powerful muscle tensing response—especially in the head muscles. In migraine headache, a vascular disorder, there is a strong peripheral vasoconstriction response. It should be noted that the disordered response may not be apparent unless some load is put on the system, that is, the client may look fine under normal resting conditions.

The training is tailored to the physiological stress profile, and the ultimate aim is to teach the client to respond less maladaptively in the afflicted system. Further details on determining a stress profile can be found in Appendix A, *A Systems Approach to Relaxation Training*, and in the section on Tension Headache (the case study on Mr. H.).

BIOFEEDBACK IN TENSION HEADACHE

Because it is a comparatively straightforward affliction, tension headache is discussed first. In this very common stress-related disorder, biofeedback techniques have successfully run the gauntlet of controlled studies and are beginning to see extensive clinical use. Since Wolff (1968) and others had experimentally determined that tension headaches involve the sustained contraction of head and neck muscles, a relaxation approach seemed *a priori* a reasonable intervention. This supposition has, in fact, been well-supported in several studies over the past decade. To demonstrate that there exists a firm empirical basis for biofeedback training in tension headache, the relevant studies are outlined briefly. For a more extensive review see Budsynski (1976 a, b).

Empirical Support

In our own work with tension headache, we have regularly found that feedback-induced relaxation is a useful treatment modality. Our pilot observations (Budzynski, Stoyva, and Adler, 1970) were later confirmed in a controlled study by Budzynski, Stoyva, Adler, and Mullaney (1973). In our pilot study, EMG feedback training was applied to the first five individuals available. With EMG feedback training these clients not only learned to produce lowered EMG activity (frontalis monitored) but showed associated reductions in headache activity. Follow-up results over a 3-month period indicated that, for these subjects, headache activity remained at a low level, especially if they continued to practice relaxation for a short time every day. An interesting collateral observation was that many subjects, when they felt a tension headache beginning to develop in a stress situation, learned to abort the headache by deliberately relaxing their upper body musculature.

In view of our favorable pilot observations, and to guard against the possibility of placebo responding, we initiated a controlled-outcome study (Budzynski et al., 1973). The design involved one treatment group and two control groups over an 8-week period. The six individuals in the *pseudofeedback* group were given the same number of laboratory sessions of relaxation training, but instead of true feedback they listened to feedback signals that had been tape-recorded from the experimental group. To help in applying the relaxation response to everyday life, all subjects in both experimental and pseudofeedback groups were told to practice relaxation at home or at work twice a day. The six subjects in the second control group received no treatment at all.

All volunteers chosen for the study suffered from frequent tension headaches and had been afflicted for an average of 7 years or more. Subjects in all three groups kept daily records of headache activity (a rating scale of headache intensity recorded on an hour-by-hour basis) during the entire experiment, including a 3-month follow-up.

Briefly, the results showed that *frontal EMG levels* in the experimental group fell to less that 40% of baseline values; those of the controls changed very little. Similarly, *headache levels* showed a significant decline in the experimental group, but little change in the controls. Experimental subjects also showed a sharply reduced *medication* usage as assessed at the end of the 3-month follow-up period. Such a reduction was not characteristically shown by the control patients.

Also of great interest, from the point of view of modifying maladaptive stress responding, is that subjects typically passed through several stages in their ability to use a "cultivated" relaxation response to reduce headache activity. At first, they were able to relax only with deliberate effort. Later, the relaxation response became easier to do, even when the patient felt under some pressure. Finally, with some individuals the relaxation response appeared to have become virtually an automatic reaction, no longer requiring conscious effort.

Of the more than two hundred clients who by now have received feedback-assisted relaxation, approximately 60% have shown marked improvement, 20% moderate improvement, and 20% no improvement.

This finding has been replicated in a number of other independent investigations (Raskin, Johnson, and Rondestvedt, 1973; Wickramasekera 1972; and others). Recently, an extensive controlled study by Hutchings and Reinking (1976) has again documented the usefulness of EMG feedback in the treatment of tension headache. EMG feedback proved significantly superior to progressive relaxation training in the reduction of headache activity. In a follow-up study, Reinking and Hutchings (1976) noted that continued practice of relaxation was significantly associated with maintenance of headache alleviation. They noted also that in the case of two subjects whose headaches had returned, there again occurred a marked reduction in headache activity after they had relearned the relaxation response.

Evaluation of Tension Headache

The basic training procedure with tension headache, a very common stress disorder, is as follows: First, our practice is to confirm that the diagnosis of the client's affliction is, in fact, tension headache. The typical symptoms of these headaches are: They are gradual in onset, are likely to occur when the individual feels under stress, are typically bilateral, are nonpulsating in nature, and the pain is dull.

The other most common variety of headache, the migraine type, has the following typical symptoms: The pain is unilateral, it is pulsating in nature, there may be nausea or vomiting, there is a history of migraine in other family members, and the client is sensitive to bright lights.

If the headache description does not fit the tension-headache category, we will ask for a medical reevaluation, since it is important that the training be tailored to the pathophysiology of the disorder in question.

After the diagnosis of tension headache has been confirmed, we explain to the client the physiological basis of his disorder and why biofeedback techniques could be helpful in alleviating it.

Explaining Feedback Training to the Tension-Headache Client

T: The problem you have is a tension headache, which is actually a muscle contraction headache. As you indicated, these headaches get worse when you're under pressure—like when you are facing a lot of deadlines at work or around income tax time, or when you are getting into arguments with your husband. In other words, your headaches are tied up with different stresses in your life.

So, maybe before we start the biofeedback training, I'd like to explain a little bit about what we are doing—what biofeedback is and why it can be useful for tension headache.

We know that tension headache is caused by muscles that are too tense. You feel under pressure so you tense up. Your head, scalp or neck muscles go into contraction for a long time. When this happens, they begin to hurt. That's why you have the dull pain that gradually builds up over the day.

C: Do you mean to say I get uptight too easily—I'm too high strung?

T: Well, I think you've ended up being a little too high-strung, although you didn't start out that way. Tensing up your muscles when you feel under pressure is a perfectly natural, normal reaction. It's part of the body's "getting ready effort"—for doing something when we feel anxious or angry. What happens most of the time is that we tense our muscles some; we do a job or run away—then relax again—as when we are resting or sleeping. But some of the time we don't relax again. The muscles stay tense. Maybe you have an argument and the argument is over, but you keep thinking about it afterward—things you should have said—winning points!—you keep carrying this conversation around in your head. You stay tensed up, so you have a headache building up. What happens with you is that your headaches usually start when you run into a lot of deadlines at work. What happens when you have many deadlines is that you tense up—especially your head muscles—and you remain that way. You get in gear for one deadline. To tense up some is perfectly natural—but before you can really relax again, the next deadline is staring you in the face.

C: Well, O.K., but it's not just tension headache I've got. Frequently I have trouble getting to sleep. And often I have indigestion also.

T: Sure, that's an important point you bring up. When you react to stress, it's not just one part of you that's reacting. It's a whole cluster of things designed to energize you—not only do the muscles become active, but heart rate increases, blood pressure goes up, there's more blood sugar in the blood—a lot of things. And, at the same time, those things to do with digestion and rest slow down—there's less movement of the stomach and intestines; digestion pretty much stops. This is something everybody has, the fight-or flight reaction. We wouldn't survive long without it.

But what happens is that some people react too strongly, particularly with some part of this reaction. *You* show the muscle reaction quite strongly when you are stressed. As you've mentioned before, there are a whole lot of things that will set off the headaches—deadlines at work, thinking about arguments, meeting someone you don't like, being at a party where there are a lot of strangers, unexpected company for dinner.

Now this is where the biofeedback training comes in. What we'll mainly be doing is a relaxation training. I imagine lots of times when you've had headaches, you've told yourself "to relax, unwind," or somebody else has told you this. But probably it hasn't been that easy to do. Well, the biofeedback training makes it a lot easier.

The basic idea in biofeedback is to use instruments to tell you what is happening inside your own body—and to tell you right away. Ordinarily, this is a hard thing to do. For example, *right now* is my heart rate going up or down? What about my blood pressure or muscle tension? It's difficult to know, but with the biofeedback instruments we can tell immediately.

O.K. Let's say we want to pick up skin temperature. What we do is to tape a temperature sensor onto your skin so that you can see what your skin temperature is from moment-to-moment. Muscle tension works the same way. We tape sensors over the muscle we are interested in. These sensors pick up the tiny electrical activity that is generated by the muscles. What the biofeedback instrument does is to convert your muscle activity into sound. See, you have a pair of headphones and when the muscle is tense you hear a high-frequency tone. As soon as you relax, the tone frequency goes down. The tone tells you immediately whether you are doing the right thing or not. This is really the most important thing in any kind of learning—to know quickly whether you have done the right thing or not. The tone tells you instantaneously if you are going in the right direction. Is the muscle tensing or relaxing? Let the tone be your guide. We've used this on a lot of people now, and it helps them to relax a lot faster.

C: But those sensors, do they hurt? Are they some needles you stick in my skin?

T: Not at all. We want people to relax! The sensors are just pasted on.

All we do is to clean the skin thoroughly first with soap— it's called Brasivol, the same stuff teenagers use for acne.

C: Does the electric current go into me?

T: No. You provide the current! Different body tissues—the heart, the muscles, the brain—are continuously producing tiny electrical impulses during their work, even when you are asleep. We pick up these tiny impulses. In the relaxed muscle there are less than a millionth of a volt. Of course, a tense person will be a lot higher than that. But with this training, people can learn to relax so well that their muscles are only a fraction as tense as they used to be.

C: It sounds like something I could use, but how much time does it take?

T: Fortunately, not as long as the older types of relaxation training. But it still takes time. We have you come in twice a week, an hour each time. Of that hour about 30 minutes will be spent with you actually working with the equipment. We also have you practice relaxation on your own at home or at work at least twice a day.

Case Study: Tension Headache

This case illustrates the straightforward and uncomplicated training sequence that can be employed with well-defined tension or muscle contraction headache in a motivated individual having no payoffs for the headaches. Mr. H. was referred by a physician who had heard of our research with tension headaches. The client reported that the headaches occurred almost daily although he would be free of them on some weekends. As an administrator working for an aircraft company, Mr. H. had the disagreeable task of laying off considerable numbers of people during slack periods. Although the particular number to be laid off was fixed by upper management, Mr. H. had to decide who would go.

T: When did the headaches first begin?

C: In my first year of college, although they were never as frequent or severe as they are now.

T: Can you tell me how often you have them now?

C: I'll have them at least 5 days each week; in fact, I seem to wake up with one and it will vary in intensity all day.

T: Your medical records indicate tension or muscle contraction headache. Would you describe how you feel just before the headache and then the pain itself?

C: I'll sometimes feel a buildup of tension in my shoulders and back of my neck. Soon there is a dull pain which builds in intensity.

T: Where did you feel it?

C: Usually on both sides in the back of my head and in front also.

T: When you have them at work, what do you do?

C: I try to take several aspirin but that usually doesn't help much.

T: Are they ever bad enough to cause you to go home?

C: Hardly ever, I feel like I should be able to live with them.

T: What happens when you have them at home?

C: I can usually carry on with most activities; however, maybe once a month it'll be bad enough to cause me to lie down in a darkened room. The headaches are really worse at work.

From this interview data it seems that the client is probably receiving little in the way of a payoff for his symptom. The headaches are likely the end-product of a habitual response to stress, that of a sustained contraction of the muscles of the shoulders, neck, scalp, and forehead. The stress of new experiences, and perhaps the more competitive atmosphere of college, apparently initiated the headaches. Present-day stresses seem to be associated with work-related problems, particularly the layoff decisions, although the headaches were there even before the layoff began.

At this point the physiology of the tension headache was explained to Mr. H.

T: Your headaches are caused by an old habit of tensing and holding tense muscles in your shoulders, neck, and head. When stresses such as difficult decisions arise, so does the tension in these muscles. With prolonged tension, probably below your awareness at first, the muscles begin to cramp. Blood flow is restricted and the pain builds.

Mr. H. is next introduced to the daily headache rating charts (see Figure 1), which he will fill out each day. The vertical intensity scale is explained, as is the medication assessment. Mr. H. will need only to keep track of aspirin ingestion. Later, when he begins the homework of listening to the cassette tapes he will be asked to rate his degree of relaxation for his two daily practice sessions. Each time Mr. H. returns to the clinic he will bring whatever charts are completed. The therapist will look them over and comment on progress. If difficulty has been encountered with the relaxation, the therapist must determine what is causing the problem and suggest changes.

In the session following the initial interview a *physiological stress profile* is determined. This is taken under three different conditions. The client is asked to relax with his eyes closed in a semi-darkened room for roughly 15 minutes. Measurements are taken each minute of forearm extensor EMG, frontal EMG activity, peripheral skin temperature, and EDR—the emotional sweating response. Clients with cardiac or blood pressure problems will have heart rate and blood pressure measured before and after the sessions. After the *relaxation period* there is a 6-minute stress period during which the client is instructed to perform serial sevens—the mental arithmetic task of subtracting 7s serially starting with some beginning number such as 700. Generally, it is easy to spot the hyperreactive response system during this period. Immediately following the 6-minute stress period the client is asked to relax again. A *recovery period* of 10 minutes follows. The object of this phase is to see if the client's responses readily return toward relaxed baseline levels. A slow recovery time may signal a difficulty in adapting to frequently occurring arousing stimuli. This, in turn, could result in chronically elevated responding in that system.

The profile defines for us the client's ability to relax given the opportunity to do so. We can see which responses, if any, appear to be excessive and maladaptive. Furthermore, it tells us whether the client does react to the imposed stresses (some do not) and whether he can recover in a reasonable amount of time after the stress. Eventually, with enough normative data, we should be able to use the profile as a fairly precise diagnostic tool. For example, our analysis of the profiles of 17 essential hypertensive clients showed that as a group, they produced lower EDR levels and slower skin temperature recovery times than did a control group of normotensives (unpublished data).

As is typical of tension-headache clients, Mr. H. exhibited high frontal EMG levels as well as high forearm tension. His autonomic responses were within the normal range. During the stress phase both forearm extensor and frontal EMG rose even higher. During the recovery phase these responses did not return to relaxed baseline levels.

After his stress profile had been taken, Mr. H. was given a set of home practice tapes. He was told to practice with Side One (labeled "Tense-Slo-Relax") twice each day for 4 days. On the fifth day he was to listen to Side Two ("Differential Relaxation") until he returned 7 days later for the next clinic session (for a brief description of the tape cassette series, see Appendix B.)

Forearm extensor EMG feedback was initiated in this next session. It should be noted that some clients have a very difficult time relaxing their forearms. Should this be the case, the arm can be grasped by the therapist at a wrist and elbow and then progressed through a random sequence of movements with the instruction, "Just let me do the moving—you do nothing." After a few minutes the therapist can feel the arm loosen and the feedback tone should indicate the onset of relaxation. These passive movements may have to be carried out several times throughout the session. The emphasis should be on "letting go" rather than "*trying* to make it relax." Mr. H., in fact, required this kind of help for only a single session. After that, he rapidly lowered forearm EMG with the help of the tone feedback and a tri-level visual display. As his EMG fluctuated, the tone frequency and the visual display tracked the changes. Thus a sudden rise in EMG would cause the tone to increase in pitch and the visual display to change from green to amber and perhaps red. Mr. H. was told to "allow" the tone to remain low and the light to stay green. If they went "up" he was to become aware of any thoughts or feelings that occurred just before this happened. This instruction begins the process during which Mr. H. will learn that very subtle and fleeting thoughts, sensations, and feelings affect his physiological functioning.

By the end of this session Mr. H. was exhibiting levels of forearm EMG below the criterion shown on the flow charts (2.0μV). Immediately after the session (and before the therapist even entered the client room) Mr. H. was asked how he felt, particularly his arm. He reported that it felt heavy, in fact all four limbs felt heavy.

> T: Were you aware of any thoughts or feelings that precipitated an increase in the tension?
>
> C: Yes, a thought intruded about seven people I have to lay off today. I became aware of the thought when the tone shot up suddenly.
>
> T: You can see how fleeting thoughts of a conflict nature affect your muscle tension— imagine what happens when you dwell on such thoughts over a long period of time.

Before leaving Mr. H. was asked how well the homework practice was proceeding (he was adhering to the twice-per-day schedule). He also turned in his headache sheets (there were daily headaches). Mr. H.'s new homework assignment was Side Three ("Limb Heaviness").

In the next session Mr. H. was told that he would receive forearm feedback as previously; in addition, frontal EMG feedback would be presented. A "mixer" system is used to present such simultaneous feedback. For example, the tone in the right headphone will reflect frontal EMG. The click rate, a common form of EMG feedback which sounds something like a Geiger counter, tracks the level of EMG activity. Some clients at first have difficulty with dual feedback, especially if they are highly anxious. Mr. H., however, handled it quite easily. As he focused primarily on the clicks from his forehead region he was also aware of the tone level tracking his arm tension. Clients find it very satisfying to be able to control two responses simultaneously. At the start of this session, Mr. H. was told to move his jaw up and down, to swallow, to clear his throat, then frown and wrinkle his brow, and finally to move his eyes around rapidly. All of these produce a change in the feedback signal. Once Mr. H. learned what these artifacts sounded like, he could discriminate them from frontal EMG signals associated with thought processes.

In order to establish further the connection between thoughts and physiological changes, the client will be asked to make the feedback go up, not by muscle movements, but rather by thinking of stressful situations. (Clients are often amazed at the extent to which these thoughts cause the feedback to change.) After a short period of raising the click rate by thinking, the client is asked to lower the click rate. This alternation is carried out over a 6-minute period after which the client is instructed to allow the click rate to decrease for the next 15 minutes.

Following the feedback practice the therapist and client will talk about what happened. For example, during the final 15 minutes Mr. H. noticed that work thoughts would intrude without his awareness at first. The increasing click rate would be his first indication that such thoughts were present. He learned that even fleeting thoughts, either verbal or visual, could cause the signal to increase. This was particualrly true of work-related cognitions. Mr. H. was assigned tape Side Four ("Arms and Legs Heavy and Warm"). Building on the prior homework exercises, this tape begins to establish control over the autonomically mediated peripheral warmth.

Returning 3 days later for his second frontal EMG session Mr. H. announced that he found a way to listen to the cassette tape at work. Since he always brought his lunch he would eat it in his car and then practice the relaxation for the last 20 minutes or so. Even sitting up in the car he was able to achieve profound relaxation as he focused on the tape message. He reported that he was feeling the warmth in his hands but not his feet. Moreover, Mr. H. stated that he was attempting to relax his shoulders and neck while at his desk. He thought his headaches were less severe, although they maintained their constancy.

Once again Mr. H. received the dual feedback of the tone and clicks. Occasionally his arm would show a burst of activity, but he was able to relax it quickly. Mr. H. was also learning fast to eliminate certain thoughts and to focus on the heaviness and warmth feelings in his limbs. At times he would shift his focus to his breathing.

T: Every so often check to make sure you are breathing out and in from your abdomen, not your upper chest—let your belly move in and out slowly, rhythmically.

Mr. H. also was learning to keep his jaw muscles relaxed because they contributed in great measure to high frontal EMG levels. The EMG readouts indicated low arm tension and some frontal readings below 2.50 μV peak-to-peak: although he averaged about 4.00 μV overall. Mr. H. was encouraged by his progress.

Since he had achieved both heaviness and warmth in his home practice, Mr. H. was told to begin Side Five ("Forehead and Facial Relaxation"). Once again this cassette builds on prior learning but focuses particularly on relaxation of the muscles in the face, forehead, and scalp areas. This tape also includes the first repetitions of the phrase, "I am calm." The client is instructed to repeat the phrase on each exhalation, but only if he feels deeply relaxed. Upon repeated association with a relaxed state this phrase becomes a semantic conditioned stimulus for relaxation.

In his next session (the third focusing on frontal EMG), Mr. H. at first had high EMG levels. Gradually, he brought the frontal EMG down, although his forearm at times showed bursts. Several times frontal EMG would increase and remain high for 15 to 45 seconds before decreasing. Toward the end of the session, Mr. H. finally came close to the criterion of 2.50 μV for frontal EMG. Afterward, Mr. H. said, "I have to layoff a good friend today—I kept rehearsing what I would have to say to him. Toward the end I was able to concentrate on the breathing and on heaviness in my arms and legs."

T: How do you feel about your friend being laid off?
C: There was no alternative. It was dictated by seniority in that section.
T: So, there was nothing you could do?
C: Yes, nothing I could do—I guess I can't worry about something that I have no control over.

When Mr. H. returned for his fourth frontal EMG session, he reported that his headaches were no longer constant. As a matter of fact, they had occurred only three times over the past week. Furthermore, the headaches were of diminished intensity. Mr. H. had settled on a daily routine of listening to the relaxation tapes in the morning before going to work and then at lunch in his car. He had a growing awareness of tensing his forehead, neck, and shoulder muscles during the day. At these times he would relax the muscles whether at work, driving to and from work, or at home. Mr. H. was quite encouraged by his progress and remained highly motivated. He was experiencing one of the most stressful periods of his life and yet was controlling the headaches. During session four he achieved levels below criterion for more than half the session.

> C: I am really keeping my mind focused on my body. Intruding thoughts seem to be far less of a problem that they were earlier.

Because he had met criterion with feedback the next session would involve a gradual "fading" of the feedback (some trials would have no feedback). When feedback is removed, the response sometimes builds up and feedback must be reinstated. This was the case for Mr. H. in the fifth frontal EMG session. However, after several alternations of feedback and no-feedback trials, his levels with feedback off were as low as with it on. Mr. H. finished the session below criteria on both forearm extensor and frontal EMG. He reported only one headache for the prior week. At this point, since he was doing so well, Mr. H. was asked to come back in 2 weeks.

His last session was the one after the 2-week interval. Mr. H. easily met criteria without any feedback and reported only three minor headaches in the past 2 weeks. He was told to remain faithful to the daily home practice and to call us if the headaches returned. Follow-up a year later revealed that the headaches remained at a low level.

This straightforward case represents the ideal in that a motivated, intelligent, flexible individual with no secondary gain or payoff complications, required only six sessions to rid himself of a troublesome habit. However, now let us look at two more difficult cases, ones that did have complications.

Case Study: Tension Headache Secondary to a Sexual Disorder

The client was a 27-year-old law student with a presenting complaint of tension headaches. Having suffered from the condition for 4 years, the client had undergone extensive medical workups, and had been treated with analgesics, muscle relaxants, and chiropractic treatments. At the time he entered biofeedback therapy he was contemplating withdrawing from law school. In the initial meeting, the therapist structured the interview to ascertain the cognitive, behavioral, and environmental determinants of headache onset.

T: Can you recall the period in which the headaches began?

C: They started to become severe the first year after I graduated from college.

T: Describe what was occurring in your life during that first year after your graduation.

C: I was in a quandary about my future. I was married two months after graduation and there was pressure to obtain a full-time job, but I wanted to go to law school.

T: How supportive was your wife about your not working and going to law school?

C: Oh, she thought it would be great if I went to law school. You see, she had a fairly good job teaching at the time. However, I felt quite a bit of guilt about her supporting me for three years.

T: So you made the decision to go into law school and this is when the headaches began?

C: No, it was about five months later that they became a weekly event.

T: Has the frequency and intensity changed over the last four years?

C: Yes, I would mainly get the headache on the weekend after an intense week at school.

T: Has your law school work become more difficult over the past several months?

C: No, in fact, I have more time than at any other period in law school. But, generally, I am more tense than ever before in my life.

T: How do you experience tension?

C: Just from the headaches and a very tight feeling in my neck. Many times it sounds like rocks rubbing together when I move my head. It is this way *before* and also when I have the headache.

T: Describe the feeling you experience when you have a headache.

C: The back of my head hurts first. Then if it is going to be a bad headache, I feel intense pain over both eyes.

T: Do you ever have sensations of nausea?

C: No, or at least it is infrequent with the headaches.

T: Do you feel the tense neck muscles after studying hard at law school or at home?

C: Sometimes, but usually they start during the evening, and the headaches are more severe during the weekends.

T: What do you take for the pain?

C: I usually take anywhere from 6 to 12 aspirins to gain some relief.

T: Do the headaches cause any problems with your law school studies?

C: Not really, they make it more difficult to study at times, but I have
managed to remain fourteenth in my class.

The judgment of the therapist at this time was that the headaches were
caused by the tension of shoulder and neck muscles. There didn't seem to
be any secondary gain involved.

The therapist explained the underlying physiology of the tension headache (see previous section, *Explaining Feedback Training to the Tension
Headache Client* , for a detailed description). Following the evaluation interview, the patient began working with the alternate tensing and relaxing
of various muscle groups that characterizes the initial phase of progressive relaxation (Jacobson, 1938). Then, toward the end of the first session, the client was given a headache rating scale (see Figure 1). The client was also given the ''Tense-Slo-Relax'' tape cassette (see Appendix B)
to practice with at home during the week.

The primary step in the training is for the client to become aware when
tension is present. In his first feedback session, the client was asked to become simultaneously aware of changes in muscle tension and tne accompanying change in the feedback signal. Training was initiated with the
forearm extensor which the client learned to control after ten 1-minute trials. The feedback was then shifted to the frontal muscle group where
EMG levels ranged from 18 to 25 μV—very high levels. The client was instructed to close his eyes and to listen to the feedback tone, and then to
reduce the frequency of the feedback rate by relaxing his facial, shoulder,
and neck muscles as he had learned to do with the progressive relaxation
procedures. Although the client made little progress on this response during his first session, he improved considerably at the second session.

C: I can recite the instructions on the relaxation tape and begin to feel
more relaxed, particularly in the shoulder and neck muscles. It feels
as if my arms are hanging loose and limp at my sides. Then the rate of
the feedback begins to reduce. I've been able to hear the feedback in
my own head during the week when my neck would become tense,
and I would relax by imagining the feedback rate decreasing. It was
successful in getting rid of two headaches over the past week.

T: Were you aware of any thoughts or feelings during the session that
caused any changes in the feedback rate?

C: No, not really—it just felt good to be that relaxed.

During the third session the therapist had the patient relate what occurred prior to the onset of headaches during the past week.

C: I can't think of anything that caused the headaches. I felt tense several times during the week so I relaxed my shoulder and neck muscles. The headache seemed to go away during the day, but I didn't have the same success at night. At night I would try to do the same things that I did during the day but the headaches would still get intense and not go away as they had during the day.

T: Were you aware of any thoughts or feelings that were different at night?

C: No, the evenings are tranquil, but my wife has a much higher sexual need than I do.

T: How does your wife's sexual need influence your headaches?

C: My wife would like to have sexual relations every other night, but I really don't enjoy sex that often. I guess to be honest with you, when I have a headache she feels sorry for me and I can get out of having sexual relations. When I tell her my headache is better, she says that is no excuse and then I get tense and usually develop a headache.

T: What types of problems do you have with sexual relations?

C: It goes back a long time. When I was in my second year of college I was dating a girl steadily. When we attempted sexual relations I lost my erection. She ridiculed me for being less than a man. I didn't even try again until I was married. Then I was troubled by premature ejaculation and the whole sexual experience was not particularly pleasant.

T: I would like your wife to come in the next session and see if we can help you with this hurdle.

C: That would be fine with me if my wife agrees.

It became evident that his headaches were a source of major secondary gain. During the first several feedback sessions he had managed to reduce his EMG tension levels, but over the last few sessions his levels had again increased. This puzzling trend was associated with a fear of success—if he got rid of his headaches completely there would be no further excuse for his not having sexual relations more frequently with his wife.

In view of the client's difficulty in maintaining an erection, the therapist decided to discuss with him the use of a penile erection feedback system (PERFS)[3]. With this instrument the user can become aware of minute in-

[3]The penile erection feedback unit developed by Biofeedback Systems, Inc., Boulder, Colorado.

creases or decreases in penile size. The therapist initially utilized the PERFS unit along with a tape cassette of a woman's voice giving verbal relaxation instructions phrased in such a way as to take the performance demands out of sexual activity.

The patient worked with the PERFS unit by himself in the familiar surroundings of his bedroom. He was able to condition himself to obtain an erection, to allow the penis to become flaccid, and then to reestablish the erection, thus increasing his voluntary control and reducing his performance anxiety. During the initial 2-week period in which the client was working with the PERFS, the therapist suggested that the client not attempt sexual relations with his wife. Instead, he was to become comfortable with his ability to obtain an erection. After the second week, the client and his wife did have sexual relations, and he reported that for the first time he didn't even experience mild anxiety that he might lose his erection.

It was evident too, that his inner speech had changed. He reported that when he began to feel concern about losing his erection he would relax for a moment and imagine the sound of the feedback and thus gain reassurance. The client had become aware of what part thoughts of failure played in his behavioral sequence. He had become aware also of what he said to himself and that he had acquired some new coping skills. Over the next month his control over his new responses had been maintained and generalized so that the sexual act became more spontaneous. The client's gains were maintained, and at a 6-month follow-up he reported that he rarely got headaches any more. Usually, he could sense his shoulders and neck getting tense and could reverse the process fairly quickly. Regarding his sexual problems, he said it was hard to remember that he'd ever had any.

Biofeedback in Migraine Headache

Although it is difficult to know how many people in the United States suffer from tension headache (estimates run as high as 65 percent of the population) there are perhaps 20 million other people who have migraine headaches. For reasons as yet unknown, females report more migraine pain than men by a ratio of roughly 3:1.

Migraine pain differs from tension headache pain in several ways. Usually, a migraine attack results in a sharp, throbbing sensation on one side of the head whereas the tension headache manifests itself as a dull, band-like sensation or pressure on both sides. Classic migraine is identified by an aura preceeding the actual pain. The aura may be visual (light or spots before the eyes, blank spots in the visual field, etc.)' or may consist of numbness or tingling in the limbs on one side. At times speech and thinking abilities may be affected, and finally there is usually a sensation of nausea. Common migraine has little or no warning signals. Auras tend to occur 5 to 25 minutes before the onset of the pain itself and probably represent the vasoconstrictive phase of the cranial arteries just prior to the rebound vasodilation that produces the pain. (Budzynski, 1976 a, b).

Empirical Support

The research in this application has been concentrated on two approaches. The first and most widely used biofeedback procedure consists of the production of peripheral vasodilation or "hand warming" by means of skin-temperature feedback. This approach was pioneered by Sargent, Green, and Walters (1972, 1973) at the Menninger Foundation. Combining the biofeedback with autogenic-like phrases, these researchers reported that of those subjects who completed the training, 74% made moderate-to-good improvement and 60% learned to abort headaches. The ability to initiate and increase in blood flow within one minute was judged important for symptom relief. Additional support for the hand-warming procedure was provided by Wickramasekera (1973), Johnson and Turin (1975), and Turin and Johnson (1976).

A second biofeedback approach, which has not yet found its way into clinic applications, is that of temporal artery pulse feedback. A reflectance photoplethysmograph senses the blood pulsing through the extracranial temporal artery. This signal when processed into a feedback display provides information as to the amount of blood flow present. The subject attempts to decrease the flow and thus abort or at least lessen the pain.

First reported by Koppman, McDonald, and Kunzel in 1974, the success of the procedure was supported by the research studies of Zamani (1974) and Friar and Beatty (1976). If the temporal artery pulse feedback research continues to show positive results we may have two effective biofeedback strategies for migraine headaches. The handwarming appears to be maximally effective during the preheadache vasoconstrictive phase, while the temporal artery pulse feedback is most useful in the later vasodilation phase. This latter form of feedback may prove to be more helpful in cases of common migraine where there is no forewarning of the headache.

Headache pain can be precipitated by a number of causes other than the localized muscle tension leading to tension headache or the vasomotor instability of the cranial arteries leading to migraine. There is an excellent discussion of the 15 categories of headache pain in the Sandoz Pharmaceuticals publication, "Headache: The Commonest Symptom." A diagnosis of the correct category should come from physicians trained in neurology so that the potentially disastrous results of a misdiagnosis can be avoided. In general, if a new headache client has not had an appropriate medical workup, our neurologist will order the tests. These may include a clinical EEG, a brain scan, and X-rays, in addition to the neurological exam.

Since migraine is reported as a pain more severe than that usually associated with tension headache, there is the potential for greater secondary gain with migraine conditions. Consequently, one must be prepared to deal with this complication should it arise. The case study demonstrates how this was handled at the clinic.

Case Study: Migraine Headache with Complications

Mrs. C. was a very attractive 30-year-old married woman with a long history of migraine headaches, which had worsened in the last 4 years. Her migraine attacks were not preceded by any aura or forewarning (common as opposed to classical type). Such headaches are considered more difficult to treat with biofeedback. In the initial interview she at first stated that she was happily married with "two lovely boys and a strong, intelligent husband." Her headaches occurred almost daily and often required her to go to bed in a darkened room. Over the years she had taken a host of medications including Sansert, Cafergot, Fiorinal, and Demerol. Stating that she hated to take drugs, Mrs. C. remarked also that she now took only Cafergot P.B. when the headache began. If she caught the headache in its early phases the drug was successful at times. When asked what situations, it any, seemed to precipitate headaches, Mrs. C. mentioned parties.

T: Close your eyes and see yourself at a party. What are you thinking and doing?

C: It's always the same: My husband, who is a Ph.D., goes over and talks to the other smart guys. Me, with my high school education, am left alone, so I get a drink and then some guy will come over and make a pass.

T: What happens when the guy does this?

C: I don't know how to handle that—most of the time I say something that gets him angry.

T: What else happens at the party?

C: Well, at some point I find myself talking to the girls. They always ask me about some book I've never read—I don't read much. Or, they'll ask if I saw a particular movie, and if so, what I thought of it. But, whatever I say, for example, "I really liked it," it's always wrong. If I liked it the critics didn't, and vice versa. I feel really dumb around those other women. Most of them have college degrees, you know.

T: When do you get the headaches connected with parties?

C: Sometimes they start before we've left home, in that case I'll just stay there and my husband will go. Often, I'll get one soon after arriving at the party, and then I'll have to lie down in a bedroom or ask to leave. My husband doesn't like to leave parties early.

T: When else do you get headaches?

C: Sometimes if I have to discipline Jimmy, my second boy—he's a devil. If my head hurts too much I can't do it and my husband will spank him when he comes home from work.

T: Is your other boy O.K.?

C: Oh, yes, he's a love, but the youngest one doesn't like me and never minds me.

T: O.K., we'll talk about that later. Is there anything else that may start a headache?

C: (Hesitating) No, I don't think so.

Later, after explaining about biofeedback and physiology of migraine, the therapist asked casually, "Did you see that long distance runner on the 'Tonight Show' last night?" (Her husband is a jogger.)

C: Yes, I did—he really looked in good condition.

T: Bet your husband enjoyed the comments that runner made on physical fitness.

C: No, he didn't see it, he was in bed.

T: Does he usually see the show?

C: No, he usually goes to bed earlier.

T: Do you wake him to tell him about some interesting guest on the show?

C: No, once he gets to sleep, he's gone.

(Note: Mrs. C. had earlier mentioned that her husband worked till 7 or 8 PM most evenings and got up at 6 AM to jog. Several weekends each month he would go fishing, hunting, or camping "with the boys.")

T: If he goes to sleep before you do each week night and he is gone half the weekends, when do you two find time for lovemaking?

C: (Somewhat flustered) Well, I guess we don't—at least not much.

T: Can you give me an honest estimate of how often?

C: Maybe once every month or two.

T: Do you get headaches connected with this?

C: I guess so. At least in past years I've not been able to go through with it because my head hurts so much.

T: Do you have any idea what's wrong here?

C: I think it's because we're both from Nebraska.

T: (Surprised) I'm not sure what you mean.

C: We only learned to do it one way—him on top—and I'd like to try different things.

T: Have you talked to him about this?

C: I think so but he still does it just the same.

T: O.K., I think we can help you with that later, but we'll focus on the biofeedback training first.

Since Mrs. C. was very tense, it was felt that she should focus on acquiring some relaxation skills before going on to more complex issues. Her physiological profile, as assessed at the next session, revealed vasoconstricted hands and high muscle tension in the frontal area. Training began with frontal EMG feedback. Since Mrs. C. saw herself as a failure in almost all areas of her life, she was given frequent praise for moving in the right direction (lowered EMG). Thus the feedback sessions became a situation in which she could succeed. Through four sessions she moved quickly to criterion for frontal EMG (her forearm extensor was below criterion from the beginning). Gaining confidence rapidly, Mrs. C. was ready for the fifth session, which was a talk session. During this hour we discussed her problem with the youngest boy.

T: What do you do when he misbehaves?

C: I punish him one way or another—or his father does when he comes home.

T: And if he does something good?

C: Well, I don't do anything cause he's supposed to do it—like his older brother.

T: Does he get an allowance?

C: Yes, both he and his brother get so much a week.

T: Is it always the same?

C: Yes, as they get older however, we give them more.

T: What are some things he should be doing?

C: Keeping his room clean, washing dishes, taking out the garbage, coming in on time, and so on.

T: How would you feel about giving them points—both of them—for doing those sort of things? At the end of the week their allowance would depend on how many points they've totaled.

C: I'll give it a try—I'll try anything.

The therapist and Mrs. C. worked out a chart that would be kept on the door in the boys' room. It would list the number of times each boy completed one of these activities. This would shift the mother's attention to the good rather than the bad behaviors of the boy. If this procedure was successful, Mrs. C. would no longer have to get a headache to avoid punishing the youngest boy. One of the required activities was remaining quiet while the mother listened to the relaxation tapes. Both boys liked the program and accomplished even more than was usually expected the first week. Mrs. C. was delighted at the dramatic change in the youngest boy. What really made her day, however, was at the end of the second week the youngest boy hugged his mother and said that he loved her.

Although Mrs. C. was into her fourth week of training and working on skin temperature feedback, her headaches had diminished very little. Thus her eighth session was another talk or "integrative counseling" session. The objective was to improve the sexual relationship between Mrs. C. and her husband.

T: Have you and your husband read any of the sex therapy books?

C: No, he doesn't trust shrinks or their books.

T: How about something like *The Sensuous Woman*?

C: Oh, no, that's too far removed from me.

T: O.K., there is one called *The Sensuous Couple* which you could both read.

C: Oh, he wouldn't read it.

T: Just leave it lying around where he might see it—say after the kids are in bed.

C: Well, I'll try, but I don't think he will.

T: If he does, be very nice to him after he reads it.

A week later Mrs. C. reported that her husband indeed did begin to read the book. After a while she had brought him a beer and some crackers and sat down on the arm of the chair. He had read some passages to her and then put his arm around her. They had enjoyed reading about the different positions.

C: Then a real surprise—he said "Let's go into the bedroom." It was really incredible, like he'd stored up five years of new ideas. We didn't come out for 2 hours.

Mr. C.'s weekend trips decreased to one per month, and Mrs. C. was no longer watching the "Tonight Show," although they watched it together on Friday nights. It is a common observation that the relaxation that comes with biofeedback training, coupled with the new found confidence, will often bring about new, more adventuresome behavior.

At this point, roughly 10 weeks into training, Mrs. C.'s headaches were decreasing both in frequency and severity. There was, however, one remaining area of her life causing difficulty, that of the party situation. Three aspects of the party scene were involved. There was the anxiety that had generalized to all social gatherings, there was the problem of men making passes at her, and finally, the other women who would try to belittle her lack of sophistication. Although she had mastered the EMG relaxation and the handwarming, Mrs. C. still encountered headaches associated with these social situations. She reported that she was unable to warm her hands at a party, or even when she was preparing to go to the party. In order to give her some alternative behaviors for coping with aggressive males, the therapist role-played her part and she pretended to be the "fresh" male. Two different strategies were played: one for the usual situation in which the male was suggestive in a subtle way, and a second in which the male was quite aggressive. In the first instance, Mrs. C. was taught to let the man know she appreciated the fact that he found her attractive (she did), but that she wasn't interested in carrying things any further (she wasn't). For the more aggressive approach, Mrs. C. learned to be quite firm and, if necessary, make reference to the fact that her husband (an exmarine) was easily angered by this sort of thing.

In the next session, these behaviors were rehearsed again until Mrs. C.'s delivery seemed natural. At this point, work was begun on her other problem, that of women belittling her. It was suggested that Mrs. C. begin to read *Time* or *Newsweek* each week and that she join a "Book-of-the-Month" club. This would give her some current events and books to talk about. Then the therapist and Mrs. C. role-modeled and rehearsed situations in which Mrs. C. expressed opinions about movies or politics and others disagreed with her.

T: Mrs. C., it is perfectly O.K. to like a movie that someone else does not. People respect you more for having your own point of view and sticking with it. It is not necessary to go into detail about exactly what you liked or disliked about it.

As a final stage or preparation for social events, Mrs. C. underwent two sessions of systematic desensitization, focusing on these two situations. In each of the visualized scenes she was to realistically appraise the situation and repeat to herself, "I can control. I can cope with this. I can handle it," and then to see herself doing just that. In each session, Mrs. C. relaxed initially with feedback in order to decrease muscle tension and to warm her hands. Then, while getting feedback between scenes, the desensitization proceeded. Between scenes, feedback was given as an aid to relaxation. In her first encounter with the imagined party situation, Mrs. C.'s hand temperature dropped. She was told to banish the scene and to relax with the help of feedback. When her hand temperature recovered she was given the next scene. By the end of the second session, Mrs. C. was able to imagine herself handling any party situation without excess muscle tension or peripheral vasoconstriction. She was advised to test herself by arranging a dinner party that posed only a minimal threat. She and her husband then hosted a dinner for four good friends. All went well.

Then, using tape Side Six—which is called "Stress Management," although it is really a systematic desensitization procedure—Mrs. C. practiced relaxation at home and imagining herself in more difficult party situations. After 3 weeks such a party did occur. Mrs. C. did her hand-warming and relaxation several times during the day and even while her husband drove them to the party. Armed with the latest in current events and being half way through her best-seller, Mrs. C. actually found herself eager to exercise her new abilities. During the party she remembered to take 5 minutes out (she went to a bedroom) in order to relax and to do the handwarming. These were successfully accomplished. After an encounter with several women, which she had coped with reasonably well, she again found her hands to be cool. Retreating to the bathroom, she was again able to relax and to handwarm. Mrs. C. had been told that with continued practice in real-life situations her control would become easier and more automatic. Although, at this party, Mrs. C. did not have an opportunity to test her skills in fending off ardent males she was successful in doing so at a later event. Most importantly, she did not get a headache either before or during this party.

This case is a good example of how secondary gain factors can keep a client from really using the biofeedback-acquired skills until she learns to cope with threatening situations by means other than getting a headache. Follow-up information on Mrs. C. indicated that her life had improved dramatically and that a headache occurred only at the time of her menstrual period.

When Biofeedback Doesn't Work for Headaches

We have found at a Biofeedback Institute of Denver that a vascular-type headache of a *constant* nature, where the pain is continuous during waking hours, is relatively resistant to biofeedback. Even though all neurological tests have been negative, neither biofeedback nor drugs seem to help. We suspect that, in these cases, deep-seated emotional problems may be the culprits.

A second category is those clients who stand to lose pensions or other compensations if their headaches disappear. In some of these instances, the welfare system is simply providing too many reinforcers. One such client appeared to be doing well; she was able to relax very well and to warm her hands, and her headaches were diminishing. But when she learned that she would have to return to work if the headaches disappeared, then the headaches began to worsen. In another similar case, a client felt trapped in a marriage with a diabetic alcoholic who suffered from a heart condition. Living in a small town filled with his relatives and having four children, she felt she could not leave. Her headaches remained constant, even though she sometimes demonstrated that she could relax for short periods at least.

A DENTAL PROBLEM: CASE STUDY OF JAW PAIN AND BITE DISORDER

This client was a 22-year-old computer operator who had been referred for treatment of severe muscular pain in the right masseter and sternocleidomastoid muscle. The pain had begun following the removal of a tumor in the splenious capitis muscle. Although the client obtained some relief from Soma, she still had difficulty in normal mastication of solid foods.

During the intake interview, the client was asked to describe the circumstances when she could detect pain sensations in her jaw.

C: Usually when I get tired, tense or when I am exposed to cold air from the air conditioner. I've learned to chew food only on the left side, because before the operation if I put any pressure on the right side there was sharp pain that nearly took my breath away. There is still some pain when I put pressure on the right side.

Her dental work-up had shown a marked atrophy of the right masseter muscle, but no direct organic cause of the pain. The atrophy was a result of not applying any pressure on the right side because of pain. After the tumor operation she had been given an analgesic for the pain, but this treatment simply exacerbated the wasting away of the muscle. Although the analgesic produced a pharmacological reduction of pain, it did not re-educate the client to the proper use of her masticatory muscles. In the treatment that followed, the therapist worked jointly with the dentist in re-educating the client in the normal use of *both* masseter muscles.

In the first EMG-feedback training session, the therapist applied EMG electrodes to the right masseter muscle and told the client gradually to increase tension in the muscle so as to increase the click rate. The purpose of this procedure was to interrupt her response chain of only using the left side of her jaw. The client was asked to describe the thoughts and feelings that preceded her biting response.

C: I'm afraid it will hurt.

T: We only want you to increase the tension a small amount so there should be no discomfort.

After a few trials of increasing the feedback rate without pain occurring, she gained confidence in the procedure. The therapist then had her bite down on the right side while saying to herself, "This is comfortable and does not hurt." The intent of this procedure was to alter her covert self-statements so that she could perform the task without experiencing any discomfort. Soon the client was regularly able to "bite down" without experiencing discomfort. Her dentist then made an insert to aid in strengthening the muscle during her home practice assignments. After eight sessions she proved able to increase the EMG microvolt level of the right masseter from 1.83 to 35.61 μV.

C: I am still aware of favoring the left side of my jaw when chewing food, but when I become aware of this I correct and chew with both sides. At first I went very slowly, but more often I am chewing on the right side without even being aware.

At the end of 14 weeks of training the chewing on both sides had become an automatic response and the client reported, "I no longer have the belief that I will be grotesque and pained forever. My face looks balanced for the first time in years."

The client continued the dental insert and portable EMG for two additional months, at which time her bite was judged nearly normal by her dentist. Four months after termination of the biofeedback therapy her dentist reported near normal electromyographic readings from left and right masseter during chewing. The bite had normalized itself, thereby eliminating the need for expensive corrective dental procedures.

The painful spasms that had been triggered by temperature change from the air conditioners were no longer a problem. One year later there had been no return of symptoms.[4]

BIOFEEDBACK IN ANXIETY DISORDERS

The systems approach described earlier is frequently useful in anxiety disorders. This is true particularly when there is a strong physiological arousal component to the anxiety. Although many anxious individuals (perhaps two-thirds) show heightened muscle tension, a small proportion have fairly low EMG levels. In these clients, however, there will usually be a high level of autonomic activity (often cardiovascular in nature). Biofeedback training for this type of client will primarily involve peripheral skin temperature and EDR feedback.

Our own research involving biofeedback for anxiety reduction began with a case study completed in 1966 in which alpha-brainwave feedback training was used as a procedure to counter the physiological arousal associated with anxiety (Budzynski and Stoyva, 1973b). A client with a severe thanatophobia was first taught to increase the percentage of alpha rhythm from roughly 15 to 70%. Then a hierarchy was developed and desensitization was carried out. The client received alpha feedback between visualizations, at which time he attempted to achieve a high-percentage alpha time. Those scenes that produced more anxiety resulted in a longer recovery time, the latter being the time required to reach an alpha level of 5 or more. Desensitization was completed in four sessions. An 11-year follow-up indicated no return of the anxiety.

[4] *Biofeedback in Dentistry* by Rugh, Perlis, and Disraeli (1977) should be consulted by biofeedback therapists working with temporomandibular joint (TMJ) disorders (see reference list).

The use of alpha-EEG feedback to counter anxiety has been largely superseded by EMG, skin temperature, and EDR feedback primarily because alpha blocking becomes confounded with visual imagery and limb movement. That is, both pleasant as well as unpleasant scenes will cause the alpha rhythms to disappear. Additionally, roughly 20% of the population have either too little or too much alpha to make feedback training feasible. These clients find the feedback training either frustrating or boring. We think, however, that alpha feedback as an aid to desensitization may be useful in those cases where there is alpha blocking in the presence of anxiety and where the level of alpha before training averages between 10 and 30%.

Because of such difficulties in working with alpha rhythms, we turned to the development of the EMG-feedback system (Budzynski, 1969; Budsynski and Stoyva, 1969). With the first prototype completed in 1967, we began to work with anxious clients who had been unable to learn to relax with the brief Wolpe–Jacobson training usually provided by behavior therapists. Over the past 10 years we have worked with a number of chronically anxious clients on a case-by-case basis (Budzynski and Stoyva, 1973, 1975). Not unexpectedly, the more pervasive or generalized the anxiety the more biofeedback training is required to reach relaxed levels.

The use of EMG feedback for anxiety has received support from a number of studies. Raskin, Johnson, and Rondestvedt (1973) found that frontal EMG training in combination with daily practice of relaxation was moderately useful for clients suffering from severe chronic anxiety. The ten clients in this study had been troubled by the severe symptoms for at least 3 years. Previous therapeutic efforts—individual psychotherapy and medication—had not been successful. After training to a criterion of 2.5 μV peak-to-peak or less on frontal EMG, one client showed a dramatic lessening of all anxiety symptoms; three others found the training to be useful in controlling previously intolerable situational anxiety.[5]

Canter, Kondo, and Knott (1975) compared the relative effectiveness of frontal EMG feedback and progressive relaxation with 28 patients diagnosed as suffering from anxiety neurosis, and having complaints of muscle tension and insomnia in addition to a high level of anxiety. Fourteen patients reported acute panic episodes associated with their condition; the other 14 were more typical chronic anxiety cases without acute panic episodes. Both EMG feedback and progressive relaxation training produced significant decreases in frontal EMG activity. However, EMG

---

[5]We have since learned in clinical practice that it is not enough simply to teach people to relax: they also must be taught to transfer this skill to everyday life situations.

feedback was found to be generally superior in producing longer reductions in muscle activity, and in producing an associated diminution in anxiety symptoms for a greater number of patients.

Frontal EMG feedback training was compared to group psychotherapy in a study of chronically anxious subjects by Townsend, House, and Addario (1975). In the feedback group, there were significant decreases in EMG levels, mood disturbance, trait anxiety—and, to a lesser extent, state anxiety—that did not occur in the group psychotherapy.

How does frontal EMG feedback compare with Valium? A partial answer was obtained in an extensive controlled study reported by a Montreal group Lavalle, et al., (1975). Forty outpatients with chronic, free-floating anxiety were randomly assigned to one of four groups in a 2 times 2 factorial design: EMG feedback and Valium, EMG feedback and Valium placebo, EMG feedback placebo and Valium, and both placebos. Results indicated that during treatment, frontal EMG feedback and Valium were additive in reducing muscle tension. Although all active treatment groups reduced their anxiety after treatment, Valium-treated subjects (with or without feedback) did less well than other subjects on measures of anxiety, adjuvant medication usage, and home practice. In general, the results showed that frontal EMG feedback treatment without Valium had a more prolonged therapeutic effect for chronically anxious subjects than did Valium alone.

It may be important to note here that all of these research studies were aimed at the production of muscle relaxation in the laboratory. Although subjects· were asked to practice relaxing at home, typically on a twice-a-day schedule, little or no instruction or rehearsal was given in the transfer of the new skill to work or social situations. Moreover, this training, even if transfer were successful, would have modified primarily the physiological component of the anxiety response. Cognitive and behavioral manifestations of the anxiety might still have been operative. In a typical clinical setting these factors are handled with more traditional behavior therapy and cognitive therapy procedure.

Looking at our therapy program as practiced in a private setting (Biofeedback Institute of Denver) it can be seen that we focus on correcting maladaptive behavior in three response systems: cognitive, physiological, and overt behavioral. Furthermore, the sequence of the therapy is one of first developing *awareness* of the maladaptive responses, next, acquiring *control* over the responses, and finally, being able to *transfer* the skill to real-life situations (Budzynski, 1973a). Biofeedback enters the picture primarily at the level of awareness and control of physiological responses.

Case Study: Generalized Anxiety

Mr. S., a 32-year-old married man, was referred to the Biofeedback Institute of Denver with the complaint of severe, generalized anxiety and anxiety panic attacks. Beginning with social situations, the anxiety had spread to other areas of his life. He could no longer go out for lunch with associates or attend the many small parties connected with his work. Mr. S. was no longer able to take overnight trips, a requirement of his work. Consequently, he was demoted and given an in-house position at less pay.

A small, rather homely man, Mr. S. complained that he was totally unable to assert himself in the presence of authority figures. In fact, on several occasions when he forced himself to do so, he experienced sudden, intense feelings of panic that forced him to withdraw from the situations. After 7 years of individual psychotherapy and 2 years of group psychotherapy he was still a very unhappy man. Although he had taken several kinds of medications through the years, none had successfully combated the anxiety. Valium left him with unpleasant ill-defined sensations, and he stopped taking it.

When questioned about the situation in which the anxiety was first noticed, Mr. S. stated that he had always been nervous even as a little boy. He had struggled with it through a business curriculum in college and in the job he assumed after graduating. Although marriage had eased the anxiety somewhat, it slowly worsened again on the job, especially in social situations involving fellow employees. Once, on an overnight trip about 200 miles away from Denver, he suffered a severe attack while alone in his motel room. He managed to phone his wife, who came to get him and drove him home the next day. Company lunches at nearby restaurants became terror-filled experiences, so he resorted to carrying a lunch.

In terms of physiological responses, Mr. S. reported that when he was anxious his hands would become very moist and cold while his heart felt as though it would jump out of his chest. His relaxation-stress-recovery profile showed a pattern of high frontal EMG, low hand temperature, and a high conductance reading on the EDR unit. The skin temperature from the left index finger read 78° F, indicating considerable vasoconstriction and high sympathetic tone. During the stress phase he produced a paradoxical decrease in frontal EMG (often seen in highly anxious people because being occupied with mental arithmetic is less frightening to them than are their usual thoughts). Temperature was already "bottomed out" and did not change under stress. Only the EDR registered a slight increase. The recovery phase produced no change in temperature, a slight increase in frontal EMG, and a slight decrease in EDR. There was little tension in the forearm extensor area. At the end of this session, Mr. S. was allowed to hear briefly the various feedback modalities in order to acquaint him with the equipment.

At the next session, Mr. S. was taught to do the "Tense-Slo-Relax" exercise. He was asked to tense up certain muscles, to become aware of the tension sensation, and then slowly—and with control—to relax the muscle group. All the major muscle groups were thus explored. Next, Mr. S. was given the cassette tape set and told to practice twice each day with Tape Side 1. He was also taught how to rate his anxiety on a 5 point scale three times a day.

On his return 3 days later, Mr. S. began training with frontal EMG feedback. He showed a pattern of momentary (1 to 2 seconds) dropping to low EMG followed by a sudden increase, not unusual in individuals who fear profound relaxation.

T: You're dropping down briefly but then tightening up again. Can you tell me why?

C: I really don't know; maybe I was falling asleep and caught myself.

T: Well, go ahead and continue to drop down. However, if you wish, you can tense and bring yourself right up again. It's alright to do that.

These instructions gave Mr. S. permission to take control should the relaxation become frightening to him, and when he otherwise might lose control and panic. Over the next several sessions of frontal EMG feedback, Mr. S. did, in fact, learn to produce low EMG levels momentarily before voluntarily "coming back." In the sixth session he was able to meet criterion for the frontal EMG (2.5 μV peak-to-peak, see Figure 7). In his homework, Mr. S. had progressed through Tape Side 3 and now began Side 4, which relates to peripheral warmth. As he progressed through training, he also reported a lessening of anxiety.

Now that he had mastered the EMG response, Mr. S. eagerly looked forward to working with temperature feedback. Actually, with relaxation training his temperature had already attained 82°F, within two temperature-feedback sessions, he learned to reach levels of over 90°F.

The one remaining response was EDR. This had already decreased somewhat from levels averaging about 12 micromhos to approximately 8 micromhos. Mr. S. was now able to control two feedback signals simultaneously. As he worked with the EDR he also "heard" either frontal EMG or temperature (whichever was furthest from criterion). A fast learner, Mr. S. relished the dual feedback and found that by the third

EDR session he could "still his mind" and thus lower both EDR and his frontal EMG levels.

Although his anxiety scores continued to decrease, Mr. S. was still avoiding almost all the situations which made him anxious. With the help of the therapist, a series of four anxiety hierarchies was developed, each dealing with one of the situations. He was also taught several cognitive coping statements such as, "I can cope because I can control" and "I can handle this because I can relax." As he visualized the hierarchy items, Mr. S. would attempt to keep the two feedback signals (EDR and either frontal EMG or temperature) at levels indicative of relaxation. The desensitization procedure was as follows:

> T: The EDR is in your right headphone and the frontal EMG is in your left. Try to keep them as relaxed as you are now. As you visualize or image the scenes, see yourself realistically appraising the situation. It may even make you slightly anxious, but then use the coping statements and wade in and handle it.[6]

Mr. S. was somewhat tense for the first desensitization session, which is not unusual (Budzynski and Stoyva, 1973). He was, therefore, asked to visualize pleasant scenes until he became relaxed. Then Mr. S. was asked to image the first scene from a hierarchy labeled "Lunch at Work." The essence of the procedure is that the client must visualize each scene without undue arousal for 30 seconds before continuing to the next scene. Allowance must be made for an initial rush of anxiety (and arousal) as the client "enters the scene." If this arousal continues the scene is terminated by the therapist. But if the client maintains relaxation, then he can progress to the next scene. As is typical of highly anxious individuals, Mr. S. was maximally responsive in his EDR. His next most reactive response was frontal EMG. An increase in either one or both of these would signal anxiety during a particular visualization. It was, in fact, necessary to terminate several scenes. In spite of this, desensitization to all four hierarchies was completed in six sessions. During this time, Mr. S. practiced his hierarchy items at home using Tape Side 6. This cassette, called "Stress Management," alternates imaging of anxiety scenes with deep relaxation for a total of 10 scenes (see Appendix C).

The final two therapy sessions were used to develop more appropriate assertive behavior. Now able to relax, Mr. S. was ready to engage in the

---

[6] Borkovec (1976) has noted that when the immediate anxiety reaction involves a strong physiological component, cognitive and behavioral interventions will be ineffective and will remain so until the autonomic component is reduced.

new behaviors. The therapist and Mr. S. role-played such situations as making suggestions to the boss, hosting a party, and telling his wife his real opinion. About this time, Mr. S. and wife went on an overnight trip to the mountains. The client experienced no panic, but only some mild anxiety that he was able to master by relaxing and thinking the positive coping statements. He also went out to lunch twice in one week and actually enjoyed it. The most difficult challenge of all was asking the boss for a raise. Unfortunately, his request was refused. The boss, however, was courteous and gave him a good explanation for the refusal.

Mr. S. has since quit his job, something he long wanted to do, and found a new position in another state. A follow-up questionnaire revealed that he had stopped using the cassette tapes and suffered some return of anxiety with the stress of his new job. He then resumed a once-per-day regimen of tape-assisted relaxation, and again his anxiety dissipated.

In a total of 23 sessions (including the initial interview), Mr. S. was able to control maladaptive anxiety. His new coping skills of relaxation and the use of positive self-statements allowed him to engage in behavior he formerly had been afraid to attempt. He no longer required any medication, instead relying strictly on self-control procedures.

SPECIAL PROBLEMS

Client Variables

Perhaps the most common problem experienced by clients is an inability to control the feedback and, therefore, to shape the physiological response in the desired direction (usually towards lowered arousal). Many clients with long histories of chronic heightened arousal have literally forgotten how to relax. Even highly intelligent clients, for example, may find it impossible to relax the forearm extensor. In such a situation the therapist should grasp the arm at the elbow and wrist, and ask the client to do nothing except allow the therapist to move the arm without resistance. The therapist then manipulates the arm through a series of movements until there is a noticeable freeing up of the muscle tension. At this point, the feedback rate will drop off sharply, even though the arm is still being manipulated. At other times the inability to relax the forearm is due to a tonic high level of shoulder tension. When the client is instructed to relax his shoulders the forearm tension decreases.

When the client progresses to frontal EMG training it is sometimes useful to gently manipulate the client's lower jaw up and down and then sideways. Before this manipulation begins the client is asked to relax and to allow his jaw to be moved. This procedure may have to be done at the start of each frontal EMG session.

In some clients dropping down to a low frontal EMG level may bring on panicky feelings of losing control. Such individuals should be given permission to "drop down" briefly but to *voluntarily* tighten up if they feel frightened. Furthermore, they are told that anxiety about seemingly unusual sensations is common for someone who has maintained a state of heightened tension over the years. Then as they become more skilled at relaxation, they are requested to "test the water" for longer and longer periods. When a client has permission to "tighten up" (he has control), he is more likely to experiment with this new state of deep relaxation.

Sometimes, when crises occur in the life of the client he may wish simply to talk rather than work with biofeedback. The therapist should always be alert for such occasions. In most instances, after a period of "ventilation" the client will wish to resume biofeedback training.

Again, it should be emphasized that the problem of transferring the new skills to real-life situations is extremely important. The ability to do this varies greatly from client to client. Often it is necessary to do an imagery rehearsal of the application of these skills in specific situations. Use of the skills must be associated with frequent events such as answering the phone, entering a car, meeting someone, entering a room, being in the supermarket, and so on. This heightened awareness is necessary until the relaxation response becomes completely automatic behavior.

There is one factor in applied biofeedback work that, although well known by the clinician, is often ignored by the researcher. This concerns the empathy developed between therapist and client. If the client is made to feel defensive or threatened, he will have difficulty lowering muscle tension and in warming his hands. When the client appears to be nervous, or in any way ill-at-ease, the therapist must attempt to remedy the situation. Often this goal can be achieved by engaging the client in a friendly and sympathetic conversation. Sometimes it may be necessary to minimize performance anxiety. Yet, at the same time, the client must be made to feel that he is in control of the learning.

Therapist Variables

Perhaps the most important therapist qualities are warmth, understanding, and a positive outlook. Next in importance might be knowledge of biofeedback principles as well as of behavior therapy or traditional psychotherapy skills. Many clients referred for biofeedback have been refractory to other forms of therapy. Consequently, they may have developed a cynical attitude about what can be done for them. So it is important that in the initial interview the therapist should be able to present a positive, credible argument for the efficacy of biofeedback in general. If biofeedback training is indicated for the client, then the therapist should be able to give probability figures of expected outcome. If such probability figures are not available, or if the client's problem does not fall into a specific category of disorders known to be treatable, then it should be carefully explained that it is not known whether or not the training will be effective for the client's particular problem. Although this reduces placebo effects, it is an ethical consideration that should not be ignored.

Further on in the training program the therapist or facilitator must be prepared to counter discouragement in the event that symptoms have not yet diminished or have returned after a period of remission. For example, it is fairly common for "breakthrough headaches" to occur after a relatively headache-free period. Usually, this is the result of a particularly stressful incident with which the client is not yet prepared to cope. Strangely enough, the relationship between the period of stress and the headache breakthrough often escapes the notice of the client. This must be brought to his attention. And it may be necessary that the client learn to reassess his interpretation of a particular stressor—it may be more stressful than he had guessed.

Finally, it should be noted that therapists who manifest a cool, detached demeanor, however skilled they may be in biofeedback therapy, often find their clients making minimal progress. Therapists of this sort usually give up on biofeedback and turn to other endeavors.

APPENDIX A

A Systems Approach to Relaxation Training

This sequence of biofeedback training (see Figures 6,7,8, and 9) was originally designed to be used with facilitators having relatively little experience in biofeedback therapy. Transition from one type of feedback to another is based on criteria developed in our laboratory and clinic over the past decade. The actual biofeedback training is carried out in parallel with a very thorough cassette-tape home training program as shown on the flow charts in Figures 6,7,8, and 9.

Note that the intake interview block includes an explanation of feedback concepts (see the section, *Explaining Feedback Training to the Tension Headache Client*). The careful instruction of the client is one of the

1. PROCEDURES COMMON TO ALL TREATMENT PROGRAMS

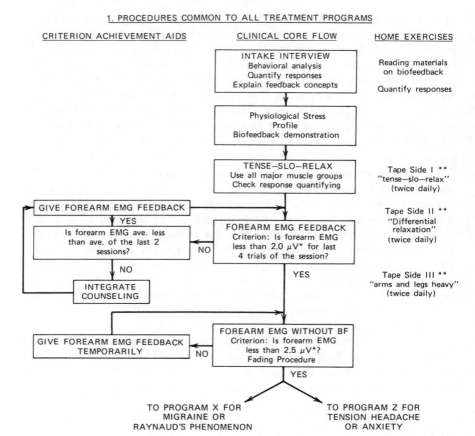

Figure 6.   Systems Approach to Biofeedback Training Flow Chart 1.

most neglected aspects of biofeedback training. It is probably, however, one of the more important phases of the program.

The second block in the flow chart is labeled *Physiological Stress Profile* and consists of three parts: a relaxation phase, a stress phase, and a recovery phase. This standardized procedure was the outcome of efforts to develop a diagnostic tool. In recent years, all clients at our private clinic

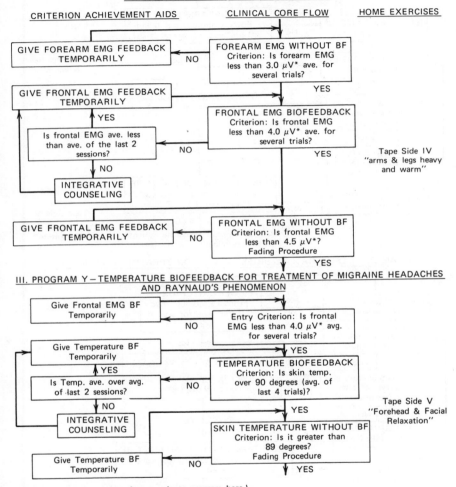

II. PROGRAM X – FRONTAL EMG FOR TREATMENT OF MIGRAINE HEADACHES AND RAYNAUD'S PHENOMENON

CRITERION ACHIEVEMENT AIDS   CLINICAL CORE FLOW   HOME EXERCISES

GIVE FOREARM EMG FEEDBACK TEMPORARILY

NO ← FOREARM EMG WITHOUT BF
Criterion: Is forearm EMG less than 3.0 μV* ave. for several trials?

YES

GIVE FRONTAL EMG FEEDBACK TEMPORARILY

↑YES

Is frontal EMG ave. less than ave. of the last 2 sessions?

NO ← FRONTAL EMG BIOFEEDBACK
Criterion: Is frontal EMG less than 4.0 μV* ave. for several trials?

YES

Tape Side IV "arms & legs heavy and warm"

NO

INTEGRATIVE COUNSELING

GIVE FRONTAL EMG FEEDBACK TEMPORARILY

NO ← FRONTAL EMG WITHOUT BF
Criterion: Is frontal EMG less than 4.5 μV*? Fading Procedure

YES

III. PROGRAM Y – TEMPERATURE BIOFEEDBACK FOR TREATMENT OF MIGRAINE HEADACHES AND RAYNAUD'S PHENOMENON

Give Frontal EMG BF Temporarily

NO ← Entry Criterion: Is frontal EMG less than 4.0 μV* avg. for several trials?

YES

Give Temperature BF Temporarily

↑YES

Is Temp. ave. over avg. of last 2 sessions?

NO ← TEMPERATURE BIOFEEDBACK
Criterion: Is skin temp. over 90 degrees (avg. of last 4 trials)?

YES

Tape Side V "Forehead & Facial Relaxation"

NO

INTEGRATIVE COUNSELING

SKIN TEMPERATURE WITHOUT BF
Criterion: Is it greater than 89 degrees? Fading Procedure

Give Temperature BF Temporarily

NO

YES

(NOTE: Migraine patients often terminate program here.)

Figure 7. Systems Approach to Biofeedback Training Flow Chart 2.

249

IV. PROGRAM Z—FRONTAL EMG BIOFEEDBACK FOR TREATMENT OF TENSION HEADACHE AND ANXIETY

CRITERION ACHIEVEMENT AIDS   CLINICAL CORE FLOW   HOME EXERCISES

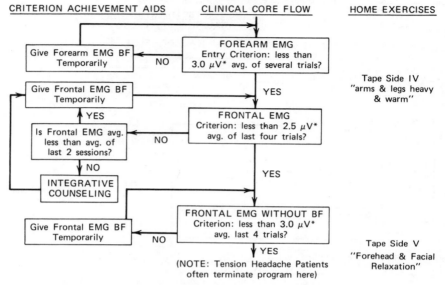

Tape Side IV
"arms & legs heavy & warm"

Tape Side V
"Forehead & Facial Relaxation"

V. PROGRAM Z—1: TEMPERATURE BIOFEEDBACK FOR TREATMENT OF ANXIETY

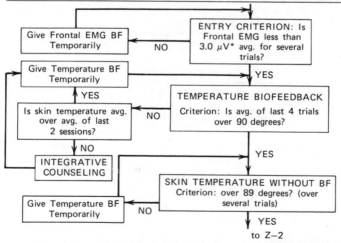

Figure 8.   Systems Approach to Biofeedback Training Flow Chart 3.

T—18 PROCEDURAL FLOW CHARTS — 4

VI. PROGRAM Z—2: EDR BIOFEEDBACK FOR TREATMENT OF ANXIETY

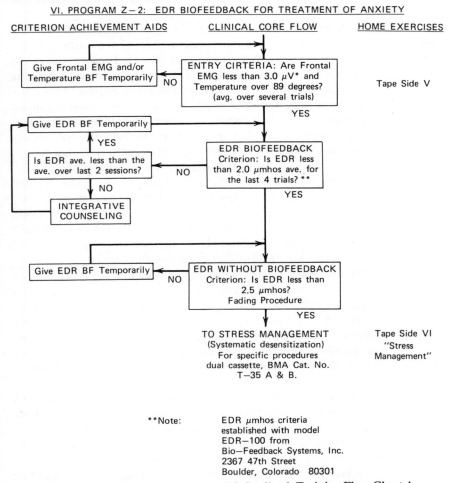

Figure 9. Systems Approach to Biofeedback Training Flow Chart 4.

and all subjects in our experiments at the Medical Center have been exposed to this combined "baseline and stress testing" procedure, since labeled a *Physiological Stress Profile*. A period of *14 minutes of relaxation* is followed by a *6-minute period of stress* (substracting serial 7s). This in turn is followed by a *10-minute recovery period* during which the client attempts to relax after having performed the mental arithmetic. We monitor forearm extensor and frontal (forehead) EMG, finger temperature, and EDR.

Generally, a client will show a "favored" response in some system (response stereotype). This may be at an exaggerated level in all three phases. But in some cases the aberrant response may be noted only in the stress phase or in the subsequent recovery phase. Slow recovery may indicate an inability to habituate appropriately. For example, compared to normotensives, individuals with essential hypertension show a sluggish finger temperature response to stress. Specifically, they show slow recovery of peripheral temperatures after they have been stressed (recent unpublished data from this laboratory). Another common pattern is that seen in generalized anxiety where clients often exhibit cool, moist palms.

Sometimes clients will relax well during the first phase of the session, but then respond dramatically during the stress phase and subsequently have difficulty recovering to relaxed baseline levels during the recovery period. It is our conviction that the Relaxation-Stress-Recovery Profile provides a useful information about the dynamics of the physiological systems measured and will become increasingly valuable.

Details of the use of the flow charts are presented in a cassette tape (catalogue number T-18, available from BioMonitoring Applications, New York). It should be noted here that the block labeled "Integrative Counseling" indicates those occasions when a more experienced professional enters the therapy sequence. Generally, this occurs when satisfactory progress has halted or when the facilitator senses that the client needs additional help. At this juncture the more traditional psychotherapy or behavior therapy procedure may need to be employed.

It may be noted that the six-part home practice relaxation cassette tapes are approximately synchronized with the phases of biofeedback training. Note, too, that clients should be questioned about their home practice at *each clinic session*. A disinclination to practice suggests a secondary gain problem.

Finally, the last flow chart indicates that systematic desensitization may be called for after the physiological criteria have been met. Details for this procedure are provided in a 2-cassette album (catalogue number T-35 from BioMonitoring Applications, New York). Usually, it is a good idea to monitor the client's "favored" (most reactive) response very carefully during the hierarchy presentations. Other responses may be monitored as well. A sustained high level (more than four seconds) of response would be cause for the termination of that scene. When the client can correctly visualize all scenes while remaining relaxed in various response systems, the desensitization is complete (see Appendix X for further deatails).

APPENDIX B

Summary and Listening Instructions for Cassette Relaxation Program

(Text by Thomas Budzynski and produced by BMA Audio Cassette Programs, 200 Park Ave. South, New York, N.Y. 10003. Summaries reprinted with permission. BMA catalogue numbers are indicated in titles.)

Tape MV3-1: Tense-Slo-Relax

The object of this tape side is to allow you to develop a "muscle sense" or conscious awareness of feelings of tension and relaxation in your muscles. Use this side for practice twice each day until you do develop this awareness. In other words, you should be able to verbalize what the tension feels like, for example, tightness, pressure, and so forth, and just where you feel it, for example, biceps, forearm extensor, and so forth. Additionally, you should be able to tell someone what your muscles feel like when they are relaxed, for example, heavy, tingly, warm, limp and so forth.

CAUTION: Do not overdo the tensing! If you have back troubles or other musculoskeletal medical problems do not aggravate by excessive tensing of the affected muscles. A moderately low sustained level of tension can be as effective as a high level.

Tape MV3-2: Differential Relaxation

This tape side is designed to give you practice at relaxing some muscles while others are tensed. This approximates the everyday situations in which you must employ certain muscles but could be relaxing others, for example, while driving a car, shopping, or giving a speech. The ability to differentially relax your muscles allows you to save considerable energy. The result is a feeling of control, less tiredness, greater energy and less tense-muscle problems.

You should try to use your differential relaxation skills in all of your daily activities. No matter what activity in which you are engaged try to relax those muscles you do not need to use. Watch particularly for tense shoulders, forearms, abdominal muscles and jaws. When you become aware of tension, relax those muscles if you can.

Use this tape side until you can feel a measure of control in tensing some muscles while relaxing others.

Tape MV3-3: Limb Heaviness

Now that you have begun to develop a "muscle sense" you can refine your ability to decrease muscle tonus to very low levels. This tape side, together with the next two sides, will deal with the use of auto-suggestive phrases that will allow you to relax very deeply. There will be no muscle tensing but you will have to become very aware of subtle sensations in the muscles.

NOTE: While using these auto-suggestive phrases you must do so in a *passive volitional* rather than an *active striving* manner. *Trying too hard* to force the suggestions often will result in just the opposite result taking place. *Allow* the suggestion to implement itself; don't force it or order it to happen. It may take a while, perhaps weeks, for the suggestion to be felt (or it could happen the first time you use this tape side). Stay with the tape side until unmistakable sensations of relaxation are felt in your arms. As usual, schedule two sessions a day and remember—*don't* dwell on intruding thoughts—this is *your time*, it doesn't belong to your work or family.

Tape MV3-4: Arms and Legs Heavy and Warm

Now you are ready to add to the phrases you practiced on limb heaviness. This tape side focusses on feelings of warmth in the arms and legs although it will be felt primarily in the hands. This warmth is due to an increase of blood to the small arteries of the skin in the hands and feet. Unlike the earlier tape sides which dealt with skeletal muscle relaxation this side and side MV3-5 will begin to develop the control over this autonomically mediated response. Specifically, peripheral blood flow is increased by *decreasing* sympathetic nervous system (SNS) outflow. This is the subsystem—within the larger autonomic nervous system (ANS)—that goes into action when you are anxious, fearful, or in some way excited. Thus by increasing hand warmth you have decreased SNS activity, or you could think of it as relaxing the Autonomic Nervous System.

As you listen to this tape side and repeat the autosuggestive phrases examine closely the webbing between each finger. The warmth is quite often felt here initially. Again, it is important to use passive "let it happen" volition rather than "active striving." If you care to try it, imagined visual scenes such as a warm sunny beach or hands in battery-heated mittens may help bring on the warmth. NOTE: Don't be discouraged if your hands and feet seem to get cooler. This is quite common at first. A number of sessions may be required to develop this skill.

Use this tape side until you can feel your hand warming reliably each time you practice. Try to keep your hands warm *all through the day*. This is especially important if you have migraine headaches.

Tape MV3-5: Forehead and Facial Relaxation

Facial muscles are among the most difficult to relax. However, they are the key to really profound relaxation. This side will continue the use of phrases already practiced while adding new phrases. It is important while listening to this tape to keep your jaw very relaxed. Keep your teeth apart, although you may wish to keep your lips together in order to prevent mouth dryness. Remember to breathe primarily from your abdominal region and not from your upper chest.

NOTE: Do not use the phrase "I am calm" unless you do feel relaxed. Moreover, do not use the phrase in everyday life situations until you have practiced it for at least 2 weeks while listening to the tape. The phrase must be paired a number of times with an actual state of calm before one attempts to use the phrase to produce calmness in everyday life situations. Remember to check your breathing many times during the day— make sure it is rhythmical and from the abdomen. Check also for feelings of muscle tenseness and cool hands. Release the tension where you can and let your hands warm by repeating the phrases including "I am calm." It is very important that you learn to use the phrases often during the day; for example, each time the phone rings think of a phrase *before* picking it up. As you are driving in traffic relax your jaw and facial muscles, lower your shoulders, and breathe from your abdomen. Learn to be more relaxed in all situations.

Tape MV3-6: Stress Management

Now that you know how to relax generally, you can begin to go to work on those situations that cause you undue stress or anxiety. It is a fact that if you can use your imagination and visualize yourself performing well in these situations while *remaining relaxed* that it will eventually transfer or generalize to the real-life situation. That is, you will be more relaxed and less tense in the real situation. Of course, the first few times that you try to imagine these situations you may feel some anxiety. If you do, try to relax it away and keep visualizing. However, if you cannot manage to relax while imaging, stop the scene, banish it from your mind, focus on the relaxation of your muscles, and repeat the phrases. This tape side will have you focus on relaxing first, and then it will alternate silent spaces with relaxation instructions. During the silent periods visualize yourself in these tough situations; however, "see yourself" using the phrases, relaxing your muscles, warming your hands, and generally coping well. If a particular scene causes too much anxiety you will need to soften it somehow, perhaps by changing it to an earlier period of time. Thus, for example, visualizing a final exam may be too much. If so, visualize yourself studying for the exam and it is one week to the actual exam. Then try a scene where it is the night before. Next, the morning of the test. Finally, you can try the actual exam scene once more.

NOTE: If you are using these tapes in conjunction with sessions of psychotherapy, behavior therapy, or biofeedback the planning of the scenes should be worked out with your therapist.

IMPORTANT! In general, try to incorporate your phrases into your everyday activities. Be aware of heightened arousal. If it is inappropriate use your phrases or relaxation abilities, or take time to listen to a cassette side. Fall back on listening regularly to the tapes if stress in your life builds up.

APPENDIX C

Stress Management (Systematic Desensitization)

BMA Catalogue No. T-35 (2 Cassettes)

The procedures described in these cassettes were evolved over a 10-year period at our laboratory in the University of Colorado Medical Center and then later refined for use in our private clinic, the Biofeedback Institute of Denver. In desensitization, the use of physiological monitoring alone, without any feedback, can be extremely valuable. With this additional information the therapist can judge his client's physiological state with much more certainty than would be possible from just subjective report. After using biofeedback monitoring in desensitization for a decade we have found it an unsettling experience to attempt such a procedure without the biofeedback.

We have also noted that when clients are provided with feedback during desensitization, their feelings of control and self-mastery are enhanced during this difficult time. Eventually, of course, clients learn to visualize the scenes without feedback so as to increase the efficiency of the transfer to real-life situations. Basically, the procedure is as follows:

1. After meeting criteria during the relaxation phase, the anxiety hierarchy or hierarchies are prepared in the usual way by client and therapist.

2. With relevant responses being monitored (we use forearm extensor and frontal EMG, skin temperature, and EDR, and sometimes heart rate), multiple feedback, for example, frontal EMG and EDR is provided for a short period to enable the client to move quickly to a relaxed state.

3. Next, the feedback is turned off and a pleasant scene is visualized by the client for roughly 30 seconds. Then he is told to banish the scene and focus on the feedback which is again provided. After the 1-minute relaxation period he is asked once again to visualize a pleasant scene. This sequence is repeated until the client can visualize the pleasant scene while remaining relaxed (he has habituated to the procedure). Levels of responses are noted for this pleasant visualization. In the ensuing hierarchy visualizations, any sustained (longer than 4 seconds) heightening of any response over that of the pleasant scene is cause for termination of the scene. During the visualizations the client is asked to make a *realistic* appraisal of the situation, to use coping statements, for example, "I can relax," "I can handle it," "I'm O.K.," and so forth, to monitor and relax his physiology, and finally to see himself as coping well in the situation and not avoiding it.

4. When the client can visualize all scenes in the hierarchy while remaining relaxed in the absence of biofeedback, *recovery training* is begun. This procedure is used to increase the client's confidence in his ability to cope with anxiety. Typically, the last scene from the hierarchy is used. It is highly exaggerated by the therapist so as to generate some anxiety sensations in the client in much the same way that a flooding scene is presented. When the client reports verbally or with a finger signal that he feels some anxiety, he is presented with the feedback and asked to relax as quickly as possible. At first, this will take perhaps 6 minutes. With repeated presentations, each of which generates some anxiety, the client learns to relax more and more quickly. Usually, less than ten presentations are required to convince the client that he can relax within 10 to 20 seconds. Finally, he is able to do so in the absence of feedback. Now the client has faith in his ability to handle his anxiety even when it flares up in real-life situations.

Also detailed on the cassette tape is the use of biofeedback in the flooding procedure. In this case, physiological monitoring allows the therapist to be sure that high arousal has occurred. He can accurately monitor the extinction process as shown by decreasing responses with each successive presentation. Finally, he knows when extinction is complete as shown by a lack of response during scene presentations. Without bio-monitoring we feel that a client could be terminated with the extinction process incomplete, leaving him in a state of some distress. Usually, we book 1½ hours of therapy time for a flooding session.

APPENDIX D

Getting Started in Biofeedback: Source Materials

Since biofeedback involves principles drawn from many disciplines, the beginner may find himself a little bewildered. The following list of source materials, although not exhaustive, is meant to guide the reader to a point where he can begin to make his own judgments about the various aspects of biofeedback.

Aldine Biofeedback and Self-Control Annuals

These annuals, edited by Barber, Kamiya, Miller, Shapiro, and Stoyva, are anthologies of biofeedback-related papers that have appeared during a particular calendar year. Since 40 to 50 articles are reprinted each year, the Annuals constitute a convenient library of work in the biofeedback area. Individual volumes cost approximately $18.00, and the series goes back to 1970. Information brochures may be obtained by writing the Aldine Publishing Company, De Gruyter,Inc., 3 Westchester Plaza, Elmsford, New York 10523.

Proceedings of the Biofeedback Society of America (BSA) Annual Meetings

Each volume of the proceedings contains abstracts of 80 to 120 papers presented at the yearly meeting of the Biofeedback Society of America. These volumes are an excellent way of getting up-to-date information on topics of particular interest. Names and addresses of the investigators are given. Information on these and other publications of the Biofeedback Society of America may be obtained from Dr. Francine Butler, Executive Director, Biofeedback Society of America, Box C268, University of Colorado Medical Center, 4200 East 9th Avenue, Denver, Colorado 80262.

Biofeedback and Self-Regulation: Journal of the Biofeedback Society of America

This journal, published by Plenum, consists of original experimental, clinical, theoretical, and review articles pertaining to biofeedback and the general area of self-regulation. Individual subscriptions are $15.00. A free examination copy may be obtained by writing the Plenum Publishing Corp., 227 West 17th Street, New York, New York 10011.

Bibliography

An extensive bibliography was published by the Biofeedback Society in 1973. The references, totaling over 100 pages, are divided into approximately 20 different topic headings. Copies are available from the Biofeedback Society of America at a cost of $6.50 for nonmembers. Ask for *Biofeedback and Self-Regulation: A Bibliography* by Butler and Stoyva.

Audio Tape Series

A useful source for practitioners is the tape cassette series on clinical applications on biofeedback published by BMA Audio Cassette Programs, 200 Park Ave. South, New York, New York 10003. Most of the authors in this series are experienced clinician-investigators, and a major emphasis of the tapes is on the actual use of biofeedback techniques with clients. The majority of the tapes provide background on the pathophysiology of the disorder in question as well as discussing specific biofeedback procedures. A catalogue may be obtained by writing Biomonitoring Applications in New York.

Workshops

Workshops designed to acquaint the clinical practitioner with biofeedback are given at various times around the country.

Our laboratory has from time to time given workshops under the auspices of the National Association of Professional Psychologists. These workshops are generally held at the New School of Social Research in New York. Information may be obtained by writing President, National Association for Professional Psychologists, 15 Columbus Circle, New York, New York 10023.

Workshops are also given by the Biofeedback Society of America. These are usually offered in October. Information may be obtained by writing Dr. Francine Butler at the office of the Biofeedback Society of America.

Information concerning other workshops can generally be obtained through the *Newsletter* of the Biofeedback Society, or in the APA *Monitor*.

Graduate Training Opportunities in Biofeedback

A survey of training programs in biofeedback can be obtained by writing the office of the Biofeedback Society of America. Ask for the survey by Cram and Warrenburg (cost is $2.50).

Biofeedback Instruments ˙

The choice of instruments is a central and often vexing question for the beginner. For most practitioners, an EMG feedback unit should receive first priority, followed by skin temperature and EDR (GSR) units. For those who would like some guidance about the electronic characteristics of instruments, a clear and sober discussion is provided by Rugh (Catalogue No. T-22, BMA Tape Cassette Series).

In evaluating instrument companies, beware of those given to flamboyant clinical claims. Happily, fewer of these are in existence than was the case a few years ago. Names of particular instrument companies may be obtained by examining advertisements in the journal, *Biofeedback and Self-Regulation*, or in the *Monitor* newsletter published by the American Psychological Association.

SELECTED REFERENCES

Malmo R.B. *On emotions, needs, and our archaic brain.* New York: Holt, Rinehart and Winston, 1975. A short but stimulating treatment of psychophysiological background material.

Sternbach, R.A. *Principles of psychophysiology: An introductory text and readings.* New York: Academic, 1966. Provides discussion of major psychophysiological concepts such as response sterotypy, activation, law of initial values, and so forth, as well as summarizing much research up to the mid 1960's.

Greenfield, N.S., and Sternbach, R.A., (Eds.), *Handbook of Psychophysiology* . New York: Holt, Rinehart & Winston, 1972. Contains authoritative contributions on many topics within psychophysiology by leading investigators in the field. Especially valuable for those wishing to research a particular topic.

Birk, L. (Ed.). *Biofeedback: Behavioral medicine.* New York: Grune & Stratton, 1973. Various investigators describe their work with clinical applications of biofeedback.

Rugh, J., Perlis, D., and Disraeli, R. (Eds.). *Biofeedback in dentistry.* Phoenix, Arizona: Semantodontics, 1977. Although it focuses on dental disorders, this book will be of use to many since EMG feedback techniques are extensively described, as are specific techniques for working with certain stress disorders. Strong empirical orientation.

Stern, R.M., and Ray, W.J. *Biofeedback.* Homewood, Illinois: Dow Jones-Irwin, 1977. A brief and readable account of the biofeedback area.

Simeons, A. *Man's presumptuous brain.* New York: E. P. Dutton, 1962. An evolutionary interpretation of psychosomatic disorders. In Simeons' view, the chief culprit in psychosomatic disorders is the frequent triggering of the individual's defense-alarm reaction.

Beatty, J., and Legewie, H. (Eds.), *Biofeedback and behavior: NATO Conference Series.* New York: Plenum, 1977. Main emphasis is on status of various research issues in the biofeedback area.

Schwartz, G., and Beatty, J. (Eds.). *Biofeedback: Theory and research.* New York: Academic, 1977. Original chapters by Mulholland, Brener, Lazarus, Black, Miller and Dworkin, Lawrence and Johnson, Harris and Brady, Taub, Rosen, Shapiro, Mainordi and Surwit, Beatty, Schwartz, Rosenfield, Sterman, Basmajian, and Budzynski cover theoretical issues as well as applications.

Wickramasekera, I., (Ed.). *Biofeedback, behavior therapy and hypnosis:* Potentiating the verbal control of behavior for clinicians. Chicago: Nelson-Hall, 1976. A series of articles exploring the similarities and differences between biofeedback, behavior therapy, and hypnosis.

Gaarder, K., and Montgomery, P., *Clinical Biofeedback: A procedural manual* . Baltimore: Williams and Wilkins, 1977. Covers some very practical issues including software and how-to-do-it clinical procedures.

REFERENCES

Benson, H. *The relaxation response.* New York: Morrow, 1975.

Borkovec, T.D. Physiological and cognitive processes in the regulation of anxiety. In G. Schwartz and D. Shapiro (Eds.), *Consciousness and Self-Regulation: Advances in Research.* New York: Plenum, 1976.

Budzynski, T.H. *Feedback-induced muscle relaxation and activation level.* Unpublished doctoral dissertation, University of Colorado, 1969.

Budzynski, T.H. Biofeedback procedures in the clinic. In L. Birk (Ed.), *Biofeedback: Behavioral Medicine*. New York: Grune & Stratton, 1973.

Budzynski, T.H. *Systems approach to biofeedback training*. New York: Biomonitoring Applications, 1976. (Tape-recorded lecture, catalogue number T 18.)

Budzynski, T.H. Biofeedback strategies in headache treatment. In J.V. Basmajian (Ed.), *Biofeedback: A handbook for clinicians*. New York: Williams & Wilkins, 1979.

Budzynski, T.H., and Stoyva, J.M. An instrument for producing deep muscle relaxation by means of analog information feedback. *Journal of Applied Behavior Analysis*, 1969, *2*, 231–237.

Budzynski, T.H., and Stoyva, J.M. Biofeedback techniques in behavior therapy. In N. Birbaumer (Ed.), *Neuropsychologie der Angst* (Reihe Fortschritte der Klinischen Psychologie, Bd. 3). München: Urban & Schwarzenberg, 1973.

Budzynski, T.H., and Stoyva, J.M. EMG-Biofeedback bei unspezifischen und spezifischen Angstzustanden. In H. Legewie and L. Nusselt (Eds.), *Biofeedback-Therapie: Lernmethoden in der Psychosomatik, Neurologie and Rehabilitation (Fortschritte der Klinischen Psychologie, Vol. 6)*. München: Urban & Schwarzenberg, 1975.

Budzynski, T.H., Stoyva, J.M., and Adler, C.S. Feedback-induced muscle relaxation: Application to tension headache. *Behavior Therapy and Experimental Psychiatry*, 1970, *1*, 205–211.

Budzynski, T.H., Stoyva, J.M., Adler, C.S., and Mullaney, D.J. EMG biofeedback and tension headache: A controlled outcome study. *Psychosomatic Medicine*, 1973, *35*, 484–496.

Canter, A., Kondo, C.Y., and Knott, J.R. A comparison of EMG feedback and progressive muscle relaxation training in anxiety neurosis. *British Journal of Psychiatry*, 1975, *127*, 470–477.

Charvat, J., Dell, P., and Folkow, B. Mental factors and cardiovascular disorders. *Cardiologia*, 1964, *44*, 124–141.

Dalessio, D.J. *Wolff's headache and other head pain*. New York: Oxford U.P., 1972.

Friar, L.R., and Beatty, J. Migraine: Management by trained control of vasoconstriction. *Journal of Clinical and Consulting Psychology*, 1976, *44*, 46–53.

Friedman, M., and Rosenman, R. *Type A behavior and your heart*. New York: Knopf, 1974.

Gellhorn, E. The influence of curare on hypothalamic excitability and the electroencephalogram. *Electroencephalography and Clinical Neurophysiology*, 1958, *10*, 697–703.

Gellhorn, E. Motion and emotion. *Psychological Review*, 1964, *71*, 457–472.

Gellhorn, E. *Principles of autonomic-somatic integrations: Physiological basis and psychological and clinical implications*. Minneapolis: Minnesota U. P., 1967.

Gellhorn, E., and Kiely, W.F. Mystical states of consciousness: Neurophysiological and clinical aspects. *The Journal of Nervous and Mental Disease*, 1972, *154*, 399–405.

Germana, J. Central efferent processes and autonomic-behavioral integration. *Psychophysiology*, 1969, *6*, 78–90.

Greenfield, N.S., and Sternbach, R.A. (Eds.), *Handbook of Psychophysiology*. New York: Holt, Rinehart & Winston, 1972.

Hess, W.R. *Diencephalon: Autonomic and extrapyramidal functions*. New York: Grune & Stratton, 1954.

Hutchings, D.F., and Reinking, R.H. Tension headaches: What form of therapy is most effective? *Biofeedback and Self-Regulation*, 1976, *1*, 183–190.

Jacobson, E. *Progressive relaxation*. Chicago: Chicago U.P., 1929.

Jacobson, E. *Progressive relaxation* (2nd ed.). Chicago: Chicago U.P., 1938.

Johnson, W.G., and Turin, A. Biofeedback treatment of migraine headache: A systematic case study. *Behavior Therapy*, 1975, *6*, 394–397.

Koppman, J.W., McDonald, R.O., and Kunzel, M.G. Voluntary regulation of temporal artery diameter by migraine patients. *Headache*, 1974, *14*,

Lavallée, Y., Lamontagne, Y., Pinard, G., Annable, L., and Tétreault, L. Effects of EMG feedback, diazepam and their interaction on chronic anxiety. Paper presented at the *International College of Psychosomatic Medicine, Third Congress*, Rome, 1975.

Luthe, W. (Ed.). *Autogenic therapy* (Vols. I-VI). New York: Grune & Stratton, 1969.

Malmo, R.B. *On emotions, needs, and our archaic brain*. New York: Holt, Rinehart and Winston, 1975.

Malmo, R.B., and Shagass, C. Physiologic studies of reaction to stress in anxiety and early schizophrenia. *Psychosomatic Medicine*, 1949, *11*, 9–24.

Mason, J.W. Organization of psychoendocrine mechanisms. In N.S. Greenfield and R.A. Sternbach, (Eds.), *Handbook of psychophysiology*. New York: Holt, Rinehart & Winston, 1971.

Meichenbaum, D. Cognitive factors in biofeedback therapy. *Biofeedback and Self-Regulation*, 1976, *1*, 201–216.

Moos, R.H., and Engel, B.T. Psychophysiological reactions in hypertensive and arthritic patients. *Journal of Psychosomatic Research*, 1962, *6*, 227–241.

Pickering, G. *High blood pressure* (2nd. ed.). New York: Grune & Stratton, 1968.

Raskin, M., Johson, G., and Rondestvedt, J.W. Chronic anxiety treated by feedback-induced muscle relaxation. *Archives of General Psychiatry*. 1973, *28*, 263–267.

Reinking, R., and Hutchings, D. Follow-up and Extension of "Tension headaches: What method is most effective?" *Proceedings of the seventh annual meeting of the Biofeedback Research Society*, 1976, 60–61. (Abstract)

Sargent, J.D., Green, E.E., and Walters, E.D. The use of autogenic feedback training in a pilot study of migraine and tension headaches. *Headache*, 1972, *12*, 120–124.

Sargent, J.D., Green, E.E., and Walters, E.D. Preliminary report on the use of autogenic feedback techniques in the treatment of migraine and tension headaches. *Psychosomatic Medicine*, 1973, *35*, 129–135.

Sargent, J.D., Walters, E.D., and Green, E.E. Psychosomatic self-regulation of migraine headaches. In L. Birk (Ed.), *Biofeedback: Behavioral medicine.* New York: Grune & Stratton, 1973.

Schultz, J.H. *Das Autogene Training: Konzentrative Selbstentspannung.* Stuttgart: Georg Thieme, 1932.

Schultz, J.H. *Das Autogene Training: Konzentrative Selbstentspannung (12 Auflage).* Stuttgart: Georg Thieme, 1966.

Selye, H. *The Stress of Life.* New York: McGraw-Hill, 1956.

Sittenfeld, P., Budzynski, T.H., and Stoyva, J.M. Differential shaping of EEG theta rhythms. *Biofeedback and Self-Regulation*, 1976, *1*, 31–46.

Stoyva, J.M. Biofeedback techniques and the conditions for hallucinatory activity. In F.J. McGuigan and R. Schoonover (Eds.), *The psychophysiology of thinking*. New York: Academic, 1973.

Stoyva, J.M., and Budzynski, T.H. Cultivated low arousal—an anti-stress response? In L.V. DiCara (Ed.), *Recent Advances in Limbic and Autonomic Nervous Systems Research.* New York: Plenum, 1974.

Stoyva, J.M. Why should muscle relaxation be clinically useful? Some data and 2 1/2 models. In J. Beatty & H. Legewie (Eds.), *Biofeedback & Behavior: NATO Conference Series.* New York: Plenum, 1977.

Surwit, R.S. Biofeedback: A possible treatment for Raynaud's disease. In L. Birk (Ed.), *Biofeedback: Behavioral Medicine.* New York: Grune & Stratton, 1973.

Townsend, R.E., House, J.F., and Addario, D. A comparison of biofeedback-mediated relaxation and group therapy in the treatment of chronic anxiety. *American Journal of Psychiatry*, 1975, *132*, 598–601.

Turin, A., and Johnson, W.G. Biofeedback therapy for migraine headaches. *Archives of General Psychiatry*, 1976, *33*, 517–519.

Watson, D.L., and Tharp, R.G. *Self-directed behavior: Self-modification for personal adjustment.* Monterey, Calif. Brooks/Cole, 1972.

Weiss, T., and Engel, B.T. Operant conditioning of heart rate in patients with premature ventricular contractions. In L. Birk (Ed.), *Biofeedback: Behavioral medicine.* New York: Grune & Stratton, 1973.

Wickramasekera, I. Electromyographic feedback training and tension headache: Preliminary observations. *American Journal of Clinical Hypnosis*, 1972, *15*, 83–85.

Wickramasekera, I. Temperature feedback for the control of migraine. *Journal of Behavior Therapy and Experimental Psychiatry*, 1973, *4*, 343–345.

Wolff, H.G. In S. Wolf (Ed.), *Harold G. Wolff's "Stress and Disease"* (2nd Ed.). Springfield, Ill.: Thomas, 1968.

Wolpe, J. *Psychotherapy by reciprocal inhibition.* Stanford: Stanford U.P., 1958.

Zamani, R. Treatment of migraine headache through operant conditioning of vasoconstriction of the extracranial temporal artery (biofeedback), and through deep muscle relaxation. (Doctoral dissertation, University of Minnesota, 1974). (University Microfilms No. 26, 259)

Zeigarnik, B. Uber das Behalten von erledigten und unerledigten Handlungen. *Psychologische Forschung*, 1927, *9*, 1–85 [cited in Woodworth, R.S. and Schlosberg, H. *Experimental psychology (revised edition).* New York: Holt, 1956].

CHAPTER 6

Paradoxical Intention

L. MICHAEL ASCHER

Temple University Medical School
Department of Psychiatry

INTRODUCTION

It is generally the case that, while most therapeutic approaches have specific treatment directives, that is, techniques, these techniques, because they result from unique sets of theoretical considerations, are not especially useful for nor relevant to alternative therapeutic systems. This chapter deals with one notable exception to this observation, the therapeutic procedure first labeled "paradoxical intention" by Viktor Frankl (1955). It is an exception because many professionals representing a wide variety of disparate approaches to psychotherapy have incorporated this intervention into their systems both practically and theoretically. While Frankl fails to give an unambiguous didactic definition of paradoxical intention, and the related technique that he labeled "dereflection," his intent is articulated in the numerous descriptions of their application in case studies that appear in his writings (e.g., Frankl, 1955, 1960, 1967, 1974, 1975) and in those of his adherents (Gerz 1962, 1966, being the most notable of these in this country).

Generally, paradoxical intention is employed when the individual's concerns focus on the frequency of a response. In cases involving clients complaining of behaviors whose frequency they would like to reduce, paradoxical intention would require that they attempt to increase the occurrence of these behaviors. For example, a client who perspired profusely under the most inopportune circumstances was requested by Frankl (1960) to perspire as much as possible on these most discomforting occasions. Thus he is instructed to increase the frequency of a response whose level is already uncomfortably high. In a similar fashion, clients complaining of behaviors whose frequency they would like to increase would be instructed, employing dereflection, to continue to inhibit the occurrence of these behaviors. It was suggested by Frankl (1960), for example, that individuals who are concerned about an inability to fall asleep with satisfactory rapidity be instructed to remain awake as long as possible. Another common problem suitable for dereflection occurs when a male is distressed by the inability to obtain or maintain an erection of sufficient quality to undertake intercourse; he is instructed to enter the sexual situation but to try not to attempt to have intercourse, or even to experience an erection (e.g., Ascher and Clifford, 1976). That is, he is to continue to exhibit less of the behavior whose low frequency is presently a source of concern. Because the dereflection procedure is identical to that of paradoxical intention and is only differentiated by the direction of change of frequency that the client desires to produce in the target behavior, paradoxical intention will be employed to denote both the prescription to intentionally increase uncomfortably high-frequency behaviors, and to intentionally decrease or inhibit uncomfortably low-frequency behaviors.

Paradoxical intention is utilized by Frankl in a logotherapy context. As such, his goal is to take advantage of the unique ability of humans to employ humor in detaching themselves from the "sorrowful concern" that they direct toward their symptoms (Frankl, 1956, 1962). Once this detachment has been accomplished and the specific complaints are ameliorated as a result of the application of paradoxical intention, other aspects of the logotherapeutic process can then be initiated.

In the past two decades, paradoxical intention has become popular with a variety of therapists. Many of these professionals (e.g., Lazarus, 1971; Fay, 1976; Jacobs, 1972) simply incorporate the technique into their repertiore of treatment procedures in an ecclectic manner. Other therapists who operate within more organized frameworks, impressed by the effectiveness of paradoxical intention and related techniques, have attempted to conceptualize this therapeutic method in such a way that it remains consistent with their system (e.g., Haley, 1963, 1967a, 1967b, 1973, 1976; Shelton and Akerman, 1974; Watzlawick, Beavin, and Jackson, 1967; Watzlawick, Weakland, and Fisch, 1976; Weakland, Fisch, and Watzlawick, 1974). While these alternative systems differ in the concepts that they utilize to explain the role of paradoxical intention, there is a great deal of similarity in the manner in which the technique is employed within the system. That is, these approaches are directive in nature and view paradoxical intention, and a number of related procedures (see Johnson and Alevizos, 1975), either as strategies designed to enhance the client's cooperation in following the prescriptions of the therapist or as techniques utilized to promote rapid behavioral change, thus enabling the client to move to other problems.

Behavior therapy, which is in some ways allied with these directive approaches, begins with a behavioral analysis upon which the therapist bases the treatment program. This program consists of behavioral techniques and assignments agreed upon by the client to be undertaken during the intersession interval. While behavior therapists have in their repertoires admittedly effective therapeutic procedures, the mere administration of these procedures is not always sufficient to produce the desired behavioral change. When progress is impeded in the context of an appropriate behavioral analysis and a correctly administered behavioral program, then enhancing the client's ability to cooperate may become the focus of attention (Ascher, 1975; Ascher and Efran, 1978; Davison, 1973; Johnson and Alevizos, 1975; Wolpe and Ascher, 1976). In the context of the difficult patient (or of resistant behaviors) in behavior therapy, paradoxical maneuvers offer a logical area for exploration because these techniques have been helpful with the difficult behavioral problems encountered in other therapeutic contexts.

During the last decade paradoxical intention has become increasingly popular as the result of a large number of articles extolling its virtues. However, this literature is composed almost entirely of uncontrolled case studies. Because of the manner in which paradoxical intention is administered, its use in better-controlled experimental investigations is often precluded. That is, the technique is most often described as being presented in a spontaneous, unpredictable style within a context of humor. Recently, however, some researchers have been able to utilize a modified paradoxical intention procedure for the purposes of research. While the less predictable aspects of the technique were necessarily deleted because of the restrictions imposed by experimental design, the explanation of the rationale and self-administration aspects remained more or less intact.

Solyom, Garza-Perez, Ledwidge, and Solyom (1972) conducted a pilot study with the purpose of testing the effectiveness of a modified paradoxical intention procedure in the amelioration of obsessive thoughts. Each of ten patients complaining of multiple obsessions were assigned a "target" thought and a "control" thought from the list of obsessions that was accumulated during initial interviews. Subjects were instructed in the rationale and self-application of paradoxical intention to the "target" thought; the control thought remained untreated. Five of the ten clients reported that the "target" obsession was greatly reduced or eliminated; for these clients the control obsession continued unabated. Two clients had to be eliminated because they were unable to apply the technique.

While there are many criticisms of the study, notwithstanding its "pilot" status, it represents the first attempt to place paradoxical intention within an experimental context.

A paper by Ascher (1975), extended by Ascher and Efran (1978), was a second successive approximation to more acceptable experimental data supporting the effectiveness of paradoxical intention. From a sample of self-referred sleep-onset insomniacs in a behavior-therapy clinic, five clients who resisted the behavioral treatment of choice were chosen for the multiple case study. These five had provided at least 2 weeks of baseline data and had been exposed to 10 weeks of a multitechnique behavioral program. At the conclusion of treatment the clients reported continued dissatisfaction with the length of time that was required for them to fall asleep. As a result, a paradoxical suggestion was administered in a manner that was more similar to that described in clinical case studies, as compared with the administration employed by Solyom, Garza-Perez, Ledwidge, and Solyom (1972). The five clients all experienced an immediate reduction of their sleep-onset latency to the point that additional therapy was unnecessary. While these data again fell far short of that required to validate the clinical efficacy of paradoxical intention, it represented a vast improvement over anecdotal case studies.

Turner and Ascher (1979) conducted what is possibly the only satisfactorily controlled experimental study to investigate the clinical significance of paradoxical intention to date. Individuals exhibiting clinically significant sleep-onset insomnia (requiring at least 1 hour to fall asleep three or more nights per week) were randomly assigned to one of three treatment groups (progressive relaxation, stimulus control, or paradoxical intention). The results indicated no differences between the two control groups, no differences among the three treatment groups, and a significant difference between the data from the control procedures versus the data from the treatment procedures. Thus when compared with progressive relaxation and stimulus control, procedures which have substantial evidence supporting their effectiveness in ameliorating sleep difficulty, the untested technique, paradoxical intention, produced equally satisfactory behavior change. The reduction in sleep-onset latency experienced by the clients in all three treatment groups was judged by these individuals to be of a sufficient magnitude to preclude additional treatment for the problem. Thus data have begun to accumulate that would suggest that paradoxical intention is a valid procedure for the production of behavioral change (at least in the area of sleep dysfunction).

Again, the major problem pervading the literature is the fact that, with the few previously mentioned exceptions, data supporting the effectiveness of the technique is derived totally from uncontrolled case descriptions. The value of such data in corroborating hypotheses regarding the effectiveness of therapeutic techniques is nil (Paul, 1969a). However, case studies can suggest hypotheses for experimental validation. In addition, those that include careful, detailed descriptions, perhaps with *verbatim* material, could serve as instruction in effectively employing paradoxical intention in a clinical context.

Unfortunately, the available clinical material relevant to paradoxical intention has largely failed to make the contribution of adequately exposing clinicians to and aiding them in the use of this technique in behavior therapy. Two types of omissions contribute to this failure. First, important details regarding the administration of the technique are not included. For example, the manner in which the assignment is introduced to the client is rarely described. This is a vital aspect of the administration of the procedure. Since the typical paradoxical instruction requires behavior on the part of clients that is diametrically opposed to their therapeutic goals, it is often difficult to present the assignment in the manner necessary to promote comfort and cooperation on the part of the client. In addition, there is little mention regarding the coordination of paradoxical intention with more conventional behavioral techniques (in those articles attributable to behavior therapists). What is the therapist to do if the client follows the instructions and fails to produce the change that the therapist expects; and, more important, what is the therapist's role in the event that the client successfully carries out the therapist's assignment? A second important class of omissions is related to the observation that many of the case descriptions end with miraculous changes in behavior, but few discuss the measures that must be taken by the therapist and the client to secure the continued maintenance of this improved functioning.

It is the purpose of this chapter to place the technique "paradoxical intention" within a behavioral context both by suggesting a behavioral rationale for its effectiveness with various complaints, and by demonstrating through case examples its utility within specific behavioral programs.

Paradoxical intention can be associated with a behavioral approach in two ways. It can be employed when the treatment of choice unpredictably fails to produce the desired results. Thus, there are occasions when an individual becomes uncomfortable about the frequency of some response. Either there is concern that the behavior appears too frequently (e.g., as in the case of excessive perspiration or blushing), or too infrequently (e.g., urinary retention, inability to experience orgasm). The resulting anxiety produces physiological changes which tend to exaggerate the frequency of the behavior in the same direction which the client finds undesirable. For example, the woman who is concerned about blushing when speaking to males will, prior to such encounters, become apprehensive, thereby stimulating the autonomic nervous system and ensuring continued blushing. Therefore, assuming no actual physiological pathology is associated with the behavior, the presenting complaint is a direct result of the anxiety related to the functioning of the specific response. In such cases, a paradoxical suggestion is introduced into the ongoing behavioral treatment in an effort to produce some rapid improvement that, hopefully, can be sustained by the continued application of behavioral techniques (Ascher, 1975; Ascher and Efran, 1978).

In an alternative fashion, paradoxical intention can be utilized as the core of "treatment of choice" behavioral programs complimented by more conventional behavioral techniques in an ancillary position (Frankl, 1975; Goldstein, 1975; Turner and Ascher, 1979). In contrast to the spontaneous manner of utilizing paradoxical intention, it is here employed as an integral part of the behavioral program. As is the case with all such behavioral programs, the patient is fully informed concerning the validity of the procedure and the rationale for its use with the client's specific problem. The two forms of utilization of paradoxical intention in behavior therapy are not mutually exclusive. In fact, as is reported in the example to follow, the spontaneous use is sometimes necessary to facilitate the utilization of paradoxical intention in a preplanned program.

Although it is beyond the focus of this chapter, there is a third manner in which paradoxical intention may be applied in a behavioral context. Several individual behavioral techniques have been developed that appear, as a whole or in part, to be translations of paradoxical intention into learning terms. "Negative practice" (Dunlap, 1928) is an obvious example since a large part of the procedure involves clients practicing the behavior which they would like to stop. Dunlap (1932, 1946) suggested that the appropriate application of his technique would result in the cessation of an incredibly wide variety of maladaptive responses. More recently, implosion (Stampfl and Levis, 1967, 1973) requires the exposure of clients to the anxiety contingent upon contact with phobic or contaminating stimuli; they are encouraged to withstand efforts to escape or avoid the unpleasant experience. Although the implosion procedure includes other significant aspects as well as an alternative dynamic and behavioral rationale, the paradoxical component of the technique is quite evident (Marks, 1973).

Presenting Problems

The literature suggests and the experience of this author corroborates the effectiveness of paradoxical intention with a wide variety of problems in most clinical contexts (e.g., Greenwald, 1967; Rosen, 1953). This chapter emphasizes the application of paradoxical intention as the nucleus of behaviorally oriented treatment programs in an outpatient setting. For the purpose of simplifying this presentation, the targets of these programs are restricted to an apparently disparate group of problems that can be fairly resistant to conventional behavioral treatments. The problems are related to complications resulting from the attempt on the part of an individual to exert voluntary control over behaviors that have a significant autonomic component. Initally the individual becomes dissatisfied with the frequency of a response and endeavors to increase or decrease its occurrence. Failure to change frequency of occurrence elicits anxiety, which serves to continue the trend of the response frequency in the discomforting direction. Some examples of behaviors in which this process can produce difficulties include excessive perspiration or blushing, sexual dysfunction, disturbances of sleep, and difficulties related to the elimination of urine or fecal matter (it is assumed that there exists no precipitating physiological pathology). These behaviors as a class differ from the typical targets of paradoxical intention (Raskin and Klein, 1976), although Frankl and Gerz have successfully applied paradoxical techniques to several of these autonomic difficulties. Thus a male with a history of erectile dysfunction will, in sexual situations, focus on and become distressed about increasing the frequency of erections. The sympathetic activity that results from the high levels of anxiety elicited by the performance demands of the sexual situation inhibit the low-level parasympathetic activity, that is, sexual arousal, which might otherwise be associated with erotic interactions. In this manner, a low-frequency response (erections) is further reduced by anxiety (Ascher and Clifford, 1976; Masters and Johnson, 1970; Wolpe, 1958). Similarly, an individual who is anxious about high-frequency blushing will experience an enhancement of this high rate of responding as the natural result of sympathetic activity upon peripheral blood flow.

It is not suggested that these and related problems are not generally accessible to behavioral techniques. For example, there is a large number of fairly well controlled experimental studies that demonstrate the effectiveness of various behavioral approaches to aspects of insomnia (Bootzin and Niccasio, in press). Rather, there appears to be an increasing concern, expressed in the literature (Wilson, 1973), that a small, but significant percentage of certain behavioral complaints do not seem to yield to conventional behavior therapy treatment programs.

It is one contention of this author that the resistance to conventional behavioral programs of some clients presenting with the previously mentioned problems is due to the complications created by performance anxiety that is experienced while attempting to control the autonomic nervous system. Sleep-onset insomnia offers an excellent illustration. A great percentage of individuals who experience this problem, either as a primary or secondary consideration, obtain satisfactory relief from progressive relaxation (Borkovec and Fowles, 1973; Lick and Heffler, 1977), often as a component of a systematic desensitization program (Geer and Katkin, 1966). With the remaining population for whom these techniques are not completely successful, ancillary behavioral procedures are employed with good results, for example, stimulus control (Bootzin, 1972, Turner and Ascher, 1977), thought stopping, and autogenic training (Nicassio and Bootzin, 1974). Yet, in spite of the best efforts of the conventional behavioral program, there exists a small but consistent percentage of individuals complaining of this and related difficulties who remain largely unchanged. There is some evidence that suggests that paradoxical intention applied to obviate performance anxiety can ameliorate the complaints of many of these resistant clients (Ascher, 1975; Ascher and Efran, 1978).

In order to illustrate the difficulties engendered by an individual's need to control certain involuntary physiological systems as well as the proposed treatment of the problem, this author has chosen a case that exemplifies the entire therapeutic process. The case to be presented is that of a male who complained of anxiety phobia. Anxiety phobia was not chosen because this problem is particularly relevant to the paradoxical intention treatment program; in fact, any one of the aforementioned difficulties could have provided an equally good illustration. Rather, the specific case was selected because it represents one of the clearest examples of the administration of paradoxical intention within a behavioral treatment program presently available to the author. The particular case is paradigmatic of the use of paradoxical intention both as the core of a behavioral program and in a more spontaneous manner.

Prior to discussion of the client and the details of the specific therapeutic program, it will be helpful to present details regarding the etiology of anxiety phobia in order to provide a context within which to administer treatment.

Etiology of Anxiety Phobia

A phobic is one from whom the conditioned response of anxiety is elicited by some environmental conditioned stimulus. Typically this conditioned response is a component of the external environment. When phobic individuals are presented with the discomforting conditioned stimulus, they begin to experience anxiety, which reaches some plateau and remains there until the conditioned stimulus and the phobic individual part. The phobic object remains the primary focus of attention; anxiety is in a secondary role. If a phobic is able to successfully avoid the conditioned stimulus without difficulty, the individual does so and either learns to adjust to the occasional mild disturbance that chance encounters might produce, or experiences apparently spontaneous remission of the conditioned response of anxiety to the environmental conditioned stimulus. If phobic individuals enter therapy it is often as a consequence of the increased restriction resulting from their attempts (whether successful or not) to avoid the phobic stimulus. The treatment of choice for these phobics is systematic desensitization in imagination conducted in the office with coordinated *in vivo* assignments between sessions.

While systematic desensitization in imagination has been of demonstrated success in neutralizing the phobic conditioned stimulus (Paul, 1969 b, c), there is a subgroup of phobics that does not seem to respond to this technique. These individuals, labeled "anxiety phobics" for the purposes of this discussion, have a conditioned stimulus and a conditioned response that differentiates them from the more common imaginally desensitizable phobics. Whereas the conditioned stimulus of the common phobic is an external conditioned stimulus, the conditioned stimulus of the anxiety phobic is some component of anxiety (an internal conditioned stimulus), and the conditioned response is further anxiety itself with profound physiological and cognitive components.

When anxiety phobics experience anxiety they become concerned about the possible catastrophic consequences that can result from high sustained levels of anxiety. There are generally three different groups of catastrophic concerns with which the anxiety phobic associates the acute autonomic changes contingent upon peak anxiety: fear of cardiac arrest, or some equally serious physiological dysfunction resulting from the perception of increased cardiac rate; loss of control, either psychologically, for example, fear of psychosis, "going crazy," or a "nervous breakdown," related to the fleeting stream of thoughts that some anxiety phobics experience at peak levels of anxiety, or loss of control over some physical system, for example, fainting or dizziness; or fear of embarrassment directly related to the anxiety itself ("everyone will see that I am afraid of something") or as a physiological reaction to extreme anxiety, for example, vomiting in public, choking, or crying out for help.

Conditioning in the anxiety phobic is probably associated with a profound anxiety attack, due to factors perhaps unrelated to the current environment (e.g., hypoglycemia), which results in exaggerated physiological reactions (e.g., increased cardiac rate, dizziness, gagging or choking, hyperventilation, vomiting). Later anxiety acts as a conditioned stimulus for a component of the original physiological or cognitive reaction to the anxiety. Notwithstanding the fact that the anxiety phobic has been conditioned to internal stimuli, this subclass of phobics often complains of fear related to external stimuli. This is possibly the result of higher order conditioning in that external stimuli, present during the initial profound anxiety attacks, become conditioned in a higher order fashion to internal stimuli. In such cases, the anxiety phobic, actually conditioned to internal stimuli, can, at first, appear as the more common phobic conditioned to external stimuli. It is most important that this critical differentiation be made before possibly inappropriate treatment is initiated.

When external stimuli do function as higher order conditioned stimuli for the anxiety phobic, systematic desensitization in imagination will not produce significant amelioration of the presenting problem. While anxiety associated with the specific stimulus focus of the desensitization procedure may be reduced, the anxiety phobia, that is, the conditioned response conditioned to the internal stimuli and the catastrophic consequence, will remain unaffected. It can be particularly frustrating to the client and to the therapist when the anxiety phobic presents with a large variety of external conditioned stimuli if an attempt is made to desensitize these stimuli one by one. Despite any minor successes, the basic anxiety will persist.

Generally, when common phobics encounter the external conditioned stimulus, their anxiety rises to some uncomfortable level and maintains a plateau until the stimulus is removed. Their attention is focused on the phobic situation, not on their anxiety. In contrast, when anxiety phobics are forced to confront the higher order conditioned stimulus, their anxiety continues to rise until the phobic stimulus is removed from their environment. At first they attend to the external stimulus. However, the focus of their attention soon shifts to the anxiety and the possibility of the catastrophe. Most anxiety phobics may be differentiated from the more common phobics when they initially describe their complaint. In those cases in which the anxiety phobic presents as a common phobic, aid in making an appropriate discrimination may be obtained from the patient's description of their experience when faced with the external conditioned stimulus for a sustained duration.

The Development of Performance Anxiety

Individuals who are concerned about the frequency of occurrence of some aspect of behavior that is specific to certain situations may tend to avoid those situations. For example, anxiety phobics who are disturbed by the possibility of experiencing some disastrous consequence outside of their home may refuse to leave their house unless accompanied by someone who could help them in the event of the predicted emergency. In a similar fashion, individuals having a history of urinary retention will avoid those bathrooms in which they are most uncomfortable (Ascher, 1977). In the extreme the businessman who cannot urinate outside of his home will drastically restrict his fluid intake during the day in order not to have to urinate until he returns home; he thereby avoids having to utilize any public facility. Men who are worried about their ability to obtain an erection during sexual activity, or women anxious about their failure to experience orgasm during intercourse, may drastically reduce any type of contact with the opposite sex.

When such individuals must enter a discomforting location they do so with the view that each confrontation is a test of their ability to remain comfortable and in control of the relevant physiological process. In anticipation of this test, the individual complaining of anxiety phobia, for example, experiences a complex of stimuli composed of the input of several sources: external stimuli that partially resemble or are components of the actual target situation (these become more prominent as the individual draws closer to the target), cognitions related to past failure (e.g., "I wonder if I will be extremely anxious and embarrass myself by having to leave in the middle of the meeting again?"), cognitions related to the impending test and to the possibility of experiencing the catastrophic consequence (e.g., "If I get on the subway I know I'll have a heart attack"), and cognitions related to the consequences of persistent failure (e.g., "How will I ever be able to lead a normal life if I have to remain in my room?"). Alternatively, the male with erective dysfunction may have thoughts similar to the following, which are related to past failures: "Last night was the most embarrassing situation that I have ever been in; I can't believe that she actually asked me if I were gay when I couldn't get an erection." And, the same male may, just before entering the sexual situation or just prior to intercourse think: "I hope that I'll be able to get it up; I know she's going to leave me this time if I can't."

In addition to these cognitive discomforts there is performance anxiety related to the maintenance of control over involuntary physiological processes. In the case of the insomniac, the ability to fall asleep at will is the goal; having an orgasm whenever she wishes is the aim of the nonorgasmic female. The anxiety phobic is concerned about maintaining control over the autonomic nervous system and the specific physiological components involved with the catastrophic contingency of high anxiety, for example, heart, throat, lungs, circulatory system. There is the implication that the individual must maintain perfect control over the relevant physical system at all times; this, of course, is an impossibility for anyone, but particularly for those with concern in this area.

The following case is presented for the purpose of illustrating the relationship of performance anxiety to the deterioration of some desirable behavior. Mr. V. was a successful salesman,; 42 years of age, whose presenting problem was sleep-onset insomnia. He was concerned about the cummulative effects of long-term sleep loss and medication intake. The problem first became evident at the age of 19 and grew progressively worse from that time. Several years ago, in addition to the lengthening sleep-onset latency, he began to awaken in the middle of the night and experienced difficulty returning to sleep. His first therapeutic encounter began at age 27; he chose psychoanalysis and remained for 8 years, three times a week. He became dissatisfied when he began to feel that the analyst was not particularly interested in his presenting problem. Subsequent to termination, he consulted a series of therapists espousing varying approaches, but could report little improvement as a result. At age 39 he began behavior therapy and obtained some amelioration of the problem, but not to a satisfactory extent. After 8 months he terminated and did not seek additional consultation for several years. Finally, he sought advice from a series of physicians, one of whom referred him to this author. At the time of the initial meeting, the client's mean daily sleep-onset latency was 2 hours. In addition, he reported awakening at least once per evening, four or five times per week, and experienced difficulty returning to sleep. Several physical examinations initiated by Mr. V. failed to reveal a physiological basis for the problem. The verbatim material was extracted from the initial session:

T: How long does it take you to fall asleep presently?

C: Some nights 5 hours. I get into bed at 11:00 and I'm still up at 4:00 AM. Other nights it's a little better.

T: How much better?

C: Sometimes it only takes me an hour or two to get to sleep.

T: How many nights per week would you estimate that you had a great deal of difficulty?

C: At least four.

T: Is there any pattern that you have been able to determine with respect to those nights on which you have a great deal of trouble versus those on which you have less difficulty falling asleep?

C: No. My last therapist had me keep a diary but we weren't able to pick out any events from the past day or the next that could be involved. . . .

T: Do you ever think about anything related to sleep during the day?

C: Yes, a lot.

T: Can you give me some examples?

C: I think about the evening and whether I'm going to be able to sleep. I think about how much I hate to lie in bed awake all night. I think my poor sleeping habits can affect my health, or my work the next day.

T: In what way do you think that this loss of sleep will affect your health?

C: I don't know, I just think it's bad for me.

T: Do you feel anxious if you are reminded of sleep during the day?

C: What do you mean?

T: Well, suppose you were to read a magazine and see an advertisement for some over-the-counter sleeping medication. Would that upset you?

C: It would make me think of my own difficulties and I would become a little upset, so I guess it would upset me.

T: Has this ever happened to you?

C: Yes, sometimes when I go into a drugstore and see _____ or _____ on the counter I get nervous. . . .

T: What do you do once you're in the bed, prior to falling asleep?

C: I toss and turn.

T: What else?

C: I try to do some of the things that I learned in therapy.

T: What were they?

C: A relaxation exercise mostly, but also some imagining.

T: Does it help you?

C: Sometimes it does, sometimes it doesn't; I don't really know. . . . .

T: What do you think about when you're lying in bed?

C: Mostly about how I'll never get to sleep and how tired I'm going to be the next day.

T: Do you have a clock near your bed?

C: Yes, I look at it once in a while and that makes me nervous too. . . .

Mr. V. reported that he experienced anxiety during the day when presented with stimuli associated with sleep. In addition, he had many anxiety-related categories of thoughts to which he attended during the day. These included concerns about the discomfort of remaining in bed for long periods of time without sleeping, reduced performance resulting from the loss of sleep, and the cummulative effects of the sleep dysfunction in terms of a deterioration of his health.

Before the individuals enter the test situation, they have already developed a significant amount of anxiety. Immediately after entering the test situation, anxiety phobics, for example, monitor their level of anxiety and the specific system related to the aversive consequence of excessive anxiety (e.g., heart rate). They will undoubtedly find both to be too high, and this will result in further increasing their level of discomfort. Insomniacs will focus on their level of "sleepiness" and judge it to be insufficient to foster the rapid onset of sleep.

Once they are actually in the sleep situation, with a high degree of anxiety, they will attempt to apply coping mechanisms in order to gain control over the specific physiological system of focus in an effort to prevent the occurrence of failure (and the catastrophic consequence in the case of the anxiety phobic). For the anxiety phobic the primary focus of these coping mechanisms is on the reduction of anxiety (Quinn and Richardson, 1971). Although different individuals develop different devices, typical examples include thinking of distracting thoughts; becoming involved in animated conversation with others, even when this requires approaching strangers; and carrying, but not necessarily using, medication or alcohol. Mr. V., an insomniac, reported the use of warm milk and certain imaginal exercises. It was also clear from the verbatim material presented that he was using a relaxation procedure in order to enhance the sleep process. While such coping responses may have worked with low anxiety, they will not work at the high levels of discomfort that the individual now experiences in the test situation. The realization that this last resort has failed to reduce the anxiety and that they have lost control of the autonomic nervous system means for anxiety phobics that the ultimate aversive consequence is insured and escape becomes imperative.

To summarize, anxiety phobics enter discomforting situations with concerns about their ability to voluntarily control their autonomic nervous system; such control is important in order to prevent the overloading of physiological processes which it innervates. These concerns are themselves related to an increase in anxiety. Prior to entering the discomforting situation, and throughout the time spent on location, anxiety phobics constantly monitor their level of anxiety as well as the specific physiological systems relevant to the hypothesized catastrophic event. Thus if these phobics are concerned about an imminent heart attack, they will monitor their cardiac rate. The perception of an uncomfortably high level of anxiety serves to further increase the amount of anxiety. The individual will then apply a series of coping strategies interspersed with self monitoring. Each monitoring event will reveal the failure of a coping response and will again serve to additionally increase discomfort.

Thus is revealed the circular performance anxiety process that is central to the anxiety phobic's problem. That is, the individual with a history of dysfunction in some area enters with anxiety regarding the performance of responses designed to control the relevant involuntary physiological process. This performance anxiety serves to exacerbate the dysfunction of the physical system. The individual becomes more anxious and attempts to further control the system. But this becomes increasingly unlikely, and each attempt fails, completing the circle by further increasing the anxiety. Therefore, concern over control produces the dysfunction and failure to successfully control it results in further dysfunction. Each time the anxiety phobic escapes from the discomforting situation, the circular process becomes stronger.

This pernicious circle is sometimes maintained by the activities of the therapist. Whenever the anxiety phobic is presented with a technique that can be used in a direct attempt to control anxiety, the therapist unwittingly makes a contribution to the circular performance anxiety process. This may be overt and explicit, or it may be implicit in the therapeutic assignment. For example, in the case presented, the therapist introduced deep-muscle relaxation in order to help the client reduce his general level of tension. If the therapist is not cautious, the patient will possibly misuse the technique by employing it as a coping response in an attempt to reduce peak anxiety. This will be experienced as one more failure for the client, but also for the therapist and possibly for therapy in general. The therapist must emphasize the appropriate use of each technique and be prepared to counter possible improper modes of utilization. Mr. V. was instructed in the use of a relaxation procedure by his previous therapist. The client inferred from these instructions that he was to employ the procedure to help him to fall asleep. Thus he utilized relaxation as a coping device that served to exacerbate the problem.

The Role of Paradoxical Intention

Given the self-maintaining circular performance-anxiety process and the potential for the therapist to perpetuate the discomfort of the client by erroneously prescribing additional control strategies, the initial efforts of the therapist must be focused on dissolution of the circle. This can be accomplished by utilizing paradoxical suggestions requiring behavior on the part of the client that is incompatible with that which has been maintaining performance anxiety. In the case of the anxiety phobic, the individual endeavors to maintain calm and thereby control the autonomic nervous system. In addition, there is an attempt to avoid the catastrophic consequence by trying to control some additional physiological process influenced by the autonomic nervous system (e.g., in the following case, the anxiety phobic is fearful that the increased cardiac rate resulting from his anxiety will result in cardiac damage).

The history of anxiety phobics will reveal that in the past they have reduced their attendance at anxiety-provoking locations to the lowest possible frequency. Avoidance becomes a powerful coping maneuver. When forced to be present at some discomforting situation, the anxiety phobic attempts to maintain control over the autonomic nervous system and related physiological processes often by employing various cognitive strategies, usually in an effort at distraction (e.g., making lists of members of various categories). When these initial responses fail, the phobic will engage in more extreme behavior going to great lengths to remain comfortable (e.g., having an intimate conversation with a stranger in order that, should the client pass out, this new found "friend" will make sure that the client receives any aid which may be necessary). When anxiety becomes too uncomfortable in the situation, the anxiety phobic leaves. Escape is the final coping response. The anxiety phobic utilizes these coping devices in an effort to reduce anxiety when, in fact, it is these behaviors that serve to maintain the performance anxiety circle and the anxiety phobic's related discomfort.

If the circular process is to be broken these coping behaviors must be subverted. Paradoxical intention accomplishes this subversion by requiring the client to perform behaviors in opposition to the coping strategies typically employed. Prior to suggesting the paradoxical intention, the anxiety phobic is exposed to the rationale of the problem. This includes a detailed discussion of the way in which the client developed the performance anxiety circle and the specific responses utilized to deal with the discomfort. The explanation includes details of the manner in which the coping behavior has been maintaining the anxiety by preventing the client from remaining in the discomforting situation long enough to learn that no catastrophic consequence follows peak anxiety. The therapist should then point out that in order for the discomfort to be alleviated the client must experience peak anxiety on a number of occasions and thereby demonstrate to himself or herself that nothing follows peak anxiety except fatigue. When the client agrees that this final step follows logically from the proceeding discussion, the paradoxical suggestion is introduced. The client is told to try to experience as much anxiety as possible and to enhance the quality of the anxiety experience. The client is instructed to seek out and enter as many discomforting situations as possible (within the confines of their anxiety hierarchy). He or she is not to avoid an opportunity to practice anxiety enhancement. The more experience obtained with peak anxiety and consequent fatigue, the less frightened he or she will become of anxiety. Therefore, when the client is in a discomforting situation, there must never be an attempt to reduce the anxiety; the goal should be that of trying to increase or enhance the feelings that anxiety produces. He or she should focus on the physiological effects of anxiety, particularly those about which the client is most concerned, and attempt to increase these experiences. Thus if the individual fears a heart attack, focus should be on cardiac rate; perhaps the individual can take his or her pulse and try to increase the number of beats per minute. If the fear is that others will learn of one's anxiety because of a flushed face, perspiration, trembling, and so forth, the requirement becomes that of increasing these symptoms of anxiety. In other words, he or she is to try to enhance the experience of anxiety by attending to those physiological processes that are most sensitive to sympathetic activity and by making every effort to increase these physical sensations. Finally, in spite of peak anxiety, the client is never to try to reduce the anxiety by employing former coping mechanisms and must never escape from the experience of anxiety. Each escape strengthens the bond between the discomforting situation and the anxiety that makes it discomforting.

If the client accepts these explanations and agrees to follow the therapeutic directives, he or she will enter previously uncomfortable situations with the intention of becoming anxious. Thus anticipatory anxiety will be obviated. No longer will they fear the possibility of impending anxiety or be concerned about their ability to maintain discomfort at a low level; in contrast, the intention will be to try to become anxious. If the therapist has been successful then for the first time, the anxiety phobic will enter the feared location without anticipatory anxiety. Now the client focuses on various physiological symptoms and tries to enhance their functioning. Just as they were unable to decrease the activity of these processes before, they will not be able to perceptibly increase these processes now. In addition, by focusing on internal stimuli, rather than on thoughts of catastrophic consequences, the client reduces the probability of actually experiencing anxiety in the discomforting situation. Therefore, when paradoxical intention operates in an optimal fashion, the client never actually experiences the expected anxiety.

To summarize, the anxiety phobic enters a discomforting situation with apprehension regarding the ability to perform behavior that will control the autonomic nervous system and related physiological processes. Responses made on behalf of this control (e.g., avoidance, self-monitoring, distraction, escape), and the techniques that the therapist might teach the client in this attempt to control the uncontrollable serve to maintain a circular performance anxiety process. In order to break this circle, a paradoxical suggestion might be presented instead, requiring the client to engage in behavior that is incompatible with the anxiety-producing responses. Therefore, the anxiety phobic is encouraged to seek out discomforting situations to try to increase the anxiety and attempt to produce the catastrophic event in the manner specifically denoted by the therapist. Just as the client was previously unable to reduce the level of anxiety (as well as the level of activity of related physiological processes), now he or she will be equally unsuccessful at increasing these systems. The behaviors that have been maintaining the performance anxiety are thus obviated resulting in the extinction of the performance anxiety.

Client Variables

The paradoxical intention procedure must be considered to be in the initial very tentative exploratory phase, as a behavioral technique. As such, the emphasis has been placed on the general presenting problems with which it seems most effective. Questions concerning the roles of specific client characteristics in facilitating or inhibiting the effectiveness of paradoxical intention require more information about the technique; such information can only be obtained from continued clinical application with a wide variety of individuals. Notwithstanding the premature nature of such considerations, there is certainly one aspect of client behavior that does appear to have some bearing on programs involving paradoxical intention.

Behavior that may be subsumed under the general label of "oppositional responding" has some influence in the functioning of paradoxical intention. Clients who appear to be uncooperative, resistive, or rebellious pose a problem for any therapeutic program. It was previously noted that paradoxical intention could be employed as the central core of a behavioral program or could be used in a more unplanned, spontaneous manner when a block in therapeutic progress made this necessary. Thus oppositional behavior can prevent the effective operation of paradoxical intention, as is true with any therapeutic procedure when that technique is utilized as the core of a behavioral program. However, oppositional behavior can be surreptitiously overcome by the administration of paradoxical intention in a more spontaneous fashion. The case described later in this chapter offers an excellent example. For several sessions the behavioral-paradoxical intention program had been ineffective in producing change in the desired direction. In session nine the therapist spontaneously employed a paradoxical startegy that eventually served to move the client to a more cooperative stance with respect to the therapist's proposed treatment program.

Another example comes from the case of a 42-year-old housewife who complained of having difficulty falling asleep and of awakening in the middle of the night and being unable to return to sleep within a comfortable length of time. She had been in analysis for some years but had decided on a "symptom-based" treatment when she consulted this author. Treatment began with progressive relaxation at bedtime and systematic desensitization to concerns about the cummulative bad effects of constant sleep loss. The rationale of performance anxiety and the role that it might be playing in her case was discussed. In spite of her professed desire to begin behavior therapy and to cooperate in home practice of the techniques, she behaved in an exceedingly resistive manner. She questioned the rationale of each technique that was proposed, was unable to practice at home for innumerable reasons, and generally felt that behavior therapy would be useless for her as it failed to deal with the basis of her problem. The following material, typical of much of the previous interaction with the client, was obtained from the fifth session.

T: Well, how did things go this week?

C: I was up for 2 or 3 hours in the middle of the night every night. It isn't working.

T: The relaxation?

C: Yes, it won't work.

T: Why do you suppose?

C: I don't see how it can help, it's got no relationship to the real problem.

T: I understand what you are saying, but as I mentioned, the relaxation technique is only one portion of the program. As I see it, the total program will, one way or another, deal with whatever material you think is important.

C: I don't see how this program will uncover the underlying anxieties.

T: Well, I believe you worked on this material when you were in an analytic context. Since it was not particularly successful, I assumed that you had decided to attempt to view your problem in an alternative fashion.

C: I have, but I don't see that there's anything which behavior therapy has which can uncover these anxieties.

T: What you seem to be saying is that you'll try behavior therapy but you'll work from an analytic frame of reference. That is, you're retaining the analytic model of behavior. There seems to be no substantial evidence that the underlying tenets of the analytic model are useful in changing behavior. Therefore, behavior therapists work with concepts that are more operational—are easier to observe and work with. Using such concepts we have been quite successful with a wide variety of problems including sleep dysfunction.

C: I see it, but I can't buy it. I just don't believe that my behavior is not influenced by unconscious thoughts and anxieties.

This was the tenor of most of the session. The following material was taken from a point close to the end of the session:

T: Well perhaps you are right.

C: About what?

T: We haven't been successful in reducing the amount of time which it takes you to fall asleep after you awaken at night. So maybe we should try to operate from your frame of reference at this point.

C: How will that be?

T: Suppose you are correct about this deep underlying material which is at the basis of your problem, how can we best get at it?

C: I don't know.

T: We could assume that the revelation of this material has something to do with sleeping. You know, you fall asleep to prevent yourself from thinking about certain things. So even though you are complaining about an inability to fall asleep at certain times, maybe you're actually falling asleep too fast. You know, too fast to latch on to the anxiety-provoking thoughts. Maybe, you are afraid to face these thoughts and use sleep to avoid them. I think you should try, in every way possible, to get at the unconscious material.

C: How?

T: Well, how do you feel about the idea that you are being protected from the anxiety-provoking material by falling alseep too quickly to allow yourself to experience these thoughts?

C: It could be; I do a lot of thinking when I'm lying in bed.

T: Sure, and the thoughts may be linked together in some manner so that the later thoughts are the more significant ones.

C: So what can I do about it?

T: Just pay special attention to the thoughts that you have closest to the time that you fall asleep.

C: But how do I know when I'm going to fall asleep?

T: That doesn't make any difference. What I'm saying is the later thoughts will be more significant than the earlier ones. So pay careful attention to all the material and the things that you remember as having experienced last; we'll discuss them here.

C: People can't usually remember what happened just before they fall asleep.

T: That is a problem. That's probably why, after all this time, you still haven't come up with these thoughts.

C: What would happen if I tried to remain awake?

T: I don't know.

C: I might have a better chance of getting to the bottom of this problem.

T: I don't know, it might work. Do you want to try it?

C: You mean just stay up?

T: Yes that's the only way I can think of.

C: It sounds silly.

T: It sure does.

C: What do I do, stay up and watch TV?

T: No. You should lie in bed, with the lights out and attend to your thoughts just as you would if you were going to sleep.

C: But I shouldn't go to sleep?

T: No, just keep thinking. Perhaps you should try to keep your eyes open to insure that you don't fall asleep.

C: But won't it be better if I have the lights and TV on, then I certainly won't fall asleep.

T: We want the situation to be as natural to sleep as possible so that you will have a better chance to get at the thoughts. So turn out the lights and do everything as though you were trying to fall asleep.

When the client returned for the sixth session she reported that she had been unable to carry out the assignment. Although she did awaken on several evenings, she could not remain awake. It had been a week in which she was very active, and we attributed her inability to remain awake to the possibility that she was unusually fatigued. She returned home with the assignment of attempting to delay the onset of sleep as long as possible the next week. She continued to report failure to remain awake on several additional sessions. Finally the client was informed that, in spite of her continued inability to delay sleep onset, she had contributed enough new material for the purpose of desensitization. It was suggested that she return to the relaxation exercises when she got into bed in preparation for desensitization. She agreed.

This case was included to illustrate the spontaneous use of paradoxical intention to subvert resistive or oppositional behavior; after the client had demonstrated an inability to cooperate with the behavioral treatment of choice, the therapist placed the paradoxical perscription, that of trying to remain awake, within a context which she could accept.

Therapist Attitude

Frankl and his coworkers suggest that paradoxical intention is best administered within a context of humor. That is, the therapist should maintain as light an atmosphere as is possible under the circumstances. It is assumed that humor on the part of the therapist will contribute to a possible transformation of the stance of sorrowful concern that the client holds toward the problem. This is an important contribution, as it is hypothesized that the depressing attitude serves in large part to maintain the problem behavior. If such is the case, then changing the client's relative view of his difficulty from one of disparagement to one of humorous indifference could enhance therapeutic progress (Allport, 1950). This is often difficult for the therapist to accomplish since many clients enter the therapeutic situation with a grave attitude of discomfort, if not of desperation, regarding their primary complaint. In the same manner that a long-term behavior problem is resistant to change, the client's accompanying view of it also represents an overlearned response that may be equally difficult to modify.

Naturally, humor must be incorporated into the therapist's approach gradually during the establishment of rapport but not before the therapist has enough understanding of the client to determine the actual form of this humor. The therapist must first develop a relationship of mutual respect, an interaction in which the client has confidence that the therapist can be of assistance, and that the therapist is truly concerned with the problem. This last point is critical. If humor is injected prematurely, it can be interpreted by the client as being an indication that the therapist either is not particularly concerned with the client or the unadaptive behavior, or that he does not have the critical understanding of the client's difficulty required to render assistance. The therapist must demonstrate that he is concerned and should communicate to the client that humor, rather than being a negative chance factor, is actually a positive, purposeful component of the treatment package.

The actual administration of the humor depends on what level the client and therapist are most comfortable. That is, humor can be presented in a subtle, tentative manner, or in a very obvious, heavy-handed way. One is not necessarily superior to the other; the decision is dependent both upon what the client seems to appreciate and which seems to have the greatest effect on him. Some initial exploration is important. On the other hand, it cannot be assumed that a therapist who is not humorous will be unable to utilize paradoxical intention. Many therapists who employ this technique either do not mention humor or do not emphasize its use in conjunction with paradoxical intention (e.g., Watzlawick, Weakland, and Fisch, 1974). A therapist who is not comfortable employing humor in the therapy session should not make the mistake of attempting its use. A stilted remark meant to be humorous could be interpreted by the client in ways that would not be congruent with a good therapeutic relationship. For example, the therapist could easily appear to be condescending. On the other hand, a therapist who presents a dour attitude toward the client's problems will certainly strengthen this same attitude in the client.

The following example of the use of humor is presented as an extreme to demonstrate an example of the range of possibilities. The material comes from the first portion of the fourth session conducted with an anxiety phobic. She was specifically concerned with the possibility of experiencing cardiac arrest when she left her apartment. She was in excellent health as attested to by her family physician and a cardiologist whom she regularly consulted. The client was instructed to enter certain mildly discomforting locations (i.e., low on her anxiety hierarchy) and attempt to experience peak anxiety and, if possible, to have a "heart attack." Although, she was initially skeptical, she soon proved to be a cooperative client after reasoning that much of the instruction was exaggerated for its humorous affect.

> T: I hope you are clear about your assignment. I simply want you to go to the _____ Shopping Center and try to have an anxiety at-

tack. When you are successful, remain until it extinguishes. Don't leave during the attack, or you will be strengthening the anxiety to the shopping center on later occasions. Okay?

C: Sure, you want me to go and become petrified.

T: Yes, that's about it.

C: This could kill me (She smiles, laughs nervously).

T: Well, in fact, I want you to try to have a heart attack. After all, it's the heart attack that you're really concerned about, not so much the anxiety. So it makes sense to try to have a heart attack.

C: But if anything happens to me who'll pay the bill?

T: Gee, that's right. Hmm. Well, I can get it from your estate.

C: I'm afraid my estate doesn't count for much.

T: Well, then I'll just have to accept the risk (The client gets up to leave). Oh, I forgot to ask the name of your local newspaper.

C: It's the _____ why?

T: When I send someone out to do this I like to keep an eye on the obituary column so I know whether to expect them on the following week.

C: Very funny. Won't you be surprised if something happens.

T: Yes.

Another example of humor employed as the context for a paradoxical suggestion comes from the case of a 39-year-old male who complained of urinary retention in public facilities. The following material was taken from the end of the third session following the presentation of the paradoxical intention instructions:

T: Do you understand what I want you to do? Simply enter the men's room when you have the urge to urinate and do everything that you would normally do—everything, except do not urinate. Under no circumstances should you allow yourself to urinate. Wait until you return home at the end of the day.

P: You mean you just want me to stand in front of the urinal and not do anything?

T: Well, you could do general relaxation, or some imaginal work, but there really isn't enough time.

P: I don't mean that, I mean you want me to stand there and not urinate?

T: Exactly.

P: What if somebody sees?

T: Sees what, your "Pee-pee?"

P: (Laughs.) No, sees that I'm just standing there and not urinating.

T: How will anyone know?

P: I don't know, someone may look and see.

T: You mean look in your urinal while you're urinating?

P: Yes.

T: Do you look in other people's urinals while they're urinating?

P: No, of course not.

T: Come on, I bet you do.

P: No, really.

T: Now we get to the real problem. You go into the men's room and are compelled to look into urinals to see who's urinating and who's not.

P: That's crazy. Besides I'd have no reason to do that. I just assume everyone is urinating.

T: Well, then why would you suspect others of displaying this unusual interest where you are concerned?

P: I guess that's right.

It is expected that the client will view the humor of the therapist as indicating that the therapist is confident about his or her ability to ameliorate the problem and that the therapist does not feel that the client's difficulty is quite as hopeless as does the client. This should serve to reduce the individual's concerns to some extent. Once the client becomes less involved with the problem, the possibility of speedy remission is increased. One reason for postulating that an attitude of humorous indifference toward one's difficulty hastens recovery is suggested by the foregoing discussion of the etiology of performance anxiety. If the client has focused a great deal of concern on a particular behavioral process in an effort to change its frequency of occurrence, it is hypothesized that the resultant performance anxiety will work in opposition to the individual's desire. If, on the other hand, the attitude of the individual toward the presenting complaint is one of humorous indifference, then the frequency of occurrence of the response will, by definition, be of no concern, and performance anxiety will be obviated.

Humor on the part of the therapist serves another purpose. The administration of paradoxical intention must be performed in a context of nonconfrontation. The therapist and the client must agree on the course of therapy, rather than the therapist setting goals which the client must achieve. If the client cannot or will not cooperate with the therapist's suggestion, then the suggestion is withdrawn or modified in order to be more comfortable for the client. If the client reports the inability to fulfill the agreement during the previous week, labels such as "failure" should never be applied. Rather, the positive aspects of the situation should be emphasized as an approximation of the agreed goal. An air of humor seems to be congruent with this permissive, accepting, nonconfrontative approach.

The following case is provided in order to illustrate the use of paradoxical intention with one of the general clinical problems which seem exceptionally well suited to the technique. The case of Mr. B., an anxiety phobic, is a particularly good example of the utilization of paradoxical intention because a paradoxical strategy was eventually required to enable the client to benefit from the paradoxical-behavioral treatment of choice. Where possible, only those aspects of the case directly relevant to the use of paradoxical intention are included.

History

Mr. B. was a 43-year-old self-employed businessman. He and his wife of 19 years had two children, a girl 17 and a boy 15. His presenting complaint was that of experiencing extreme anxiety whenever he drove. He indicated that this was the only time when he experienced anxiety of this type.

The problem had persisted for approximately 20 years in spite of the efforts of various psychotherapists. At first he experienced only mild discomfort while driving, but prior to the initial meeting with this author the anxiety had reached peak levels with almost every driving event. As a result, he restricted his driving to those circumstances that were absolutely essential, that is those related to work or to some dire emergency. In an attempt to reduce the discomfort while driving, Mr. B. often pulled to the side of the road and "double parked" with his engine running; he remained in this stationary position until the anxiety subsided substantially before resuming his itinerary.

The reason for originally consulting the author was Mr. B.'s realization that the frequency and duration of these stops were becoming unmanageable. The primary role that Mr. B. assumes in his business is that of salesman, since it is in this way that new accounts are acquired and old accounts are persuaded to increase their orders. Each day, Mr. B. has a list of customers or prospective customers to call upon in the early mornings. Prior to these visits, he engages in some administrative activities, and when he returns in the late afternoon he must record the orders to be sure that they are properly filled. Because of his increasing need to pull off the road while driving it was becoming impossible for him to complete his responsibilities within the normal working day. An additional difficulty related to this anxiety was his need to use only small streets that were not heavily trafficked; for obvious reasons, these restricted routes served to further increase the length of time necessary to complete his scheduled appointments. At the time of the initial interview his average working day was approximately 12 hours and would sometimes be extended to as long as 15 hours. He objected to the extended duration because he was becoming fatigued and was not able to engage in avocational activities. In addition, the reduction in time spent with his family was becoming a source of difficulty between Mr. and Mrs. B.

During the initial two sessions the behavioral analysis was completed. In addition to details of the presenting problem, Mr. B. indicated several areas of discomfort. His relationship with his wife was a major source of concern. Mr. and Mrs. B. seemed to argue constantly and had several important conflicts, not the least of which related to sexual behavior. A second family-related problem involved his son. Mr. B. was upset by what he described to be a poor relationship between the two of them. Further, he was not pleased with important aspects of his son's behavior and felt that his son was often out of Mr. B.'s control. With respect to this last concern, he felt that his son sometimes displayed inproprietous behavior and disregarded his father's attempts to correct and instruct him. At work Mr. B. felt somewhat unhappy about his interactions with his employees. He did not feel that they were using what he felt to be a fair standard and had difficulty cirticizing them, or being as stern with them as he wished. Mr. B was also uncomfortable in dealing with both established customers and with prospective clients. He attributed his discomfort to a desire not to be a "typical pushy" salesman, but, in fact, would not engage in behavior that was appropriate to his goals and certainly fell well into the range of propriety.

Session Three

> T: Tell me again, what will happen if you should become anxious while driving but be unable to pull over?
>
> C: I'd pull over no matter what.
>
> T: What I mean is that I want you to imagine that you are forced to continue to drive; it's impossible for you to pull over or to stop driving.

C: Then I'd have an accident.

T: I don't understand. How would the accident occur?

C: It'd just happen. I'd get nervous and anxious and would get into an accident.

T: Well, under the circumstances that I suggested, an accident might not definitely occur.

C: I'm sure, that I'd get so anxious that I'd get into an accident.

T: Let's forget about the accident for a minute. What would happen as your anxiety increased but you found that you could not pull over?

C: I'd just keep getting more and more anxious.

T: Then what?

C: Then that accident.

T: Well, I want to forget about the accident for a moment because as I mentioned, this may not occur, but your increased anxiety certainly would.

C: Yes.

T: But what would happen as your anxiety increased and you still were unable to get out of the situation?

C: It'd keep increasing until I lost control of the car.

T: Well, how would you lose control?

C: I don't know; I just would.

T: If I were observing your behavior, what changes would I see as you lost control?

C: Shaking, sweating.

T: Would you experience any dizziness?

C: I don't know, maybe. If I got that anxious behind the wheel I might faint.

T: So, what you're afraid of is some loss of control which you feel will lead to an accident.

C: Yes, and my heart, I'm afraid of a heart attack.

T: Why is that?

C: Because when I become very anxious, my heart beats real fast. I think someday something's got to give there.

T: Is there anything else?

C: No. I don't think so.

T: Do you then feel apprehensive before you enter your car?

C: Yes, really.

T: What kinds of things do you think about?

C: The anxiety that I'm going to have. How uncomfortable I'll be and how much I don't want to drive.

T: What happens after you begin driving?

C: I get more anxious.

T: What do you think about?

C: I think more about my anxiety because I'm getting more anxious; and when I get anxious enough I start to feel my heart beat, and this makes me more anxious.

T: And then what do you think about?

C: About a heart attack, getting into an accident.

T: All kinds of pleasant thoughts!

C: Yes, and then I think about what'll happen if I do have a heart attack—the accident, injury, ambulances, crowds, it's terrible—and the longer I drive the worse it gets.

T: Then what happens, do you continue to become anxious until you reach a peak?

C: No, I try to think of other things—my next appointment, concentrating on the scenery—I play games.

T: What kinds of games?

C: Well, like I'll pick a category and go down the alphabet trying to think of one example for each letter.

T: I see, and does that help?

C: It used to help more than it does now.

T: What do you mean?

C: I used to be able to keep the anxiety down by using these things until I reached my next appointment. Lately I haven't been able to make it to the next appointment. I've had to stop during the trip, and lately these stops have been increasing.

T: And what would happen if you didn't stop?

C: I would have more anxiety and then some bad problems.

Preparing the Client

The enlistment of the patient's cooperation is a crucial factor in any therapeutic program, the present one being no exception. However, the unusual nature of the proposed paradoxical intention approach necessitates some discussion of the manner in which such cooperation may be obtained. It is first assumed that the therapist has endeavored to build rapport with the client in order that the paradoxical prescription may be given in the context of a relationship which the client perceives as comfortable, supportive, and reinforcing. For this reason, the present author rarely employs paradoxical strategies in the aforementioned spontaneous manner before attempting to promote behavioral change with conventional behavior therapy techniques. Thus if it becomes necessary to utilize an unplanned paradoxical suggestion the therapist will have established an appropriate trusting therapeutic relationship and will, therefore, be working with a cooperative patient.

Although the importance of humor was previously mentioned in another context, humor can also serve to enhance the client's willingness to undertake the paradoxical directive. There is literature to suggest that prognosis improves when a patient becomes able to view their problem within a humorous context (Allport, 1950; Frankl, 1955). It was for this reason that Frankl originally included humor as a component central to paradoxical intention. Once the patient is able to laugh at his or her anxiety phobia, it takes on less of the life and death aspect with which it was originally invested.

Initially the client entered therapy with the fear that anxiety would lead to some catastrophic consequence. Certainly, if this is to be the case, the client will not tempt fate by purposefully increasing anxiety. But the therapist makes a two-pronged attack on this belief: first, by explaining that there is no data (from the specific case history of the client) to support the catastrophic contingency of peak anxiety, and second, by himself viewing the problem and reinforcing the client for viewing the problem in a humorous manner. Thus as it has been described in the literature (especially by Frankl), paradoxical intention requires the use of humor with patients who are often quite dour, if not depressed with regard to their problem. This, after all, is understandable, since from the client's perception the anxiety could lead to fatal consequences. It, therefore, becomes advisable that the therapist who employs paradoxical intention be comfortable in utilizing humor in his relationship with his clients. Further, humor must be a pervasive element of therapy and should not be introduced only at the point at which the therapist is to administer a paradoxical suggestion. The therapist should model and reinforce the use, by the client, of humor, in relation to the presenting problem throughout the course of therapy.

Since no data has been collected to support the importance of humor in the success of paradoxical intention, its use by the therapist can be only suggested tentatively. In fact, as mentioned previously, a good deal of literature related to paradoxical intention fails to mention humor as a component in producing a successful therapeutic outcome. Therefore, the inability of an individual therapist to function comfortably in a humorous therapeutic context does not necessarily preclude them from realizing favorable results from the utilization of this technique.

A third factor in gaining the client's cooperation involves the demonstration that they do have some control over their anxiety. This can be accomplished in the therapist's office by suggesting to the client that she or he try to have an anxiety attack and attempt to produce the catastrophic consequence. The therapist can point out that the client is in an optimal situation to have such an attack, the rationale for this statement being based on the client's particular concerns. Thus if the client is afraid of physical damage, and the therapist is a physician or maintains an office in a medical center, it can be pointed out that in case of any difficulty the client can receive immediate assistance. Under these circumstances, the client either will or will not be able to have an anxiety attack. If the client reports that he or she is experiencing increased anxiety, the therapist should guide the client in an attempt to increase that feeling without panicking. It is this author's experience that the client will be able to produce a manageable increment of anxiety before the discomfort subsides. The therapist should point out that if the client approaches discomfort in this manner on location, it can be assumed that the outcome will be similarly satisfactory, that is, a reduction in anxiety rather than some catastrophic event.

In the event that the client cannot become anxious, the therapist should suggest that this results from the client's direct attempt to increase his or her anxiety. Whereas when the client finds himself or herself in uncomfortable surroundings, attempts to reduce anxiety serve actually to increase the experience. In either case, the therapist has helped the client to feel somewhat more comfortable with his or her discomfort. With all of this as a foundation, the therapist should then assign the client the task of increasing anxiety in an *in vivo* setting that is discomforting yet manageable. In order that the therapist be able to make *in vivo* assignments that are appropriate to the client's level of comfort, an anxiety hierarchy should be established similar to that used in systematic desensitization (Wolpe, 1974). By employing such a hierarchy, the therapist can control the relative difficulty of each assignment. This reduces the probability that clients will enter situations that evoke so much anxiety that they will be in danger of becoming panicky and escaping. Each time the client escapes from an assigned situation while experiencing anxiety the escape response increases in strength. The possibility exists that, through reconditioning, therapeutic advances which the client experienced may recede. As the third session continued, the therapist prepared Mr. B for the paradoxical assignment.

T: I want to tell you about some research that has been done in experimental psychology. If you take a rat and put it in an operant chamber—do you know what an operant chamber is?

C: Uhmmm.

T: A Skinner box.

C: Yes.

T: With a grid floor and a lever on one wall, with a food cup and a water spout. . . .

C: Yes, I've seen one.

T: Well, if you take a rat and put it onto the grid floor, and after a short period there is a tone followed after 10 seconds by high intensity shock, it will keep bouncing around until it hits the lever. At that point the shock is terminated. The rat then explores the chamber, grooms itself, and after awhile, say 60 seconds after termination of the last shock, there is another tone. Ten seconds after the tone, there is another continuous shock. Again the rat bounces around until it hits the lever and the shock is terminated. This same sequence occurs a number of times, and if you look at the data you find that the latency between the onset of shock and the rat's pushing the lever, decreases. In other words, the rat is learning to escape from the shock faster and faster. After additional trials, the rat starts to push the lever in response to the tone—the tone that has consistently occurred 10 seconds prior to shock onset. At this point, he is avoiding experiencing any of the shock.

C: So this is why I'm having trouble driving?

T: I don't want you to draw an analogy yet. I just want you to listen to this isolated from your particular situation. The rat will continue to press the bar to the tone even though the shock apparatus has been turned off. It never waits long enough to find out that there is no more shock. Perhaps it does not press the bar as soon as the tone is sounded, but it never waits the full 10 seconds. Now suppose the rat is prevented from pressing the bar after the tone. This can be done by removing the bar or locking it in place, or putting a plexiglass wall in front of it. Now the buzzer is sounded and the bar is locked in place. The rat continues its normal post-tone behavior until it is time for it to press the lever. At this point it finds that the lever cannot be pressed. Its behavior changes radically. It begins to cower, quiver, crouch, squeel, urinate, defecate, all behaviors from which we infer anxiety and fear. Every once in a while, it goes to the lever to press it; failing, it returns to the fearful behavior. This will continue for some time even though it does not receive any shock. The next time it hears the tone, the whole thing will begin again. But after a number of similar trials of tone without shock, the tone will return to being a neutral stimulus. When it is sounded the rat will not change its behavior. Now I want to draw the analogy between what has happened to the rat and the situation in which you find yourself. Each time you go into a setting that is associated with anxiety by you, you attempt to make an avoidance response. Your anxiety is similar to the rat's tone in that each functions as a signal for a future disaster. In the case of the rat, it is the shock; in your case it is loss of control, or rather hypothesized loss of control. The rat will go on escaping from the tone indefinitely if it is permitted, even though the shock has been turned off. Just as you have for many years escaped from the anxiety, thinking that you have been avoiding some disastrous consequence. But just as shock does not follow the tone for the rat, heart attack, loss of control, and an accident do not follow your anxiety. The rat is forced to experience the fact that shock no longer follows the buzzer. But, I cannot do this for you; you must set up your own procedure to allow yourself to experience the fact that you can have anxiety without losing control.

C: How?

T: By entering the situations that make you as anxious as possible and not leaving until your anxiety disappears.

C: But why should it disappear? It would probably keep getting greater and greater until I don't know what.

T: Have you ever actually been in a situation where you became anxious but could not leave? You had to stay no matter how uncomfortable you became?

C: Yes, several times. I've been at meetings where I got very anxious and wanted to leave.

T: Why couldn't you?

C: Once it was because I had to give a report; another time I was sitting in the middle and didn't want to draw attention to myself.

T: So what happened?

C: I got very anxious.

T: How long did it last?

C: A long time.

T: Well, did you remain anxious for the entire duration of the meeting?

C: No. After a while the anxiety left me.

T: How did you feel then?

C: More comfortable and tired after all that anxiety. It really makes me tired.

T: Then you didn't experience the heart attack and the loss of control after peak anxiety that concerns you?

C: No, but I was worried about it.

T: I'm sure, and what I'm suggesting is that the anxiety is maintained by your concern about what will follow the anxiety. At any rate, why do you suppose that you are still concerned about the consequences of anxiety when you had those two incidents in which nothing happened following peak anxiety?

C: I don't know. I guess I just thought that I was lucky and next time I'll really have some trouble.

T: Actually, those two examples are good representatives of what will happen to you following anxiety, rather than two lucky exceptions. Let me tell you what occurs when you become anxious. Your brain, acknowledging something dangerous in the environment, is instrumental in increasing the level of adrenalin in your blood. The adrenalin serves to prepare you for dealing with the danger by increasing the activity of certain processes and cutting down the activity of less essential processes. Thus you breathe faster, and your cardiac rate increases in order that you can oxygenate more blood and that it can be sent more quickly to your extremities for running and fighting. Your digestion is reduced in order that the blood needed for this can be sent to more important areas temporarily. Because this activity increases your body temperature, you begin to perspire in order to cool off. Thus you experience your heart racing, increased breathing, perspiration, unsettled stomach. Now, your system can maintain this high pitched activity for only a short time, and then it becomes fatigued. This fatigue occurs long before any damage can be done. So when you were at the meeting and couldn't leave, your anxiety reached a peak that couldn't be maintained and just calmed down. You felt tired because the anxiety had actually fatigued you. I'm suggesting that this is what will happen every time. You will become anxious, reach a peak, fatigue will develop, and you'll calm down. What you have done most of the time is to become anxious but escape before you reached the peak and the subsequent period of relaxation. Each time you escape you strengthen the fear, and it becomes more uncomfortable on the next occasion.

C: Then what am I supposed to do?

T: Well, when you get into a situation that makes you anxious I don't want you to leave. I want you to remain in it as long as possible—until you calm down. Once the anxiety has completely subsided, then you can leave. I'm really asking you to do nothing more than what you have already done on those two occasions when you couldn't leave a meeting despite high anxiety. And I'm suggesting that the same thing will happen; you will get anxious but then calm down.

C: I really don't have many of these chances.

T: What about the various situations that you mentioned during the first session?

C: They don't bother me any more—only driving.

T: Okay, what about driving?

C: Oh, I couldn't do it when I drive.

T: Why not?

C: Because I might get into an accident.

T: But driving is the same as any other situation. You'll become anxious for a while, and then you'll calm down and that'll be it.

C: Well suppose I do it, how many times will it take?

T: I don't know. Several. Until you no longer are afraid of the anxiety. When you realize that nothing follows the anxiety, then you'll be able to drive and not be concerned about your anxiety. Anxiety is not pleasant, I grant you, but eventually you'll be able to say that it doesn't matter whether or not you have anxiety: you have somewhere to go and you have to get there in a limited amount of time, and the heck with the anxiety.

C: It sounds real hard.

T: I know, but you told me it's becoming increasingly more difficult for you to function at work. And, you can't drive anymore unless it's a dire emergency. So, you have a choice. You can either live with gradually decreasing freedom, not a pleasant possibility, or you can try the approach I described. I realize that it's not going to be easy to break out of this prison, but you had better do it now because it's not going to get easier if you wait.

C: All right, I'll try it. What do I have to do?

T: I want you to drive on your regularly appointed rounds each day, but continue even as the anxiety builds up. Do not stop. The purpose is to let the anxiety build up. Further, I want you to make every effort to experience the anxiety, do not try to distract yourself. In fact I want you to try to increase the anxiety. The faster you get to peak levels, the faster you will experience the calm; this will enable you to have a shorter period of discomfort.

C: How can I increase the anxiety?

T: By trying to make the experience of anxiety as vivid as possible and by concentrating on your heart and trying to make it beat faster, try to perspire more, try to get the blood coursing through your system faster and faster.

C: But how can I do that?

T: I can't explain to you how this is done; all I can tell you is that one can control his cardiac rate. For example, are you familiar with biofeedback?

C: Yes. My last psychiatrist used biofeedback to help me to relax.

T: How did it work?

C: There was a staticky noise that was stopped when I relaxed.

T: Okay, there is also a device that monitors cardiac rate and sends out a similar signal. By increasing or decreasing your cardiac rate you will increase or decrease the feedback signal. Was the feedback effective in helping you to relax?

C: Yes, very helpful.

T: Did you have one at home?

C: No.

T: Well, you said you practiced at home, how did you do it?

C: I don't know, I just did.

T: I don't understand; if you couldn't hear any signal how did you know you were becoming relaxed?

C: I could feel it.

T: Well, possibly what was happening was that during the biofeedback sessions you were learning to correlate various muscle sensations with an increase and decrease in the feedback signal; as you learned which sensations you could control to reduce the feedback, you were able to relax successfully without the aid of the signal. Now that's the same thing that would happen in the case of the cardiac device. Eventually you would learn to correlate certain sensations with an increase and others with a decrease, with the aid of feedback. After a while you would no longer need this aid. This is what I want you to do. Practice at home and try to do it while driving. Do you think that you can do that?

C: I'll try.

T: Now you pointed out that there were some driving situations that were less discomforting than others.

C: You mean that list we made up from 0 to 100?

T: Yes.

C: Yes. Some things are better than others.

T: Well, I want you to try this procedure only in situations which are low on the list, say 20 to 25.

C: Okay, but when I drive I might be in several situations with different amounts of anxiety.

T: In that case, make sure you try this only when you can control the particular trip. For example, try this on your way home, and if things get out of hand, you know you'll be ending your driving for the day anyway.

C: Okay.

T: So, when you feel anxious just let yourself go. Don't try to stop the anxiety; keep driving and try to increase your heart rate.

C: What do you mean when you say, "Don't try to stop?" How can I stop the anxiety?

T: Well, you really can't, you just think you can. You have maneuvers that you use while driving in an attempt to keep the anxiety under control. The most obvious of these is the constant stopping, but even before you reach this point you try to distract yourself by talking to passengers if you have any, thinking about something related to your business, trying to compile the lists you mentioned. You do these things in an effort to reduce anxiety, right?

C: Yes, I suppose.

T: And does it work?

C: I'm not sure.

T: Of course it doesn't work. If it did you wouldn't take the time to come here. You would be using these devices to control your anxiety and continue working.

C: So you don't want me to do that?

T: No. When you attempt to use them in an effort to control your anxiety you're already fairly anxious. They fail to be effective, and you become even more anxious realizing that your last hope has gone down the drain.

C: Yes. I guess that's true. I sometimes do feel that way.

T: So when you go driving, in an attempt to increase your anxiety I don't want you to use these maneuvers. They don't work anyway, so what difference does it make if you stop using them? I want you to increase any behavior that you have experienced as increasing as a result of anxiety except one. You mentioned that you perspire, feel unsettled in your stomach, feel your heart pounding, breathe more rapidly, and sometimes feel dizzy. Well, the dizziness is probably related to your increased respiratory rate. Try it now and see if that is true. Breathe rapidly. (Mr. B. breathes rapidly and deeply for less than 1 minute.)

C: Yes, I feel dizzy.

T: Okay, good. Stop breathing rapidly. Now you can avoid this aspect of your discomfort when you are driving by simply keeping your mouth closed when you become anxious. When your mouth is closed it becomes very difficult to hyperventilate to the extent that you become dizzy. Now do you understand what you are to do? Just get out there and let yourself go. It's like falling off a cliff; there is nothing you can do about it, so just let the anxiety grow until it increases and dissipates.

Notes on Session Three

During the third session the behavioral analysis was completed, and Mr. B. was presented with the therapist's rationale for the presenting problem, that is, anxiety phobia. Much of the description of Mr. B.'s anxiety attacks which he had detailed during prior sessions contained many of the features typically observed in the anxiety phobic. He entered each driving event with some anxiety that was related to concerns about his ability to remain relatively calm during the trip. Once actually engaged in the driving activity he would become more anxious, and his thoughts would turn to the possibility of undergoing extreme anxiety and of suffering a heart attack as a result of the anxiety. He would then presumably lose control of the car and would become involved in an accident. Sometime before he reached a panic state, Mr. B. would attempt to regain control of his thoughts and of his level of anxiety by distracting himself in various ways. These maneuvers usually did not reduce his discomfort, but rather served to increase the anxiety, necessitating escape from the situation which, in this case, meant stopping the car. After his anxiety was sufficiently reduced, he would drive for a short distance, experiencing the same discomforts and attempts at control, and would be forced to escape again.

A significant aspect of this third session consisted of the presentation to Mr. B. of the therapist's conception of his problem and the consequent treatment plan. Once the explanation is presented, it is important to determine the extent to which the client can agree that it fits his or her particular example. In most cases anxiety phobics are comfortable with this explanation since it is typically corroborated by their experience. Added confidence in the therapist thus accrues when the client feels that the therapist "understands" the problem and can explain it. This is especially the case if the client has been exposed to therapists who were both unsuccessful and did not exhibit knowledge regarding the specific difficulties of the anxiety phobic.

With respect to the treatment program, the paradoxical intention follows logically from the rationale of the problem. The therapist should emphasize the fact that the strategies that the client had been employing in an effort to control the anxiety had not been effective. Therefore, the client is asked not to make any attempt to control the level of comfort. In order to insure that this prohibition is observed, the client is asked to undertake a goal that requires behavior incompatible with responses designed to control anxiety. Thus it was suggested that Mr. B. try to increase his anxiety by focusing on the changes that take place when he becomes anxious, attempting to increase the feelings that these changes produce and specifically to increase the rapidity of his cardiac rate.

The purpose of the paradoxical intention is to involve clients in attempting to produce in themselves, when engaged in the discomforting activity, precisely that which will occur anyway. In this manner, these clients will be successful whether their anxiety increases or decreases. In the event that it increases, then they have accomplished that which was expected of them, and they are closer to the time when they will be able to enjoy greater freedom. However, in the more typical case, clients become so absorbed in attempting to increase their heart rate that they will not experience anxiety in the previously discomforting situations. The therapist's response to the client's report in this event is critical, and is discussed at a more appropriate point in this case presentation.

When the paradoxical suggestion is given, the client is instructed as to the location in which the assignment is to be attempted. The selection of this assignment is quite important. In order to reduce the possibility of failure, an anxiety hierarchy similar to that which is employed in systematic desensitization (Wolpe, 1974) should be constructed. The situation that is then recommended to the client will be one that is very low on the hierarchy. With situations that produce a low level of discomfort, the possibility is increased that the client will not experience anxiety. On the other hand, if the client is sent into a situation associated with a moderate or high level of concern, the probability will be greater that there will be the experience of a discomforting level of anxiety with the resulting unwillingness to attempt to increase this anxiety for fear of producing the catastrophe. This invariably results in the need for an escape response and an increase in the client's resistance to make a second attempt at the paradoxical intention.

In the present case, Mr. B. denied experiencing discomfort in situations other than those of driving. Therefore, the only way in which anxiety could be manipulated was by concentrating on the activity of driving. Mr. B. was more comfortable on small roads than on large streets or highways. He was more comfortable with no traffic and became increasingly anxious as traffic became more concentrated. Thus it was possible to set up an organized hierarchy of driving assignments. Unfortunately, during the course of any trip Mr. B. would move frequently among high and low-anxiety situations. Because of the inability to limit Mr. B.'s exposure to situations associated with high levels of discomfort while driving, the initial course of therapy was hampered. In the following sessions, the therapist tried to modify the assignment in order to prevent Mr. B. from attempting the paradoxical intention in a high-anxiety location.

Session Four

During this session, the client reported that he was unable to carry out the paradoxical suggestion. He was too anxious while driving, and although he tried not to stop, he would continue to worry about loss of control and continued to stop as frequently as he had initially reported. Desensitization in imagination was directed towards various aspects of Mr. B.'s concerns about driving. After further encouragement, Mr. B. again agreed to try the paradoxical intention. Then he suggested:

C: Maybe if I relax while driving it will help.

T: It would probably be better if you did not do your progressive relaxation while driving. If you want to do it before you get into the car, that will be all right, but don't try to use the relaxation to keep yourself from becoming anxious; it won't work. Just let yourself go once you feel the anxiety begin.

Notes on Session Four

As was mentioned in the introduction of this paper, the therapist must be careful, when assigning the practice of techniques to certain clients, not to exacerbate the circular performance anxiety process. This unintended intensification of anxiety can occur if the client perceives the assignment of techniques as the therapist's attempt to bolster the client's repertoire of coping responses. The effect will be that of encouraging the client's continued attempt to control autonomic functioning. Behavior of this type is diametrically opposed to the intent of the paradoxical program and can serve only to protract and/or subvert treatment.

Thus in the present case, Mr. B. was taught deep muscle relaxation and encouraged to practice this technique regularly. However, the therapist was careful to caution Mr. B. against the use of deep-muscle relaxation in an attempt to control anxiety which he might experience while driving. Mr. B. was to try to increase the experience of anxiety while engaged in this activity. He was not supposed to look for new methods of controlling the discomfort. Deep-muscle relaxation was to be used prior to driving and for nondriving related tension.

Session Five

Mr. B. again reported that he was unable to follow the therapist's suggestions. Desensitization was again directed towards concerns about driving and to discomfort related to visiting clients. Assertive training including role playing was introduced during this session and focused on interactions with clients and with his wife. The paradoxical suggestion was modified for the succeeding week; that is, Mr. B. was asked to attempt to experience the anxiety on short drives that he would take on the weekend rather than on his visits to clients.

Notes on Session Five

The purpose of changing the *in vivo* venue to pleasure drives taken on weekends from business-related drives taken during the week was to provide Mr. B. with greater control of the locations in which he might practice the paradoxical suggestion. Desensitization complemented this by focusing on the amelioration of anxiety to any driving situation.

Session Six

Desensitization and assertive procedures were continued during this session. Again, Mr. B. reported that he could not get himself to drive during the weekend and that his work-related driving had not improved. The following dialogue occurred during the last phase of the session:

T: What do you suppose we might do to make it a bit easier for you to follow through with the driving assignment?

C: I don't know, I just can't do it—too much anxiety.

T: Well, maybe that is the problem. Maybe you are too anxious, and your system is telling this to you by forcing you to stop and relieve the anxiety.

C: Yes. . . .

T: And by my asking you to cut down on this stopping, which I'm sure you're trying to do, your system is protecting itself by stopping even more.

C: So what can I do about it?

T: Perhaps we've been approaching this aspect of the problem in the wrong manner. If we're correct that you are building up too much anxiety and your body is acting to relieve this stress by forcing you to stop the car, then perhaps you should continue to stop. However, it seems obvious that the method that you employed in the past was not particularly effective in relieving the anxiety. Perhaps that was because you didn't stop for the length of time sufficient to allow enough anxiety to dissipate. So, why don't we try to modify it? I want you to continue to stop just as you have been doing, but rather than double parking and standing with the engine running for a couple of minutes, I want you to park the car, turn off the engine, and rest for 5 minutes. During that 5-minute interval, I want you to think of pleasant, relaxing scenes, like the beach scene. Every time you get the urge to stop, don't try to fight it off. Stop. Park the car in a legal spot—I don't want you to spend the time worrying about the possibility of getting a ticket. Turn off the engine, and think about a restful, pleasant scene for 5 minutes. Do you think that you'll be able to do that?

C: I guess so. You're just asking me to continue stopping as I have been but just for a longer amount of time?

T: Well, that's right, in addition to the modifications that I just mentioned.

Notes on Session Six

Mr. B. continued to complain of an inability to carry out the paradoxical intention. The refusal of the anxiety phobic to perform the anxiety-enhancing assignment, a circumstance that is fortunately not particularly common, places the therapist in a difficult position. If the phobic were able to carry out the task, the course of therapy would lead rapidly to a successful conclusion. However, when the anxiety phobic seeks the aid of the therapist, implicit in this contract is the phobic's inability to face the anxiety-provoking situation. It is expected that by adequately preparing the client and carefully selecting appropriate assignments, the client will be able to do something that he or she could not do before. But if the therapist fails to gain the client's cooperation, then an alternative program must be instituted. In other words, the client, after failing to expose himself or herself to the anxiety-provoking situation, may want to continue therapy based on the following implied question: "I would have performed this obvious solution to my problem (i.e., exposure to the anxiety-provoking stimuli) had I been able prior to entering therapy, and, therefore, do not need a therapist to propose this approach. What new alternatives can you as the therapist offer based on your professional training and experience?" The modification of the paradoxical suggestion, which the therapist instituted, took advantage of a special feature of Mr. B.'s problem.

Mr. B. was an interesting client because he illustrates the group of anxiety phobics who must enter the anxiety-provoking situation while trying to maintain their level of discomfort as low as possible. That is, anxiety phobics who must go to work but are afraid of being trapped in crowded public transportation, or who are fearful of attending business meetings, are forced to enter these situations and to use maneuvers in an effort to remain at a low level of discomfort. This group can be contrasted with the more common anxiety phobics who are uncomfortable in various situations that they would like, but are not forced, to enter. Mr. B. was required to drive each day as a condition for maintaining his business; he performed this anxiety-provoking behavior while utilizing methods he felt were aids in controlling his discomfort. On the other hand, he avoided noncompulsory driving and did not participate in recreational travel by automobile. The major component of the paradoxical program for anxiety phobia is the prescription of the *status quo*. That is, the client complains of anxiety in various locations, and the therapist suggests that they go into these situations and try to enhance the experience of anxiety. This requires nothing new of the clients except that they no longer try to reduce or escape from their anxiety when they experience this discomfort. In the case of Mr. B. (and similar resistant anxiety phobics) he had to enter the anxiety-provoking situation, but refused to carry out the paradoxical intention; the avoidance component of this behavior can provide an alternative paradoxical assignment.

Mr. B. avoided peak anxiety while driving largely by stopping his car frequently, thereby allowing the anxiety to dissipate. The price that he had to pay for this relief was a protracted work day about which he complained bitterly. Naturally, of even greater concern is the fact that as long as individuals continue to perform the avoidance behavior they will maintain high levels of anxiety in the significant situations. The therapist's task was therefore to prevent Mr. B. from making this avoidance response. Since cessation could not be obtained voluntarily it was necessary to increase the cost of the stopping behavior. This was accomplished by lengthening the duration of each stop. Successive sessions brought increases in the assigned duration of each stop and additional complaints from Mr. B. However, in order to remain within the therapeutic context, Mr. B. had to comply, since the stopping behavior was already in his repertoire; he was no longer being required to perform behavior that specifically aimed at increasing his anxiety. The therapist was, therefore, offering Mr. B. two alternatives, one that was vital for his therapeutic progress and one that, while initially attractive, was becoming increasingly disadvantageous. When the cost of the second alternative becomes too high, the patient opts for the initial therapeutic choice.

Session Seven

T: Were you able to carry out the driving assignment last week?

C: Yes, but it didn't help.

T: What do you mean?

C: I stopped as many times as I had the past several weeks.

T: Well, its purpose was not to reduce the number of stops that you make, but to reduce the anxiety which you experienced while driving. Did it help in that respect?

C: Yes, when I stopped the anxiety disappeared and I felt better when I went back to driving again, but then the anxiety would build up and I would have to stop again.

T: And each time you stopped you did as we had discussed? You parked the car, turned off the engine, and thought about a pleasant scene for 5 minutes?

C: Yes.

T: Then I think that we should continue with this procedure, temporarily, but this time I want you to stop for 10 minutes each time you experience anxiety. This should serve to increase the period of comfort between each urge to stop. Go easy on yourself. Stop as often as you need to in order to reduce the anxiety.

C: Okay. There's one thing though. I have a heck of a lot of things to do every day. I hope this won't prevent me from getting everything done.

T: Yes, I see. That is a problem. But it is most important for you to work on your anxiety. Do you agree?

C: Yes.

T: So perhaps you can get everything done if you work a little later. Is that possible?

C: Yes. I like to head for home by five at the latest, but I could work later. I had to do that this last week anyway.

Notes on Session Seven

Mr. B. reported that he was not experiencing so much anticipatory anxiety before driving and that he felt that he was more comfortable with clients. We continued to work with imaginal techniques on reducing anxiety related to driving and to his interactions with clients and spent a great deal of time on assertive training with clients and with his wife.

Session Eight

On the eighth session, Mr. B. indicated that he was more comfortable while driving and in his interactions with clients. Much of the session was devoted to concerns about his relationship with his wife; this included incidents of sexual dysfunction. As no improvement was observed in his driving behavior, Mr. B. was asked to stop for 15 minutes. He again complained of the difficulty of completing his work within a reasonable time, but agreed to continue with the assignments.

Session Nine

The ninth session was devoted mainly to the interaction of Mr. B. with his wife. Assertive training and role play was now directed toward this interaction and toward reducing some of Mr. B.'s discomfort in the marital relationship. The driving problem persisted unchanged. The following material was initiated by a complaint of Mr. B. about the program:

T: Well, it's working in that you're feeling more relaxed once you return to driving after each stop, right?

C: Yes, but it's taking a heck of a lot of time to get around.

T: I understand that, but I can't see any other way of ameliorating your anxiety. Can you?

C: No, I can't either.

T: I think that we may be at a crucial point, however. I think that we are on the right track as far as producing greater driving comfort for you. The problem is that you still are not allowing enough anxiety to dissipate on each occasion. It occurred to me that the cues in the car having been associated with anxiety are maintaining the anxiety even when you are parked and thinking about something else. Now I know you're not going to like my next suggestion.

C: What is it?

T: I think that you should increase the time of each stop by another 5 minutes. But this time I want you to get out of the car and walk around for 20 minutes out of sight of the car.

C: What? I can't do that. I might as well give up my business.

T: Well, you have been able to accomplish everything that you planned each day. Is that correct?

C: Just about, but I've been working till seven and eight each night.

T: I know. I wish that there were another, quicker way. I'm sure that it's not pleasant having to work so late each evening.

C: It isn't. And I'm not getting to do the chores around the house until the weekend, and there goes my weekend.

T: Yes, that's something I never thought about. You have to work 7 days virtually. I wish that there was some alternative.

C: What about the first thing we tried?

T: What do you mean?

C: You know, where I try to become anxious while driving. It sounded like that would be quicker.

T: I'm sure it would be much quicker, but I don't think that we should try it again just yet. You experienced too much anxiety when you tried that method.

C: But I seem to have gotten a little better; maybe I could try again.

T: I don't know. I would be afraid to jump back to that at this point just to save some time. Things seem to be going fairly well with this procedure. I'm pleased. I think that in a few more sessions we could begin to see real progress.

C: But it takes so long. . . .

T: Yes. That's the only trouble. But, bear with it a little longer if you can.

C: . . . and, the other way seems a lot faster.

T: Yes, but remember that you had a lot of trouble attempting it before, and if you had trouble this time you could set yourself back a
good deal. So I would suggest doing the same thing that you have
been doing—each time you feel anxious, park the car, turn off the engine, and take a 20-minute walk. During the walk try to think of calming, pleasant thoughts. I really think that this is the way to go at this
point. I don't feel that you're ready for the other method.

Notes on Session Nine

By session nine, the cost of continuing with the second spontaneous, paradoxical suggestion, that is, lengthening the duration of each stop, was
too great for Mr. B. He seemed to be opting for the initial paradoxical intention suggestion, that is, increasing the experience of anxiety. The therapist thought it best not to encourage Mr. B. in his discussion of the possibility of switching to the alternative assignment. One reason for this was
the absence of a definitive reason for Mr. B.'s failure to follow this program initially. Perhaps at that time the relationship between client and
therapist was not sufficient to foster in Mr. B. security in the therapist's
guarantee that no catastrophic consequence would follow peak anxiety.
Or the situation that existed at the time, that is, Mr. B.'s discomfort with
his clients and/or his wife, might have played a role in maintaining the
anxiety phobia. Now that these discomforts were largely reduced, the
driving anxiety could be more readily handled. Another excellent possibility is that neither the therapist nor the client had sufficient control over
the *in vivo* settings. Thus Mr. B. was forced to engage in assignments with
which too much anxiety was associated for him to reasonably handle at
that point in the program.

The issue of control must also be considered in the present case. Perhaps Mr. B.'s initial failure to comply with the paradoxical intention
suggestion concerned a need to obtain dominance in the therapeutic
program. This could not prevent him from complying with the second
paradoxical assignment if he wished to appear "cooperative" with the
therapist, since he had already demonstrated his ability to perform this
behavior. If control were an important issue and the therapist encouraged
Mr. B. in his decision to expose himself to the anxiety, this might result in
influencing Mr. B. to delay or cancel his intended switch. The therapist,
by remaining a neutral observer or perhaps a weak adversary, obviated
this disastrous possibility.

Session Ten

C: I've got to tell you what happened.

T: What?

C: Monday I started out and got anxious, so I did what you said; you know, stopping the car and walking around for 20 minutes. Then I got back in the car and drove for a while and started to get anxious again. So I was about to stop again when I looked at the clock in the car. It was real late and I had an important call to make. I knew I had to do something with the anxiety or I would be setting myself back.

T: What do you mean?

C: You gave me two things to do; either make it worse, or stop for 20 minutes. If I did neither and just kept on driving and trying to stop the anxiety in the old way I used to, then I might as well stop coming here if I'm not going to use either method.

T: I see. That's a good point.

C: So, I couldn't stop because I was really late for a very important appointment, so I tried the other thing.

T: What did you do?

C: I tried to become more anxious.

T: How did you do that?

C: By letting go and trying to sweat more and make my heart beat faster.

T: What happened?

C: It didn't work.

T: What do you mean?

C: I wasn't able to become more anxious.

T: Really?

C: Yes, and the anxiety kind of disappeared.

T: Kind of?

C: Well, it did disappear, but I couldn't believe it, so I wasn't sure if it would stay away.

T: I see. So what did you do about it?

C: Nothing, I got to my client and got a great order. I spent so much time there that when I left I decided to go home, since there wasn't much of the day left. I didn't have any anxiety on the way home.

T: That's very interesting. What happened during the rest of the week?

C: On Tuesday, I got up and wondered whether I would be anxious driving. I was very anxious. I tried the stopping, but when I got back and drove again, I got anxious again. So I did the other thing, trying to increase the anxiety. For a while it didn't have any effect; my anxiety stayed at the same level. But then it went down again. I did it for the rest of the day and couldn't get anxious.

T: So you were not able to get anxious throughout Tuesday?

C: That's right. And the rest of the week was pretty much the same story. I tried to get anxious but couldn't.

T: I guess that makes you feel pretty good.

C: It sure does. I finally found something that works.

T: Well, while you have good reason to be encouraged, that's the problem. It's supposed to make you more anxious, and if the rationale of your problem that I discussed with you before is correct, then you must get anxious in order to learn that you don't lose control and have a heart attack. So, next week I want you to redouble your efforts at trying to enhance your anxiety. Of course, if this becomes too troublesome for you, you can always return to the anxiety-relieving technique of stopping for 20 minutes.

C: I don't think that'll be necessary.

T: Well, whatever you say. You seem to know what's best for you so you make the choice. I just don't want you to push yourself.

Since Mr. B. no longer reported discomfort while driving or with interacting with clients, the administration of imaginal techniques was discontinued in the office, although he was advised to maintain a modified imaginal practice program when relaxing at home. His relationship with his wife had improved greatly, and he felt that he and his wife were enjoying each other's company more. We discussed areas of further improvement in their marital relationship.

Notes on Session Ten

It was no surprise that Mr. B. disregarded the therapist's words of caution and plunged ahead with his own program. The great success which Mr. B. reported was not greeted by encouragement or reinforcement by the therapist. Two considerations went into the therapist's decision to omit this type of response. First, based on the concern regarding control, the therapist's encouragement may very well have had an effect opposite to that which was intended. Perhaps if Mr. B. began to feel that he was actually doing what the therapist expected of him, Mr. B. might have ceased further participation in the program.

On the other hand, the therapist's verbal reinforcement might actually have been perceived by the patient as a reinforcing event, leading to an alternative problem. If the client is concerned about the effects of his performance on the responses of the therapist, performance anxiety can once again adversely influence the client's behavior. For example, Mr. B. was able to report that during the week prior to the tenth session he experienced no anxiety while driving. If it is important to obtain therapist approval, Mr. B. may feel it necessary to present a report as good or better on the eleventh session. That is, he must be able to report that he had no anxiety while driving, and perhaps that he undertook to drive more than he did the previous week. Thus, between the tenth and eleventh sessions, he may very well be concerned that he not become anxious in order that he not have to present a poor report and disappoint the therapist. Therapist reinforcement in this case can serve to present the client with an anxiety-provoking goal that might negate progress to that point. For this reason, the therapist took an apparently neutral stance with regard to the client's achievements. While the conjectures of control and reinforcement are opposed, it is not always certain which is operating; the therapist's neutral response is appropriate in either case.

The possibility of the client developing performance anxiety despite the lack of therapist reinforcement can be reduced by suggesting that the client did not really achieve that which was assigned. In the present case, Mr. B. was told that he was supposed to have attempted to increase his anxiety based on the rationale that he and the therapist had discussed on previous sessions. The week in which he was free of anxiety provided a pleasant respite and even a glimpse of things to come, but now he must return to the goal of attempting to increase his anxiety. This serves to reduce the possibility that Mr. B. will provide himself with a performance goal requiring the continued experience of less anxiety than previously reported.

Actually, when paradoxical intention can be properly employed by the anxiety phobic in the discomforting setting the client will experience little or no anxiety. One indication that the client has been unable to fully perform the paradoxical intention maneuver is his or her report that he or she has tried to increase his or her anxiety and was successful, that is, he or she became more anxious. In most cases, increased anxiety results when clients actually try to increase their anxiety but they are simultaneously afraid of the consequences of that increase. On such occasions the therapist must return with the client to the rationale of the problem in an effort to increase the client's understanding and feeling of security.

Mr. B. attended three more weekly sessions reporting less driving-related anxiety each time. Progress continued for two biweekly sessions and four monthly sessions. After almost two years, Mr. B. reports no driving difficulties or additional problems.

Conclusion

Mr. B. manifested many of the behaviors typically observed in cases of anxiety phobia. He was apprehensive prior to engaging in discomforting activity. While driving, his discomfort would increase and he would begin to think of the catastrophic consequence of peak anxiety (i.e., heart attack, loss of control, accident). As his concern intensified, Mr. B. attempted to maintain some control over it in order to avoid the possibility of a heart attack. The devices that he used (e.g., distracting thoughts) failed to reduce his level of arousal, and, instead, his anxiety rose unabated. The last resort for the anxiety phobic is escape from the difficult situation. Because the anxiety phobic rarely experiences the actual consequences of peak anxiety, that is, fatigue, he remains fearful of a disaster and continues to avoid this possibility.

The case of Mr. B. was also instructive because it illustrates two approaches to the administration of paradoxical intention suggestions. Initially the treatment choice, a program composed of paradoxical intention and behavioral techniques, was presented. This was accomplished by explaining the therapist's conception of the problem, which logically unfolded into the principles upon which treatment would be based. The best alternative would have been to pair imaginal behavioral techniques with carefully selected *in vivo* assignments. The *in vivo* assignments would be chosen from a hierarchy of increasingly discomforting situations. By preparing the client in imagination for a gradual entry into the *in vivo* situation, clinically significant levels of anxiety are largely prevented. Insuring success for the client in the *in vivo* situation, that is, low anxiety, increases the probability of therapeutic progress. In contrast, if the client enters an *in vivo* situation and experiences a high level of anxiety, there is an excellent possibility that he will escape and avoid the future encounters prescribed by the treatment program.

This latter difficulty was observed with Mr. B. He denied experiencing anxiety in any circumstances that did not involve driving. Each driving event required Mr. B. to expose himself to a random patchwork of situations associated with varying degrees of discomfort.

It is possible that this inability to control the *in vivo* assignments produced the initial failure of the treatment program. This occurred in spite of the extensive use of systematic desensitization and covert conditioning directed toward those aspects of driving that were discomforting to Mr. B. In a further attempt to correct this difficulty, Mr. B. was advised to carry out the *in vivo* program only in the least anxiety-provoking driving situations. This mainly meant that he would engage in the paradoxical intention exclusively in recreational driving during weekends. Unfortunately, this modification was not effective since Mr. B. found driving so aversive that he would only do that which was vital for the maintenance of his business. In fact, it was this latter factor that suggested an alternative approach to the administration of the treatment program.

If Mr. B. could have completely avoided driving, he would probably have chosen this course in dealing with the problem, as opposed to seeking therapeutic aid. However, driving was an exigency of Mr. B.'s business; he was required to drive extensively, 5 days a week. In order to remain as comfortable as possible, he attempted to utilize the previously described methods for controlling his anxiety, and often employed escape as the last resort (i.e., pulling to the side of the road and remaining until his anxiety abated). He entered therapy because his discomfort was increasing, and these devices were taking more of his time and working less effectively. In other words, these responses cost too much. Although the initial treatment program was designed to obviate the need for anxiety reducing behavior, Mr. B. was unable to cooperate with the program. For several weeks he failed to participate in the treatment program, possibly because the *in vivo* situations elicited too much anxiety. In response to this anxiety Mr. B. persisted in utilizing the various escape responses that served only to maintain the anxiety.

In order to help Mr. B. relinquish his escape tactics, the therapist employed imaginal techniques to reduce Mr. B.'s anxiety and employed a strategy that increased the cost of escaping. The therapist suggested that Mr. B. continue to stop when he experienced discomfort while driving and extended the duration of those stops in successive sessions. Mr. B. was then left with two choices in order to remain within the context of therapy. He could continue employing the responses and thereby make life incredibly inconvenient, or he would opt to participate in the initial treatment of choice (for which he was now better prepared).

Since Mr. B. was not participating in the first alternative, he had no option but to accept the second choice. When this second alternative became sufficiently troublesome, Mr. B. went back to the original treatment program. His ability to return to and experience success with the original treatment program was probably due, in part, to the reduction of anxiety resulting from the administration of imaginal techniques as well as to the assertive training that permitted him to deal with clients and with his wife under conditions of greater comfort and reinforcement.

SPECIAL PROBLEMS

Maintaining the New Behavior

An examination of the clinical literature reporting the effectiveness of paradoxical suggestions reveals the general failure of these studies to discuss the methods instituted to maintain the adaptive behavioral change. That is, once the appropriate modification has been observed, what insures the permanence of the alteration? Certainly there are circumstances under which paradoxical suggestions might be sufficient to produce relatively permanent modification. This is possible, for example, in cases where behavior is assumed to be functionally autonomous; that is, in learning terms, the response no longer produces those desired effects in the environment that originally served to strengthen and maintain the behavior. In other cases, changing the behavior abruptly may have the effect of influencing the environment in a manner that feeds back to maintain the behavioral change.

Notwithstanding those situations in which paradoxical suggestions alone might prove to be sufficient to produce a lasting behavior change, there are many more cases in which specific programs must be instituted in order to maintain the modification produced by the paradoxical maneuver (e.g., Graziano, 1978). This is based on the assumption that most behavior is maintained by the favorable effect that it produces on the environment. If the maladaptive response is altered, then the favorable environmental condition that was produced by this altered response must be generated in a more adaptive manner if possible; otherwise, an alternative reinforcement must be provided. The behavioral analysis presents the therapist with the contingencies of the maladaptive response in order that he may consider this aspect of the behavior in the total therapeutic program. Since paradoxical maneuvers are quite effective in rapidly changing unwanted behavior, it is tempting for the therapist to design a program aimed at the spectacularly rapid amelioration of a troublesome response. In his haste, the therapist may overlook the contingencies associated with the behavior; one or more of several undesirable consequences can be expected to follow such an incomplete program. For example, if the response were instrumental in achieving a specific event that the client still valued, then the failure of the therapeutic effort to provide an alternative reinforcement might result in the equally rapid reappearance of the maladaptive response in order to regain that reinforcement. Or if the therapist neglects to guide the client in selecting a more adaptive behavior for achieving the reinforcement, the client may select an alternative means that is as unfavorable as the response that was successfully changed.

The behavior therapist who employs paradoxical techniques does so within a complete behavioral program that has been based on a careful behavioral analysis. As such, attention has been directed to the contingencies of the target behavior and the consequent effects on the individual of the successful removal of this behavior from his response repertoire. A major component of the behavioral program involves either providing the client with an adaptive alternative behavior to enable him to obtain the necessary reinforcement (e.g., Goldiamond, 1974) or providing a satisfactory substitute reinforcement.

In the case of Mr. B., his dilatory manner of driving resulted in reducing the number of clients whom he could contact each day and limiting the amount of time available for his wife. Since he was anxious about these interactions one might hypothesize that in addition to the difficulties associated with Mr. B.'s driving behavior, there were salient reinforcement contingencies. A significant aspect of the therapeutic program focused on these interpersonal difficulties and discomforts that Mr. B. experienced. Partially as a result of this therapeutic effort, Mr. B. reported that his interactions with clients were much more rewarding than they had been previously and that he and his wife were enjoying an excellent relationship. Mr. B. indicated that his general level of discomfort was substantially reduced. Shortly after, Mr. B. was able to resume relatively normal driving behavior. It is thus hypothesized that the part of the therapeutic program relevant to the amelioration of Mr. B.'s interpersonal difficulties constituted the measures taken to ensure the stability of the adaptive changes in his driving behavior.

For example, Ascher (1975) and Ascher and Efran (1978) report the successful use of paradoxical intention in the reduction of sleep-onset latency. In the course of treatment, clients were first administered a behavioral program appropriate to their individual needs. Paradoxical intention was utilized after this program failed to produce the degree of change required. However, subsequent to this change, the behavioral program was again employed in order to maintain the satisfactory behavior.

REFERENCES

Allport, G. W. *The individual and his religion: A psychological interpretation.* New York: MacMillan, 1950.

Ascher, L. M. *Paradoxical intention as a component in the behavioral treatment of sleep onset insomnia; A case study.* Paper presented at the *Association for the Advancement of Behavior Therapy,* San Francisco, California. December, 1975.

Ascher, L. M. *A paradoxical program for the treatment of urinary retention.* Paper presented at the International Congress of Behavior Therapy, Uppsala, Sweden, August, 1977.

Ascher, L. M., and Clifford, R. E. Behavior considerations on the treatment of sexual dysfunction. In M. Hersen, R. M. Eisler, and P. M. Miller (Eds.), *Progress in behavior modification* (Vol. 3). New York: Academic, 1977.

Ascher, L. M., and Efran, J. S. The use of paradoxical intention in a behavioral program for sleep onset insomnia. *Journal of Consulting and Clinical Psychology,* 1978, *46,* 547–550.

Bootzin, R. Stimulus control treatment for insomnia. *American Psychological Association Proceedings*, 1972, 395–396.

Bootzin, R., Niccasio, P. M., Hersen, M., Eisler, R., and Miller, P. Behavioral treatment for insomnia. In *Progress in behavior modification* (Vol. 6), New York: Academic, in press.

Borkovec, T., and Fowles, D. Controlled investigation of the effects of progressive and hypnotic relaxation on insomnia. *Journal of Abnormal Psychology*, 1975, *82*, 153–158.

Davison, G. C. Counter-control in behavior modification. In L. Hamerlynck, L. Handy, and E. Mash (Eds.), *Behavior change: Methodology, concepts and practice*. Champaign, Ill.: Research, 1973.

DiCassio, P., and Bootzin, R. A comparison of progressive relaxation and autogenic training as treatments for insomnia. *Journal of Abnormal Psychology*, 1974, *83*, 253–260.

Dunlap, K. A revision of the fundamental law of habit formation. *Science*, 1928, *57*, 360–362.

Dunlap, K. *Habits, their making and unmaking*. New York: Liveright, 1932.

Dunlap, K. *Personal adjustment*. New York: McGraw-Hill, 1946.

Fay, A. Clinical notes on paradoxical therapy. *Psychotherapy: Theory, Research and Practice*, 1973, *13*, 118–122.

Frankl, V. E. *The doctor and the soul: From psychotherapy to logotherapy*. New York: Knopf, 1955.

Frankl, V. E. Paradoxical intention: A logotherapeutic technique. *American Journal of Psychotherapy*, 1960, *14*, 520–535.

Frankl, V. E. *Man's search for meaning: An introduction to logotherapy*. Boston: Beacon, 1962.

Frankl, V. E. *Psychotherapy and existentialism: Selected papers on logotherapy*. New York: Washington Square, 1967.

Frankl, V. E. Paradoxical intention and dereflection: Two logotherapeutic techniques. In S. Arieti and G. Chrzanowski (Eds.), *New dimensions in psychiatry*. New York: Wiley, 1974.

Frankl, V. E. Paradoxical intention and dereflection. *Psychotherapy: Theory, Research and Practice*, 1975, *12*, 226–237.

Geer, J., and Katkin, E. S. Treatment of insomnia using a variant of systematic desensitization: A case study. *Journal of Abnormal Psychology*, 1966, *71*, 161–164.

Gerz, H. O. The treatment of the phobic and the obsessive-compulsive using paradoxical intention. Sec. Viktor E. Frankl. *Journal of Neuropsychiatry*, 1962, *3*, 375–387.

Gerz, H. O. Experience with the logotherapeutic technique of paradoxical intention in the treatment of phobic and obsessive-compulsive patients. *American Journal of Psychiatry*, 1966, *125*, 548–553.

Goldiamond, I. Toward a constructional approach to social problems: Ethical and constitutional issues raised by applied behavior analysis. *Behaviorism*, 1974, 2, 1–84.

Goldstein, A. J. *The treatment of agoraphobia*. Paper presented at the *Association for the Advancement of Behavior Therapy*, San Francisco, California. December, 1975.

Graziano, A. M. Behavior therapy. In B. Wolman, J. Egan, and A. Ross (Eds.), *Handbook of treatment of mental disorders in childhood and adolescence*. Englewood, N. J.: Prentice Hall, 1978.

Greenwald, H. (Ed.). *Active psychotherapy*. New York: Atherton, 1967.

Haley, J. *Strategies of psychotherapy*. New York: Grune and Stratton, 1963.

Haley, J. Marital therapy. In Harold Greenwald (Ed.), *Active psychotherapy*. New York: Atherton, 1967a.

Haley, J. *Advanced techniques of hypnosis and therapy*. New York: Grune and Stratton, 1967b.

Haley, J. Strategic therapy when a child is presented as the problem. *Journal of the American Academy of Child Psychiatry*, 1973, 12, 641–659.

Haley, J. *Problem solving therapy*. San Francisco: Jossey-Bass, 1976.

Jacobs, M. An holistic approach to behavior therapy. In A. A. Lazarus (Ed.), *Clinical behavior therapy*. New York: Brunner-Mazel, 1972.

Johnson, S. M. and Alevizos, P. N. *Strategic therapy: A systematic outline of procedures*. Paper presented at the *Association for the Advancement of Behavior Therapy*, San Francisco, California, December, 1975.

Lazarus, A. A. *Behavior therapy and beyond*. New York: McGraw-Hill, 1971.

Lick, J. R., and Heffler, D. Relaxation training and attention placebo in the treatment of severe insomnia. *Journal of Consulting and Clinical Psychology*, 1977, 45, 153–161.

Marks, I. M. New approaches to the treatment of obsessive-compulsive disorders. *Journal of Nervous and Mental Disease*, 1973, 156, 420–426.

Masters, W. H., and Johnson, V. E. *Human sexual inadequacy*. Boston: Little Brown, 1970.

Paul, G. L. Behavior modification research: Design and tactics. In C. M. Franks (Ed.), *Behavior therapy: Appraisal and status*. New York: McGraw-Hill, 1969a.

Paul, G. L. Outcome of systematic desensitization II: Controlled investigations of individual treatment, technique variations and current status. In C. U. Franks (Ed.), *Behavior therapy: Appraisal and status*. New York: McGraw-Hill, 1969b.

Paul, G. L. Outcome of systematic desensitization I: Background procedures and uncontrolled reports of individual treatment. In C. M. Franks (Ed.), *Behavior therapy: Appraisal and status*. New York: McGraw-Hill, 1969c.

Raskin, D. E., and Klein, Z. E. Losing a symptom through keeping it: A review of paradoxical treatment techniques and rationale. *Archives of General Psychiatry*, 1976, *33*, 548–555.

Rosen, J. *Direct psychoanalysis*. New York: Grune and Stratton, 1953.

Shelton, J. L., and Ackerman, J. M. *Homework in counseling and psychotherapy: Examples of systematic assignments for therapeutic use by mental health professionals*. Springfield, Ill.: Thomas, 1974.

Solyom, L., Garza-Perez, J., Ledwidge, B. L., and Solyom, C. Paradoxical intention in the treatment of obsessive thoughts: A pilot study. *Comprehensive Psychiatry*, 1972, *13*, 291–297.

Stampfl, T. G., and Levis, D. J. Essentials of implosive therapy: A learning theory-based psychodynamic behavioral therapy. *Journal of Abnormal Psychology*, 1967, *72*, 496–503.

Stampfl, T. G., and Lewis, D. J. *Implosive therapy: Theory and technique*. New Jersey: General Learning, 1973.

Suinn, R. M., and Richardson, F. Anxiety management training: A nonspecific behavior therapy program for anxiety control. *Behavior Therapy*, 1971, *2*, 498–510.

Turner, R. M., and Ascher, L. M. *A methodological and statistical analysis of behavior therapy treatments for insomnia*. Presentation at the *49th Annual Convention of the Eastern Psychological Association*, Washington, D. C., March, 1978.

Turner, R. M. and Ascher, L. M. Controlled comparison of progressive relaxation, stimulus control, and paradoxical intention therapies for insomnia. *Journal of Consulting and Clinical Psychology*, 1979, 47, 500–508

Watzlawick, P., Beavin, J., and Jackson, D. D. *Pragmatics of human communication*. New York: Norton, 1967.

Watzlawick, P., Weakland, J., and Fisch, R. *Change: Principles of problem formation and problem resolution*. New York: Norton, 1974.

Weakland, J., Fisch, R., and Watzlawick, P. Brief therapy: Focused problem resolution. *Family Practice*, 1974, *13*, 141–168.

Wilson, G. T. Innovations in the modification of phobic behaviors in two clinical cases. *Behavior Therapy*, 1973, *4*, 426–430.

Wolpe, J. *Psychotherapy by reciprocal inhibition*. Stanford: Stanford U. P., 1958.

Wolpe, J. *The practice of behavior therapy*. New York: Pergamon Press, 1973.

Wolpe, J. and Ascher, L. M. Outflanking "resistance" in a severe obsessional neurosis. In H. J. Eysenck (Ed.) *Case histories in behavior therapy*. London: Routledge and Kegan Paul, 1976.

CHAPTER 7

The Treatment of Agoraphobia

DIANNE L. CHAMBLESS AND ALAN GOLDSTEIN

Temple University Medical School
Department of Psychiatry

INTRODUCTION

Definition of Problem

We are devoting a chapter of this handbook to the treatment of agoraphobia for several reasons. First, agoraphobic problems are common presenting complaints in the practice of behavior therapy. Extrapolating from a population incidence in a Vermont community (6.3/1000), one can estimate that over 1 1/4 million Americans suffer from this problem (Agras, Sylvester, & Oliveau, 1969). Agoraphobics make up from 50% (Marks, 1970) to 82% (at the Behavior Therapy Unit in recent years) of clients seeking therapy for phobic complaints. Second, this syndrome has been particularly difficult to treat. The symptoms generally run a life-long fluctuating course with only about 20% of such phobics achieving lasting relief (Marks and Herst, 1970; Roberts, 1964). Poor results have been reported with treatments as diverse as analysis (Weiss, 1964), individual and group psychotherapy (Gelder, Marks, Wolff, and Clarke, 1967), and desensitization (Gelder and Marks, 1966). Thus agoraphobics diverge from other phobics in that they do not derive much benefit from desensitization. This brings us to a third point of interest; agoraphobics report a variety of symptoms not found with other phobias. These include, most importantly, spontaneous panic attacks, but also claustrophobia, high levels of general, persistent anxiety, experiences of depersonalization, and depression. This confusing array of symptoms makes agoraphobia a complex, challenging problem for the behavior therapist. Understanding and learning to treat the agoraphobic syndrome teaches one diagnostic and treatment skills that are appropriate to related complaints such as anxiety states, hypochondrical neuroses, and social anxiety.

Description of Specific Behavior Pattern

Most agoraphobics have a wide assortment of fears including fears of crowds whether on the street or in shops; fears of enclosed places such as elevators, airplanes, high buildings; fears of means of transportation over which they have little control such as buses , trains, and airplanes; fears of being away from home beyond a certain circle of safety; and fears of being alone. The common theme is that of feeling trapped in a situation, whether by distance, crowds, or physical barriers, so that they cannot easily return to a place of safety or to a person who symbolizes safety. Most agoraphobics report that they feel more secure and can enter some of the situations they would normally avoid if accompanied by another adult or one particular person known in the literature as the "obligatory companion" or "phobic companion." It is interesting to note that the great majority of complex agoraphobics are women [For an analysis of this phenomenon see Fodor, 1974]. The syndrome is essentially the same for those men who do become agoraphobic, but frequently their disabilities are less severe, perhaps because familial and societal pressures militate against men becoming extremely dependent and helpless.

The therapist cannot expect the agoraphobic to come to the first session and present a complete list of his/her fears. Commonly they initially describe one particular fear but upon questioning can readily identify the other fears. Consequently one may be referred a client with a fear of driving who is actually not afraid of driving *per se* but rather of driving out of her/his safe zone unaccompanied. Similarly a client may complain of excessively frequent urination, which closer examination reveals is a result of fear of leaving home. Fear of flying may be just that or may be only one part of an agoraphobic package of fears. Therefore, the therapist must be alert and search for the presence of agoraphobic problems when faced with any phobia that can be part of that complex.

Inversely there are times when, because a client avoids leaving home or leaving home alone, she/he is labeled agoraphobic, although this is inappropriate. For example, a man who is so fearful of dogs that he hesitates to leave his home for fear of encountering the neighbors' dogs is probably not agoraphobic. Similarly, a woman with fears of being raped who refuses to exit unaccompanied from her apartment after having experienced such an assault is not accurately described by the label of agoraphobia proper. We cover how one makes the proper behavioral analysis in the section on data gathering.

In a previous paper (Goldstein and Chambless, 1978) we have described two types of agoraphobia proper. The majority of agoraphobics fall into the category that we have labeled *complex agoraphobia* which is defined by the presence of four elements.

1. Low levels of self-sufficiency whether due to anxiety or actual lack of skills. Complex agoraphobics are generally unassertive people with marked social anxieties (fears of criticism, being disapproved of), fears of responsibility, and difficulty coping with life tasks particularly when problem solving is involved. Consequently they are very dependent on the significant people in their lives, particularly their families, and perceive themselves as incapable of functioning without someone to take care of them. In fact, the onset of the phobias is usually when these people are at life stages that raise the specter of independent functioning. Two such times are adolescence, when deciding on career goals and separating from parents are primary tasks, and adult life, when a marriage is going poorly and one begins to consider separation or divorce. Since real separation seems impossible to people who feel so incompetent, this situation generates considerable conflict.

2. Onset under conditions of conflict, generally interpersonal conflict. Agoraphobia rarely begins with the kind of conditioning event that often produces other phobias. For example, they do not become afraid of driving a distance from home territory after being in an automobile wreck. It is the absence of such conditioning events that should alert the therapist to the presence of the kind of conflict described above. Usually because of his/her unassertiveness the agoraphobic has found himself/herself in an unhappy seemingly irresolvable relationship under the domination of a spouse or parent. The urges to leave and the fears of being on her/his own balance out, and the agoraphobic is trapped in this conflict, unable to move and lacking the skills to change the situation. The word "trapped" is a key one here; recall that we have noted that agoraphobics feel fear any place in which they feel trapped. Their definitions of what constitutes a trapped situation are extremely subjective, but what is important is that this is the way they label a given situation, not the validity of this label to an outsider. This may appear rather nebulous; it is helpful to view it as a semantic generalization on their trapped feeling in the conflict situation.

3. A tendency to misapprehend the causal antecedents to emotional distress. The life events described previously are not unique to agora-

phobics; other people find themselves in irresolvable, conflictual situations and do not form phobic symptoms. Another personality characteristic seems essential to the formation of this syndrome, and that is a certain repressive response style. Agoraphobics usually do not connect their high levels of anxiety to relationship variables, and in fact will generally report, for example, that their marriages are fine. With persistent gentle exploration and sufficient development of the therapeutic relationship, the patterns emerge. Consequently, it is often a breakthrough experience for them when they recognize the source of their conflict. Until that time they report that anxiety attacks, which reliably follow situations where they have been in conflict with someone, "comes out of the blue." They often show a striking inability to label feelings such as anger and hurt and experience such feelings as diffuse autonomic arousal, which is then labeled as inexplicable anxiety. Alternatively, they may briefly experience a feeling, for example, anger, but quickly suppress it and deny it, only to become anxious instead. This anxiety that comes "out of nowhere" is all the more frightening for its mysterious nature, and they often explain it as being afraid of whatever place they find themselves when experiencing the anxiety. It is the inconsistent nature of the anxiety felt in particular places that points to the holes in this explanation. While an elevator phobic is typically afraid of elevators in a consistent fashion, an agoraphobic may be fine on an elevator one day and in sheer terror the next depending on (one eventually finds) other events in his/her life.

4. Fear of fear as the central phobic element. The hallmark of the agoraphobic syndrome is the panic attack. Panic attacks are terrifying experiences during which the victim experiences a number of possible symptoms that most frequently include heart palpitations, dizziness, a sense of inability to breathe, and for some people a heaving stomach and an urge to urinate or defecate. During such attacks there is a strong feeling of loss of control and impending doom, such as death by a heart attack or stroke, or madness. Panic attacks seem to be engendered by high levels of conflict, although physiological predispositions probably play some role. After experiencing such noxious events, people with sufficient personal resources will generally move to resolve the offending situation, but the agoraphobic, who does not have such resources and who misinterprets the causes of such feelings, cannot do so. Sometimes one or two panic attacks are sufficient; sometimes a whole series is necessary. Eventually the agoraphobic, convinced of eventual loss of life or sanity during a panic attack, begins to avoid situations that are interpreted as dangerous. Now it should be clear why a trapped situation is to be avoided. A trapped situation is dangerous because she/he will not be able to get to safety in the event of a panic attack. In any trapped situation agoraphobics

are so anxious about the possibility of a panic attack that they inevitably bring one on. This is why we define the fear of a panic attack, or fear of fear, as the phobic core in this syndrome. Thus while someone with a simple fear of flying may well fear an airplane crash, the agoraphobic fears flying because there is no way out in case of a panic attack. The role of the "phobic companion" also makes sense now. Agoraphobics can travel more freely when accompanied by a trusted person because they rely on the companion to take care of them in the event of the feared consequences of a panic attack. Of course, these fears only increase the dependency and helplessness felt by agoraphobics, which in turn increase chronic anxiety. Another consequence is that they then become even more unassertive because they cannot afford to alienate those they must rely on for mobility and because they feel even less self-confident than before the onset of panic attacks. These are the essential elements of the syndrome that we have labeled complex agoraphobia. In our experience, neglecting the treatment of any of these important aspects will lead to eventual relapse. It follows that successful treatment of complex agoraphobia is comprehensive and rarely effected by short-term therapy. Therapy of 2 years duration may be required for lasting gains.

Simple agoraphobia is considerably less difficult to treat on the whole. We have given this label to those agoraphobics who do not show the personality characteristics or the conflictual environment of complex agoraphobics. Fear of fear forms the core of the phobias for this group as well, but these people first experienced panic attacks as a result of physical conditions such as hypoglycemia or endocrine imbalance or due to a bad drug experience with hallucinogens. Once any underlying physical disorders have been controlled, the fear of panic attacks and consequent avoidance will usually yield readily to the treatment interventions described later without the extensive interventions in the interpersonal arena and in developing coping skills required by complex agoraphobics.

Theory and Research

We have described the situation faced by most agoraphobics in which intense conflict is experienced because the desire to leave a noxious situation is blocked by fears of being on one's own. This sets up a situation analogous to laboratory studies on experimental conflict in that the client experiences anxiety created by competing response tendencies. Once panic attacks have begun and fear of fear is established, the agoraphobic begins to interpret feelings of mild-to-moderate anxiety as signs of the dreaded event—a panic attack—and gets so anxious about being anxious that the attack is triggered. This may be conceptualized as a condition in which the sensations created by anxiety become conditioned stimuli for the threatening conditioned response of a panic attack, particularly in the presence of discriminative stimuli such as being alone or in a trapped place. Thus agoraphobia is distinguished in part from other phobias in that the important conditioned stimuli are interoceptive ones, for example, rapid heart beat, queasy stomach, body tension. If this is the case, then it is understandable that therapists who have focused on desensitization to the external situations, for example, supermarkets, in which they report anxiety have had little success (reviewed by Goldstein and Chambless, 1978). The typical finding is that some progress is made (this is to be expected as the actual situations may become higher order conditioned stimuli) until the client experiences a panic attack that wipes out all gains. Consistent with this formulation are the findings that flooding, a treatment that emphasizes feeling and mastering anxiety, has led to improvement with agoraphobics (reviewed by Goldstein and Chambless, 1978). This is also consonant with the authors' clinical experience that paradoxical intention (Frankl, 1960), which also stresses facing and coping with the anxiety experience itself, shows great promise in treating fear of fear. For a more complete treatment of the theoretical underpinnings of our approach to the treatment of agoraphobia and review of related research findings, the reader is referred to Goldstein and Chambless (1978).

THERAPEUTIC PROCESS

Therapeutic Setting

Environmental Variables

In general, behavioral interventions seem most effective when tailored to the specific problems presented by an individual client. When faced with a problem as difficult to crack as agoraphobia, it is especially important that the therapist not fall into following the routine most convenient for her/him but rather remain flexible as to the setting for and length of sessions. Therefore, while the procedures described in this chaper often assume a weekly session in the therapist's office, it is frequently preferable to make changes in this format. For example, extra-office sessions are desirable when *in vivo* techniques are more powerful in breaking up a pattern; if homogeneous clients are in treatment concurrently, the time required for *in vivo* procedures may be reduced by a group approach (Hand, Lamontagne, and Marks, 1974). In the case of an agoraphobic incapable of traveling to the office even if accompanied, the therapist must be willing to abandon formality and begin treatment in the client's home or choose the alternative of having the client hospitalized at a convenient institution. The latter is undesirable on a number of grounds: the expense, the unnecessary stigma of psychiatric hospitalization, and the problem of generalization of gains made in a supportive hospital environment to the home setting. When treatment begins in the client's home, the focus may be at first on the limited goal of helping the client become capable of reaching the therapist's office.

Many behavior therapists habitually work only with the person presenting the complaint. Given the interpersonal matrix within which agoraphobia is developed and maintained, it is always helpful and frequently essential to involve significant family members in the therapy. Depending on the severity of the interpersonal problems and on practical factors, this involvement may vary from one session with a spouse or parent to elicit cooperation with the planned program to weekly sessions with a couple or family for a time. Sessions with significant family members also may be conducted in a group format.

Agoraphobia is usually a powerful habit maintained by many factors. In relying on a conventional 1-hour session per week the therapist attempts to set about changes in 1 hour that will counteract the reinforcement for this maladaptive pattern incurred in the approximately 110 other waking hours that remain in the week. This seems a feeble weapon indeed, and we would suggest more frequent meetings when possible. If this is not feasible, the therapist may want to incorporate a schedule of telephone contacts so that the client receives more immediate feedback and reinforcement for attempted changes.

These suggestions should not be viewed as exhaustive or restrictive. The point here has been that the therapist needs to intervene as powerfully as possible and should be attentive to the possibilities suggested by whatever resources can be mustered in his/her particular setting.

Therapist Attitude

Typically the agoraphobic client's first need upon entering therapy is to feel that he/she is understood. The therapist will further the cause of the therapy if she/he implicitly conveys the following message, "I understand your problem, what it is like for you, and I will be available to you as you need me. There is a remedy which has been applied successfully to others with the same problem, and I will make clear to you what is needed."

This message is transmitted by giving information and, more importantly, by the therapist's attitude toward the client and her/his needs. Particularly important points are dealing with dependency needs, needs for structure and understanding. Structure is provided by the explanatory process of therapy preparation (see "Preparing the Client for Therapy"). The other points are elaborated in the following.

Dependency. The therapist's attitude that is most facilitative is one that, at first accepts, even *encourages* the client to depend upon the therapist. By allowing this dependency to occur the therapist conveys acceptance of a powerful need and gains leverage to motivate the client during difficult times in therapy. Thus one may give the client one's phone numbers, including a home number, and encourage the client to call whenever he/she feels the need to do so. It is also helpful to be as flexible as possible about appointment hours, allowing changes and extra time during sessions if needed. In short, any steps that say "I'm available when you need me" are helpful in the early stages of therapy. The therapist needs to understand from the outset that agoraphobic clients will make more demands than most other clients and will have an overwhelming need to know that the therapist cares. Of course, it would be destructive to promote permanent dependency; however, meeting these needs at the outset is helpful to the progress of therapy. Having established oneself as a supportive, nurturant figure, one can more easily encourage and reinforce independence as the client progresses.

The feeling of being different. Most agoraphobics have made it a point to hide their problem from all but a few people in their lives. They have not had the experience of meeting others with similar problems even though they probably know one or more people who are agoraphobic and also hiding it. They are convinced that no one else would understand how they could be afraid of commonplace events like eating in restaurants or going grocery shopping. They are sure that others would think them "crazy" if they knew. Most have been to one or more therapists who also seemed not to understand their problem. Consequently, a strong bond develops with a therapist who can show he/she truly does understand the syndrome.

The therapist may convey understanding by making empathetic statements such as, "It must really frighten you to find yourself unable to do things that it seems everyone else can do," and "It makes you feel alone in the world when no one else seems to understand what you are going through." Less obvious than the value of accurate empathy is the helpfulness of being able to make statements about the client's experience *before* the client does. Because certain aspects of the syndrome are almost always found, the therapist can be quite confident of being accurate if he/she says, "I suppose that the more a situation precludes your getting away quickly, the more you fear it," or more specifically "I guess that the longer a line at the grocery store, the more difficult it is for you," or "I suppose that you would rather sit on an aisle seat rather than in the middle of a row at a movie." This communicates that one understands the experience from the client's perspective.

Need to be accepted. Unfortunately, most people who have tried to be helpful to the agoraphobic, including many therapists, have adopted attitudes which are in one way or another nonaccepting. A common one is based on the assumption that people always do what they *really* want to do, and if the agoraphobic does not go out, it must be because he/she really does not want to, consciously or unconsciously. Such helpers will say things like, "When you really want to you will get over this," or "You don't go out because you really want to punish your husband." A second common interpretation is that the client lacks will power. The helper will say "If you really try, you will be able to lick this thing," or "It only requires the courage to face it." Both of these assumptions are circular in nature since they cannot be disproved by anything the client does. Thus an agoraphobic who rushes home, defeated by a panic attack, may be told, "You didn't try hard enough," or "You must not have *really* wanted to go." A much more productive attitude is that the client cannot get out because it is *normal* to avoid situations that feel life-threatening and that lack of progress has been due to a misunderstanding of the problem and its solution. It then becomes the therapist's responsibility to furnish the necessary ingredients for progress. If the client does not improve, it is the *therapist's* fault, not the client's. The prevalent attitude of placing the responsibility on the client just adds guilt and further reduces the client's self-esteem.

Data Gathering

The process of data gathering proceeds in two steps. First, the therapist collects information about the topography of the symptoms. That is, where and how do the problems occur? Second, she/he expands on that information by seeking to make a functional analysis of these maladaptive responses, that is, establishing a consistent chain of events that precede, include, and follow the complained-of response. The functional analysis determines the treatment interventions appropriate for a particular client. One needs to keep the various components of the syndrome in mind as a structure for data-gathering interviews, for these clients are usually unable to identify important sources of distress. Thus one seeks information not only about the reported fears but also about possible sources of stress, for example, physical factors or interpersonal problems. The appendix contains a structured interview that may be used to guide data gathering over several sessions. The client's responses on the Fear Survey Schedule (e.g., Wolpe and Lang, 1964), a Life History Questionnaire, and an Assertiveness Inventory (e.g., Gambrill and Richey, 1975) are frequently helpful in amassing relevant information in a short space of time. The Fear Survey Schedule, for instance, includes a number of "fear of fear" items such as anxiety about mental illness, loss of control, and heart palpitations. The collection of topographical data is illustrated by segments of initial interviews with two clients.

T: I understand you've been referred to me because you have some fears that are bothering you.

C: Yes, street fears. I'm afraid when I'm out on the street by myself, especially at night.

T: What bothers you about being by yourself on the street?

C: Well, about six months ago I was raped, and it took me a long time to calm down again. Then last month when my girlfried and I were walking in center city, we were mugged. A gang of kids robbed us and beat us up. Since then I've been afraid to go out alone.

(Not a case of agoraphobia! Note the clear-cut conditioning events. The current fear was one of being attacked again, not a panic attack. Also her Fear Survey Schedule showed fears of being alone but no travel restrictions and no fear of fear components. Contrast this to the following case of a woman presenting with a fear of flying.)

T: Tell me what brings you in to see me.

C: Well, my husband's new job involves traveling a lot on business trips. I want to go with him, but I can't get on an airplane.

T: Have you always been afraid of flying?

C: No, it never used to bother me, only the past few years.

T: What happened to make it change?

C: I don't know. I just don't want to get on a plane anymore.

T: I see. I notice on your Fear Survey Schedule that you also are afraid of other kinds of public transportation. When did that begin?

C: I'm not sure. Around the same time, I guess.

T: This has been going on for a few years. What made you decide to get treatment now?

C: Well like I said, my husband's new job takes him out of town, and I don't like to stay alone, so I want to go with him.

(Obviously we have a lot more than fear of flying here, and with the help of the Fear Survey Schedule eventually uncover the usual rash of agoraphobic fears. We consequently suspect panic attacks are playing a role. Rather than ask a question as leading as "Do you have panic attacks?", we can usually obtain that information by asking about the beginning of the phobia.)

T: Can you remember how all these fears began?

C: We were moving here from _____ (a small town in New Jersey), and when we started to drive over the Benjamin Franklin Bridge (a very long, very tall bridge over the Delaware River, connecting New Jersey and Philadelphia) going into Philadelphia, I all of a sudden got this horrible feeling that something terrible was going to happen. I pleaded with my husband to turn back, but he said I was being stupid and went ahead. I thought I would die the whole time I was on that bridge. I don't know what happened; I must have been over that bridge a hundred times before, and it never bothered me.

T: Can you describe that feeling to me?

C: Oh, yes. It was the worst thing I ever experienced. My heart was beating so hard I thought it would burst, and I felt funny in my head, like I would pass out.

T: That sounds really frightening. Have you had any more experiences like that?

C: Not so much anymore. I had them a lot for a while.

T: What made them stop?

C: I don't know, they just have.

(Usually this means the client is very successfully avoiding anything that might produce anxiety. The therapist now moves to make the connection between the panic attacks and the avoidance behavior.)

T: If you were to get on a plane, how would it be?

C: I wouldn't get on one.

T: Well, just suppose somehow you found yourself on one; imagine yourself right now being on a plane.

C: (Closes eyes, then shudders) I wouldn't be able to get out. I'd have to wait until we got to the airport.

T: What would make you need to get out?

C: Well I always have to know that I can get out if I should get that feeling (panic attack).

T: (Smiling to break tension) You certainly can't run out of there at 30,000 feet.

C: Right. That's it. I always feel like I have to be able to get out.

T: Is that why you always sit at the back of auditoriums?

C: Yes, if I have to run out, I don't want everyone to notice.

T: (Making the generalization for client) So you seem to be avoiding places you can't get out of easily like crowded streets, buses, and so on.

C: You know I never really thought of it that way before, but you're right. Any place I get that trapped feeling.

T: What would happen if you couldn't get out?

C: (Getting visibly anxious at the very thought) Well I know it sounds silly, but I'm afraid I might go crazy.

T: What would you do?

C: I'd lose my head and start screaming and trying to get out. My husband would never forgive me.

T: So rather than take that chance, you avoid going any place you might get panicky?

C: I guess that's what I've done.

T: Do you have a safe place you head for when you get that feeling?

C: Yes, how did you know? I have to get home. It doesn't make sense, but I know if I get home I'll feel better.

Agoraphobics almost always assume they are the only person so afflicted and think therapists who ask pertinent questions are brilliantly insightful. While this is gratifying, it is helpful to let them know one asks the right questions because there are many other people like them. This reduces their feelings of being crazy.

Next the therapist asks for more information about the circumstances of the client's life around the time of onset. The goal here is partly to help sort out whether this is simple or complex agoraphobia. The remaining emphasis is on beginning to set the stage for the connection of other events to the panic attacks and phobias if this turns out to be a case of complex agoraphobia.

T: You've told me this all started when you were moving to Philadelphia. What were things like for you at that time?

C: Well, moving was really a hassle for me. I was really upset and worn out.

T: Yeah, moving is always tough. Coming to a big city from a small town is a big switch. How did you feel about the move?

C: I hated to leave. I lived in _____ all my life, and it's just not the same here.

T: That must have meant moving away from people you cared about.

C: Yes, all my family is there, and we've always been very close, and my friends.

T: Did you want to move?

C: No, but that's what my husband wanted to do.

T: Did he know how you felt about it?

C: Well, I guess so. My mother told him I didn't want to go, but he just said we had to go.

T: It sounds like you were pretty upset with him when you had that first attack.

(There are clues here that the client may be unassertive with her husband, and that this may play a role in the phobic symptoms. The therapist does not push this connection too strongly at this point, but leaves it for the client to mull over.)

Another part of the topography the therapist wants to explore is whether there is a phobic companion, and if so to begin to make this person's role clear. There are a few agoraphobics who feel more comfortable when alone, and this is important information to have in arranging the sequence of assignments to be made later in the course of treatment. For most, however, some important person is closely involved in providing them with mobility.

T: Is it easier for you to go out of your safe territory if someone is with you?

C: Mainly my husband. There's no one else here I feel close enough to. Sometimes when my mother visits I can go places with her.

T: Can you go any place with your husband? It doesn't seem like you can go on planes with him.

C: No, I can drive almost anywhere in the city with him as long as there's not a traffic jam, but I still wouldn't get on a train or plane even if he's along.

T: So having your husband along increases somewhat your mobility but doesn't give you complete freedom.

C: (Nods) Mm-hmm.

This is a fairly typical picture in that another person adds enough reassurance to increase freedom of movement, but not enough to remove all restrictions. There is great variability in the range of movement agoraphobics have. Some we have seen can travel anywhere within the city of Philadelphia, which is quite a large land area, but not to outlying suburbs. Others cannot go out the door of their homes if unaccompanied, but may travel to a foreign country with a trusted companion. The most common pattern is one where there is a "circle of safety" around their homes within which they can freely travel unaccompanied. The circle may have a radius of a few blocks or a few miles and is generally marked by boundaries of broad or heavily trafficked streets the agoraphobic is particularly hesitant to cross.

T: What is helpful about having another person along?

C: Well, the psychiatrist I saw for a while said it's because I'm like a child and don't want to grow up.

T: I'm not sure it helps much to think of it in that way. I'm sure there are times when you feel like a child, most of us do when we're very frightened. Can you think of any other reason?

C: No, not really.

T: Would you feel able to drive around the city with me?

C: Yes, I think so.

T: How come?

C: Well, you're a doctor.

T: So?

C: Well, if anything happened, you would know what to do.

T: If anything happened?

C: If I started to go crazy.

T: I see. So if you have someone along that you trust to handle the situation if you have a panic attack and go crazy, then you can go into places you can't go alone?

C: Yes (with some surprise) I guess that's really it. I think that's why I don't like to be home when my husband is out of town (now putting connections together for herself). I don't know who I would call if I started to panic. When he's in town, I can call him at the office. He doesn't like it, but if I'm in bad enough shape, he will come home.

T: I'm getting the feeling that if we could do something about this fear of panic attacks, I call it fear of fear, then you wouldn't need to have your husband with you so much.

C: You know, I remember now I told my old therapist just that once—that it was the fear of being afraid that bothered me. But he said I just had to make my mind up to go out and face it like an adult.

T: Easier said than done, huh?

C: (Heatedly) You said it! I didn't need to pay him to tell me that. That's what my husband tells me constantly. If I could just go out and face it, I would!

T: Well, there are ways I can teach you to handle these panic attacks, and once we've done that you will be able to go out yourself.

C: (With tears in her eyes) You mean you think you really can help me?

T: Yes, I think if we work together we can change this; (pauses) that seems to be hard for you to believe.

C: I felt so hopeless after I left the other doctor. It seemed like I was so messed up that nothing could be done for me. He kept telling me I just didn't want to stand on my own two feet.

T: What do you think?

C: I really do want to get better.

T: I believe you. I think you just don't know how, and that's what I'm here to help you do.

The therapist has accomplished several things in this segment. First she has made an analysis for herself and the client of the function of the phobic companion. Again she is demonstrating to the client that her behavior is reasonable, not "crazy," given the underlying fears that have now been repeatedly exposed. Frequently previous therapists, due to frustration or to an orientation that emphasizes pathology, will have given a client derogatory explanations of her/his behavior, as happened with this woman. This only exacerbates the client's low sense of self-worth, so the second intervention was to debunk this view of her behavior. In using the phrase "most of us feel that way sometimes" the therapist attempts to convey a feeling that both of them are members of the human race; she is not perfect, and the client is not a sick member of some other species. The therapist implies that she knows the client does want to get better and expects that with some help she will follow through on a program that should lead to improvement. In many cases one does find that an agoraphobic is deriving some secondary gain from her/his phobias, as we explore in greater detail later. This does not mean, however, that he/she would not trade "sick" behavior for other patterns if the therapist can teach other ways of getting one's needs met.

The third major point about this tape segment is that the therapist, by making the functional analysis clear to the client, has set the stage for the client to understand the rationale for the treatment interventions on fear of fear which will follow. It is extremely important that this be accomplished at every step of the therapy, since otherwise the client will not be motivated to work cooperatively for change. She has also begun making it clear to the client that this therapy is a joint venture. Many clients come to behavior therapists expecting to be "done to" while they maintain an essentially passive position. Given their tendencies toward passivity and dependency, agoraphobics particularly will adopt this stance if it is not continually corrected.

It is important to have information about a client's particular pattern of anxiety, as this information determines what coping tactics the therapist will suggest later in treatment.

C: I was slowly walking along the aisle with a grocery basket and all of a sudden I felt like I *had* to get out of there—I just ran out the door. I felt like I had to get home.

T: I see. That must have been frightening for you—when you felt as though you had to get out, what did you notice in your own body that told you that you had to get out?

C: I felt like I was going to faint, dizzy and shaky in the legs.

T: Anything else? Any tingling feeling in your fingers?

C: I don't remember any feelings like that, but sometimes my heart beats a mile a minute.

T: So when you feel anxious or nervous, what you notice is that you are dizzy and your legs shake and your heart pounds?

C: Yes.

T: Is that what usually happens when you get scared?

C: Yes.

The client's symptoms sound like those caused by hyperventilation. This is commonly a part of anxiety attacks which will continue to spiral out of control as long as the client continues to gasp for air. Consequently, we explain hyperventilation immediately and instruct clients to keep their mouths closed and breathe through their noses when anxious.

In the interpersonal area the topography of problematical responses may be explored through encouraging detailed and concrete accounts of interactions. Here is a segment from the third interview with an agoraphobic woman.

C: I really feel that my problem is due to my husband's lack of respect for me.

T: How's that?

C: If he would say nice things, be affectionate instead of always being critical.

T: There are times when he is critical and withdrawn emotionally and at these times you are feeling that he doesn't respect you?

C: Uh-huh.

T: When is the last time that happened?

C: Just this morning.

T: What exactly did he say and do this morning?

C: He was his usual grumpy self; he didn't pay any attention to me at all.

T: What did he do that made you feel that he was not paying attention to you?

C: He sits there at the breakfast table reading his newspaper, doesn't speak to anyone, and just slams out of the house.

T: What were you feeling at the breakfast table while he was reading?

C: That he doesn't care.

T: That's what you thought, but was there some feeling also?

C: Just that he didn't care about us.

T: Well what did you feel like doing at the time?

C: I wanted to yank that paper right out of his hands and scream at him.

T: Then you were feeling angry?

C: Yes.

T: Well how did you respond to his sitting and reading?

C: I didn't say anything. It wouldn't do any good anyway, we would just end up arguing. So, I just swallow it.

It is unlikely that information of the type elicited here will occur in the first few interviews in a case of complex agoraphobia due to the unusually high level of anxiety triggered by discussions of interpersonal conflict. In fact such conflicts are usually out of awareness in the early stages of therapy. As is usually the case, data gathering is a part of the therapeutic process and proceeds hand in hand with intervention throughout the course of therapy. Here we learn that in this particular interaction the client's belief that her husband lacks respect for her stems from feelings of anger and hurt that she is unable to express effectively. This gives us a hypothesis to pursue during the functional analysis—that her anxiety may be connected to a lack of assertiveness. Further details of her reactions in a number of situations related to anger will either support the hypothesis or force us to abandon it. It may turn out, for example, that she has difficulty in any situation where either she is angry or other people are angry. On the other hand, she may have no difficulty with people other than her spouse, or perhaps she is unable to express herself appropriately only when her anger is likely to be met with withdrawal of affection on the part of her spouse. The definition of her idiosyncratic response pattern will be aided by records the client is asked to keep.

Record keeping is introduced as a part of orienting the client to self-observation and to insights based on cause-effect relationships that occur in the here and now. This is an extremely important method of gaining needed information with all types of cases, but particularly with agoraphobics, for they are markedly unable to report accurately their experiences. For example, we both interviewed an agoraphobic woman for a study we were conducting, and when one of us saw her shortly after her arrival at our offices, she was still crying hysterically in the aftermath of the panic attack she had experienced on the drive over. Forty-five minutes later she had an interview with the other, who asked when she last had a panic attack. "Oh, not for years," she replied! Not every case is this dramatic, of course, but a therapist frequently has to rely on conviction about the presence of antecedents to panic attacks until the client begins to remember or keeps good records.

The rationale for record keeping can be presented to the client in the following manner.

T: It seems pretty clear from what we have discussed that your distress is sometimes better, and some days you can go shopping without concern and on others the thought of going out causes anxiety. Such changes do not occur out of the blue—without causes—but at this time we are not clear about what antecedent events lead to your feeling scared when out. My guess is that it has something to do with what goes on between you and your husband or perhaps other people; but in any case, it would be helpful if we could get a more accurate picture of the connection between how you feel and what precedes it, as well as what follows it. How about making some notes this week—whenever you feel discomfort, write it down. Specify what feelings you are having—pounding heart, sweating, whatever, also note what is going on around you at the time, where are you, who is with you, whether you were already upset about something else. It is also important to note any persistent thoughts that you are having. What thoughts after first noticing being afraid and your first response to those thoughts?

The first attempt at such record keeping will not be particularly informative but usually may be used productively by going over the incidents recorded during the past week in detail. It is important that such homework assignments be inquired about and given attention, as it is destructive to the client's motivation if the therapist gives homework and then forgets about it. Whatever attempts have been made should be praised, and further suggestions for improving record keeping given without criticism.

Preparing the Client for Therapy

As noted above, data gathering, especially with agoraphobics, continues throughout the course of therapy, and the introduction of the proper intervention usually follows smoothly from this interaction with the client. The client is given feedback on how the therapist understands the structure of his/her problems at this time and is informed as to what treatment procedures have been helpful with such problems. The therapist endeavors to present the treatment rationale at a level appropriate for the client at that point in therapy and to elicit her/his active cooperation. Early in the therapeutic process, explanations will center on how fear of fear is operating in this particular case.

The following segment comes from the first meeting of a group of agoraphobic women who will be going out together to confront their phobic situations (see "Group *In Vivo* Exposure"). The members are either simple agoraphobics or clients who will be receiving individual and marital therapy for other aspects of complex agoraphobia. Members of the group have been sharing their problems with each other and expressing how important it is for them to meet others who understand, who do not find their fears to be "crazy." The leader breaks in at this point to explain the rationale for the treatment program in which the group will be engaged.

T: Well, really it's not so weird. All of you seem to be saying that you've been avoiding going places because you're afraid you'll have a panic attack there. Actually that's pretty natural. People tend to avoid things they're afraid of; if our ancestors hadn't done that they would have been eaten up by animals or have fallen off cliffs, and none of us would be here today. Don't you know anyone else who has phobias?

C1:   Yeah, my husband is afraid of water; he won't go swimming and now my little boy is starting to be afraid too.

C2:   Mine won't go up a ladder. When we painted the house, I was the one who had to do the second-story windows. But he's not stuck in the house like I am.

T: Yes, you're right. That's an important difference. You're doing the same thing they are, avoiding what you're afraid of. The difference is that for you to do that means your life is severely affected. Whereas if you were afraid of one situation you could get away with it. So avoiding isn't working for you, or is it?

C3: No, it's only getting worse. Every month I can do less than the month before (other members generally agree).

C5: But trying to go out doesn't work either. Everybody tells me to force myself, but when I do, I just feel worse and have to run home like a fool.

T: Well, I agree with you. Forcing yourself isn't the answer either.

C5: (Looks relieved) What are we going to do then?

T: Let me show you how I think it works (draws on blackboard). Let's say you're going someplace where you had a panic attack like the grocery store. Now you probably get anxious just thinking about going to the store. You may go ahead, getting more anxious all the while until you're in the store. Then you think, "Oh my God, what if I have an attack. I'll never be able to get through the checkout line." Maybe you leave then or maybe you stay, but you've made yourself more anxious. When you feel that anxiety you say to yourself, "This is it, this time I'll never make it, I'll die, go crazy, or whatever." Naturally, you scare yourself into a full-blown attack.

C2: Then I head for home.

T: Sure, and say to yourself "I'll never go back to that store." So because you're afraid of it, you bring it on.

C4: Yes! I always say that. I do it myself, but I can't help it.

T: So after you go through that cycle a few times, pretty soon you won't even consider going to the store again. So there are a couple of problems—the way you think and the way you act. The more you try to avoid the scary feelings and thoughts and the situations where you may have them, the more you've reinforced your fear, the more you're a prisoner. So we have to help you learn not to avoid the frightening thoughts and feelings.

C1: That doesn't sound good.

T: Well, you're right, it won't be easy. I wish there were an easy way, but I don't know of one. See, if you were afraid of water, then I could lead you in the water bit by bit until you weren't afraid. Dogs the same thing, height the same. But you're afraid of panic attacks, afraid of fear. So what you have to expose yourself to is fear.

C2: Makes sense. I've always said it's the attacks I'm really afraid of.

T: Okay, so what I'm going to ask you to do is break up this cycle of fear you've got going. First place to break in is to stop avoiding, to stay wherever you are until the anxiety goes down. Second place is instead of saying, "Oh God, I musn't get panicky," I want you to break up that pattern by confronting those thoughts and feelings. The more you break the pattern up, the less anxious you'll be in the long run. Once you realize you can handle panicky feelings and that nothing bad will happen to you—you won't die or go crazy or faint—then you can go anywhere.

So we're going to do the opposite of what you have been doing. We're going to try to find ways of getting you panicky so you can practice these different ways of coping with it. When you can cope with the panic, then you'll be free women. I'm going to act as a sort of coach, to teach you ways we've found make it easier to deal with high anxiety and to remind you of these methods when you get frightened because it's easy to forget and go back to fighting anxiety when you're scared.

C5: But will I ever be really *rid* of these fears?

T: That depends on you. If you work hard and learn to handle panic attacks, you'll be able to go where you want to go with the confidence that you can handle the anxiety if it comes. Now, you probably started having panic attacks because you were under some kind of stress. Some people get ulcers, some get migraines, you get panic attacks.

C4: I'd rather have an ulcer!

T: Unfortunately nobody asked for your preference, so you're stuck with panic attacks. To the degree that this stress still exists in your life and you don't deal with it, then you'll continue having attacks. Eight times out of ten, it's family problems, like troubles with a husband or mother-in-law.

C1: How about both!

T: Or both. So if you want to get free of the attacks, you'll have to work on the source of the stress. If you've already resolved the stress, then just dealing with the fear will be sufficient.

The therapist has set the stage for treatment by introducing the philosophy that anxiety is not to be avoided, rather it is to be confronted. She has engaged the clients in agreeing to tentatively adopt this hypothesis to learn if this new approach leads to improvement and has emphasized the importance of persistent effort on their part.

She has also raised the notion of panic attacks as a symptom of conflict in a way that de-emphasizes the idea that such attacks are the reflection of deep-rooted disturbance or "craziness." This makes it easier for clients to identify and report sources of conflict. The tenor of her entire presentation communicates that the clients are not "sick," but are responding in normal ways given their experiences.

With most cases of complex agoraphobia clients become open to examining the nature of their conflicts only when some symptomatic improvement has begun. Once avoidance behavior has diminished, day-to-day variations become more salient. These variations are frequently entrees for continuing the functional analysis into the conflict arena. This part of the functional analysis is particularly therapeutic in that seeing one's behavior as predictable and understandable usually results in a diminution of anxiety. However, this rarely suffices for a problem such as agoraphobia; most agoraphobics we have seen have had extensive prior therapy that led to much "insight" but little in the way of lasting behavior change. The following interaction illustrates the close connection between functional analysis, preparation, and therapeutic interventions.

C: While driving in to see you I had an anxiety attack. I'm still shaky—I don't understand it—I have been driving in by myself the last 3 weeks without feeling uncomfortable.

T: Tell me what happened.

C: I was about halfway here when I stopped at a red light—my heart started pounding and I felt as if I wanted to turn around and rush home. I did as you suggested—concentrated on making my heart beat even faster—and in a few minutes it passed. All the while I just kept on driving here.

T: I'm sorry that you had to go through that; I know how scary it is for you.

C: It sure is. I thought, "Oh, no! here it comes again," and I had this feeling that something awful was going to happen to me.

T: What do you suppose would happen if you could not control the panic?

C: I don't know! Just something horrifying!

T: Well would you close your eyes for a moment and go through a fantasy of the worst possible consequences? First start by imagining yourself back in the car and feeling afraid—let it go where it will from there. . . .

C: I can't continue driving, I'm out of the car running and screaming. . . .

T: What happens next?

C: That's all, I can't go further.

T: Try to imagine this, I'll never be the same again! They will lock me away. I'll be completely out of control, crazy!

C: (Showing visible signs of distress) Yes, I'm really afraid of being insane!

The therapist reassures the client that these fears are groundless because people with this problem *do not* ever go crazy and that she has none of the thought disorder that accompanies insanity. He pushes his point by stating that, in fact, she cannot be crazy even if she wants to, just does not have it in her. When the client feels less distressed, she and the therapist pursue in detail the antecedents leading to her panic attack.

T: As we have seen before these episodes of anxiety have antecedents. Let's explore what may have preceded this one—have you any ideas?

C: No, it seemed that it came from nowhere.

T: Well, tell me what your morning has been like from the time you got up until you came in here.

C: Well, I got up feeling O.K., went into the bathroom, showered, and got dressed as usual.

T: Art (client's husband) was up or still sleeping?

C: He was asleep. I went down and got some coffee and was reading the paper when he came down. I prepared breakfast for us both and we ate.

T: Tell me about your conversation with Art this morning.

C: Well, we got into an argument—well, he did anyway.

T: What did he say that was argumentative?

C: He asked me what I was doing today, I said that I was coming to see you, and he said he wished I would stop seeing you. He said we can't afford things that we need because of all the money I am spending in therapy and that its not doing any good anyway.

T: How did you feel when he said that?

C: Well, he's right about the money. It is expensive and I don't earn any of it.

T: You were feeling guilty?

C: Yes, so I couldn't argue about it.

T: Has Art noticed that you are driving about the city pretty freely these days?

C: He hasn't said anything about it; in fact, he's getting more insistent that I quit therapy, but I am improving! He's *always* critical no matter what I do.

T: It may be that he's feeling uncertain about the changes, perhaps he would like to come in with you or by himself sometime. Anyway I'm glad that you see that it's not necessarily so that you are always wrong; but, in fact, Art is at least sometimes critical as a result of his own insecurities. What happened next?

C: I didn't answer; went into the bedroom, straightened up a bit.

T: What were you feeling . . . any thoughts at the time?

C: I was really feeling bad about myself, why do I have to be so weak, to go to a psychologist, I'm not much good. I'm just a drain on everyone.

T: What then?

C: Well, Art left and I got into the car and drove here.

T: So you were feeling guilty about coming, perhaps having mixed feelings about it . . . guilty for Art's sake and feeling that coming here means you are weak . . . on the other hand wanting to come because it has its positive aspects for you.

C: Yes, I enjoy being here. I feel better when I leave, and I really don't want to give it up.

T: (Noticing apparent change in client's sensation level) How are you feeling now?

C: Much better! I see that I was anxious because of what happened with Art.

While this may be viewed as information gathering, it also serves the purpose of reorienting the client to a view of anxiety that is orderly, not crazy, and allows us to proceed to face the interpersonal problem directly. The therapist may sensibly suggest that they work on how she might handle a similar situation when it comes up again.

During this segment the therapist has made a functional analysis of the antecedents of this panic attack, which the client first thought came out of the blue. He has also, however, set the stage for a crucial part of the treatment of complex agoraphobia—teaching the client to express herself in effective, appropriate ways. Having clear connections between the conflict with her husband and the panic attack while driving, the client is now probably motivated to engage in role playing with her therapist other ways of interacting with her husband.

Course of Therapeutic Intervention

We have outlined (see "Description of Behavior Pattern") four broad areas that require intervention in most cases of complex agoraphobia. For conceptual purposes it is useful to think of the course of therapy as a combination of discrete interventions for each problem area. In reality the therapeutic process is a complex gestalt with progress in each area having impact on the status of the other problems. The success of technical interventions depends on sensitive timing and the consistency of a caring relationship with the therapist (see "Therapist Attitude"). With that caveat in mind, the reader is encouraged to use Table 1 as an overall guideline for the case example which follows:

Table 1

Problem	Intervention
Dependency, lack of self sufficiency	Assertive training, desensitization to fears of rejection and criticism. Shaping of autonomous behavior, for example, encouragement to begin volunteer work, then part-time, then full-time employment. Training in problem-solving skills.
Conflict, generally interpersonal	Couples or family therapy with emphasis on communication training and support for spouse when threatened by progress of identified client. If necessary, removal from noxious climate to a temporary home with relatives and friends, or residential setting.
"Hysterical" response style	Using diary of daily events and feelings as well as incidents in therapy sessions to teach clients to identify sources of distress rather than reacting superstitiously.
Fear of Fear	
a. Panic attacks	Paradoxical intention and other self-instructional sets to break habit of avoiding anxious feelings; imaginal flooding.
b. Avoidance behavior	Homework assignments, *in vivo* exposure.

Case example

This client was referred to us for treatment after terminating with her previous therapist after 5 years. She agreed that material from her sessions could be used for training purposes and to being seen by AG while therapists in training observed on closed-circuit television. Transcript material from her sessions is used to demonstrate the interpolation of behavioral techniques with relationship psychotherapy (T, therapist; C, client; H, husband; L, lover).

T: This started a couple of years ago?

C: It didn't start 2 years ago, it got worse 2 years ago. I just stopped traveling altogether. But I guess it started about 6 years ago. I just sort of feel anxious even if I go half an hour or 20 minutes away.

T: So distance is an important factor no matter where you are going?

C: Unless I'm really familiar with the place to which I am going.

T: The unfamiliarity of it is important—so sometimes you can travel a good distance if you were very familiar with where you are going?

C: Yeah, 45 minutes, half an hour, if I knew the place that I'm going to.

T: A friend's house?

C: Yeah, it usually doesn't bother me. Even if it is familiar and it is a distance it would bother me, like Delaware. It used to be when I left Delaware to come home I would be very upset.

The increase in fear when returning home suggests that there are factors of conflict at home that contribute to the symptoms.

T: Can you remember the first time you got upset?

C: Yeah, I was in the car, it was very crowded and I was driving. I had two girlfriends and all their kids; there were about eight kids in the car. And at that particular time I had been smoking marijuana. I was smoking back then; it was about 6 years ago and that was the very first time.

T: Where were you going?

C: We had been out for a ride and we were coming back. It was on the way home.

Again she was returning home, which supports the hypothesis, although other factors such as the effects of marijuana need to be explored.

T: And you were stoned at the time? Was there something that set it off?

C: Just that the kids were very noisy, nothing else in particular. The three of us had gone places before, and I had done it stoned before; marijuana never made me anxious before this happened.

T: You had done essentially the same thing before? You were returning home?

C: And I was driving.

T: And I guess being stoned made it even more intense.

C: Yeah.

T: What specifically happened? Did you all of a sudden start to feel uncomfortable?

C: Just all of the sudden.

T: Did you have the awareness of anything that you were thinking at the time?

C: It was a long time ago.

T: Can you remember what it felt like? How the sequence of events went, were you mildly uncomfortable at first or did it hit you all at once?

C: I felt—I guess I felt trapped.

T: Trapped?

C: I felt like I couldn't get home fast enough. I was away from home and I felt I was responsible for the people in the car and there were a lot of kids. That made me uncomfortable. I was in control—it was up to me to get everyone home safely.

T: The burden of that responsibility was most salient.

C: I guess that was when it was.

T: But you had done this before.

C: Yeah, I think it might have been the marijuana.

(Onset of fear of one's own sensations is frequently associated with drug-induced experiences; even though the anxiety reaction was probably not triggered by the marijuana in this case (she had smoked many times before), the perceptual distortions and intensity of feelings being linked to panic leads to a conditioned fear of perceptual distortions and strong feelings.)

T: The combination of the two.

C: Yeah, because a couple of days after that I was smoking again and I was at home, and the panic attack that came over me was worse than what I had had in the car.

T: Even though you had smoked on a number of occasions without any problem? Were you at that point in time feeling trapped generally or did you have responsibilities that were particularly difficult?

(This is a probe into the interpersonal situation at the time of onset; most often there is a flat denial of any difficulties at first questioning, but the therapist needs to return to the subject periodically, since a little later in therapy there will very likely be an awareness of feeling, for example, a need to escape the marriage that was too anxiety provoking to be conscious. In this case, the client has had a considerable amount of insight-oriented therapy and is immediately able to report conflict at onset.)

C: Well, my child was 2 years old then. You know the terrible two's; I guess it was a bad time and I was only 21. Plus I don't know this may be just a coincidence, but this guy, L, that I had been engaged to before I met my husband, was in Germany and he was coming home then at any time and I'm not sure but I think maybe the two things are connected. I don't know how.

T: In what way, can you give me any idea how that may be?

C: Well we had been staying in contact with one another, and my husband and I weren't getting along really great at that time.

T: You were not?

C: No, and he said that when he came back he would like an answer from me one way or the other. I had been writing to him and he had been writing to me the whole year he was away; so I guess that I may have felt trapped in that I was going to make a major decision and I just felt that I wasn't ready to make it. I don't know if that makes sense to you.

T: Yes. That sort of conflict can lead you to be generally very upset throughout the day and much more susceptible to panics.

C: Again, I was smoking, the last one I ever smoked as a matter of fact, and my husband was on the phone, we had just finished dinner, the kids were in their room, and I sat down, and I was smoking by myself, and this surge of panic just rushed over me. My heart was pounding rapidly, and I just felt like I had to get out. I felt trapped in the apartment, and yet when I rushed outside I would feel like I was by myself and that feeling of being alone and by myself brought on just as much panic as being inside. So I'd run back in.

T: It must have been very frightening for you.

(To the extent that they are presented sincerely, empathetic statements are very useful in building the bonds of trust and rapport that are essential to progress.)

C: And I grabbed onto my husband and I said, "I can't stay in here but you have to come out with me," and he would come out with me.

(This episode of anxiety at home—needing to get out—and then anxiety about getting out is an excellent microcosmic look at the overall conflict situation frequently found in agoraphobic cases.)

T: How long did that go on?

C: I couldn't quiet myself down, and it went on until I took a tranquilizer that my husband had. I'd never taken them before and he gave me one and I went to sleep, but I woke up in the middle of the night with just as much panic.

T: By then you were no longer stoned, just really afraid?

C: Yeah.

T: So how long did that go on before you calmed down?

C: I was really depressed. For about three days after that I couldn't do any work, I slept a lot. I didn't eat anything—I never want to go through that again. It was terrible. I was on medication, I was taking tranquillizers and some other things that were prescribed to me by our family doctor. And then I guess my husband just said, "Get up and start doing something," and on that third day when I did, I started feeling better. That is when I started seeing a psychiatrist.

(This description of several days to several weeks of agitated depression accompanying the onset of panic attacks is typical.)

T: Okay, what else did you notice besides your heart pounding? What other physiological sensations?

(Here the therapist attempts to get at as many as possible of the subjective cues that now signal "it's happening again," which in turn leads to repeat episodes of panic.)

C: That was the most intense. I thought maybe I was having a heart attack. I'd never had anything like that before. I went and looked in the mirror, and I looked at my eyes and it frightened me.

T: Why?

C: Because I didn't recognize who I was, and that scared me.

T: There was a sense of being a strange person.

C: Like I didn't know who I was and what I wanted. That scared me.

T: And that was when you were in the midst of that panic?

C: Yeah, when it first hit me.

T: Just sort of checking yourself out.

C: I still don't know why I did that, it was strange.

T: Because you were feeling so strange—it might have been reassuring but it wasn't, it frightened you. You didn't look like yourself.

C: Right.

(Depersonalization is a symptom of high anxiety not necessarily associated with psychosis. Too frequently, therapists, like agoraphobics, err in viewing this as a sign of "craziness.")

T: You were feeling bad for a long time, so you took a tranquillizer and that calmed you.

C: Yes.

T: Did you have any other fears at the time that you thought you might have been having a heart attack?

C: Well, I thought I was dying.

T: You thought you were going to die?

C: Yeah, I didn't know what was happening to me and I thought this is death; this is it, this is what it feels like.

From this description of the subjective experience at onset, it is clear why there is such profound fear of fear subsequent to the first panic attacks. Since she did not have any cognitive structure within which to understand what was happening, the experience was all the more terrifying. The prophylactic aspect of therapy is establishing an understandable and reasonable rationale for anxiety. It will be important to link these experiences with antecedent conflicts that the client can effectively work toward resolving. In this case, if the client had been aware that high levels of anxiety are *normal* when there is severe psychological conflict, many of the fear of fear aspects (fear of death, fear of heart attack) might never have developed.

T: So there was a sense of unreality about it.

C: Yeah, I think from the marijuana too. I'm afraid that if I take any kind of medication that it is going to bring on the same kind of reaction. I'm afraid to take anything now.

T: You are pretty comfortable as long as your husband is with you when you go out?

(Feeling more comfortable with her husband along is almost entirely predictable, and when the therapist asks questions of this sort without the client revealing it first, it often serves to get across the message that the therapist *understands*, which, of course, is very helpful in establishing a working relationship.)

C: Yeah, it shows, huh?

T: How is that?

C: Well, he came with me today. I wouldn't have come if he didn't come with me because I think that if I am feeling bad then he can sort of take over.

T: It must be very important for you to have someone that you can trust.

C: Right, I drag him along to the dentist with me.

T: Is there someone else who can also fill that role for you?

C: No, just him usually. I feel uncomfortable when my father goes away. He has always been somebody that I leaned on.

T: Does he live here in Philadelphia?

C: He lives about 2 minutes from my house.

T: So that is very reassuring for you, huh?

C: Yeah, unfortunately.

T: Was that the case even before these attacks?

C: I don't think I thought about it before. But I guess, yeah, it probably is true. It wasn't conscious to me then.

T: So are there other things now that you are afraid of?

C: No.

T: Are there any particular places that you avoid going to—theaters, and so forth?

C: I used to but not so much any more. Depending on how far away they are, and this is getting back to the traveling. I haven't gone to baseball games in a while downtown, but I think it is more because of the traffic.

T: The crowds don't bother you?

C: To a certain extent. Like if it is a crowd and it is moving along it's okay, but if it is standing still it bothers me, I feel trapped.

T: So anything that makes you feel trapped?

C: Yeah, especially a traffic jam.

T: I can see that that would impede you from getting back to your safe base, home. Even when your husband is in the car, does a traffic jam upset you?

C: Yeah, the expressway going to Delaware is a great one, bumper to bumper for an hour.

T: Do you make that trip often?

C: Not any more. I haven't been there in 2 years. I'm kind of getting sick of explaining why I don't go.

T: Elevators bother you?

C: Not really.

T: Good.

C: Because I know that I can stop on the next floor and get out. Usually I can rationalize things even when in a situation. Even in a traffic jam I know that I can pull off the road.

T: So cars aren't as bad. Do you drive?

C: I always drive, I don't like being a passenger. That is another thing that bothers me—I just remembered.

(Agoraphobics vary on this point. Some feel more comfortable driving because they control the vehicle like C. Others are so fearful of losing control, fainting, and so forth, that they prefer someone else to drive, as long as that person can be trusted to turn home should panic strike.)

T: It is a sense of being out of control.

C: Yes. You are finding out too much about me.

T: Do you feel that way?

C: Yes, well I'm used to talking to Dr. P. He already knows where my head is, and I don't feel embarrassed. But with somebody new, I mean, I don't go up to strangers and tell them these things. He is the only one that knows about them.

(Here we see indications of the often-encountered aspect of keeping the problem secret. This is usually related to the client's thought that if anyone *really* knew what her thoughts and feelings were he/she would discover what the client already believes—that she is crazy.)

T: Do you feel a little bit uneasy about sharing these things?

C: Yeah, right. When I say them they sound absolutely absurd. But they are very real when I'm experiencing them.

T: You would rather not have to confront it this concretely by talking about it.

C: It just makes me feel a little uneasy. Starting over with someone new after all this time.

(The therapist respects C's discomfort and stops questioning about the phobia until she is once again ready to go on. In effect, he allows her a sense of control over the interview.)

T: I can really understand that. You've really had a hard time of it, haven't you?

C: Really, I feel lucky because I think that all these situations have made me grow in one way or another. I don't feel that I've stopped growing. After this situation when I started going to a psychiatrist, to Dr. P., I went back to school; I really started feeling better about myself.

T: So you really got some very positive things.

C: I was a straight-A student, I became a dance instructor, I really got involved. I finally felt as though I started living. I can't remember how I felt before this.

(It appears that she is already well along in doing an important aspect of the therapeutic work—developing a sense of independence by developing activities that are separate from her spouse (Goal 1).

T: You were not very active?

C: No.

T: Are you still active now, do you do a lot?

C: Yes.

T: What sort of things do you do?

C: I was a camp director for a dance camp over the summer. But that presented a problem because I had to travel 40 minutes to get there, which made me uneasy.

T: I see. You went by yourself?

C: Yes. I'm teaching gymnastics right now. I'm also taking a yoga class.

T: Do you get there by yourself?

C: Yes.

T: You are fairly free of anxiety about going to these places at this point?

C: It bothers me sometimes. I just go anyway.

T: How about the anticipation?

C: The anticipation of coming here today was worse than actually coming.

(Here we see another frequently encountered event: the anticipatory anxiety remains long after the client no longer experiences anxiety in the actual situation. This is related to the fact that she can never feel completely sure that an event that she interprets as catastrophic, that is, anxiety, will not occur again. Our task here is to help her reinterpret anxiety as a *normal* process that signals something is in need of her attention.)

T: Yeah.

C: About an hour or so before I had to leave it was, "Well, I have to go. I just have to do it."

T: You really want to get therapy.

C: Yes, it is really a pain. I haven't had a vacation in 2 years.

T: I think that is really what is holding you back. Well, when does your husband have to go with you, when you go someplace new?

C: I guess that over the last 2 years I've noticed that if I have to go a distance I just won't go unless he is with me.

T: How about grocery shopping?

C: No, that never bothers me. I'm saying never, when we moved about 6 months ago, that whole thing was a bad experience for me. I guess you can understand why now.

T: You were acclimated to the area you were in.

C: Yeah.

T: Do you still have concerns about having a heart attack?

C: No, I'm healthy.

T: Would it be fair to say that the thing that frightens you the most is that you might get frightened?

C: Yeah.

T: What do you think would happen if your fear got out of control?

Here the therapist probes for the expected fear of being crazy; the client is reluctant to reveal this fear, and when she does so, she immediately negates it. This suggests that (a) she is not very afraid of it anymore, or (b) it is too frightening to deal with yet. The therapist takes this as a cue that it is frightening to deal with and moves off the topic.

C: I ask myself that all the time; I say, "Well what is the worst thing that could happen?" And I really don't know.

T: Well could you have a little fantasy about that?

C: I think I am afraid of things getting out of control and passing out, and if I pass out then I'm not in control anymore.

T: Yeah, then what will happen to you?

C: And then someone else will have to come and help me.

T: Then?

C: I may have to go to the hospital or something.

T: What would happen in the hospital? You would be out of control now.

C: Okay, they would give me a shot of some kind of medicine that I won't have any say over because I am not conscious.

T: Okay and then?

C: I don't know it never goes any further than that, that is where the surface fear is.

T: All right, now suppose they do give you a shot.

C: Having to do something I don't want to do, against my will, I think.

T: That is really a helpless position they are putting you into?

C: Yeah, that is how I feel.

T: Do you ever have any concerns about going crazy?

C: Oh yeah! (Looking agitated) I've been assured though that that won't happen.

T: Good. That would be the ultimate loss of control, huh?

C: Yeah, becoming psychotic.

T: And then what would happen to you?

C: When I think of something like that happening to me I think, "Well now someone else can take care of me." So maybe its the old wish behind the fear.

T: Where did you get that idea?

C: That's what Dr. P. told me it was about.

The client is next asked about how her relationship with her husband is currently, and she replies that all is well—better than ever. Further information about the onset and the course of her fear development is elicited. She reported that there were a number of panic attacks during the first year after onset and that they had decreased over subsequent years until 2 years before coming into therapy. At that time she began to again have more frequent panic attacks and increased limitations.

The following verbatim exchange illustrates the process of giving information to clients who suffer from this problem.

T: We all get anxious at times, we all get fear sometimes, it is absolutely inevitable. And there is no way that we can avoid fear and still live in the world. With you, it seems that when that happens it brings out sort of additional fears; it spirals out of control.

C: Yes.

T: So the first sensations that you get, maybe your heart beats a little fast or some other signals from your body come along, and you interpret this as "Here it comes again" and that makes it worse.

C: Yeah, I get thrown into panic.

T: The panic is set off by something that you think.

(T plants the suggestion that panics do not come "out of the blue" but arise from definite stimuli, which implies the possibility of controlling them.)

C: Right.

T: What kinds of thoughts come into your head when you are afraid?

C: Being alone, I guess. All right, the very recent—I was on my way home from work; being at work, the only thing that I would think about that would make me afraid being at work is having to leave and come home again, is if there would be a traffic jam on the way home, and I felt panic.

T: First of all you were feeling a little bit uncomfortable?

C: Right, because I was in this traffic jam I was trapped, and there was no place to go. If I wanted to get home, I had to stay where I was. There was no one to help me. I always think well, I can pull off the road and use the telephone.

Note how C rehearses avoidance behaviors covertly. Such habits maintain fear of fear.

T: So you were thinking these things?

C: Yeah, right.

T: And at the same time getting more upset?

C: Right, I get to the point where I do almost pass out; I roll down the windows and try to calm myself down.

T: Let's see if we can go through that and see each step in detail. A traffic jam occurs and you get some sensations. It comes first when you start to think, "There is no one to help me, I'm in a traffic jam and I can't get any help now" and then the sensation?

C: I always thought of this happening simultaneously. I never thought of them as happening one and then the other.

T: Okay, then you think of a way that you can get out of it—pull over to the side of the road, make a telephone call.

C: Usually I think of fleeing, get out; that is always my first reaction. But then when I realize that there isn't a way out, I realize that I'm going to have to deal with it.

T: Then what?

C: Then I just sort of talk myself out of it by saying, "Well in 5 minutes you'll be out of here you can just sit here it will be all right."

T: And then you feel all right?

C: Yeah, usually.

T: So what you say to yourself is really important. You say that sometimes you feel as though you are going to pass out.

C: From hyperventilating.

T: And that is under control?

C: Yeah, I start concentrating on my breathing. Take deep breaths and hold it and let it out slowly. It usually helps, but it is hard to do when you are in a panic.

T: Another thing you can do is to breathe through your nose then you can't get enough air to hyperventilate. Do you get a sensation of dizziness too?

C: Dizziness, lightheaded, dry mouth.

T: Do you sometimes have the feeling that you are the only person who goes through this?

C: I look around at people and say, "Look at them they can go anywhere they want and they don't even think about it." And I think here I am stuck with living within 10 miles of my house. I don't want anyone to know that I go through these things because its kind of silly to tell somebody, they can't understand. Even my husband doesn't understand. And I feel embarrassed.

T: In spite of the fact that you have looked around and you haven't seen anyone else feeling the same way, what you describe is fairly common: a lot of people experience it.

C: Really, this type of thing?

T: There is a name for it, agoraphobia; probably 35,000 people in the Philadelphia area have it.

C: Really!

T: Yes, up to now it has been very difficult to deal with in the traditional types of therapy, but we have a program here that is really quite effective for most people.

C: Why didn't this other therapy work? It helped me in other ways, but never even got close to helping me with this.

(Most people come to us feeling discouraged by the failure of former therapies. Giving them a positive expectation for this new therapeutic endeavor is important in raising motivation for the difficult tasks ahead.)

T: Well, I'll be able to tell you a whole lot more after we spend more time together. But one thing certainly is clear: you developed a type of conditioned fear out of the very experience itself, out of having those first panics. Certain events take on the capacity to trigger it off again: body sensations, certain thoughts, the thought of being out of control, and so forth. This is independent of anything else that has happened to you in your life. It is purely an emotional learning experience formed out of that first series of traumatic panic events, and no amount of talking about it is going to change it.

C: So it wasn't from something in my past?

T: Maybe the first panic attacks were brought about by interpersonal events and the situation that you were in at that time, and perhaps you are still in need of resolving some of those interpersonal conflicts. The fact that you did not know what was happening to you when you panicked, that you interpreted them as physical disorders or as going crazy, was important in the development of the fears as you now experience them.

C: Hum—why or how is this therapy different from the other?

T: We are going to work specifically with some technical interventions that are designed to reverse that emotional learning experience related to those events. For example, we will work on ways that you can feel under control when you're feeling frightened—ways in which you can reverse it. Different controls work for different people; we will find what works best for you. If you can handle the anxiety situations, then all of the anticipatory anxiety goes away.

C: O.K.!

T: And what that involves is to reorient ourselves as to what the problem is. At this point, I think you probably are operating on the assumption that it is best not to get afraid and just stay away from places that are going to make you afraid, because as long as you do that, you won't have these panic attacks and generally feel better off. The problem with avoiding places is that you tend to avoid more and more places. Then you build up fears, and that goes on your list, and ultimately it spreads to different areas. I have seen people completely housebound.

C: Really?

T: It just gets worse when you get into the habit of avoiding the situations. On the other hand, if you just keep going while continuing to panic, well, that isn't good either, you just keep going through the terrible experiences without much let up.

C: You would think, "Well, if I go the next time, it will be easier for me because I will have realized that nothing happened." But it doesn't work that way.

T: It is not the place and not the distance that you are afraid of; it's being out of control or that you may pass out or go crazy. The only way you are going to feel comfortable is when you get a little scared, and you are able to reverse it. That is the thing that is going to be very important. Instead of avoiding places that you think will make you scared, I am going to tell you to go out and get scared. Not go any place in particular, just get scared.

C: (Sarcastically) Terrific!

T: Each time you go out and get a little scared and you are able to control it, that is therapeutic. Our role together will be to work on ways that you can get the control. My role is to be your ally in developing these ways. Your role will be to go out and try your new armament and see how it works. So there will be some emphasis on travel: not to just push yourself into situations but rather to set up opportunities just to practice being in control. The next couple of sessions I would like to get more information about the interpersonal aspects that went along with the development of the fears that we talked about.

(T does some "socialization" of C concerning her part in the therapeutic process. C needs to understand that she will be an active partner in treatment.)

C: I just thought of something. Is it possible that this would have come about because I no longer see L? I have noticed that it has gotten worse just since I haven't been seeing him.

T: How long has that been?

C: Two years.

T: So things got worse when you broke off with him?

C: Yes, I never put those two things together before, but I just happened to think of it now.

T: It does sound as though your relationship with him is implicated from those two bits of information. It is usually the case that these fears develop as a result of interpersonal conflict.

In the second session the client reported that she had been anxious in anticipation of making the trip into the therapy session and that her anxiety led to a lack of communication between her and her husband on the way into the session. Exploration of the details of their interaction was attempted, but little information was forthcoming. A continuation of the history of the problem and conditions at its onset was pursued. The following edited verbatim interaction brings out some important information.

T: As I recall, you were 21 at the time and there were a couple of occasions when you had panic attacks. One was in the car while you were driving, and there were some friends and a lot of kids in the car, and you had a sort of sense of being responsible for these people. Also as I recall, at that time a man who had some previous involvement with you was returning from the service, and you were worried because you had to make a choice between him and your husband at that time. Can you tell me about that?

C: I had stayed in contact with him throughout the time he was in the service.

T: You knew him for a long time?

C: In high school.

T: He was your high school boyfriend?

C: We were very close, and I wasn't too happy at home with my parents so I kind of looked to him for all the guidance and reassurance that I would have looked to my father for. I guess.

T: Because your father was not available in a sense?

C: He was there—physically. So we had this very heavy relationship, and we had planned to get married.

T: This was while you were still in high school?

C: Yes. We planned to marry after high school. We had all of these big plans, but things just didn't work out. That is when I met H.

T: What do you mean, it didn't work out?

C: He was taking me for granted. He was being nasty. I took it for a long time and would say "Maybe things will get better." I just kept putting it off doing something about it. I guess I reached a point where I just said, "I don't need this anymore," and then I met H who was older.

T: Were you still in high school at this time?

C: Yes, I guess this was my junior year, the end of my junior year in high school. H and I started dating. But I still felt a lot for L; I still felt very close to him and felt that we could talk.

T: What kind of things were going on at home at this ume?

C: When I was in high school?

T: Yes.

C: Well, I was just not getting along with my parents at all, and I felt that I just wanted to get out and just get away, and I saw H as this way of getting out. He had a good job. He had been in the service, and he was out. He had gone through school and was 7 ½ years older than I, and I just saw this as an escape.

(This pattern of going from one situation of dependency (on parents) to others (L then H) is typical.)

T: How did it turn out?

C: When I met H, I decided that I wanted to go out with him, but this didn't terminate it with L. He would still come over and he would still call. I thought I was sure, and yet there are times I had doubt.

T: And over a period of time you eventually gravitated toward H? When did you get married, when you were out of school?

C: Nine years ago—I was in my senior year.

T: In high school?

C: Yes.

T: What kind of relationship did you have with H?

C: I would say that we were getting along. You know that first year, after we got married, yes, we were getting along pretty well.

T: You didn't have doubts about the relationship at that time?

C: I had doubts the day I got married. It must have been that I was telling myself something, and it wasn't right. When I was getting married, I was thinking, if this doesn't work out, then I am making a mistake. But I think everyone feels that way. I don't remember exactly what the circumstances were, but I saw L about a year later. Oh yes, he was going into the service a year later and he came over to tell me he was going into the service, and that he was going away and wanted to let me know that he was leaving.

T: How did you receive that?

C: I don't really remember. I really didn't think about it very much. It didn't bother me. I guess that I had decided that this is it, and this is my responsibility. When L showed up, I still had feelings for him, but I wasn't upset about it.

T: And you had contact with him while he was in the service?

C: Yes, when he would come home on leave, he would get in touch with me. And I guess it was then I started doubting my true feelings about what was really happening.

T: You were in conflict at this point. Did that affect your relationship with your husband?

C: Oh yes.

T: In what ways?

C: I would find fault with the things that H was doing. It definitely put a strain on the relationship.

T: Were you feeling that you didn't want to be there anymore or were you not sure?

C: I was thinking maybe I didn't want to be there. At the same time I wasn't sure, I didn't know what I wanted. I still don't.

(There is a strong suggestion here that the conflict which was present at onset still remains and will have to be dealt with in the therapy. In some cases the original conflict has since been resolved and the fear of fear operates autonomously; in such a case it may be possible to get lasting positive results without having to focus on the interpersonal aspects of the client's life.)

Paradoxical instructions (for goal 4) are given in this session as follows:

T: Okay, we talked a little bit the last time about the fact that what seems to be happening is that you are *apprehensive about getting afraid* rather than afraid of places. What we need to do is find ways for you to get control.

C: I was pretty upset when we came here, and I have been feeling that way anymore. I don't know. I'm so used to suppressing and trying and trying to get away from that feeling that reversing it—trying to make it come on is hard.

T: When you are upset, what actual physical sensations are you most aware of?

C: Usually my heart pounding. I try and make myself aware of what my body is going through. My muscles tense up.

T: What muscles?

C: My facial muscles. I had to drive downtown everyday for a week last March, and sometimes I would feel like I couldn't breathe, my throat would tighten up. Sometimes, all of my muscles would tighten up so I would feel that I wouldn't be able to stand up.

T: Is there one cue that you get that panic is coming, heart pounding for example?

C: Probably, that bothers me too.

T: How is that?

C: My heart pounding. The other things are all just symptoms, and that is more a physical thing than the others.

T: And what is that an implication of?

C: Well, your heart does so many things, pumping blood through, and maybe because I am putting so much stress on it that something is going to go wrong (C shows signs of increasing anxiety).

T: This is a scary topic for you?

C: Yes.

T: Are you afraid that you are going to have a heart attack or stroke?

C: Yes, I really don't dwell on that, but I am aware when my heart pounds.

T: What are you worried about?

C: Just that it is going to stop.

T: From the stress?

C: Because I feel that I go through this so many times, the stress situation, that one time, you know, one more and that will be it.

T: So as soon as you start getting a little bit uncomfortable, you start to worry, well I have to get it under control otherwise this may be the time?

C: Yes.

T: So, for you, some sensations of uneasiness spiral into panic.

C: Yes, even being physically ill, not a cold but maybe a flu or fever, that is a frightening thing because maybe there is some kind of disease.

(Thus agoraphobics may develop general hypochondriacal concerns in addition to fear of fear. This is a generalization of anxiety to any "abnormal" interoceptive stimuli.)

T: What kind of disease?

C: I don't know; it is just a feeling that I don't have control over that kind of thing, getting sick. (Reacting to T's facial expression) Are you stuck?

T: As I mentioned before, I would like you to gain additional control so that when you get a little frightened, you will have a sense of being in control. This means that we have to look at your fears in a different way than you have before. The task becomes *not* going to distant places or a new place and *feeling comfortable*, but what we have to do is focus on what you do when you feel uncomfortable. Whether it is at home or here or while traveling. The therapy is actually done every time you are able to be anxious and stay with it *without avoiding your sensations or escaping the place in which you find yourself*. This week, instead of trying to distract yourself, try and make the anxiety worse. In other words, I want you to try and give up the struggle to control it directly. As soon as you get into that fight about control, and watching yourself to see if it works there is no way you can win. So what I would like you to do instead is make it worse. There are two advantages in this. The first is that you really have to find out— my telling you isn't going to be sufficient and nobody else telling you is going to be sufficient—that you can't die from this, and as long as you are healthy and your heart is healthy, no amount of stress is going to drive your heart into stopping. But my telling you just isn't going to make a difference. There is a cycle that is normal and begins with a surge of anxiety, perhaps because you are anticipating panic; if you don't fight it, it subsides very quickly. Thoughts of disaster that follow this first feeling, in fact, perpetuate your fears. If you don't feed it, the fear will subside. It is important for you to find out that it will terminate on its own if you don't do the things you usually do—fight it, have catastrophic thoughts such as "This may get out of control, I may get out of control, I may end up in a hospital."

C: That is the first thing, I get that feeling, and all of these things start running through my head.

T: And what you do is try to distract yourself with other thoughts because you are saying that you must control it. You don't have to control it because as soon as you give up control, you also do away with the thing that perpetuates it. Does that make any sense?

C: What I am to do is give into it?

T: Yes, and even try to make it worse. You will find out that if you really adopt this attitude, it is not so awful, it will be over sooner because it has a natural tendency to reduce. A way that you can try to make it worse is concentrate on your heart and try to make it pump faster.

C: I should do this even though it feels like it is coming through my ears?

T: Yes, now this is easier said than done because you have a high habit strength in response to this event. So I want you to go out and just keep going until you get anxious, and when you do, stop there but do not turn back. *This is very important. You do not turn back until you feel calm and that is a primary rule.* If you turn back then you further perpetuate the problem and increase the probability of getting upset the next time. Everytime you do that you reinforce retreat as a method of dealing with it. Getting back to safety becomes the only thing that counts. But if you stay out there, wherever it may be, and try to force your heart to beat fast and let it go through its cycle, then on that occasion you will have done something very therapeutic. It is only through those kinds of activities that you can begin to deal with it. Remember, your task is not to go out comfortably; you have been operating with that set and you have to give that up. If you get anxious, that is good, if you don't get anxious, keep going until you do.

In the third session the client reported that she had tried to increase her heart rate when she got anxious traveling and that, much to her surprise, the uncomfortable feelings diminished. She continued to drive on that occasion and was unable to bring the symptoms back. She made other trips during the week but avoided situations that she felt might be overwhelming such as expressways. We again discussed the necessity of not avoiding, but instead putting herself in situations that she feels would most likely cause anxiety.

We agreed that she would keep trying during the ensuing week and that she would drive to the next session by herself. We talked about her feelings about trips to Delaware to visit H's parents. She said that she was uncomfortable there and felt like an outsider even though H's parents treated her well. She said that she liked them and was glad to have them come to her house. However, her first panic attack was on a trip to Delaware to visit them and therefore she would not go back because of her "sickness."

During the week she called to say that she had gone out driving by herself at night, which she had not done in years, but that she was upset because H was upset with her and they were not speaking. The therapist assured her that she had done well with the traveling and encouraged her to keep it up. He suggested that H might come into the session with her next time, but to come to the fourth session alone.

At the beginning of the fourth session C said that she had driven in by herself, but it was a horrible experience.

T: What happened on the trip? Did you try to make your heart beat faster?

C: It seemed to get better. It is not a comfortable feeling.

T: Well tell me how it went from the beginning.

C: It wasn't too bad from the beginning.

T: Did you have any concerns about it before you left?

C: Oh yes!

T: You were worried?

C: Well H and I are still not speaking; I don't know what I have to give up of myself in order to get along with him. I just started realizing it. I don't know why, but I just feel that I don't want to do that any more. I tried to talk to him the other night, and he said "If you want to be self sufficient and independent, go right ahead because you don't need me." I kind of get the feeling that he is as much afraid of it as I am.

T: Of your becoming independent?

C: Yes, I just feel that in order for him to get along with me that he needs me to be dependent on him. I have been feeling this week, and I don't know why this week, that I have been sacrificing so much of the way that I feel about myself. Like coming here today—just before I left he said "If I didn't know any better, I would swear that you were going out today and getting laid." So I get the feeling that that is the way he thinks of me if he is not with me. I know it shouldn't bother me—the way he thinks about me—because I should be more concerned with the way I think about myself and that is what I am trying to get into.

It is frequently the case that as the symptomatic partner starts to become more independent, the other becomes distressed and exerts pressure to return to the previous state of equilibrium. It is apparent here too that the conflicts in the relationship come into awareness as the travel fears decrease, possibly due to the fact that obsessing about symptoms and the ensuing dependency calms the waters in that the symptomatic partner's dependent behavior reassures the other. When the symptomatic partner begins to act more independently, the fears of the other are again triggered.

T: What led to this?

C: Nothing. I felt perfectly calm this morning, and I said that I have an appointment, and I have to leave now, and that is all I said.

T: And you hadn't been speaking since last Friday?

C: Since last Friday.

T: Can you go back over that? I would like to get a clearer picture of that.

C: His parents were going to spend the weekend, and I don't know, I just, we always seem to argue before they come. Things seem to settle down once they get there. But that didn't happen.

T: You were at odds, but things didn't settle down?

C: Yes, I was uptight and not really understanding why. I was really feeling uptight when his parents were there. I am not sure, but I think it is the way I feel towards his mother. When H and I told them that we were going to get married, she was really upset, I mean really upset. She would call me and cry over the phone. She said a lot of really bad things to me. My father saw that I was really upset, and he said that no matter what happens, don't you say anything back to her because then you won't have anything to feel sorry for or anything to apologize for later, but she will.

(One can readily see how the client learned to inhibit the expression of feelings.)

T: What was she so upset about?

C: She was upset because I was getting married to H.

T: Why would that make her so upset?

C: Because he was Jewish and I was Catholic.

T: It was a religious issue then?

C: Yes. She said that I am comparing you to Hitler and this is the worse thing that could happen since Hitler. So it ruined everything. She wouldn't come to the wedding, and it was a terrible thing for me.

T: It must have been very difficult for you to have to go to their home in Delaware.

C: Well, he went out there just before we were going to get married and my father said to me "Don't go and leave yourself wide open because she is going to have all the relatives there and you are leaving yourself vulnerable to her feelings"; and I went anyway because H wanted me to go and it was a disaster. It was terrible. I came back with a really bad headache, a migraine, all the way home. I know that you are supposed to forgive and I have. She has been really nice to me, but I can't forget.

T: I understand.

C: I have never said anything to her, but I think I wanted to.

T: Yes, I don't know how you held it back this long.

C: Well, what good would it do?

T: Well, I guess it wouldn't do any harm if you told her how upsetting it was for you.

C: But it is over now—what good would it do telling her now!!

(Here the therapist tries to begin some assertiveness training, but the client is not yet ready.)

T: Okay.

C: So I think that is why we had so much trouble in the beginning.

T: I can understand why you were so anxious when you went to their house that time for the holidays. It really puts it in context. So they came this weekend, and you were feeling a lot of the old pain and anger for her that goes way back.

(T points out how feelings about her mother-in-law were antecedents to the panic attack C ascribed to the distance from home (Goal 3).)

C: Sunday, I told H that I didn't want to go with him because his cousin was supposed to come along with us.

T: Had his parents gone back yet?

C: No, they were going to go to New Jersey, it was like a family reunion, and we were all going to go over to New Jersey. H's cousin had called, and she said that she needed a ride, and I don't like her because she is sort of a pushy and snobby person, and I just didn't want to be in the same car with her especially under those circumstances. If I did get upset, I wouldn't be able to verbalize it and I would have to keep everything in, and I didn't want to put myself in that situation; so I told H that I didn't want to go especially under those circumstances. He was furious, and he started to carry on. I walked out. My son had told me that H had made a big thing in front of his parents. He told them that I wasn't going and that I was playing a game, but it was really because his cousin was going in the car, and I didn't feel comfortable with her. So I was ready for anything and if anyone had come near me or said anything to me, I was ready to bite their head off.

(Clients with social anxiety may be markedly more likely to panic in the presence of a person they perceive as particularly judgmental.)

T: You weren't feeling scared, you were feeling angry?

C: Right. I was really angry. I was just waiting for his mother to say something to me; it would have given me the opportunity to let all of those feelings go. His father had said something to me, but I had said that I really didn't want to go. Well, I guess that is about all. I asked H if we should sit down and talk about it, and he said "No, I don't want to talk." So I started to think that it is always on his terms, you know, that we always have to get things straightened out when he is ready. We have never let things go this long without discussing it. The scary thing was, the night before last he called me from work. He started to talk about our son, and I said "Do you want to talk?" He said "I don't feel like talking," and I said "Well, I don't want to talk either, goodbye!" and I hung up. I really started feeling scared about that. Because I am alienating him, and the more I push him away, the more I have to stand on my own.

T: It is scary to be on your own. What scares you?

C: Well, when you think about it, I lived with my parents until I was eighteen, and then I married H, and I never have been on my own, never. And I keep thinking that I want to try it.

T: But you have to find out if it can be done?

C: Right, I think now, that I can, but I am not sure about giving up 9 years work of marriage.

T: Sure.

C: Just to see if I can be independent, but I'd like to be independent, but still be with H. It is possible for me, but I don't know if it is possible for him. So it is like a really big decision for me to make. You know, go ahead and try it, be daring, but at the same time I have to remember that I might be losing something.

C's ambivalent state is clear here, one that was so actively in evidence at onset of the problem. Having again come clearly in touch with the conflict, it can be expected that the client may find herself in the same avoidance condition with a new rash of phobias about traveling. It is important that the therapist not allow this to occur. He/she must continue to encourage the client to stay in contact with the conflict and attempt resolution. The client will need a great deal of help in making connections between the interpersonal events and outbreaks of symptoms.

T: You called to tell me about one evening when you went out all by yourself, and drove by yourself. What was his reaction to that?

C: I didn't tell him.

T: He still doesn't know? Has he, in some way, seen you act more independently?

C: I certainly feel that I have been.

T: In terms of what? Your interaction with him?

C: Yes, standing my ground for a change.

T: And driving here today by yourself.

C: I think not giving into him for once; he would start saying something and trying to pull me into an argument just so we could have some conversation, and I would not answer him. I wasn't short with him; I just was very calm.

T: Ordinarily, you would give in?

C: Well, that is the way I see it. He may not see it that way.

T: I am interested in *your* perception and how you feel.

C: As far as our relationship, yes, that is how I see it.

T: When you told H this morning that you were coming yourself, how did he respond?

C: I don't know, but anytime I go out, and I haven't done it in so long I had forgotten about his reactions, but that is always his reaction. I used to feel that, well, hell, if he is really going to think that, then I may as well go out and do something like that. Since he already thinks that way about me, then I may as well go out and do something, whatever it is he thinks I am doing. I can see that now, so what, it is his problem if he wants to think of me, you know, he has to deal with that, but I don't have to.

T: That had really scared you because the feeling that something terrible will happen if he gets angry enough.

C: Yes.

T: What do you suppose will really happen?

C: Well, like before, I might go and do what he says I am doing.

T: So your fears are related to what you are going to do and not what he is going to do. And what might you do?

C: Well, I might have an affair with someone.

T: Do you feel a need for an affair?

C: No, I don't know, yes and no. I can feel it, and then I can rationalize it. I can feel, yes, I do, and then if I think about it, I will think, well, all I am doing is just replacing H. I am just giving into my fear again of being on my own. I am seeking someone else.

T: So someone else takes the place of that support system? It will be important for you to stand on your own two feet to get over this.

C: But I don't want to stop dealing with other people either; that is what confuses me.

T: I am not sure that I understand.

C: I don't want to go out with someone else, even though I feel that I would like to; I'm not sure that I understood what I said either—I just don't want to get those two things confused and say "Well, maybe I am just using that person as a substitute for H."

T: I see.

C: I think maybe what I am going to have to look at is how I see that person and if I see that person as a crutch, someone that I need to know where they are all of the time that type of thing, then it is a substitute for H; but if I really enjoy being with that person and just enjoy the company that is the other side.

T: I think that it is going to be important too to learn to deal with H and feel good about yourself with him. Whether or not the relationship works, it is important for you to come out of it feeling good about yourself.

C: Yes, I thought about that too. I have to have a better self image.

T: Are there issues now with H in need of dealing with?

C: No, I haven't just been thinking about just one issue—it is the total relationship; I think maybe I should just kind of slow down a little bit and just take one thing at a time. It is really hard to deal with one big lump. It seems like such a sudden change. I didn't feel this way last week. Why? There is a lot to think about.

T: Yes, what happens is, you have focused on your fears of going out, which keeps you from thinking about these things; also not going out has reduced the conflict in the relationship. Now that you are acting more independently the old conflicts come back into focus. It will be important for us to work toward resolution of these interpersonal problems so that you don't fall back into obsessing about your symptoms.

C: I had asked H earlier if he would come with me. I didn't even get all of the words out.

T: What did he say?

C: He got really angry, which didn't surprise me because I had asked him to go when I used to go to Dr. P, and he did go for a while and then he came away from it saying "That is silly and if it works for you, fine you go, I don't need it." And he still feels that way; he doesn't want to help me with my problems. So I don't push him; I just say okay.

T: What did you say to him when you asked him to come?

C: I just said that Dr. G would like to see both of us together. I think that it would be a good idea under the circumstances because of what is going on. Usually I would wait until the right moment to say something to him, but there was no right moment at this point. But I haven't felt as bad as I had felt before. You know, I just haven't felt as bad about myself, and I haven't felt that I have to have him on my good side or I have to have him with me in order to feel good about myself. I can go and do things I want to do and not necessarily have his approval. He comments on the clothes that I wear, the way the covers are arranged, everything, how I drive, and I never noticed it before. That is what really puzzles me the most; why I never noticed it before.

(This is probably not accurate. C has probably noticed these things before but pushed them out of awareness, as too threatening to attempt to resolve.)

T: All of these things are springing into awareness?

C: Yes, all at once. And usually his working at nights would bother me more than when he works during the day, but it hasn't bothered me this week. During the day I am really busy doing the things that I have to do, but at night I have a lot of time to myself. So being there by myself should really bother me if he were working nights this week, but it hasn't. I have been doing my yoga and reading and doing some Christmas shopping and taking the kids someplace, and no problem. So where do we go from here?

T: We are on the right track. Could you tell me more about what the trip was like for you, coming here? When you left the house, you were already upset because H had been on your back.

C: I tried to overlook that. I didn't want to come down here feeling angry and saying to myself "Well, I'll show you." I didn't want to do that, I wanted to do it for me, and it didn't bother me until I got about 10 minutes from here and then I started to think "I am getting upset and maybe I will do something to hurt myself." That went through my mind and that was very scary. I thought that if it gets so bad that I can't stand it, maybe I will run out in front of a car or something trying to escape the feeling, and I thought about that and that seemed to be the scariest thing, and then when I got on the expressway, and I saw the traffic backed up, and I said "Oh terrific!, this is the ultimate test," and when I was sitting there I could feel my heart pounding, and I thought "Okay, what are you going to do? All of these people are going to honk their horns at you. If you just stick with the flow of traffic and just hang in there, you can see up ahead that the traffic is starting to move, and everything is just going to be fine, so, if you are just uncomfortable for a short time, it will be over." That is talking myself out of it, isn't it? It is not facing it. I have to.

T: Or else?

C: I have to fight it. I know this sounds ridiculous, but otherwise it is going to take over. That is just the way I feel, and then I won't be me anymore.

T: What will happen?

C: I don't know.

T: Who will be you?

C: I won't be anybody (with tears forming in her eyes).

T: What will it be like?

C: Do you have any tissues?

T: Yes (T hands box of tissues to C).

C: I don't know what will happen.

T: Something right now is really upsetting for you.

C: Whatever it is that is making me upset, I want to face it; but it's too frightening now.

T: Something inside of you is taking over?

C: There is definitely something taking over. There is something there.

T: What is the feeling?

C: I feel bad that I haven't faced it, but I thought I had.

T: There is no need beating yourself. You are working hard at this.

C: Yes, but I had felt that I had gotten stronger.

T: You have.

C: Not if this thing is still forcing me down, I haven't.

T: Well, we haven't gotten rid of your habit, but you still got yourself here. You are standing up for what you feel and what you say, and what you are, even though that is causing conflict, these are important and difficult steps.

C: Is it worth it? I keep asking myself that. Is it worth it and all of these things that are happening. It is coming down here and being that upset, is it worth it? I think that I have said for too long it is not worth it, and I have given into it. But I wish I could face what it was.

T: We will find out. I promise you that nothing is going to sweep you away; we will just take it as it comes, huh?

C: But I am not young anymore. What do I have to do to deal with what is there?

T: You have to let it take over and find out that it is not something to be scared about. It seems really scary, I know.

C: Just let go?

T: Yes, just let go and not only let go, but help it along. I know that that is very hard.

C: It is so easy for you to say it, and sit there and tell me just let go.

T: I know that it is very hard for you—absolutely terrifying.

C: But when it is happening, all I want to do is stop the feeling. That is all, that is all that is on my mind.

T: I know that is what makes it so hard, that it is so extraordinarily terrifying. The way to feel better is just to let it go until you get rid of it. The way you are doing it, you avoid it, and it will always come back.

C: I don't like things that I am unsure of. I am afraid.

T: Can we imagine the worst possible catastrophe? Let's get back into the car and into the traffic jam, can you do that?

C: Okay.

T: Okay, let's get back into the car and into the traffic jam and lets see what happens. Could you put yourself back into that situation? You

are driving along and you get onto the expressway and you see the
traffic mounting up ahead and you say "Oh no! great"; and the traffic
is practically standing still and the car is pulling up behind, and there
is no way out. Do you see that?

C: I can see it, but I am holding back. I just can't get into it. I keep
thinking to myself, here if I do get upset. . . .

T: Go ahead.

C: If I do get upset, then I am too far away from anyone that can do
something.

T: And how will you ever get help? And all of those terrible things
that you are afraid of will happen.

C: That is it.

T: And all of those terrible things will take over. He won't be there
and you will lose all control. What will you do? What will this state of
being do? Is it evil, is it dangerous, does it kill?

(C avoids the tack T is pursuing and succeeds in diverting T onto another course. It was probably best to let it drop here, as her trust in T was
insufficient in the face of her fear; however, T would have done better to
simply recognize that fact and empathize with the feeling, suggesting that
at a later time C would overcome her fear.)

C: It is not that bad. I am thinking about my parents. When I get too
far from them, I will be alone and if I leave—that is like telling them I
don't need their help anymore. And if I don't need their help anymore, I won't be able to ask them for help. If I am not able to ask
them for help, then I will really be alone.

T: Have you ever thought about the fact that they will die some day?

C: But then they are leaving me, I am not leaving them.

T: How did they feel about you leaving them?

C: My mother has to know what I am doing so she can decide whether
it is right or wrong. And if it has to do with another man, then it is
wrong. Like anytime I go someplace, she will ask me where I have
been and what I was doing. So I guess that I feel guilty about the
things that I do when I am away from her.

T: If she is not there to sort of keep checks on you and H is not there
to check on you.

C: Then I might do something that they would consider wrong.

T: Well, what would that be?

C: I just told you. Going out with someone else.

T: And being away from that sort of protection is making you vulnerable?

C: Yes, I was stuck. On the inside lane and there was a guardrail and I was just kind of closed in with no way to the people that would help me and that is how I felt.

T: And without that help, what would you do?

(T attempts to get back on track.)

C: Lose control and start yelling and screaming. I guess, I don't know.

T: People would gather around you?

C: Yes. But no one there would be able to help me.

T: And what would happen then? Maybe they would call an ambulance and sedate you and rush you off to the hospital. Then you wouldn't be in control.

C: Right, I might stay that way forever. I don't know.

T: You would be crazy then and they would lock you away.

C: Yes, and I wouldn't be able to get out, and that to me is just as scary as being stuck in a traffic jam.

T: You would be locked away for life. In the hands of people that don't really care about you. Your parents wouldn't be able to come to your rescue. And you would have to stay that way the rest of your life in that horrible state of panic.

C: And that is the way I feel a lot of the time.

T: Like you are crazy?

C: Yes.

T: And that something else will take over. This desire of another man.

C: I don't know.

T: What is there about you that is crazy?

C: My feelings that when I get upset or depressed then I think that other people are not like that, and that I am the only one who feels that way. It is not the normal way to feel.

T: Feelings of depression? Feelings of anger?

C: When I was younger, I remember being ridiculed a lot and there wasn't very much praise, and now that I am away from that, H tells me all the time that I am crazy.

T: How is that?

C: He tells me all of the time.

T: That you are crazy?

C: Yes, he comes right out and says "You're crazy and your whole family is crazy."

T: What do you do to make him say that you're crazy?

C: He just tells me that my whole family is crazy.

T: Who in your family?

(Again the diversion occurs.)

C: Everybody.

T: What do they do that makes them seem crazy?

C: I don't know, I guess its just the things that go on everyday.

T: Do you think that they are crazy?

C: No, they are just people trying to live. I don't think that they are any different from other families.

T: What are the things that happen to upset you?

C: I don't know. It is just that my sisters had a hard time getting along when they lived there. I have two younger sisters, so a lot of times I would talk to them and try to help them because I remember what it was like to go through that, and he would hear me talking to them, and he would shake his head and say "All of you girls are crazy." It's just that, all of the time, and then I guess I put his opinion of me over what I thought of myself. I would listen to him, and I started believing it. I guess if I believe it, then I have to feel that way, right?

T: You have to be on guard against your own feeling, so it doesn't take over, that the craziness doesn't take over.

C: It would make me angry when he said it, but I could see myself getting angry at him and looking crazy at the same time.

T: You see anger as being crazy?

C: Yes, I can see myself getting really angry with him and I would start screaming and I would say, you know, I am, look at me, I am crazy. Yelling and screaming and carrying on, now that is crazy.

T: Does any one in your family yell?

C: My father yells, and my mother is very quiet. My father yells all of the time.

T: So for you, being angry is being crazy.

C: I get scared when I get angry, yes.

T: It must be hard for you to sort out if you are angry or scared. Sometimes when you get angry you get scared?

C: Maybe I really am angry.

T: Well, we all experience anger. You would be the exception if you didn't. I sure would be angry if I was told I was crazy all of the time.

C: That is silly to listen to that. I wouldn't get angry if I didn't listen to it, and then he wouldn't do it. He does it because it really hurts me. It hurts and then I get angry.

T: It sounds perfectly normal to me.

C: Then those things that people said about me would not bother me.

T: I think it is hard not to let things bother you from people who you really care about. It you felt stronger about yourself, you could stand up for yourself and confront issues and perhaps change that interaction. But you are not going to be left indifferent. How do you get your feelings met by someone caring about you, you know those kinds of things that we all have needs for?

C: I would say that the only thing I can think about is sex. The way I think of it is if you have sex with a person that you really care about, then that is your way of showing that you really feel something for lationship? Just treating the other person like a person.

T: This role is important. And ignoring it is not going to make it much better.

C: Well, why can't you just say "Oh well, that is their problem and they will have to learn to deal with it?" "If they want to say those things, then they can." You shouldn't make it so that you take it so personally.

T: You have basiç needs that need to be met that come from a relationship. And it sounds like those are not being met particularly well, and it is important for you to get what you can, to get what you need.

C: I don't know what I need right now; I am like right in the middle.

T: I understand that what you are experiencing now is that a few things are pretty bad that I wasn't even aware of. That is a lot to deal with and expect yourself to come out with a clear head and having all of this sort of coming down on you at this point. But you are not powerless in this situation. Hopefully we will find ways to get more good things from your husband. If that is what you want. Of course there is a lot of anger right now. That is okay and I wouldn't want you to deny that. I don't suppose that it has any impact, but I can assure you that you are not crazy, that you don't have what it takes, there is a certain precondition for craziness that you don't have. What you have is a fear about your own feelings.

C: When you are in high school, and someone says that they are going to a psychiatrist, you think that that person is crazy, but I think a lot of people still think that way, and maybe I feel bad about myself because I am here. Like H said the other day, everytime the bills come, he says "Oh you should have married a shrink, at least your bills wouldn't be so high.'' I guess that I am supposed to feel guilty about that and I said "You should have married a surgeon," because he has been in the hospital several times. I wanted to show him that just because I go to a certain doctor and you have to doesn't make any difference. Is that the way I should deal with those situations? Or should I just ignore them.

T: Did you feel better after you got through?

C: I felt fine.

T: Then you did all right. That is the criteria for how you handle it. How you feel about it.

C: Well normally that would make me angry—his saying it would make me angry, and I would start yelling and then I would feel bad about myself. I am doing it, I am creating the hurt that made me feel guilty.

T: It is important for you to be able to communicate to him the pain that it causes you and the hurt.

C: Communicate to him! I think that is what he is looking for.

T: Then why don't you speak to him?

C: I don't want to give in to that.

T: Okay, I am sorry that he won't come in.

C: I think he thinks about that.

T: These are going to be hard times if you won't deal with them, and he is going to put a lot of pressure on you.

C: I can see that.

T: To revert back to your more dependent stage.

C: But I don't know how to get out of the situation that we are in now. I have approached him saying "Let's talk." I am not going to bend over backwards, and it could go on like this.

T: Can you hold your feelings back?

C: Well, if I have held it this long, and I felt good about holding it too, really. Not just out of anger, but because the way I really believe. But there has been no human communication, there has been no. . . .

T: It has been really lonely, huh?

C: Yes, I think that is what bothers me the most, and I think that is what I miss the most, and I think that's why I had given in in the past.

T: And everytime you give into that you reinforce his methods of getting you to comply. So it seems that the hands have changed. Then it is important for you to get what you need rather than triggering off your guilt and fears. This would work better for both of you. His putting more pressure on you to become more dependent and to quit therapy and those kinds of things aren't necessarily because he is evil or wants bad things for you; but things have been a certain way for a long time, and any change in the system makes for a discomfort. He loses his sense of predictability of what is going on, and there is a kind of natural tendency to push things back into the old shape.

C: Maybe when he said that this morning, he expected me to say "Well, if that is the way you feel, then maybe I won't go." Maybe because that is what I have done in the past.

T: And the fact that you don't react predictably makes him feel less in control. Incidently. if he really wants bad things for you, it is in terms of his being, and it is his concern. It is important for you not to revert back to being so destructive. And when they are destructive for you, they are also destructive for the relationship, and it will be destructive for him, and everybody suffers, and everyone gains when things get better. It is the nice thing about relationships, it is not a win or lose proposition. So you are not being evil, and your feelings are not crazy and it is perfectly appropriate for you to experience these feelings. And the problem is not that they are going to get out of hand and take you over, but you will repress it to the point that it will make you bubble up inside and scare you. It probably would get expressed in other ways, or indirectly; they will make other problems for you. Next week, would you take note of your interactions with H, your mother, or anybody and notice how you come away from each one and make some notes about it? (Goal 3)

C: I did that last week, and I marked it down.

T: That is great. Next time let's go over that in detail, shall we? And then you can start talking about ways that you can deal with these situations, so that you can start feeling very good about yourself. The changes are going to come your way, taking each thing in turn, a little bit at a time. It is not going to be an overnight change.

C: I know.

T: And the way you feel about yourself and the satisfaction you get in your relationships are all dependent on little things, you know. And it is the accumulation of all of those little things which give an overall tone or view. How do you feel about going home?

C: No problem, the way I feel right now.

T: If you start getting scared, just try to make it worse. I know that it is hard . . .

C: It just doesn't sound like it makes sense. If you start feeling bad, try to feel worse. I know what you mean though.

T: Yes, try and focus on some part of your body that you are aware of, like your heart pounding, sweating, or whatever you are aware of.

C: When I came down here I felt like I was having trouble breathing and I was thinking "Oh my God, I am going to stop breathing."

T: Well, try and stop breathing, hold your breath for as long as you can when you get that way.

C: When I am driving! You want me to pass out in the middle of the road!

T: No, I don't want you to pass out in the middle of the road, because I am confident that you won't pass out in the middle of the road. If you intentionally hold your breath, you are going to dissipate that feeling of not being able to breathe because your body will take over. It is not going to let you stop breathing, but if you try and fight it, that sensation will remain.

C: And it usually gets worse.

T: It is like saying, do not think about purple elephants.

C: And that is all you think about right?

T: If you believe that your life depended upon you not thinking about purple elephants for the next hour, what chance would you have?

C: Yeah.

T: And that is essentially what you do. I know that this is a really hard time for you, I hope that you will feel free to stay in touch with me and if you want to talk, just give me a call. Probably you will be very tempted to just chuck it all, but you probably have the hardest part done already, even though there is a lot of work to do yet.

(By predicting C will want to "chuck it all," T reduces the likelihood she will do so, for she will now view such feelings as part of the process of change.)

C: I feel like I have done so much.

T: You have.

C: When I am sitting here and going through this, I feel like I haven't done anything yet.

T: You have done a lot.

C: Well, you didn't see me in the beginning.

T: From the time I last saw you until now, you have done a lot.

C: Yeah, I feel that way too, even though I haven't overcome coming here by myself.

T: Well, please keep going out and trying to become scared.

C: Okay.

If we now organize the information thus far obtained, it can be seen that C's problems include several factors:

1. *Avoidance behavior.* A functional analysis of her avoidance behavior suggests the following: C prepares to go out ⟶ anticipatory anxiety ⟶ thoughts of impending doom, such as, heart will stop, will go crazy, won't be able to get help ⟶ increasing anxiety ⟶ decision to avoid by not going ⟶ anxiety reduced.
   Or C goes out and finds herself in "trapped" situation, such as heavy traffic ⟶ catastrophic thoughts ⟶ increasing anxiety ⟶ turning back toward home ⟶ decrease in anxiety.

   Intervention. It is important to continue to help the client develop and use tools for feeling more in control when anxious. In this case the therapist has employed paradoxical intention, which also has the effect of interrupting the cognitive habits of catastrophic thoughts. Second, it is necessary to block the avoidance behaviors, in this case turning back or deciding not to go out. T has stressed this point and has constantly encouraged C to keep traveling, particularly when anxious. This will be a continuing effort. If it becomes apparent that she cannot do it by herself, then T will take C into particularly difficult situations. *(In vivo* techniques are described in a later section.) In this case the client is doing well at traveling so far.

2. *Making connection between antecedent events (conflict) and anxiety.* The client is not making connections between her interpersonal conflicts and her fears, but she has reached the point of being aware that the conflicts do exist when she acts more independently. As we have seen, interpersonal events can lead to a pattern of fear and avoidance as follows: criticism or anger from spouse as a reaction to the client's independent behavior ⟶ anxiety. At this point the client is "set up" for a panic attack. When she goes out or otherwise behaves independently, she is in conflict, for she fears alienating her husband but also wants to be more independent ⟶ increasing anxiety ⟶ catastrophic thoughts ⟶ panic. As we shall see, other interpersonal conflicts can lead to symptoms.

   Intervention. The therapist will take every opportunity presented to trace the antecedent events for each episode of anxiety and panic that the client reports; this generally leads to encouraging alternative ways of dealing with these antecedent events. Often a lack of assertiveness is involved.
   T will employ cognitive restructuring emphasizing the danger of attitudes that imply that submissive behavior is appropriate, and supporting the belief that in the long run mutual respect and greater hap-

piness result from being assertive and expressive of one's needs. At this point it seems reasonable to plan both assertiveness training and systematic desensitization of themes of criticism, anger (his and hers), and suggestions that she is crazy.

3. *Fear of fear.* There is a fear of becoming "crazy" that makes any strong arousal sensations frightening, as they are interpreted as the beginning of craziness.

   Intervention. The particular feelings or thoughts that the client interprets as crazy are as yet unclear. Flooding to scenes of being crazy is a possible approach to exposing these stimuli. Initial attempts at this have not been particularly successful; however, this particular approach will be tried again.

4. *The effect of C's changing upon the marital relationship.* It seems that C's husband has begun to express discomfort about C's therapy and will undermine her progress if ignored.

   Intervention. It is important to give him support throughout the therapy process. Plans should be made to include H in future sessions or to have an individual session with him to make him feel more a part of C's changes.

Each of these four factors was dealt with in subsequent sessions. The therapist had these in mind as goals to be accomplished, and the process of therapy was one of dealing with each factor as problems presented themselves. Throughout the therapist attempted to move on each front at a pace that took into account the client's readiness to do so. While having such a plan of action is important, therapists also need to retain sufficient flexibility and open mindedness to deal with other issues as they arise.

Blocking Avoidance Behavior. As the therapy progressed, C was repeatedly urged to continue going out. Over the next couple of months she became able to travel to more and more places, but continued encouragement remained necessary. A typical interaction follows:

T: Well it looks like you are traveling to a lot of places now.

C: Yes, I still get scared in anticipation of going some places, but I can usually do it.

T: Are there places that you don't go now—places that you avoid?

C: I have a friend who lives in _____ (a small town about 30 miles from C's home). She called me and asked me to come visit, but I didn't go.

T: Why not?

C: Well, I've had lots of things to do, I haven't seen her in a while, you know, and you just don't have much to talk about after not being together for so long.

T: Even so, how do you feel if you think about making that trip?

C: I really didn't consider it (silence). I guess I'm afraid of being that far from home.

T: It seems that this is a good opportunity to practice traveling to places that you suspect will upset you. We have to keep looking for such opportunities until you *know* that you can go everywhere.

C: Sometimes it's hard to know if I'm avoiding, or I just really don't want to do something.

T: When in doubt assume that you are avoiding—at least until you *do* it comfortably a couple of times. How about going to see her?

C: All right, I'll try it.

T: When can you go?

C: I'll do it Saturday.

T: Good, and *try* to get anxious, will you? If you do, then see if you can make it worse. Okay?

During the next session the therapist inquired about the trip and found that C had a little anticipatory anxiety but no discomfort once under way.

Involving the Spouse. In the sixth session C's husband (H) came in with her, and the therapist spent the first 45 minutes talking to him alone. He confided that he was angry at C because she would not go to visit his parents and that such family gatherings were important to him. T stressed the importance of letting C decide when she was ready to make the trip, for if traveling more freely resulted in pressure from H, we could expect she would stop progressing. A second issue was that he did not know how to deal with her demands that he accompany her many places and that he be "on call" all the time. He always had to let her know where he would be throughout each day in case she needed help. T suggested that H respond to such requests based upon *his* needs. That is, if he really wanted to be helpful at a particular time, then he should make himself available. If, however, he felt resentful about accompanying C on a particular occasion, this was a time to express that and to refuse. For example, if he were feeling that he was being taken advantage of, then he should say so and let C know that it is important for him to be able to say no sometimes without feeling guilty. T cautioned that H might be tempted to use refusal as a way of punishing C when angry about other things and suggested that he deal directly with the other issue instead. Joint sessions with C were offered as a way of discussing these issues with T's facilitation. H agreed to attend a limited number of sessions.

Over six conjoint sessions, agreement was reached as to H's handling C's demands by taking his own needs into account. The second primary issue was H's concern about C having an affair if she could travel freely. While no guarantees could be given that this would not happen, T emphasized that in the long run that C's increasing resentment about his punishing her progress was more likely to lead her to seek companionship elsewhere. In fact, T asserted, H's best chances of having her affection would come from his being supportive of her becoming more independent. This was concretized by working out specific ways in which he might contribute to her growing independent functioning, resulting in his maintaining his stance of being needed but doing so in more positive, constructive ways. Specifically he was encouraged to help her set increasingly difficult traveling goals and to encourage her to stick to these goals. This plan was later changed, as C felt that it was important to set up her own goals independently and that H was in fact the person from whom she needed to declare her independence.

Making Connections and Encouraging Expression. In order to help C stay in touch with antecedents to her high anxiety states, T asked that she keep a diary in which she was to record every occurrence of high anxiety and then to note whatever was going on in her environment at those times. These records were reviewed at each session but were not fruitful. C generally reported she had no idea what she was responding to. T was more successful at making such connections when C came into sessions feeling more anxious than usual. An excerpt from the beginning of such a session follows:

T: Hi, how are you?

C: Horrible! I was really upset driving here today—I really didn't think that I would make it.

T explores what had transpired between C and H over the last 24 hours, but nothing significant emerged.

T: When did you get anxious?

C: I was on the expressway, nothing unusual, and all of a sudden it just hit me.

T: Well, this is a mystery! Let's see if we can recreate the circumstances when you got anxious; you were driving on the expressway?

C: Yes.

C was asked to close her eyes and imagine entering the expressway; details of the passing scenery were suggested, and she was asked to just let her thoughts wander as she relived the trip. At a point in the fantasy trip she opened her eyes.

T: Where were you on the expressway?

C: Hmm—I'm not sure really—probably near the Girard Avenue exit. I know what I was thinking about!

T: What?

C: I'm not sure that I can talk about it—it really scares me.

T: Well, please don't feel that you have to, the main thing is that you are aware of what set off your anxiety.

C: My heart is really racing right now—why can't I get over this—will I *ever* be better!

T: It seems that your automatic avoidance behavior of obsessing about your symptoms is getting going—I think that it will be more productive if we can just stay with whatever thoughts are bothering you. Perhaps you could tell me what you fear will happen if you did talk about the thoughts that you were having.

C: It's more feelings than thoughts—I don't know why I have to get so upset.

T: Uh-huh, what do you suppose will happen if you talked about it?

C: I guess you wouldn't approve—I don't want you to see me this way.

T: Well, I can see how that would be scary—to think that I would reject you for what you are feeling. I suppose that you would have the expectation then that I, too, would be intolerant of any sexual feelings you may be having.

(T guesses that the forbidden feelings are sexual and helps facilitate C's talking about them by introducing the subject.)

C: Yeah—I thought that I was over these feelings—and here they are coming back again.

C went on to talk about an extherapist who called her the "id kid" and insisted that she needed to get more control over herself. C interpreted his position as one of disapproval of certain feelings, particularly sexual ones toward anyone but her husband.

T: It sounds like you *buried* them or awareness of them anyway, but as you get out into the world, you are bound to experience such feelings—and there is no effective way to not have feelings—you always have choices about what you *do* with them, but little choice about their cropping up. When they are unacceptable to you, they can easily trigger off anxiety, and then it gets confusing as to what you are experiencing. By the way, the psychotherapeutic situation is very likely to produce some of those feelings—you confide the most intimate details of your experience, and the therapist is usually accepting and empathetic. Most people have such feelings when in therapy.

C: I thought you would be upset if you knew how I felt.

C went on to talk about her sexual feelings about T, and how she gets anxious when such feelings occur. T again assured her that such feelings are normal, and that he felt comfortable about having them. He added that his personal rules precluded acting on them in any way, as he felt such an involvement would be destructive to a therapeutic relationship. T commented that C was likely to feel somewhat rejected and urged her to talk this out. He suggested that any time these feelings were interfering with the therapy process she bring them up again.

This process does not necessarily lead to resolution of this issue, and it may come up a number of times. However, making the issue overt in this way prevents the client and therapist from becoming stuck in the therapy process. If not dealt with, such issues can lead to "resistance" in the form of loss of interest in homework assignments and a general state of anxiety in the therapist's presence, which precludes cooperative interaction.

Identifying and Resolving Feelings of Craziness. In spite of additional attempts of resolving C's fear of going crazy through flooding to scenes of "craziness," hospitalization, and related themes, she still expressed feelings of sometimes being on the verge of insanity. In order to explore these feelings further, the therapist switched to a gestalt model, as he had noted that C frequently showed conflicting stances, alternating from one to the other as she spoke.

C: I feel scared and despair that I will ever get better!

T: (Noting sad expression as she says this) It must leave you feeling really sad and alone.

C: I don't like that part of me—I should be through with all this now. I'm just feeling sorry for myself—you won't respect me if you see that part.

T: It seems that one part of you has a hard time accepting the other.

(T implies that C's fear he will reject her is based on her own rejection of that part of herself.)

C: What do you mean?

T: Well, as soon as you start to express sad feelings or loneliness, immediately there is a switch to another part of you that puts down what you were experiencing.

C: Yes, I know, but I ought not be having feelings like that; I thought I had that all worked out.

T: It seems to me that this conflict between these two parts of you keeps you from resolving something, so I suggest that we try to get a clearer picture of each side—sort of get to know each side more thoroughly. Would you be willing to give it a try?

With this information the therapist decided to employ a gestalt approach to help C get more in touch with and accepting of her thoughts and feelings.

C: What do I have to do?

At this point the therapist and C agreed to "split" C into two people which they agreed to identify as "critical C" and "needy C." Critical C was assigned one seat and "needy C" another, and C was asked to switch chairs depending upon who was talking.

T started with "critical C" and asked her what she thought about "needy C." In a lengthy exchange T elicited the following information. "Critical C" stated that it was "needy C" who is always anxious, and who embarrasses her around some men by overcoming her with sexual feelings. She does not like "needy C" and sees it as her task to get rid of her; she is the weak one, the sick one, and if she could be stamped out, all would be well.

T asked C to change chairs so that he could get to know "needy C." C complied, but found it very much more difficult to stay in this role— "critical C" kept intervening; however, with continued encouragement she was able for the first time in therapy to allow expression of her sadness without having to cut off. As she did so, she became increasingly upset and began to cry as she blurted out how she missed L (her former boyfriend). She exclaimed, "My God, this is my craziness!" She acknowledged that this was her first awareness that these thoughts and feelings were what had been frightening her. The remainder of the session was spent talking about the emotional support she had received from L and how much she missed him and his nurturance.

In the next session C again took two roles and continued expressing her sadness about what was missing in her life. Over the next two months C was markedly less anxious and rarely thought of herself as being crazy; however, she seemed more depressed than usual. This was interpreted as a normal period of grief over her loss. She noticed that as long as she was able to allow thoughts of missing L, she had no phobic symptoms. From these sessions there arose a discussion of the necessity of meeting her needs for emotional support, and C chose to continue trying to get it from her husband, H.

Becoming More Expressive with H. It became clear that C had difficulty expressing herself with H. At first she felt that she had no right to be upset with H even though he was, at times, abusive and acted in ways which left her feeling bad. For example, she frequently complained of how H interrupted her, finished her sentences for her, and derided her for her opinions, particularly in the presence of others. She, at first, concluded this was evidence of her stupidity. As therapy progressed, she began to see that she was entitled to express her feelings. However, as she began doing so, it became clear that she was inhibited by her high anxiety in face of his anger. A two-session desensitization to scenes of H's angry face, loud voice, and cutting statements was successful in reducing this anxiety sufficiently so that she could begin to be more expressive.

Conclusion. After about 1 year of therapy C was traveling freely, no longer having panic attacks, and was attempting to work out her relationship with H. She was discontent in the relationship but not willing to give it up. She remained mildly depressed. At this point she terminated therapy, but 6 months later returned, still in conflict about her relationship with H. She has continued to struggle with the marital situation and vascillates between leaving and staying. On an irregular basis she comes in for follow-up sessions.

Other Treatment Techniques

C's treatment has illustrated many of the important aspects of behavioral psychotherapy with a case of complex agoraphobia. A number of interventions that are frequently required for the treatment of agoraphobia, however, were not necessary for C's improvement. The most important of these are *in vivo* and imaginal flooding; when necessary, medication may also be a substantial adjunct.

In Vivo Exposure. *In vivo* exposure is a powerful tool in breaking down the habit of avoidance, yet it is often ignored, perhaps because it seems so simple. Essentially it means, if you're afraid of it, do it! Effective exposure can be accomplished through the use of homework assignments such as those given to C. Frequently, a therapist's encouragement is not sufficient to induce a client to enter avoided situations, and in such cases *in vivo* treatment under the therapist's guidance is essential. The therapist may actually accompany clients when they are fearful of a particular situation even with a companion. Other times the therapist acts as a starter motor by sending clients into feared situations and awaiting their return.

For economic reasons, homework assignments are prefered to therapist-assisted *in vivo* work. However, the expense can be reduced by forming groups. The use of groups is discussed later, as they are important in providing emotional support and boosting motivation. Even when *in vivo* work must be done on an individual basis, we would suggest it under the following circumstances:

1. When clients are so frightened or so entrenched in avoidance behaviors that they do not carry out homework assignments despite all attempts to make initial steps small enough to conquer. The presence of the therapist on initial excursions is reassuring and provides the extra motivation required to take those first steps. Clients who are totally housebound (unable to go out even with a companion) usually require such assistance.

2. When clients get stuck at a particular point in therapy. Frequently progress is made at an acceptable rate until a particular barrier is encountered, and it seems like the client just cannot get beyond that point. This becomes frustrating and lowers motivation to continue therapy, so that it is useful for the therapist to intervene at such times and get things going again. One client, for instance, had conquered the use of trains and other public conveyances within the city of Philadelphia but had failed repeatedly to overcome anticipatory anxiety about going any further than Trenton, the next major city. After his therapist made one trip with him beyond this point, he was able to repeat the step with his wife. This led to a major breakthrough, and he rapidly began taking his family on vacations all over the East Coast after 30 years of confinement. •

3. Another time when *in vivo* work is valuable is with clients who are completing homework assignments regularly but whose anxiety is not extinguishing, that is, they still get panic attacks despite repeated attempts to stop fighting their anxiety. Often in these cases, the client is unaware of some behavior that is blocking extinction, and the therapist may, through observation, solve the problem. Frequently, clients do not grasp the notion of paradoxical intention unless the therapist can give them instruction while they are actually panicky. Finding it useful at that moment usually cements learning this approach rapidly. Some clients can make themselves panicky in the therapist's office, but others must wait for it to strike in an avoided spot. Another kind of problem occurred with a particularly difficult client who had not improved despite a year of treatment with a student. Her anxiety about being alone in stores, for example, never dropped. Upon accompanying her to a store, the therapist eventually realized that her reports of getting lost and confused were quite real. This client was so constantly obsessed with her bodily symptoms that she was literally unaware of her surroundings. When she was taught to focus on the physical environment sufficiently to identify her whereabouts, she became much more confident and able to increase time outside her home.

4. Occasionally clients are not amenable to verbal therapy because they are unwilling or unable to focus on problems other than somatic complaints. Such clients tend to drop out of therapy when it is confined to the office, and sessions are more fruitful if the therapist quickly shifts to mostly *in vivo* work. During this work, defenses often drop, and the client will let the therapist in on important conflicts which were previously denied. As rapport builds during casual conversations, the therapist may be able to form a contract to work on other trouble areas.

5. *In vivo* exposure is sometimes rejected by our students as somehow beneath their dignity as psychotherapists. We have found, however, that significant data may emerge from such sessions which are difficult to obtain in the office. We have often had the experience of introducing a situation in which the client has reported anxiety and finding that the response we observe is what most people would label something else, usually sadness or anger. For instance a client emerged from a department store in tears. She reported that the sense of aloneness she felt was like that experienced when her mother died. As she related the circumstances surrounding her mother's death, it was clear that the onset of her problems (previously mysterious) was a case of unresolved mourning. While she had probably had this insight before, she had never reported it and indeed forgot it happened by later the same afternoon. This instance led to a productive shift to imaginal flooding on her mother's death.

Our approach to *in vivo* exposure is somewhat different from that described elsewhere in the literature. The idea is not simply for the client to go in a particular place and remain a certain period of time. Rather it is essential that each exposure experience be used as an opportunity to learn to accept anxiety and not fight with it. Clients who grit their teeth and fight their way through an experience often emerge with even more conditioned anxiety and a stronger tendency to avoid. Eventually most clients who continue to go into situations where they have anxiety develop some coping mechanisms which allow them to be more comfortable. However, many coping techniques for avoiding the experience of anxiety fail at times, and when panic attacks break through, the client is resensitized. We have found that, for reasons outlined above, providing clients with an adaptive coping mechanism like paradoxical intention from the outset is more conducive to faster progress and less likelihood of relapse.

Procedure for Therapist-Assisted In Vivo Exposure. *In vivo* work is necessarily tailored to the needs of a particular client and the pace suited for her/him. Nevertheless, some general guidelines can be drawn.

1. Choose tasks that, if accomplished, will have some impact on the client's daily life; this increases motivation for further work. For instance, if learning to use an elevator would be important so that the client can accept a promotion to an office on the 23rd floor, then tackle the elevator before the shopping mall. One exception to this rule is the pessimistic, easily discouraged client whose motivation would be boosted by the rapid accomplishment of a fairly easy step.

2. If possible, work in the client's own environment, at least occasionally. This reduces the tendency some clients have exhibited to view accomplishments during a session as somehow unreal and not connected to their day-to-day lives.

3. Most tasks can be broken down into smaller steps. Encourage clients to attempt the largest steps they will tolerate; this is not an *in vivo* desensitization procedure. If they balk at a particular step despite urging, try to shift to the next lower level of the same task.

4. The therapist repeats the particular coping instructions worked out for the client before beginning the task and also repeats instructions for the client to remain in the situation until comfortable. If the therapist is accompanying the client, the therapist repeats paradoxical instructions whenever the client reports anxiety.

5. The therapist phases herself/himself out of the situation as quickly as the client will allow, until the client can handle the situation alone.

6. The therapist reinforces progress at every point and particularly praises the client's having panickly feelings and resolving them. This is much more important than breezing through a situation calmly. (Panic attacks are absolutely not to be viewed as failures but as opportunities to practice coping with one's feelings.) Clients are also encouraged to self-reinforce to break up a common habit, which is to say to oneself, "Well, I did it today, but tomorrow I probably won't."

These principles can be applied to many situations of which a typical example is a large supermarket because of long check-out lines, high ceilings, and bright fluorescent lighting. The therapist and client may select this as a target problem because the client completely avoids these places (principle 1) and, in the case of a traditional woman, feels considerable guilt about abdicating her domestic responsibilities. If possible, a particularly threatening store in the client's neighborhood is selected (principle 2). In the case of a very avoidant client, the therapist may accompany her when she first enters the store (principle 3). Otherwise the therapist will attempt to remain outside and send the client in with instructions to have a panic attack and practice coping with it, for example, "Now see if you can go in and make your heart beat as fast as possible. Try to make it pop out of your chest." Once being alone in the store itself has been mastered, waiting in line is tackled. If necessary the therapist may wait part of the time in line with the client, repeating the instruction to resist fighting with the anxiety. Everytime the client reports panicky feelings the therapist responds, "Good! this is another opportunity for us to change your habit of avoiding the feelings. (Then depending on the feeling reported) Go ahead let your legs wobble, see if you can let them wobble so much you just fall down. (If the client has a sense of humor, the therapist might add) You may as well go ahead and collapse. Get it over with instead of worrying all day." The metamessage here is that twinges of panic are to be accepted. Anxiety is not awful! After successfully navigating this task, the client is asked to go back into the store, go through every aisle again, select the longest line, and wait in line alone while the therapist waits in the parking lot. If the client reports remaining through panics and not fighting the anxiety, the therapist responds with praise. A client reporting having dealt with anxiety through distraction, and so forth, will be met with an empathic "I know it's really hard to break the habit of fighting it. See if this time you can increase the feelings instead of trying to push them away." When a client mentions having completed negatively anticipated tasks without anxiety, the therapist is not to respond with "Hey, that's great. You didn't get anxious." This would reinforce the cognition that anxiety is to be avoided. Instead one might reply, "It sounds like you must have gone in with a different attitude. That's interesting. When you go in and try to get panicky, it doesn't happen. Does that tell you anything?" With different clients this might be delivered differently. Often a humorous style works well, for example, with the therapist replying "Gee, you're really making me a failure today. I can't get you anxious." Repetitions of this assignment are to be carried out several times before the next session. Generally the session with the therapist requires 1½ hours.

Once the habit of fighting anxiety has been broken, the therapist can switch to the use of homework assignments for the necessary exposure work. The therapist may also train a spouse, family member, or friend to assist in the completion of homework tasks. Mathews, Teasdale, Munby, Johnston, and Shaw (1977) have used this work with some success in England. We find, however, in particularly pathological relationships the spouse or parent may actually punish rather than reward progress. Consequently, a careful analysis of the relationship is advised before including a "significant other" in this way.

This combination of *in vivo* exposure and paradoxical instruction is usually sufficient to quickly reverse cases of simple agoraphobia. In other settings *in vivo* exposure is also used as the primary treatment for complex agoraphobic cases as well. Our experience warns that for these cases exposure is only a part of the necessary therapeutic program if stable change is to be achieved.

Group In Vivo Exposure. The use of groups for *in vivo* work has been a major innovation, first reported by Watson, Mullet, and Pillay (1973). This approach is now used in most centers for the treatment of agoraphobia. Groups offer a number of advantages. First it is possible to give more clients access to this important form of treatment both by increasing the numbers of clients who can be treated and by decreasing the cost of such treatment.

Second, there are significant therapeutic reasons for using a group approach. Most agoraphobics feel that they have a unique form of "disease" and that no one else could possibly be so "sick", "crazy", and so forth. This adds to their emotional distress, and we find most group members experience a dramatic sense of relief in actually meeting someone else with the same fears, someone who does not ridicule or pooh-pooh one's anxieties. Probably because of this sense of sameness, group members can push each other, motivate each other in ways nonagoraphobics cannot. It is quite different to be urged to take a risk by someone who knows how hard it is, firsthand. "Priming" a group with a member who has gotten the hang of paradoxical intention provides a facilitative modeling effect. Thus we have seen improvement in group clients who were viewed as impossible to motivate by their individual therapists. The group also provides a powerful incentive through amplified reinforcement power; a group of people who can sincerely cheer for completion of a difficult assignment has more impact than an individual professional. Frequently some friendly competitiveness arises which also spurs increased risk taking.

While it is not a focus of *in vivo* work, members usually talk informally about how their problems started. Occasionally, this is a less threatening way to begin making connections about antecedents of anxiety. Commonly, members begin to see themes, such as that of the spouse who is threatened by independence and who, therefore, punishes improvement. The group leader can facilitate this if desired by asking at the beginning of a new session, "Did you tell the folks at home what you accomplished last time? What kind of reaction did you get?"

There can be a detrimental aspect of groups that the leader must watch for and counter. This is the tendency for members to teach each other maladaptive habits they have been using as coping mechanisms; most commonly, some type of distraction is involved. The leader can prevent this by asking members to talk about ways they have tried to cope. This gives her/him an opportunity to point out the problem with the distraction approach. Instead each member is asked to remind a panicky companion not to fight or run away from the anxiety. Once this has been set up as a group contract, members generally adhere to it.

Groups may be run on a once-a-week basis for an extended period of time or may meet for a short-term intensive contract. We started out treating short-term clients for five full-day sessions with only a weekend break. This tended to be too strenuous for therapists and clients, and we now suggest eight 5-hour sessions in blocks of two days with several days alloted for rest and homework practice in between. For instance, eight sessions may be spread over the course of one month. The blocks of two sessions have an important function in keeping momentum going.

One therapist can comfortably handle a group of about five clients; for larger groups two leaders are suggested. The co-leader position may be ably filled by a student or paraprofessional worker. In fact, such groups are most economically run with trained paraprofessionals. Marks, Hallam, Philpott, and Connolly (1975) report that behaviorally trained nurse therapists in England achieve the same results as psychiatrists and psychologists.

A typical short-term group at our unit was run by DLC and a medical student. It was comprised of five women who had been restricted by their agoraphobia from 1 to 30 years. Mary, Carmen, and Lottie were being seen in individual therapy by colleagues; Maureen and Joanne were on the waiting list for treatment. All were unable to leave home alone, and several could not stay home without a companion.

Day 1. Clients met each other for the first time; all had had at least a brief interview with the leader. The women needed little encouragement to tell each other of their fears, and all expressed excitement and relief at the commonality of their experience. With the help of the leaders they constructed a list of activities or places that they all feared. Each woman then shared her particular feared catastrophe with the rest of the group. Three women feared fainting most strongly, one a heart attack, and one losing her mind. Generally they all had milder fears of the other catastrophes as well.

Next the leader gave a mini lecture on the evils of avoidance habits and how fear of fear develops. Once each member understood the concept, everyone was asked to induce her personal catastrophe. Mary had the most difficulty with this assignment. The others shortly laughed and declared it impossible within the safety of our classroom. As soon as they insisted that they could have panicked if only they were outside, the leaders directly took them out to the grounds of the building. Everyone was given the instruction to scatter, and when alone, to bring on her catastrophe. Eventually, the women returned with each reporting her amazement at having remained calm despite challenging herself to panic. This concretized the concept of paradoxical intention, and the group was ready to take on the outside world.

In view of an approaching thunderstorm the first site selected was the area's largest shopping mall. The therapists drove on this occasion. Group members and therapists lunched in a restaurant together, insisting on a table in the center (most threatening part) of the room. Clients who were convinced they could not swallow when anxious learned otherwise by being instructed to keep chewing and not attempt to swallow (we are indebted to Claire Weekes for this useful suggestion). Mary ordinarily had alcoholic beverages in restaurants to control her anxiety, but was asked to refrain during the group. Each woman practiced leaving the dining room alone to go to the ladies room (walking across a room where people might see wobbly legs is frequently anxiety provoking). Each stood in line to pay her check having been instructed to try to collapse in line or shake so hard she dropped her money. Some mild panicky feelings were reported, but everyone felt successful and a bit powerful. The group members then tackled the mall at large. One leader walked with the most anxious clients, while the other remained a stationary point for more ambitious members who went exploring on their own, first walking, then entering stores, then trying on clothing. The last step is rather difficult because of the confinement of dressing rooms and the fact that running in a panic out of a store with unpurchased clothing on would lead to arrest for shoplifting! The stationary therapist provided reinforcement for clients' efforts and encouraged panicky members to go out again and not fight the anxiety this time. The "walking leader" encouraged her charges to wobble through the mall, get dizzy, and faint. Once they realized this was not likely to happen, they too began to venture into stores alone.

At the end of the day the group reconvened at the office and shared experiences. Everyone was astonished at her progress, and several felt rather confident that this "weird" approach to dealing with panics was going to work if they could avoid getting overwhelmed and starting to avoid or fight anxiety. Mary continued to label panic attacks as failures and was encouraged to change this approach. Other members helped out by telling her of times they panicked during the day but managed to stay and then felt fine. Lottie was convinced that all of her accomplishments were a strange aberration that would never reoccur. The leaders picked up on this and predicted that all members would feel some of this and fear the second day, perhaps even more than the first. They were told that such feelings were to be expected but to not let it prevent them from returning the next day.

Day 2. The women returned in a typically pessimistic frame of mind, assuming that yesterday's accomplishments would never be repeated. Mary reported having been belittled by her husband, who discounted the gains she had made. The relationship between her lack of progress in individual therapy and her marital problems was becoming clear to her despite previous denials that this was the case. Carmen had also been greeted abusively by her husband, who insisted she had been out looking for men. The other women got no reaction or more positive ones. After some discussion of how change may be viewed as threatening by an insecure spouse, the leaders began a discussion of the day's goals. With some encouragement everyone agreed to attempt public transportation, which was used on this and subsequent days.

The group took a commuter train for the 10-mile ride into center city Philadelphia, where the tall buildings, large stores, and bustling crowds elicit high levels of anxiety. At first most of the women were only willing to attempt walking half a block alone. Joanne had progressed so rapidly the first day, however, that she accepted an assignment to meet the group some nine blocks away in unfamiliar territory. The other women were encouraged to increase their tolerance of anxiety symptoms when alone, and by the day's end, all but Mary could negotiate four city blocks alone. Joanne, Maureen, and Carmen were by now shopping in stores with little discomfort, while Lottie had difficulty only when going to upper floors in department stores where elevators were the only means of access to the outside. Mary was reluctant to venture too far from the entrance to a store and would only go in if one of the leaders was outside. Her progress, while slow, was still significant, but she continued to try to avoid panic attacks and to regress when she did experience one. Carmen and Maureen were having attacks rather frequently on difficult assignments, but handled them without avoiding and were comfortable again in a brief time. Joanne was rarely anxious and avoided only one assignment, to stay on the 20th floor of a tall building until she was no long uncomfortable. The general mood at the end of the day was exhiliration.

Day 3. On the third day most of the patients returned in good spirits, although Lottie was apprehensive of what might be asked of her that day. Mary was agitated, as her husband was becoming more abusive and threatened to refuse to bring her to group. She now realized that her progress would continue to be undermined unless she could effect at least a temporary separation from her husband, who refused all attempts to involve him in therapy. She found that even the day's separation from him in the group left her calmer, so that she was able to sleep without alcohol and tranquillizers. Maureen's husband, on the other hand, was so proud of her progress that he sent her a bouquet of roses.

In view of Joanne's successes on the previous day, she was sent out by bus to tour a section of the city she was unfamiliar with and told where to meet the group for lunch. The others took the train into town after being asked to sit in separate cars and to practice getting panicky. Once in center city Maureen and Carmen were able to go off on their own for periods in excess of an hour and a half. Lottie had particular difficulty with large open spaces and went with one leader to such a site to practice walking in it, while Mary worked on remaining alone or walking on a busy street. Gradually she came to tolerate being alone with no knowledge of where to find the leader for a period of 15 minutes, while if she knew where the leader was waiting, she could wander away for about 30 minutes. Though her confidence had increased, she was not able to cope with more than mild attacks without seeking assistance. Much of her fear of being alone seemed to result from her tendency to ruminate at such times about her unhappiness and the impossibility of resolving it. She tried to avoid these thoughts by continual chatter with a companion.

Day 4. On the fourth day Carmen, Maureen, and Joanne were able to fend for themselves for half-day periods, reporting in at lunch time. Joanne and Maureen were now using public transportation without any problem, while Carmen still avoided it. Consequently, Carmen, Mary, and Lottie worked on public transportation. Joanne was sent to try remaining in a tall building again, and Maureen elected to work on being alone in a restaurant. At the end of the day Maureen had completed her tasks and journeyed 2 hours to her home on a series of buses. Joanne had avoided her assignment, and the other three were handling public transportation more comfortably, though Mary still would not attempt more than a few blocks if alone. At the end of the day the leaders requested that members make up homework assignments to carry out once the group had ended and bring these lists on the next day.

Day 5. On the fifth day each member practiced giving herself tasks to accomplish that day. Mary and Lottie worked on shopping in grocery stores with a leader remaining outside. The other leader accompanied Joanne to make certain she attempted the tall building; once pushed into the situation she had no trouble remaining an extended time alone and returning alone. Carmen felt her greatest difficulty was walking alone on crowded streets and practiced trying to faint while doing this, and Maureen traveled the city on her own, becoming anxious only when caught in a large crowd of political demonstrators.

At the group's end Maureen and Joanne were able to accomplish anything the leaders could dream up, while Carmen was faring as well with the exception of public transportation. Carmen was concerned about how well her gains would generalize to driving; she had so far avoided testing her limits on this. Lottie could now shop comfortably in stores and navigate crowded streets and open spaces on her own, and take public transportation to familiar spots on her own. She reported considerable anxiety yet about driving on crowded streets. Mary had definitely increased her tolerance for being alone in all situations, but she remained extremely limited. She had, however, resolved to do something about her marital conflict.

The leaders reiterated the principles stressed in the group practice and encouraged members to continue daily practice on their problematical situations. Those members in individual therapy for marital and other problems were exhorted to continue to work on resolving such conflicts if they wanted to maintain their progress.

At six-month follow-up a mixed picture emerged. Joanne and Maureen were symptom free and had returned to work. Maureen reported her marriage had improved as a result of her ability to travel and attend social functions. Joanne was now proceeding with plans to marry that had been disrupted by her "illness." Neither of these women have had further treatment. The three other women have continued in individual therapy with other therapists. Lottie is seen infrequently because of financial problems and the considerable distance she must come for treatment. She is hampered by her continued fear of driving on busy streets and does not actively seek out opportunities to be alone in her formerly fearful situations. When she does find herself alone in a store, however, she has little difficulty.

Carmen maintained progress she made in the group, but had only slowly increased her ability to drive a distance from home. This prevented her from returning to work so that she was poorly prepared to cope when she precipitously left her husband. During the separation she was quite depressed and panicky and has now returned to her husband. As a result of her departure, he is more willing to work on their difficulties, hopefully opening the way for a more stable improvement for her.

Mary did make some efforts to change her situation. Family members, unfortunately, rejected her requests to live with them while she overcame her fears of living alone. The only residential setting possible for her was an in-patient unit at our hospital. Because of her fears of mental illness and "crazy" people, she has so far refused hospitalization. She has made no further progress and has returned to alcohol and other substance abuse. Her husband continues to be extremely abusive and impervious to therapist's entreaties to consider marital therapy. Mary is severely depressed. Under the circumstances, we fear it is impossible to help her without a residential treatment setting.

Thus we find that with an approach only aimed at the phobic behavior, the two women diagnosed as simple agoraphobics before treatment (Maureen and Joanne) were cured. Lottie and Carmen made significant improvement, but were blocked by their trouble with driving, which was not dealt with in the group; this was a major deficit in the group experience for them. Mary, whose marital situation is the worst we have ever seen, improved the least. This is in line with Hafner's report (1976, 1977) that marital conflict correlates negatively with progress for *in vivo* exposure.

The only lasting value from the group for Mary has been the insight she gained, which has helped her be less self-deprecatory.

Imaginal Flooding. Since *in vivo* exposure is generally more potent than imaginal exposure, flooding in fantasy is not required for the treatment of fear in most clients. Some clients however have strong obsessions that persist even though they are no longer behaviorally avoiding any "trapped" situations. Frequently, the content of such obsessions is some type of loss of control for example, going crazy, running about screaming. In these cases we have found a series of imaginal flooding sessions to be beneficial. The reader is referred to Chapter 3 in this volume for detailed instructions on this technique. The following excerpt is presented to illustrate some of the themes used in flooding with clients who fear loss of control. The client is an agoraphobic male who was generally miserable at social gatherings due to his fears that he would lose control of himself. He dreaded embarrassing himself and his wife and also feared that he might hurt someone and/or end up in a mental hospital. The therapist introduces all these themes over the course of a 90-minute session.

T: You are there in the room with all those people, everyone seems to be having a good time. They are all drinking, talking, joking. There are quite a number of people around that you know. You know that the room is very large, but right now the room seems small because there are so many people there. You are standing by Alice, and you are just drinking soda so you stay in control. You are wondering what the hell you are doing there in the first place. You are forcing yourself to be there. You can hear your heart beat really fast. You are feeling dizzy and light-headed. You are trying to listen to what people are saying, you are trying to find a way that you could have some fun too. But you know that having fun is only for other people. All the people are normal, and you are not. And that is what you tell yourself all the time. You keep comparing yourself to other people, and they always end up being okay and you don't, but right now it is worse than ever. You are feeling so uncomfortable, you wish you could run out of the place. And that is really scary when you start feeling that way. You're feeling like you don't belong here. It is so uncomfortable to stand there at a party with 220 people always feeling different, like you don't belong there, you are different, you are abnormal, you're crazy; but that is what your life is all about, that is how you always feel. But right now it is worse than ever because you have all those sensations, you have all those feelings, all those fears. You wonder if they know, if they know that you are frightened. You wonder if they know that you are feeling so abnormal. You keep thinking how you would like to slip out. But there are a lot of people between you and the exit. You are standing there, and you are getting more and more uptight. It feels as though you are going to jump out of your skin; it is very uncomfortable, and you are feeling very dizzy, very light-headed, very hot, very uptight. You look around, and you know the people, and you can hear their voices, you can see their mouths move when they talk; but it doesn't make sense to you anymore. It is as if things are unreal to you—it's like in a dream—you are standing there, you know the people, you know the place, everything around seems familiar, but nothing makes sense. Everything is distant, you are feeling really detached, very removed from everything and everyone, and you are feeling very uptight.

The therapist elaborates these stimuli until the client reports diminished anxiety; this took about 45 minutes in this session. She then introduces the loss of control fantasy previously reported by this client.

T: Obviously, you are looking very strange right now because they are looking at you, and they have a very puzzled look on their faces, and they really don't know what is going on; they want you to tell them. You can't, you just cannot find the words that will explain to them what is happening to you. You realize that this is how people who belong in hospitals feel! This is how they feel all the time, being with people and at the same time they are not really there. That is exactly how people in state hospitals feel. That is how you feel right now. You knew that one day this would happen. You've been trying to push that from your mind for so many years, but that very thing that you've been so scared of for so long is happening right now. You've known all along that the craziness was there, but now you feel as if you can not keep it in. Now everything is going to come out. You feel very unreal, and you feel as if your body is going to explode into pieces all over the room. You are on the verge of freaking out. Suddenly you throw your glass up in the air, and you start running. You can see the door; it is very far because there are so many people. You are running, you are pushing people. You need to get out, and you don't have time to explain. You push Bill and Frances. Frances tries to stop you, and you push her down. You see that she is bleeding, blood is coming out of her mouth, you just hit her! You didn't mean to, but you just couldn't stand being there and giving reasons. You are pushing people, you can feel your hands pushing people right and left, and you are trying to make a way out for yourself. Everyone is looking at you, looking surprised and shocked. You can hear someone saying "But that's Bob F _____, what's happening to him? This guy's gone crazy, he must be crazy.'' You can hear people cry, you can hear people scream, you can hear someone that you don't even know say "This guy is crazy; let's call the police, this guy is crazy." You are looking at the exit, you want to get out of there, get in your car and just drive somewhere and never see those people again because it is so embarrassing. You are running through the place, you are running, you are screaming "I want to get out of here," you are screaming! All these people are normal, you don't belong here, you are abnormal. They never should have invited you; they always knew there was something wrong with you anyway. You can hear the sound of a police car coming, the police are coming, they are going to get you.

When this scene has been fully elaborated and the client's anxiety has lessened considerably, the session is terminated for the day. During subsequent sessions the theme is repeated and extended to a scene of the police carrying the client to a state psychiatric hospital.[2]

Another case in which imaginal flooding is likely to be employed is that of clients whose anxiety masks unresolved grief. In these cases clients are usually unaware of the connection between the buried grief and their present state of anxiety. It may be that the loss occurred years before and that little conscious thought of the deceased[3] occurs at all. Instead, when the grief begins to break through, the client begins to obsess about the possibility of heart attack, craziness, and so forth. The obsessive thought acts as a diversion from memories of the loss, and in this way, obsessive thoughts are reinforced and become a fixed avoidance pattern. This pattern is sometimes discovered when a client reports he/she is having a panic attack, but appears to an observer to be profoundly sad. The following vertabim account details the interaction between a therapist and client while they are in a car during an *in vivo* exposure session. The client is driving, and up ahead there is a line of cars waiting at a busy intersection.

C: I am starting to get anxious.

T: What sensations are you having that tell you that you are anxious?

C: My legs are shaky, I feel a tightness in my chest . . . a pressure in my head.

T: Just focus on those sensations, and let whatever happens happen. Don't fight it or try to stop it.

C: My God, this is it! I'm really panicked.

T: (Noting expression on C's face) You look sad to me, not anxious. You seem to be fighting back tears. What are your thoughts now?

C: I don't know why, but I'm thinking about my mother (she begins to cry).

T: What about her?

C: How I *miss* her.

The therapist asked C to pull over to the side of the road and tell him more about her mother. She talked about her mother's death, which had occurred 16 years before when C was 12 years old. Even though C had mentioned this during the initial history taking, she had not shown any affect about it at that time. It was clear now that she had not completed mourning her mother and that the affective state she feared was one of profound sadness. This was her "craziness," and she felt as if she would be out of control if it developed further. She described it as feeling as though she were falling into a bottomless pit from which there might be no return. Several subsequent sessions were spent in going over and over the events leading up to her mother's death and the funeral. These memories were accompanied by a great deal of sadness and crying. She was urged to dwell on these memories as much as possible between sessions and to expect that she would feel upset while going through this process. The therapist told her that she was having a normal, if delayed, mourning reaction and that it would be finished in time if she did not avoid the process and its attendant feelings.[4]

She experienced about 5 weeks of increased depression followed by considerable relief of the pervasively anxious state that was constant for several years prior to treatment. Treatment was continued as avoidance behaviors persisted, and she still became anxious when going into grocery stores and so forth. With continued *in vivo* exposure, she improved rapidly.

The case of Mrs. J is one that illustrates the possibility of defining the presenting problems as the result of incomplete mourning right from the first session. Mrs. J, a 32-year-old married woman, presented with anxiety and depression and complained that she was the victim of frequent panic attacks. She associated the onset of this condition to an adverse reaction to a sedative 6 years before. She had just returned from the hospital following delivery of a stillborn infant and was distraught and guilt-plagued over the loss of the baby when her physician gave her a tranquilizer.

In the interview, whenever she talked about the baby or children, she began to cry and reported she was having an "attack." Questioning revealed that she was subject to attacks when confronted with television programs about children, children on the street, baby carriages, various thoughts such as how old the child would be now, and other baby-related events. She had never been aware of the connection between the loss and her feeling of sadness and presumed that something was physically wrong with her such as a brain tumor. Through the years she had sought a number of medical opinions and had fairly consistently been told that it was her nerves and that she had to get hold of herself. This led her to believe that she was perhaps going crazy. From this information we can hypothesize that Mrs. J's agoraphobia developed secondarily to an incompleted mourning reaction and that treatment might best focus on this issue.

Therapy consisted of encouraging her to get into the mourning reaction with assurances that it was a normal process that would lead to recovery if not suppressed. There were a number of flooding sessions to specific memories and relevant themes. A brief excerpt from such a session follows. She was also encouraged to facilitate the mourning process at home by allotting time to think about the things that made her sad.

T: Imagine that you are arriving home from the hospital. You're very aware that something is wrong. You should have a baby in your arms. But the baby is dead. Your arms are empty as you walk up the steps into the house. Let yourself realize fully that there's no baby to bring home with you. What are you feeling as you realize this?

C: Like I'm choking. I can't breathe, my throat and chest are so tight.

T: You're fighting back the tears and choking on them. Let yourself cry. It's okay to let go and let the hurt out.

C: (Sobs for a while and then becomes quiet.)

T: Where are you now?

C: I'm thinking about the nursery, hoping they already took the furniture away before I see it. All that furniture I bought . . . (starts to cry again).

T: Of course you want to avoid seeing the nursery because it'll hurt. But it's important that you go in there. The only way through this is through it.

C: I can't (sounding panicky).

T: You're feeling afraid because you're trying to get away from the sadness. But it's okay, walk down the hall and enter the nursery. You see the white crib from the doorway, the empty white crib.

C: My chest hurts.

T: That's right. That crib is empty just like that raw place in your chest that aches. Look at the crib. Think of how you dreamt it would be, but the baby's dead.

Over the next few months her depression gradually lifted with concomitant reduction in her fear of going out of the house.

Medication. Most agoraphobics have been through a variety of drug re-
gimes before finding their way to a behavior therapist. Generally a family
doctor will have prescribed a minor tranquillizer like Valium or Librium;
this commonly lowers general anxiety sufficiently to reduce the probability of panic attacks somewhat. Occasionally agoraphobics have been
maintained on such large doses that they become addicted to these drugs
and require a detoxification program. On the whole we find minor tranquillizers helpful for periods of unusual stress but not for chronic use.

Frequently major tranquillizers, for example, Stelazine and Mellaril,
are prescribed when minor tranquillizers have little effect. These drugs
have an adverse effect on agoraphobics (Klein and Fink, 1962) who will
usually refuse to continue the medication. Unfortunately, such bad experiences with medication often increase fearfulness about taking drugs
that might prove useful. Stimulants like caffeine and amphetamine also
are likely to exacerbate general anxiety as well as panic attacks.

Until recently, imipramine (Tofranil), one drug that is likely to benefit
agoraphobics, was rarely prescribed because it is known as an antidepressant, and most agoraphobics complain largely of anxiety symptoms.
There is, however, a growing body of evidence that imipramine, which
belongs to the tricyclic family, and the monoamine-oxidase (MAO) inhibitors (another family of antidepressants) are beneficial (e.g. Ballinger,
Sheehan, and Jacobson, 1977; Zitrin, Klein, and Woerner, 1978). These
drugs are purported to reduce the frequency and severity of panic attacks. While there is clinical evidence to support this proposition, there
are few controlled observations on this particular question. Data from
controlled trials does indicate, however, that across groups, clients receiving antidepressant medication improve more quickly or more extensively.

We have also found imipramine useful in working with clients who no
longer have frequent panic attacks but present a picture of chronic
depression that makes it difficult to engage them in carrying out an effective treatment program. In these cases the drug seemed to help primarily
by lifting the depression with a concomitant increase in motivation.

Only in rare cases of brief duration have we found medication to effect
a miracle cure. Almost always the avoidance habits remain difficult to
break even though panic attacks may be less frequent. Fully 25% of our
clients refuse to take imipramine because of their fears of medication in
general and of side effects experienced with this drug specifically. Com-

mon side effects are dizziness and rapid heart beat—two dreaded signs of panic attacks. Consequently, clients may refuse to continue the drug saying they may not be panicky but feel so scared all the time that they would prefer the possibility of panic.

Our preference is to avoid the use of drugs when progress is being made without them, for the following reasons: (a) the number of clients who experience adverse side effects; (b) use of medication fosters the notion that the client is "sick"; (c) relapse after withdrawal of medication is to be expected unless the client has learned effective ways of coping with panic attacks; and (d) medication requires the expense of psychiatric consultation, which is not readily available to all therapists.

When imipramine is prescribed, it is used in the fashion suggested by Klein (see Zitrin et al., 1978). The client begins with 25 mg at bed time and increases the dosage every other evening in increments of 25 mg until an effective dose level is reached. Clients known to be particularly hypochrondriacal start with a dose of 10 mg and go up by 10 mg increments. The therapist and client check in with each other several times a week during the initial stages to insure the client's using the medication in the prescribed manner. This is initially time consuming, but necessary to combat fears about side effects. Questions about side effects are checked with the consulting psychiatrist, who talks with the client periodically. Generally side effects subside in a few days, and less intervention is required to keep clients on the medication. Klein (Zitrin et al., 1978) has noted that 20% of agoraphobics are extremely sensitive to the drug, and 25 mg may be an effective dose level for such people as opposed to the more usual 150 mg. This finding has been replicated in our experience.

SPECIAL PROBLEMS

Client Variables

Agoraphobia is rarely effectively treated in isolation from the resolution of other significant problems facing the client. In general, the more "intrapsychic" and/or reality problems a client experiences, the more difficult his/her treatment will be. Thus while we note some of the more frequent difficulties we or our students have encountered, the list of possible problems is endless.

1. A significant number of clients are put off by paradoxical suggestion due to their concrete approach. Most of these clients respond well to an alternative route to the same attitude. We ask them to simply con-

centrate on whatever they are feeling without making any effort to make the feeling go away, whether it be dizziness, wobbly legs, or a tight throat. They are not to deflect their attention from this sensation until it has ceased to be frightening. While we prefer the more active approach implied by paradoxical suggestion, the focusing exercise, if diligently pursued, achieves the same goal, keeping the client occupied in a way that she/he does not fight or avoid feelings of anxiety.

2. Common sources of stress that disrupt progress include financial difficulties, physical illness, and hormonal fluctuations such as those during and after pregnancy, during menopause, and phases of the menstrual cycle. Bad weather that keeps an agoraphobic confined for a period of time will lead to regression, as will having to care for sick children, which also leads to confinement. Separations such as having a close friend move, a therapist leave for vacation, or even threatened separations as when a close person becomes ill, may lead to intense anxiety reactions. Situations like these are not avoidable. Instead, the therapist may predict that such times will be ones that will heighten phobic anxiety. When the anxiety is predictable and understandable, clients experience it as less threatening. Also the therapist may continuously exhort the client to keep feelings focused on the actual causes of affect, for example, sadness about losing a friend, rather than worrying about bodily sensations. Additional support and encouragement to resist resurgence of avoidance patterns is helpful, perhaps taking the form of more frequent sessions or telephone contact between sessions.

3. All agoraphobics are somewhat obsessive about their symptomatic concerns; some are extremely so. For these people slight changes in body sensations such as those stemming from circadian cycles become the objects of rumination and resultant distress. Numbness in the finger tips becomes a neurological disease; a headache must result from a brain tumor. These clients are particularly difficult to work with. Our sample has not been large enough for generalization, but some seem to become less obsessive when taking imipramine. With others we have employed paradoxical intention, suggesting they dwell on any anxiety-provoking thought and attempt to think of nothing else for a period of 5 minutes or longer, until distress is no longer experienced with this particular thought.

4. The importance of the therapeutic relationship with agoraphobics has been emphasized. Some clients, however, are unwilling to form a close attachment with the therapist, which lowers considerably the leverage one has in treatment. Usually these clients are males who resist intimacy and find dependency on a therapist or anyone else very threatening. One useful approach is to avoid these issues at the beginning through the use of extensive individual *in vivo* work. During the

progress of this work the therapist may slowly build up a trusting relationship with the client, who may then begin to share fears about closeness and so forth.

Therapist Variables

Agoraphobics are particularly sensitive to the interpersonal environment of psychotherapy. They respond strongly to the therapist as a person, and the success of the therapy often hinges on this relationship. Consequently, certain therapists consistently fail, mostly by having clients drop out of treatment. These seem to be therapists who are unwilling or unable to engage warmly with clients or who find dependency repugnant. A different kind of problem exists with the therapist who fosters dependency on a continuing basis, the therapist who does not urge the client to begin separation at the appropriate time. His/her clients will improve but need to stay in therapy to maintain improvement.

Obviously the easiest way to avoid such problems is by selective referral. An alternative solution is to treat clients in groups when possible. Since group members provide so much support and encouragement, the therapist may remain more aloof with less deleterious effects. Also, less dependency develops on the therapist as an individual in a group setting. Since members often develop competition over improvement rates, there is a natural push toward termination.

Other Variables

1. Perhaps the most commonly encountered problem is that of virulent interference by family members. The example of Mary in the *in vivo* group typifies this problem. Family members may refuse to bring the client for treatment when he/she starts improving, or may create intense conflict as a more indirect way of blocking continued treatment. While we can usually avoid total breakdown by involving family members in the treatment process, some people refuse to join sessions and continue to undermine progress. A particularly clear example of this was a young woman who had been severely phobic since age 16. Unable to leave her house, she functioned as a live-in maid for her parents. Her parents insisted there was nothing abnormal about Susan's behavior and that it was a waste of time and money for her to seek treatment.

   Milder levels of such problems may be partially resolved by having volunteers who can provide transportation to therapy or by having the therapist meet the client within her/his safe territory so that transportation is not an issue. In more difficult situations a temporary relocation to a residential treatment setting seems a promising avenue;

however, we have not had the resources to test this hypothesis.
2. Since it is widely accepted that behavior therapy is the treatment of choice for phobias, one may be called upon by therapists of other orientations to treat the phobias of an agoraphobic person while the other therapist handles the ''real neurosis.'' Such a partnership is feasible for isolated problems, but is difficult, if not impossible, with agoraphobia. This situation puts the client in conflict, with divided loyalties to two therapists, and prevents the development of the kind of relationship necessary for progress. In addition, the client may receive encouragement from the other therapist to fight or avoid anxiety that dilutes the impact of the treatment program we have advocated. If the client adheres to the model of working only on the phobias with the behavior therapist, the integrated approach breaks down. For these reasons we suggest avoiding such contracts when possible, perhaps by suggesting to the client and referring therapist that they take a temporary break with the client set to return when she/he has overcome the fears.

REFERENCES

Agras, W. S., Sylvester, D., and Oliveau, D. The epidemiology of common fears and phobias. *Comprehensive Psychiatry, 1969, 10,* 151-156.

Ballenger, J., Sheehen, D., and Jacobson, G. *Antidepressant treatment of severe phobic anxiety.* Paper presented at the meeting of the *American Psychiatric Association,* Toronto, 1977.

Fodor, I. G. The phobic syndrome in women. In V. Franks and V. Burtle (Eds.), *Women in therapy.* New York: Bruner/Mazel, 1974.

Frankl, V. E. Paradoxical intention: A logotherapeutic technique. *American Journal of Psychotherapy, 1960, 14,* 520–535.

Gambrill, E. D., and Richey, C. A. An assertion inventory for use in assessment and research. *Behavior Therapy,* 1975, *6,* 550–561.

Gelder, M. G., and Marks, I. M. Severe agoraphobia: A controlled prospective trial of behavior therapy. *American Journal of Psychiatry, 1966, 112,* 309–319.

Gelder, M. G., Marks, I. M., Wolff, H. H., and Clarke, M. Desensitization, and psychotherapy in the treatment of phobic states: A controlled inquiry. *British Journal of Psychiatry, 1967, 113,* 53–73.

Goldstein, A. J., and Chambless, D. L. A reanalysis of agoraphobia. *Behavior Therapy, 1978, 9,* 47–59.

Hafner, R. J. Fresh symptom emergence after intensive behavior therapy. *British Journal of Psychiatry, 1976, 129,* 378–383.

Hafner, R. J. The husbands of agoraphobic women and their influence on treatment outcome. *British Journal of Psychiatry, 1977, 131,* 289–294.

Hand, I., Lamontagne, Y., and Marks, I. M. Group exposure (flooding) *in vivo* for agoraphobics. *British Journal of Psychiatry*, 1974, *124*, 588–602.

Klein, D. F., and Fink, M. Behavioral reaction patterns with phenothiazines. *Archives of General Psychiatry*, 1962, *7*, 449–459.

Marks, I. M. Agoraphobic syndrome (phobic anxiety state). *Archives of General Psychiatry*, 1970, *23*, 538–553.

Marks, I. M., Hallam, R. S., Philpott, R., and Connolly, J. C. Nurse therapists in behavioral psychotherapy. *British Medical Journal*, 1975, *3*, 144–148.

Marks, I. M., and Herst, E. R. A survey of 1,200 agoraphobics in Britain. *Social Psychiatry*, 1970, *5*, 16–24.

Mathews, A., Teasdale, J., Munby, M., Johnston, D., and Shaw, P. A home-based treatment program for agoraphobia. *Behavior Therapy*, 1977, *8*, 915-924.

Roberts, A. H. Housebound-housewives: A follow-up study of phobic anxiety states. *British Journal of Psychiatry*, 1964, *110*, 191–197.

Watson, J. P., Mullet, G. E., and Pillay, H. The effects of prolonged exposure upon agoraphobic patients treated in groups. *Behaviour Research and Therapy*, 1973, *11*, 531–545.

Weiss, E. *Agoraphobia in the light of ego psychology*. New York: Grune and Stratton, 1964.

Wolpe, J., and Lang, P. A fear survey schedule for use in behavior therapy. *Behaviour Research and Therapy*, 1964, *2*, 27–30.

Zitrin, C. M., Klein, D. F., and Woerner, M. G. Behavior therapy, supportive psychotherapy, imipramine and phobias. *Archives of General Psychiatry*, 1978, *35*, 307–316.

NOTES

1. While C's fear of "craziness" was based on her rejection of sexual attraction to men other than her husband, this does not mean that all agoraphobics fear sexual impulses. Rather they often fear strong feelings in general—anger, sadness, sometimes even exhilaration—and particular clients may be more fearful of one emotion than others.

2. The authors thank Genevieve Roy, the therapist in this segment.

3. Actually it makes little difference whether a separation occurs because of death, divorce, or physical distance, as the impact on the person left behind is much the same.

4. For a more complete illustration of the treatment of a delayed mourning reaction that was presented as pervasive anxiety see Goldstein, A. J. in R. J. Corsini (Ed.) *Current psychotherapies* Itasca, Ill.: Peacock, 1973, or Chambless, D. L. and Goldstein, A. J., in R. J. Corsini (Ed.) *Current psychotherapies* (2nd ed.). Itasca, Ill.: Peacock, 1979.

APPENDIX
Evaluation of Agoraphobia

I.   *Fear Inventory* (NB: Objectives are to get a sense of the degree of limitation and to draw to the client's attention how this jumble of fears is quite consistent, that is he/she fears any place where there is a sense of being "stuck".)

What are the major fears troubling you? (Check the fears that are especially significant to this patient.)

	Alone	Accompanied
1. Driving (if yes, how far from home)	_____	_____
2. Waiting in line (e.g., supermarket)	_____	_____
3. Crowds (e.g., department store)	_____	_____
4. Elevators, escalators	_____	_____
5. Public transportation:		
a. airplanes	_____	_____
b. buses	_____	_____
c. trains	_____	_____
6. Being at home	_____	_____
7. Auditoriums, churches, movies		
(Does client sit near exit?)	_____	_____
8. Bridges	_____	_____
9. Tunnels and other enclosed spaces	_____	_____
10. Open terrain; parks, stadiums	_____	_____
11. Other	_____	_____
_____		
_____		

Where else do you feel stuck or trapped?   _____

II. *Panic Attack Data*

A. Establishing Basis of Fears (NB: Objective is to establish presence or absence of "fear of fear")

What concerns you about being in (typical avoided situation)?   ____
_____

What do you feel will happen?   _____
_____

(Elicit panic information if present such as "I'll get one of those spells." Other phobics would describe fears of external consequences such as the plane crashing.)

B. Phobic Companions's Role—if there is an indication that the presence of another is comforting, ask the following:

How does having someone with you reduce your fear? What can that person do for you? _____

(Objective here is to show how this is not "silly" either if one is expecting disaster in the form of feared catastrophes such as heart attack, etc.)

C. Onset

When did you have your first attack? _____

Description of client's general life circumstances at onset. _____

_____

_____

(NB: If there is no clear precipitant such as a bad drug experience, this is a cue for complex agoraphobia. Look for interpersonal triggers— Check all applicable descriptions)

Drug trip___ Hormonal fluctuations___Death of significant person ___

Postpartum _____ Interpersonal conflict hypoglycemia _____

Illness _____ Post operative _____ Other _____

When searching for interpersonal conflict it may be helpful to inquire: Was there anything going on in your life then that made you feel particularly trapped? _____

_____

D. Description of Attack

What happens to you when you have an attack? What do you feel in your body? (Check all applicable descriptions)

Shaking _____ Derealization _____ Heart palpitations ____

Dizziness _____ Can't breathe _____ Depersonalization ____

Nausea _____ Need to urinate _____ Need to defecate ____

What runs through your mind (feared catastrophe) at such times?

_____

What could happen to you other than you would be stuck for a while? (Check all applicable descriptions)

Heart attack _____   Going crazy _____

Stroke _____   Loss of bladder control _____

Pass out _____   Loss of bowel control _____

Screaming _____   Other comments _____

What do you usually do when you have an attack? (Check all applicable descriptions)

Run home _____   Stick it out _____

Never go anywhere that may   Call for help _____

cause one _____

            Other _____

E. Cycles of Attacks

Do you find you have fluctuations in the severity of panics and

fears? For example, do you ever just wake up and know it's going to be a bad day? _____
Length of cycles (check one)
Days _____ Months _____ Years _____
(If female patient) Do you find the panics are more likely at certain times in your menstrual cycle? _____
What is going on in your life when these fluctuations occur? NB: Objective—the client probably does not know but this gives the therapist a chance to open this issue and perhaps suggest keeping a journal—check all applicable descriptions)
Deaths _____   Interpersonal conflict _____
Illness or surgery _____   Hormonal fluctuations _____
Birth _____   Other comments _____

III. *Current Results of Condition* (NB: Objectives—gather information and build motivation for change)
A. Interpersonal Aspects
How have people reacted to your problem (spouse, parents, children, lovers, friends)? How does this affect your family and social life? ___
_____
_____
B. Vocational Adjustment
Have you been able to work since this problem began? _____ (if yes) How has it affected you in your work? _____
C. Leisure Time
Have you given up doing things you used to enjoy? _____

IV. *Current Physical Data*
A. General Condition
Have you had a physical? _____
What has your doctor told you about (e.g., your heart)? _____
_____
(Give assurance that you understand how powerful these physical symptoms are, that they're not "just nerves". Explain how anxiety and hyperventilation cause these sensations.)
If person hasn't had physical, suggest he/she get one for reassurance.
B. Hypoglycemia or endocrine disorders? _____
(NB: Panic attack sensations can be caused by such problems. If there is reason to suspect any physical disorder, it should be corrected before assuming psychotherapy is required.)

C. Current drug use (dosage and reactions)

1. Caffeine _____ (In excess can cause panics)

2. Amphetamine: _____ (Extremely detrimental to agoraphobics)

3. Hallucinogens (LSD, marijuana, mescaline, etc.): _____

4. Minor tranquilizers: _____ (Can be somewhat helpful for general anxiety but will not stop panics)

5. Major tranquilizers: _____ (Exacerbate agoraphobic symptoms)

6. MAO inhibitors or trycyclic antidepressants: _____ (In proper dosage can be very helpful)

7. Other (specify): _____

V.   Prior Treatment

A. Psychotherapy—what type and of what duration? _____

"What did you gain from this treatment?" _____

B. Drug therapy (Note whether there was improvement, no change, or exacerbation of symptoms)

1. Minor tranquilizers: _____   2. Major tranquilizers: _____

_____   3. Tricyclic antidepressants or

MAO inhibitors _____

How long: _____   What dosage: _____

C. ECT? _____ If yes, how many treatments? _____

D. Expectations for this therapy: _____

(NB: Give a tentative treatment plan for how you will proceed if patient comes in for treatment. Educate the patient about behavior therapy.)

CHAPTER 8

The Treatment of Obsessive-Compulsive Neurosis

EDNA B. FOA

Temple University Medical School
Department of Psychiatry

and

ARND TILLMANNS

Rehabilitationsklinik Windach
Federal Republic of Germany

INTRODUCTION: THEORETICAL CONSIDERATIONS AND TREATMENT MODALITIES

Definition of Obsessive-Compulsive Neurosis

The concept of obsessive-compulsive neurosis has been discussed for over one hundred years. Esquirol provided the first written account as early as 1838, but it was not until the beginning of this century that attempts to reach a formal definition were made (Lewis, 1936; Schneider, 1925). In spite of ongoing controversy on certain issues, there is considerable agreement that the obsessive-compulsive disorder is characterized by a "recurrent or persistent thought, image, impulse, or action that is accompanied by a sense of subjective compulsion and a desire to resist it" (Carr, 1974). Similarly, the DSM of mental disorders published by the American Psychiatric Association (1968, p. 40) defines this disorder as "the persistent intrusion of unwanted thoughts, urges or actions that the patient is unable to stop."

Within this population of obsessive-compulsives, there are several classes. For instance, it is common for patients to suffer from recurring disturbing thoughts or images without manifesting repetitive actions, and a few patients will manifest persistent repetitious behaviors in the absence of recurring thoughts. However, a large proportion of obsessive-compulsive patients complain of having intrusive disturbing thoughts and of performing repetitious, stereotyped actions. This chapter describes a treatment plan designed for the latter patient population.

It is customary to refer to thoughts and images as "obsessions" and to repetitious actions as "compulsions." We find this classification unsatisfactory, as it is based on the modality rather than on function. We suggest instead a distinction based on the relationship between anxiety/discomfort and each class of symptoms. Thoughts, images, and actions that *elicit* anxiety or discomfort are called obsessions. On the other hand, behaviors and (more rarely) thoughts or images that *reduce* anxiety are termed compulsions. Both obsessions and compulsions share such characteristics as high frequency of occurrence, persistence, and repetitiveness, as well as internal resistance to these symptoms. There is, however, a prevalence of thoughts over behaviors in obsessions, while the opposite is true for compulsions.

Obsessive-Compulsive Patterns: Description and Case Reports

Neurotic thoughts and behaviors occur in a variety of forms. Two very common types of compulsive behavior are washing and checking (Rachman, 1976a). *Washers* are patients who feel contaminated when exposed to certain objects or thoughts; their compulsive behavior consists mostly of excessive, ritualistic washing and cleaning. *Checkers* are patients whose compulsions consist of repetitious checking and/or ritualistic stereotyped actions that they perform to avoid future "disasters" or punishment. Sometimes, the rituals are related to the anxiety-evoking obsessions in a direct, rational way (e.g., checking to see if the stove is off in order to avoid possible fire); other rituals are not rationally related to the obsessions. Both washing and checking can be found in the same patient. For our purposes in outlining a treatment plan, however, it is more convenient to treat them separately. We begin by describing two cases from each group; later, we outline the various stages of treatment, using the two washers as case examples.

Washers

Case 1. Steve is a 19-year-old, single male who complained of becoming contaminated (a distinctive sensation on his skin accompanied by strong anxiety and discomfort) when exposed to the odor of chicken soup or the body odor of other people. The fear of becoming contaminated generalized to every object that might have been touched by other people. When Steve came for treatment, he was avoiding contact with the outside world whenever possible, and for the most part stayed home. Even at home, he felt contaminated by his parents and the objects they had touched. Moreover, certain words such as "chicken soup," "odor," and so forth had the power to contaminate him. Somewhat excessive washing had started at age 12; in the year previous to treatment, the amount of time he spent washing and the number of rituals involved in his washing behavior had increased, taking up about 8 hours of his day.

Case 2. Sara is a 33-year-old married female, with two children. She felt contaminated (a nonspecific feeling of being dirty, accompanied by extreme anxiety and discomfort) when in contact with her mother. Her symptoms started 10 years prior to treatment when she was pregnant with her second child after her mother had touched her once in order to feel the movements of the fetus. Sara felt highly anxious immediately after that touch and was relieved after a normal shower. She came for treatment when she felt contaminated by everything that could have been in contact with her mother, even remotely: persons living in the area where her mother lived, persons who were in contact with her mother, mail from the area where her mother lived, and so forth. She avoided "contaminated" places and controlled her husband's and children's movements to avoid being contaminated through them. In spite of all attempts to avoid contamination, she gradually increased hand washing to about 50 hand washings and three 30-minute showers per day.

These two cases are typical of "washers." The stimuli that produce feelings of contamination differ for different patients, but they all experience high levels of anxiety after having been in contact with these stimuli, and they all get some relief—a sense of relative comfort—after washing or cleaning. It is important to remember that when obsessive-compulsive patients complain about "feeling dirty," they are not necessarily referring to actual dirt. Rather, what they often experience is a subjective experience of some discomfort on their skin. Even when they avoid touching places which are considered by most people to be dirty, such as floors, it is not concern for "normal dirt" that makes them do so. Sara, for example, could not touch the floor because it was possible that somebody who had been in contact with her mother (through a chain of people) might have walked on it. Ironically, some obsessive-compulsives will not clean their rooms for years in order to prevent the rooms from being contaminated.

Checkers

Case 3. Mike, a 32-year-old patient, performed checking rituals that were preceded by a fear of harming other people. When driving, he had to stop the car often and return to check to see whether he had run over people, particularly babies. Before flushing the toilet, he had to check to be sure that a live insect had not fallen into the toilet—he did not want to be responsible for killing any insects. At home, he repeatedly checked the doors, stoves, lights, and windows—making sure that all were shut or turned off so that no harm, such as fire or burglary, would come to his family due to his "irresponsible" behavior. He particularly worried about his 15-month-old daughter, repeatedly checking the gate to the basement to be sure that it was locked. He did not carry his daughter while walking on concrete floors in order to avoid killing her by accidentally dropping her. He performed these and many other checking rituals for an average of 4 hours a day. Checking behavior started several months after his marriage, 6 years prior to treatment. It increased 2 years later, when his wife was pregnant with their first child, and continued to get worse over the years.

Case 4. Jeff is a 45-year-old, single male who complained of intrusive negative thoughts about God. Although he did not imagine God as a person, thoughts such as "God should be bald" and "God should break his leg" would intrude frequently. He considered these thoughts to be sinful and was afraid of being punished by God. To prevent punishment, Jeff had to undo the thoughts by repeating whatever he had been doing when the "bad thought" entered his mind. He repeated the action continuously until he was sure that he had done it without having the bad thought. In addition, he was counting the number of times he repeated the action to avoid repetition of multiples of three—because of his preoccupation with the Holy Trinity. For example, Jeff was combing his hair when the thought "God should be bald" came into his mind. He then had to comb the exact spot on his head in exactly the same manner several times until he was satisfied that the last strokes of the comb were not accompanied by the thought. If, however, he counted 3, 6, 9, and so forth strokes, he would have to start the ritual again to avoid multiples of 3. Jeff reported having had these thoughts from early childhood, but they only began to evoke anxiety at age 22. He developed the rituals after becoming incapacitated by fear of punishment. The rituals helped him to keep the anxiety at a tolerable level that would allow him to work, but they consumed a great deal of his time and hampered his functioning in social situations.

Mike is a clear case of a patient who developed checking rituals to prevent catastrophe from happening because of his irresponsibility. Jeff used a different technique for the prevention of catastrophic events—being punished by God or self-harm; he belongs to the group of repeaters.

Rachman (1976a) suggested that the underlying motive for all checkers and repeaters is the need to avoid criticism either from others or from oneself. For checkers, unlike washers, the anxiety-evoking stimuli are either objects or events that evoke thoughts of disaster or the thoughts themselves, which often occur in the absence of "real" stimuli. As one patient told us:

> I was lying in bed and was thinking to myself that probably I had forgotten to turn off the stove and the house was going to catch on fire. This will happen when I am asleep and I won't know that there is a fire in the house. By the time I wake up, the children's rooms will be on fire and the children will be dead.

This patient would immediately jump out of bed and run to check the stove. His behavior is defined as compulsive because of the way in which the checking had to be performed, and the number of times it had to be repeated. Each part of the stove had to be touched, or turned on and off several times. Before leaving the kitchen he would glance again at the stove and often go back to repeat the same actions.

As suggested by these clinical examples, checking behavior increases when the patient is in a position of responsibility, and thus occurs most often at work or at home. Repeaters, on the other hand, will behave ritualistically when the appropriate stimuli are present, which may happen anywhere.

Two processes seem to take place as the symptoms develop:

1. For washers, the number of contaminating stimuli increases with time. In the beginning, Sara felt contaminated only by direct contact with her mother or her mother's personal belongings. Later, a person who lived close to Sara's mother "contaminated" the whole factory where her husband worked, so that both the products of this factory and all its employees, including Sara's husband, became contaminators. Generalization can expand to such an extent that some patients become nonfunctional, and even completely isolated from the outside world.

2. In an effort to counteract the multiplication of anxiety-evoking stimuli, the number of rituals, their duration, and their intensity tend to in-

crease with time. Washers often end up using strong detergents and disinfectants. They wash in a stereotyped way that has to be repeated exactly before they feel relief. Rituals may include cleaning the soap, preparing a special water temperature, cleaning in a special order, and so forth. Sara, who began by feeling relieved after just regular washing, eventually developed a complicated ritual that included cleaning her nails first, followed by washing each finger for a "magic" number of times. Often, washing rituals include the cleaning of faucets (which in turn leads to an additional repetition of hand washing), cleaning the entire bathroom before taking a shower in a prescribed manner and order, and so forth. Another patient, a checker, had to undress and dress hundreds of times per day in order to reduce the anxiety elicited by the thought that her husband might be killed in a car accident; in the beginning, performing the ritual only once was sufficient.

A Theoretical Model of Obsessive-Compulsive Disorders

Maintenance of Avoidance Responses

The learning models we use to explain the etiology and maintenance of obsessional-compulsive behavior apply equally well to the acquisition of fear responses, or phobias. Therefore, in the following theoretical analysis, specific distinctions between these two classes of symptoms are omitted.

Mowrer's theory (Mowrer, 1960) does not account for *all* avoidance responses (Beech and Perigault, 1974; Rachman, 1976b; Teasdale, 1974). Nevertheless, it is a widely accepted model of avoidance learning because it seems to account satisfactorily for the maintenance of obsessional-compulsive behaviors of both washers and checkers, and we discuss this theory at some length. According to the two-factor theory, avoidance responses are acquired in two stages. In the first stage, a neutral stimulus that does not evoke anxiety becomes associated (by pairing) with an unconditioned stimulus (UCS) that innately evokes discomfort or anxiety. By the process of classical conditioning, the neutral stimulus acquires such aversive connotations that its presence will result in anxiety; it now becomes a conditioned stimulus (CS) for fear response. When this CS is paired with yet another neutral stimulus, the latter also acquires aversive overtones and its presentation will also elicit anxiety. Through this process of higher order conditioning, many concrete stimuli, as well as words, images, and thoughts, acquire the capacity to evoke anxiety. At the same time, the original anxiety response tends to expand into a general feeling of discomfort.

Anxiety or discomfort is experienced as an aversive or unpleasant state. The second stage, then, consists of developing or learning responses that decrease or terminate the discomfort arising from the presence of the conditioned stimuli. Such responses are termed avoidance or escape responses.

Avoidance and Compulsions

In obsessional-compulsive patients, avoidance or escape responses take the form of ritualistic-compulsive behavior (Dollard and Miller, 1950). These responses are reinforced by the anxiety reduction that results from their performance. How are *specific* compulsions learned? The phobic patient who responds with anxiety to elevators successfully organizes her or his life in such a way that the use of elevators will be eliminated. The obsessional-compulsive patient who feels contaminated by her mother will attempt to avoid any contact with her. The high degree of generalization and higher order conditioning that takes place in obsessional-compulsive neurosis progressively reduces the effectiveness of mere avoidance that may remain effective for the phobic patient—there are just too many stimuli to be avoided. Specific behavioral *patterns* are then developed to terminate or reduce discomfort. Even in the initial stages, passive avoidance never works as well for the obsessive-compulsive patient as for the phobic. It is possible for the latter to shun threatening places and situations, but how does one escape from an expected disaster, such as a disease, or punishment in the after-life? Active avoidance *patterns* are required for the obsessional-compulsive patient in order to reduce anxiety to a tolerable level.

Often, the rituals that the obsessive-compulsive develops are logically related to the source of discomfort. The person who feels discomfort because of "dirt" develops washing rituals; those who are afraid of harming their families by neglecting to lock the door or shutting off the stove will resort to checking. Sometimes, however, specific behaviors may lead to relief by chance when first performed in the presence of the evoking stimuli, and are then repeated every time the discomfort-arousing stimuli are present. They seem "senseless" and "superstitious," but they do produce relief. The longer patients engage in "relief-producing behavior" the more convinced they become that only this specific behavior can bring them relief. They feel that anxiety "will stay forever and even worsen" if they behave in specific ways. Moreover, they are convinced that "something terrible" will happen to them if they do not perform their rituals. As rituals become more complicated and elaborate, the difficulty of completing them successfully increases. Sometimes patients forget several steps, or more often, they don't remember if they followed the proper sequence in full. Then they have to start again and redo the entire procedure. Even when the rituals become more and more disabling and aversive, patients continue to depend on them for handling discomfort and usually do not learn more appropriate ways to relieve their anxiety.

Performance of Rituals and Level of Discomfort

The drive-reduction model described predicts that discomfort level immediately after completion of a ritual should be lower than level before the ritual was performed. While this appears to be the case for the majority of obsessional-compulsive patients, some investigators (Wolpe, 1958; Walker and Beech, 1969) have shown that in certain cases anxiety may increase rather than decrease following the performance of rituals. Why are rituals maintained in such situations? Herrnstein (1969) suggests that avoidance behavior will persist when the state of the organism after its performance is less aversive than it would have been had the organism not emitted the avoidance response.

One possible source of discomfort after completing rituals is the avoidance-avoidance conflict (Teasdale, 1974). While patients are motivated to perform rituals because of their discomfort-reduction properties, such performance may also be aversive: it consumes time and energy, it is a source of ridicule by significant others, and it makes the patient feel ashamed. When the drive to reduce discomfort is stronger than the rituals' aversive consequences, they are likely to be maintained; nevertheless, the patient is left tense and shameful after performing them. Another source of tension, found mostly among patients who perform checking rituals, is the difficulty they report in deciding when to stop (Walker and Beech, 1969) and in deciding whether or not earlier checking was adequate. Roper, Rachman, and Hodgson (1973) found that on 7 out of 36 occasions checkers reported higher anxiety following the rituals, while on no occasion was such an increase reported by washers. Herrnstein's theory predicts that refraining from checking would result in more discomfort than being subject to doubts about termination and effectiveness of the ritual. Many checkers, as well as washers, try to maintain environmental conditions that will minimize their need to perform rituals because of their aversive implications. Washers attempt to "stay uncontaminated," while checkers "allocate responsibilities" to other people. For example, a patient who was concerned with spots and wrinkles on his clothes and, therefore, found himself checking them repeatedly, allocated the responsibility for his clothes to his wife; another patient who was afraid that his baby daughter would be hurt if he did not "secure" her physical environment, finally allocated the responsibility for her well-being to his wife and refused to take care of her during her waking hours. Invariably, as we mentioned earlier, such attempts at passive avoidance fail, and in spite of the aversion associated with performance of such rituals, they still seem necessary to the patient to reduce discomfort to a "tolerable level."

The Etiology of Obsessional-Compulsive Behavior

According to the two-factor theory, avoidance behaviors presuppose the presence of anxiety conditioned to objects or thoughts. One of the more popular learning models for the genesis of phobias (Eysenck and Rachman, 1965) suggests indeed that phobias are learned by classical conditioning. Their persistent nature is attributed to the fact that avoidance responses prevent prolonged or repeated exposure to the conditioned stimulus, in the absence of the unconditioned one, and so do not allow for extinction.

The classical conditioning model for acquisition of fears has been criticized on several grounds. It is rarely possible to identify a specific traumatic event when the phobic stimulus was paired with an unconditioned stimulus. Moreover, stressful events often appear to precede the onset of phobias, rather than being paired with the phobic stimuli.

Teasdale (1974) presents an alternative model, which was suggested by Watts. This model proposes that phobias develop as a result of some stress event that sensitizes the person to stimuli having an innate tendency to elicit fear responses. To explain the persistence of phobias in the absence of stress conditions, Watts adopted Eysenck's proposition that presentation of a conditioned stimulus without the unconditioned one can result in either extinction or enhancement of the conditioned response. Watts suggests that a phobia will persist under conditions where the tendency for response enhancement outweighs the tendency for extinction. While this proposition merits attention, it is compelling only if the differential conditions for transient versus persistent fears can be specified. In addition, as pointed out by Teasdale (1974, p. 225), it is not necessary to postulate that only innate fears are susceptible to sensitization; learned anxiety responses and early experiences may also be enhanced by stress.

This formulation may relate to the acquisition of obsessions. However, neither the two-factor theory nor Watts's theory can adequately account for the ritualistic character of compulsive behaviors as well as for the development of multiple rituals in the same individual (Carr, 1974).

Attempts have been made to explain "senseless," "fixated" rituals using paradigms developed in animal research (Metzner, 1963). Stereotyped behavior was induced in rats under three experimental conditions: (a) when a previously rewarded response later served to avoid an aversive event, (b) when an avoidance or escape response was punished, and (c) when noncontingent shocks were administered and produced "superstitious" escape behaviors. It is not clear whether fixated, stereotyped behavior in animals is in fact analogous to compulsive behavior in human beings, particularly since patient reports seem to indicate that "senseless" repetitious behavior continues to be effective in reducing anxiety across a variety of situations comparable to the experimental conditions just described.

An interesting hypothesis about early differential experiences of cleaners and checkers was put forward by Rachman (1976a), who suggests that both groups share experiences of excessive parental concern and control; cleaners' parents are over-controlling and over-protective, while checkers' parents are over-controlling and over-critical. Furthermore, he suggests that while washers fear objects or situations, checkers are largely motivated by fear of criticism or guilt. This latter hypothesis, mentioned before, has important implications for treatment, which is discussed later.

In summary, while it is clear that the two-stage theory is unable to account for the acquisition of obsessive-compulsive disorders, it seems to provide an adequate explanation for their maintenance. Either through classical conditioning or events that sensitize innate or previously learned tendencies, anxiety is elicited in the presence of previously neutral stimuli. Performance of rituals successfully terminates or decreases the aversive state of discomfort/anxiety. Rituals are maintained because of their discomfort-reduction properties. We now describe some experimental results that are relevant to the maintenance of compulsive behavior.

Research Findings Relating to the Two-Factor Theory

The drive-reduction hypothesis predicts that exposing an obsessional-compulsive patient to certain stimuli or situations will result in an increment of anxiety or discomfort; performance of compulsions should decrease discomfort. In a set of experiments, Hodgson, Rachman, and Roper obtained support for such predictions. In the first experiment Hodgson and Rachman (1972) studied 12 patients who displayed clear-cut washing rituals related to fear of dirt or contamination; after having touched a contaminated object they were exposed to the following experimental conditions: handwashing immediately after contamination, a half-hour delay before washing after contamination; handwashing after the delay, and interruption of the hand-washing ritual after contamination. Pulse rate and subjective anxiety discomfort were recorded before touching the contaminated object, after touching the object, half an hour after touching or after interruption of the ritual, and after completion of the ritual.

Self-rating of discomfort/anxiety were significantly higher after touching the contaminated object and decreased significantly after washing. Pulse rate data followed the same trend, but the differences were not significant. Thus the data supports the proposition that washing rituals are maintained because they successfully decrease discomfort. As to the failure of pulse rate to reach significance, there are several possible explanations. The authors confronted the patients in this study with items of moderate "contaminatability;" it could well be that objects more strongly contaminated would have produced greater differences in pulse rate. Moreover, not all people react with increased pulse rate; if several patients were GSR (galvanic skin response) reactors, for example, they would have reduced differences across experimental conditions. When the ritual was interrupted or delayed by half an hour, the expected increase in discomfort failed to materialize, perhaps because patients knew that they would eventually be allowed to wash; in the meantime they were asked to spread the contamination, that is, to touch other objects or their own clothes. Clinical observations of washers are in accordance with these results; these patients can often delay their washing for several hours and tolerate high degrees of contamination as long as their "safe," "clean" places are not contaminated, and if they can clean themselves before contacting those places (e.g., bedroom, bed, chair they use, etc.). Had those patients who were interrupted in their rituals been told that they could not wash for several days, anxiety/discomfort after interruption probably would have arisen.

Disturbed by Beech's (1971) observation that rituals sometimes increase anxiety and by their own clinical observations of the differences between self-reports of checkers and washers, Roper, Rachman, and Hodgson (1973) repeated the original experiment with a group of twelve checkers. Patients were asked to perform an act that produced discomfort and were allowed to check under the following conditions: immediately after completing the urge-producing act, half an hour later, immediately— but in each case checking was interrupted. Subjective rating of anxiety/ discomfort and pulse rate were reported. The results were similar to those found in washers: checkers experienced an increase in anxiety/discomfort after carrying out a "potentially harmful act." Completion of the appropriate act of checking was usually followed by a decrease in anxiety/ discomfort. However, two differences between the two groups of patients were noted:

1. Washers who were requested to delay their ritual stayed anxious,

while checkers reported a significant decrease in anxiety during this period.

2. In some instances checkers reported an increase in anxiety/discomfort after ritual performance, while no such increase was reported by washers. This result gives some support to the view that a ritual can increase discomfort; in general though, the discomfort-relief model is supported for both checkers and washers.

Recognizing that the conditions of their experimental environment were not likely to produce much discomfort in checkers: that is, responsibility could be transferred to the experimenter who was present during the experiment, and the hospital was relatively safer than home, Roper and Rachman (1976) replicated this study with 12 additional checkers. This time, they elicited the compulsive urges, and patients performed their checking rituals in natural environments, with and without the presence of the experimenter. The response-prevention period was extended to 2 hours. Their results showed that discomfort and compulsive urges in natural situations were considerably more pronounced than those reported in their earlier experiment. They were even stronger when the experimenter was absent. Checking rituals reduced discomfort, but not as effectively as washing rituals for washers. Only 2 of the 12 checkers who participated in this experiment reported an increase in discomfort on some occasions after their ritualistic behavior.

On the whole, these three experiments show that the discomfort-reduction hypothesis provides a satisfactory explanation for the maintenance of checking and washing rituals. Similar results were reported by Carr (1971).

From Theoretical Considerations to Choice of Treatment

The theoretical model presented here states that (a) a neutral stimulus acquires properties of arousing anxiety or discomfort, and (b) this discomfort is reduced through the performance of rituals. These propositions suggest three possible strategies for treatment:

1. *Reduction of Anxiety/Discomfort: Systematic Desensitization.* This first strategy focuses on breaking the bond between the conditioned stimulus and anxiety (Stage a). Once the stimulus does not arouse discomfort the compulsions should no longer be needed as relief-producing tactics and should, therefore, be extinguished. Specifically, this strategy suggests that the use of systematic desensitization will eliminate the conditioned fear response and thereby obviate the rituals (see Chapter 2).

In general, the literature on the use of systematic desensitization in obsessional-compulsive patients reports conflicting results. Some report success (e.g., Haslam, 1965; Rackensperger and Feinberg, 1972; McGlynn and Linder, 1971), while others report failure (e.g., Furst and Cooper, 1970; Marks et al., 1969).

Cooper, Gelder, and Marks (1965) report the use of desensitization *in vivo* and in imagination with ten obsessional patients. Only three showed improvement, and a control group treated with supportive psychotherapy and drugs showed more improvement. Wolpe (1964) used systematic desensitization with a washer. After 100 sessions, the patient was unable to transfer to real-life situations. He then tried desensitization *in vivo*, which did result in decrease of washing.

Walton and Mather (1963) distinguished between cases of recent onset, when compulsions are elicited by conditioned anxiety, and chronic cases when compulsions become "functionally autonomous" and independent of anxiety. They hypothesized that the former group but not the latter would respond to systematic desensitization. They tested this hypothesis with a sample of six patients with severe obsessional-compulsive neurosis. For two patients whose symptoms were of recent onset, the compulsions were extinguished; for two of the patients with long-term, chronic symptoms, desensitization decreased anxiety but left the compulsions unchanged. In another chronic case, compulsions were the focus of treatment; here, treatment achieved a temporary remission of rituals, but anxiety increased. In still another chronic case, both systematic desensitization and retraining to actual "performance hierarchies" did not yield results.

Marks and coworkers (1969) treated a patient whose fear of contamination by dogs was accompanied by ritualistic washing with 62 sessions of systematic desensitization. They succeeded in lowering anxiety, but rituals were not affected nor did improvement transfer to other situations.

In summary, reduction of anxiety by systematic desensitization is costly in terms of number of sessions, and its success appears to be limited to cases with recent onset of symptoms. Desensitization *in vivo* seems more successful than desensitization in imagination.

2. *Eliminating the Ritualistic Behavior.* The second strategy suggested by the drive-reduction model focuses on eliminating the functional relationship between the ritualistic behavior and relief. This behavior is maintained because of its effectiveness in decreasing discomfort produced by given stimuli or situations. If the contingencies could be re-arranged so that the compulsive behavior will be associated with *increase* rather than decrease in discomfort, it should extinguish. Thorpe, Schmidt, Brown, and Castel (1964) reported on the use of aversion-relief conditioning with a patient who was a compulsive hand washer. Presentation of the anxiety-evoking stimulus was fol-

lowed by electric shock. Shock termination was contingent upon presentation of non-obsessional material. After a few days (two sessions per day), hand washing disappeared. However, anxiety level between sessions was high, and the patient cried frequently. After 2 weeks the patient relapsed and declined further treatment. The use of aversion-relief technique was also reported by Marks and coworkers (1969) and Rubin and Merbaum (1971). In these studies, electrical shock was made contingent on washing and was terminated when the patient came in contact with the "contaminated" object. Thus the patient experienced discomfort when performing the ritual and relief when touching the object—the opposite of the conditioned response symptom. Aversion-relief treatment together with desensitization reduced the compulsive washing somewhat. Desensitization alone was not effective.

Another form of this treatment method uses aversion alone (Kenny, Solyom, and Solyom, 1973). The authors divided each compulsion into distinct steps. Each step was then performed by the patient in imagination and was followed by electrical shock. They dealt with obsessions in the same manner. Three out of the five patients so treated improved. However, the follow-up interval was too short to yield conclusive data.

Use of aversion therapy usually results in rapid suppression of the target behavior, but Eysenck (1960) has warned against "cures" that extinguish motor responses but fail to affect conditioned autonomic drives. Walton (1960) also reports relapse in a case in which only the motor responses were treated. We encountered similar difficulties in the treatment of sexual deviations by aversive techniques alone (Foa, 1976). On the other hand, Taylor (1963) suggested that maintenance of compulsive acts depends on positive reinforcement rather than on their anxiety-reducing properties. Therefore, treatment should concentrate on the compulsion itself. This procedure may be valid when disorders involve repetitive motor habits such as nail biting or trichotillomania. As shown by the studies of Hodgson, Rachman, and Roper discussed earlier, the treatment proposed by Taylor is not effective with checkers and washers.

Meyer, Levy, and Schnurer (1974) reviewed studies and case reports of sixty-two patients who were treated by techniques based on the two strategies described so far: elimination of anxiety and extinction of compulsive behaviors. These authors dichotomized the outcomes into "improved-unimproved" and concluded that 55% of the patients were improved. This figure is quite impressive when compared with the results of traditional psychotherapy, for which Kringlen (1965), for example, reports a 21% improvement rate. However, the same 55% figure is disappointing when compared with reported improvement of phobic states (e.g., Wolpe, 1958, 1973).

3. *Flooding and Response Prevention—The Treatment of Choice for Obsessive-Compulsive Disorders.* A third strategy uses techniques that deal with anxiety as well as with the elimination of the compulsions that cause it. As we have said, the high degree of generalization in obsessive-compulsive disorders prevents patients from avoiding anxiety-evoking stimuli for very long. They repeatedly find themselves having an urge to check, wash, or repeat a ritualistic act—an urge that is extremely difficult to resist. Under these circumstances, traditional outpatient treatment of once-a-week therapy sessions, which leaves the patient free to carry out her/his passive and active avoidance responses in between sessions, has to be unsatisfactory.

With this in mind, Meyer (1966) developed a therapeutic program later on labeled "apotrepic therapy" (Meyer, Levy, and Schnurer, 1974, p. 245), which consists of "prevention of rituals for a long period of time while the patient is required to remain in the situations which normally evoke anxiety and ritualistic activities." The authors reported results on 15 patients, all of whom were washers, checkers, or repeaters; all but one were inpatients. Treatment involved continual supervision to prevent patients from carrying out their rituals. After rituals were totally eliminated, the patients were exposed to anxiety-evoking situations in hierarchical order from the least to the most stressful. The reported results are impressive; of the 15 patients treated with this program, ten were rated as much improved or symptom-free, and five were rated as improved. Only two patients relapsed during the follow-up period.

Meyer's apotrepic therapy consists of two basic components: (1) exposure to discomfort-evoking stimuli; and (2) response prevention, that is, blocking the compulsive behaviors. What do we know about the effects of these two procedures?

Exposure

Maier (1949) reported that the only technique he found successful in eliminating stereotyped behavior in animals was "guidance", that is, guiding the animal manually toward the previously avoided situation. This procedure is essentially exposure *in vivo* to anxiety-evoking stimuli. Almost two decades later, Stampfl (1967) formulated a clinical technique labeled "implosion," which consists of prolonged exposure in fantasy to anxiety-evoking situations (see Chapter 2). Studies have since demonstrated the efficacy of flooding in fantasy and flooding *in vivo* for treating phobias, the latter being especially effective (Marks, 1972, 1975).

Exposure in Fantasy Versus Exposure in Vivo. While Stampfl (1967) reported success by exposing an obsessive-compulsive patient to her/his

most dreaded situation, Rachman, Hodgson, and Marzillier (1970) concluded that implosion had no therapeutic effect, while exposure *in vivo*
combined with modeling was shown to be effective in their comparative
study. (However, the number of exposures in imagination was smaller
than in *in vivo*.)

No Exposure Versus Exposure In Vivo. Encouraged by Meyer's success,
Rachman, Hodgson, and Marks conducted a series of investigations in an
attempt to find which form of exposure will yield the best results with
obsessive-compulsive patients (Hodgson, Rachman, and Marks, 1972;
Rachman, Hodgson, and Marks, 1971; Rachman, Marks and Hodgson,
1973). Subjects were 20 patients who suffered from chronic obsessive-
compulsive disorders and whose performance of rituals was triggered by
identified stimuli. These patients were given 15 sessions of relaxation
training over 3 weeks. This treatment yielded no improvement in obsessive-compulsive symptoms, although it did produce reduction of self-
reported anxiety and depression. All patients received 15 additional sessions of exposure *in vivo*, after which nine improved significantly, five improved moderately, and five patients failed to improve. Follow-up investigations showed continued improvement, but these results are equivocal
since some patients received additional therapy.

In another investigation (Roper, Rachman, and Marks, 1975), ten
obsessive-compulsive patients watched for 15 sessions while a therapist
was exposed to contaminating situations with response prevention. The
patients themselves were not contaminated at this stage. In the next stage
they were taught muscular relaxation exercises, modeled by the therapists. In the third stage of treatment, they watched the model exposing
himself to contamination, and were then exposed *in vivo* and instructed in
response prevention. The order of presentation of the three stages was
randomized across patients. The results indicated that the greatest effect
was obtained in participant modeling, actual exposure of the patient with
response prevention.

Duration of Exposure. The actual length of exposure of obsessive-compulsive patients to discomfort-evoking stimuli varies from one study to
another. Mills and coworkers had washers touch contaminating items
several times a day. Items were touched for 30 seconds in each trial. In
the studies conducted by Rachman and his colleagues, length of exposure
was 40 minutes per day. We must remember, of course, that the "subjective exposure" for these washers was longer than the actual 40 minutes.
Prevented from washing off the contamination, they suffered from it for

many hours during which they still felt exposed. The subjective experience for checkers is less easy to identify.

Prolonged exposure *in vivo* was found to be more successful than brief exposure for agoraphobics (Stern and Marks, 1973) and in obsessive compulsives (Rabavilas, Boulougouris, and Stefanis, 1976). Similarly, exposure in imagination is necessary to obtain habituation of subjective anxiety (Foa and Chambless, 1978).

Gradual Exposure Versus Rapid Exposure. In one study (Hodgson, Rachman, and Marks, 1972), patients were exposed to discomfort-evoking situations gradually (e.g., by desensitization *in vivo*) after watching the therapist model each step. Other patients were exposed immediately to the situation at the top of the stress hierarchy, again after watching the therapist modeling. The two groups were treated for 15 sessions over a period of 3 weeks. Both techniques were equally effective in reducing obsessive-compulsive symptoms.

Exposure With and Without Modeling. When modeling is not followed by the patient's exposure to the feared situations, its efficacy is reduced significantly (Roper, Rachman, and Marks, 1975). Moreover, when flooding with and without modeling were compared, modeling did not improve efficacy of treatment. This does not mean that individual patients did not benefit from modeling. Some patients reported that modeling by the therapist helped them to be able to experience discomfort-evoking situations. However, other patients did not feel that modeling assisted them in overcoming their resistance and fear of exposure.

In summary, it has been shown that exposing the patient to discomfort-producing situations *in vivo* is more successful than fantasy or modeling alone. The manner of exposure—graduated versus rapid, with or without modeling—does not modify its effect.

Response Prevention

Response prevention is the other treatment strategy. It is analogous to an experimental procedure that has been used successfully in eliminating avoidance behavior in animals. Baum (1968, 1969, 1970) trained rats to escape or avoid electrical shock by jumping from one side of a box into a safety compartment. Following the avoidance training, rats continued to jump into the safety compartment despite the removal of the shock. Preventing this response by blocking the path to the compartment extinguished the escape-avoidance behavior. The longer the animal stayed in the shock-related situation, the faster the jumping response was eliminated.

Supervised versus Nonsupervised Response Prevention.

The "apotrepic therapy" described by Meyer, Levy, and Schnurer (1974, p. 246) involved inpatient treatment and "continual supervision during the patient's waking hours, by nurses who were instructed to prevent the patient from carrying out any rituals." The staff engaged the patient in alternative activities, discussions, and also used persuasion. Only one patient required mild physical restraint. When the rituals were repetitions of normal necessary behaviors some judgment was exercised as to how often and for how long the patient should engage in the particular behavior involved. Exposure was gradual and was accompanied by encouragement, social reinforcement, modeling, and physical guidance. When total suppression of symptoms was maintained in spite of the stress caused by exposure, supervision was gradually relaxed.

Rachman, Hodgson, and Marks (1971) instructed their patients to refrain from carrying out their rituals, but did not supervise their behavior.

Mills, Agras, Barlow, and Mills (1973) systematically studied five obsessive-compulsive washers in order to determine the effect of supervision on response prevention. They found that instructions to stop rituals were effective, but complete elimination of rituals did not occur unless response prevention was used. Indeed, most of the failures reported by Rachman and coworkers (1973) and Marks and coworkers (1975) were attributed to failure on the part of the patients to carry out response prevention. A comparison of Meyer's results with those reported by Rachman and coworkers suggests that Meyer's success was due to complete response prevention.

Duration of Response Prevention.

In the investigation by Meyer and coworkers (1974) time for response prevention varied from one patient to the other, ranging from 1 week to 2 months. Rachman and coworkers (1973) treated all patients for 3 weeks, during which they were instructed to refrain from carrying out rituals. (Some patients, however, were given additional treatment sessions; although the authors did not report the nature of the instructions given through this latter period, we assume that response prevention instructions continued with treatment.) Mills and coworkers (1973) implemented response prevention in their patients from 10 to 14 days.

In general, these studies showed that for most patients a period of 14 to

21 days of response prevention is sufficient to achieve marked improvement; some need additional time.

The Differential Effect of Exposure and Response Prevention

All studies, as well as case reports, that used flooding with obsessive-compulsives combined exposure and response prevention. From the failures reported by Rachman and coworkers (1974) we can conclude that exposure without response prevention does not result in much improvement. Indeed, Mills and coworkers (1973) found that exposure to the discomfort-arousing situations without response prevention resulted either in no change or in an *increase* in compulsions and subjective urges. However, these authors also found that extensive exposure during and after response prevention was necessary to eliminate avoidance responses associated with the compulsions. Similarly, exposure was found to be useful in reducing the subjective feeling of discomfort associated with the previously avoided situations of phobics. Thus both exposure and response prevention seem necessary to eliminate both the discomfort evoked by the salient stimuli and the rituals. Thus exposure seems to reduce subjective discomfort and passive avoidance; response prevention is effective in eliminating compulsions. An alternative hypothesis (Marks, personal communication)—that response prevention is only useful as a means of prolonging exposure to the discomfort-evoking stimuli—merits investigation. However, some of our partial successes do not tend to support it; despite continual exposure to discomfort-producing stimuli, only those rituals that were actively prevented disappeared. Other rituals, although evoked by the same stimuli, remained unchanged.

THERAPEUTIC PROCESS

An Overview of a Treatment Program for Obsessive-Compulsives

In the first part of this chapter we have summarized the theoretical and empirical considerations that have led the senior author to construct a treatment program for patients who (a) manifest compulsive rituals; (b) express a desire to get rid of them; (c) can identify and report a set of stimuli, thoughts, or objects, that precede emission of, or urges to, emit the compulsive rituals. To this date, 25 patients have completed the program; these patients have provided us with the experience and the insights that we will share here.

There are three stages of treatment in this program:

1. *Information gathering period (about four sessions).* Each patient is seen by a therapist for several sessions during which:

a. Information about the obsessions and compulsions is collected.

b. The patient is informed about the treatment.

c. A verbal contract is made between therapist and patient regarding the role of each in carrying out the treatment plan.

d. The program for the next stage of treatment is outlined, including (1) preparing the environmental setting for treatment and designating individuals to supervise response prevention; (2) defining the scenes for flooding in fantasy; (3) delineating and preparing situations or objects to which the patient will be exposed *in vivo*, and (4) listing the target rituals that are to be the focus of the response-prevention regime.

2. *The flooding-response prevention period (about two weeks during which 10 therapy sessions are conducted).* During this period, the patient is usually seen every day by the therapist, excluding weekends. In each session, several minutes are spent discussing the patient's mood, his/her urges to perform the target rituals, and the degree of discomfort he/she experiences when exposed to discomfort-evoking situations. Flooding in imagination follows this discussion. The fantasy scenes may be composed of anxiety-evoking situations which had not yet been introduced *in vivo* and/or obsessional content of "disasters" that may follow nonemission of rituals. Exposure *in vivo*, with or without modeling (depending on the patient's need), is introduced following the flooding in fantasy. Finally, the therapist gives the patient further instructions for exposure *in vivo* in the next 24 hours, usually in writing.

Response prevention is continuous during this period, and is designed to eliminate any anxiety-relief experience associated with emission of rituals. Washers are not permitted *any* contact with water, towels, or tissues with which they can wipe their hands. Checkers are instructed to omit any checking behavior, to think about situations that elicit checking behaviors, and to expose themselves to such situations *in vivo*. When the self-reported urges to perform the rituals have diminished considerably, the therapist requests the patient to perform the "prevented" behavior in a normal way. Washers are instructed to take a quick shower and, in order to avoid any long-term relief, to immediately follow it with deliberate contamination. Checkers are allowed to check designated items such as stoves or entrance doors only once; they are instructed not to check items that can be realistically judged to be safe without checking.

Individuals in the patient's own environment who were designated as supervisors by both the therapist and the patient are responsible for response prevention.

Exposure in fantasy is conducted by the therapist, who describes the previously prepared scenes to the patient, providing him with the relevant imaginative cues. Some patients report that their imagination is enhanced by their own participation in describing the scenes—in these cases, the therapist aids the patient only occasionally. The therapist records subjective discomfort level every 10 minutes on a scale of 0 to 100 (Wolpe, 1973, pp. 120–123). When the patient reports considerable reduction in discomfort, flooding is terminated (about 90 minutes). The content of the scenes is modified as additional fantasy material is provided by the patient. The procedure is repeated every day until the cues evoke little or no discomfort.

Exposure in vivo is another treatment modality used throughout this stage of treatment. Discomfort-evoking items are carried around by the patient continuously, starting with items that elicit a moderate degree of discomfort and gradually proceeding to more disturbing ones; each item is carried continuously until it ceases to evoke discomfort and is then replaced by a more disturbing one. Thus, whenever possible, the patient is kept in continuous contact with discomfort-evoking stimuli.

At the end of the 2-week period of response prevention and exposure the therapist evaluates (a) the frequency and intensity of the urges to emit the ritualistic behaviors, (b) the frequency and intensity of the obsessional thoughts, and (c) the degree to which anxiety-evoking situations are being avoided by the patient. In some instances, additional periods of exposure and response prevention are required. However, it has been our experience that when considerable improvement has not been achieved by the end of 1 month, the therapist should re-evaluate the suitability of this program for the patient.

3. *Follow-up therapy.* Once the compulsions decrease or are eliminated and the obsessions do not occupy as much of the patient's attention, two sets of problems may arise:

a. Patients usually report difficulty in judging how much of the ritualistic behavior is emitted by normal people. Therapist modeling of normal washing, dressing-up, or checking is helpful in teaching patients "normal" behavior. In addition, very specific instructions are given to patients to be followed for several weeks. These may include a limit of six hand washings per day, a 10-minute shower once a day, a list of items that they are allowed to check once a day, and so forth. During these weeks, patients are also instructed to deliberately expose themselves to previously avoided situations that are not usually encountered in their everyday lives.

b. The elimination of ritualistic behavior leaves patients with the need to change their life styles and expand their activities. Situations that had been previously avoided because they arouse anxiety related to the obsessive-compulsive disorder become approachable—yet the patient may have lost the skills required to successfully participate in these situations. Often, anxiety evoked by increased interpersonal contacts is a major problem and may be appropriately treated with assertiveness training (Chapter 9) and desensitization (Chapter 2). Therapist coaching is often useful in helping patients enter previously avoided settings such as work and recreation facilities, and marital therapy is often necessary in order to change patterns of interaction that the partner may have established in order to cope with the "sick" spouse. Treatment is continued once or twice per week until the previously designated treatment goals are achieved.

Therapeutic Setting

Environmental Variables

Information Gathering. The therapist usually implements this first stage of treatment in an outpatient setting with once or twice-a-week sessions. Leaving the patient in his/her natural environment during this stage allows patients to continue everyday confrontation with discomfort-arousing stimuli. In addition, patient reports about the intensity and frequency of compulsions experienced are more accurate if the patient stays in his/her natural environment during this period. This is especially important for checkers who experience more discomfort in an environment where they feel personal responsibility for the consequences of neglecting checking rituals. By contrast, information provided by patients who stay in an inpatient setting will reflect their current subjective state in a "protected" rather than in a natural environment. However, in rare cases when the interpersonal atmosphere at home is so strained as to prevent patients from providing coherent information about their symptoms, hospitalization may facilitate information gathering.

Flooding and Response Prevention. This stage may be carried out in an outpatient setting when the following conditions are met: (a) at least one family member, a close friend, or a nurse is available to prevent the performance of compulsive behaviors and to ensure that exposure is enforced consistently in a positive, supportive, but firm atmosphere; and (b) the patient can be trusted to follow instructions scrupulously because of a personal determination to eliminate the obsessive-compulsive symptoms.

When these conditions cannot be met, it is advisable to treat the patient in an inpatient setting. Before the patient is hospitalized, it is important to ensure the cooperation of the staff in the total treatment plan. Such cooperation is facilitated by providing all staff members with detailed information regarding the nature of the treatment, regular reports on its rate of success, and specific instructions as to what is required of the staff in terms of time, duties, and the atmosphere to be fostered.

Treatment may be carried out in a hotel room when neither the patient's home nor hospital facilities provide the conditions necessary for treatment. We have chosen this environment for patients who refused to be hospitalized, but at the same time expressed fear of becoming too irritable or depressed during treatment to remain with their families.

In summary, the environmental setting for the flooding period should guarantee consistent exposure and response prevention by a firm but supportive supervisor.

When treatment is not carried out in the patient's natural environment, it is extremely important that the patient be returned to the home environment during the last stages of exposure and response-prevention treatment. Nontransfer of improvement from hospital to home is a common phenomenon and can be prevented by the therapist's accompanying the patient to his/her home for a few days and personally setting up the response-prevention and exposure regime. During this final stage of the flooding period, the therapist should actively seek help from family members and friends and model a firm yet supportive attitude.

Follow-Up Treatment. This final stage is most effectively implemented in an out-patient setting. Its goals are to help the patient function at work, in the family, and in social situations. The patient's experiences in the natural environment will reveal remaining problem areas that need to be dealt with in therapy—areas that might not be apparent in the relatively secure setting of an inpatient unit. Those patients who had completely isolated themselves from most social functions before treatment began may benefit from a day center facility as a transitional environment, in combination with individual and/or group therapy.

Therapist's Attitude

This treatment, and especially its anticipation, places patients under considerable tension. An internal conflict is developed between the wish to get rid of the problem behaviors and fear of complying with the "harsh" program and its possible "damaging" effects. The patient's trust in the therapist is, therefore, a basic requirement for success in treatment and for the patient's compliance with its demands. Throughout the first two stages of treatment (information gathering and flooding-response prevention), it is important that the therapist express empathy and sympathy with the tremendous "tortures" that the patient is enduring. As far as possible, the therapist's attitude should counteract the harshness of the treatment, as illustrated by the following verbatim material:

T: Now let me describe the treatment. You will be forbidden to wash at all for at least several days.

P: Well, I can't touch water at all? Can't take a bath, oh dear God, I take three a day. Do you know what you are asking of me? If I could do that, I wouldn't be here.

T: I know exactly how you feel. It is very difficult to imagine that you can do without washing when you have felt that washing is absolutely necessary for your survival.

P: Right. In my imagination I will go crazy if I don't wash when I touch these things.

T: Yes, I know, but most patients report that it was much easier for them not to wash than they had imagined. I know it is not much of a consolation right now; but you probably will find it easier than you think. Right now it is very difficult for you, and I respect your courage and determination. I do know how impossible it is for you to imagine yourself with no washing.

P: But I am afraid I'll go crazy if I am contaminated and I can't wash at all.

T: I understand how you feel, but I will take your feelings into consideration. I will support you all the way. At every stage of the treatment we will decide together what items you can touch without going crazy. You will have my telephone number so that you will be able to call me at any time.

P: This will be very helpful. I really appreciate it.

Expressions of warm support are extremely important. No less important, however, is for the therapist to be firm in carrying out the different steps of treatment, in spite of the patient's pleas to be allowed to avoid or delay exposure to anxiety-evoking situations. For example:

P: I can't touch the chicken soup. I just won't do it.

T: What you are telling me is that touching the chicken soup will make you very anxious. I know how difficult it is for you, but we can do it together. We shall start with just a drop of chicken soup. You might find it less difficult than you thought. Let's start now, okay? (A drop of chicken soup is spilled on one finger).

P: It feels bad but not as bad as I thought it would.

T: What is your anxiety level?

P: I thought it would be 100 but it's not so bad. I guess it's about 50 maybe 55.

T: You see, I told you. Most of the time, anticipating contact with these "horrible" situations is much more difficult than actually being there. So let us proceed and have some more chicken soup on your hands. I can't tell you how pleased I am with your cooperation. You should be proud of yourself because I know how difficult it was for you to allow me to spill chicken soup on your hands.

As demonstrated by this conversation, flexibility on the part of the therapist contributes to the success of the program. Such flexibility should not be confused with weakness or retreat from the original plan; a delicate balance between firmness and determination on the one hand, and warmth and flexibility on the other, is necessary to insure treatment success. The therapist should not react to hesitation on the part of the patient to expose himself to discomfort-evoking stimuli with accusation and criticism; instead, the patient must be treated with understanding and respect. It is important for patients to express their fears and hesitations—yet such expressions should not deteriorate into prolonged arguments and "negotiations." Here again, the therapist's attitude should combine acceptance of the patient and her/his discomfort with determination to follow the treatment program:

P: One thing was bothering me a lot, I wanted to talk about. It was bringing my girlfriend up and my dad was planning on calling tonight. How long would I have to see her? What should happen in that time? I am very upset about it because I think it is going to affect the relationship. I don't mind seeing her, touching her, and being contaminated; yet I very very much mind her seeing me. Doctor Foa said it was important, you said it was, I will do it, but by then I'm pretty sure I'm going to be pretty raunchy and so on. I don't want having to spend a whole day with her. I think it will scar our relationship.

T: Yeah, I understand how you feel. It must be difficult to see your girlfriend when you are not clean. It is difficult for everybody, but especially for you. Yet she knows that you undergo special treatment and that it is important for you to see her and touch her when you feel contaminated.

P: That's the thing. When I say she knows. She has known about me seeing a psychiatrist, and I was surprised until this Saturday I didn't tell her really what I was going for. I told her for aggression and stuff like that and anxiety. But I didn't tell her why and I had to. And I said "You mean you haven't guessed? Because of cleanliness. You know, I wash often." She said that doesn't bother her. She didn't think it was that bad. And so I explained to her that with me it is not just a wash. I have to wash. So she knows to that extent. And I told her that for the next couple of weeks I would be guarded and not allowed to wash. But I don't think that she is prepared to the extent that I haven't been touching water for like 5 days and stuff like that. That I am going to be in the same clothes. She doesn't know. She really doesn't know. She really doesn't have the details of it.

T: Are you afraid that she might leave you after seeing you somewhat less clean than usual?

P: Yeah, I think she is very clean and very that way. I guess it is going to have some effect on the way she feels about me. Especially like then. When she sees me, how I look and smell, I don't think she is going to want to be near me. And I think she is going to remember. It is not something I forget and I don't know how she will. It even bothers me about my father. He is my father and I don't think he would desert me. But I know that he even asked me if he should take a shower and everything like that. And I told him yeah, because I want him to be normal because I don't want to compete with him to see how long we both can go. And who is going to get upset. And I wouldn't want to be around anyone like that. And I don't see how anyone else is going to stand it.

T: I do appreciate your concerns. It is, however, important that she sees you untidy because one of the fears you expressed is that people will reject you if you are less than perfectly clean. You don't really think that avoiding seeing her will help your treatment, do you?

P: Except you see most people, I mean, you know, I've heard, my family is clean and I've heard like someone says to me you know like Bonnie or like, my God, this lady came into work today and she smelled so bad I didn't want to let her help me try on the clothes, she works in a clothes shop. And to me that is a natural reaction. What I am aiming at is not to feel contaminated. When I smell someone who has body odor I should say to myself "Oh my God," but not be contaminated. Or I should not be afraid of losing my friend if I am not super clean.

T: That is our goal in therapy. Therefore, it is important that you see Bonnie. She loves you, and she does not become contaminated by body odor. Therefore, she will be less intimidated by your appearance than you expect.

P: I agree with you. My father said he would explain it in more detail. She really doesn't know why I am not washing for 5 days. I talked it over with him, and he said I don't give her enough credit.

Occasionally patients will direct anger and even rage towards the therapist whose instructions cause frustration and a high degree of anxiety/discomfort. Such expressions may reach extreme levels in rare cases, but expressions of anger should be handled with understanding and compassion for the suffering that causes them.

On the fifth treatment session Steve, who had been contaminated with canned chicken soup for 3 days, felt that the soup was spoiled. He was enraged with the therapist, yelled at him, and accused him of inflicting unfair treatment:

P: I am telling you that I go through hell. And I think I am getting undue anxiety. I am getting undue, unfair treatment. Okay, it is enough to have chicken soup. Warm chicken soup, at least it is not cold and clammy, which has nothing to do with my feeling. Before, I never thought of the difference of cold chicken soup or hot chicken soup but now. I've never felt it. It has nothing to do with that. It has to do with feeling of stuff that is not bothering me or that I shouldn't or is not contaminating me. It is not really my problem. We've never talked about dog crap. But I don't want to, and it is going to cause me great anxiety, and I am going to get very upset if you brought some into this room and wanted to rub it on my body. It is not fair. It's just not fair. I think I have to do enough with my own problems with the things that bother me. Not to take in the stuff that has nothing to do with my problem. I feel sheer, pure anger about doing things with no logical reason.

T: You are upset because you have chicken soup on you, and you do not understand the reason. Well, the reason is that I want to make sure that you get used to the odor of chicken soup. If you wash it off, you won't get used to it.

P: This was not chicken soup. It doesn't smell like chicken soup, and it doesn't feel like chicken soup. It is just rancid stuff, and if you didn't tell me that it is chicken soup, even my dad wouldn't guess that it is chicken soup; it is rancid. I have never smelled that smell before in my entire life except from that can. And I have never associated it with chicken soup. It is different. I don't know how contaminated it is compared to regular chicken soup. But it bothered me more than regular chicken soup. That smell, because I've never had it before. I've never smelled rancid crap like that, and I've never had it put on my body. And so it did bother me more and I guess that if you went out and got dog crap, I've never had that on my body before either, I'd be just as mad and just as upset and if something like that were brought in here I just wouldn't do it. I'd say forget it, you know. At this point this smell I think it bothers me more than my body odor. More than chicken soup and more than anything that I've ever had on my body. More than vomit, more than dirt, more than dog crap. I'm sure that there are a lot of of other smells that I've never smelled before, and if put in front of my nose and rubbed on my body, it is going to make me mad, upset, and anxious, and I don't want people to go searching for smells that are going to upset me.

T: Why would they upset you?

P: I don't know. I don't classify as anxious. I classify as personal because I think I was treated unfairly. I was mad at you, I still am because I am going through more hell than I deserve.

T: I didn't know that the soup was spoiled, and I agree with you. You don't have to do any unnecessary things. It was unfair to spill spoiled soup on you. Believe me, I would not have done it had I known. I apologize for upsetting you so much. But did it bother you because it was spoiled or because it was chicken soup?

P: Because it was spoiled, I think.

T: Did it just bother you because it was spoiled and unfair, or did it arouse anxiety?

P: Really I was so confused and upset that I couldn't make the distinction if it bothered me. I knew it was unfair, but I couldn't make the distinction if it contaminated me anymore or if it bothered me, I can't now. I was so mad about doing it that I didn't think of anything else. I was so upset I had it all in my mind, all the answers. "No it doesn't bother me," I was going to say. But it did bother me. I didn't want to touch anything. I think I was so upset and mad at you because I realized that I am still bothered by chicken soup even if it's not spoiled. Of all the days that I have gone through this treatment this has been the hardest. This morning I got up, and I wanted to die.

T: I am sorry that you felt bad. Why didn't you call me? You have my telephone number at home. I wish you had called me.

P: Thanks. But I was so mad at you.

T: Now that you know I didn't plan to spill spoiled chicken soup on you, are you still angry?

P: No, I really am not.

This exchange demonstrates yet another important issue in the therapist-patient relationship—open strategy. Throughout the treatment, the therapist should not give instructions or expose the patient to situations without discussing them first. Steve was angry because he felt that he was forced to handle a situation (i.e., spoiled chicken soup) that had not been discussed with him ahead of time. He lost confidence in the therapist's honesty and became angry. In our experience, outbursts of rage happen only when patients are confronted with unexpected demands and perceive the therapist to be "tricky," disrespectful, and arbitrary. This extreme anger can be avoided if the therapist adopts an open-strategy attitude, sharing with the patient the plan for the next day, as well as its therapeutic rationale.

Data Gathering

In the first session it is desirable to concentrate on investigating the presenting state of the neurotic pattern. Most patients are quite upset when they finally seek treatment, especially when the obsessions and compulsions are greatly impairing normal daily functioning. It is only natural that they are eager to discuss their symptoms in detail. Later on, we collect more general information about family background, religious beliefs, performance at school, sexual development, and so forth (see Wolpe, 1973). In this chapter, we do not discuss gathering of such general information unless it is directly related to the presenting problem.

Information about the history of the complaint and its onset does not usually prove specifically helpful in designing the treatment program. However, it should be collected in order to acquire a comprehensive picture of the severity and duration of the problem. Occasionally, the beginning of the disorder is related to specific stresses present in the patient's life at the time of onset, such as separation from family, added responsibility (e.g., giving birth or marriage), and so forth. This information might provide clues about specific patient deficiencies in dealing with certain life functions. Treatment of these problems is deferred until the final stage of treatment—after the presenting obsessive-compulsive symptoms have been eliminated. Occasionally, events that precipitated the onset of symptoms may provide hypotheses concerning the nature of specific fears and can be incorporated into flooding in imagery.

Earlier, we stated that the program described in this chapter is appropriate for patients who experience anxiety/discomfort when in contact with certain stimuli (thoughts or objects) and when such discomfort decreases following the performance of specific rituals (washing, repeating words, thoughts, checking, counting, etc.). Therefore, the purpose of the first session is to establish whether or not the patient's complaint follows this pattern, thus indicating the implementation of a flooding/response prevention program. Three sets of data are gathered in this session:

1. The stimuli that elicit discomfort, feelings of contamination, or anxiety.
2. The repetitious, stereotyped behaviors (e.g., rituals) that the patient emits to relieve the discomfort and the patterns of avoidance that he/she has established.
3. The relationship between the discomfort-evoking stimuli and the rituals.

The initial interaction should start with a general question such as "What can I do for you?" or "What is the problem that brought you here?'' A typical answer is ''I wash all the time. See my hands, they look terrible from all this washing. I know it is crazy to spend all this time washing and worrying, but it seems I can't help it. It is as if I have to do it.''

Discomfort-Evoking Stimuli

At this point, the therapist can interrupt and begin to gather systematic information. First we need to know the set of stimuli that elicits discomfort. We can get this information by asking ''What makes you wash?'' ''What are the thoughts that make you feel 'dirty'?'' In the case of a checker, the key question will be ''What are your thoughts just before you feel the urge to check?'' Examples of answers to these questions are:

You see, everything that has to do with cancer makes me feel that I have germs all over me, and then I have to wash.

When I touch something that other people have touched, I get this feeling of being dirty and I do not feel comfortable until I wash.

I drive on the highway and suddenly I find myself thinking ''What if I ran over somebody and I killed him?'' Then I have to pull over to the side of the road, and I have to check if there is a body lying on the highway. After I have made sure that nobody is dead, I can go on driving.

Throughout the course of the session, the therapist's questions should become more specific in order to get more concrete information. For example, in the case of a hand washer, we may ask for a list of ''dirty'' items, starting with the most ''contaminating'' one. The question should use the terminology of the patient: ''What are the things that make you feel *dirty*?'' or ''Can you tell me what is the thing that *contaminates* you the most?'' With checkers, one can list the ''disasters'' that would follow nonchecking or the situations that precede the urge to check. In order to facilitate ranking of stimuli, the therapist introduces the notion of the above mentioned subjective anxiety/discomfort scale, ranging from 0 to 100. Two separate scales are useful in treating obsessive-compulsives, the dirt-contamination scale (for washers) and the discomfort scale for both washers and checkers:

T: Imagine that you could rank all things in your physical environment according to how dirty (or how contaminated) they make you feel. Certain things don't make you feel dirty at all, so you can say that they are 0 on this scale. Some things make you feel extremely dirty so you could rate them as 100. What is the thing that will make you feel the dirtiest you have ever been?

P: Touching things coming from the lab at Temple Medical School.

T: So let us call the lab 100 on the scale of dirt. How dirty are things in the laboratory?

P: About 90 to 100.

The therapist then asks the patient to rank the same items according to how much discomfort or anxiety they evoke. (Although a high correlation exists between the two scales, it is not always perfect.)

Once we have a list of several items that arouse feelings of contamination in the patient, we are able to abstract the dimension along which generalization takes place. We can then try to guess what are some of the contaminating items that were not mentioned by the patient and can phrase them as additional questions. Understanding the dimension along which generalization takes place enables the therapist to point out internal consistency in the patient's behavior and to explain that the behaviors are not "crazy," because in fact they are predictable. The patient has undoubtedly heard many times, from friends or relatives, that her/his fears and behaviors are "crazy" and senseless. When patients realize that the therapist understands and respects them and does not perceive their patterns of behavior and thought to be "crazy" they gain a sense of trust and some relief from anxiety.

The following verbatim material is from the first session with Sara:

T: Miss Stringer told me that you feel contaminated by certain things, especially your mother and your husband. And when you touch them you have to wash. Is this accurate?

P: Well, yes. But not only things from my mother and my husband. There are a lot of other things that make me feel dirty. Oh God, there are so many of them.

T: Why don't you start by describing to me a normal day, from the time you wake up in the morning.

P: My husband is the first one awake, and he gets ready for work by going into the bathroom and shaving and so forth. Well, then I get up just as he is finishing up, because I have to escort him to the door. Then he goes downstairs and gets a little orange juice or whatever. And then he kisses me and then he goes down to what he calls the dungeon, the basement because I have a wardrobe there, and he keeps all his clothes down there.

T: So he dresses before?

P: No, he dresses just before he is ready to go out the door. And he keeps anything that is connected with work down there. And I wait upstairs, and about 10 minutes later when he is ready, I open the door for him. And then I go up and take a shower, and then I get ready and get dressed to get the children up and get them ready for school and everything is pretty normal except for, say, washing a lot.

T: What about the children, do they dress in their rooms?

P: They used to dress in specific areas, but I have brought that under control, and now they dress in their rooms and their clothes are in their closets where they belong, and there is no problem there.

T: Can you touch the children's clothing?

P: Yeah, the only thing that I am not too crazy about, say, their coats. If they put their coats on, I prefer not to have much contact after that for some reason, and that happens with their shoes. When they get to the foyer, I help them tie their shoes and so forth. I don't touch anything else until I go and wash my hands. And then I am alone for most of the day.

T: Your husband doesn't touch the door; do you open the door for the children?

P: Yes.

T: Before we go any further, let me see if I understand you. It seems that the clothes your husband wears to work are extremely contaminated and, therefore, he has to dress in the basement. Is this the way it is?

P: Yes. You see, my husband works in this factory. And one of the people there lives on the same street as my mother, about three houses from her. So, they must shop at the same supermarket, they walk on the same street. And then he comes to work, and he walks on the same floors as my husband, they eat in the same cafeteria. That's where the dirt comes from.

T: Now it is clear. So that means you cannot invite your husband's friends from work home because all of them are contaminating.

P: That's exactly what happens. I don't invite them.

T: Now, let's see. It is very difficult to describe how much discomfort you feel when you touch different things. So let's imagine a scale from 0 to 100. 0 means a situation where you feel completely relaxed and 100 would be a situation of almost panic.

P: I understand.

T: Let's start using this scale in describing what you feel in different situations. It may be difficult in the beginning, but when you become accustomed to it, it will be helpful in our communication. So, when you help the children tie their shoes, that makes you feel dirty?

P: Yes.

T: How much?

P: Just maybe 10%. It is really when my husband gets ready to go to work or comes home.

T: How dirty would you feel if you touched your husband's clothes?

P: Oh God, I don't know, maybe 80% or even more.

T: Can you imagine a situation where you would feel 0 anxiety?

P: I suppose when I am sleeping, I don't think even then, because I wake up most of the time feeling a bit of anxiety. I find myself dreaming more than I would like. I suppose about the lowest would be 10%. When I think about it I don't think that I am completely free of anxiety ever.

T: That must be awfully difficult for you. But hopefully we will be able to help you. So the highest discomfort you feel now is about your husband's working clothes.

P: Yes, but that's because I avoid other things. Like I haven't seen my mother for five years now. And I don't see any of my relatives, because that would be 100.

T: I see, touching your mother would be the most disturbing thing for you. Is this true?

P: Yes, even if on TV they are talking about Montgomery County, it is almost as though they are reaching out, and I want to turn off the TV, and I haven't been able to control that. And there is a little bit of jumps in the chest sort of feeling. And I don't have any friends. I never had any friends for years and years. I only met one girl in therapy, and now I don't even want to see her. Because I've learned that she has associations out toward where my people live. And she wanted to bring Christmas gifts, and I hadn't been answering the phone and was sort of getting around her more and more and more. And she came over Christmas Eve, she forced herself, and I really was uncomfortable and went around scrubbing everything after she left. I had to make her a cup of tea, and I washed her dishes and the chair, and her presents haven't been opened or touched. And I have really been avoiding her, which makes me angry at myself.

T: It must be very difficult for you, all these constraints. How much discomfort did you feel when this girlfriend visited you?

P: About 80 or 90%, like I feel about my husband's clothes or when he comes back from work.

T: So you avoid contact with people and with your husband when he comes from work. What else do you avoid?

P: When it comes time that I have to sort the mail and send a check to whomever, I go through great pain of being in the foyer and taking the stamps with me and taking whatever envelopes and a pen, whatever I might need, and making it out and quickly running to the mailbox and getting it out of my hands. Come back and take a rag with disinfectant, clean the doorknob, both ways, then I'll go upstairs and take a shower.

T: Is that only your mail or mail for your husband and your children?

P: No, any mail that would come to the house.

T: Okay, and what makes the mail dirty? Is it because it comes from the area in which your family is living?

P: Some of it comes from where my husband works. Like the other day I got a Christmas card, it said Jenkintown, and instantly I got panicky. It is out that way, and I have relatives, and it is out that way even though I have no relatives in Jenkintown, I instantly got terribly upset. I didn't even open it. I didn't want any part of it. And it did bother me terribly. Now I haven't since, but it has been on my mind to wash out the mailbox, although I'll still go through the same thing. But it's especially something from where my relatives are. Mostly it is because of my mother.

T: And what happens when you would get a letter from San Francisco?

P: Well, only because it comes with the same mail.

T: I understand that the contamination spreads from your mother to your family, and to the area where she lives. That sounds logical.

P: I've had a hard time convincing other people.

T: It is generalizing.

P: That's what it is; it's the generalizing of my mother, a chain reaction it all goes back from one link to another to my mother.

T: So that is why when you have contact with the mail, you have to wash yourself.

P: Yes.

T: Okay, how contaminated are you when you touch the mail?

P: About 60%.

By now, the set of stimuli that elicits discomfort in Sara is quite clear: everything and any person that has been in contact, directly or indirectly, with Sara's mother is a potential source of contamination. The more direct the contact, the more contaminating the object or person is.

A more complex pattern of contaminating stimuli was presented by Steve:

T: I understand that there are certain things that make you feel dirty. What is the dirtiest thing you can think of?

P: The things that always contaminate me are the smell of chicken soup and perspiration.

T: Is it perspiration or body odor?

P: I guess it would be body odor. It is a general body odor. If someone has a really strong odor, that would make me feel contaminated, and then chicken soup. If I were in a room which smelled of chicken soup, it would surround me.

T: Imagine a scale of contamination from 0 to 100. 0 means no contamination and 100 is the most contaminated you can become. How much is body odor?

P: Body odor would get 100 and the chicken soup would get 99.

T: In what situation will you be 0?

P: After I just took a shower.

T: Are there other things that make you feel dirty?

P: Money. My brother-in-law told me that colds are caused from handling money. Kids put it in their mouths and drop it on the ground.

T: Do you mean to say that you are afraid of germs that can make you ill?

P: Yes, germs that come from other people or animals. Except I know that it does not make sense to be afraid of the germs.

T: What do you think can happen to you if you get these germs into your system?

P: I don't have any idea. The only thing I feel is this dirty feeling.

T: I understand. Well, how dirty do you become when you touch money?

P: 80%, public doorknobs—85%, touching garbage can—95%.

T: Anything else?

P: Bugs and flies. 97% flies and bugs and most insects.

T: Is this touching them, or seeing them?

P: Just touching them is so high. Even seeing a bug is 60%. If I see a bug, I make a point not to touch the bug or where it has gone, it makes me feel dirty. Even if I say "bug," it would make me feel dirty; or if I think "chicken soup," I'll feel dirty.

T: To what degree does the word "chicken soup" bother you?

P: Probably 60 or maybe 70. Of all words, chicken soup is the worst.

T: Let's see if I have got the picture clearly. There are things that can make you feel dirty. The dirt comes from insects, animals and people, and some kind of germs.

P: It is not the germs. Just dirt, and then everything that was touched by people or insects become dirty. And everything that was around chicken soup is also dirty, like restaurants, or supermarkets.

T: I understand that people and insects are spreading dirt. But why is chicken soup dirty?

P: I really don't know. Maybe because it smells kind of similar to body odor, and body odor means that the person didn't wash, and he is dirty.

T: Oh, I see, now it makes sense to me. So that means that you avoid contact with almost everything in the world. That must be very difficult for you.

P: That is exactly true. Now, that's why I left school, and I don't see any of my friends, and I almost never go out anymore. Even at home I can't touch most of the things, because my parents and my sister touch them. But at least my room is clean and my bed too.

Steve felt contaminated by dirt of people and animals. His situation was more uncomfortable than Sara's, since even thoughts and certain words, through higher order conditioning, acquired contamination power for him; more stimuli disturbed him. At the same time, the intensity of contamination was higher for Steve than for Sara; there was hardly a stimulus in his environment that elicited less than an 80% feeling of contamination. Words and thoughts caused less contamination than real objects. Odors were a high source of contamination feelings—especially perspiration and chicken soup.

Identifying Compulsions and Avoidance Patterns

After the "contaminating dimension" has been established, the therapist proceeds to collect information about the rituals that are performed by the patient and the avoidance patterns that he/she has established. Delineation of the avoidance patterns and identification of the contaminating objects is important for establishing a program of gradual exposure to discomfort-evoking stimuli. Information about compulsions or ritualistic behaviors is necessary to specify response-prevention instructions. It is helpful to have patients describe in detail daily activities, so that ritualistic behaviors that are no longer recognized as such by the patient can be realistically defined.

The following verbatim material—taken from the first interview with Sara—illustrates the ritualistic nature of her washing and the complex pattern she had developed to avoid touching items that had come in contact with her husband's place of employment.

T: I understand now that everything that comes in contact with your mother is contaminated. Like the mail, and your husband's work, and many other things. If you cannot avoid touching these things what do you usually do?

P: I'll go and wash.

T: How often do you wash your hands?

P: It can vary—in the course of the day?

T: Yes.

P: At least 30 times, maybe more—plenty of times when I think about it. Everytime I go into a room, say I'm vacuuming, and I finish a room I'll go and wash my hands before I do anything else. That may be more than 30 times. (Pause) Maybe, yeah, Probably without realizing it, I'd say closer to 50, figuring the course of the whole day.

T: And for how long do you wash?

P: It depends on how dirty I feel.

T: Do you keep special soap?

P: No, not hand soap. I don't like to go back and take the cake of soap—I'd rather pour it from a bottle, a liquid soap. I even wash the bottle when I wash my hands. I wash the spigot every time, because I had to touch it to put it on. I'll wash the bottle of soap several times during the day, but whereas for a cake of soap you can't do much for it. You can't wash a cake of soap.

T: So you don't use a cake of soap because it is not clean enough; how does it become dirty?

P: Well, touching it.

T: So when you touch the soap you contaminate it.

P: Right, because I've used it to wash my hands. I've often thrown out a cake of soap. And I've really needed to get to a sink, and if there happens to be a cake of soap and not a bottle of soap, I will run the soap under water and then throw it away after I've washed my hands.

T: Can you give me an example of what actually happens after you touch the mail or money?

P: I have a tremendous urge to wash. Now if my husband will leave the money to put in his bank and the food money, he'll leave it on top of his wardrobe, so I must go there to get the money once a week. I wait until they are all gone and then I get out a plastic trash bag, I have a rag with a lot of disinfectant, and another rag for rinsing and one to dry. I have on the least amount of clothes that I can, because I am going to wash. I get the money very carefully, put it on top of the trash bag, I usually do it on top of the dryer. Then I'll go up and wash my hands because I've gone into the room and the cabinet and so forth, and I'll carefully take the bills and lay them out. I take the disinfectant and wash one side, then wash my fingers, turn the bill over, wash the bill, and again each finger. When I have them all washed, then I take the other rag and dry them because I've been having trouble. People in the store will look at the bills and will say: "Oh my goodness, what is wrong with this money?" They think it might be counterfeit. I can hardly say "I wash my money," so I play dumb. They say "Do you have another $20 bill?" So now I've wised up to that, and I rinse them with a good rag, and I dry them quickly so the green part doesn't fade. So after I've washed the money, I bring it up and put it in a can on top of the ice box. And I then quickly go and take my shower. Now I can handle the money afterwards, just put it in my purse or whatever. It is clean. But it is only because it comes from where my husband works.

T: Do you sometimes avoid handling this money?

P: Oh sure, I avoid emptying the mailbox, or I'll take my son's allowance out of his jar and say I'll give it back to you—I'll borrow $20 for the store—he has 60-some dollars, and he gets mad because I'm always borrowing money. He knows he'll get it back. But this avoids my having to go to the cabinet at that moment. I can put it off to another day. But then when he runs out of money, and I run out of money, I have to go down to the cabinet and go through this ritual.

T: That is really a hard thing.

P: It is ridiculous.

T: It is annoying.

P: I hate it the whole time I am doing it. And I say to myself why are you doing it? The feeling is if I don't do it I'm going to climb the wall.

Another pattern of "ritualistic avoidance" is illustrated in a sequence of events that repeats itself everyday when Sara's husband returns from work:

T: Okay, and what happens when your husband comes home?

P: Well, I'm always there to open the door.

T: Does he ring the bell?

P: No. He rings the phone so I know that he is on his way, and I know exactly how long it will take him. And I watch for him. And it drives me crazy if he is held up in traffic and he is late. Here I am wasting all this time standing at a window watching for his car when I could be doing something constructive—cooking, just sitting down and reading a book. But no, I'm at the window driving myself crazy watching for the headlights of his car. And then when he comes, he is now allowed to park in front of the house. This is what makes me think that I can overcome all this. Because now I am able to allow his car in front of the house. Before I used to make him park his car a half block away. But now I say to myself—I said it to him "Don't listen to me. Park in front of the house," and he does. And those feelings aren't there any more about the car. I've been able to overcome it. But he comes in and as he is coming up the walk I go to the door ready to open it. We used to have a storm door and a gate, but we don't anymore, because I would have to run out and open the gate for him and the storm door. The neighbors started looking quite a bit. They would see me standing there opening the door every night and every morning, and I began to wonder what they were wondering. Fortunately, the storm door broke in a storm last year, and I was tickled, because now all I have to do is stand in the foyer and open the door. And it looks as though he is opening it himself. He comes in and goes right downstairs to his wardrobe and undresses completely all the way down. And then he comes up and wipes his feet in the foyer real good, and then he goes up to the bathroom, and I have the basin filled with a certain amount of water and strong disinfectant with ammonia, and he must wash his hands before he is allowed to touch the shower and marble. So then he goes and takes a shower, and he dries, and I take my shower; but I make sure that he gargles while I take my shower. By that time he is getting dressed, and I quick hurry and get dressed and we can eat dinner. But I don't want to do that. I want to be cooking dinner when he comes in and say "Hello." I don't even set the table, because he has to walk by the dining room table to go upstairs and I'm afraid of the dirt, so I have to wait until we are all clean; then we can come down and wipe the table; then it is clean to set the table. I would prefer to have the table set a half hour beforehand.

T: It must be very hard for you.

P: I make things so hard on me when I don't have to.

T: Yes, it is very difficult. Besides taking long showers of about 1 hour each, scrubbing each part of your body several times, and washing your hands 50 to 60 times a day and cleaning carefully the contaminated things like money and door knobs, do you have other rituals?

P: No, that is all that I do. Believe me, that is keeping me quite busy.

T: Do you have any thoughts or special words that can decontaminate you?

P: No, it's only washing and cleaning.

Sara presented a clear picture of elaborate attempts to avoid contact with "contaminated" objects. When those attempts failed, her rituals consisted of excessive cleaning and washing.

Steve exhibited a more complicated pattern of compulsion; he performed both cognitive and behavioral rituals. The washing rituals were explored in the following exchange:

T: What would you do if you touched somebody's hands?

P: If I could, I would wash them and generally longer and more, and I may wash them 4 minutes. With newspaper, it would be a normal wash. Like after someone's hands, I would be thinking that I have to wash my hands to get them clean.

T: And how long would you wash in this case?

P: Maybe 8 minutes.

T: Do you follow a special ritual?

P: Usually I will change the ritual if something bad has happened to me when I was following that pattern. So I will start a new one. There is a pattern. For the last four weeks, I turn the water on and maybe for a minute I will wash my hands and I'll count in intervals of 4. I may go 1, 2, 3, 4, 5, 6, 7, 8, and I may stop at 8 or I may stop at 16.

T: Do you count in order to know how long you wash?

P: No, I guess it is just a plan. If I count, I know that my hands are clean, and everything went according to plan. Like I'll get the soap and rinse my hands, then I'll put the soap back. Then I'll wash my hands with the soap. That is one time. And then like I make sure the water is the right temperature, and that goes on for four times, and then the lather, wash, rinse, and rinse, and that will be exactly four times all the time. Then the cold water just till my hands cool down. Then I don't count anymore.

T: That is the normal procedure. If you want to prolong it, which part do you prolong?

P: Usually when I prolong it, I'll do the whole thing and then turn off the water and then turn it back on and repeat the whole thing. Usually I repeat it twice, but occasionally it was as many as four or five times. When I have a pattern, I never interrupt a pattern. If it's interrupted, I'll start all over again.

In addition to the washing rituals Steve had some cognitive rituals as well:

T: Last time you told me that you have a special pattern for washing your hands; do you have any other similar patterns?

P: Yeah, really with counting, and to make everything set and sort of secure. Like I might say "Palmolive green soap" and I might say it to myself two times, and then like count to four, before I do almost anything. Getting up, taking paper towels off the roll, taking toilet tissue off the roll, turning on the TV, turning on the radio.

T: Must you always count?

P: Yeah, always something. Like when I turn on the washer, I may say "Palmolive green, Palmolive green," and that sort of sets everything, and I'll turn it on. The words clean everything, because they are clean words, and now I think or say the words, and that gives it order, and everything is clean and in order, and everything is set. I feel everything is calm and collected.

T: Does the number of times you repeat a clean word depend on the situation?

P: It varies a lot, but at certain times it will stay the same, for 2 days I will use the same pattern. Then I'll switch, but that basic pattern I will keep for usually 2 days. I have several clean words. Clean words are usually something that I guess for clean, and then maybe they sound good. Maybe the name of a shampoo or something that sounds earthy and natural. Like herbal essence, or something that sounds to me very natural. I like the outdoors and nature and all that stuff, and to me that is clean. Everything like that: mountain streams and junk like that. So something earthy like that, something that sounds like that to me. It is usually a brand name that I buy.

T: So I understand that you wash when you feel contaminated, and use clean words when you think about dirty words. Is this really the case?

P: Yes, but washing especially. That is something I always have a pattern for. But really I have a pattern for everything I do; when I go to bed now, I make sure the light is off, the alarm is set, the shade is down. But I don't just sort of look around. It is not a casual sort of making sure everything is okay. It's a definite ritual.

T: What makes it a ritual, the order?

P: No, that switches. Just as long as I make sure. The order switches a lot. The order—one pattern becomes unclean or not good anymore, it becomes too old. Maybe I thought of something bad, or had a bad experience while I was using that pattern, so I'll switch it. Including the name of the soaps. If something bad happens, I'll switch it.

T: What bad things can that be?

P: Being contaminated is the first. Or maybe just thinking of words— chicken soup or something like that. A commercial about it. Or over a period of time, I guess 2 weeks, everything has been okay but it hasn't been super clean. So I'll switch the order. Except for being contaminated, that is the only definite reason for switching around.

Relationship between Discomfort Evoking Stimuli and Rituals

Once the nature of the discomfort-arousing stimuli is discussed and the ritualistic behaviors are clearly identified, the relationship between them must be explored, as demonstrated by the following verbatim material taken from the second session with Steve:

> T: Let's suppose that you have just touched chicken soup, and you can smell it all over you. What will happen?
>
> P: I'll feel very anxious and contaminated, as you know.
>
> T: And what would you usually do?
>
> P: Well, I'll wash my hands or maybe take a shower in the same pattern I told you about.
>
> T: How do you feel after you have washed yourself?
>
> P: I am clean again, and relaxed, and the anxiety and contamination disappear.

It becomes obvious from this conversation that indeed certain stimuli evoke discomfort for Steve, and the ritualistic behavior serves to decrease or eliminate anxiety. The therapist is then justified in implementing the exposure-response prevention program and should proceed to prepare the patient for this treatment.

Preparing the Patient for Treatment

Usually by the end of the second session of behavioral analysis, it becomes apparent whether or not a patient may benefit from a treatment program of exposure-response prevention. When this type of program has been decided upon, the therapist provides the patient with a full description of its procedure and rationale, thus allowing the patient to be an equal partner in the treatment.

First, the therapist should summarize the information that has been collected, and should explain the functional relationship between the obsessions and the compulsions. This summary helps the patient to understand the connection between the treatment and the nature of the obsessive-compulsive disorder and can serve to reduce his/her resistance to the treatment's somewhat rigorous requirements. The following verbatim material is from the third session with Sara:

T: I understand now that everything that was in indirect or direct contact with your mother is contaminated. Being in touch with those things arouses considerable discomfort, and this is unpleasant. Well, nobody likes to be in a state of discomfort. We all try to avoid it, or to do something that will reduce this feeling of discomfort. What you have learned to do in order to restore a state of comfort is to wash, and to clean things that you consider to be dirty, and to manage your life in such a way that you minimize your exposure to those dirty things. For example, all the ritualistic ways in which your husband must clean himself when he comes home from work, and washing the money he brings home.

P: This is amazing. I've never heard anyone explain it in such a way. That makes sense.

T: The problem is that everytime you wash you feel much better, and the feeling of relief you experience after washing reinforces this behavior. So the more relief you feel after washing, the more you wash. You have never tried to see what will happen to you if you touch "dirty" things and you don't wash.

P: I feel that if I don't wash, I'll go crazy, I won't be able to tolerate the stress and something horrible will happen to me.

(It is important here to reassure the patient that she is not "crazy.")

T: I understand that the situation concerns you. It may make it easier for you to know that there are a lot of people that suffer from the same problem.

P: It is hard to believe. It seems that I am the only one.

T: Very often people who have a problem like yours feel that they are strange or crazy. Other people don't understand why you feel anxious when you touch certain things and that you have the urge to wash.

P: Right.

T: Just because they don't have a similar urge to wash, they think you are crazy. I can assure you that you are definitely not mentally ill. You have just learned to feel anxious when you touch certain things, and you learned to achieve some comfort by washing. It's all learned.

P: That is very interesting. It makes me feel much better.

T: It helps to know that it is learned. Other people did not learn it, but you did. Now the essence of our treatment program is to help you unlearn this behavior.

P: It seems more or less a bad habit. I thought it was a disease of the brain.

T: You are not psychotic.

P: How about that. Like my mother or my mother-in-law will say to me on the phone "You don't appear to be wacky; you sound so normal," and I'll say to my husband afterward "What am I supposed to sound like?" They expect that you talk the way you act.

T: You *are* normal, you just have acquired a maladaptive habit. About a month ago, I had a patient who suffered from this problem.

P: Really!

T: Yes, and he was cured, and I think you will be cured too.

P: How encouraging. How did you do it?

T: That is what I intend to discuss with you now. As I said, you have learned to achieve relief by washing. So you touch certain things, you become contaminated, you feel anxious, you wash, and then you feel fine again. We have to break up this chain of events, this relationship between anxiety and washing. Also, we have to stop all attempts to stay "clean." It means confronting you with situations in which you will experience a lot of contamination and not allowing you to wash at all.

It is important to impress upon the patient that the demands of the treatment program may seem harsh, that they will probably cause a high degree of discomfort, and that instructions regarding exposure and response prevention must be followed scrupulously to ensure treatment success. The patient should be told that exposure and complete response prevention will teach him/her that discomfort-decrease can be reached without rituals emission:

T: As I said, we will forbid you to wash, or to do anything relating to cleaning. This might be very difficult for you.

P: Well, I can't touch water at all? Can't take a bath, oh dear God, I take three a day!

T: No shower, no bath, no washing your hands.

P: Oh, dear God! And this does end?

T: It does end. It ends when you think it is no longer necessary to wash.

P: You do believe that you do come to a point where you do feel that way.

T: Yes. I know that it is impossible for you to imagine that now. But I can assure you that it will happen. I've had patients who didn't believe it either but they came to the point where they could say "So what if I touched the floor."

P: Oh my God!

T: It is really hard, and you need a lot of courage to go through that, but it is only 2 weeks compared to the rest of your life. It might not be as unpleasant as you think. I will support you so you are not alone in this struggle. Most of it will be done by you.

P: How do you know that this treatment will not make me worse?

T: We have a lot of experience with this treatment, and so do other people around the world. The success rate is about 75%; that is quite high. In most cases that I have seen, after 2 weeks the discomfort decreased, and the problem was over, or much improved after the 2 weeks. Occasionally, it takes a week or more.

P: So I understand I can't wash at all. Do you know what it means to me?

T: Yes. As I said, it is going to be very difficult for at least 3 days. I wish there were an easier way for you to rid yourself of this problem.

P: The only thing that I look forward to is telling myself that there is going to be something better at the end of 2 weeks than when I begin the 2 weeks. I can't believe that I am not going to feel worse and worse where I am not sure of what I'm doing. I feel that I'll suffer a terrible amount of anxiety and dizziness and trembling. I have experienced it in the past, but it will probably be more intense during this time.

T: As I said, it will be difficult for the first few days, because we will contaminate you with all the things you have been avoiding so carefully. Your husband will touch you when he comes home from work without washing; you will have to touch the mail and the money he brings home. Eventually, you will have to touch your mother, and she will touch everything in your home.

P: Oh my God! I often wondered what would happen to me should I confront myself with my mother. Nothing. But I'm afraid of being so bad that I'll lock myself in a room.

T: That will not happen. We will do it gradually, and I will support you. As I said, you will feel very anxious in the beginning but the anxiety will decrease.

P: I'll take your word for it. I am partially convinced, but not completely.

T: Your doubts are not surprising. You have had this problem for such a long time that it is impossible for you to believe that it will be over in 2 weeks. I will try to make it easy for you. Every day we will have a session in my office where I will present you with scenes that you will have to imagine. In these scenes you will get completely contaminated. You will experience a lot of anxiety while you imagine the scenes, but eventually it will decrease. This way you will learn that anxiety decreases without washing. Then we will construct a program of touching contaminating objects all day. We will start with objects that you can tolerate and gradually progress to more contaminating ones. Do you agree to participate in such a program?

P: I can't stand the way I am living, restricted, and it is hard on my family. I get mad for everything. They just touch things that are normal, and I get agitated. I can't go on like this forever. I was in therapy for 8 months and nothing happened. And I can't let my family suffer because of my problem. My son got into oil, and he put it on the floor in the foyer; I just went wild hollering and screaming, and he said "If you were normal that would not have bothered you," and I got mad. Then my son doesn't want to talk to me. I'll do anything to be cured.

All obsessive-compulsive patients who seek treatment genuinely want to get rid of their symptoms. In this respect, they are highly motivated. However, it is important to impress upon them the need to relinquish control and to obey the therapist's instructions rigorously. Patients should be told that the program will be discussed with them in advance and that there will be no "surprises" involved. The therapist should take into account the patient's discomfort level in his/her decision as to when to proceed to items higher on the discomfort-arousing hierarchy. However, this schedule should be determined by the therapist and *not* by the patient. It is important to get a firm verbal agreement on this point from the patient in order to effectively deal with later arguments, pleadings, and anger.

Moreover, it is important to explain to the patient that the treatment will be successful only if complete trust between the patient and the therapist can be assumed. This means that if rituals are performed, the patient must report them to the therapist. Similarly, if patients realize during treatment that certain disturbing stimuli had not been mentioned by them, these stimuli must be reported to the therapist so that these stimuli can be incorporated into the treatment program.

The following verbatim material from Sara's third session illustrates such a verbal contract:

T: At no time are we going to lie to you, play tricks on you, or surprise you by suddenly exposing you to things that might contaminate you that we have not discussed. In the last part of the session today we will construct the program together. I'll try to make it as easy as I possibly can by exposing you to things which are progressively more disturbing. But once the treatment starts, you will have to follow my instructions.

P: I appreciate that a lot. It is a lot better for me to know than for you to put me through something that I don't know. I don't respect that at all, you know, being tricked or something.

T: During treatment you might remember certain things that bother you which have not been included in the program. It is very important that you tell me about them so we can expose you systematically to those things. Is this agreeable to you?

P: Sure. I have to get rid of this problem, and I promise to cooperate.

T: Also, if you wash your hands because you cannot resist the urge, I want you to let me know about it. I promise that I won't put you down for washing, but it is important that I know should this happen.

P: I'll do that, but I hope it won't happen.

T: The last thing I want to discuss before we start to construct the program is the fact that I will be the one to decide when you touch each of the things that contaminate you. I realize that sometimes you will want to delay touching certain things. This will just prolong your agony and will not help your treatment. Do you think you will be able to go along with my decision?

P: If you leave it up to me, I'll never touch any of these things, you know, my husband's clothes and the mail. So I'll just go along with what you say; I hope I can do it.

T: Very good. I am sure you will be able to follow the program. So let's start planning your treatment.

Forming the Treatment Program

After the patient agrees to participate in the treatment program, the environmental setting should be negotiated with the patient. As mentioned earlier, there are three settings that can be offered: an inpatient setting with response prevention supervised by nurses; an outpatient setting where family members supervise the treatment program; and in rare cases, a situation where patient self-control may be sufficient.

Sara was one of the two washers who we felt could assert self-control:

T: We have discussed the difficulty that you will experience when asked to refrain from any washing. You will probably have strong urges to wash, since you will be constantly contaminated. I would prefer that you be admitted to the psychiatric ward in the building next to us so that whenever you want to wash, someone will help you to overcome the urge.

P: I have three children. The youngest is 6 years old, and that would be very difficult for the family. I really would prefer to stay at home.

T: Can your husband take 2 weeks vacation and be with you at home to help you overcome the urge to wash?

P: I don't think so. He just had 2 weeks vacation 2 months ago and I don't think they will let him have 2 more weeks. But I think I can do it on my own.

T: This will be very difficult. Do you really think you can control yourself during the 2 weeks?

P: I guess, sure, if you use enough will power. It's just that you feel like you are going to faint or perhaps go crazy; you get to a certain point where you start to tremble, and you are not so sure because your body seems to take over. I can control a certain amount of anxiety, but I found that I try to go along with it rather than try to fight it. But I do want to try it on my own.

T: I will be here to support you.

P: That will help, because in my worst moments I've been alone.

T: But I will see you everyday.

P: I think that will be tremendous.

T: And you have my number at home, so you can call me any time. I will give you every support that you need. The last patient I had said that he could not control himself. With a washing compulsion, one has an immense urge.

P: Everything you touch is contaminated.

T: There will be a problem with the kitchen and the household work. I mean you will not be allowed to touch water, or do any cleaning. How will you handle that?

P: Well, I just won't clean, someone else will do whatever is necessary. My husband and the children. He does the dishes, I never touch a dish. Actually, the only thing I mind is cleaning the bathroom; but I guess they can keep it together for whatever amount of time.

When a self-control situation is chosen, it is important to impress upon the patient the need to be completely honest in her/his reports and to create a nonpunitive atmosphere where reports of failure will be met with understanding rather than blame. This strategy allows the implementation of supervision if needed.

Steve, in contrast to Sara, did not trust himself, and preferred being hospitalized; however, after a visit to the ward he changed his mind. His father agreed to take 2 weeks vacation and supervise response prevention. Steve felt that he should be supervised 24 hours a day and suggested that he sleep at night in the same bed with his father. He even insisted that his and his father's wrists be tied together with a rope to prevent him from washing while his father slept. Both Steve and his mother preferred that she move out for this first 2 weeks of treatment. They both feared that she would hinder the treatment by being too concerned and overprotective.

Constructing Scenes for Flooding in Fantasy

The therapist should use flooding in fantasy to anticipate later exposure *in vivo*, and/or to provide exposure to stimuli and situations which cannot be produced *in vivo*, but which are part of the stimuli-complex that evoke anxiety and maintain the ritualistic behavior. Prolonged flooding in fantasy aims at extinguishing anxiety to the imaginary consequences of exposure to the specific stimuli involved. Thus washers who are afraid of becoming infected with a disease following exposure to dirt would be asked to imagine that they have actually become sick; checkers who fear causing death or harm to other people are asked to imagine that indeed such harm has actually been inflicted.

The subjective experience of these "disasters" follows an imaginary exposure to situations that usually evoke the urge to emit compulsive behavior; it occurs because the rituals are not performed. Thus the fantasy scenes that the therapist evokes include imagining exposure to potentially real situations, response prevention, and the occurrence, in fantasy, of the expected "disasters."

Two or three scenes are constructed, increasing incrementally in terms of how much anxiety they would evoke if they were indeed to really happen. The first scene should evoke about 60 SUDs (subjective units of discomfort), the second scene 80 SUDs, and the final scenes should be the highest on the hierarchy, evoking 100 SUDs. We have found that this gradual increase in anxiety provocation facilitates habituation and reduces stress during treatment.

Three scenes were constructed for Sara's treatment: (1) picking up the "Inquirer" and reading it, and spreading it on her bed and other places in her home, knowing that it is contaminated by her mother's neighbors; (2) hugging her husband when he comes home from work without his changing his clothes or washing; and (3) touching her mother, who then "contaminates" her whole home.

Steve's treatment involved first asking him to imagine touching flies, while following scenes included being in a restaurant where chicken soup is spilled on him.

Other examples of therapist-patient constructed flooding scenes are as follows:

One patient, a washer, who was afraid of being contaminated by a local Medical School (100 SUDs), generalized his fear to downtown Philadelphia (70 SUDs), and to being touched by people in the railway station (60 SUDs). He was first asked to imagine that he was standing in line at the station. He hears two persons behind him talk about their work; they turn out to be two physicians who work at Temple Medical School. They continuously touch him as they are standing in line. In the last scene, he imagines himself being in the most "contaminated" place—a lab that contains a substance that will infect him with incurable cancer.

Still another washer was asked to imagine that her hands were contaminated by urine and feces. She did not wash her hands, and her being uncareful about this caused her baby to be very sick. The baby was hospitalized, and all her family accused her of causing harm to her daughter through being negligent about personal hygiene.

The inclusion of induced fantasies about disasterous consequences is of particular importance in the treatment of checkers. For this group of patients, the prevention of disasters is often the most salient reason for performing checking rituals. A patient who was constantly making sure that her telephone was on the hook was instructed to imagine that she neglects to check the telephone, and indeed the telephone is off the hook. Her sister calls to ask her help; one of her children is very sick and needs immediate hospitalization. She desperately needs the patient to babysit the baby. Since the telephone is off the hook, the patient cannot be reached and her nephew dies.

The content of the scenes to be imagined should be based on fearful situations reported by the patients. The cooperative efforts of the therapist and the patient are required to compose effective fantasy scenes.

Preparing a Hierarchy of Situations for Exposure In Vivo

On the basis of information collected in early sessions, a list of anxiety-producing situations, objects, or persons is prepared with the patient. Often patients have been avoiding certain objects to the extent of eliminating them completely from their immediate environments. Arrangements should be made to have such objects available before commencement of treatment.

Following is the hierarchy of situations constructed for Sara's treatment:

1. The newspaper: holding it; putting it on her face, hair and the rest of her body; wiping her entire home with it; spreading it on her bed; carrying it with her constantly; sleeping at night with it in the bed with her.
2. The mail and money: holding the mail; holding money that her husband brought from work.
3. Her husband: wearing her husband's shirt that he had worn to work; touching him immediately after his return from work; having him touch everything at home without washing.
4. Her mother: wearing her mother's clothes that were sent to her by

mail (this garment had been sent to the therapist's office before the beginning of treatment); her mother coming to visit, touching Sara, and "contaminating" her home.

Steve was exposed to the following situations:

1. Touching flies and cockroaches collected by the therapist.
2. Smelling a shirt worn by the therapist, who had not taken a shower for several days; wearing this shirt for several days and nights.
3. Smelling boiling chicken soup prepared by his father.
4. Having chicken soup spilled on his hair, face, hands, clothes, and bed several times per day.

These situations are defined and anticipated in collaboration with the patient, who consents to being exposed to them in the prescribed order. The patient is told that the therapist will use his or her judgment in deciding when to introduce a new situation and will take into account the progress made by the patient (i.e., how much reduction of discomfort is achieved) in each stage.

Listing the Target Rituals to be Prevented

From information collected in early sessions, a list of rituals is prepared. Such a list may seem to be quite simple to construct for washers; it usually consists of cleaning and washing behaviors. However, some patients may substitute wiping their hands for washing. They may also develop avoidance responses, such as using paper to touch contaminated objects. It is, therefore, useful to anticipate such substitutions and avoidances and to definitely specify in writing what behaviors are to be prevented. Lists of rituals for checkers and for patients who are using cognitive rituals are necessarily longer and more complicated.

A written list of rituals proves helpful for patients as a device that clearly structures their tasks. It is also useful for those who are designated to supervise response prevention and to help the therapist follow the progress of the treatment. Sara's list was short and simple:

1. Refraining from cleaning.
2. Refraining from being in contact with water.
3. Refraining from wiping hands.

Steve's list was as follows:

1. Refraining from cleaning.

2. Refraining from washing.
3. Refraining from using paper to touch objects.
4. Refraining from wiping hands.
5. Refraining from thinking or uttering "clean words."
6. Refraining from checking things before going to sleep.
7. Refraining from counting in intervals of four.

Course of Therapeutic Intervention

Once the treatment program has been constructed, it is best to follow it as strictly as possible. A rigorous implementation of the program decreases the likelihood of arguments between patient and therapist, as well as decreasing the amount of tension and frustration experienced by the patient during therapy. Occasionally, however, it is necessary to introduce changes in the program in order to include exposure to disturbing items that have not been mentioned by the patient earlier.

Exposure-Response Prevention Phase

During this period, treatment consists of daily (excluding weekends) sessions that last about 2 hours. Most patients show significant improvement within a period of 2 weeks, or ten treatment sessions. An additional week or two of this regime should be considered when the patient has made considerable progress, but discomfort has not been extinguished to high discomfort-evoking items on the hierarchy. Let us follow Sara's progress in treatment during this 2-week treatment:

First Session

Sara came to the first session completely decontaminated. She had taken an extended shower before starting treatment. Excessive washing prior to treatment is typical of most washers; they seem to take advantage of their last opportunity to indulge in ritualistic behavior. Most patients experience a great deal of anticipatory anxiety prior to treatment and feel some relief when treatment begins. Sara expressed it as follows:

> T: Well, finally we are starting treatment today. How do you feel now?
> P: Well, I thought this morning would be a lot worse; I didn't sleep. I slept about 3 hours. I went to bed about 3:30, I felt this terrible need to clean last night, and I swear my toilet bowl is clean enough to drink out of—that may be a slight exaggeration—but I really just cleaned and washed and washed everything trying to get ahead of things,

ironing—but then when I went to bed I was so tired and so nervous knowing that morning was approaching so quickly that I didn't sleep. I felt very anxious. Anyway my husband got up, and I thought "I'm going to panic," but I didn't. It wasn't as bad as I thought it would be. I let him out the door, but I didn't take the shower. I haven't washed my hands since last night.

T: Very good.

P: So I did cook the kids' breakfast and things like that. I let them do some of the things like going out to pick up some trash that was out on the patio; I don't want to go out to do that without being able to wash my hands.

T: For the time being, you don't have to touch the trash, but you will have to do that later. At the present, we will concentrate on touching the newspaper. Later on, you will be able to touch other things that you now avoid.

P: They did wash their hands right after.

T: It is okay if they do that on their own, but you should not tell them to do it. You did well this morning. It will take some time until you get accustomed to handling situations in a normal way. You may find yourself violating some of the rules we have set, but this will happen less frequently during the course of the treatment.

In the first days of treatment, most washers tend to avoid contact with dirt. They should be reassured that these habits will diminish as they get less anxious when in contact with the contaminating objects.

Throughout treatment, but especially in the first few sessions, issues concerning ambivalence toward response prevention may arise; some flexibility is in line without violating the "rule" of no contact with water. The following verbatim transcript illustrates this point:

P: Can I use mouthwash?

T: I would rather that you don't.

P: Oh yuk. Nothing. I can't brush my teeth.

T: You may use a towel just to wipe your teeth.

P: How about a dry toothbrush without the toothpaste?

T: You may use a toothbrush, but no toothpaste and water.

P: Okay. I can't rinse with just plain water?

T: No, you shouldn't be in contact with water at all.

P: I can't drink it?

T: Yes, you can drink it, but let somebody else pour it. You see, being in contact with water may tempt you to wash your hands.

P: That happened this morning a little; I was pouring something out of a pitcher and I got kind of damp and was conscious of it.

After the initial conversation, flooding in imagination was introduced. Sara was asked to imagine that she was buying a newspaper, bringing it home and contaminating the entire house, including the food in the refrigerator, which the children then ate. (Verbatim material of 15 minutes of flooding in imagination, given in the fifth session, is presented later.) She was able to imagine the scene very clearly, and reported a high level of anxiety. This fantasy scene was continued to 110 minutes, and Sara's subjective anxiety level was monitored every 10 minutes. The fantasy session was terminated as soon as she reported a discomfort level of 30, a considerable reduction in anxiety; her SUD reports throughout the session were: 50, 95, 90, 90, 85, 80, 50, 70, 50, 45, 40, 30. The therapist followed this flooding in imagination with exposure *in vivo*, by "contaminating" Sara's clothes, hands, and face with the "Inquirer," the local daily newspaper. Finally, the patient was instructed in the "homework" techniques required by the treatment:

T: At home I want you to do exactly the same things that we did here. I want you to sit with a newspaper on your lap and to carry it at all times. Put it in your bed, your closets, on your clothes, and on your skin. I also want you to contaminate your underwear. Do not change the clothes that you are wearing now for the next 24 hours.

P: No.

T: It may seem unnecessary to you, but I would like you to wear the contaminated clothes so that you don't experience relief by changing them. From now on, you are not allowed to wear uncontaminated clothes, and you are not to wear gloves.

P: Do I have to touch everything with the newspaper?

T: Yes. And you must be in contact with it all the time. I mean you must put the pages of the newspaper in the closet and in your bed and leave them there. Okay?

P: Okay.

T: Do you anticipate a great deal of difficulty in following these instructions?

P: I know people who work for the Inquirer; my husband tried to comfort me by saying that the newspapers were bundled and that not every newspaper was touched. But to me they were still on the truck and were contaminated by the people who work there.

T: How do you feel now?

P: Well, anxious at the prospect; I think I will feel better if I buy it around the corner. I'm not too choked up about that either but I have no choice.

T: Just give me a call at any time if you feel you need support.

P: Thank you.

Second Session

At the beginning of the second session, it is important to find out how closely the patient followed the homework instructions:

T: What happened when you came home yesterday?

P: Well, I didn't buy the paper on the way home. I went out to get it about 2 o'clock. I laid it on the floor and didn't mind it as much as I thought I would. Afterwards, I made a game with the kids and threw the newspaper over their heads, and they thought it was a riot. They didn't know what was going on. I told them, "Mommy is going to play a game," and I went around touching everything with the newspaper, and they thought that it was a riot. Then I went upstairs and and put it over my clothes and in my drawers; that I really didn't want to do, but I made myself go through it. I ripped it up into pieces and put it between the underwear, and it is in the closet, and I laid it on the bed.

T: Under the covers?

P: I laid it on top of everything, and then eventually when we were getting ready for bed, my husband took it and put it underneath, and I said it wasn't necessary, but he said yes it was. I didn't have as much courage as he did. He said "I never thought I'd see an Inquirer in my house, let alone in bed with us." That was really something. They all enjoyed seeing a paper in the house.

T: Was that helpful for you?

P: To a point, yes. My husband enjoys reading the paper, and he had to read it in work before. I imagine he would like to have a newspaper all the time.

T: How do you feel about having a newspaper every day?

P: It doesn't matter if it is the "Bulletin" does it? (The "Bulletin" is another local daily paper.)

T: What is the difference between the "Inquirer" and the "Bulletin?"

P: Well, the "Bulletin" is an evening paper. I never did like the "Inquirer," but the "Bulletin" is truly more contaminating to me. I know that it would be better for me. I did shy away from the "Bulletin" last night, although I wanted it today more than the "Inquirer." I used to read the "Bulletin."

T: Well, if you like to read the "Bulletin" and if you feel that it contaminates you more than the "Inquirer," I don't see any reason why you should not buy it.

After reaching a firm agreement with the patient that he/she will continue to maintain normal contact with the item to which he/she has already been exposed, the therapist can then inquire about other peripheral avoidance habits that had not been included in the original hierarchy; the therapist encourages gradual change of these habits, with their elimination as the ultimate goal:

T: So your son came home at 2 o'clock. Did he change immediately?

P: No, he took his shoes off, but he didn't take a shower at this time. Well, I could tell him to put the same clothes back on; he usually puts on dungarees. I told him to leave his school clothes on. He took off his shoes and then automatically out of habit he washed his hands. They automatically wash their hands. Yesterday, they left their clothes on and they stayed dressed; they had snacks and watched TV.

T: They are used to taking off their shoes and to washing their hands. You can tell them that you don't mind if they wash their hands only when they want to from now on. If they wash their hands before they eat, that is basic hygiene. But if they are allowed to touch you only after washing their hands, then you avoid contamination, and that should stop.

P: Should I tell them to leave their shoes on in the house?

T: Yes. Moreover, do you think it is necessary to have a mat inside the house?

P: Not if it were for the sake of you know—my thought was for the sake of contamination, for no other reason.

T: So why not get rid of it?

P: The mat outside the door is not big enough. Shall I buy a new one now? Well gosh, I hate leaving it there. It is bringing so much of the outside in; I guess I could go along with your suggestion.

The therapist now proceeded to discuss the next step on the hierarchy:

T: Tell me again, what happens when your husband comes home from work?

P: He phones me, and I wait at the door. Then he beeps his horn, and I go to the door and open it for him. Then he gets changed in the basement, and I fill the basin for him, but I don't touch him.

T: What do you do next?

P: I put some soap in the basin because of the spigots.

T: I would like you to change this procedure. Does your husband have a key?

P: I don't want to hear it; I know what you are going to say. Yes, he has a key.

T: So he can open the door by himself.

P: He doesn't wash his hands?

T: Only when he takes a shower.

P: Okay, can I turn the shower on?

T: No, let him take a normal shower without preparing anything for him.

P: This will be very difficult.

T: Did you contaminate the bathroom and the kitchen with the newspaper?

P: Yes.

T: So the bathroom is contaminated. Will your husband contaminate it more?

P: Much worse; I feel that it is contaminated 50%. But his coming into the house without my having opened the door, and then having to use the door tomorrow would make it about 90%. The remaining 10% would be the difference between my mother and other things.

T: So, today your husband will touch the door knobs, outside and inside, then he will go immediately upstairs by himself and prepare his own bath. This way he will not contaminate everything today.

P: Yeah. On one hand I think it would be better for him to contaminate everything, but on the other hand I think it would be comforting to see him take a shower. I think that tomorrow he could contaminate everything. It's bad enough with the kids and their shoes. I usually ask them to take their shoes off at the bottom of the steps. I guess you know that you are not going to win a popularity contest with me?

T: I know. I realize how difficult it is for you to go through this program and I respect your courage. I also know that as we proceed with the treatment you will not feel as uncomfortable as you do now.

P: Yes. Like the kids and the newspaper I thought were on the same level, but they are not. It bothers me much more with my husband than with them.

After agreement has been reached on the exact situation for the next stage of exposure, the therapist introduces this new situation with flooding in imagination in order to achieve some degree of habituation. (This procedure seems to facilitate subsequent exposure *in vivo*.) Sara was asked to imagine that her husband contaminated the entire house with the clothes he had worn to work. After 90 minutes, she was able to imagine the scene with only 15 SUDs.

At the end of the session, Sara reported that she had washed her hands once accidentally. Such reports are characteristic in the first days and should be met with an attitude of understanding. However, such behavior must be discouraged:

P: By the way, I washed my hands last night accidentally, I didn't even know I was doing it. It was about 7:30, and I was upstairs talking a mile a minute, and I picked up the soap and turned on the water and my husband said "What are you doing?" I was really startled. I dropped the soap as though I had burned myself and said "Oh God, it was an accident."

T: It happens in the beginning of treatment because washing has become such a strong habit for you. Don't worry about that time, but try to make sure that it doesn't happen again.

Third Session

As treatment progresses, conflict develops between the continuing tendency to avoid contact with "contaminated" objects and a beginning realization that the discomfort evoked by such contact does diminish with time. Whenever the patient reports avoidance behavior, the therapist can introduce exposure to the situation involved immediately in the office:

T: How was your day yesterday?

P: Okay, until my husband came home. Then I avoided him and everything he touched. I stayed pretty much in the chair, and I was careful.

T: Did he shower?

P: Yes, he did what he was supposed to, and he came down, and I stayed downstairs, and he wanted to kiss me and I said "No." I just made sure I didn't come into contact with him. And then when we went to bed he said, "What, no kiss?" and I said "No." So he didn't push it. And the first time I touched anything was a doorknob on the way up. I was tempted to put my gloves on, but I knew that it was something I had to do.

T: Did you touch yourself with your hand?

P: No, I guess I will have to eventually.

T: Can you do it now? Please do it.

P: (Touches her face with her fingers) How is that?

T: That is not enough. Touch your face with both hands.

P: How about that?

T: Watch me do it, and then touch your face exactly as I do (modeling).

P: Oh God! (Models after therapist.)

T: How are you feeling?

P: Ucky, dirty, I would like to wash my hands.

T: It is quite natural for you to feel this way, but the feeling will subside gradually.

To illustrate that habituation does occur with time and continued exposure, the therapist may point out that items that were lower on the hierarchy and that have been introduced in therapy already evoke less anxiety:

T: How was it when you bought the newspaper?

P: It was okay. I didn't buy the newspaper until late, and I bought it around the corner where I am quite disturbed about the place. I thought it would be a good idea to go there. I avoided the shop since just after I moved in because I saw a car pull in ahead of me with tags of the firm where my husband works. So after I saw that, I pulled out and never went there again. So yesterday I thought it would be a good idea to go there and buy the paper. I even bought a piece of candy, and I didn't find it that disturbing to eat it.

T: That was very good. What was your level of anxiety when you went into this place?

P: Not really bad at all, 10%.

T: How did you feel when you brought the newspaper home?

P: I really enjoyed reading this paper because the "Inquirer" was more of an effort because I didn't enjoy reading it. And the "Bulletin" I found interesting. I put it down to go back to it after dinner.

T: It is very encouraging that you are not disturbed anymore by the newspaper. What about the children? When your daughter came home did she take her shoes off and then wash her hands?

P: She took her shoes off and well that is all. She said "Can I leave my dress and stockings on?" and I said "Yes, stay as you are."

T: Did she want to take her shoes off?

P: Well, it is just a habit. Now today she wore dress shoes, and I know she doesn't want to take those off, because she said to me

"Can I leave my shoes on after school?" because I know she likes to wear them, and I said "Yes."

T: How did you feel when she didn't wash her hands?

P: I don't pay too much attention. I don't think that it bothers me as much the second day. It really seems to bother me the first day. Like you said, the anxiety does decrease.

T: Yes, it does. I am glad you noticed it.

P: Those things seem little to me now compared to Bob. The newspaper seems like nothing. His touching the doorknob seems like a major thing to me.

The therapist then outlined the next step of exposure:

T: We have two days left to work on contact with your husband. So today, he may still change his clothes, but his shower will be delayed, and he will touch you before he takes a shower.

P: Well yeah, I guess it is better to get it over with—say he doesn't have to take a shower right away.

T: How about before he goes to bed?

P: Just as long as he changes his clothes.

T: He comes home, changes his clothes, and then touches you.

P: Okay, touches me just like that (demonstrating minimal contact).

T: Well, we have to make sure he contaminates you; therefore, he has to touch you more like this.

P: O.K.

During flooding in imagination, the scene of the previous session's scene was repeated. This time, reported anxiety diminished after 45 minutes. General discomfort level during the third day of treatment was 50 SUDs. Anticipatory anxiety about her husband's touching her before showering was 75 SUDs.

At the end of the third session, it is advisable to plan ahead for the next few sessions and discuss homework for the weekend:

T: How contaminated do you think you will feel when your husband touches you?

P: 75% at least, maybe higher. I think he is the most second to my mother and relatives. I think if I can get over Bob—I think that will be a big step.

T: Yes, you must first be contaminated by Bob before you meet with your mother. I would like you to meet with her this week.

P: This week.

T: Yes, before the weekend.

P: I thought that was going to be last.

T: If we expose you to your mother at the end of the week, then at the end of the second week you may not feel contaminated anymore.

P: I see; where shall I meet her?

T: There are three possibilities. You could meet at her home, you could meet at your home, or you could meet her somewhere else. Each possibility has its advantages and disadvantages.

P: Do you think one place is better than the other for one reason or another?

T: I think that it will be best if your mother comes to your house.

P: I was afraid you were going to say that. I think that is the worst. Don't you think that is the worst? That means everything.

T: Okay, we don't have to start with her coming to your house.

P: Oh good.

T: Does your mother know about the treatment?

P: Vaguely. She knows that I'm coming, and this type of therapy is more helpful than what I've been through in the past years. I told her the type of therapy I was going to be going through was drastic. I didn't get explicit. I thought that they wouldn't understand. I guess for the first meeting we could meet here? Because it's so traumatic; it's been 2 years.

T: Okay, we could have the first meeting here on Friday. On Saturday she will come to your house, and on Sunday you will go to her house. Ask her to bring a garment with her on Friday that you can then take home with you.

P: Oh God! Let me leave. I don't want to.

T: We did discuss the program before, didn't we?

P: It's probably worse in my mind. Because even buying the paper I thought I couldn't handle, and now it does not bother me anymore.

T: A week from today, you may feel the same way about your mother.

P: That's what you keep telling me; I can't imagine it; oh my God! Today is Wednesday, Thursday, and then Friday. What time would you like her to come here?

T: I have time on Friday afternoon.

P: I'll call her. I don't foresee any problem.

Although the treatment program was clear to Sara, it seemed important to discuss again in advance the most anxiety-evoking event—meeting her mother. This extra step helps to avoid arguments on the day before this final step is to be implemented.

Fourth Session

By the fourth day of treatment habituation to major sources of contamination start to generalize to other objects in the environment. Patients then begin to approach situations that they had avoided before. This generalization process was experienced by Sara:

T: So you had a busy day yesterday.

P: Yes.

T: Did your husband come home early?

P: Yes, just after I got in, he called and said that he would be home in a few minutes, he wasn't feeling well. So actually, he didn't have his bath at all. He didn't feel well enough to take a shower at all. It all worked out for the best.

T: How did you feel when your husband touched you?

P: Not as bad as I thought I would, actually. It was even better today.

T: How did you feel?

P: He just hugged me. I was conscious of his hands on my back but we didn't have too much contact yesterday because he didn't want me catching anything he had. Yesterday I went for the paper about 4:00, and I stopped at the grocery store and bought four Amorosa rolls. We had them for dinner, and I felt no anxiety at all. It didn't faze me; it was just like buying anything else. And today, after 5 years, I allowed the dog to sit on my lap.

T: This is very good. How did you feel about the dog?

P: Fine, it didn't bother me a bit.

T: So how much do you feel contaminated?

P: I went to the mailbox on my way out and I thought "I wonder if I can reach into the mailbox." I opened the lid of the mailbox and took the mail out and felt nothing. I looked through at a few of my bills and then threw them on the counter in my kitchen, and nothing, I didn't feel anything.

T: Did you have the urge to wash?

P: Well, I do feel contaminated.

In some cases, obsessive-compulsives are not able to differentiate between "normal" dirt and contamination, nor between anxiety and a sense of contamination. When avoidance responses diminish, they can learn to make these distinctions if taught by the therapist, as illustrated in the following:

T: Contaminated or dirty?

P: Well, I'm beginning to feel like I would like to take a shower. Now I feel a lot of perspiration. I would like to use deodorant.

T: Is that because you are dirty or is it because you feel contaminated?

P: No, it is because I feel dirty. I just feel like I need a bath after 4 days.

T: So what is your contamination level?

P: Well, I don't know because I've been thinking a lot about my mother and how I'll actually—she seems to me like the ultimate—so I would say I will be 90%. Right now I don't feel like there is anything I couldn't touch.

T: How is your anxiety level—the overall anxiety level?

P: Fine, about 20%.

T: How much would you say your house is contaminated now?

P: Well, I guess I'm trying to think if my mother were to come, I don't know. I'm still skeptical with her, but as far as—I was talking last night about bringing up the boxes and furniture that are in the basement, I'm anxious to rummage through them now and bringing up some of the things now.

Flooding in imagination concentrated on preparing Sara for contact with her mother. It lasted 80 minutes, with the following SUDs reported at the usual 10-minute intervals: 30, 30, 75, 100, 75, 50, 25, 25.

The fourth session terminated with further instructions for homework:

T: How about your husband's clothes, are they still in the basement?

P: We've already ordered, well we have twin closets that slide over. They really aren't big enough. So we ordered a huge wardrobe, and they are delivering it this week sometime, so we were waiting only to bring the clothes up to put them in the new wardrobe.

T: Is there some space in your closet now?

P: Well, we could squeeze them in there.

T: Can you do that today?

P: Yeah.

T: And let your husband wear his working clothes, not his home clothes, even though he is not going to work. Be sure that he touches you while wearing his work clothes. How do you feel about being touched by your husband while he is wearing his work clothes?

P: I don't know. Because I've found that thinking about those things are worse than doing it. I thought that a lot of these things would be terrible mountains, but they turned out to be very small molehills. So I think the best thing is just to do it and then see what kind of reaction I have.

The realization that anticipatory anxiety is often more intense than the actual discomfort experienced during exposure is of utmost importance and should be reinforced. Such recognition motivates the patient to attempt self-exposures to additional situations that had not been practiced during treatment.

T: It is important that you have noticed that you are not as disturbed by touching things as you thought you would be. If you remember that, you will not hesitate when you try to touch things you have not yet touched.

P: I think the only things would be those things that would be directly completely with my mother.

T: Well, you are going to see her on Friday.

P: That is still frightening.

Fifth Session

This session was most difficult for Sara, since she was about to meet with her mother, the main source of contamination. Her anxiety was very high, and caused an increase in the level of feeling contaminated. Because of the high level of arousal, she was not able to discriminate between these two subjective feelings, although she had learned to do so previously.

T: How do you feel today?

P: It just hit me on my way home from my visit with you. I started to feel achy, and as soon as I got home I took some aspirin. I think it will pass; I think I will be able to get rid of it.

T: How anxious are you?

P: Terrible, 80%.

T: How high is your contamination level?

P: About 90%. I wasn't feeling so good yesterday, and my husband had everything ready. He had candles on the table. I think he is trying to boost my morale, knowing what was coming, and so then last night we carried up all his clothes, and I did as you instructed, leaving some on the bed and I intermingled his clothes with mine.

T: How did you feel about his clothes?

P: When I think about it, I felt just fine. I even carried his shoes for him which I considered worse than carrying his clothes.

T: That's very good. Aren't you proud of yourself?

P: Yes, but I feel terrible.

T: How strong is your urge to wash now?

P: A lot today.

T: What is the reason for this?

P: I guess it's because I am going to see my mother. I keep thinking "Two and a half years. What am I going to say to her?" Does she have to touch me?

T: Yes, it is absolutely necessary. Anything special about yesterday or today? What about the mail, could you touch that?

P: No problem. Last night I made out some checks, and today I went to the post office because the postage went up. I had to get some 13-cent stamps. And I thought I'll mail them at the post office, and I thought I'd never have the mail in my pocketbook. But there was no problem for me. And I avoided the bank all along and no problem. The only thing I minded was not having any makeup on.

T: You did make tremendous progress, and that's very encouraging. How did you sleep?

P: I was thinking about today. So I went downstairs, and I just sat there and read, and I wasn't interested in reading. So I just sat there and sat there until 4:30. Then I went to bed and tossed and turned. I fell asleep finally toward morning when it was time to get up.

T: I am really sorry that you have to go through all this pain and discomfort. But you have realized by now that the only way to get rid of your problem is to confront the feared situations. I assure you that after you meet with your mother you'll feel better. Now, your mother will come here in about an hour and I would like to rehearse with you again in your imagination being in contact with her.

P: Okay.

The transcript of the first 15 minutes of flooding follows. It illustrates the persistence of the therapist in maintaining in fantasy the image of the most salient and anxiety-evoking stimulus—Sara's mother holding her hands. It also demonstrates the patient's attempt to avoid the discomfort-evoking images and the therapist's efforts to block such attempts.

T: I want you to imagine that you are sitting here in the chair, and I am with you. The door opens and your mother comes in. She enters the room, she sees you, and she says "Hello it has been a long time." She comes to you, and she touches you. She wants to hug you. Your mother is astonished that you let her hug you, and she says "I am allowed to hug my daughter again." Now you feel the contamination spreading all over you. You can feel her hands on your back. And you begin to feel that it will never go away. It can never be washed. You would like your mother to leave, and you want to take a shower or a bath so you can feel clean again. You can't say anything. You can't move; you are overwhelmed by the feeling of being contaminated. Your mother is standing beside you, and she is holding your hand and you can feel how she becomes even more contaminating. You would like her to take her hand off. And she is asking you "Are you afraid of me?" And you would like to explain to her how much afraid of her you are, but you don't say anything. You just let her hold your hand and let her hug you. You let her sit beside you, real close, and she is contaminating you. You can feel the contamination all over your body. You wish you could run out and scream and never come in contact with her again. But you stay here, you stay beside her as she contaminates you more and more. You feel that you will never be clean again. You realize that your mother is contaminating you. You feel the contamination on your skin. You feel the burning spots on your back and hands. It is the feeling of contamination, creeping up your arms, creeping up your face, it's all over your body. You try to keep your hand close to your body to make sure that the parts which are not contaminated now will remain clean. But it is spreading over your whole body. And your mother is still sitting beside you, still contaminating you. She is contaminating you more and more. She is telling you something but you can't really listen to her. You are so upset, your heart is beating, you can feel your heart beating really fast. You feel as though you are going to faint. But something forces you to stay and listen to her. You would like to run to the next room, but you realize that you have to face the fact that you can't avoid your mother any longer. You feel trapped. She will never go away, she will go on contaminating you forever, more and more. You will never feel free again. You have the urge to leave the room and to forget everything about your mother. But her touch is everywhere on your body. How are you feeling now?

P: 75%.

T: Can you describe to me how you feel?

P: I can tolerate being insane, but I can't tolerate her touching me.

T: You would like to take her hand and push her away but you can't, you can't move, you can't say anything. She has her hand on your arm, and she takes your hand, and she holds it. And all the time she is holding your hand, she tells you how happy she is. You feel terrible, you would like to push her away, you would like to take your hand away.

P: She is touching me!

T: You don't want her to touch you, but you can't do anything about it. She is touching your hand. You don't want it, but she is touching your hand.

P: Yes, she is touching me! She is touching me, and I don't want her to.

T: Yes, but you can't do anything about it. She is touching you.

P: No!

T: Yes, your hand is in her hand; she is holding you.

P: No!

T: She is sitting near you, and she is holding your hand. Keep on feeling your mother is holding your hand.

P: No, I don't want to.

T: How do you feel?

P: Like my hand is going to fall off.

T: And she takes your hand now. . . .

P: Don't touch me!

T: But she *is* touching you, she is contaminating you. She is contaminating you all over. You don't want her to touch you, but she does it.

P: Don't let her touch me!

T: But she is touching you, and you can't do anything about it. Let her touch you. She is touching you.

P: God, she wants something. She is putting something on me.

T: What is she putting on you?

P: I don't want her to touch me.

T: What is she putting on you?

P: I don't know. I don't want her near me. I have to wash it away.

T: No, you can never wash it away.

P: If she touches me, I can't get rid of it.

T: That is true, you will never wash it away. Your hand is burning. You can see a big red spot, and it must be feeling like this. She is touching you, she is touching your hand. Don't keep your hand away from her.

P: Oh, God, no!

T: Feel it on your hand, you don't want her to, but she is touching you.

P: I can't stand her, I can't stand her.

T: Imagine how she is doing it.

P: I can't stand her, I can't stand her! God, if she touches me, I won't be able to do anything with my hands.

T: She is touching your hands. She is not only touching your hand, she is holding your hand.

P: God, I'll die, I'll die. I will! I will! I don't want her to touch me. I don't want her near me. I don't want her near me.

T: She is sitting beside you. She is holding your hand.

P: No!

T: Yes, she is holding your hand. She sits beside you, and your arms are on the chair, and she holds your hand. She contaminates you. She puts something on you. You will never get rid of it. You can't avoid her anymore. She is touching you, she is holding your hand. She keeps your hand in between both her hands. She is not only touching you, but she is holding your hand.

P: It will fall off, I'm telling you. You don't know it will, I can't do it, I want to run away.

T: But you don't. There is a force which keeps you in this room. You would like to leave the room; you would like to run away and never see your mother again. But you stay in the room, and you let her touch your hand. You let her touch, and she touches your hand.

P: Her hand is touching mine.

T: Yes.

P: Don't touch me!

T: But she is touching your hand. Feel how she is touching your hand. She has got it between her hands.

P: She is contaminating me.

T: Yes, she is. She is contaminating you all over. Don't pull your hands away. You can't do anything about it, she is touching your hand. Describe how she is touching you.

P: Holding my hands, and they feel so dirty, contaminated. When she is touching me, I can't get it off of me. It is there permanently, forever. And I can't turn my hand away. And she is touching me. She is squeezing my hands. It seems to make me more contaminated when she puts pressure on me. It seems to penetrate more.

T: It penetrates the skin, goes into the blood, which carries the contamination to your heart.

P: She is holding my hands in her hands, and I am contaminated all over, especially in my hands. It feels like she has left something there, something I can't wash off. Something I can't scrape off.

At the end of flooding in imagination, Sara reported 25 SUDs. Her mother then entered the office. Upon meeting her mother, Sara again felt highly anxious (90 SUDs) and refused to let her mother touch her. The therapist then suggested graduated exposure. First, her mother touched her with one finger and gradually increased contact. Within 5 minutes, with a great amount of support from the therapist, Sara's mother was holding both her hands. This exposure to body contact with her mother lasted 45 minutes, after which discomfort decreased considerably.

T: How are you feeling now?

P: A little bit better, 50%. This is something I would never have done on my own. I'm going to take a 5-hour bath after this is over.

T: Well, you know you are not allowed to wash yet.

P: Right, I was joking.

T: I would like you to hold the sweater that your mother brought for you continuously for the next 24 hours. Tomorrow, when your mother comes to visit you, let her act normally. Let her sit wherever she likes, and let her touch the children. Can you do it?

P: Yes, I think I can.

Sessions Six through Ten

On Saturday Sara's mother visited her home, and on Sunday Sara and her family went to visit her mother's home. The second week of treatment focused on reinforcing the progress that had been made and carefully monitoring Sara's behavior, so that the habit of avoiding contact with previously contaminating situations were completely extinguished. In addition, habits of normal washing and cleaning were introduced.

A whole new world opened for Sara in a few days. She described her new feelings to the therapist:

Saturday while we were out, Bob and I, as a matter of fact yesterday, we took the kids to see the Liberty Bell on the way to my mother's. We had to go through center city, and I hadn't seen it in years. So we took the kids in there, and we took some pictures, and that was fun. Saturday, since Bob and I were out, we stopped at a department store, and we were walking around, and it didn't upset me. It is amazing how good I feel. And you keep waiting for something to happen to you, and nothing happens. I just couldn't believe it. It has only been a week ago that we actually started this, but you know, you were right. Last week I would not have thought it was possible. I wish that everybody that has the same problem I had knew about this and could do something about it. (Sixth session).

Yesterday we went down in the basement, and I got the boys to unpack a lot of things. I couldn't help it, I got into a lot of things myself. It was like opening surprise packages, because I hadn't even known what was in some of them. We brought a lot of old things up, and it was nice to see them again, and my husband turned on an old record; it was called "You Were Meant for Me," and we danced, and my older son said "How corny," and we had a lot of fun. And I didn't hear from my mother until 7:00 last night. She said she couldn't make it today, but she said she would be here tomorrow. (Seventh session).

Last night Bob and I had sex, and it was different, it was like taking a shower, and it wasn't because of the absence of a week or two, because that has been before. It was just that I could feel that I was much more relaxed. I hadn't realized that I had so much anxiety. It was just great (Tenth session).

Residual Avoidance

Habits that have been strengthened by years of constant reinforcement rarely extinguish completely in 2 weeks of treatment. Patients should not be led to expect the occurrence of such miracles, or they will become discouraged and revert to their old habits. It is important to emphasize the strength of compulsive habits and to stress that patients must continue to be "on guard" and continue the regime of deliberate exposure to discomfort-arousing situations for several months after treatment.

Sara experienced a residual tendency to avoid contact with her mother and described her feelings to the therapist in the ninth session. She noticed no such tendency after her mother's first two visits to her home. Sara made the following observation after her mother's third visit:

P: My mother was coming, and I was touching everything, and I thought I'll never be able to handle all that. When she came, I was very conscious that she touched everything at first. I thought "Gee, I wonder how I'll feel about touching that chair after, or that pillow?" But after a while, they sat down, and we started telling stories. We got to laughing, and it became a very relaxed atmosphere. We really enjoyed last night. It was fun talking to someone I've known way back. I kept myself so restricted to people I've just met, where this way it was enjoyable. We had coffee. The only part that upset me was at the end of the evening my mother said she had to go to the bathroom. I said "All right, I'll show you where it is." I had shown her where it was before, and I thought "I wonder if it is just because I don't want her to touch the light switch upstairs. Am I making excuses?" Anyway, I was conscious of the fact that she was touching the wall all the way up, and after they left I avoided the railing. I changed the towel in the bathroom, and I wouldn't use the toilet paper. But then this morning, I made sure I went up and down the stairs. My son said "What are you doing, Mommy, going up and down the stairs?" I didn't tell them. I wanted to make sure I went both back and forth with both hands up and down the rail. Then I went back to the hamper and got the towel out and hung it up this morning and made sure that I did use the toilet paper.

T: You did the right thing. How did you feel after you touched the rail and the towel?

P: O.K. today. Last night I felt nervous, and I thought "Now, I didn't use the towel yet, I just hung it up before I left for here." I know that I did experience some great feelings after I fished them out. I kept thinking "I will," but I didn't. I don't know why I avoid some things. I mean, she sat on the sofa and chair and different things, and that was okay.

T: How did you feel when she came in and touched you and kissed you?

P: O.K.

T: Did you have a feeling of contamination?

P: A little, maybe a touch. Afterwards nothing; I think I was anticipating that something would happen, but nothing really happened.

T: From your description I understand that you still experience some anticipatory anxiety. How afraid were you before your mother came?

P: I was pretty anxious before she came. I think about 40 to 50%.

T: What were you anxious about?

P: About how I would react to her touching me, sitting and moving around my house. I guess I had some doubt. Last night she touched the top of my washing machine, and I wasn't crazy about the idea. I would rather she didn't. But today I will feel better touching the washing machine. But why does it bother me in the first place?

T: Contact. Your mother provoked so much anxiety for years, and it is only 1 week since you first renewed contact with her. In time, with many contacts with your mother, feelings of discomfort will disappear. It is important that you don't wait too long between visits. It is also important that you don't yield to temptation to avoid things she has touched. Like today, you may shower, but use the soap your mother used.

P: I knew you were going to say that.

T: You cannot expect such a strong habit to disappear in 1 week. So you have to keep on fighting it.

P: I guess you are right.

Resuming Normal Washing and Cleaning Activities

On the eighth day of treatment, Sara was allowed to take a 7-minute shower, but was instructed to "recontaminate" her whole body with her mother's sweater. The first shower may be introduced after the third or fourth day, provided that the level of contamination has decreased considerably (to about 0 to 20%) beforehand, and that the patient is recontaminated with the most discomfort-evoking object to which he or she had been exposed before showering. It is not advisable to allow contact with water when patients still experience a great deal of contamination and discomfort. Thus each step of exposure should be followed by response prevention until habituation to this step occurs.

Whenever possible, showers during treatment should be supervised in order to block ritualistic behavior (e.g., certain order in washing the different parts of the body, repetition of scrubbing, or cleaning the faucets). Modeling of "normal" showering may facilitate elimination of such rituals.

Hand washing is introduced at the end of treatment. Six to eight hand washings per day are prescribed—after defecating or urinating, and before eating. The patient is asked to wash her/his hands while the therapist observes. If excessive lathering and washing is apparent, the therapist models normal hand washing (about 20 to 30 seconds) and then asks the patient to wash again. This sequence is repeated until the patient demonstrates that he/she has learned a normal handwashing routine.

Some obsessive-compulsives engage in excessive cleaning and straightening. It is more difficult to establish norms for cleaning than for personal washing. Yet some agreement between the patient and the therapist can be reached regarding the actual time spent on cleaning activities. The following material illustrates how such an agreement was reached with Sara.

T: How many hours did you spend on cleaning the house?

P: Too much, I think. I can't stand seeing lint or crumbs on the carpet. I know that I go and visit my girlfriend, and it disturbs me to see crumbs on her carpet. It doesn't bother her, but it bothers me. I will go over and pick up a piece of lint if I see it lying on the carpet. That is excessive, I think. I have been more relaxed lately, but I don't know if I will go back to that. A lot of these things didn't bother me because I couldn't do them while I was in treatment, so I sort of ignored it. I knew the carpet would get vacuumed eventually. I do think it would disturb me more if I knew someone was coming. Only because I wouldn't want them to think I wasn't a perfect housekeeper.

T: Basically, it is nice to live in a clean house. Having breadcrumbs on the floor is not dangerous, so they don't have to be removed immediately—that is the problem with habit. Can you wait without feeling anxious or upset?

P: Well, I haven't been able to do anything since the treatment began, so now we will have to see.

T: In general, how many hours per day would you normally spend on cleaning and straightening the house?

P: I think I can manage with 5 hours, because I don't like to rush when I clean.

T: That seems reasonable, and it does leave you time to do other things.

P: Yes, I would like to start painting again, I haven't painted for over 2 years.

Final Instructions

In the last session, the patient is given a list of exposure activities and a written schedule for washing. The specific instructions given to Sara were as follows:

T: I would like to suggest that for the next 2 months you follow the washing schedule that we have discussed. Here, I have written it down for you. You are allowed to take one shower per day for 7 to 10 minutes, and you can wash your hands for no longer than 30 seconds about six times per day. I would like your mother to visit your house once a week for the next 2 months. On the days that your mother visits you, you can wash before she arrives, but do not wash for the rest of the day after she leaves.

P: Not even my hands?

T: I suggest you don't. It may sound somewhat disappointing. You were hoping that after therapy you would not have any more constraints. It is important to insure that you will be in contact with your mother until you feel comfortable around her. That does not mean that in the future you will have to see her even if you don't feel like it. It just means that you will have the freedom to see her whenever you want to see her and that you will not be controlled by irrational fears.

P: O.K., I guess it is a good idea.

Follow-Up Therapy Phase

During the first phase of treatment it became apparent that Sara needed assertiveness training in order to deal effectively with her relatives and friends. She expressed the fear that her mother would become dependent on her again and would request more time than Sara would be willing to spend with her or with other members of the family. Ten additional weekly sessions focused on teaching Sara assertive behaviors (see Chapter 9).

At a 1-year follow-up Sara was asymptomatic. She resumed her artistic activities (painting and pottery) and showed no need for therapy. Sara reported one instance of mild relapse; about 8 months after termination of therapy her mother visited her house, after which she experienced difficulty in using the towel her mother had used. She was anxious for several hours, but then decided to touch the towel and refrained from washing for the next 24 hours. This was the only episode of feelings of contamination that she could recall in the follow-up interview.

SPECIAL PROBLEMS

Client Variables

Indications for Failure

After treating over 30 obsessive-compulsives, 21 of whom were evaluated before treatment by an independent assessor (Foa and Goldstein, 1978) we have arrived at three predictive variables for failure or relapse: noncompliance with treatment instructions, overvalued ideation, and severe depression.

Noncompliance with Treatment Instructions. High motivations and a determined attitude to comply scrupulously with treatment demands seems to be crucial for success. No less important is compliance with the final instructions to maintain continuous deliberate exposure to the relevant stimuli, and restricted washing, cleaning, or checking.

The only patient who did not improve in our study was a 58-year-old unmarried woman who lived with her parents. In spite of repeated instructions and daily supervision by her parents, she did not refrain from the symptomatic ritualistic behaviors, except for praying. At follow-up, after 3 years, she was slightly improved, but she attributed this improvement to the dynamic therapy she had been receiving for the last 2 years.

Another patient who did not comply completely with treatment instructions felt contaminated by body secretions. Before beginning treatment, he used to wash for several hours a day and to engage in ritualistic cleaning of the ward, especially the bathrooms. While agreeing to refrain from washing, he refused to stop his cleaning rituals. At the present time, he maintains normal washing behavior, but his cleaning rituals have not diminished. These cases of partial compliance suggest that response prevention must be specific and does not generalize to neurotic responses that are not actively prevented.

While these patients did not comply with instructions regarding response prevention, others refused to expose themselves to the discomfort-evoking stimuli. These patients may be persuaded to cooperate if exposure is introduced in smaller increments, that is, by increasing the number of steps. Such an approach, however, is time consuming. The first author spent over one hundred 2-hour sessions with a patient who refused exposure. The treatment was successful, and all obsessions and compulsions were eliminated. However, post-treatment instructions were not followed, resulting in partial relapse.

It seems, therefore, that when the therapist does not obtain a promise of total commitment to treatment demands during the outlining of the treatment program, therapy should not be continued. The therapist should leave the patient the option of returning at a later date. In fact, three patients who initially refused a total commitment returned later and were treated successfully.

Overvalued Ideation. Most obsessive-compulsives realize that their rituals and ruminations are irrational, although they are unable to control or resist them. Bob expressed this as follows:

> I know that the man with strong body odor waiting in line with me is not dangerous and can't harm me, but I still get anxious. It is not logical to feel this way, but I can't help it.

Few patients maintain that their fears are *realistic* and that their ritualistic behavior really prevents the occurrence of disastrous consequences, but some may express varying degrees of such conviction. When asked "What is the probability that if you abstain from your rituals, the feared consequences will actually happen?" the response may vary from 0 to 100%. A case report of treatment with a patient who experienced some degree of irrational conviction follows.

Judy is a 37-year-old artist, married to a businessman. They have three children, ages 8, 6, and 3. She was afraid of being contaminated by leukemia "germs," which she would then transmit to her children and her husband. While she was not afraid of dying of these germs, she was convinced that her family would die of leukemia unless she took the right precautions.

The following material is from the first interview with Judy:

T: I understand that you need to wash excessively everytime you are in contact, direct or indirect, with leukemia.

P: Yes, like the other day I was sitting in the beauty parlor, and I heard the woman who sat next to me telling this other woman that she had just come back from the Children's Hospital, where she had visited her grandson who had leukemia. I immediately left the place—I still had the rollers on my head. I took a cab and registered in a hotel. I first took a shower for 2 hours. Then I called my husband and told him what happened. I told him I couldn't come back home before I am clean. I washed for 3 days, and then he bought me new clothes because I could not wear the ones I had had on when I was at the beauty parlor.

T: What do you think would have happened if you did not wash?

P: My children and my husband would get leukemia and die.

T: Would you die?

P: No, because I am immune, but they are particularly susceptible to these germs.

T: Do you really think people get leukemia through germs?

P: I have talked with several specialists about cancer. They all tried to assure me that there are no leukemia germs. But medicine is not that advanced. I am convinced that I know something that the doctors have not discovered yet. There are definitely germs that carry leukemia.

T: What is the probability that if you don't wash, your family will get leukemia?

P: One hundred percent. They might not get it immediately, these germs could be in their bodies for 5 or even 10 years. Eventually they will have leukemia. So you see, if I don't wash, it's as if I murdered them.

Judy, as well as three other washers who were characterized by strong beliefs that their fears were realistic (e.g., overvalued ideation), improved only slightly with respect to obsessions and fears, despite their adherence to treatment demands. They all improved initially with regard to their rituals, but relapsed in varying degrees several months after treatment.

Severe Depression. Obsessive-compulsive patients who are also severely depressed do not show the typical reduction of discomfort despite prolonged exposure *in vivo* and in imagination (Foa and Chambless, 1978). Although rituals diminish after treatment, discomfort associated with contaminants does not decrease. However, behavior treatment followed by the administration of tricyclics resulted in marked improvement for two depressed patients (Foa and Steketee, 1977). The treatment order that yields the most success is yet to be investigated; whether this sequence—behavior therapy preceeding drug treatment—is the most effective remains to be determined.

Special Problems in the Treatment of Checkers

In this chapter we have referred mainly to washers, since they constitute the majority of the obsessive-compulsive population. The treatment of checkers and repeaters follows the same pattern as the treatment of washers with a few exceptions. As noted in the introduction, checking rituals are often performed in order to avoid future "disaster," punishment, self-criticism, or guilt. These imagined consequences, then, constitute a crucial part of the total configuration of discomfort-evoking stimuli. For obvious reasons, they cannot be realized *in vivo*, so that it is necessary to rely on flooding in imagination for the exposure phase of treatment with checkers. These patients are asked to imagine scenes in which their negligent behavior results in the disastrous consequences they fear, and in which they are punished or criticized by significant others or by God.

For checkers, more than for washers, compulsion to perform their rituals is weaker when they do not feel responsible for the safety of their environment. In the hospital, for example, they may believe that other people are responsible and will then relax and refrain from checking locks or stoves as they would do at home. In these cases, treatment should be conducted on an outpatient basis, ideally in the patient's home. For example, a patient who was afraid of leaving her stove burning was accompanied by the therapist to her home, the stove was lighted, and was left burning for 2 hours after the patient left the apartment with the therapist.

The hospital is not the only situation in which checkers may feel that they are no longer responsible for the safety of themselves or others. They may personally allocate responsibility to another person (e.g., a spouse). The therapist may also become responsible in their view by the very fact that she/he instructed them to relinquish their rituals. The goal of treatment is not to relieve patients of feelings of responsibility, but to enable them to assume responsibility without the urge to behave ritualistically. In order to avoid such transfer of feelings of responsibility, the flooding scenes should include repeated reminders that it was the patient's *choice* to relinquish the rituals so that the imagined consequences of their "negligence to check" remain their own responsibility.

This difficulty is less likely to arise when rituals consist of repeated behaviors different from checking, since intensity of the urge to perform such rituals, as well as their frequency, does not change across environments. However, the "disastrous" consequences that patients expect to follow neglect of rituals are crucial stimuli for repeaters as much as for checkers. We treated a patient who was both a repeater and a checker; her repetitious ritual of dressing and undressing in order to "protect" her family from dying in a car accident continued in the hospital and was treated there. However, prevention of checking had to be conducted at her home, since she had no urge to check at the hospital. During her hospitalization, she was accompanied daily by the therapist to her home, and these response preventions were accompanied by flooding in imagination. She was asked to imagine that her family died in a car accident because she had been "selfish" enough to rid herself of her rituals.

The Treatment of Cognitive Compulsions

Some patients, such as Steve, develop cognitive rituals such as rigidly prescribed numbers, words, sentences, or images to be emitted in the presence of discomfort-arousing stimuli (which may be tangible events or thoughts). These rituals do not differ functionally from the overt ones: both decrease discomfort. Therefore, response prevention should be implemented for these cognitive compulsions also. Since the control of such rituals is totally in the hands of the patient, motivation is especially important for successful treatment. Suppose, for example, that a patient becomes disturbed every time the number 5 is present in his thoughts or when he encounters it in reading. His rituals might consist of repeating the sequence 4, 8, 10, after which his discomfort diminishes. We instruct him to avoid thinking about these numbers, and if they do come up in his thoughts he should immediately follow them by repeating several times the number 5 (the discomfort-evoking one)—in fact, to undo the undoing. This procedure is then practiced in the therapy sessions. For continued practice between sessions we must rely on the patient's commitment to becoming symptom free, since it is obviously impossible to implement outside supervision.

Therapist Variables

If the treatment program and its rationale are clear and simple, why do patients need a therapist's help to follow it? All patients are given full information about the treatment in the preliminary sessions. For some of them, several weeks elapse between these initial sessions and their final decision to enter treatment. Yet most of them do not attempt to carry out the program on their own. This suggests that most obsessive-compulsive patients require the support of a firm but warm therapist in order to endure the fears and suffering treatment necessarily involves. A very bright patient had the following insight on this issue:

> It is very difficult to stick with an object when you feel contaminated, are sick inside, and your panic keeps increasing, if you do not know that the feeling will pass. There must be a depth and trust in the therapist the patient can "feel" that will permeate that barrier of doubt and fear as the treatment moves along. It seems that the therapist is important during the high-anxiety periods because the anxiety makes one want to return to one's usual way of dealing with anxiety—avoidance.

When the therapist fails to maintain the delicate balance between warm support and firmness, is unable to tolerate anger directed toward him or her during treatment, or is drawn into arguments and "bargaining" discussions, progress is slower. Both lack of rapid progress and lack of support during the earlier and more painful exposures may cause the patient to terminate treatment prematurely.

The following guidelines may help to avoid difficulties in patient-therapist relationships:

1. *Open strategy.* Patients should be fully informed of and actively consent to the demands of the treatment program.
2. *Support and firmness.* Some flexibility is necessary, but the treatment program should be followed rigorously. It is advisable that patients be able to reach the therapist by telephone at any time during the first 2 weeks of treatment.
3. *Avoiding arguments.* A clear and firm agreement should be reached at the very beginning of treatment that the therapist and not the patient will make the decisions regarding the pace of treatment.
4. *Responsibility.* It should be established that the implementation of the treatment program is the responsibility of both the therapist and the patient.

Environmental Variables

Generalization from the Hospital to the Home Environment

When treatment is carried out in an institutional setting, progress achieved there may not generalize to the home environment. Sometimes patients habituate to the "contaminated" institution, yet on returning to their homes resume their active and passive avoidance behavior. To avoid this, the last stage of treatment should be conducted in the patient's natural environment; it should include contamination of the home and, if necessary, of their place of work. As a rule, our therapists accompany the patients to their homes and conduct therapy there for 2 or 3 days. This period also provides an opportunity for modeling to relatives a warm, firm approach. They are taught how to support the patient when urges to ritualize are expressed and how to help him or her to carry out follow-up instructions.

Interference from Significant Others

A great many patients seek behavioral treatment several years after onset of symptoms (the mean of our sample was 11 years). During this long period, neurotic patterns of interaction with significant others are established and related to the obsessive-compulsive symptomatology, and, when left unchanged, are likely to reinforce its resumption following a successful treatment. In our practice the following three problem areas have been observed:

1. *Compliance with the patient's demands to participate in neurotic patterns.* Family members, especially spouses, have been "trained" by the patient to cooperate in their ritualistic behaviors. These may include participation in excessive washing and cleaning, helping the patient in checking rituals or avoidance behaviors, providing repeated reassurances that the "disastrous" consequences will not materialize, and so forth. It is important to support the family in the first few weeks of treatment in order to block attempts by the patient to maintain the above patterns and to resume former behavior. The family should be warned that the patient may be initially upset by their refusal to "help" in a relapse.

2. *Helping the patient resume previously avoided activities.* Patients should receive emotional as well as practical support in reentering leisure and work activities and resuming a normal life-style. The spouse and other relatives who have already established life-styles separate from the patient may find it difficult or nonrewarding to change them. The following case illustrates this point:

> Susan was 35 years old when she entered treatment and had started washing and cleaning rituals 15 years earlier. During the 10 years before treatment, she had refused to live in her own home because she was overwhelmed by the amount of time she had to spend decontaminating it. She moved in with her mother, while her husband

bought a mobile home and spent only some nights with his wife. However, he visited her everyday, showing a definite commitment to their marriage and to her recovery. Yet when Susan became asymptomatic after treatment and expressed a desire to resume normal married life, her husband did not help her to carry out the follow-up instructions and did not take the initiative in finding a permanent home for them; she lived in a motel, while he continued to reside in the mobile home. Her fear of resuming activities from which she had withdrawn for many years kept her confined to her room, and she maintained her previous life-style although she no longer feared contamination. Nine months later, she relapsed partially. Unfortunately, Susan lived a hundred miles away from our clinic in a rural area where family therapy, which might have helped in facilitating normal interaction between her and her husband, was not available.

3. *Tension at home.* Numerous investigators have noted the relationship between obsessive-compulsive symptoms and mood states, notably depression (Beech and Perigault, 1974; Marks, 1965). Indeed, the lifestyle imposed on families by the patient often results in tension and overt anger directed at him or her. This resentment, built up during years of frustration, often continues after successful treatment. Patients who have gone through weeks of agony and discomfort in therapy return hoping that their families will show appreciation for their efforts and their determination to change. When these expectations are not met, depression and tension may result. One of our patients who had been released asymptomatic from the hospital resumed 30% of her rituals during the course of 3 months of unrelieved tension at home. She noticed that on "good" days when her husband was pleasant to her, she did not ritualize, whereas when she was the target of his insults, she resumed some of her compulsive behaviors. These, in turn, triggered more anger and derogatory remarks from him. Here again, family therapy was indicated, but the husband refused to participate in treatment.

Thus securing understanding and cooperation from the family is extremely important for maintaining improvement achieved during formal treatment. Nevertheless, even in cases where such cooperation could not be obtained, relapses were partial and fluctuating, and even these patients benefited from treatment.

REFERENCES

Baum, M. Efficacy of response prevention (flooding) in facilitating the extinction of an avoidance response in rats: The effect of overtraining the response. *Behavior Research and Therapy*, 1968, 6, 197–203.

Baum, M. Extinction of an avoidance response following response prevention: Some parametric investigations. *Canadian Journal of Psychiatry*, 1969, *23*, 1–10.

Baum, M. Extinction of avoidance responding through response prevention (flooding). *Psychological Bulletin*, 1970, *74*, 276–284.

Beech, H.R. Ritualistic activity in obsessional patients. *Journal of Psychosomatic Research*, 1971, *15*, 417–422.

Beech, H.R. and Perigault, J. Toward a theory of obsessional disorder. In H.R. Beech (Ed.), *Obsessional states*. London: Methuen, 1974.

Carr, A.T. Compulsive neurosis: Two psychophysiological studies. *Bulletin of the British Psychological Society*, 1971, *24*, 256–257.

Carr, A.T. Compulsive neurosis: A review of the literature. *Psychological Bulletin*, 1974, *81*, 311–318.

Cooper, J.E., Gelder, M.G., and Marks, I.M. Results of behavior therapy in 77 psychiatric patients. *British Medical Journal*, 1965, *1*, 1222–1225.

Dollard, J., and Miller, N.E. *Personality and psychotherapy: An analysis in terms of learning, thinking and culture.* New York: McGraw-Hill, 1950.

DSM. 1968, p. 40.

Esquirol, J.E.D. *Des Maladies Mentals* (Vol. 2). Paris: Bailliere, 1838.

Eysenck, H.J. Learning theory and behavior therapy. In H.J. Eysenck (Ed.), *Behavior therapy and the neurosis*. Oxford: Pergamon, 1960.

Eysenck, H.J., and Rachman, S. *Causes and cures of neurosis*. London: Routledge and Kegan Paul, 1965.

Foa, E.B. Multiple behavioral techniques in the treatment of transvestism. In H. J. Eysenck (Ed.), *Case histories in behavior therapy*. London: Routledge and Kegan Paul, 1976.

Foa, E.B., and Chambless, D. Habituation of subjective anxiety during flooding in imagination, *Behaviour Research and Therapy*, 1978, *16*, 391–399.

Foa, E.B., and Goldstein, A. Continuous exposure and complete response prevention in the treatment of obsessive-compulsive neurosis. *Behavior Therapy*, 1978, *9*, 821–829.

Foa, E.B., and Steketee. G. Emergent fears during treatment of three obsessive compulsives: Symptom Substitution or deconditioning? *Journal of Behavior Therapy and Experimental Psychiatry*, 1977, *8*, 353–358.

Furst, J.B., and Cooper, A. Failure of systematic desensitization in two cases of obsessional-compulsive neurosis marked by fears of insecticide. *Behaviour Research and Therapy*, 1970, *8*, 203–206.

Haslam, M.T. The treatment of an obsessional patient by reciprocal inhibition. *Behaviour Research and Therapy*, 1965, *2*, 213–216.

Herrnstein, R.J. Method and theory in the study of avoidance. *Psychological Review*, 1969, *76*, 49–69.

Hodgson, R.J., and Rachman S. The effects of contamination and washing in obsessional patients. *Behaviour Research and Therapy*, 1972, *10*, 111–117.

Hodgson, R., Rachman, S., and Marks, I.M. The treatment of chronic obsessive-compulsive neurosis: Follow-up and further findings. *Behaviour Reseach and Therapy*, 1972, *10*, 181–189.

Kenny, F.T., Solyom, L., and Solyom, C. Faradic disruption of obsessive ideation in the treatment of obsessive neurosis. *Behavior Therapy*, 1973, *4*, 448–457.

Kringlen, E. Obsessional neurosis: A long-term follow-up. *British Journal of Psychiatry*, 1965, *111*, 709–722.

Lewis, A.J. Problems of obsessional illness. *Proceedings of the Royal Society of Medicine*, 1936, *29*, 325–326.

Maier, N. *Frustration and conflict*. New York: McGraw-Hill, 1949.

Marks, I.M. *Patterns of meaning in psychiatric patients*. London: Oxford U.P., 1965.

Marks, I.M. Flooding (implosion) and related treatments. In W.S. Agras (Ed.), *Behavior modification: Principles and clinical applications*. Boston: Little Brown, 1972.

Marks, I.M. Behavioral treatments of phobic and obsessive-compulsive disorders: A critical appraisal. In M. Hersen, R.M. Eisler, and P.M. Miller (Eds.), *Progress in behavior modification*. New York: Academic, 1975.

Marks, I.M., Crowe, M., Drewe, E., Young, J., and Dewhurst, W.G. Obsessive-compulsive neurosis in identical twins. *British Journal of Psychiatry*, 1969, *115*, 991–998.

Marks, I.M., Hodgson, R., and Rachman, S. Treatment of chronic obsessive-compulsive neurosis by *in vivo* exposure. *British Journal of Psychiatry*, 1975, *12*, 349–364.

McGlynn, F.D., and Linder, L.H. The clinical application of analogue desensitization: A case study. *Behavior Therapy*, 1971, *2*, 385–388.

Metzner, R. Some experimental analogues of obsession. *Behaviour Research and Therapy*, 1963, *1*, 231–236.

Meyer, V. Modification of expectancies in cases with obsessional rituals. *Behaviour Research and Therapy*, 1966, *4*, 273–280.

Meyer, V., Levy, R., and Schnurer, A. The behavioral treatment of obsessive-compulsive disorders. In H.R. Beech (Ed.), *Obsessional states*. London: Methuen, 1974.

Mills, H.L., Agras, W.S., Barlow, D.H., and Mills, J.R. Compulsive rituals treated by response prevention. *Archives of General Psychiatry*, 1973, *28*, 524–529.

Mowrer, O.H. *Learning theory and behavior*. New York: Wiley, 1960.

Rabavilas, A.D., Boulougouris, J.C., and Stefanis, C. Duration of flooding sessions in the treatment of obsessive-compulsive patients. *Behaviour Research and Therapy*, 1976, *14*, 349–355.

Rachman, S. Obsessive-compulsive checking. *Behaviour Research and Therapy*, 1976a, *14*, 269–277.

Rachman, S. The passing of the two-stage theory of fear and avoidance: Fresh possibilities. *Behaviour Research and Therapy*, 1976b, *14*, 125–131.

Rachman S., Hodgson, R., and Marks, I.M. The treatment of chronic obsessive-compulsive neurosis. *Behaviour Research and Therapy*, 1971, *9*, 237–247.

Rachman, S., Hodgson, R., and Marzillier, J. Treatment of an obsessional-compulsive disorder by modeling. *Behaviour Research and Therapy*, 1970, *8*, 385–392.

Rachman. S., Marks, I.M., and Hodgson, R. The treatment of obsessive-compulsive neurotics by modeling and flooding *in vivo*. *Behaviour Research and Therapy*, 1973, *4*, 463–472.

Rackensperger, W., and Feinberg, A.M. Treatment of a severe handwashing compulsion by systematic desensitization: A case report. *Journal of Behavior Therapy and Experimental Psychiatry*, 1972, *3*, 123–127.

Roper, G., and Rachman, S. Obsessional compulsive checking: Replication and development. *Behaviour Research and Therapy*, 1976, *14*, 25–32.

Roper, G., Rachman, S., and Hodgson, R. J. An experiment on obsessional checking. *Behaviour Research and Therapy*, 1973, *11*, 271–277.

Roper, G., Rachman, S., and Marks, I.M. Passive and participant modeling in exposure treatment of obsessive-compulsive neurotics. *Behaviour Research and Therapy*, 1975, *13*, 271–276.

Rubin, R.D., and Merbaum, M. Self-imposed punishment versus desensitization. In R.D. Rubin, H. Fensterheim, A.A. Lazarus, and C.M. Franks (Eds.), *Advances in behavior therapy* (1969). New York: Academic, 1971.

Schneider, K. Compulsive states and schizophrenia. *Archiv für Psychiatrie und Nervenkrankheiten*, 1925, *74*, 93–99.

Stampfl, T.G. Implosive therapy: The theory, the subhuman analogue, the strategy, and the technique: Part 1. The theory. In S.G. Armitage (Ed.), *Behavior modification techniques in the treatment of emotional disorders*. Battle Creek, Mich.: Veteran's Administration, 1967, 22–37.

Stern, R.S., and Marks, I.M. Brief and prolonged flooding: A comparison in agoraphobic patients. *Archives of General Psychiatry*, 1973, *28*, 270–276.

Taylor, J.G. A behavioral interpretation of obsessive-compulsive neurosis. *Behaviour Research and Therapy*, 1963, *1*, 237–244.

Teasdale, J.D. Learning models of obsessional-compulsive disorder. In H.R. Beech (Ed.), *Obsessional states*. London: Methuen, 1974.

Thorpe, J.G., Schmidt, E., Brown, P.T., and Castell, D. Aversion-relief therapy: A new method for general application. *Behaviour Research and Therapy*, 1964, *2*, 71–82.

Walker, V.J., and Beech, H.R. Moods states and the ritualistic behavior of obsessional patients. *British Journal of Psychiatry*, 1969, *115*, 1261–1268.

Walton, D. The relevance of learning theory to the treatment of an obsessive-compulsive state. In H.J. Eysenck (Ed.). *Behavior Therapy and the neuroses*. Oxford: Pergamon, 1960.

Walton, D., and Mather, M.D. The application of learning principles to the treatment of obsessive-compulsive states in the acute and chronic phases of illness. *Behaviour and Therapy,* 1963, *1,* 163–174.

Wolpe, J. *Psychotherapy by reciprocal inhibition.* Stanford: Stanford U.P., 1958.

Wolpe, J. Behavior therapy in complex neurotic states. *British Journal of Psychiatry,* 1964, *110,* 28–34.

Wolpe, J. *The practice of behavior therapy.* London: Pergamon, 1973.

CHAPTER 9

The Treatment of Communication Problems with Assertiveness Training

IRIS GOLDSTEIN FODOR

New York University

THE CLINICAL USE OF ASSERTIVENESS TECHNIQUES

More than any other behavioral procedure, assertiveness-training techniques have been adopted by the general public and publicized in the popular press and media. Assertiveness training (AT) workshops have not only been offered as self-improvement courses at "Ys" and for college credit in extension programs, but have been incorporated into many college counseling programs, integrated into management training programs in the business world, and considered by some as "essential" for the liberated woman. There has even been a recent AT consumer's movement. Assertiveness training may be the only behavior therapy procedure that has generated its own professional organization (The International Organization of Assertiveness Trainers) with over 600 members; a monthly newsletter reporting on new techniques, workshops, and publications (*Assert*); and its own code of ethics for trainers (Alberti et al., 1977).

Assertiveness training has stimulated a publishing and research deluge as well. As of this date, professional behavior therapists, serious researchers, and popular journalists have produced over 20 books on assertiveness, including a few best sellers. A recent bibliography (Moore, 1977) lists 250 references, most of them published within the past 5 years. Judging from the correspondence this author receives from doctoral students and from reports at professional meetings, doctoral dissertation research in this area is proliferating. At present, it is no longer possible for even a serious practitioner or researcher to keep up to date with current literature.

Much of the popularity of assertiveness techniques may be attributed to the thrust of the human potential movement and its associated philosophy of therapy as growth. However, while the crest of its popularity may wane, there is no question that the strength of the interest in AT reflects the fact that these behavioral techniques address themselves to a class of problems that are central to the lives of many different types of people.

BACKGROUND AND DEFINITION OF ASSERTIVE BEHAVIOR

Salter (1949) and later Wolpe (1958) are both credited with the clinical development of assertiveness techniques within the context of learning theory. Salter spoke of "inhibited" people with a pattern of shyness for whom he recommended "excitatory" training in expressiveness. Wolpe first used the term "assertive" to refer "not only to more or less aggressive behaviors, but also to the outward expression of friendly, affectionate and non-anxious feelings" (Wolpe, 1958, p.114).

Following a reciprocal-inhibition-theory model, Wolpe taught assertive responses to his patients as one of three types of responses antagonistic to anxiety. This concept was further elaborated by Wolpe and Lazarus, who recommended assertiveness training for the person who has "unadaptive anxiety response habits in interpersonal situations and the emotion of anxiety inhibits the expression of appropriate feelings and the performance of adaptive acts" (Wolpe and Lazarus, 1966, p.38).

Alberti and Emmons popularized the concept of assertiveness as a human right and provided the most frequently cited definition of assertive behavior: it is "behavior which enables a person to act in his (her) best interest, to stand up for himself (herself) without feeling undue anxiety, to express his (her) honest feelings comfortably or to exercise his (her) rights without denying the rights of others" (Alberti and Emmons, 1970, p.2).

In many respects, leading assertiveness trainers such as Lazarus, Alberti, Emmons, Colter, Jakubowski, and others essentially espouse an assertive philosophy of life that supports open, honest interpersonal communication styles. This philosophy reflects the underlying assumption that unassertive people lead a self-denying life that causes them to suffer in interpersonal relationships and sometimes leads to emotional and physical consequences.

A central issue in the definition of assertiveness has been the distinction between "assertive" and "aggressive" behaviors. Both the public and the popular press, not to mention some assertiveness trainers,[1] have tended to confuse these two concepts. The terms are used interchangeably by

Gelder (1967) and Palmer (1972) among others. Lazarus (1973) speaks of "more or less aggressive behavior" as one aspect of assertion, and Rathus (1973) included many aggressive items in his assertiveness scale (e.g., "Most people seem to be more aggressive and assertive than I am").

Currently most trainers follow the three-category distinction of assertive, nonassertive (passive), and aggressive behavior originally proposed by Alberti and Emmons (1970). Table 1 presents an elaboration of this scheme by Jakubowski (1973).

While early work focused on the distinction between these three categories of behavior, other distinctions have been more recently suggested. For example, McFall (1973) suggests that what may be called appropriate assertive behavior can only be measured according to its effect on others. Galassi and Galassi (1978) state that an "adequate conceptualization of

Table 1. A Comparison of Non-Assertive, Assertive, and Aggressive Behavior

	Nonassertive Behavior	Assertive Behavior	Aggressive Behavior
Characteristics of the behavior:	Emotionally dishonest, indirect, self-denying, inhibited	(Appropriately) emotionally honest, direct, self-enhancing, expressive	(Inappropriately) emotionally honest, direct, self-enhancing at expense of another
Your feelings when you engage in this behavior:	Hurt, anxious at the time, and possibly angry later	Confident, self-accepting at the time and later	Righteous, superior, deprecatory at the time, and possibly guilty later
The other person's feelings about her/himself when you engage in this behavior:	Guilty or superior	Valued, respected	Hurt, humiliated
The other person's feelings about *you* when you engage in this behavior:	Irritation, pity, *disgust*	Generally, respect *(but possibly also resentment)*	Anger, desire for *revenge, resentment*

Modified by Patricia Jakubowski-Spector, Facilitating the growth of women through assertive training, *The Counseling Psychologist*, 1973, *4*, [1], from Robert E. Alberti & Michael L. Emmons, Your perfect right: A guide to assertive behavior, 2nd Edition. San Luis Obispo, California: Impact, 1974.

[1] To get around this confusion some trainers use other terms for assertiveness training, for example, "personal effectiveness training" (Lieberman, 1976) or "interpersonal communication skills training" (Fodor and Wolfe, 1975, in workshop descriptions).

assertive behavior involves separation of the components of a behavioral, personal, and a situational dimension." Rich and Schroeder (1976) stress reinforcement. They feel that "assertive behavior is the skill to seek, maintain, or enhance reinforcement in an interpersonal situation through an expression of feelings or wants when such expression risks loss of reinforcement or even punishment." Going further into the social learning and cognitive areas, Bandura (1977) raises the issues of expectations and intent, thus focusing attention upon such questions as: What do you expect to do? What is your intent in self-expression? What do you expect the other person to do?

Jakubowski (1973) and Wolfe and Fodor (1975) also stress cognitive aspects of unassertive/aggressive behaviors. Attuned to the sets of "irrational beliefs" delineated by Ellis (1962), they attend to their clients' internal dialogues as well as their external response.

Other writers (Cheek, 1976; Jakubowski, 1973; Wolfe and Fodor, 1975; Osborn and Harris, 1975) stress the social-cultural context of appropriate assertive behavior. For example, Cheek suggests that the assertive message of a black ghetto person will have a different impact when addressed to a middle-class white or a black peer. Additionally, female assertiveness that goes beyond traditional sex-role learning will be defined differently by people having different expectations of what is and is not appropriate feminine behavior for that context.

OVERVIEW OF MAJOR ASSERTIVENESS TECHNIQUES

While the concept of assertiveness remains somewhat global and complex, most trainers today use some variant of a flexible treatment package that allows them to take all of the preceding into account. Such treatment packages generally include skills training and/or help in developing new responses antagonistic to anxiety. More recently such packages have included cognitive-restructuring techniques as well.

Essentially, most treatment programs, whether individual or group, include the following components:

1. *Assessment:* Initial assessment of assertiveness problem(s). Use of self-report questionnaires. Setting up behavior role playing situations. Training clients to self-monitor their own and others' behavior.
2. *Instruction:* Introduction to assertive philosophy and the distinction between assertive, aggressive, and unassertive behavior. Examples and instruction in how to behave more assertively. Discussion of

rights. Setting assertive goals. Format may include lectures, group demonstrations and discussions, work books, or programmed materials.

3. *Skills training:* Direct teaching, practicing and integrating of behavioral skills judged to be poorly developed or lacking in the client's repertoire. The components of skills training are *modeling,* where the participant observes the trainer, another participant, a coached actor, or an audio or visual tape demonstrating assertive behavior; *role playing,* where the participant acts out an assertive response; *behavioral rehearsal,* where there is active practice of assertive responding with the trainer or other participants. After such practice there is *feedback,* where the trainer and other participants give explicit descriptions of how they viewed the response; *coaching,* where suggestions for improvement are provided; and *reinforcement,* from the trainer and other participants for aspects of the response which were well executed.

4. *Anxiety reduction:* When the client has the skills in his or her repertoire, but expression is inhibited by anxiety, some variant of relaxation training or systematic desensitization is used. Sometimes direct *in vivo* exposure and practice in the feared situation may help, (e.g., when the client is afraid of expressing his/her own anger or fears other peoples anger, direct practice in anger expression or standing and facing someone who is making an angry outburst helps the client to master the anxiety). At other times the focus may be on controlling anxiety.

5. *Cognitive restructuring.* When client's values, cognitions, or attitudes inhibit assertive expression, client's thoughts about himself/herself and expectations about the consequences of assertive behavior need to be modified. Standard procedures include discovering and challenging irrational beliefs or self-statements (Ellis, 1963; Meichenbaum, 1977); paying attention to societal sex role programming and other social learning variables (Jakubowski, 1973; Wolfe and Fodor, 1975); and discussing expectations about the effects of new assertive behaviors on others (Bandura, 1977).

(Steps 3, 4, and 5 are usually carried out simultaneously.)

6. *Practice—follow up—generalization:* Having the client practice the new behaviors and integrate them into his/her repertoire and interactions in everyday life. One may bring in significant others, make adaptations where necessary, or select new goals. Use of self-monitoring procedures and homework assignments, typically involving more practice.

THEORETICAL AND RESEARCH BASIS

Although heavily influenced by Salter's and Wolpe's work on condition-ing theory and behavioral procedures, assertiveness training as it is cur-rently practiced leans more closely toward theoretical formulations de-rived from social learning theory. The research and theorizing of Bandura (1977b, 1977) on modeling and on self-efficacy has been most influential. Other current research efforts have been heavily influenced by Kelly's (1955) fixed-role theory, Ellis' (1963) rational-emotive theory, and Ser-ber's (1972) work in the nonverbal area, which has roots in Reichian therapy.

RESEARCH ON ASSERTIVENESS

After a slow beginning, interest in research on assertiveness and asser-tiveness training has gained increasing momentum. Generally, such re-search has tended to be atheoretical in nature and has been limited to either college student or inpatient psychiatric populations, focusing on training from nonassertive to assertive and generally ignoring problems of aggression. Special categories of nonassertiveness have also been singled out for special study, particularly heterosexual anxiety (deficits in dating behavior and related social skills) and refusal behavior.

For a general review of research findings, detailed presentation of key studies, and critical evaluation of the literature, the reader is directed to Galassi and Galassi (1977), Rich and Schroeder (1976), Rachman (1976), and to Curran (1976) for a review of the literature on heterosexual anxiety and social skills training.

To date research efforts have primarily focused on the following ques-tions:

1. What is assertiveness and how is it measured?
2. Is assertiveness training successful?
3. What components contribute to the success of assertive behavioral training programs?
4. What are the cognitive aspects of assertiveness? Does cognitive re-structuring enhance assertive responding?
5. Does assertiveness training generalize to untrained situations? Are results maintained on follow-up?
6. What other personality and situational variables are related to prob-lems in assertiveness?

7. What types of clinical problems lend themselves to assertiveness training?

Research Findings

What is Assertiveness and How is it Measured?

Generally, most major researchers in the area of assertiveness have focused on assessment issues. An impressive array of both self-report and behavioral measures have emerged from this area of research. To date, at least 17 self-report questionnaires and numerous behavioral measures and scales have been developed.

In general, research using these scales on various populations supports clinical and theoretical claims that assertiveness is not a unitary personality trait, but is more situationally specific. For example, factor analysis of Bates and Zimmerman's (1971) Constriction Scale resulted in 13 factors for males and 14 factors for females. Gambrill and Richey (1975) found 11 generally weighted factors that accounted for 61% of the variance in their assertion inventory. Research by Eisler and coworkers (1975), Galassi and coworkers (1974), and MacDonald (1975) also supports the situational specificity of assertive behavior.

Is Assertiveness Training Successful?

Major research studies containing various behavioral training packages have been conducted by Eisler, Hersen, and Miller (1973) using psychiatric patients, and by Galassi and Galassi (1974), Gambrill and Richey (1975), Rathus (1972), McFall and Lillesand (1971), and McFall and Twentyman (1973) using college student populations. Generally, all of these studies and others report significant changes on self-report and behavioral measures following behavioral treatment.

What Components Contribute to the Success of these Behavioral Packages?

The bulk of the research on assertiveness training, as opposed to assessment, has focused on trying to determine which components of the training package and/or which presentation or type of models contribute to the overall success. Such research takes many forms. For example, McFall and colleagues conducted a series of studies that examined the contribution of various rehearsal, feedback, instructional, coaching, and modeling components (McFall and Lillesand, 1971; McFall and Marston, 1970; McFall and Twentyman, 1973). Galassi and Galassi in reviewing this literature (1977) report there is support for the effectiveness of rehearsing appropriate behavior followed by therapist coaching (a form of behavior rehearsal) in the modification of nonassertive responses, and that the research also suggests that overt rehearsal may be somewhat more effective than covert rehearsal, while the contribution of performance feedback and consequences that follow rehearsal to assertion training remains unclear.

The contribution of live, videotaped, audiotaped, and imaginary models has also been studied (Fensterheim, 1972; Kazdin, 1976; Rathus, 1973; Wolfe, 1975). It is unclear whether such modeling contributes significantly to the learning of assertive skills. Mode of presentation has also been studied and there is a suggestion that anxiety reduction is aided by graduated presentations (Bandura, 1977).

What are the Cognitive Aspects of Assertiveness? Does Cognitive Restructuring Enhance Assertive Responding?

Recent research has focused attention on identifying cognitive aspects of unassertive behaviors (Schwartz and Gottman, 1976; Ludwig and Lazarus, 1972), as well as adding cognitive components to the behavioral treatment packages (Loo, 1971; Thorpe, 1974; Wolfe and Fodor, 1977). The latter research suggests that the cognitive components added to the behavioral packages are as effective in shaping up assertive responding as the behavioral packages alone, and, additionally, may serve to aid in anxiety reduction. Eisler, Frederiksen & Peterson (1978) report that high assertive patients expect more favorable consequences from others in social situations than low assertive patients. Glass (1978) also reports an interesting finding on heterosexual anxiety. The combined treatment package worked best for those less skilled and more anxious, while the cognitive approach worked best for those more skilled and least anxious.

Does Assertiveness Training Generalize to Untrained Situations? Are Results Maintained on Followup?

As Galassi and Galassi (1977) stress, there are four aspects to the generalizability issue. First, do the results generalize to similar but untrained situations? Generally, the majority of experimental studies support this type of generalization. Second, does training on one dimension of assertion (e.g., refusal) result in changes in other dimensions (e.g., initiating requests)? There appears to be little generalization across these categories in the few studies reported. Third, is there generalization from the laboratory into the real life situation? While research here is crucial, it has been difficult to carry out. Galassi and Galassi report that only one out of six major studies (McFall and Twentyman, 1973) supports such a transfer for assertive behavior. However, the research on heterosexual anxiety specifically addresses itself to this carry-over, and the results of thirteen studies reported by Curran (1976) are more positive.

Finally, there is the question of long-term maintenance. Generally, there are few studies that have long term followup. Of the few studies reviewed by the Gallassis, with follow-ups from 3 months to a year, the changes are maintained.

Summary of Research

Rachman (1976, p. 210) has summarized the results of modeling and AT research as follows.

"The quality of the evidence appears to be sound as far as it goes . . . particularly demonstrating effectiveness of participant modeling . . . but there is a strong tendency for research workers to rely entirely on demonstrations of an acute (short term) effect. The longer term value of modeling has rarely been studied . . . Another weakness is the brevity of the treatment . . . sometimes no more than an hour. Lastly, the problem of poor generalization from the experimental situation to the natural environment must be overcome . . . particularly attention to the extent and duration of treatment effects."

What Other Personality and Situational Variables are Related to Problems in Assertiveness?

Personality and situational variables are a growing area of research, particularly since self-report or personality inventories lend themselves to dissertation research. Most popular are studies of sex differences, aspects of sex-role stereotyping, attribution, interpersonal perceptions and their relevance to aspects of assertiveness, and readiness to succeed in assertiveness programs.

To date, there appears to be male/female differences, with men generally being more assertive at work than women, and women being able to be more assertive in emotional expressiveness (expression of love, affection, etc.) (Hollandsworth and Wall, 1977; Gambrill and Richey, 1975).

What Types of Clinical Problems are Suitable for Assertiveness Training?

Generally, there has been little systematic research using outpatient clinic populations. Most of the research relevant to this issue involves single-case designs or case descriptions. Such work describes the utility of AT for urinary retention problems (Barnard, Flesher, and Steinbook, 1966), the aged (Corby, 1975; Edinberg, 1976), homosexual pedophilia (Edwards, 1972), sexual offenders (Laws & Serber, 1970), alcoholics (Hirsh, 1975; Montorano, 1973), juvenile delinquents (Kornfield, 1975), depression (Maish, 1972), and obesity (McMillan, 1977). Assertiveness training for children and adolescents is also a growing area.

Research Applications for Clinicians

For the clinician, the research limitations in the populations studied leave a gap of knowledge for the bulk of clients coming for help, such as neurotics or more normal people with specific life-stress situations. Further, the brief automated treatments are usually a "turn-off" for most clinicians. A split has occurred between researchers and clinicians. Researchers tend to use standard assessment and treatment procedures, often with very limited treatment goals, and the clinician relies more on experience, intuition, and clinical judgment using assessment only where it furthers the therapeutic outcome.

Suggested References

Given the proliferation of work on assertiveness training over the past few years, it is often hard to know where to begin to read, with over 20 published books and more than 250 articles, not to mention substantial chapters in most behavioral tests by leading practitioners. See Table 2 in the appendix for this author's suggested guide through the maze of AT publication. It is divided into professional books, popular books, general, self-help workbooks, and women's assertiveness books.

INDICATIONS AND PRESENTING PROBLEMS: WHO COMES FOR ASSERTIVENESS TRAINING

As both researchers and clinicians have pointed out (McFall, 1973; McDonald, 1976), nonassertiveness is not a unitary personality trait, and problems are often situationally specific. McDonald (1976) proposes that a person is functionally unassertive for at least one of three reasons: (1) a genuine skill deficit—not knowing how to be genuinally assertive, (2) inadequate stimulus discrimination—not knowing the circumstances for which assertion is appropriate, or (3) fear of irrational or rational consequences.

How do these relate to the sample of people coming for help? Generally, given all the publicity, the majority of people asking for assertiveness training are self-identified. However, in the course of working with clients with other presenting problems, or of the need for assertiveness will sometimes make itself apparent. Generally, most clients can be grouped under the following categories:

A. Skills deficit—unassertive person

1. Severe skills deficit. People who are slow to learn, disabled, or mentally retarded. (Often these people are seen in institutionalized settings, schools, or brought in by family members.)

2. Schizophrenics and schizoids. People who have real difficulty in relating to people and whose bizarre behaviors, aloofness, withdrawal, unusual affect or paranoia interferes with interpersonal communication. (These people are seen frequently in institutions or as outpatients in a day hospital setting.)

3. Excessively shy people. Avoidance of social situations has resulted in a real skills deficit appropriate to age (e.g., a 30-year-old man who has never dated). This population usually consists of excessively shy young men and women, although more typically males seek help for situations relating to dating, initiating relationships, and so forth. Such people are seen as outpatients or in college counseling centers.

4. Women wishing to break out of the stereotypic feminine role. While, the content of their assertive messages are in the new mode, they consider themselves soft, frail, and so forth, in getting their message across. Such women may be assuming new leadership roles at work, wishing to initiate more in social situations, or be taken more seriously by significant others. Such work is often in shaping up more assertive styles in communication: fullness of voice, learning how to express anger, not smiling all the time, and so forth. This work is done in outpatient clinics, private practice, or university counseling centers.

5. Another similar category are people who are beginning to develop assertive skills, but they need further help in the nonverbal areas of assertiveness (e.g., a man who can now initiate conversations with women, but his wishy-washy way of talking turns them off). Again, more work in the nonverbal area and learning about communication style is stressed. These people are seen primarily as outpatients.

B. Skills deficit—Too much aggressive behavior

1. Problem with loss of control of aggressive feelings—occasional temper outbursts or impatience. Such people may generally be in control. They may be unassertive people who hold everything in and then the anger comes out in the form of tirades and tantrums.

2. Impatient, irritable people—who are always blowing off steam,

getting pissed at minor incidences, a sort of short-fuse behavior, or rebellious people who always look for a fight. Usually these people are seen as outpatients, although some delinquents and others in institutions fall in this category.

3. Severely impulsive people whose angry outbursts lead to trouble or violence. Such people are usually seen in institutions, prisons, juvenile detention centers, and so forth. They may include parents of battered children, spouses of battered wives, and so forth. When frustrated, upset, or angry their major response is a hostile, aggressive attack.

C. Fear or loss of control of feelings inhibits assertive responding

1. Fear of loss of control of intense feelings—anxiety, fear, hostility, love, dependency, and so forth, inhibits the assertive response. The person is anxious about showing the feeling (particularly hostility or caring) or is anxious about not being able to control the intensity of the response or both. Usually, there is not a skills deficit, but the anxiety over the loss of control inhibits the response (e.g., "When it really counts, I can't be assertive." "I know what to say to my boss[/]lover, I just can't say it, do it," etc.).

2. Related to the fear of loss of control is the fear of the consequence of assertive responding either rational or irrational. (e.g., "If I tell my boss how hard I'm working he will fire me, he will get mad, won't like me," etc.) These fears are usually situationally specific. Some aspects of women's assertiveness inhibitions fall into this category (e.g., "Men don't like assertive women." "If I'm assertive, I won't be liked, be considered a bitch," etc.).

3. A third inhibition is fear that other people cannot control their feelings. There may be reality here—for some people to be assertive with a person who is overly aggressive and prone to violence may be dangerous.

Other Assertive Problems

In the course of work with almost any client, the therapist will run into a problem of inhibition of direct expression when an issue of major importance crops up. Sometimes, people in crisis would rather avoid expressing themselves, since they do not wish to face, compromise, or perhaps move out of an unhappy situation. Additionally, behavior therapists while treating patients with phobias, overeating behavior, alcoholism, sexual problems, psychosomatic complaints (particular, headaches, asthma, fatigue) as well as depression may discover that unassertive behavior in an important area is a prevalent pattern that directly relates to the maintenance of the maladaptive behavior.

Assessing the Problem

Since there are so many different assertiveness procedures and treatments and clients coming with a variety of different presenting problems, assessment needs vary. It is important to keep in mind that assessment is an ongoing process. There is initial assessment for determining the appropriate intervention, assessment of progress during the course of training and assessment for studying behavioral change, generalization and follow-up.

The questions a therapist generally keeps in mind include the following:

1. Is this a nonassertive person (passive, inhibited) or is the problem one of being too aggressive?
2. Which categories are most problematic? Does the problem involve many categories or just a few? Is the problem one of being a responder to other people's assertive and aggressive responses, or does the person primarily need help in initiating the response? Lang and Jakubowski (1976) list the following categories of assertiveness: (1) initiating interactions; (2) refusing unreasonable requests; (3) expressing disagreement, displeasure or criticism; (4) speaking up in groups, expressing opinions and suggestions; (5) being able to receive criticism; (6) giving and receiving feedback. This author would add an additional category: asking for help, letting someone else know specifically what you'd like them to do for you.
3. Does the person know what he/she is feeling, what he/she wants, what are their rights in the problematic situation? Can he/she articulate goals?
4. Is this a general skills deficit. (If so, is it the verbal message or is work on body language necessary, facial expression, stance, voice, tone, etc.?)
5. Does the person know when to be and when not to be assertive?
6. What are the social and cultural factors operating in the person's background? In the present situation?
7. What are the consequences of being more assertive? Is the person aware of these consequences and willing to take a risk? (For example, will a wife get beaten if she is too assertive with an abusive husband? Is she willing to risk separation or change?)
8. In what ways does anxiety and other strong feelings inhibit assertive responding? Can the person handle intense feelings and still respond

assertively? How does the person feel about their own anger/other people's hostility, and so forth?

9. What does he/she say to himself/herself when he/she does or does not engage in appropriate assertive behavior. Is lack of self-assertion related to self-downing and poor self-appraisal.

Assessment Scale

During the past 5 years, there has been an increasing interest in assessing assertiveness. There are at least 17 assertiveness questionnaires available in various stages of development.[2]

Most of these questionnaires are self-report inventories that provide information on the frequency with which a trainee believes that he/she asserts him/herself in situations that require such behavior. They are especially useful to clinicians in getting objective scores, comparing different types of clients, seeing categories of problems, and assessing change. The most frequently used instruments are the Wolpe-Lazarus Assertiveness Questionnaire (1966), the Rathus Assertiveness Schedule (1973), the Conflict Resolution Inventory (McFall and Lillesand, 1971), the College Self-Expression Scale (Galassi, DeLo, Galassi, and Bastien, 1974), and the Assertion Inventory (Gambrill and Richey, 1975). Generally, these scales are useful in group prescreening, for research, and for assessing pre- to post-treatment change. Most of the scales address themselves to defining the extent of the unassertive problem, identification of problematic categories, and assessment of discomfort in varying situations.

The following are descriptions of the most frequently used scales.

Wolpe-Lazarus Scale

The Wolpe-Lazarus Scale is administered by the therapist. There are 30 social-situational questions such as "Do you protest aloud when someone

[2] Action Situation Inventory (Friedman, 1971), Adolescent Assertion Discrimination Test (Shoemaker, 1973 as in Bodner, 1975), Adolescent Self-Expression Scale (McCarthy and Bellucci, 1974), Adult Assertion Scale (Jakubowski and Wallace, 1975, as cited in Lange and Jakubowski, 1976), Adult Self-Expression Scale (Gay, Hollandsworth, and Galassi, 1975), Assertion Inventory (Fensterheim, 1971), Assertion Inventory (Dalali, 1971), Assertiveness Inventory (Gambrill and Richey, 1975), AQ Test (Phelps and Austin, 1975), College Self-Expression Scale (Galassi, DeLo, Galassi, and Bastien, 1974), Conflict Resolution Inventory (McFall and Lillesand, 1971), Constriction Scale (Bates and Zimmerman, 1971), Lawrence Assertiveness Inventory (Lawrence, 1970), Rathus Assertiveness Schedule for Junior High (Vaal and McCullagh, 1975), Rathus Assertiveness Schedule (Rathus, 1973), and Wolpe-Lazarus Assertiveness Questionnaire (Wolpe and Lazarus, 1966). For a fuller review of Assertiveness Scales see Galassi and Galassi (1977) and Bodner (1975).

pushes in front of you in a queue?" "Are you inclined to be overapolegetic?" "If a friend criticized you do you express resentment there and then?" "Do you generally express what you feel?" "Do you find it difficult to begin a conversation with a stranger?" "Do you usually keep quiet for the sake of peace?" "If a friend makes what you consider an unreasonable request, are you able to refuse?" "Are you able to contradict a domineering person?"

Instead of trying to elicit a simple "Yes" or "No" from the client the therapist can ask questions such as the following: "How much of a problem do you have responding in this situation?" "How are you most likely to act in this situation?" "If that failed, what would you do?" "What would you like to be able to say?" "What stops you from acting this way?" These questions elicit patterns of unassertiveness. While there is no normative data or test[/]retest reliability, research use by McFall and Marston (1970), and Eilser, Miller, and Hersen (1973) demonstrates the scale's usefulness in identifying unassertive and assertive people. It is also useful for clinical interviewing during the first session.

Rathus Scale

The Rathus Scale consists of a 30-item questionnaire derived from the Wolpe & Lazarus scale. It is a 6-point scale, going from +3 (assertive) to −3 (unassertive). It was tested on college students and correlates with other ratings of assertiveness (.62 and .70). The questions include "I don't know what to say to an attractive person of the opposite sex." "There are times when I look for a good, vigorous argument." "To be honest, people take advantage of me." The Rathus Scale has been criticized by Galassi and Galassi (1975) for not distinguishing between assertion and aggression. (Thirteen of the items were correlated significantly with semantic differential ratings of aggressiveness.)

Conflict Resolution Inventory

McFall's Conflict Resolution Inventory (CRI) (35 items) is one of the most widely used researched instruments for assessing refusal behavior. High correlations have been found between refusal behavior (behavioral ratings) and the CRI.

College and Adult Self-Expression Scale

Galassi and coworkers have developed both the College and Adult Self-Expression Scales (1974 and 1975, respectively). The Adult Self-Expression Scale is a 48-item questionnaire designed to tap the expression of seven behaviors: expressing personal opinions, refusing unreasonable requests, initiating conversations, expressing positive feelings, standing up for legitimate rights, expressing negative feelings, and asking favors. These behaviors cover six interpersonal situations: parents, the public, authority figures, friends, intimate relations, and unspecified persons.

Assertiveness Inventory

The Assertiveness Inventory developed by Gambrill and Richey (1975) has an unusual format. It collects three types of information for each of 40 items: how uncomfortable a person feels in specific assertion situations, how likely the person is to react assertively in the situations, in what situations would the person like to act more assertively.

BEHAVIORAL ASSESSMENT

Behavioral Sample

Most clinicians prefer behavioral samples to paper and pencil measures. Behavioral assessment is a necessary auxiliary to self-report in assessing the extent of the social skills deficit or anxiety based inhibitions. The clinician can choose from standardized situations developed for research purposes generally using film or videotaped presentations (Galassi and Galassi, 1973; Eisler, Hersen, and Miller, 1975; Wolfe, 1975; Jakubowski, 1974). Usually the film or recording sets the content of the situation and there are prompting statements for the client to respond to. More typically, the therapist asks the individual to set up his/her own behavioral situation based on a problematic area.

Rating Scales for Behavioral Assessment

Most of the researchers cited have developed rating scales for the verbal content of the message. Additional self-ratings are also used, particularly for the anxiety response and self-appraisal of assertiveness. The SUD (Subjective Units of Disturbance Scale, Wolpe, 1969) is often used to assess anxiety while the client is engaged in trying to respond assertively. Similarly, a therapist may ask a client to rate his/her response for assertiveness on a 0 to 5 scale (0) being nonassertive and 5 being assertive). Colter and Guerra (1976) have developed several useful self-rating forms both for initial appraisal and homework assignments.

Evaluation of Nonverbal (Paralinguistic) Aspects of Assertive Responses

Eilser, Miller, and Hersen (1973), following the work of Serber, developed a rating scale for paralinguistic variables for distinguishing nonassertive and assertive responding. For research, the person's behaviors are usually videotaped to assist in the quantitative ratings:

1. Duration of looking—length of time that the group member looks at the person asserting himself/herself (from the delivery of the statement to the end of the response).
2. Duration of reply—length of time the member speaks to the person in role play.
3. Loudness of speech—loudness rated on a five-point scale (1 is low, 5 is very loud).
4. Affect—affect rated on a five-point scale (1 is very flat, unemotional tone, 5 is full and lively tone that is appropriate to the situation).

Cognitive Variables

To evaluate cognitive variables, Schwartz and Gottman (1974) have developed an Assertion Self-Statement Test (ASST) to measure cognitive aspects of assertiveness problems. This is a 34-item self-report questionnaire rated on a five-point scale. It has such items as the following:

1. "I was thinking that I would probably feel guilty later if I refused to do the person a favor."
2. "I was worried that the person might become angry if I refused."
3. "I was thinking that a friendly person would not refuse in this situation."
4. "I was too busy to say yes."

Other cognitive assessments might include discovering which, if any, of Ellis' (1962) irrational beliefs apply to AT. Those related to assertion include the need to be loved and liked, avoidance of unpleasant situations, guilt arousal, taking care of others before oneself and fear of being imperfect.

ASSERTIVENESS TRAINING IN GROUPS

Unlike most other behavioral procedures, assertiveness training can be done with individuals, with small closely related groups (couples, families, dyads within families, work colleagues), or with larger groups. The equipment used can vary from nothing other than the imagination of the therapist to a cassette tape recorder or elaborate videotape-playback equipment and packaged stimulus materials. Assertiveness training can also be seen as covering a continuum from the one-day workshop to long-term individual treatment. Group training, however, has certain distinct advantages over individual therapy:

1. The 1-day workshop provides an excellent format for introducing standardized procedures to large numbers of people; it can be primarily didactic, for professionals and students, or experientially oriented. For many people afraid to commit themselves to other forms of treatment, the 1-day workshop provides, so to speak, a "dip into the water."

2. A group provides for shared problem solving among people with similar concerns: defining one's rights, distinguishing between aggressive and appropriately assertive behaviors in problematic situations, reconciling "femininity" and assertiveness, dealing with the stress associated with common life-cycle shifts.

3. A group provides a natural laboratory for the assessment of assertiveness problems. Participants do not need to describe their unassertive behaviors; they become readily observable. A "shy" nonsmoker seated next to a cigar puffer may show signs of discomfort, cough, and sneeze for a full hour before meekly venturing to ask the therapist "Is smoking allowed here?"

4. The situations that occur naturally in a group reflect a broader range of real-life situations than those that usually occur in a therapist's office. People often come to AT groups because they have difficulties in expressing both positive and negative feelings, and particularly feelings of frustration. Group interactions produce a number of annoyances and satisfactions: one participant may sulk over not getting his or her "fair share" of the time; another may seethe in angry silence over being interrupted; yet another may wish to compliment or thank someone and be too "shy" to do it. As these situations occur, the group can focus then and there on learning to express these feelings directly and assertively.

5. Since a group will often include people of various ages, occupations, and social positions, a further "real-life" dimension enters into the playing of roles. A real employer or parent can play opposite members having difficulties in relationships to their own mothers, fathers, or "bosses." Or it may happen that one member, by some mannerism, reminds another of the significant person with whom he or she wishes to behave differently.

6. The group often can devise creative assertive responses that might not occur to the trainer.

7. Members have the opportunity to find out how it is to be on the other end in role playing; a participant who tends to be aggressive may perceive how this is experienced by being on the receiving end of bullying or sarcasm.

8. Groups can be composed of people with differing problematic areas of assertiveness. However, most people's unassertive behaviors affect many situations in their lives. In exploring the problems of others, participants often gain "bonus" skills.

9. Group support and reinforcement are crucial elements in risking new behaviors. The group provides both in giving feedback. Further, it provides objective and constructive feedback on how well homework assignments are working out. This is particularly important to clients risking, for the first time, incurring displeasure as they learn to assert their rights.

The importance of the group to an individual's progress can best be seen in a clinical example:

Paul, a 55-year-old man, suffering from low self-esteem, came to an on-going AT group at a clinic complaining of a host of real-life problems. Foremost among them was his concern about finding a new job, since he was one of 17,000 teachers recently excessed in New York. In presenting his problems to the group, his unassertive style was noticably whining and complaining. "What's the use? I'm getting too old. Why try? There just aren't any jobs," were phrases he used repeatedly.

The group immediately took up his job situation as a problem, suggesting practical steps: Had he tried to get reassigned? What exactly were the procedures for finding another position? He was given the assignment to find out where and how teachers were being rehired. The next week, he came in knowing all the bureaucratic procedures, which he presented with a hopeless, defeated air.

In role playing a job interview, he sat slouched, his chest collapsed, his shoulders rounded, cupping his hands as though he were about to beg. He pleaded, "I'm one of the laid-off teachers. Do you have a job in your school for a social studies teacher?" When questioned about how he thought the interviewer would react, he reported he was hoping the other person would immediately take pity on him and take care of him. Several other group members offered to take on his role. He heard them say such things as "I'm a specialist in social studies. I've heard you have some openings in your school. I've worked in various schools and am an experienced teacher. Can we get together for an interview?" Paul tried out some similar scripts and the group gave him feedback on his behavior and body language: his voice needed to be steadier and louder; he needed to sit straight, maintain eye contact; "tell what you want instead of pleading."

Each week, Paul reported back to the group, from the stage of making phone calls to going for interviews. Each week he rehearsed what he would do next. By the end of the 6-week group, he had a job assignment.

Even if the outcome had not been so fortunate, Paul's behavioral changes resulted in an immense growth in self-esteem, which was commented on by the entire group.

One-Day Workshops

Typically, such a group runs 4 to 8 hours, often with a follow-up session after a week's time. There are usually 12 to 20 participants. Often, in a clinic, it is used to help clients assess their assertiveness problems. Then if more work is needed, they are directed to another group or treatment procedure. Homework is often assigned, to be discussed during the follow-up. In a 1-day workshop, part of the time is spent teaching, using structured exercises and role-play demonstrations to convey the basic concepts of assertiveness.

Special workshops are also conducted in work settings with such various groups as nurses, dieticians, mental health professionals, executives, federal employees, and teachers. Generally, the 2- to 4-hour workshop format is followed. What is striking is how quickly people are able to articulate their work problems. In a recent workshop with dieticians, within half an hour, over 30 people identified about four types of recurring, frustrating problems that occurred in settings as disparate as universities, homes for the aged, and large, urban teaching hospitals. Interestingly, the problems identified were not with the clients of the institutions, but rather were problems of power, status, and authority within the staffs.

On-Going Groups

These groups usually meet for 1½ to 2 hours over a period of 6 to 8 weeks. Sometimes groups are theme oriented, such as groups for women only, couple assertiveness, parent-child groups, or groups around specific social or work situations. Often a mixed group will work well if participants with severe deficits in social skills are also seen individually for supplemental work. Usually, follow-up is built into the program. There may be periodically scheduled "reunions."

The leader is highly active in structuring the beginning sessions of an on-going group: setting up exercises, suggesting role-plays, choosing volunteers, instructing, and commenting to give feedback and support. Gradually, as the group learns AT procedures, the participants themselves take over the work of the trainer. By the end of 6 to 8 weeks, the group is often ready to work without the leader, who then remains available as a consultant.

Assessment in on-going groups may consist of the use of standard assertiveness questionnaires such as the Rathus scale. Assessment may be for the purpose of prescreening or for helping clients defining assertiveness problems in the early sessions. More typically, assessment is accomplished by going around the group, asking participants to state their main assertiveness problems, and is clarified by the behavioral samples that emerge within the early sessions. Assessment is an on-going process.

The following procedures for running on-going groups illustrate the treatment process. They have been adapted from guidelines developed in trainers workshops at the Institute for Rational Therapy by Janet Wolfe and the author. Clinical examples exemplify work at various stages, with the identities of participants disguised.

The Therapeutic Process in On-Going Groups

Beginning the Group. In the opening session, group members are seated in a circle and the leader asks individual members, in turn, to give their first names and to state briefly why they have come into the group. Participants are also asked to cite a recent situation that specifically illustrates their main assertiveness problem. Approximately 3 to 5 minutes are spent with each person.

The following initial problems were cited by an interracial group of males and females in an outpatient clinic. The majority of the clients were referred by their therapists for specific work, so no pre-assessment procedures were carried out.

Bob (a stockman in his 30s, who maintains a wide grin while talking): I have trouble meeting women socially. Like to fool around a lot instead of being upfront. I have no trouble at first but keep getting the runaround after a while.

Cathy (a thin, stylish, 25-year-old, who appears tense, jaw clenched as she smiles while speaking): I work in an ad agency as a copywriter. It's difficult for me to show feelings—not only angry ones, but happiness too. Sometimes I feel like I'm not alive or real.

Fran (in her mid-40s, Fran keeps her head down, and words trail off as she speaks so softly as to be almost inaudible): I got divorced last year, and I have so many problems. My boss is abusive. She puts you down and assumes you don't know anything. I'm a bookkeeper and I don't say nothing. Have a lot of medical problems—so many tests and they don't tell you nothing, like I should leave the worry to him. And my daughter now—she moved out this summer and she don't talk to me. (The therapist gently stops her, commenting that it sounds like she has a lot of problems.)

Larry (mid-20s): I'm a writer . . . and I'm shy . . . I have trouble meeting people. . . . If I see a pretty girl at a party, I couldn't go over and talk to her. . . . I feel so stupid about it. . . . At this age . . . you think I'd know how to do these things.

Bill (late 20s, speaking slowly and hesitantly, intent on looking at a spot on the floor, very tense): I'm an accountant . . . it's hard for me to come into this group. . . . Almost didn't come today . . .

Therapist: It's good you were able to make it.

Bill: I get afraid in groups—hard for me to look people in the eye. It makes me feel nervous. I don't speak up, go along with what everyone says. And now, at work—I may get a promotion, be a supervisor. Worry that I can't be bossy.

Fay (mid-30s, thin, blond, with a frightened look in her eyes as she talks in a restrained monotone): I'm afraid to express my anger. My feelings of anger stay frozen inside. My therapist told me to come to the group. Worry a lot—maybe men think I'm a bitch. My husband tells me I'm bossy. Have a lot of trouble with him.

Sally (mid-30s, sits slouched in the chair, shoulders hunched, looks wearily at the therapist as she talks in a complaining tone): My problem is assertiveness on the job. I take on an unwarranted amount of work and can't say no. My boss is very aggressive and I'm no match for him. I cry a lot—come home feeling worn and frustrated—feel he takes advantage of me.

Mary (50s, speaking above a bare whisper): I've been hired as a secretary. Feel O.K. on the job so far, but worry if I'll be firm enough. I'm the first woman on the job. I was hired just as a trainee, but now they expect me to do bilingual translations. I just can't cope on what they pay me with all the extra work it takes.

Sue (appears thin and fragile, talking in a high childlike voice, looking around the room and smiling frequently): I feel like a marshmallow. People walk all over me. When my boyfriend says "jump," I say "how high?" I do need assertiveness training. I've been reading about it.

Lynn (tall and stylish, Lynn looks like an executive, speaks in a husky voice, but appears cool and self-confident as she maintains good eye-contact with the therapist): I have a tense situation at work. I have a management position, but I'm treated like a secretary. Some of the men say I'm too aggressive. Came into this group to see if that's so.

Hilda (large and strongly built, generally phlegmatic, speaks slowly and quietly): I'm a dietician and have trouble at work—dealing with the kitchen help and the nurses on the floor. I get it either way, feel defeated. It's a lousy situation—I come home worn out.

John (mid-30s, speaks with deference to the therapist): I have trouble meeting people. I just recently split up with my girlfriend. I'm lonely—would like to meet more people. Also, my boss is a terrible bully.

I have a hard time at work.

Lucia (mid-30s, she looks haggard): I'm a teacher—having problems with my students. Other teachers sure seem to handle them better.

Louis (mid-40s, puts his hand over his mouth as he talks, rubs his chin and rocks back and forth, looking weary): I've just been promoted. My boss told me to go to a group. He wants me to be more pushy. I'm not sure what he wants me to do.

Rose (late 50s, has disheveled gray hair and a nagging quality to her voice): I know people take advantage of me. My landlord doesn't give me enough heat. I just got laid off from my job. That landlord just gives me the runaround, and I call them and call them but they don't listen. My social worker sent me here, says I need this help before I can go back to work. (Rose rattles off a long list of complaints until the therapist stops her, commenting that she seems overwhelmed by her problems, she agrees.)

Jo (a male in his 30s, speaks seriously and intently in a heavy accent): Have trouble with my superiors at work, worry a lot, how I do, how I am doing. Feel I don't get along too good, worry about my English.

As the participants are speaking, the therapist sketches a circular seating chart and jots down the names of each and the problematic situation they've mentioned.

Introduction to the Main Concepts of Assertiveness. Using the material the group has just brought up, the leader proceeds to talk for about 10 to 15 minutes about assertiveness and the types of problems people have. Books and readings are recommended (see Table 2 for self-help books). To aid the group in learning more about the distinctions between nonassertion, aggression, and appropriate assertion, Table 1 is handed out and discussed. The group may be given an example of role-play so that behavioral samples of the various categories can be concretely presented to the group and discussed.

A married couple has agreed that one partner will do all the cooking for a week. The other, however, continually comes home late. What would be an assertive response by the cook?

In volunteering to be unassertive, several people produce clearly aggressive responses: "Late again, you louse!" Others produce such passive-aggressive responses as "Would you like some burned chicken now, dear?" The avoidance of confrontation is discussed, and many members reveal their fears of a "fight," or their worries about "divorce." The discussion turns to irrational beliefs, rights, and goals. Finally, the group is able to construct an assertive script: "I'm upset that you're late again, and haven't called. We have a problem. Let's eat now and talk about our schedules after supper."

A Presenting Problem: Initial Role Play. As the next step, the leader next selects a member willing to present and work on his or her problem. It is better to start with a more general problem (such as learning to be more comfortable in a social situation or with your boss) than a more idiosyncratic personal problem. The volunteer briefly describes the situation and the other significant person involved, whom another volunteer will play. The group is prepared for the role play by presenting the guidelines for effective behavior (Wolfe and Fodor, see Appendix).

However, we do something different now: since it is time for a coffee break (we have been going for 1½ hours at this point), people are asked to select someone in the group (men and women are both asked to initiate) and begin a social conversation while having coffee. (Another variant of this exercise is to ask the socially anxious people to initiate two or three conversations during the coffee break.) What is interesting to observe is who initiates and who waits to be picked.

Group discussion follows this exercise, and from this experience Larry agrees to present a problem. He chooses one that he has also often experienced at cocktail parties: he can approach some women, but not those who appear "cool and self-assured," yet these are the women who attract him. Cathy in the group appears such a person to him, but he has not been able to approach her. He is asked if he would like to try that now and he agrees. Cathy agrees to role play with him. Cathy sits in the middle of the room, and Larry goes over to her:

Larry: Er . . . Hello. My name is Larry (long pause). What is your name?

Cathy: Cathy.

Larry: Er . . . er . . . I don't know too many people here besides George and Alice. Do you?

Cathy: Not too many.

Larry: Do you . . . er . . . live in this neighborhood? I . . . I (swallowing, fidgeting) . . . I live in the Village Er . . . May I sit down? I like the Village. I'm a writer and work weird hours and things are open there all night. What do you do?

Cathy: I work in advertising.

(The role-play continues for 2 to 3 more minutes.)

Assessment of the Role-Play. Both participants are asked how they felt during the role-play. Also the subject is asked to self-rate his/her assertiveness, focusing first on what he/she liked about it. Possible questions to help the subject clarify the issues are: What really went on? What are your rights in this situation? Were they being violated? What would you like to say to the other person? What were you telling yourself? How do you think the other person experienced you?

Larry: I feel good that I was able to do that. I was so nervous. I could never do that before in front of all these people.

T: How did you rate yourself? Let's use a scale of 0 to 5, 5 being assertive.

Larry: I'd rate myself a 3, because I did it. It's a start, but it could be better.

T: What were you feeling?

Larry: Very anxious and excited, afraid my nervousness showed. I could feel my voice crack, and my hands started to shake.

T: What were you saying to yourself?

Larry: What am I doing making a fool out of myself in front of all these people? Idiot! You're doing it? Then I was afraid I was being boring—wasting the group's time. Can't I think of a more interesting conversation? Of course, in real life, I'd be expecting her to reject me, to walk away.

T: What did you like about your performance?

Larry: That I did it and was able to think of something to say, and that I saw it wasn't too awful.

T: (to Cathy) What did you like about Larry's interaction?

Cathy: He came on straight, didn't give me a line. I even liked his nervousness. I felt like he was someone I'd want to get to know better. I didn't find him boring. (Larry swallows and smiles.)

T: What might be improved?

Cathy: Well, his standing over me was awkward. I kept wanting to ask him to sit down. Also, I felt pulled to take care of him. He paused a lot, as if he was waiting for me to move in. It would be hard to reject him. I have a hard time saying no to people anyway.

Involvement of the Group in Giving Feedback. Next, other group members are asked for positive feedback to reinforce the good components of the behavior—content, tone and body language. Then suggestions for improvement can be asked for. The group is directed to talk directly to the subject when giving feedback and to avoid saying "You should . . ."

With a shy group, the therapist may have to model a positive statement. In this example, the participants could begin themselves:

Bill: It was good he came on straight.

T: Say that to Larry.

Bill: It was good you came on straight, like, I would have joked around, made some remarks.

Fran: He was nice and sweet. I would go out with him.

Bill: I really could identify with him . . . with, er . . . you, Larry. Not sure I could have done that. Now, maybe next time I'd know what to do. Good that you looked her in the eye. And your voice was O.K., like you were sure of yourself.

Faye: I liked the sincerity, not giving you a line. Reminds me of Jimmy Stewart. You know, the strong but silent type.

Sally: I wish I could meet someone like you at a party. I liked the way you started out slow, took time to get to know her. I wouldn't find you boring (smile).

John: I like what you did. I'd like to try it next, have the same problem. I liked the way you finally sat down and looked her in the face and told her about yourself.

Hilda: You looked like you had confidence.

Louis: It was good that you volunteered and asked lots of questions. She made you ask questions. I sure have trouble initiating.

Joe: It took guts to do that with an attractive girl who gives you almost no response . . . and . . . er . . . just smiles in that cool way. But you kept talking.

Rose: I couldn't relate to this—keep thinking of my own problems. He's a sweet boy, reminds me of my nephew.

Jo: You remind me of my problem, good that you could do it. I worry so much about making a good impression.

Larry had already indicated that he thought there could be improvement. He elaborated, saying he could have talked more, kept up the questions. The therapist proceeds:

T: I liked your persistence and the fact that you kept in good contact, but you seemed to swallow your words. Maybe if you took a deep breath like this before you begin a sentence, it might help (therapist demonstrates and Larry tries it). O.K., now, what else might Larry do?

Mary: Well, it's hard to criticize . . . er . . . but he should have sat down without asking.

T: See if you can make suggestions without using "shoulds." Tell him in a positive way.

Mary: It's hard to do it . . . er. It would have been better if you had sat down without asking earlier. It was awkward seeing you stand.

Sue: You need to work more on controlling your voice. Like I know when I'm nervous my voice shakes too, but it sounded nice.

Lynn: Stand up straighter. Don't stoop so much. Don't sit so stiffly . . . er (laughs).

T: What are you doing Lynn? (laughs).

Lynn: I sound like I'm giving commands! Try to be more relaxed in the way you stand and sit.

Jo: Maybe it'd help if you plan what to say in . . . er . . . maybe in advance.

John: You might try what I do. What I find it hard to do, I mean—talk more about yourself. What you do, instead of asking so many questions.

Lynn: She wasn't helping you much, just answering questions, briefly. You had to do all the work. Maybe better if you just talked more about yourself.

Sue: I would have liked it if I heard more about what you felt about the party. I like it when I hear someone else is having my problem too.

Feedback for the Role-Playing Partner. The partner is often revealing a great deal about his or her style of relating. In this group, Cathy had already received some feedback about her "not helping much," although the focus had been on Larry. The group focused on her responses:

Lynn: Cathy, you didn't let go much with him, give him much to work with.

Cathy: Yes. That's my problem. I felt more interest than I guess I showed.

Joe: I couldn't tell what your smile meant, seemed like it made it harder to approach you—not knowing.

Others repeated that she had made Larry do all the work and commented on her stiff, cool responses. Cathy stated that the feedback was "good for her," smiling, but her voice was shaking, and the leader directed the group to focus on giving her positive feedback.

At this point, the group could turn to help Cathy with being more emotionally expressive, or that could be saved for another time.

Setting Goals. When the subject has been given sufficient feedback, he or she is asked what it would be best to do differently the next round. In this group, Larry stated that he would like to try to keep more of a flow of the conversation and avoid asking Cathy questions. He would try to relax more and use the technique of taking a deep breath, so that the words could flow. He would try to push out thoughts about being boring and anticipating rejection.

Second Role Play. The subject now attempts to role play a second time, following the same procedures. The therapist's work at this time is to keep all group members as involved as possible and to be on the alert that the group does not dump more negative feedback and advice on the subject than he or she can assimilate, since the goal is self-directed behavior change.

It may be more appropriate to ask a second group member with the same problem to attempt a similar role-play. It may be equally valuable to ask for a volunteer who feels confident in the particular area to model his or her handling of the situation, although a super-competent model can prove intimidating to the original subject. The leader exercises judgment in which direction to take the group at this point. In an on-going group, the same or related themes are usually continued through the session. Toward the end, a topic is selected for the following week or weeks.

Homework Assignments. Whether the group is a 1-day workshop or an on-going group, appropriate assignments are given to each member, specific to the problematic behavior of each. The group as a whole is instructed to self-monitor and observe their particular assertiveness problems and to set small goals for change.

The on-going group described previously has chosen the topic for the next session of dealing with authority figures at work. Assignments are given in that area. In addition, Larry is to try to initiate conversations with women, practice making "I" statements, and told where to obtain a relaxation tape. Cathy is to try to express more positive feelings, and, to become aware of how she reveals her feelings, to practice in front of a mirror.

Standard assessment or self-monitoring forms (see Table 3) may be given out to assist in homework assignments.

Homework Follow-Up. The next session begins with a review of the homework assignments, which provide the material for further work. (As homework, participants had monitored their interactions at work.)

In self-monitoring, Jo has found that his problematic area is in attempting to please everyone at work. His position is one of mediator, and consequently he is bound to displease someone. This paralyzes him. This week he was to get the programmers to redo a program, quickly, since data had been omitted. He found it difficult to order the work, since he so much wants everyone to like him.

Lynn finds that she takes on too much responsibility and then can't do all the work. She then becomes "pissed off at her boss." She says "He's brilliant and affable, but he's also dogmatic and doesn't listen when I try to talk to him. He interferes with administrative issues that aren't his province. I'm so angry with him! He's my consultant but he acts like he's my boss. But sometimes I find myself saying, 'I guess he must be right.' "

T: What makes you feel that way?

Lynn: He's so sure! He's got such conviction. However, when I speak up and am assertive, he says I'm aggressive . . .

Hilda: I had two problems this week. A doctor changed a diet, and the nurse wouldn't listen to me and wouldn't let me call the doctor.

T: How do you feel?

Hilda: So frustrated . . .

T: You seem weary as you tell me this.

Hilda: Yeah, I feel what's the use. I get no respect in that place. And my supervisor, she don't care—all she wants is the menus circled and the forms filled out.

Sally: I sure never took such a good look at work before. My job is too much and my boss is impossible. He wants me to type and answer phones. They keep ringing, and then he yells because the typing isn't done. I feel I ought to quit. Men are impossible! I don't think he'll ever change.

T: But you can change.

Sally: But I feel the situation is hopeless.

John: I sure let my boss bully me. He's on my back all the time and I just keep my feelings in.

Lucia: My boss is a tyrant, too. He yells and screams. Last week I got in trouble for using the Xerox machine for class work. I had to spend my own money instead.

Bill: My boss talks to me in a condescending way.

T: What do you do?

Bill: I get tongue-tied. I can't think of anything to say, so he gets the upper hand.

Faye: My boss is ineffective, uncommunicative and cold. I never noticed that before. He's a lot like my father in many ways. My father was of German descent and very authoritarian. My boss is a perfectionist, but disorganized. I have to call up and look for him when he has an appointment. He forgets. He also gets very angry when I do any work for anyone else. But I wouldn't dare say how I feel.

After more sharing and discussion, someone is asked to volunteer. Sally elects to role play her problem. Louis, who has trouble being a boss, volunteers to play the role of Sally's boss: Sally briefs Louis about what her boss is like and how he typically behaves.

Louis: What were you hired for? (speaks in a good firm voice)

Sally: Typist. Now I'm doing record keeping, have no lunch hour. I'm answering phones all day (complaining tone of voice).

Louis: What do you want?

Sally: I really can't handle all this work you pile on me (voice is cracking and she is close to tears).

T: What did you want? What are your goals?

Sally: I want him to know there's too much work for one person. We need an extra person.

T: Did you tell him that?

Sally: I can't. Oh, it's so hopeless.

Since Sally feels so defeated that she cannot express herself, the leader asks another participant to role-play the situation. Lynn volunteers and is firm in telling Louis what her feelings are about the situation, and makes suggestions, setting priorities. The group feels that Lynn was very firm and positive. Sally now replays the role, trying out Lynn's responses. The group gives her feedback, and she feels encouraged to attempt approaching her boss in a different way.

As the group is finishing work on Sally's problem, Lucia asks what to do if you are really dealing with such a "monster" as she has for a boss. "What do you do when you feel so anxious you can't deal with the situation?" Lucia is then asked to be more specific about her situation. She reports that she is a new teacher in a school with a bully as principal, and provides information about her situation. John, who has stated that his boss is a bully, agrees to take the part to see what it is like to be such a person. They set up an encounter about using the Xerox machine:

John: (as Principal) What the hell are you doing with all that paper? Things are tight now. What are you doing? Don't you know the school can't afford this?

Lucia: (Small voice) This is for the workshop tomorrow.

John: What workshop? I never heard about a workshop.

Lucia: The workshop I'm conducting for the Board of Ed.

John: Screw the Board of Ed. Go across to the Xerox shop and make your copies there.

Lucia: (Aside to the group) I'd better get out of here before I start crying. I'm already tearful.

T: What's happening?

Lucia: I feel small. I want to stand up for myself. What should I do?

In order to answer Lucia's question, someone else takes Lucia's role, and the scene is replayed. After participants have been given feedback, Lynn, who had been able to present herself assertively previously, admits that "it cost her a lot of anxiety." The leader uses this opportunity to present the stages of anxiety experienced by those at different levels of assertiveness.

Stage 1: In the face of a perceived threat, the individual experiences acute anxiety and is unable to be assertive.

Stage 2: In the face of a threat, the individual experiences anxiety but is able to carry through assertive behavior.

Stage 3: Through repeated practice, the individual responds to the threat assertively and anxiety is reduced to a minimum.

The leader and group members then help Lucia get in touch with her rights in this situation. Keeping in mind one's rights is a potent check against anxiety. Lynn further suggests that knowing she was dealing with a "bully" helped her stand up to him. Other means of strengthening responses with a threatening person were discussed, and the group came up with the following:

1. Be aware of your rights. Say them to yourself.
2. Use back-up authority (e.g., the Board of Ed).

3. Recognize the other as a bully.
4. Learn how to distance yourself emotionally.
5. Observe others as they interact with the person.
6. Appeal to the person's own self-interest if that is reasonable.
7. Use relaxation procedures.

The Use of Specific Auxiliary Exercises. In discussions of role-plays and giving feedback, often a particular concern is voiced by a number of group members that lends itself to further exercises. Sometimes the problem centers on worries about appearing foolish in social situations. For these situations, shame-attacking exercises are useful. (e.g., get in touch with what you would be most ashamed for anyone to see or know about you and act it out or pick an embarrassing assignment, such as begging in the street, and do it). In this group, several people reported they feared a "bully" yelling at them. An experiential exercise might be useful at this point to help the person become more aware that his own response to the bully is the major problem, not the bully himself. A scolding exercise followed.

The participants pair up facing each other. At first one line scolds their partner non-verbally (pointing a finger, grimacing, etc.), while the other partner is instructed to stand up to the scolder while getting in touch with what they are experiencing. Then the other line scolds. During the next round, or at the same time, one can add yelling. The group really got into this exercise, and many members reported feeling very childlike and inhibited. Lucia spoke of "freezing" and not knowing how to respond. She also cannot get into the role of the "bully." A few people seemed undaunted and were willing to demonstrate their stance toward a "bully" and reveal what they were saying to themselves to shore themselves up. Helpful discussion followed about how hard it was to continue "bullying" someone who managed to remain unruffled. The entire group practiced again, they loosened up, and there was much laughter and even some mock fighting. Lucia is now asked to role play herself again, standing up to the bully boss, and to try to imitate some of the gestures and body language she has observed. Discussion followed, and Larry commented "I guess you are showing us that we are more frightened about not knowing how to take what the bullies are dishing out, than the bullies themselves. If we can handle ourselves, we can handle them better."

Jo asked "But how can we stop them from behaving that way. We are still getting yelled out." The therapist said "Why not tell them . . ." Again the group agreed that it was hard to really "be aggressive back." Again, there was a feeling that only by yelling back, would a bully stop yelling. Another exercise was introduced at that time. It involved saying "I resent_____." The group practiced such statements as "I resent your yelling." Then it was suggested that they try during the week to let at least one person who is annoying them know that they resent it. (Again, the importance of starting with less important persons or situations is stressed.)

Continuous Feedback. As participants try out assertive skills *in vivo*, there is a need for continuous feedback. Each session in an on-going group begins with reports of how things are going. For example, we might begin the next group with Lucia relating progress in standing up to her principal or the groups' experience in expressing resentments. The following illustrates the importance of on-going monitoring in translating skills developed in role-play to real social situations.

Mary, had been hired as a trainee translator at a low salary. However, she was doing the work of a bilingual secretary and getting no further training or salary raise for it. She wishes to talk to her boss about the matter, and after role playing her situation and rehearsing an improved response, felt ready to try it out at work. The following week, she came in depressed and disgusted, saying "it didn't work." She was asked to "show" what happened. What she did was fine, but it turned out that she had selected a very busy morning to deal with her supervisor, when she had been called in extra early to prepare a special report for her supervisor to present to a U.N. official. Her boss was frantic and blew up at her. The group discussed the importance of taking into account the situation and timing, and Mary was encouraged to try again at a more appropriate time.

Another issue that frequently comes up is how persistent to be in self-assertion. Sometimes, a person develops an adequate assertive response, but keeps "harping" on it rigidly. On-going groups provide for monitoring where this is a problem. Clients become progressively aware of how to assess the impact of their assertive messages and how to determine when they must give up and compromise. Group problem solving aids in learning to compromise.

Themes in Succeeding Weeks. In an on-going group, a new topic or theme might be introduced weekly. Generally, as in the examples given, groups begin with work problems and social inhibitions. As the group continues, more personal issues are introduced, and nuances of assertive styles are taken up. A great deal of time may be spent on working on the cognitive aspects of assertiveness, or self-statements. It is always important to emphasize that as one learns assertive responding, it may increase the probability of others responding differently in turn. But there is no guarantee that others will change. An important and related issue is that of the cause and effect of one's feelings. At the beginning of groups, members often state "He makes me so mad; she makes me nervous." As the group progresses, members make a distinction: the behavior of another affects them only insofar as they allow it to do so. Some members come into groups from very difficult life situations. Group support helps give them the choice to behave differently themselves.

Special Groups

Groups for Women Only

The majority of assertiveness-training workshops still attract a preponderance of females. Generally, women's groups are closer knit, move more quickly into dealing with intimate issues, and often are vehicles for group problem solving of role realignments in difficult life situations. The general format is the same as for other groups, with an emphasis on discussing sex-role messages.

Most women coming for assertiveness training are in a work situation where they feel subservient to males. Such similar complaints are voiced by secretaries, managers in industry, and physicians that, if one were to listen to the content of tapes of sessions, it would be hard to distinguish a female secretary confronting her boss from a doctor confronting the ward administrator. A small group of women who have administrative responsibilities also come to AT workshops seeking guidance. In women's only groups, with a woman leader they feel free to explore their insecurities about assuming power and their fears that their tendencies to protect and nurture may interfere with their exercise of authority. The therapist's style is closely observed by members of women-only groups. She is viewed as a role-model who is struggling with the same issues.

Whatever their position at work, women struggle with developing a feminine assertive style. In a recent workshop, a young women lawyer was upset at what she perceived as male aggression in the courtroom. Yet, she knew that she must stand up for her client, to "attack" the opposing attorney's case. She worked on role plays with the group to develop an assertive style that felt comfortable to her and would be effective in court. Subsequently, this woman organized AT groups specifically for women lawyers.

Problems with males that come up for frequent discussion in women-only groups include the following: establishing an equal relationship, insisting on paying one's own way, risking inviting a man out or initiating sex, setting limits on sexual conduct, speaking up when dissatisfied, and shifting power in an on-going relationship. Even traditional women now want more equality and bring in assertiveness problems ranging from wanting an "evening out" to establishing an independent checking account.

No matter what type of women are in the group, on-going issues between women and their mothers are constantly brought up. Such problems lend themselves easily to role play when the group comprises a range of ages. Recently, the dyadic treatment of mothers and daughters has been tried (Fodor and Wolfe, 1977). The following case illustrates one of the problems involved when a mother and daughter struggle to work out an adult to adult relationship. The group was composed of six mother-daughter dyads and was run as a 2-day workshop with follow-up a month later.

Case Study: Anita and Rosa

Anita, a single woman in her early twenties, had been in individual assertiveness training for 6 months when it became apparent that her struggles with her lover, for which she entered treatment, were paralleled by ongoing hassles with her mother. From Anita's self-monitoring of phone conversations with her mother, the following problematic patterns of interaction were articulated.

1. Even though Anita had lived away from home for 4 years, taking a B.A. in English and working as an editor, upon her return to the city her mother expected her to check in with her daily by telephone. Anita felt that her mother did not respect her as a separate person, grown-up, entitled to her own life.

2. Her mother "criticized" her too much about small things, such as gaining weight, staying out late, and working too hard. Further, their values differed over Anita's life-style.

3. Anita felt pressured to attend family affairs, visit sick relatives, and send birthday cards even to distant relatives; her mother became "upset" if she refused or forgot, making Anita feel guilty.

Until recently, Anita had handled her mother generally by "tuning out." However, she had become progressively aware of how angry she felt. She was worried she might fly into a rage at her mother.

Anita's mother, Rosa, agreed to attend a mother-daughter assertiveness group. In her initial description of the problems, she emphasized that "she just wanted what was best for Anita" and that keeping in touch by phone and going to family gatherings together was "so little to ask for." She described Anita's lover as "not having the right intentions." She complained that Anita wouldn't even "let me take care of her when she is sick and needs me." Asked for a recent conflict, both described an incident when Anita had a dental problem. Rosa had wanted to accompany Anita to the dentist. They reconstructed the following phone conversation for the group (Rosa, R; Anita, A):

R: (Walking toward Anita) Anita, I want to take you over to the dentist today.

A: (Pushing hands out, palms up, backing away) It's all right, mama, I can go by myself.

R: (Still walking closer, smiling) Well, maybe. But I'd feel better if I went with you. And maybe the doctor has to cut you and give you anesthesia. You can't drive home by yourself.

A: (Still backing off, frowning) Don't worry. I can go alone. I don't live far, and I can always take a taxi (words are racing out).

R: (Moving even closer) I don't feel that's right. I'd feel better if I could go. . . .

A: (Puts arms up in front of her—slouches, head down) Look now, I can take care of this myself. There is no need for you to come into the city for this.

R: I'll be worrying all the time about what's happening. I'll never be able to relax (voice gets louder).

A: I can get there by myself (voice begins to peter out).

R: I'd much rather go with you.

A: (Slouching) I don't want you to (voice barely audible).

R: (Smiles) I won't even go in, if that's what you want. I promise. I'll just stay in the waiting room and you can go in by yourself (conciliatory tone).

A: (Gritting her teeth) O.K., then. You can come (Looking away).

The leader asked Anita how she was feeling, and she said she felt furious and defeated. She said she also felt guilty because she had no right to be angry. Rosa said she felt unhappy because she knew Anita had not really wanted her to come. She also said that she felt really worried about the dental work. She was asked how she would feel if Anita told her she was angry about giving in. Would she be hurt? She did not answer directly, saying only that she didn't think Anita realized how really worried she was.

The group gave some constructive suggestions, and both thought about how they might again approach the situation. They tried it again:

R: (Again approaching Anita) Anita, you know I worry so . . .

A: (Stands ground . . . Looks at her mother) Sure, mama, I know you're worried about this, but I'd like to be alone to have this work done. I'd like you to understand that. I understand how you're worried. How about if I call you as soon as it's all over? I'll be sure to do that.

R: (Looks at Anita . . . Seems serious) Well, I guess I'll worry, but that will be O.K.

T: (To Anita) How does that feel?

A: A lot better. Hey, I'm not mad even having had to discuss it. I'm not mad. Why is that?

R: I felt better about that.

Group member: Maybe you both feel better because you both listened to each other.

T: But what if one of them had not listened and the compromise hadn't worked? Let's continue. Rosa, this time keep insisting.

R: (Begins to press herself next to Anita) Still, I want to come with you.

A: (Faces ahead, but twists her knees around as if to run) I'm upset that you won't accept what I just said.

R: (Moves forward) But, I will worry so much . . .

A: (Turning away with more of her body) I said I'd call you as soon as I could. Please! (Exasperated tone) Let's leave this matter now. I've made up my mind (hands push Rosa away).

R: Gee, what a difference. When I press—I guess I have a lot to learn.

It is clear that change will not be instant. Some of the anger between mothers and daughters results from life-cycle shifts: for mother to realize and accept that the daughter is grown and separate and for the daughter to not feel that she has to give in to the mother's demands. It will take a while for Rosa to accept that Anita is becoming stronger and means to set boundaries. Finding the right line between staying with one's own feelings and trying to see the other's view of the situation without rationalizing or denying is often hard. At the next session in the group, Anita and her mother worked on the situation of "dropping in to visit":

A: Gee, it's nice to see you, but I have lots of work to do today. Let's just have a cup of coffee and a brief visit, and I think we have to talk about your dropping in on me (sinking voice, eyes down).

R: But Anita, I just never see you anymore. And I want to hear about the new article you're working on (hurt tone of voice).

A: (Aside, blowing out air) Oh, damn, I'm already feeling guilty and pressured (exasperated voice tone).
(To mother) I know, but I get upset when you just drop in anytime (in whining voice with a sigh).
(Aside) Such rage—it's reaching the boiling point. She is blackmailing me with guilt . . . (Talking to the therapist, hands to cheeks) I'm boiling. (Continues to look away from her mother.)

T: What are you saying to yourself?

A: She'll never see. She'll never change. So what the use (starts to cry).

T: Aren't you demanding too much at once. She's here and trying.

A: (through her tears, nods toward her mother.)

At this point, another mother and daughter bring up a similar problem that they feel they have been working on with some success. They role play (voluntary) Anita and Rosa, while the latter pair pull back to watch. In the feedback on the difference between the two interactions, the group notices body-language differences. The more successful pair stay put and face each other. As Anita comments, "It's not a 'push-flee' response."

The group then discusses the problems involved in talking directly face to face when there are strong feelings involved. The daughters in particular felt they talk themselves out of direct expression by assuming responsibility for not making their mother upset, but then feel resentful and want to flee. Facing their mother at this time is particularly painful.

The leader suggests a group exercise to help deal with this problem. Each mother-daughter pair faces each other, about arms length apart, and begins a dialogue with such sentences as: "I like it when you _____, I would like you to _____, or I don't like it when you _____, I resent it when you _____." The group begins the exercise, and there is some crying and hugging when the women begin to talk face to face. Acceptance of the mixed feelings is hard. The group needs to learn that one can express resentment about aspects of a person's behavior without it meaning "I don't care about you anymore." For the next few weeks, Rosa and Anita were instructed to practice talking more directly and listening to each other. The therapist reminded them that they were under no obligation to comply with any request. In addition, they are both to keep records of these interactions for discussion at the follow-up session. One month later, at follow-up, Anita and Rosa bring in their records and compare notes. During this conversation, they look at each other, Anita stays put, and they demonstrate an improved facility in talking and listening. It is a beginning for them. Anita still needs more help in being comfortable saying "no," and Rosa still has a hard time accepting (although she can now hear what Anita is saying) that Anita wants to spend less time with her than she would like. Rosa at this point could use help in finding other friends and new interests. At 6 months follow-up, Rosa is involved in a women's organization, there are fewer hassles, and Anita is initiating some more of the contacts. Change is slow, but Anita and Rosa are on their way to shift from parent-child roles to beginning an adult friendship.

Special Problems in Running Assertiveness Groups

Refusal to Participate or Role-Play

In every group, there is at least one person who has "really just come to watch," will say little, and generally refuses to participate if pressed to do so. Sometimes such people can be encouraged to join in by trying "private" exercises (such as choosing one group member with whom they feel they can practice talking to during the break). If after encouragement they still remain silent, it is best not to urge. Over time, these people will often come to other workshops and feel comfortable in participating more actively.

In almost every group and occasionally in individual work, someone refuses to role play, declaring it "silly" and "unreal." They want instead to talk about their problems. Since role playing is a potent vehicle for changing unassertive responses, discussion about problematic behavior is relatively unproductive. Watching others in the group role-play often is the needed incentive for reluctant participants, but there are some who will leave in disgust saying that the workshop or group was not the "lecture" or "class" they had expected. Again, gentle and gradual suggestions to "show" aspects of a problem may help them get in touch with their inhibitions. Most unassertive people are initially self-conscious about role playing, and slow entry is necessary for some.

Very Disturbed People

In workshops at outpatient clinics, there are usually one or two people with a multitude of problems who need a lot more therapy than a 1-day workshop can provide, or whose problems are so general that assertiveness training is not really a suitable starting point. Lonely and preoccupied with their suffering, they cannot relate to other people's problems, cannot define one problem or stick to one topic, and do not wish to role-play. Referral to an individual therapist may be necessary; yet, for lonely people who can listen quietly without engaging in constant and inappropriate interruptions, continuation in the group can be helpful. Further, such people are often important to the group, helping other participants articulate their feelings toward relatives and others in their lives who act this way. Recently, a woman with a disorganized hodge-podge of endless complaints came into a group, loaded down with shopping bags, which she spilled, talking a blue streak, and disrupting an on-going role-play. One of the group members who had reported having particular trouble in expressing resentment was able to successfully and gently point out to this woman that she was being intrusive.

About three or four times a year, usually in a clinic, an extremely paranoid individual shows up in a group. For the most part, assertiveness training groups can be very helpful to some types of schizophrenics, helping them to stay focused on and articulate about specific problematic situations. Usually, group members prove patient and supportive to these people. In one particular group, a very distraught young schizophrenic woman reported problems with her beautician. She had suspicions that he was trying deliberately to burn up her hair every time he put her under the dryer. She asked for help in dealing with him, since she really did not wish to change hairdressers; she liked the way he styled her hair. The group was empathetic and helpful: several women reported problems in asserting themselves with their hairdressers (making sure that they did not cut their hair too short, resisting pressure to have expensive conditioning treatments, and asking for having their hair blown dry instead of setting in rollers). They modeled and role played situations with laughter and gusto. At the follow-up, the woman reported feeling less terrified at her weekly beauty parlor appointments.

Sometimes, however, a paranoid person can be highly disruptive in the group. In one, a young man came in, sat in the middle of the circle with a tape recorder in his lap, and turned it on. When the leader asked what he was doing, he said that he had to tape the group so he could remember everything and that this was the best position in which to place himself for taping. He was angrily resistant when asked to move. Finally, he was given the choice of joining the circle or leaving the group, and told, firmly, that the group would have to agree to the taping. On the first go-round, he reported that he had come into the group because he felt that people did not like him. He then again asked permission to tape, but the group refused his request. He sat fuming, saying he had been "rejected again," and left at the coffee break.

Unless the leader is a paranoid's therapist or communicates with his or her therapist, caution is in order. Another man came to a group also initially stating that he was there because people did not seem to like him. His general behavior did not suggest paranoid trends. In the middle of the first go-around, he interrupted the leader's comments, injecting an off-color sarcastic comment. Perhaps without having adequately sized up the situation, the therapist gave him feedback on how she experienced the interruption and asked if this might not be part of his general difficulties with others in other situations. The man withdrew, evidently hurt, and did not speak again for the rest of the workshop. During the break, the therapist attempted to discuss the situation privately with him, but he just commented that she "didn't seem to appreciate his sense of humor." A few days after the workshop, the therapist received a paranoid hate letter. Luckily, this individual was in therapy with a colleague who was able to work on the issue with him subsequently. The case illustrates the importance of pre-assessing the referrals of individuals with paranoid tendencies and the importance of caution in giving feedback early in a workshop to provocative individuals. When people's first complaint is that others dislike them, it can be a tip-off that paranoia possibilities exist.

Effects of Assertiveness Training on Client's Relationships

More so, perhaps, than with other behavioral procedures, assertiveness training has impacts on significant people involved with clients. An unassertive husband or wife who becomes more assertive in the marital relationship will disturb the *status quo* of the marriage. It is important to explore the consequences of new behaviors and ways of relating. Involving significant others as group members is the most productive solution, but this is often unfeasible. An interesting and recent problem is that some women are now being "sent" by their husbands, who claim to want "more assertive wives." The very fact that these women come constitutes a form of compliance in itself, an issue that can be tricky to make explicit and work on.

Therapist Attitudes

As with all therapy, the attitude of the therapist is important. Since assertiveness trainers put a premium on assertive behaviors, they may be judgmental, either covertly or overtly, when clients do not change in the expected direction. For example, a feminist therapist may put pressure on a passive, dependent woman to behave more assertively in areas in which the client has expressed no desire for behavioral change. A traditional male therapist may tend to call in the husband if such a woman's emerging assertive behaviors threaten the dominant-submissive aspects of the marital relationship. As Broverman (1970) has suggested, mental health professionals have their own sets of sex-role stereotypic attitudes.

INDIVIDUAL THERAPY AND ASSERTIVE TECHNIQUES

While group training is often the treatment of choice, the use of assertiveness techniques can also be extremely valuable in individual work with clients. It can be used as an adjunct to other behavioral training procedures for helping clients master difficult life situations or interpersonal conflicts. It can also be used more ambitiously, often in conjuntion with dynamic therapies and gestalt techniques, to work on personality or characterlogical problems or maladaptive defensive structures.

More so than in group work, the therapist working with an individual uses himself/herself as the instrument for change. The interactions between the client and the therapist are the natural material for assertiveness training. The deferent client who smiles at a therapist who is 10 minutes late or who talks on the phone during sessions reveals more about his manner than when he tells about his deference with others. Likewise, the passive person who sits and waits for the therapist to initiate all conversations is graphically demonstrating his style of relating to important people in his life. Further, since most therapists quickly become authority figures or people about whom the client has strong feelings, the therapeutic relationship is a natural area for the emergence of assertiveness issues with others whom the client respects, fears, or loves.

Clients watch and use the therapist as an assertive role model. It is important, then, that at some point in therapy the client receive feedback on how the therapist experiences his style. The therapist who allows himself/herself to become upset or annoyed by such things as homework assignments left undone, appointments cancelled at the last minute, bills unpaid, important issues raised only in the closing minutes of a session, and who does not express how he is experiencing such behavior provides a poor model for the client working on assertiveness issues. Further, clients need to see that the therapist can take the risk of displeasing them. For many, a therapist who can be open enough to risk doing so provides a needed role model for confronting others in an appropriately assertive way.

Finally, therapy sessions may be the only time when a client can get such honest feedback in a helpful way. For example, an anxious, sexually inhibited man complained of poor peer interactions and of not having found a satisfactory sexual relationship. During desensitization for his anxiety reaction, the therapist became aware of his chronic fussiness. He complained that she was not doing this or that right, and she found herself dreading his coming and feeling drained after his sessions. She felt under pressure to do everything just right for this man. After a few sessions, she shared her feeling of irritation with him and questioned if his demanding, critical manner might not be what was interfering in his interpersonal relationships. He had never focused on that before, and it became the target behavior for the next piece of work. Here, the therapist's use of her own reactions served as a catalyst for the client's exploration of alternative modes of relating.

Types of Assertiveness Problems in Individual Therapy

Assertiveness techniques can be used with virtually every client a behavior therapist sees. Just about everyone at some point in individual work brings up someone important with whom he or she is having an interpersonal conflict. A therapist who is sensitive to such issues can see how they reflect communication styles, specific anxieties, and inhibitions about self-assertion that keep clients in repeatedly unsatisfying relationships and recurrent, problematic life situations.

Often it is only after a presenting problem has been alleviated that some people are ready to face their more pervasive problems in getting along with others. Initially, work begins with the phobia, the overeating behavior, the sexual inhibition, the headache, but as these are mastered, issues around self-assertion come to the fore. Often the presenting problem itself has served to mask interpersonal difficulties. An agorophobic, tied to home by her fears, may become aware of marital conflicts only when the need for "protection" is lessened. A socially inhibited person may master his social anxiety and then find the need to work on communication skills as he is able to enter into more intimate relationships. As therapy progresses, people who have always attempted to please others may become aware of how out of touch they are with their own feelings. Working on assertiveness for some clients becomes a life-long process of self-exploration, risk taking, and the acquisition of a richer repertoire of modes of interacting with others.

Some of the most intensive problems in assertiveness relate to natural life-cycle shifts that require role changes. A child's emergence into adolescence poses new issues of power struggles with authority: issues around autonomy and separation from home enter the life of the young adult and marriage poses problems of establishing traditional or nontraditional roles for husband and wife. Clinical problems often reflect life-cycle issues that were not adequately resolved at the appropriate time. An extreme case in the author's recent experience involved a 45-year-old single woman living at home with her 75-year-old mother. They had remained deeply entrenched for 25 years in communication patterns that were an exaggeration of the adolescent power struggle.

Additionally, men and women come for assertiveness training with prototypical problems related to their different socialization histories and the cultural expectations of assertiveness associated with sex-role behaviors. Stereotypes about the "shoulds" and "oughts" of sex-role behavior and assertiveness function as internal belief systems or schemata through which their own and others' behaviors are evaluated. When their own behavior deviates from what they believe it ought to be or from what they imagine others expect it to be, feelings of anxiety, guilt, and confusion ensue. Loss of self-esteem then perpetuates problems of self-assertion.

For men, not to be "assertive" is not to be a competent male. Many men berate themselves for not being masculine enough even when to be yielding is appropriate. Further, in our culture assertive and aggressive modes are not always differentiated. Men often come for help with problems related to aggression and the under-control of anger for which they need to substitute alternative assertive behaviors. Yet another group of men are entrapped in "Be brave, be cool" sex-role messages and come to learn how to express more readily their tender, vulnerable feelings. The largest group of men undertaking assertiveness training are in their 20s or early 30s and have problems with lovers or wives.

For women, sex-role programming has taught them to associate unassertive behavior with being appropriately feminine. Such early messages as "be nice," "don't be selfish," "don't make waves" insure an unassertive style. To be assertive means being selfish or masculine. To express legitimate anger brings out fears of being bitchy, castrating, or witchlike. A further problem arises when women attempt to break out of ingrained stereotyped behaviors. Feelings that have been "sat on" emerge, often in the form of hysterical or aggressive outbursts. When this is the case, some women tend to be particularly self-doubting, berating themselves for their irrationality. Fears of "sounding just like my mother" plague the woman attempting to break out of a mold. For the most part, women coming for assertiveness training are struggling with one of several prototypical situations. Young wives or mothers may sink so far into self-abnegation that others complain of their passivity; others are trying to shift role alignments within the family and are meeting resistance and disapproval. Some mothers of adolescents find that they cannot deal with rebellion. Many young women need help in becoming more strongly assertive in both work situations and close emotional attachments. Older women, often divorced or widowed, feel lonely, depressed, and unable to adjust to the self-assertion a single life requires or that relationships with their grown children entail.

Thus assertiveness training with individual men and women involves more than in group work. In addition to attention to body language, speech, and the content of communications, familial learning patterns need exploration. It is useful to obtain a history of how parents interacted with clients and what their modeling experiences were. The trainer then can provide a more adequate role model, giving more appropriate feedback messages and reinforcements for assertiveness. For many women, it is especially important to work on self-reliance as opposed to reliance on the response of male partners and others as the prime base of self-approval and esteem.

Progress in Becoming Assertive

In working individually with clients as they become more assertive, careful attention can be focused on specific areas of deficit.It is useful to think of assertive behavior as representing a hierarchy of stages, with skills to be acquired at each level. Individual clients may require work at one or more of these levels when presented with a problematic situation.

1. The clients learn to become aware of what they feel at the time the event occurs.
2. The clients learn to become aware of what they want at that time to happen.
3. The clients learn to be aware of their rights in that situation.
4. The clients learn to risk expressing their feelings and wants by
   a) learning to communicate clearly and directly,
   b) listening to and trying to understand the response of others,
   c) taking into account the cultural milieu.
5. The clients learn to communicate clearly in the face of meeting possible disapproval or rejection.
6. The clients ned to learn to deal with their anxiety, anger or other strong emotions while responding assertively.
7. The clients need to deal with their own anxiety and self evaluation after an assertive response is attempted.
8. The clients need to recognize when they have reached an impass with another and need to learn to compromise, accept disappointment

about not getting what THEY had wanted, or when to look elsewhere for this type of satisfaction.

At each stage, the clients will need help in learning to define their rights, to set realistic goals, to assess their own behavior and significant others behavior realistically (to be aware of irrational beliefs and self statements that interfere with progress toward learning assertive behaviors) and to continue to reevaluate and monitor their progress and responses to the problematic situations.

The following case material has been selected to highlight problems in one or more of these stages. The cases are composites of individuals seen by the author over the past 7 years. Identities have been carefully disguised especially when one individual's progress in a stage has been followed closely. The composites represent differing presenting problems and personality styles. All are types of cases likely to occur in the practice of behavior therapists.

Alice presents a problem at stages 1 and 4. She was often unaware of what she was feeling and wanted to blame others for her problems. Her assertiveness training involved more emphasis on self-awareness than is usual, to help her change a passive, reactive style. As she improved in knowing what she wanted, treatment shifted to helping her risk expressing her feelings. Hal describes work with a man who knew what he wanted but was afraid of risking expressing himself too directly. His assertiveness training involved work in risk-taking and direct communication (stages 4 & 5). Angela is a woman who seemed to know what she wanted and to possess abilities to assert herself. However, she could not use these abilities in the face of strong emotional feelings (stage 6). As she progressed, problems in stage 8 became paramount in her treatment. All of the cases illustrate how goal setting is interwoven with work at the various stages, as is the need to take into account the responses of others and to deal with the problem of stage 8.

Case Study: Alice

Background

Alice was a short 32-year-old woman with medium-length bleached blond hair. About 20 pounds overweight, she wore baggy jeans and a loose-fitting blouse. She applied makeup heavily, and carelessly, often smudging lipstick on her teeth. Alice was married and at home full-time with her two preschool children. The family lived in a middle-class Brooklyn neighborhood adjacent to a deteriorating area. Alice hoped to take courses at a community college the following year, when her children would start school.

Presenting Problem

Alice came for behavior therapy for a transportation phobia of 2 year's duration. It confined her to walking a few blocks around her neighborhood; she was only able to go farther with her husband if he drove. He brought her to the therapist's Manhattan office.

Behavior During the Initial Interview

Alice slumped back heavily in the chair and avoided looking at the therapist while she rambled on aimlessly about her inability to cope and her hopeless feelings about her incompetence. She talked about how overwhelmed she felt with all her responsibilities and wondered aloud if the therapist could possibly help her. Her voice was whiny as she pleaded for help, and she cried easily. Passive, weak, and put-upon by the world, Alice was only too willing to let the therapist take control and direct her.

Behavior During Desensitization

The initial phase of the treatment involved standard desensitization (Wolpe, 1959). Alice was suggestible and again only too easy to direct during her weekly sessions. It was difficult for her to do some of the *in vivo* exercises alone. Nevertheless, with the help of graduate student therapy assistants she began riding subways and buses, and at the end of 25 sessions over a period of 6 months she was able to come to the therapist's office alone. It was at that point that she began complaining about her husband and asked the therapist to help her with her marriage.

Assessment of the Marital Problem (Session I)

Alice felt that she and Ted were together only for the sake of the children. She wasn't sure why she had married him. It had just been "time to get married—all my friends were getting married—no way of earning a living." Alice had felt she couldn't have done better than marry Ted. She sensed that they were both afraid of alternatives to being married.

Alice reported their current sex life as terrible; their only close contacts consisted of bickering. Ted had taken on an extra job some evenings. She was lonely in the evenings, but when he was there "he's always on my back—expects me to have supper ready." She complained that the children were "a handful" and that all the housework was beyond her. "I feel awful all the time, and he's always picking on me."

Also, Ted's parents lived in the neighborhood and were always dropping in. His relatives were always dropping their kids off too. When she would tell Ted she didn't want to take care of them, he would complain that she didn't care for his family. She also said that she hated living in the city, but her husband wouldn't consider moving.

Preparing the Client: Self Monitoring (Sessions 2 and 3)

The first assertiveness-training sessions were spent teaching self-monitoring skills. Alice was told to keep track of the situations that she felt she would like to handle differently. In view of her disorganization, it was important to start on a general level with a list of the problematic situations and what she did about them, instead of conducting a more multifaceted assessment. The next week she came in stating that she had lost the self-monitoring form we had constructed, searched in her overfilled pocketbook, and then read from little bits of paper a long list of complaints about her problems with her husband. These included the following: While she was preparing supper, he told her she was not doing things in the right order; another day he came into the kitchen and barked that she had left the dishes too close to the edges of the counter. She had handled both of these situations by crying. Most of the situations depicted Alice as a reactor or respondent to her husband's orders or comments. She did initiate one situation. She wanted to take a course and couldn't find the courage to ask her husband for the extra money for a babysitter. Finally, when she did bring it up meekly, he was on his way out the door. He said they should talk about it later, but she did not mention it again. Generally, she presented herself as meek, submissive, fearful, and put upon and her husband as critical, authoritarian, and cold. As we talked further about the marital situation, she began to cry, saying she was too scared to think of a divorce and seemed in a daze for the rest of the session.

Since the therapist viewed the marital situation as too emotionally charged for initial assertiveness training, Alice was given another homework assignment: that of monitoring other problematic situations. She brought in several situations the following session, all involving neighbors or relatives and refusal behavior. It was hard for Alice to focus during this session and give details of the upsetting incidents. In the early phase of work with such clients who have a strong desire to talk, it may be necessary to set aside time or sessions for talking, even though it means therapy will take longer. The therapist may be one of the few people who really listens to and accepts such peoples' feelings.

What emerged as a pattern of refusal was the following. First, as with her husband, Alice was a responder to other people's demands, had trouble saying "no," and would rarely initiate. Most of the problems involved the neighbors dropping children off, and Alice typically said that she was available. Relatives asked her to run errands (now that she could go out more), and she usually complied. However, as Alice was talking about these situations, when asked what she would want, it became clear that Alice often didn't know what she wanted in these situations. Sometimes it was nice to have people drop in; other times she didn't realize she was upset or resentful until later. Hence, the interim goal, before work on assertiveness training could begin, was to work on helping Alice get more in touch with what she was feeling as these situations occurred and what she wanted, so that she would know when to say "yes" or "no," for a start.

Self-Awareness Training (Sessions 4 to 9)

For the next month, work focused on developing self-awareness and articulating wants. The therapist used Gestalt-awareness exercises during this time. Alice was directed to pay attention to what she was feeling during the therapy session. The therapist would ask such questions as "Do you feel cold? Do you feel hungry? What do you feel like eating? Are you anxious? Does this make you nervous? Is this hard to do?" Focusing on herself produced a great deal of self-consciousness and anxiety, but since Alice was highly compliant, she would try. At this time, a session might begin with "I feel . . . (fill in the blank).

Following this training, Alice was given the homework assignment of monitoring problematic interactions and taking her "emotional temperature" randomly during the day. Was she enjoying being alone? What if someone were to ask her to babysit now? How did she feel at the instant the phone rang? To these questions, Alice's initial responses were "I feel so weak," "It's hopeless." It took a month for Alice to get in touch with some of her feelings of resentment and relate them to her problematic situations.

Alice was then asked to select a recent situation to work on. For this work, a variant of a Gestalt exercise (Polster and Polster, 1973; Perls and Heft-Erline, 1951; Goodman, 1951) was used. (Stevens, 1971, p. 75):

Begin by paying attention to the thoughts going on in your head. Now begin saying those thoughts, but like a very soft whispering, so the words get barely past your lips. . . . Say them a bit louder . . . and keep increasing the volume until you reach your normal speaking level. Imagine that you are talking to someone. Continue to say your thoughts and pay attention to what is communicated by the sound of your voice. What is your voice like? Is it strong or weak, clear or harsh or mellow? Is it whining, complaining, pleasing?

Alice's early thoughts about her neighbors involved wishing they would go away, would not bother her, and involved envy that they had such "nerve." As Alice began to express her thoughts, a tape was used so that she could begin to hear how many of her utterances were complaints and to what extent they were statements blaming others. "You should go away. You are selfish. You don't care about me." Alice began to see that by continually saying "you" instead of "I" she was avoiding her own responsibility in the problem. At this point, another fill-in-the-blank assignment was added, beginning with "I want . . ._____" What she felt about the therapist and wanted from her was included in this exercise.

Typically, the more charged the situation, the more Alice reverted to her old style of responding. When the therapist stated that she would be raising her fee after the summer vacation, Alice responded with her eyes down, complaining in a whiny voice about bills and debts. The therapist then gently asked what she was feeling. Alice said that she felt hurt and worried and anxious and that maybe Ted would make her stop coming. The therapist then asked her to tell her that directly. As Alice started to express her feelings, she began to apologize and say that she knew the therapist had a lot of expenses, too. At this point the therapist asked her "Who are you taking care of now?" Alice then was able to approach discussion of the fee more directly.

Three months into assertiveness training, Alice still tended to say "I'm upset" rather than "I'm annoyed or angry," but she had made progress.

Defining Goals for Assertiveness (Session 10)

As Alice became more aware of her feelings, she began to complain less about her life during the sessions and had begun to see the relationship between her burgeoning feelings of hurt and resentment, her behavior, and other people's responses to her. She was now ready to work on shaping refusal behaviors with her neighbors and relatives. Alice selected a recurrent situation with her sister-in-law to begin with. The initial role-play entailed an assessment about whether to proceed next to one of three alternatives: work on skills training, work on anxiety control, or work on cognitive restructuring.

Behavioral Assessment: Initial Role Play. (Alice provided details for the therapist to play the role of the sister-in-law)

T (as sister-in-law.): Hey, Alice, I'm going to stop at A&S to return the stuff I bought the other day. I figured you'd be home and wouldn't mind taking the kids. I'll be right over. O.K?

A: Yeah . . . er . . . I can't go on (stops).

T: What are you feeling?

A: Like I don't have a choice. Like I'm going to be home, so like I have to babysit.

T: Is that a feeling?

A: No . . . er . . . I guess I feel defeated, like to have to.

T: What are you saying to yourself?

A: Like if I don't, I'm selfish. What does it matter?

T: Does it matter?

A: Well, I guess it does, cause I feel bad.

T: What do you want to do?

A: I don't want her to drop over and take me for granted. I don't even like her kids . . . er . . . they stir mine up, make so much noise. I don't mind it once in a while, but almost everyday it's too much?

T: Why don't you say that to her?

A: No, I can't.

T: Why not?

A: It sounds too selfish.

T: What do you mean?

A: If I refuse, she'll think I'm selfish, won't like me, maybe be mad at me.

T: I think we lost *you* again. What do you want?

A: (Starts to cry) I wish people would leave me alone.

From this behavioral sample, it was clear that part of the problem related to Alice's being more concerned with what other people want than with what she wants. Alice now knew what she wanted in this situation, but was fearful of taking the risk of telling her sister-in-law not to drop in. She felt it was "selfish" for her to act in her own self-interest, and she feared risking another's displeasure. Thus the problem in assertiveness now was less in helping Alice state what she wanted, but in working on some of her underlying beliefs around refusal. The therapist acted somewhat as an "ally" in giving Alice permission to change.

Work on Beliefs About Selfishness (Sessions 11 to 13)

The next three sessions dealt with Alice expressing what she wanted without labeling herself or these wants as "selfish." The therapist first elicited what Alice did want: "I want my mornings free; I don't want to take care of everybody else's kids; I don't want to run errands for my in-laws."

Once she had clearly expressed these goals, she was instructed to say to herself "I have a right to have my mornings to myself; I have a right to peace and quiet in my house. I'm still O.K. if I don't do everything everybody wants me to do. It's O.K. to displease other people." The latter self-statements are not easily established since women like Alice have a long history of socialization in pleasing others and have been reinforced for self-sacrifice. If therapy bogs down at this point, a women's assertiveness-training group or a consciousness-raising group may be in order. Alice had shown that she responded well to experiential treatment, so rather than the use of some of Ellis' techniques for cognitive restructuring to attack her irrational beliefs, a more structured, behavioral risk-taking approach was chosen.

Behavior Rehearsal: Problematic Situations with Neighbors (Sessions 14 to 20)

At this point, it was finally possible for Alice to work on producing actual refusal statements. The therapist again played the role of the problematic person (here a neighbor).

T: Hi, Alice. I'm dropping the kids off while I go downtown.

A: Well . . . er . . . you see. This afternoon . . . er . . . I was going to wash my hair, and . . . er . . . well, you know . . . um . . . so much work (in a low voice, occasionally holding her hand over her mouth, looking toward the floor).

Alice stopped the role play saying that she couldn't go on. The therapist decided to help her by presenting a model response.

T: (as Alice) Gee, Sally, I'm sorry to disappoint you. I need some quiet this afternoon, and having four kids in the house is too much for me today. Perhaps later this week.

Alice practiced this response.

T: (as Sally) But I was counting on you.

A: I feel I should say yes.

T: But say what you *want* to say.

A: O.K. I know, Sally, but maybe you could take the kids with you since it's not too cold out. I'm sorry, but today is impossible for me.

T: That was much better. How did you feel?

A: I'm not sure I could do it again.

T: Let's try.

As Alice tried again, her voice became firmer, she began to maintain eye contact, and her manner began to command more respect. She still feared trying it out with the neighbor in real life.

T: What's the worst thing that could happen?

A: She'll never speak to me again.

T: What's there to lose? A friendship with a selfish person?

A: Gee, I never thought . . . er . . . I worry so much about my being selfish. I keep forgetting *they* are taking advantage. Oh, I'm so hopeless!

The homework assignments for the next few weeks were for Alice to practice saying "no" to neighbors and to report on her progress. She was also instructed to stop berating herself for less than perfect responding. Sessions were used to rehash her experiences, both the ones that had seemed effective and those that had worked out poorly. This constant feedback is essential to maintaining the new behavior.

As Alice was better able to deal with neighbors and relatives, work was undertaken on a similar situation—ending telephone conversations. Her neighbors had been calling Alice frequently to tell her their problems. She had always been willing to listen. Now that she could get out more, however, she felt too busy to talk on the phone. Again, initially Alice could not come up with an assertive response on her own. Again, the therapist needed to model "I'd like to talk more, but I have things to do. It's nice to talk to you, but I have too much work." Again, Alice worried that people would not call her if she were "rude" on the phone. She felt her friends would get angry or feel she didn't care about them. Alice was finally able to use the therapist's modeled responses in a strong, firm voice. The therapist congratulated her for the improvements. Close to tears, Alice remarked "I feel I get my passivity handed down from my mother. She didn't teach me anything—to drive, to swim, to stand on my own two feet—and now I have to be in therapy to learn these things." It was an emotional moment, and the therapist gave Alice a warm hug.

Marital Assertiveness

Preparing Alice for Couple Work. The previous work had prepared Alice to be more in touch with what she was feeling and what she would like to have happen. She was now able to be an accurate observer of the marital interactions and was more in touch with what she was experiencing. Her major complaint was that her husband was still "picking on her a lot," for example, he would walk in from work while she was making supper and remark what a mess she was making in the kitchen, or he would work late and be furious to find her sitting in bed with the children watching TV, commenting on her laziness. When Ted criticized her she immediately felt hurt and resentful, felt he didn't care, believed she should try to be a better housewife, and either withdrew (feeling badly about herself) or became weepy.

Alice was asked what she would like to have happen in the situations when Ted comes home from work and she feel criticized. What would she like him to do?

A: When Ted comes home I would like him to give me a kiss, relax, unwind, and let me do things my own way in the kitchen.

T: Tell him that. Let's role play Ted coming home and I'll play Ted.

A: This is hard. I'm not sure I can do it.

T: Let's try.

A: O.K.

T: (as Ted walking in the door) What a mess this place is.

A: er . . . er.

T: Tell him what you are feeling. Make an "I" statement.

A: er . . . Ted, I feel upset when you come in and harp on me.

T: That's really good. Your voice was firm, and I heard you. How did it feel saying it?

A: It felt good, but it's one thing to practice it here with you and another to deal with him at home. He's impossible, and I'm not sure he can really change dominating me.

After a few meager attempts at assertion at home, Alice seemed defeated and discouraged. I suggested that Ted come into our sessions. At first, Alice said such things as "He's too busy; he won't come. He sees the problem as mine. I'm the 'nut'." However, she agreed to talk to him (we role played this situation) and much to Alice's surprise, since she was so unused to initiation, expecting defeat, he very much wanted to come. However, Ted requested a session privately first, and Alice agreed.

Preparing Ted for Couple Work. Ted immediately congratulated the therapist for her "good work" with his "hysterical" wife. "I know she's been a handful for you" he stated. While there had been some improvement in the situation at home, he felt she still "grated" on his nerves. He came home from work, often late and exhausted, and instead of supper being totally ready, the house was a mess, the kids were running around, and he felt totally disgusted. He felt like screaming "Why am I with this woman who can't do anything right." He felt he was carrying everything on his shoulders, and he often started to harp on Alice. That made everything worse.

T: What else might you do?

Ted: Try to relax and let her get supper ready in her own way. Things usually work out if I can do that. Before she started therapy, I used to stay out late and just come home to sleep, but I don't want to do that.

T: What do you want for yourself?

Ted: I would like to tell her how burdened I feel. Everything is on my shoulders. I would like some comforting.

Ted knew what he felt and wanted, but he was also into blaming and avoiding direct expression of his feelings. It was easier for him to be critical than tell Alice what he wanted (This is often typical of traditional male/female relationships.)

Direct Expression and Listening. The therapist presented AT work to the couple as helping them understand something about their temperamental differences and communication styles. She pointed out that the wife's scatteredness and the husband's cool criticisms seemed to clash. The way in which they handled their differences might prevent their listening and willingness to communicate.

T: (To Alice) What do you want from Ted when he comes home?

A: I would like Ted to come home and leave me alone in the kitchen. He should either set the table, play with the kids, nap, read the newspaper, but not harp on me (in a slow, hesitant voice, looking at Ted, tearfully).

T: (To Ted) What would you like to have happen at dinner time?

Ted: I would like Alice to drop all the work in the kitchen and sit down and listen, let me tell her about my day, rather than rushing me with her accumulated problems while she's also rushing around trying to get supper ready. I would like to tell her how hard things are.

T: (To Ted) You're talking to me, not Alice. Tell her that.

(Ted repeated that he wanted more of a show of caring and listening, and talking. He was looking at Alice, and they hugged, and Alice cried.)

Further sessions involved working out specific assignments to talk about: child care, sharing discipline, how much time to spend with Ted's relatives, moving and so forth. It had now taken about 9 months of weekly work (not counting the initial work with Alice alone) to get this couple to begin to learn to communicate. The therapist felt at this point that she could fade out more, be available as a consultant and continue to help them set goals, and be available for support and feedback.

Change is slow and hard. Alice was still easily discouraged by setbacks. In some sense, she still expected to get little, felt Ted did not want to stop dominating her, and still called the therapist for support and help in minor crises. Still, she struggled, and 2 years later she had changed a lot. Alice now moves about the city more independently, is enrolled in a community college, handles her children better, and seems happier and looks better. She has also worked with the therapist on dealing with her weight. At least she now knows more about herself and is able, most of the time, to hold her own with Ted. Ted feels more listened to and taken care of and is, therefore, less critical. What they can express is the fact they care and that helps a lot. The work continues.

Case Study: Hal

At the beginning of treatment, Hal was further along than Alice in knowing what he felt and wanted. However, he had trouble in being direct and open about expressing himself. His style of communicating was, as he aptly described it, "wishy-washy." Assertiveness training involved working on his taking the risk of being direct, providing training in constructing scripts and dialogues, and providing structured practice with supportive feedback.

Background

Hal was a tall, slim 25-year-old whose tenseness lent a sharp quality to his good-looking features. He was an only child who had lived at home in the suburbs of New York until he finished graduate business school. An accountant, he had been living alone in the city for the past 3 years. He was still very close to his parents, particularly his mother, visiting home weekly for dinner. He described his mother as the "boss" of the family and his father as a "worrier" who rarely initiated anything.

Presenting Problem

Hal came into therapy for a depression of 2-months duration that he connected to the breakup of a relationship with a woman. A neighbor of his parents had recommended the therapist. Hal stated that he needed "assertiveness training" and that he had read several popular books about it before contacting the therapist, although he was not sure that his problem "fitted." He reported no problems at work. Indeed, he had recently passed his CPA exam and was under consideration for the position of assistant treasurer in his small firm. His major problem was in relationships with women.

Behavior During the Initial Interview

Hal sat stiffly, holding his hands clenched tightly in his lap or at his sides. He waited for the therapist to initiate questions. When responding, he had trouble maintaining eye contact, and he barely opened his mouth while speaking. He spoke breathlessly, and often his sentences petered out and his voice became barely audible. His depression was most apparent by the hesitancy with which he spoke, occasional deep sighs, and the self-deprecating quality of his statements about himself.

Hal was asked to describe his last relationship. He had dated Lois, a nurse, regularly for about 6 months. At first, he said, everything was fine; they were sexually turned on to each other, and they liked to do such things as play tennis together. But after a few months of seeing each other two or three times a week, Lois seemed to give him excuses whenever he wanted to see her, and they dated less frequently. Finally, without warning, 2 months previously, she had announced that she had met someone else and didn't want to see Hal anymore. He had handled this announcement by not saying anything. He had felt very hurt, humiliated, and puzzled. "It was pretty stupid of me not to see she was getting turned off." It had happened to him before.

Since that time, he had been lonely, depressed, and hadn't wanted to try to go out again. He had even tried getting a roommate. That was a "disaster," with the guy moving out still owing him money. He felt it was "now or never" for getting help for his problems, and he felt so awful he had asked his parents' help in finding a therapist.

When pressed for further details about other relationships and the types of women to whom he is attracted, Hal reported that he usually would stick to one relationship at a time. They generally lasted from 3 to 6 months, "starting out great, madly in love, and then I always seem to get hurt." He described women who interested him as exciting, energetic, bright, liberated. When asked if he had heard any complaints about his behavior, he admitted that Lois had mentioned a "lack of spontaneity." Hal was worried that he might be "boring."

Assessment of the Problem (Sessions 1 to 3)

To begin the assessment, Hal responded to some of the items from the Wolpe-Lazarus (1951) questionnaire. It revealed that he was inclined to be overapologetic, would find it difficult to begin a conversation with a stranger, would keep quiet for the sake of peace, and would smother his feelings rather than express resentment. Generally, the pattern that emerged strongly was one of fearing to take risks, particularly where doing so might incur displeasure. In exploring Hal's assertiveness problem, the therapist was struck by Hal's speech: it was long winded, imprecise, and, in fact, boring. Since it was clear that he was fairly globally nonassertive, it was decided to pinpoint specific situations for further work. Hal was given a self-monitoring sheet modeled after Colter (1976)

At the next two sessions, Hal brought in a very detailed sheet covering problematic interactions over two weeks. From the discussion of these situations, the following problematic areas emerged:

Behaviors: Hal is accommodating, doesn't like "to make waves," sits back and lets others take charge. He has a deficit in open expressiveness, communicated indirectly so that it is hard to tell what he means. He has a tendency to be indecisive.

Feelings: Most of the time Hal is in touch with feeling sad, depressed, anxious, tense, drained of energy. He is not yet aware of his resentments and angry feelings.

Cognitive factors: Hal wants to be the "nice guy" who is liked. He has strong fears of rejection, of risking displeasure, of other's anger.

Self-evaluation: Hal continually puts himself down and calls himself "wishy-washy" when he is unassertive. He does praise himself for positive assertive attempts and successes.

Hal kept his self-monitoring form almost like an accountant's careful ledger. He made meticulous notes, filling sheets with elaborate detail. In view of his problem with spontaneity, the therapist discontinued his keeping formal self-monitoring records beyond the assessment period. Hal was already looking at himself too objectively and weighing each remark he made too critically.

Behavioral Assessment (Session 3)

Since Hal had read several books on AT and used some of the language from the literature, the therapist asked for some sample role-plays of nonassertive, aggressive, and assertive responding to try to further clarify the problem. Hal was asked to role play the situation discussed in the group session previously: a partner coming home late at night and the other partner expecting him earlier and having dinner ready. In the role-play it was clear that Hal was particularly confused on the distinction between nonassertive and assertive.   When he tried to respond nonassertively, passive aggressive features predominated. He gave indirect digs like "What a nice night it is to sit by the window, lucky there's nothing else to do but wait for you to walk down the street before dinner gets put in the oven." This was spoken with a smile and in a placating manner. When Hal tried to act assertively, he was also indirect, never stating directly what he felt or wanted, and tending to blame his partner. There was also a striking absence of "I" statements.

Assertive Training: Communication Style (Session 4)

Hal was instructed to bring in a problem related to his "wishy-washy" style. He selected the situation with his ex-roommate who had moved out and left him in the lurch. A tape recorder was used as he described the situation:

H: He left me . . . er . . . holding the bag. And that . . . er . . . was 2 months ago. He would pay me his . . . er . . . share of rent. He was supposed to . . . er . . . pay me until I found another roommate. But . . . um . . . he moved out and didn't give me any money. I . . . er . . . talked to him about a week later, asked how his parents were doing, and he said . . . oh . . . I'm really hard up now. Can I give you $40? He owes me $150 and . . . er . . . he is working. And so I said . . . er . . . O.K., I understand. Then I didn't hear from him again, and finally two weeks ago I . . . uh . . . wrote him a note.

T: Could you tell me what was in the note?

H: In the note, I . . . er . . . said I know you've been busy and I know your family has been a major concern, but, you know, if you recall, you said (voice barely above a whisper) you would pay me the rent. You would pay me the rent, so please let me know what the story is and send it to me in . . . er . . . batches if you . . . er . . . can't give it to me all at once.

T: How would you rate that as an assertive letter?

H: Maybe a . . . er . . . two on a scale of one to five. I guess I could have come on much stronger. I thought to myself, well, rather than call . . . er . . . that's what I could have done, I'll write him a letter. But I guess it's pretty wishy-washy.

T: I want you to get in touch with what you do that is wishy-washy. Are you comfortable listening to this tape now with me?

H: Yes (fidgits in chair).

The tape is replayed

H: Gee, it sounds so wishy-washy. Er . . . I was so evasive, like I kept stalling. Gee, it's awful hearing how I sound (begins to slump into chair).

T: This is very hard. To listen to your voice and get feedback. You're doing fine. Do you want further feedback?

H: Yes.

T: Well, it was good that you were able to raise the issue and you were persistent. But you could focus more on yourself. You're into your roommates structure and problems. "How's your family, I know you're busy." Where are you and your agenda? Second, while you were persistent and as you mentioned it takes you a while to get to the point, but when you do, instead of saying I want my money now, you give him an out. Third, it could be better to begin with your request, also you put the whole burden on him, and part of the wishy-washyness is the plea for him to take care of you—"you promised," and so forth. You need to work on what *you* would like him to do.

H: Wow, I can see all that now.

T: What do you really want?

Hal: I feel that the ball is in his hands. If he can't pay, at least give me a straight story.

T: You let him have the ball. Why not put it in your hands. What would you like to say to him?

H: Listen, Jim. You made these promises before you moved in, signed a lease with me (voice starts to waiver). You definitely said you would give me at least 2 months rent . . . er . . . (looses breath, voice peters out).

T: Is that what you really wanted to say to him?

H: Yeah.

T: That sounds like pleading again. You said you'd do it and now you won't. It seems to me that you are unwilling to take a risk. Stay with your feelings and state what you want. What do you feel?

H: I'm exasperated . . .

T: Take a deep breath, relax, and then express that. Tell him what you want.

H: (In a stronger, firmer voice) I want a large sum that is due to me (bursts out laughing. The laughter is not unusual as a first breakthrough. It often serves as a release and it is encouraged).

T: Let's continue.

H: (Takes another deep breath). Er . . . er . . . you know, we're not talking about nickels and dimes here. It's a substantial amount of money (begins speaking more decisively).

T: Be more direct. Take a deep breath and begin.

H: I want my money now (laughs aloud). I would like this money and would like it now.

T: Say it again.

H: I want you to sit down and write me a check (slightly waivering voice).

T: Now say it to me as your exroommate. Could you please sit down right now and write me a check.

(H. Repeats it over and over and begins to laugh.)

T: (Also laughing) How does that feel?

H: So much better.

T: Why?

(As Hal is laughing, he begins to choke.)

T: What are you choking on? You've just been firm and stayed with yourself. What did you start to feel?

H: God damn it. This guy gave me a damn runaround on this thing. Why can't he be a responsible adult?

T: What are you feeling now?

H: I don't know.

T: Are you feeling angry. I would be feeling angry at someone who gave me a runaround and made me stoop to begging them for the money. It's his responsibility to pay. Are you choking on anger?

H: Yes . . . er . . . you're right. I'm angry.

T: Can you say it?

H: Er . . . I'm . . . angry with you. No, I'm really annoyed that you didn't do me the courtesy of giving me the money, so pay me the money now (starts to look at his watch).

T: Do you want to be let off the hook?

H: Er . . . this is uncomfortable (begins to laugh again). In fact, it's good to realize I don't have to start swearing. I can just say I'm angry.

T: I guess it's hard for you to lay the cards on the table.

H: I'm afraid I'd be so angry and shaking and the words won't come out the way I want them to.

Since the time was up for this session, Hal was given a homework assignment: to review the tape and try to draft a letter or phone conversation for dealing with Jim. The therapist noted that laughing and choking suggest an area for further work: the release of strong feelings.

The following week, Hal came in with a script and reported a sense of relief and accomplishment at figuring out a way to handle this situation. He role played the situation over and over again with the therapist, coming up with various responses on the part of Jim. Finally, Hal felt confident in following through on this assignment and felt good about himself for doing it. What he got in touch with as work on this problem ended was his insecurity in exercising his power.

Work on Communication: Social Conversation

The previous work suggested that the therapy sessions were a good arena for direct work on Hal's communication style, but it might be easier to begin work in a less charged area than expressing anger. In the week following the successful confrontation with his exroommate, Hal reported that he had gone to a few parties over the weekend. However, what began to come back were some old problems. While talking to the therapist, he appeared excited, sitting on the edge of the chair; his hands were in his lap clenched together, his body was stiff, and despite his excitement, his lips barely moved while he was speaking. Hal stated that when he meets a new woman, he is often unsure as to how to begin the conversation. Should he say that he is an accountant or an assistant treasurer to be—which sounds better? He feels so lost when he goes to a party in New York. There are so many people; one has to do so much sorting and he isn't sure what the other person wants to hear. He is always trying to sound out the others and program himself to say or do the right thing. This creates tension until he finds the "right track." When the therapist asked what would be wrong in being himself and talking spontaneously, Hal said that it would make him too nervous and he worried about being boring.

The therapist then asked Hal to just start talking about anything—the weather. The goal was to try to shape up spontaneous speech and to understand more about what Hal does to inhibit conversational flow. The following was taped:

H: Er . . . heard on the radio . . . er . . . before I came into the session that there might be a storm . . . er . . . er . . . a lot of snow, maybe a blizzard coming . . . er . . . (looks at therapist, who is experiencing a plea for rescue).

T: Is that so?

H: Well, I heard them say that the . . . er . . . Farmer's Almanac . . . er . . . said this was going to be a hard winter.

T: Let's stop now. How are you experiencing this?

H: I'm worried about whether I'm doing this right, making it interesting enough, not sure what you want to hear.

T: It feels like you're not sure what I want to hear about the weather, so what's coming across is your tentativeness. I realize I haven't given you much, but what I miss is there's none of you in there. You tell me about the news, Farmer's Almanac, rather than, Gee, it'sure feels like snow today. How about doing that?

H: Er . . . I find that hard, might be wrong . . . er . . . surer about the other.

(During the tape-replay, Hal began to hear how worry slows him down.)

Exercises to Increase Spontaneity (Sessions 8 to 10)

Over the next few sessions we worked on some ways of helping Hal become less self-conscious. Exercises included talking to the therapist nonverbally. He was pretty inhibited, and it was hard for the therapist to do it too. This time together evoked a lot of laughter. The next step was talking gibberish. "I want you to express yourself in gibberish—any sounds or noises that are not words in any language you know. By talking in gibberish, you can express your feelings fully without getting stuck in causes, reasons, justifications, arguments, and so forth. As you get in touch with your feelings, let them flow into nonsense noises of gibberish" (Stevens, 1971).

Hal had never done anything like that before, and it was difficult for him to start. Again, the therapist revealed her own self-consciousness about doing this exercise, and after some initial hesitation Hal was able to do the exercise. He began to laugh more and showed more liveliness and verve than the therapist had seen in him previously.

Another exercise involved "telegrams." Since Hal was apt to be wordy, he was instructed to communicate only using words or short phrases, then single words for a minute, then gibberish, then sounds, then only words again, then phrases or short sentences, then complete sentences. He was asked to talk about what that experience was for him. Out of this exercise, Hal came to an awareness that he tended to think aloud. His hesitancy and pauses and long-windedness came from not taking the time to plan.

A final exercise in the series consisted of sentence completions of the following sorts: "I'm trying to give you the impression that _____. What I'm saying now is _____. I refuse to _____. I'm afraid you'll think I'm _____. If I went crazy right now I would _____. If I get angry with you I _____. I try to please you by _____". (Stevens, 1971, p. 204–205).

Risking Social Situations: Initiating Conversation

Since the therapist was beginning an on-going assertiveness group, Hal was asked to participate. The group turned out to be an excellent auxiliary to weekly treatment. During the first session, the group dealt with social anxiety (very much like the group discussed previously).

Hal was one of several volunteers who initiated a conversation. He was asked about the experience.

> H: When you announced the assignment, I felt anxious and when I went to approach someone . . . er . . . I felt my knees shake. I picked Phyllis because . . . er . . . she also was an accountant, and I felt it might be easier to talk to someone with similar interests. I felt good at this point.
>
> T: (To Phyllis) What was your experience in working with Hal?
>
> P: Well, it was good that you approached me Hal, but I felt once you did, I had to do all the work. You just stood there.
>
> T: (To Hal) What kept you from keeping the conversation up?
>
> H: I was worried that I might be boring her, or that I would get feed-back—worried—maybe if I told her too much about myself I might get rejected.

From that exercise in initiating conversation, Hal was led into taking some risks with strange women and into trying to make a conversation flow while they did not respond or seemed turned off. This exercise engaged the whole group. Some inhibited people can actually be quite funny and creative playing these roles. As Hal began, he immediately said "I don't know how good this is going to be," then caught himself and laughed with the group.

> H: Nice party.
>
> Woman: Oh, I don't think so. I think I'll go get a drink.
>
> H: Er . . . er . . . I'll get you a drink . . . er . . . my name is Hal (woman walks away).

As Hal stood in the middle of the "rejecting" group, he experienced that "maybe it's not so bad." Then the group shared with him their own experiences and feelings around rejection, with everyone agreeing that to be alive, one has to risk. In later sessions, Hal reported that this particular exercise was a turning point in his therapy and helped him to do further risk taking.

Behavior Rehearsal: Persistence in Dealing with Evasive Woman Friend

At the end of the third month of treatment, Hal now appeared more relaxed and at ease within the therapy sessions. He had been practicing Yoga daily, could move his body more freely, and was more expressive non-verbally. He opened his mouth more, and his conversation was more fluent. Still, there was much work to be done. Hal had begun dating again, and after a few dates with the young woman, Peggy, she began to be less interested in seeing him. Hal brought the situation to the attention of the therapist, who had him plan the conversation he was planning to have on the phone that evening.

H: Er, I'd like to see you next week.

T: (As Peggy) Er . . . I'm so busy. I have so much work to do.

H: (With some irritation in his voice) That's nonsense. No matter how busy one can always find time if one wants to do it (somewhat louder, less defeated voice tone and stance).

T: What's happening?

H: I'm not sure!

T: I experience us as arguing. Also, you're being indirect. You say "one" when you mean "you" and again, you're into her structure. However, most importantly, it seems like a tug of war. Let's try it again.

(We see an interim stage of AT development. Before, Hal was fearful of putting out his wants, now that he is more direct, he needs help in going a further step.

T: Make a suggestion to get beyond this tug of war.

H: Peggy, I'd really like to see you this week.

T: (As Peggy) I'm so busy, have so much work to do this week, term paper due next Monday. I'm way behind in correspondence, and my mother may be coming in sometime this week for dinner. Maybe . . . er . . . in 2 or 3 weeks from now if I can breathe, I can find some time.

T: What are your feelings—like I'd like to believe her—yet feel I'm getting the runaround. Let's continue.

H: I'm under a lot of pressure too. But surely we can find some time this week to get together. It's just a matter of deciding that you want to.

T: (As Peggy) I really want to see you—no question about that. Just don't know when to find the time.

H: I think you can find the time. How about if I just come . . . er. . . . drop in, or call you and see if you'd like to go out for coffee or a drink. It doesn't have to be that long.

T: (As Peggy) O.K., give me a call. I'm not making any promises.

T: (To Hal) How did that feel?

H: Somewhat better. At least I made a suggestion and eventually stopped the tug of war. I still don't feel satisfied somehow.

T: If she continues to be evasive, we have to do more work on your directly stating what you want and asking her where she is at.

H: That will be hard! I guess I'd feel hurt, and don't want to really hear her reject me. But I think I can take that risk.

Risking Direct Communication: Confronting the Therapist

Around the 15th session, Hal announced, "Er, I've been thinking. I want to work more on my own, would like to come only twice a month—a lot of progress so far, and I'm in the group. It's expensive and I need time to practice. Besides it's close to tax time, and I'm busy at work." Hal did not look at the therapist while talking, his breathing was shallow, his voice petered out, and his hands shook while he said this. He continued "Er . . . so, if it's O.K. with you and fits into your schedule, I would like to come, maybe not every week.

T: What are you feeling right now when you are telling me this?

H: (Still no eye contact) Er . . . tense. Maybe you're not going to like what I'm saying—your income.

T: Can you look at me? I'm experiencing you as wishy-washy again. You worry a lot. You could have stopped a long time ago. Now tell me directly, and try to look at me.

H: Er . . . well, I've made lots of progress. And I now feel I would like to work on my own, so would like to come only every other week. Is that O.K.?

T: How did that feel?

H: It felt good to say it short and to the point.

T: You are right about making progress, and I can see that every other week with the weekly group sessions seems like a good plan, but how about if I resist? What will happen? Do you care to try it?

Hal agreed and repeated that he wanted to cut down individual sessions to twice a month.

T: Well, I could see how you might feel that way, but I feel our work has just begun. You are in a new relationship, and the same problems are occurring and you're still having problems dealing with your mother, not to mention problems at work.

H: Well . . . er . . . I feel I've made a lot of progress. Part of the reason I want to cut back is to work things out more on my own (voice starts to waiver).

T: What are you saying to yourself now?

H: That you have a good point there. I got into believing what you said, and I couldn't immediately think of a counter-argument, so I lost my center.

T: What else could you have done?

H: Well, as you've taught me, I could have said . . . er . . . wait a minute, let me collect my thoughts, or I'll think about it. Let's try it again!
Er, well, I feel I made a lot of progress. I've been studying people and how they talk and . . . er . . . interact. And I've been feeling good about . . . er . . . the way I've been able to converse better. And I will still be doing more work here. So let's try it.

Both Hal and the therapist broke into a smile, and the therapist was able to convey nonverbally her praise and acceptance of Hal's fine progress.

Hal continued in a group for the rest of the year and maintained biweekly sessions for about 6 months. By the end of therapy, he was feeling better about himself, more energetic, lively, and more confident in sustaining conversation and contact with people important to him.

Case Study: Angela

Angela's case illustrates the problem of how to maintain assertive responding while strong feelings are being held in check. Like Hal, Angela worried about herself and occasionally, like Alice, she was out of touch with her feelings. She was more able than the others to assert herself, but she feared losing control of her feelings; she worried particularly about maintaining control of her anxiety while responding assertively. In this, Angela is typical of many contemporary women seen in practice in New York, women who in trying to transcend aspects of the stereotypically "feminine" role fear any show of dependency, vulnerability, anxiety, or irrationality.

Background

Angela looked somewhat older than her 26 years, although she dressed in a skirt, sweater, and boots with her dark hair worn long and straight and no make-up, like a college student. She held a Ph.D. in biology and was working as a University research assistant. A single woman, she was living alone in New York after having attended college and graduate school out of town. Angela was the eldest of two daughters from a first-generation working-class family. Achievement pressures from her family had been strong. Angela described her mother as domineering, critical, and perfectionistic. "She was always putting my father and sister down and holding me up as the perfect child." She also remembered her mother as hysterically out of control with crying and outbursts of temper. Angela had learned to placate her mother by "not making waves," which meant being the good, achieving child. She was never allowed to "really" express herself. In fact, she vividly remembered once trying hard to keep her feelings hidden but being punished by her mother for making faces. Angela's father provided a different role model of calmness and reasonableness, although occasionally he had violent outbursts that terrorized everyone. Thus the familial communication message came through strongly to Angela: Feelings are bad. I don't want to lose control of them. I don't want to be like my mother—hysterical. I must be a good girl. Mild anxiety for Angela conjured up the possibility of getting out of control. She then panicked and fled from situations where anxiety might arise.

Presenting Problem

Angela was an emergency referral with a presenting problem of public-speaking anxiety. As a scientist, she had particularly sought out a research position that required no teaching. She had worked in the laboratory out of the limelight. Now, her supervisor, a prominent biologist, insisted that she begin to attend a biweekly staff meeting and present some of her research findings to the group. Additionally, in 6 weeks, she was to substitute for him at a professional meeting to present a paper on the work of the project.

Behavior During the Initial Interview

Angela's face was almost expressionless, except for an occasional, nervous flicker of a smile. She sat rigidly against the back of the chair, occasionally twiddling her fingers. Although she faced the therapist, for most of the session she studiously looked to the side at a wall of books. Her voice quivered noticeably, and her hands trembled, but overall her demeanor was one of keeping a cool front. She noticed "feminist" books and stated that she "already felt better." Yet her quick trust in the therapist did not establish close contact. Her sidewise glance gave a remoteness to her manner of relating. On practical matters such as the fee and in discussing the treatment strategy, she asked no questions and raised no objections.

Assessment of the Assertiveness Problem

In view of the emergency nature of the referral (Angela had 2 weeks to get ready for the informal conferences and 6 weeks for the major presentation), work on assessing the performance anxiety was undertaken immediately. For anxiety states, the therapist routinely begins with hierarchy construction and relaxation training. In ascertaining when Angela was tense and relaxed, it became clear that she was out of touch with her own body. She was not sure where her tensions were and if she were ever really relaxed. It was clear that anticipatory anxiety was one of the major components of her problem, but her reactions during the actual presentation could not be predicted. Consequently, she was asked to bring in material for an informal speech. Angela was frantically worried about what to bring in and arrived at the session highly anxious. Yet she did well in giving the sample speech, and although she was slightly stiff and her delivery stilted, her anxiety did not show.

When asked to describe what the experience had been like, Angela said she had worried a lot about her worries. She believed she must be cool and generally can be cool once in a situation. The problem was all the worrying beforehand. Also, if she felt well prepared, she knew she could function well, but she still was worried that she might not be able to deal with any questions or surprises that might come from the audience.

Treatment for Speech Anxiety

From the preliminary interviews, it became clear that the standard treatment for speech anxiety was not enough for Angela's problem. In addition to relaxation and desensitization, she needed help in shaping up responses to possible questions or comments from the audience and to deal with the anxiety related to this uncertainty. So the first stage of treatment involved having her bring in situations or questions that the members of the audience might ask and having her field these (Angela was seen two to three times a week during this time). With the therapist throwing questions at her, she became increasingly anxious. Again, when asked what she was saying to herself, she said "I'm worried that the audience will see how anxious I am, or how little I know, or that I'm not prepared." Angela most feared being the helpless female or getting out of control like her mother. Her worst fear was that she might become hysterical and cry on stage when attacked or criticized.

The next stage of treatment involved work in relaxation procedures and involved shaping up openness in admitting that she couldn't have all the answers: also, work on admitting that she was anxious to herself and that it was all right to let others see that she was anxious. At this point, Angela stated that she felt she could never be comfortable letting others see her anxiety, since men didn't show anxiety. (We then got into a discussion about whether or not men felt anxious.) Angela commented that all the men she knew seemed so "cool." She was asked to interview men she knew about how they felt in similar situations and discovered similar fears, much to her surprise.

It was further suggested that Angela join an on-going group the therapist was conducting for professional women. Several sessions were devoted to Angela and her problems. The women in the group were journalists, college professors, psychologists, and lawyers struggling with similar issues. (The problem of a woman lawyer experiencing similar problems prior to her first courtroom trial was helpful for Angela.) Does a woman have to adapt the male style of coolness under fire? Does a woman have to be tough during the answer period? Does she have to be perfect? The group collectively worked with Angela on what she could say when asked a difficult question and came up with such statements as "Let me collect my thoughts. That's an interesting question, I'm not sure, what do you think about that data?" Gradually with help from the group, relaxation procedures, a few sessions of desensitization, and a lot of behavior rehearsal, Angela was able to adapt a more natural style for her presentations.

Phase II: Beginning Social Contact

Once Angela had successfully given her speech, she began to talk about being ready to deal with not being so afraid of men. During this phase of treatment, the therapist saw Angela once a week for 1-hour sessions.

Angela had avoided most social contact with males. Initially, she was afraid she wouldn't know what to talk about. From role playing initial conversations, her fear of rejection and feelings of being unattractive and not "sexy" emerged. She agreed to go to a half-day AT workshop run by the therapist. Once she saw that other people had similar problems and following some practice in initiating conversations with men, Angela took the risk of attending socials and began to go out with men. Early AT scripts centered on her insistence on paying her own way and handling male sexual pressures.

As Angela began to go out more comfortable and learned how to deal with closer contact with people and her sexuality, she signed up for additional workshops, including one on sexual enhancement for women. At this point, summer vacation came. Angela felt she had gained tremendously and was ready to stop therapy. (She had been seen for seven months.)

Phase III: Maintaining Assertive Responding in an Intimate Relationship

About mid-October, the therapist received a frantic call from Angela. She was very upset and needed help. She was madly in love. This time, in contrast to her first unemotional interview Angela cried and said she was depressed and unhappy. She looked it. She had thought she had met the perfect man—good looking, brilliant, intellectually stimulating—a professor at a medical school. He had come on strong. Even sex was good after her initial fears. She did not know why he liked her, but he did, and she had become so preoccupied with the relationship she could barely function. This was the first time she had ever let herself go so. She reported him to be very domineering, critical, and selfish, and she felt so dependent that she served herself up to him. In telling this, Angela starts to cry, commenting "That's some predicament for a feminist."

Assessment

Angela was requested to self-monitor typical interactions that upset her, paying special attention to what he was saying to her, what she felt like saying or doing and what she actually did, and how she felt afterwards.

In a week, she brought in a long list of situations and said that the monitoring was an eye opener. "Why he's a typical male chauvinist pig! How did I get into this?" Examples from Angela's self-assessment follow:

1. She had to work late and rushed home to get dressed. Tom was kept waiting a few minutes and commented as they went out the door about her inconsiderateness. She felt like crying, but said nothing.

2. They went to a party. A lot of her friends were there, and she spent a lot of time with them. He seemed bored and told her they had to leave, and while she wanted to stay longer, he wanted to go home. She was feeling irritated, but didn't say anything. The previous week when the situation was reversed, they ended up staying on for at least a few more hours. (When questioned, it turns out she did not make a strong case for leaving and only now felt irritated at the inequity.)

3. Saturday, she had cleared the whole day to be with him at his place. First he went to work in the morning and then spent the afternoon on the phone. She tried to tell him how she felt, and he said she was being impossible and inconsiderate.

4. One night, they went out to dinner with some friends, and he made a

comment about her hair looking awful down and suggested she put it up. (She immediately complied, even though she does not like to wear it up.)

5. He told her not to wear pants with his friends. He wanted her to be "more feminine" and "stylish."

6. The cleaning woman was at her house yesterday, and in the evening when he visited, he casually commented about the dust on the dresser, and she felt like she had to apologize for not supervising the woman more.

7. On Wednesday, he made some comment about the way she was loading the dishwasher, and she began to cry and then was called touchy or hysterical. She was a wreck when she had to cook for him; he was quick to find flaws.

8. In bed, when she went to give him a massage, he commented that her fingers were not pressing hard enough.

It became apparent from the long list of small things that Angela felt continually anxious about when a criticism might be sprung on her. She feared telling him how she felt because she worried that he might be angry and leave her. Losing him would be terrifying to her since she was so emotionally attached. She felt since it was so hard for her to begin going out, this might be her only chance at a relationship.

Risks of Assertiveness Training for this Class of Problems

In changing, Angela had to face the risk of her male friend not accepting the change and the possibility of the relationship being terminated. If this happened, Angela might be in for even more misery—that of getting over losing a relationship and being lonely. The risks were spelled out to Angela. She still felt she wanted to change, since she was so miserable now and also feeling badly about herself for not knowing what else to do. We proceeded in this case. In a beginning relationship there is more room to explore the possibility of change and for Angela to look elsewhere if she cannot get what she wants from Tom. The situation is more complex, if we are dealing, for example, with a married woman, who is economically and emotionally dependent and whose social status is dependent on her staying in the relationship. If she has started off compliant and subservient, she may be risking more than Angela by changing. In this case, we proceed more cautiously, spelling out risks along the way, and may try to involve the husband in this work, providing support for his changing as well.

Assertiveness Training

We select one of the situations from the list that was recurrent and bothered Angela.[3] There are two issues here: First, to learn how to stand up for herself and risk displeasing Tom; and second, to learn how to respond when she is feeling dependent, needing love and fears even further loss of control. (The second problem is similar to her problem with controlling anxiety while speaking in public.)

Situation: Put Your Hair Up. Angela wants the right to wear her hair as she pleases and for Tom to accept her decision. She selects that situation to work on. Angela coaches the therapist to play Tom. The following role play occurs.

T: (As Tom) Angela you look nice tonight, but you know we are going to a special party at the Plaza, and I want you to look terrific. When you wear your hair up, it's so elegant. So please go in and take care of it (playfully putting her hair up for her).

A: Yes, it looks better that way (smile on her face).

T: What are you feeling? What are you saying to yourself?

A: Maybe he's right. What right does he have to tell me how to wear my hair? Oh, I'm so confused, and I worry about crying and making things worse. Also, it's one thing to do it here, and another in the situation when my feelings are churning even more.

T: O.K., let's do it again. This time try to stand up for you, what you want.

T: (As Tom) Put your hair up.

A: (Starting to cry) Stop criticizing me. You're always picking on me. I went to the beauty parlor today, and I thought I looked O.K. Aren't you even pleased? (Loses control and sobs.)

T: How would Tom respond?

A: Probably he would hug and reassure me, although more recently, as we're having more of these hassles, he says "Oh, God, why do you have to be so impossible? I'm only trying to help you look better." He sounds contemptuous.

(Angela was now too upset to go on, and seemed paralyzed to come up with a response.)

---

[3]In emotionally charged situations, it is often best to find the simplest, least complex situation to begin practice on. We are less likely to get side tracked, and the problems in maintaining assertive responding will usually surface with any prototypical situation.

T: Let's get in touch with your goal. What do you want?

A: I want to tell him I like my hair this way.

(The therapist models a response for her and suggests a role reversal with Angela as Tom.)

T: (As Angela) I really feel my hair looks good this way. I've had it done today, and when it's down and set it feels right with the long dress and these earrings.

A: (As Tom) Well, I think it ought to go up. It's more elegant that way and shows off the good bones in your face.

T: (As Angela) I'm upset that you don't allow me to wear my hair as I please. I told you I feel good about myself now, and I feel you are being critical. We have a problem here. Do I have to do everything that suits you?

A: Gee, while playing Tom's role and having you stand up for yourself, I feel on the defensive. I never saw before that my not standing on my ground gave him permission to keep this up.

T: What are you afraid of? What might happen if you resist?

A: That he would stop loving me.

T: Is that all?

A: No, that he might yell at me. Sometimes I feel like he's yelling and I'd do anything to get him to stop.

T: Let's try this again. What are you feeling now about the situation?

A: I'm starting to feel resentful—that he treats me like a child.

T: What would you like to tell him?

A: To let me be (this time she's not smiling and her voice reflects her rising anger).

T: Anything else?

A: Wow, my cheeks are burning. I guess I'm really getting angry at him and feeling it for the first time. Wow, I guess I would like to tell him that . . . that . . . his harping is making me angry.

T: It's good that you are able to focus on how you are feeling. However, it would be better if you could make an "I" statement. It sounds too much like blaming, the other way.

A: God, there are so many things to focus on.

T: Take a moment to get in touch with what you're feeling. Take a deep breath. Now try to construct a script in your head, and take another deep breath before beginning. Are you ready?

A: Yes, I'm . . . er . . . getting tired of your harping on me, I would like it if you let me be.

T: Now I'll play Tom. What might he say? (Angela makes a suggestion.) (As Tom) I'm tired of your resisting suggestions. I'm only trying to help you look better.

A: I don't find it helpful. It makes me feel like a child.

T: (As Tom) Well, I still think you look better with your hair up.

T: What's happening?

A: I guess we are arguing, which is what I really expect to happen if I stand up to Tom. Wow!

Angela can not approach expressing herself while remaining aware of her partner's attitude. Work begins on how to compromise.

Angela is given a homework assignment to select a few of the problematic situations, write some scripts in advance, compromise in other areas, and yield in some others. We spend the next three sessions going over this material. (Angela is now coming again twice a week during this crisis.) She is also assigned some readings including a rereading of "Your perfect right" again (Alberti and Emmons, 1970).

Learning to Compromise

Angela comes into the sessions over the next few weeks feeling very discouraged. All they seem to be doing is fighting. Angela reports that Tom does not want her to change. She is asked to replay with the therapist a recent argument. From the enactment of the situation, it appears that Angela and Tom are entrenched in a power struggle. Tom is resistent to hearing what Angela is saying or following her suggestions. Angela tries to compromise, but more typically, keeps insisting that she is right and is angry at Tom for not accepting her point of view. They both fight until Angela breaks down into tears, which provides a way out since Tom immediately responds to comfort her, and then Angela feels worse. She likes the cuddling, but hates herself for giving in. An additional problem is that Angela is looking to Tom for praise for her assertive skills and instead receives attacks or comments that she is aggressive.

Again, we try to select a recurring situation to work out a compromise. It is suggested that Tom come in for couple work, but he resists. Angela begins to stop insisting that Tom see that she is right, instead pointing out how upset or frustrated she feels about the power struggle. She is also encouraged to stroke herself after assertive responding and not look toward others. After about 6 weeks, Angela sadly comes to the conclusion that the relationship is causing too much misery for the small amount of "making" up pleasure she gets. She now believes that Tom would rather have her docile and submissive in spite of what he says to the contrary and may not be able to yield the power necessary for a more equalitarian relationship. Angela does not want to be the sort of woman Tom seems to want. She begins to see and hear what he wants and decides to end the relationship.[4] More work involves saying goodbye.

Dealing with Disappointment

For the next month, assertiveness training came to a standstill and we dealt with the disappointment. Angela was often depressed, cried a lot during the sessions, and often the therapist was just there to provide comfort.

As Angela became less depressed, she was willing to rehash the situation with the therapist. She was encouraged to articulate just what she was still holding on to and what she still wanted from Tom as a way of finally saying goodbye. Angela reported being most angry that Tom who said he loves her wouldn't change. She wanted him to admit that it was his fault that the relationship didn't work. As Angela allowed herself to become enraged, she became anxious worrying that if she expressed her anger she would become just like her mother whom she describes as an hysterical shrew, looking like a witch with her long dark hair and bushy eyebrows. Again, this problem is similar to the fear of loss of control of anxiety, only this time Angela allowed it to emerge. Angela's response is not untypical of many "nice, good girls" who "smile through their tears." Once they begin to experience their anger, it is very frightening to them.

Training in Acceptance, Expression, and Control of Anger

As a stage in learning how to accept and modulate angry feelings, Angela needed help in accepting these feelings as all right so that she could better learn to express and control them. She also needed to learn more about what she did to suppress angry feelings. Self-assessment revealed that she talked herself out of petty annoyances as well as real resentments. Angela intellectually believed she shouldn't feel angry. The result often related to feeling hurt or defeated. Most of the situations that Angela reported from studying her interactions with others centered around what

---

[4] With a couple like this, who are into power struggles, sometimes helping them learn to see that they are both enjoying the struggling and helping them to be comfortable with it might be useful. But in this case Angela was too frightened and upset, and Tom was still too dominating for them to take a step back and look at the struggle another way.

she felt to be "injustices" or situations in which she felt she was being dominated and not allowed to express herself (a similar pattern to the issues involving Tom).

To further evaluate anger expression, a Gestalt exercise was used. The therapist played a "parent," shaking a finger and scolding a child. Angela was asked to respond resistively in any way she could. Angela hardly moved her body. All she could think of was to shake her finger back at the therapist with a few yells of "no, I won't" thrown in. Facial gestures were also restricted. When given feedback, Angela admitted that she couldn't even think of what to do. When the therapist modeled some behaviors (e.g., kicking, sticking one's tongue out, grimacing), Angela became aware that she had never been allowed to ever do such things.

Thus the next stage of treatment (always working toward the goal of appropriate assertive responding in expressing resentments) was work on training anger. We followed techniques developed by Palmer (1972), where Angela was taught to grimace, growl, show her teeth, make angry sounds and so forth. In a tug of war with a towel Angela was to show her strength and demand in a loud voice "Give it to me." In group we tried out these exercises, and Angela began to see this work as fun. She showed a playfulness for the first time in therapy.

As Angela learned to be more in charge of her hostile feelings, she reported being less preoccupied with the relationship with Tom, began to report feeling her "old energy" again, and was ready to begin going out again.

Therapist Patient Interactions During the Course of Therapy

In the beginning of therapy, Angela was the "good girl," deferring and passive, who allowed the therapist to pace the sessions, never voicing annoyance or giving critical feedback. Toward the end of our work together, the therapist began to point out how she experienced these interactions. This was done carefully, since clients like Angela are often overly sensitive to feedback. Once the phone rang, and the therapist picked it up. Angela sat back in the chair, eyes downcast, not saying anything. When asked how she felt, she responded with a smile on her face that she figured it was an important phone call. When the therapist commented that she seemed too "nice," she admitted that she felt annoyed. Previously when an appointment had to be changed, Angela accommodated herself to the new schedule. Toward the end of therapy, she reported feeling "pissed" at the therapists lack of evening hours. She became persistent in insisting I find an evening time for her, and I listened and we compromised. It is important not to be defensive or upset as formerly meek patients practice critical skills on the therapist. They are often the only people with whom they can safely express anger. It is important for the therapist to be honest, let them know you understand how they feel. Sometimes it is important for the therapist to hold her own ground or to try to negotiate (in this example we found a late evening time that was feasible since Angela lived in the neighborhood). If we couldn't compromise, helping Angela deal with frustration might have been useful at this point.

Followup

Two years after termination of therapy, Angela has accepted an academic position. She feels more in control of her feelings and her life, viewing the therapy as helping her find her way as a nontraditional woman. She has continued to use peer group support, is still an active member of a CR group, and calls the therapist for consultation in crisis. She has also become involved with a man again, this time not allowing herself to fall "madly in love," but proceeding more cautiously. She believes that a more equalitarian relationship is possible with him.

Case Study: Bill

Introduction: From Angry to Assertive

Men much more often than women come for assertiveness training with problems of too much aggression or an inability to separate assertion and aggression. Rimm (1977) reports two types of anger problems: some patients show a characteristic pattern of over-control. They have been taught not to express anger, and they keep their anger in until it reaches volcanic proportions, at which point they may blow up, possibly engaging in violent behavior. Another pattern is under-control. A minimal instigation to anger results in virtually instant aggression. While women and some men need to be taught to express feelings (as in the case of Hal and Angela) and even to learn how to make angry sounds, most of the work on the other side is in helping people respond assertively to anger-producing cues. Bill's case illustrates how getting in touch with feelings (stages 1 and 2) and working on direct communication (stage 4) apply equally to the process of going from aggressive to assertive. It particularly exemplifies the process of maintaining assertive behavior while dealing with strong emotions (stage 6).

Background

Bill was a 42-year-old man with an athletic build. He held a responsible position as supervisor in a large public health agency and was an active volunteer in community work. Bill was the eldest son of a hard-working union leader in the building trades. His father rarely spoke to his children, but he encouraged the boys to be physically active and rough-housed a lot with them. Bill had generally felt good about his "masculinity" as he was growing up, and he saw his father as a "good, strong" person he wanted to emulate in almost every way, except for his father's temper tantrums. His father had rarely shown his feelings, but he had a terrific temper. He would occasionally go on a rampage through the house, breaking things, bullying his wife, and harrassing the kids. Bill's mother was given to a lot of moralizing. Her values included hard work, charitableness to the "underdog," and unselfishness.

Presenting Problem

Bill came into treatment at the suggestion of his wife. He came for help with a possible drinking problem and "temper outbursts," which he feared might wreck his career.

Behavior During the Initial Interview

Bill leaned forward, elbows on his knees, in a posture of eagerness to begin. He talked in a rush of words, moving around energetically, and gesticulating to emphasize points. He described his situation as follows:

T: What brings you to seek help at this time?

B: Well, I am assistant director at my agency and will probably get another promotion this year, maybe even become the director. I worry about my low frustration tolerance—occasionally let loose with a temper tirade and then feel awful. I'm afraid it's out of control and may wreck my career. Also, my wife, Sally is complaining that she's getting tired of my tantrums at home. I'm under a lot of tension at work, and after work I go out with a bunch of the guys, the staff we deal with, hassling agencies for money. Started to have a few drinks before I went home. Not sure if drinking is a problem or not, but now I need too many drinks to unwind in the evening and occasionally booze it up on the weekend. Not sure if I have a drinking problem.

T: How do you feel about the temper problem and the drinking?

B: Well, I hate myself for the temper. After all, I'm supposed to care so much for people, and yet the way I berate the people who work for me in the office, I'm ashamed. Also, I worry that Sally has had it. Certainly none of this makes me feel good about myself.

T: Could you tell me about your most recent tirade? Particularly what set if off? How you behaved, and what happened afterwards.

B: Well, we have this guy, Peter, who works under me, who never gets his work in on time. Had a grant application deadline, under pressure from my boss to apply, and he was supposed to do the necessary research and I was gonna do the writing. And I kept asking him for the material, and he kept putting me off, sort of avoided the issue. I couldn't look at him, we didn't talk, but I felt myself getting more and more angry. I didn't say anything. At first I said I wouldn't let this bother me. But I felt myself getting more and more angry as the deadline approached. Finally, the guy asked me to sign a form for a day off. He even had a valid excuse, and it was for sometime after the deadline. And I exploded and hit him with everything in the book.

T: What did you do exactly?

B: I yelled, ranted and raved, stamped my feet, cursed—I was totally out of control. And I couldn't stop it. I just went on and on. This guy ran out of my office, and I can see that he starts to badmouth me. And I feel that I handled it badly. Now he's gonna get revenge on me by screwing up the project, and everyone else will think I'm a nut and picking on him. I feel really shitty about the way I handled things when this happens.

T: What do you say to yourself when the situation is building up?

B: Well, I hold the feelings in—feel I shouldn't make a fuss, and then, Pow! It comes out, and I feel like a bad person. And at my age, I should know how to handle it better. I get anxious about it happening again. That's where I'm at now. The deadline's been extended, and this guy still hasn't done his work.

T: Is this a typical pattern of interaction—avoidance of dealing with the situation and then a blowup, out of control?

B: Yes.

On the basis of the self-assessment and during the next few interviews the following patterns were discovered:

Problematic Behaviors: Bill is over-controlled. He is often not aware of how angry he is until the situation builds up, and then he has his temper outbursts. Usually he becomes very anxious as the first clue that he is enraged. He is inconsistent. Sometimes, he is very accommodating and placid, and other times he is snappy and sarcastic. He avoids confrontations most of the time. He drinks heavily prior to blowing up or after blowing up.

Cognitive factors: Bill is very moral. He has a belief that people should live by the rules. He is often self-righteous. If he works hard, others should. Everything has to be just so. He is a perfectionist, yet he wants to be the good guy in the office. He wants others to like him and to appreciate what a good, caring person he is.

Self-Evaluation: Bill continuously evaluates himself, mostly negatively, and particularly berates himself for his temper. Self-statements: "I shouldn't be so upset. If I was really a good person, I shouldn't act angry." He rarely expresses positive feelings about himself.

Feelings: Bill is often out of touch with his feelings. He is unaware often of what he feels, confusing anxiety and irritation. Often he doesn't know he is angry until he is in a rage. He rarely feels good about himself.

Assertiveness Goals—Behavioral: The major goal was to help Bill get in touch with his irritations and annoyances earlier, to know what he feels and have these feelings be less pressing and more under his control. For example, work on saying statements like "I'm upset and angry that you have not submitted a report" early in the week, instead of blasting his coworker later.

Cognitive Restructuring: Work on belief systems, that is, his setting rules for everyone to follow, the world should be the way I want it, and when it is not I can't stand it, and so forth.

Other: Simultaneously with work on assertiveness issues, self-control procedures should be worked out for drinking behavior. Even though drinking and assertion issues are related, they generally have to be worked on separately, since drinking takes on its own set of patterns. (Many clients whose main presenting problem is heavy drinking or overeating have patterns of anger control similar to Bill's.)

To train Bill in direct behavioral expression, he was asked to select an ongoing problem. He brought in a situation with Peter to work on: Peter is late again and Bill would like to talk to him about it, instead of following his usual pattern of avoiding confrontations and blowing up later.

T: (As Peter) Hello, Bill (walking in late again). Got . . . got to get a new car. Took a half hour to get it started this morning (low voice, head down, slouched body posture).

B: Hello. I can't even think of what to say.

T: What are you feeling?

B: Anger.

T: What are you saying to yourself?

B: It isn't fair. Why should I have to have all the worry and responsibility and do all the hard work when this guy collects his salary for goofing off.

T: What would you like to do?

B: I don't know (has no response in his repertoire).

T: Let's try it again. Stay with your anger—express it.

B: Thanks for showing up (nasty voice tone, firm voice, eyes glaring).

T: (As Peter) Did you get up on the wrong side of the bed this morning?

B: (No response, disarmed.)

T: What would you like to do?

B: Slam him. Afraid of my anger. I can't even begin to role play.

T: What are you saying to yourself?

B: What's the use? What good will it do to get angry. It'll only make me feel worse.

T: Look at how you talk yourself out of a legitimate feeling.

(At this point, Bill was invited to attend a 1-day workshop before the next session.)

At the workshop a similar situation was raised by several other members. Bill volunteered to play the shirker and get in touch with what it feels like from the other side and the manipulation involved. He really got into the role.

Supervisor: (To an employee, who is late continuously, and whose work is overdue) I would like to discuss your work with you. Your reports are never in on time. You know we have to file these reports to the state at the end of the month, and half the time I end up doing your work.

Shirker: (Played by Bill) You don't understand all the problems I've been having (gives a long list of complaints).

Supervisor: (Listens but tries to press her point) I know you've had a lot of problems lately (but gets caught up in trying to protect the shirker as Bill continues with pressing his luck, voice waivers, indecisive).

Someone else role plays. The therapist suggests that if you can't deal with your feelings now, write out a script later.

New Supervisor: Look, I know you've had a lot of problems this fall, but we have a job to do in this office and you are not pulling your full share. It isn't fair that I who also have a lot of responsibilities often have to do your work and mine. I'm not sure what the problem is, but I think we should get together each Monday morning and go over your schedule for the week.

Bill as shirker tries to interrupt, but supervisor doesn't let him.

Supervisor: And if this problem continues, I will have to take it up with my boss. So, come in on Monday, and we'll go over the work plan.

(Bill was asked how it felt role playing with someone more like himself who is easily disarmed and this other firmer supervisor.

Bill: The other person was more like me. I felt I could put anything over on her. This guy was more centered. He knew that he had to face the consequences of what he was doing.

In the next session, Bill and the therapist replayed the roles, and Bill was able to incorporate some of the features that were modeled in the group and actually was able to carry out this task.

Bill demonstrated adequate assertive skills. He was so afraid of losing control of his anger that he sat on his feelings. During the new role playing in the following session, he was able to express his annoyance and still be reasonable and firm.

The next situation Bill brought up was the reverse—dealing with his boss. Bill was always the last one in his office to put in for vacation, raises, and so forth, and felt that he was too responsible to be taken advantage of.

T: What do you want to say to your boss?

B: I'm very upset, annoyed, irritated at the way you treat me, like my feelings don't matter, like I'm a nothing . . . a blob . . . nonentity. You miserable louse, good for nothing bastard. All you're interested in is yourself, your reputation, your career, money-grubbing, exploitation of other people (amazed at all the things that came out).

T: How do you feel?

B: Boy, that sure is hostile. That's . . . us . . . why I clam up.

T: Is there anything that you could tell him?

B: He wouldn't like to even hear mild criticism.

T: Who are you taking care of? Him or yourself?

B: I could never start anything. If I let the door open just a bit, the whole thing would blow out of control.

T: How do you rate yourself in the previous encounter?

B: Very angry.

T: O.K., let's go over why it's angry: one, hostile tone; two, blaming or attacking. Another try. Let's go over the Novoko self-statements for dealing with anger and see if we can learn another response (See Appendix III to VI, Table III; Novoko, 1975).

Gradually, Bill worked on modulating angry feelings, turning from a tirade to an expression of irritation, upset, and constructive comments for better working arrangements. This took about 2 months with many ups and downs.

Cognitive Restructuring for Self-Statements that Keep Bill Enraged

As Bill begins to get more in touch with his feelings as they occurred on a moment-to-moment basis, instead of tuning out, deadening himself and then being overcome by the feeling of rage, he begins to be aware of how angry he was most of the time. The following illustrates his awareness of these situations:

Bill began to be aware of how he was constantly getting himself irritated by small things and how low his frustration tolerance was. For example, if a cab driver splashed him in the street, he cursed at the car and couldn't stop burning. He described a recent incident in his building with his hands full of bundles going up the elevator with his neighbor. The neighbor walked out, and the door slammed as he was trying to get out. He was still so furious that he would not talk to his neighbor, and worried about how to control his feelings if they should meet in the elevator again. The situation lent itself to role-playing leaving the elevator.

B: Thanks a lot (nasty, hostile voice tone).
T: What are you thinking and feeling?
B: What sort of crumb is this woman? Can't she see I've got a bundle in my hand. I have to do everything myself. People just don't give a damn in this city. (has a hard time getting in touch with self-statements.)

Role playing the situation again, the therapist plays the neighbor in the elevator when the door slams.

B: Thanks a lot (nasty tone).
T: Thanks for what?
B: (Furious, actually role playing holding the bundles, brought up all the feelings of this situation that has kept him boiling for weeks.) Thanks a lot for helping your fellow man who had a handful of bundles, is exhausted, and just had a door slammed in his face.

T: Why didn't you ask me to help you? I would have held the door for you. I was lost in my own thoughts and didn't notice your situation.

B: I shouldn't have to ask? You should see! (By this point furious.)

Bill was overwhelmed by the insight that he expects other people to be mind readers and doesn't spell out his needs and wants. He felt it was obvious that he needed help, and he was in a fury because he felt no one cares. He selectively attended to negativity.

As he worked on these smaller, less important daily situations, he began to realize that the same patterns emerged in the work situation and in the relationship with Sally. He began to bring in situations from home. He comes home from work exhausted, irritated and aggravated that Sally's not there. And he wants supper now. It's her turn to cook. So he starts to drink, and the minute she walks in he explodes (saying to himself "If she really cared for me, she'd be there, and dinner would be on the table"). In the evening he gets into bed, and Sally is still doing some work. He gets angry when she doesn't come into bed when he's ready, yet he doesn't ask her to. When asked to do more monitoring of self-statements, he came up with the fact that he wants things his way: *He is* ready for bed now. What right does *she* have to work? He began to see how he was setting rules for people and when they didn't follow them, he was upset and felt they didn't care. He practices telling Sally what he wanted.

When I come home and you're not there, I get upset, I'd wish you'd let me know if you're going to be late.

It would be nice for us to go to bed together. I would like that. How do you feel about that? I'd love it if you'd rub my back. That feels good.

Without bringing Sally in, Bill was at least putting out what he wanted instead of withdrawing, sulking, or giving her the silent treatment and then blowing up. He and Sally were communicating more.

One issue that kept emerging was that Bill didn't really feel comfortable expressing what he wanted. He felt dependent and vulnerable and worried about rejection. More work in this area was done, particular work on the relationship with Sally: the progression could be seen as aggression to assertion to "tenderness" training. With men like Bill, it is helpful to get them in touch with male problems in that area. Books such as Warren Farrell's *The Liberated Male* can be assigned, and a men's consciousness-raising group might be in order. Except for Sally, Bill had few people whom he allowed to take care of him. He could have used help in not putting such a burden on Sally to be there so much for him, but to develop other friendships where he could fulfill his needs for "stroking."

While the drinking improved somewhat with work in assertiveness, separate work was on-going in that area.

Therapist/Client Interactions

With aggressive patients, the therapist must be particularly ready to use the therapist/client interactions for further work. Does the client express minor irritations? What sort of power plays get set up? How comfortable is the client in allowing the therapist to be nurturant? Is he angry, upset, and not expressing these feelings? Is there too much focus on the negative and critical and not enough on the positive.

For the first phase of the treatment (3 months) Bill rarely expressed any feelings toward the therapist whether positive or negative. Once the therapist had become an important person, he would avoid talking about how he felt until he was about to boil. It was important to deal with those issues as they came up.

For the seventeenth session, the therapist was stuck in the subway returning to her home office, and Bill was kept waiting in the lobby for 10 minutes. She anticipated that Bill would be furious, and she was right. No sooner did she enter the elevator with him did she see that he was about to explode. He let loose with a tirade that was out of proportion to the situation. He said that she didn't care. He rushed to get there on time; what right did she have to keep him waiting? The therapist acknowledged that she knew that Bill would be upset and that this was to be an important extra session for him, but where was the evidence that she didn't care? She said that she had given him an extra appointment when he requested it, and she apologized for keeping him waiting and said that she would make up the time at the end of the session. What came out of that discussion was the fact that if she really cared she had to be perfect, and how Bill set up tests for people who may not even know they are being tested, and they often failed to meet his expectations.

Once Bill had calmed down, he was asked if he had been annoyed previously. It turns out that about a month ago, he had made a request for an hour more convenient for him that didn't fit the therapist's schedule. He seemed to accept too readily and was too nice when the therapist could not give him that time, yet now he admitted he was burning about it. As he began to talk about these issues, he produced a list of slights. The therapist took a phone call during a session in the middle of an important role-play. She didn't do enough monitoring of his drinking lately, and so forth. As he began to talk about these situations, the therapist experienced the feeling of a tug of war. Bill appeared to be insisting that the therapist see that he was right, and wanted her to acknowledge her "faults." The therapist admitted to Bill that she felt under pressure from him to be the "perfect" therapist, and he was again setting up rules for perfectionism. What emerged from this session was to set aside a portion of the regular therapy session for Bill to talk about his feelings about the session, the therapist, his progress. As he began this work, Bill readily focused on the negative, and had to work on noticing that and learning to give positive feedback, which was much harder for him to do (e.g., "I feel you've been here for me today; your suggestion about Jo last week was helpful"). The therapist also modeled such feedback (e.g. "I feel we've had a good session, we've really communicated today").

Termination and Follow-up

After 9 months of weekly sessions, Bill terminated therapy. He felt more in control of his life, stating what he wanted and was better able to stand the frustrations involved when he didn't get just what he wanted. He looked more lively and energetic, liked himself more and was less hard on himself and others around him. Most of all, what he learned was how to handle the day-in day-out daily irritations. On 2-year follow-up both severe temper outbursts and heavy drinking were just about gone. He is now the director of his agency, and his relationship with Sally continues to be positive.

SPECIAL PROBLEMS

Client Variables

In the process of changing from nonassertive to assertive, some clients become too aggressive as an intermediate step. Clients should be warned about that possibility.

As some clients change from keeping their feelings buried or tuning out the environment to being more aware of themselves and relevant stimuli, they report that everything seems to bother them. They feel irritable, grumpy, disagreeable and may snap at others, fly off the handle, and so forth. Again, they need to learn that such changes represent an intermediate change in awareness, and special help in preparing and dealing with this stage may be necessary.

As some people change from nonassertive to assertive and are aware of their "rights" in a particular situation, they may become self-righteous, rigid in insisting that someone else listen or understand their point, or press for an acknowledgement that their view of the situation is correct from significant others. Again, since new behaviors are emerging, the clients may need help in exercising restraint here. This type of behavior can lead to power struggles or the entrenchment of an ongoing struggle. For example, a married woman is just beginning to be in touch with the unfairness of the assignment of household chores. She becomes rigid in her insistence that her husband see that his not doing the dishes on Tuesday evening is another example of his wanting her to continue doing the dirty work. She continuously harps on the subject, while he insists that he views the situation differently. In these cases, awareness of the power struggle and learning how to compromise and accept change more slowly are an essential feature of the work.

For some people, change is too slow, and they become impatient to try out their newly acquired assertive skills on everyone. It is important to train clients to tackle situations using small steps and to use escalating assertion when necessary.

Some clients need help in learning when *not* to use their newly acquired skills. Since the facility to be assertive is so new, they feel it important to assert themselves in any situation when they feel their rights are being violated. Help in selection of appropriate situations (in some job situations one could use all one's energies pointing out violations of rights) and appraisal of the consequences. In some work situations, rather than individually tackling the bosses with a list of grievances, joining with other workers or forming committees might be more productive. For example, in an engineering office all of the female clerical help reported being upset by one engineer's handling their breasts. In a group, it was presented as an individual problem, and after a role play of the situation the secretary felt she could deal with him better. However, she realized it was a continuing problem. Following a suggestion of a group member, she called a meeting of the other women in the office, and they dealt with the situation as a group.

Sometimes, more realistic appraisal of the consequences of assertive responses is needed. For example, in an ongoing group a member became increasingly anxious during the session and finally left the group to "inspect his car." Upon his return he reported that he had driven several members to the group and had parked his car in front of a building where the doorman asked him not to park. When he responded that it was a legal space and there weren't any other vacant parking spaces on the block, the doorman cursed him and said he'd be sorry. Even though he felt good about standing up for his rights and received support from his friends for his behavior, he worried that the doorman might do something to his car. In such a situation, a fuller appraisal of the risks and one's own tendency to worry might call for the choice of not exercising one's right (although one can be assertive in letting the doorman know how you feel about what he is doing). Some people, particularly as they are struggling to stand up to authority, might turn such a situation into a power struggle, insist on calling the police, or escalating the situation into a fight. Realistic assessment of risks is essential.

Some clients may need help in standing up to disapproval from significant others for their assertive behavior. A family doctor may still prefer to have the patient docile and not questioning his authority. Some men are hostile to assertive responding on the part of women. The clients need to learn to appraise these situations and to make suitable choices.

Therapeutic Problems

In work on assertiveness training, there are few failures. Most people who continue to work in assertiveness-training programs do change. Most of the problems develop as the clients begin to try out their not quite developed assertiveness skills.

The largest group of problems involve clients who are too impulsive in trying out assertive skills. They may try to tackle a difficult life situation after just one role play and without adequate preparation. For example, after a first session where the client was told to monitor her interactions with an authoritarian boss, she came to the following session to report that she got so angry at her exploitation by the boss that she "told her off" and was fired. In this case, the therapist might have been sensitive to the client's impulsive tendencies and given a warning about trying things out too quickly.

People often come for assertiveness training with unrealistic goals, or they have so many other problems and they expect "miracles" from this procedure. For example, an inhibited young man came into a group for social skills training for shyness. He practiced making social conversations and began to go out more. A few months later, he called the therapist discouraged stating that the assertiveness training "didn't work." Upon further evaluation, he reported that he hoped to be more comfortable in intimate relations and found that maintaining intense contact with women was frightening. In groups, particularly, it is important to stress that learning better social skills may or may not lead to better ability to relate intimately. Additional work may be needed at that stage.

Sometimes assertiveness problems are not the main issue. For example, an older married woman with a husband who is chronically ill and who also cares for a physically handicapped child full time may find that increased communications skills is only a partial remedy for her many problems. Sometimes, lonely unhappy people come into workshops to make friends and complain and burden the group or the therapist with all their problems. They resist help in delimiting problematic situations stating that they have so many other problems. In these cases, it is important that the therapist point out that the person seems to want more than the group could offer or just wants a place to come to and complain. Such people may do well in ongoing group therapy at clinics.

Clients may come to expect too much from the development of assertive skills and become disappointed and depressed when they become more assertive and they don't get what they want. For example, a woman client asked for help in asserting herself with her male friend. She took the risk of telling her male friend that she wanted a commitment of marriage. Now that she put the issue on the table, he felt free to tell her that he didn't want to get married. She became preoccupied with the situation, didn't want to believe where he was at, and became depressed. Preparation for accepting disappointment must be a feature of training in these situations. More work on accepting alternatives, self-reliance, and looking elsewhere in such cases is an auxiliary part of the treatment.

Sometimes clients are unwilling to take risks at the time they work on a problem and need more support in sitting with a situation until they are ready. For example, Sue and Rhoda who live together were caught in an intractable mother-daughter conflict that had been going on for 25 years. In a mother-daughter group, the difficulty of the situation became apparent. The mother's message was "You are free to leave anytime, but I will probably have to go into a home." In the group, the mother wouldn't see any alternatives. Sue began to be more aware of the issues and was more aware that she wanted to move, but even with the group's support was not yet ready to do it. Further work with Sue in helping her deal with guilt and fears of living alone had to proceed. Similar situations occur in rocky marriages. Clients use the role-play of telling their spouse they are leaving as a preparation to get ready to leave. In most of these cases, at some later date, usually within a year, the clients will call again for help in coping with the final break.

Therapist Variables

More so than with other behavioral procedures, therapists use more of themselves in assertiveness training. Furthermore, all therapists have had to struggle with their own development in the area of assertiveness. It is important that trainers know themselves, know what they are feeling, know what their assertiveness issues are, and be able to take risks. It is particularly important for therapists to be able to communicate feelings and receive feedback.

The author has been training trainers in assertiveness groups and has discovered from this work recurring problems that may interfere with effectiveness as trainers. These include the wish to be liked, problems in giving negative feedback, and a tendency to take care and nurture interfering with a clients' struggles for self-help.

It is recommended that trainers begin work in assertiveness training by participating in a training group as a participant (Alberti et al., 1977). Gestalt therapist-training groups might also be helpful since such groups stress self-awareness, nonverbal communications, and taking risks as well as providing direct training in emotional expressiveness.

From work with therapists and assertiveness trainers, the following problematic areas are delineated.

1. Problems in exercising authority: One group of problems relates to worries that they don't have all the answers (behavior therapists in particular are often given some of the most difficult cases to "change"). They worry about putting up a good show of knowing what to do. Helpful for problems in this area are discussions about the qualities of a good therapist/trainer, acknowledging that there is no "perfect" way of dealing with a case, and admitting when faced with a difficult problem, impossible client, or situation that one isn't sure what to do. Discussion in the groups about the therapist as a role model is also helpful to enable them to be freer in being a more vulnerable, coping model whom the clients view as more like themselves.

2. Many therapists have struggles exercising power and providing direction when it conflicts with nurturing and protection of clients. Letting a client know that they are overstepping a limit (problems in setting fees, being firm about ending on time, etc.). In assertiveness training the wish to protect may interfere with the therapist's ability to provide honest feedback.

3. Many therapists bring up issues of not being able to say "no" to clients, students, and supervisors who want more of their time. A common complaint of therapists is "I have no time for myself." It is important for therapists to reconcile self-interest and being available to others, since these are problems often presented by clients.

4. Some therapists will prefer to sit out a trainers group and avoid directing a role-play or taking charge of the group. Often these trainers are wanting "intellectual" knowledge or are themselves rather inhibited and/or intellectually oriented. While an inhibited therapist might

be effective in helping a client be more assertive, awareness of how difficult it is to role play, take risks, give feedback, and direct a group may help such a therapist be an even more effective role model.

Conclusion

Assertiveness training is not the panacea for solving life's problems as the media suggests. While most people struggle with assertiveness issues at some point in their life, assertiveness training is usually too complex to be handled by a "how to" book or attendance at a 1-day workshop. Assertiveness techniques can be viewed when used by a sensitive, experienced therapist as a valuable tool to help people become more aware of what they want, and to select appropriate goals and the skills necessary for them to deal with problematic interpersonal situations. When clients after such training still do not get what they want, they need additional training to handle disappointment, to learn to compromise, or encouragement to turn elsewhere for satisfaction. Additionally, assertiveness techniques can be viewed as clinical tools to work on improved communication between couples, parents, children, and work with colleagues. Since most clients at some point in therapy will discuss problematic situations lending themselves to assertiveness training, most therapists regardless of orientation will need to work with these issues. This paper presents to therapists a model for the development of clinical assertiveness techniques, a necessary addition to the repertoire of essential clinical skills.

REFERENCES

Alberti, R.E., and Emmons, M.L. *Your perfect right.* San Luis Obispo: Impact, 1970.

Alberti, R.E. *Assertiveness innovations, applications, issues.* San Luis Obispo: Impact, 1977.

Alberti, R.E., Emmons, M.L., Fodor, I., Galassi, J., Galassi, M., Garnett, L., Jakubowski, P., and Wolfe, J. A statement of principals for ethical practices of assertive behavior training. In R. Alberti (Ed.), *Assertiveness, innovations, applications, issues.* San Luis Obispo: Impact, 1977.

Assert: The newsletter of assertive behavior. San Luis Obispo, Calif.

Bandura, A., Adams, N., and Boxer, J. Cognitive processes mediating behavior change. *Journal of Personality and Social Psychology,* 1977, *35.*

Bandura, A. Self-efficacy: Toward a unifying theory of behavioral change. *Psychological Review,* 1977, *84,* 191–215.

Bandura, A. *Social learning theory.* Englewood Cliffs, N.J.: Prentice Hall, 1977

Bandura, A., and Adams, N.E. Analysis of self-efficacy theory and behavioral change. *Cognitive Therapy and Research*, 1977, *1*, 287–310.

Barnard, G., Flesher, C., and Steinbook, R. The treatment of urinary retention by aversive stimulus cessation and assertiveness training. *Behaviour Research and Therapy*, 1966, *4*, 232–236.

Bates, H.D., and Zimmerman, S.F. Toward the development of a screening scale for assertive training. *Psychological Reports*, 1971, *28*, 99–107.

Bloom, L., Coburn, K., and Pearlman, J. *The new assertive woman.* New York: Delacourt, 1975.

Bloomfield, H.H. Assertive training in an outpatient group of chronic schizophrenics: A preliminary report. *Behavior Therapy*, 1973, *4*, 277–281.

Bodner, G.E. The role of assessment in assertion training. *Counseling Psychologist*, 1975, *5*, 90–96.

Bower, S.A., and Bower, G.H. *Asserting yourself: A practical guide for positive change.* Reading, Mass.: Addison-Wesley, 1976.

Broverman, I.K., Broverman, D.M., and Carlson, F.E. Sex role stereotypes and clinical judgments of mental health. *Journal of Consulting and Clinical Psychology*, 1970, *34*, 1–7.

Butler, P. *Self assertion for women: A guide to becoming androgynous.* San Francisco: Canfield, 1976.

Carmichael, S.R. The use of self-instruction in an assertion training program with chronic, institutionalized patients. *Newsletter for Research in Mental Health and Behavioral Sciences*, 1976, *18*, 20–22.

Cheek, D.K. *Assertive Black . . . puzzled white.* San Luis Obispo: Impact, 1976.

Cotler, S.B. Assertion training: A road leading where? *Counseling Psychologist*, 1975, *5*, 20–29.

Cotler, S.B., and Guerra, J.J. *Assertion training.* Champaign, Ill.: Research, 1976.

Corby, N.H. Assertion training with aged populations. *Counseling Psychologist*, 1975, *5*, 69–74.

Curran, J. Skills training as an approach to the treatment of heterosexual social anxiety. *Psychological Bulletin*, 1977, *84*, 140–157

Dalali, I.D. The effect of active-assertion and feeling-clarification training on factor-analyzed measures of assertion. (Doctoral dissertation, University of California at Los Angeles, 1971).

Edinberg, M.A. Behavioral assessment and assertion training of the elderly. *Dissertation Abstracts International*, 36/09, 4685-B. (University of Cincinnati No. 76-5960).

Edwards, N.B. Case conference: Assertive training in a case of homosexual pedophilia. *Journal of Behavior Therapy and Experimental Psychiatry*, 1972, *3*, 55–63.

Eisler, R.M., Hersen, M., and Miller, P.M. Shaping components of assertive behavior with instructions and feedback. *American Journal of Psychiatry*, 1974, *131*, 1344–1347.

Eisler, R.M. Assertiveness training in the work situation. In J.D. Krumboltz and C.E. Thoresen (Eds.), *Behavioral counseling methods*. New York: Holt, Rinehart & Winston, in press.

Eisler, R.M., Hersen, M., and Miller, P.M. Effects of modeling on components of assertive behavior. *Journal of Behavior Therapy and Experimental Psychiatry*, 1973, *4*, 1–6.

Eisler, R.M., Hersen, M., Miller, P.M., and Blanchard, E.B. Situational determinants of assertive behaviors. *Journal of Consulting and Clinical Psychology*, 1975, *43*, 330–340.

Eisler, R.M., Miller, P.M., and Hersen, M. Components of assertive behavior. *Journal of Clinical Psychology*, 1973, *29*, 295–299.

Eisler, R. Frederkisen, L. and Petersen, G. The relation of cognitive variables to the expression of assertiveness *Behavior Therapy*, 1978, *9*, 419–427

Ellis, A. *Reason and emotion in psychotherapy*. New York: Lyle Stuart, 1962.

Ellis, A. *A new guide to rational living*. New York: Prentice-Hall, 1975.

Farrell, W. *The Liberated Man*. Bantum, 1975.

Fensterheim, H., and Baer, J. *Don't say yes when you want to say no*. New York: McKay, 1975.

Fensterheim, H. Behavior therapy: Assertive training in groups. In C. J. Sager and H.S. Kaplan (Eds.), *Progress in group and family therapy*. New York: Brunner/Mazel, 1972.

Fodor, I. *The phobic syndrome in women*. In V. Franks and V. Burtle (Eds.), *Women in therapy*, New York: Bruner/Mazel, 1974

Fodor, I., and Wolfe, J. Assertiveness training for mothers and daughters. In R. Alberti (Ed.) *Assertiveness, innovations, applications, issues*. San Luis Obispo: Impact, 1977.

Flowers, J.V., Cooper, C.G., and Whiteley, J.M. Approaches to assertion training. *Counseling Psychologist*, 1975, *5*, 3–9.

Foy, D.W., Eisler, R.M., and Pinkston, S. Modeled assertion in a case of explosive rages. *Journal of Behavior Therapy and Experimental Psychiatry*, 1975, *6*, 135–138.

Friedman, P.H. The effects of modeling and role-playing on assertive behavior. In R.D. Rubin, H. Fensterheim, A.A. Lazarus, and C.M. Franks (Eds.), *Advances in behavior therapy, 1969*. New York: Academic, 1971.

Galassi, J.P. Session by session assertive training procedures. Appendix A from final progress report on NIMH Small Research Grant, MH 22392-01, 1973.

Galassi, J.P., DeLo, J.S., Galassi, M.D., and Bastien, S. The college self expression scale: A measure of assertiveness. *Behavior Therapy*, 1974, *5*, 165–171.

Galassi, J.P., and Galassi, M.D. Relationship between assertiveness and aggressiveness. *Psychological Reports*, 1975, *36*, 352–354.

Galassi, J.P., and Galassi, M.D. Assessment procedures for assertive behavior. In R. Alberti (Ed.), *Assertiveness: Innovations, applications, issues.* San Luis Obispo: Impact, 1977.

Galassi, M.D., and Galassi, J.P. *Assert yourself: An assertion training workbook.* New York: Human Sciences, 1976.

Galassi, M.D., and Galassi, J.P. The effects of role playing variations on the assessment of assertive behavior. *Behavior Therapy*, 1976, *7*, 343–347.

Galassi, M.D., and Galassi, J.P. Assertion: A critical review. *Psychotherapy, Theory, Research and Practice*, 1978.

Gambrill, E.D., and Richey, C.A. An assertiveness inventory for use in assessment and research. *Behavior Therapy*, 1975, *6*, 550–561.

Gambrill, E.D., and Richey, C.A. *It's up to you: Developing assertive social skills.* Millbrae, Calif.: Les Femmes, 1976.

Gay, M.L., Hollandsworth, J.G., Jr., and Galassi, J.P. An assertiveness inventory for adults. *Journal of Counseling Psychology*, 1975, *22*, 340–344.

Gelder, J. The use of psychological learning theory in the development of assertion. *Canadian Psychiatric Association Journal*, 1967, *12*, 207–208.

Glass, C., Cochran, Jr., and Shrurak, S. Response acquisition and cognitive self statement modification: Approaches to dating skills training. *Journal of Counseling Psychology*, 1978.

Goldstein, A.J., Serber, M., and Piaget, G. Induced anger as a reciprocal inhibitor of fear. *Journal of Behavior Therapy and Experimental Psychiatry*, 1970, *1*, 67–70.

Hersen, M., Eisler, R.M., and Miller, P.M. An experimental analysis of generalization in assertiveness training. *Behavior Research and Therapy*, 1974, *12*, 295–310.

Hollandsworth, J., and Wall, K. Sex differences in assertive behavior. *Journal of Counseling Psychology*, 1977, *24*, 217–222.

Hirsch, S.M. An experimental investigation of the effectiveness of assertion training with alcoholics. *Dissertation Abstracts International*, 36/06, 3044-B. (Texas Technical University No. 75-26843)

Jackson, D.J., and Huston, T.L. Physical attractiveness and assertiveness. *Journal of Social Psychology*, 1975, *96*, 79–84.

Jakubowski, P. A discrimination measure of assertion concepts. Unpublished manuscript, University of Missouri, St. Louis, Mo., 1975.

Jakubowski, P. Assertive behavior and clinical problems of women. In D. Carter and E. Rawlings (Eds.), *Psychotherapy for women: Treatment towards equality.* Springfield, Ill.: Thomas, 1976.

Jakubowski-Spector, P. An introduction to assertive training procedures for women. Film available through the American Personnel and Guidance Association, 1607 New Hampshire Avenue, N.W., Washington, D.C.

Jakubowski, P.A., and Lacks, P.B. Assessment procedures in assertion training. *Counseling Psychologist*, 1975, *5*, 84–90.

Jakubowski-Spector, P. Facilitating the growth of women through assertive training. *The Counseling Psychologist*, 1973, *4*, 76–86.

Jakubowski, P., and Wallace, G. Adult assertion scale. Unpublished manuscript. University of Missouri, St. Louis, Mo., 1975.

Kazdin, A.E. Effects of covert modeling, multiple models, and model reinforcement on assertive behavior. *Behavior Therapy*, 1976, *7*, 211–222.

Kelly, G. *The psychology of personal constructs*. New York: Norton, 1955.

Kornfeld, J.L. Assertive training with juvenile delinquents. *Dissertation Abstracts International*, 1974, *35*, 1501–02. (University of Southern California No. 74-17, 354)

Lawrence, P.S. The assessment and modification of assertive behavior. Doctoral dissertation, Arizona State University, 1970.

Laws, D.R., and Serber, M. Measurement and evaluation of assertive training with sexual offenders. In R.E. Hosford and C.S. Moss (Eds.), *The crumbling walls: Treatment and counseling of prisoners*. Urbana, Ill.: University of Illinois, 1975.

Lange, A.J., and Jakubowski, P. *Responsible assertive behavior*. Champaign, Ill.: Research, 1976.

Lazarus, A.A. Behavioral rehearsal vs. nondirective therapy vs. advice in effecting behavior change. *Behavior Research and Therapy*, 1966, *14* , 209–212.

Lazarus, A.A. *Behavior therapy and beyond*. New York: McGraw-Hill, 1971.

Lazarus, A.A. On assertive behavior: A brief note. *Behavior Therapy*, 1973, *4*, 697–699.

Liberman, R.P. Behavioral methods in group and family therapy. *Seminars in Psychiatry*, 1972, *4*, 145–156.

Liberman, R.P., King, L.W., DeRisi, W.T., and McCann, N. *Personal effectiveness: Guiding people to assert themselves and improve their social skills.* Champaign, Ill.' Research, 1976.

Linehan, M., and Goldfried, M. Assertive training for women: A comparison of behavior rehearsal and cognitive restructuring therapy. Paper presented at the Association for the Advancement of Behavior Therapy, San Francisco, 1975.

Ludwig, L.D., and Lazarus, A.A. A cognitive and behavioral approach to the treatment of social inhibition. *Psychotherapy: Theory, Research, and Practice*, 1976, 13.

MacDonald, M.L. Teaching assertion: a paradigm for therapeutic intervention. *Psychotherapy: Theory, Research, and Practice*, 1976, *12*.

Maish, J. The use of an individualized assertiveness training program in the treatment of depressed in-patients. *Dissertation Abstracts International*, 33/06, 2816–B. (Florida State University No. 72–31, 413).

Martorano, R.D. Effects of assertive and non-assertive training on alcohol consumption, mood and socialization in the chronic alcoholic. *Proceedings of the 81st Annual Convention of the American Psychological Association*, 1973, 8, 393–394.

McFall, R.M., and Lillesand, D.B. Behavior rehearsal with modeling and coaching in assertion training. *Journal of Abnormal Psychology*, 1971, 77, 313–323.

McFall, R.M., and Marston, A.R. An experimental investigation of behavior rehearsal in assertive training. *Journal of Abnormal Psychology*, 1970, 76, 295–303.

McFall, R.M., and Twentyman, C.T. Four experiments on the relative contributions of rehearsal, modeling, and coaching to assertion training. *Journal of Abnormal Psychology*, 1973, 81, 199–218.

McMillan, M. Assertiveness as an aid in weight control. In R. Alberti (Ed.), *Assertiveness: Innovations, applications, issues*. San Luis Obispo: Impact, 1977.

Meichenbaum, D. *Cognitive behavior modification*. New York: Plenum, 1977.

Novaco, R.W. *Anger control: The development and evaluation of an experimental treatment*. Lexington, Mass.: Lexington, 1975.

Nydegger, R.V. The elimination of hallucinatory and delusional behavior by verbal conditioning and assertive training: A case study. *Journal of Behavior Therapy and Experimental Psychiatry*, 1972, 3, 225–227.

Osborn, S.M., and Harris, G.G. *Assertive training for women*. Springfield, Ill.: Thomas, 1975.

Palmer, R.D. Desensitization of the fear of expressing one's own inhibited aggression: Bio-energetic assertive technique for behavior therapists. In *Advances in Behavior Therapy*. New York: Academic, 1972.

Paulson, T.L. The differential use of self-administered and group-administered token reinforcement in group assertion training for college students. *Dissertation Abstracts International*, 36/01, 435B. (Fuller Theological Seminary No. 75–5979).

Perls, F.S., Hefferline, R.F., and Goodman, P. *Gestalt therapy*. New York: Rand McNally, 1951.

Phelps, S., and Austin, N. *The assertive woman*. San Luis Obispo: Impact, 1975.

Polster, E., and Polster, M. *Gestalt therapy integrated*. New York Brunner/Mazel, 1973

Rachman, S.J. Observational learning and therapeutic modeling. In R. Feldman and A. Broadhurst (Eds.), *The critical and experimental bases of the behavior therapies*. New York: Wiley, 1976.

Rathus, S.A. A 30-item schedule for assessing assertive behavior. *Behavior Therapy*, 1973, 4, 398–406.

Rathus, S.A. An experimental investigation of assertive training in a group setting. *Journal of Behavioral Therapy and Experimental Psychiatry*, 1972, *3*, 81–86.

Rich, A., and Schroeder, H. Assertiveness training. *Psychological Bulletin*, 1976.

Rimm, D.C. Assertive training and the expression of anger. In R. Alberti (Ed.), *Assertiveness: Innovations, application, issues*. San Luis Obispo: Impact, 1977.

Rimm, D.C., Keyson, M., and Hunziker, Jr. Group assertiveness training in the treatment of anti-social aggression. Unpublished manuscript, Arizona State University, 1971.

Rimm, D.C., and Masters, J.C. *Behavior Therapy: Techniques and Empirical Findings* (Chapter III). New York: Academic, 1974.

Satir, V. *Peoplemaking*. Palo Alto, Calif.: Science and Behavior, 1972.

Schwartz, R., and Gottman, J. Toward a task analysis of assertive behavior. *Journal of Consulting and Clinical Psychology*, 1976, *44*, 910–920.

Seattle-King County NOW. *Woman, assert yourself!* New York: Harper & Row, 1974.

Serber, M. Teaching the nonverbal components of assertive training. *Journal of Behavior Therapy and Experimental Psychiatry*, 1972, *3*, 179–183.

Serber, M., and Nelson, P. The ineffectiveness of systematic desensitization and assertive training in hospitalized schizophrenics. *Journal of Behavior Therapy and Experimental Psychiatry*, 1971, *2*, 107–109.

Serber, M., and Wolpe, J. Behavior therapy techniques. *International Psychiatry Clinics*, 1972, *8*, 53–68.

Stevens, J. *Awareness: Explaining, experimenting, experiencing*. Moab, Utah: Real People, 1971.

Taubman, B. *How to become an assertive woman*. New York: Pocket Books, 1976.

Thorpe, G.L. Short-term effectiveness of systematic desensitization, modeling and behavior rehearsal, and self-instructional training in facilitating assertive-refusal behavior. *Dissertation Abstracts International*, 1974, *34*, 5123–14. (Rutgers University, The State University of New Jersey.)

Twentyman, C.T., and McFall, R.M. Behavioral training of social skills in shy males. *Journal of Consulting and Clinical Psychology*, 1975, *43*, 384–395.

Vaal, J.J. The Rathus Assertiveness Schedule: Reliability at the junior high school level. *Behavior Therapy*, 1975, *6*, 566–567.

Wallace, C.J., Teigen, J.R., Liberman, R.P., and Baker, V. Destructive behavior treated by contingency contracts and assertive training: A case study. *Journal of Behavior Therapy and Experimental Psychiatry*, 1973, *4*, 273–274.

Wolfe, J. Short-term effects of modeling/behavior rehearsal, modeling/behavior rehearsal plus rational therapy, placebo and no treatment on assertive behavior. Unpublished dissertation, New York University, 1975.

Wolfe, J.L., and Fodor, I.G. A cognitive-behavioral approach to modifying assertive behavior in women. *Counseling Psychologist*, 1975, *5*, 45–52.

Wolfe, J.L., and Fodor, I.G. Modifying assertive behavior in women: A comparison of three approaches. *Behavior Therapy*, 1977, *8*, 567–574.

Wolfe, J.L., and Fodor, I.G. *Leaders guidelines for assertiveness training*. New York: Institute for Rational Therapy.

Wolfe, I. *Assertiveness training for women tape*. New York: Biomonitoring 1978.

Wolpe, J. *The practice of behavior therapy*. Elmsford, N.Y.: Pergamon, 1969.

Wolpe, J. Supervision transcript: V. *Journal of Behavior Therapy and Experimental Psychiatry*, 1973, *4*, 141–148.

Wolpe, J., and Lazarus, A.A. *Behavior therapy techniques: A guide to the treatment of neuroses*. New York: Pergamon, 1966.

Wolpe, J. The instigation of assertive behavior. Transcripts from two cases. *Journal of Behavioral Therapy and Experimental Psychiatry*, 1970, *1*, 145–151.

Wolpin, M. On assertive training. *The Counseling Psychologist*, 1975, *5*, 42–44.

Young, E.R., Rimm, D.C., and Kennedy, T.D. An experimental investigation of modeling and verbal reinforcement in the modification of assertive behavior. *Behaviour Research and Therapy*, 1973, *11*, 317–319.

APPENDIX I

Table 2. Selected References on Assertiveness

Professional Books	Self Help for Clients
Lang, S., and Jakubowski, P. *Responsible assertiveness behavior*. Research, 1976. A comprehensive, well written 'how to' book for trainers.	Bower, S., and Bower, G. *Asserting yourself: A practical guide for positive change*. Addison-Wesley, 1976. Well written self-help book for clients; full of useful exercises.
Alberti, R. (Ed.) *Assertiveness, Innovation, applications*. Impact, 1977. Articles by leading practitioners on various aspects of assertiveness training.	Alberti, R., and Emmons, M. L. *Your perfect right*. Impact, 1970. Excellent introduction to AT.
The Counseling Psychologist, Vol. 5., No. 4, 1975. Entire issue devoted to articles on assertiveness training. Also published as a book by	Gambrill, E.D., and Richey, C. *It's up to you: Developing assertive social skills*. Les Femmes, 1976. Basic introduction to social skills training.

Table 2 (continued)

Professional Books	Self Help for Clients
Whitely, J., and Flowers, J. (Eds.) *Approach to Assertion Training.* Brooks/Cole, 1978.	Galassi, M. D., and Galassi, J. P. *Assert yourself: An assertion training workbook.* Human Sciences Press, 1976. Comprehensive self-help manual, discusses AT in various situations, numerous exercises.
Liberman, R. P., King, L. W., De-Disi, W., and McCann, M. *Personal effectiveness: Guiding people to assert themselves and improve their social skills.* Research Press, 1976.	

Popular Books General	Women's Assertiveness (Professional Books)
Fensterheim, H., and Baer, J. *Don't say yes when you want to say no.* David McKay, 1975. Comprehensive coverage of AT.	Butler, P. *Self-assertion for women: A guide to becoming androgenous.* Canfield, 1976. Good discussion of sex-role stereotyping, powerlessness.
Taubman, B. *How to become an assertive woman.* Pocket Books, 1976. Through interviews with leading trainers, Taubman integrates women's issues with useful suggestions for change.	Phelps B., and Austin, N. *The assertive woman.* Impact, 1975. Clearly written, emphasis on self-awareness, self-help.
	Osborn, S. & Harris, G. *Assertive training for women.* Thomas, 1975. Stresses problems of AT relevant to women: Offers suggestions for helping women organize their own groups.

APPENDIX III

Table 3. Examples of Self-Statements for Dealing with Anger[a]

Preparing for Provocation

This is going to upset me, but I know how to deal with it.

What is it that I have to do?

I can work out a plan to handle this.

I can manage the situation. I know how to regulate my anger.

If I find myself getting upset, I'll know what to do.

There won't be any need for an argument.

Try not to take this too seriously.

This could be a testy situation, but I believe in myself.

Time for a few deep breaths of relaxation. Feel comfortable, relaxed, and at ease.

Easy does it. Remember to keep your sense of humor.

Reacting during the Confrontation

Stay calm. Just continue to relax.

As long as I keep my cool, I'm in control.

Just roll with the punches; don't get bent out of shape.

Think of what you want to get out of this.

You don't need to prove yourself.

There is no point in getting mad.

Don't make more out of this than you have to.

I'm not going to let him get to me.

Look for the positives. Don't assume the worst or jump to conclusions.

It's really a shame that she has to act like this.

For someone to be that irritable, he must be awfully unhappy.

If I start to get mad, I'll just be banging my head against the wall. So I might as well just relax.

There is no need to doubt myself. What he says doesn't matter.

I'm on top of this situation and it's under control.

Table 3 (continued)

Coping with Arousal

My muscles are starting to feel tight. Time to relax and slow things down.
Getting upset won't help.
It's just not worth it to get so angry.
I'll let him make a fool of himself.
I have a right to be annoyed, but let's keep the lid on.
Time to take a deep breath.
Let's take the issue point by point.
My anger is a signal of what I need to do. Time to instruct myself.
I'm not going to get pushed around, but I'm not going haywire either.
Try to reason it out. Treat each other with respect.
Let's try a cooperative approach. Maybe we are both right.
Negatives lead to more negatives. Work constructively.
He'd probably like me to get really angry. Well I'm going to disappoint
  him.
I can't expect people to act the way I want them to.
Take it easy, don't get pushy.

Reflecting on the Experience

When conflict is unresolved:
  Forget about the aggravation. Thinking about it only makes you upset.
  These are difficult situations, and they take time to straighten out.
  Try to shake it off. Don't let it interefere with your job.
  I'll get better at this as I get more practice.
  Remember relaxation. It's a lot better than anger.
  Can you laugh about it? It's probably not so serious.
  Don't take it personally.
  Take a deep breath and think positive thoughts.
When conflict is resolved or coping is successful:
  I handled that one pretty well. It worked!
  That wasn't as hard as I thought.
  It could have been a lot worse.
  I could have gotten more upset than it was worth.
  I actually got through that without getting angry.
  My pride can sure get me into trouble, but when I don't take things too
    seriously, I'm better off.

Table 3 (continued)

Reflecting on the Experience

I guess I've been getting upset for too long when it wasn't even necessary.

I'm doing better at this all the time.

---

[a] Reprinted by permission of the publisher, from R.W. Novaco, *Anger control: The development and evaluation of an experimental treatment.* (Lexington, Mass.: Lexington Books, D.C. Heath and Company. Copyright 1975, D.C. Heath and Company).

APPENDIX VII

Table 4. Guidelines for Effective Assertive Behavior[a]

1. When expressing refusal, express a decisive "no"; explain why you are refusing, but don't be unduly apologetic. Where applicable, offer the other person an alternative course of action.
2. Give as prompt and brief a reply as you can, without interruptions.
3. Insist on being treated with fairness and justice.
4. Ask for an explaination when asked to do something unreasonable.
5. Look the person you're talking to in the eye. Check your other body language for things that might convey lack of self-assurance (e.g., hand over mouth, shuffling feet.)
6. When expressing annoyance, remember: Comment on the person's *behavior*, rather than attack him/her.
7. When commenting on another's behavior, try to use "I-statements": Example: "*When you do* such-and-such, *I feel* such-and-such." When possible, offer a suggestion for an alternative behavior.
8. Reward yourself in some way each time you've pushed yourself to make an *assertive* response (whether or not you get the desired results from the other person).
9. Don't beat yourself over the head when you behave nonassertively or aggressively; merely try to figure out where you went astray and how to improve your handling of the situation next time. You don't unlearn bad habits or learn new skills overnight.

---

[a] Developed as a handout by J. Wolfe and I. Fodor.

CHAPTER 10

The Behavioral Treatment of Sexual Deviation

KELLY D. BROWNELL AND DAVID H. BARLOW

University of Pennsylvania (KDB) and State University of New York at Albany (DHB)

Throughout the past decade there has been a substantial increase in the number of experimental investigations involving sexual deviation. Behavioral techniques have been the most popular and thoroughly studied approaches in this area. Traditional psychotherapy has yielded discouraging results in the elimination of sexual arousal in homosexuals (e.g., Curran and Parr, 1957; Woodward, 1958, Bieber, Bieber, et. al., 1963), and there has been a paucity of evidence supporting the use of traditional psychotherapy in the treatment of other types of deviant sexual behavior. This has led to the conclusion that behavioral interventions are statistically and clinically the most effective in the treatment of sexual deviation (Barlow and Abel, 1976, Marks, 1976; Barlow, 1974; Bancroft, 1974). Coincident with the mounting evidence supporting the behavioral approach to sexual deviation has been considerable debate regarding which sexual behaviors, if any, can be ethically labeled deviant. Any sexual behavior can be considered deviant depending on the frequency, location, time, and choice of partner. For example, heterosexual intercourse is "normal" in only a minute number of the circumstances in which it may occur. If either partner is a child, if done in public, or if done to the complete exclusion of other activities, the context changes, and the behavior is labeled deviant.

THE ISSUE OF DEVIANCE

A multitude of factors converge into a decision to label a particular behavior deviant. Such a label connotes the sociocultural context of the behavior rather than any properties inherent in the behavior itself (Ullmann and Krasner, 1975). Sexual behavior is no exception, and many behaviors considered deviant in one culture are accepted as commonplace in others (Ford and Beach, 1951). There are several frameworks from which to judge deviance (Ullmann and Krasner, 1975). Legal definitions of sexual deviance are often used, but discrepant laws from state to state rule out consistent defining criteria. Religious definitions vary widely, as do popular definitions across subgroups within our culture. Ullmann and Krasner (1975, p. 421), provide a statistical definition of abnormality: ". . . the therapist makes the best first estimate he can of typical behavior for a person at the age, sex, and socio-economic status of his client. In this instance, normality is behaving like most of the people in that particular person's subgroup." Deviance then is defined as behavior that occurs with low frequency in the client's population. This definition will vary across subcultures, will vary within a culture over time, and is only as accurate as the sampling procedures employed, yet seems to offer the best criterion to date.

Homosexual behavior provides an illustrative example of the difficulties involved in defining and labeling deviant behavior. The traditional psychoanalytic view of sexuality holds that genital intercourse with the opposite sex under a very rigid set of circumstances is the only "normal" sexual behavior. Any deviation from this standard is considered symptomatic of fixation at one of the early psychosexual stages of development (Freud, 1932; Bieber et al., 1963). Therapy is then aimed at resolving the intrapsychic distress that inhibits psychosexual growth. Although maintaining a different etiological view, behavioral clinicians have also implied the abnormality of homosexual contact by aiming their efforts at eliminating homosexual arousal in order to change the individual's sexual preference (e.g., Feldman and MacCulloch, 1971). More recently, behavior therapists have postulated that attempts to decrease homosexual arousal may be appropriate only in a minority of cases, and therapy aimed at increasing heterosexual responsiveness or decreasing anxiety to a homosexual life style may be more appropriate (Wilson and Davison, 1974). This movement has also occurred in psychiatric circles, with the American Psychiatric Association recently excluding homosexuality from its list of deviant sexual behaviors. Davison (1974) has suggested that attempts to decrease homosexual arousal necessarily imply its deviance, and traditional efforts to suppress homosexual arousal should be abandoned in favor of shaping society's view of that behavior as more socially acceptable. It is possible that this notion will be applied to other sexual behaviors now labeled deviant (e.g., fetishism or transvestism).

Behavior therapy attempts to provide a technology to assist individuals desiring behavior change and does not attempt to define which behaviors are "normal" (O'Leary and Wilson, 1975). Within this framework, behavior therapy "is a system of principles and procedures and not a system of ethics" (Bandura, 1969, p. 87). The therapist acts as a consultant to help achieve the goals set by the client. The statistical definition of deviance and abnormality is the most popular among behavior therapists and is the model adopted by the authors. That is, deviance is a term describing behaviors that occur with low frequency in the client's population, that are rarely sanctioned legally or socially, and that often prompt the individual to seek treatment. It is important to note that even though a behavior may occur with little frequency, the client decides whether it requires change except when considering treatment administered under forced circumstances (e.g., prisons, involuntary hospitalization). Behavior therapists are attempting to develop techniques to alter behaviors and to enhance an individual's behavioral repertoire in those cases where change is appropriate.

ETIOLOGY OF SEXUAL BEHAVIOR

Ullmann and Krasner (1975, p. 32) state that ". . . abnormal behavior is no different from normal behavior in its development, its maintenance, or the manner in which it may be changed. The difference between normal and abnormal behavior is not intrinsic; rather it lies in a societal reaction." It appears that sexual behavior is no exception, and the fact that certain sexual behaviors appear more often than others could be because a majority of people are exposed to similar learning processes (Simon and Gagnon, 1970; Ullman and Krasner, 1975; Wilson and Davison, 1974). This formulation of sexual behavior was proposed by Kinsey during the years of his pioneering work in this area.

"Learning and conditioning in connection with human sexual behavior involves the same sorts of processes as learning and conditioning in other types of behavior. . . . The sexual capacities which an individual inherits at birth appear to be nothing more than the necessary anatomy and the physiological capacity to respond to a sufficient physical or psychologic stimulus. . . . As a result of its experience, an animal requires certain patterns of behavior which lead it to react positively to certain sorts of stimuli, and negatively to other sorts of stimuli. . . . The type of person who first introduces an individual to particular types of socio-sexual activities may have a great deal to do with his or her subsequent attitudes, his or her interest in continuing such activity, and his or her dissatisfaction with other types of activity." (Kinsey, Pomeroy, Martin and Gebhard, 1953, pp. 644–646).

The importance Kinsey placed on early sexual experience is consistent with the theory of McGuire, Carlisle, and Young (1965), which maintains that early sexual experiences provide fantasy material for later masturbation, which in turn determines subsequent sexual practices. The exact role of early experiences and masturbatory fantasies in the development of sexual behavior is not clear, but the development and maintenance of sexual behavior (normal or deviant) seems to abide by the same principles of social learning as other behaviors.

A NEW MODEL OF SEXUAL BEHAVIOR

Most experimental and clinical attempts to alter sexual deviation have focused on the suppression or elimination of deviant sexual arousal. Treatment, therefore, has been defined as successful by the absence or reduction of deviant arousal. Recent advances in behavioral assessment have revealed important behavioral excesses and deficits sometimes associated with deviant arousal (Barlow, 1974). The myopic view of sexual deviation as only deviant arousal has precluded evaluation and treatment of these other areas of functioning. Associated problems may be the most important targets for the therapist, and the direct reduction of deviant arousal may play little part in improvement by the client. The movement to eliminate deviant arousal is predicated on the notion that heterosexuality is the only "natural" sexual behavior, and if deviant sexual arousal could be reduced, the prepotent heterosexuality would emerge and blossom (Gagnon and Davison, 1974). Bond and Evans (1967, p. 1162) state "It is probable that if they can abstain from their deviant behavior for a sufficient period of time, normal outlets for the control of sexual arousal will develop." This hydraulic model of sexual functioning has led to the belief that heterosexual responsiveness will increase if deviant arousal is decreased or that by increasing heterosexual responsiveness, deviant arousal will automatically decrease. Little experimental evidence exists to support such a view (Barlow, 1973). There is no reason to believe that deficits in appropriate functioning will be remedied by reduction of deviant arousal or that an increase in heterosexual responsiveness will make deviant behaviors any less pleasurable.

Sexual behavior can be conceptualized as a multifaceted phenomenon consisting of several distinct components. These four areas of sexual functioning may occur independently and each requires individual evaluation and intervention. The four areas are: (1) deviant sexual arousal, (2) appropriate sexual arousal, (3) heterosocial skills, and (4) gender role deviation. Each area is discussed individually, and the development of treatment in each area is considered.

Deviant Sexual Arousal

Sexual arousal is considered deviant if it involves inappropriate behavior or object choice. The most common manifestations of deviant arousal are: arousal to inanimate objects (fetishism), sexual contact with children (pedophilia), arousal when dressed in clothing of the opposite sex (transvestism), arousal when exposing one's genitals (exhibitionism), arousal when covertly viewing sexual behavior in others (voyeurism), arousal to pain inflicted on others (sadism), and arousal to pain suffered by oneself (masochism). In addition to the nature of the arousal, deviation is defined by a variety of other factors including frequency, magnitude, location, relationship between partners, and societal values. For example, if a woman undresses in a window and a passing gentleman pauses to inspect, he will risk incarceration as a voyeur ("Peeping Tom"). If the same gentleman undresses in the window and the passing woman looks, he will be jailed as an exhibitionist. Therefore, the social context in which arousal occurs is important to evaluate.

Historically, aversion therapy has been the most widely used approach in the treatment of sexual deviation. A variety of procedures have been used in aversion conditioning including peripheral electric shock (e.g., Feldman and MacCulloch, 1971), chemical aversion (McConaghy, 1969), covert sensitization (Cautela, 1967; Brownell and Barlow, 1976), shame aversion (Serber, 1972; Wickramasekera, 1972), and olfactory aversion (Maletzky, 1973; Colson, 1972). Of these procedures, electrical aversion has been the most widely utilized (Barlow, 1973; Marks, 1976) and offers the most impressive body of experimental evidence from which to evaluate the efficacy of aversion conditioning in the treatment of sexual deviation.

Electrical Aversion

Electrical aversion has typically involved the pairing of a painful electric shock with a stimulus designed to elicit deviant sexual arousal. It has been employed in avoidance, escape, classical fear conditioning, and backward conditioning paradigms (see Barlow, 1972, for a review of aversion procedures). Although electrical aversion has yielded the most impressive clinical findings to date (Barlow and Abel, 1976), the diversity of ways in which it has been applied makes its use difficult to evaluate. Deviant stimuli have included videotapes, audiotapes, slides, verbal descriptions, imaginal situations, and written material. In addition, aversive stimuli and deviant stimuli have varied in intensity, frequency of presentation, and time of application.

The goal of electrical aversion therapy is to reduce deviant arousal. The earliest report of electrical aversion was an attempt by Max (1935) to reduce homosexual arousal. There ensued a 30-year period in which these techniques were rarely reported in the literature. Feldman and MacCulloch (1971), using electrical aversion in the treatment of homosexual behavior, report the most impressive findings to date. In this study, ten homosexuals were assigned to groups receiving either electrical shock in an anticipatory avoidance paradigm, electrical shock in a classical conditioning paradigm, or traditional psychotherapy. Those in the anticipatory avoidance condition could avoid shock and request the presence of female slides on a variable-ratio schedule. At a 1-year follow-up, interview and rating scale measures revealed significant improvement in 6% of aversion-conditioning subjects and 20% of the traditional psychotherapy subjects, with no differences between the two aversion-conditioning groups. These results are consistent with the findings of Feldman and MacCulloch (1965) and are encouraging in light of traditional approaches yielding substantial therapeutic benefit in 10 to 30% of a large number of homosexuals (Curran and Parr, 1957; Woodward, 1958; Bieber et al., 1963).

McConaghy (1969) found electrical aversion and chemical aversion to be more effective than a no-treatment control group in prompting a change in sexual orientation as measured by penile circumference changes and subjective reports. In this sample, 6 of 18 subjects changed their sexual orientation. Birk, Huddleston, Miller, and Cohler (1971) reported that a combination of group therapy, psychotherapy, and electrical aversion was more effective than group therapy and psychotherapy alone in reducing homosexual arousal. Subsequent to treatment, five or eight subjects receiving electrical aversion, and no subjects in the control group were improved significantly according to reports of behavior. At a 2-year follow-up, 25% (two of eight) were exclusively heterosexual. These findings are further confirmed in a study by McConaghy and Barr (1973) in which 46 homosexuals were randomly assigned to classical-conditioning, avoidance-conditioning, or backward-conditioning experimental groups. There were no differences between the three aversion conditions, and at a 1-year follow-up only 25% of the sample reported a decrease in homosexual behavior.

Covert Sensitization

Covert sensitization, in which aversive scenes are paired imaginally with deviant sexual stimuli, has been used successfully in a number of studies dealing with sexual deviation. Cautela (1967) first employed this technique in a case study and successfully reduced homosexual arousal. Barlow, Leitenberg, and Agras (1969) utilized two single-case A-B-A reversal designs to evaluate whether covert sensitization was responsible for changes in deviant arousal. In the treatment of one homosexual and one pedophile, deviant images were paired with noxious scenes of nausea and vomiting. Arousal dropped during presentation of the noxious scenes, rose when the aversive scenes were removed, and dropped again when the scenes were reintroduced. Four homosexuals were treated in a similar fashion by Barlow and coworkers (1972). In their study, a penile circumference measure was added, and the effect of therapeutic instruction was evaluated. Significant decreases in homosexual arousal were noted and could be attributed to the aversion procedure rather than nonspecific influences. An experimental analysis by Brownell and Barlow (1976) found covert sensitization useful in the treatment of multiple sexual deviations. In this case study, a multiple baseline design was employed to evaluate the successive application of covert sensitization to different sources of deviant arousal (exhibitionism and sexual contact with a subject's adolescent stepdaughter). Arousal to each source declined only upon pairing the aversive scene with that particular deviant scene.

In the only attempt to compare covert sensitization to electrical aversion, Callahan and Leitenberg (1973) treated two exhibitionists, one transvestite, two homosexuals, and one homosexual pedophile in a within-subjects experimental design. All subjects received both treatments with the order of presentation being counterbalanced across subjects. The results revealed no difference between the treatments on the penile circumference measure, but a superiority of covert sensitization on subjective measures of sexual arousal.

Considering that covert sensitization requires no expensive apparatus, can be self-administered, and is publicly palatable, it may be more practical than electrical aversion. However, the long-term efficacy of both procedures has yet to be determined.

The bulk of the experimental literature describes electrical aversion or covert sensitization, most often in the treatment of homosexuality. However, other deviant arousal patterns have been treated with a variety of aversion procedures. In the treatment of transvestism and fetishism, Marks and Gelder (1967) and Gelder and Marks (1969) employed electrical aversion and produced results superior to those gained with homosexuals (e.g., Feldman and MacCulloch, 1971). Covert sensitization, and other variants of aversion conditioning (e.g., olfactory aversion and chemical aversion) have been used successfully in the treatment of exhibitionism (Evans, 1967; Maletzky, 1974), fetishism (Kolvin, 1967), incest (Harbert,

Barlow, Hersen, and Austin, 1974), and multiple sexual deviations (Brownell and Barlow, 1967a, 1967b).

In the mid-1960s, researchers were enthusiastically propounding aversion therapy as the treatment of choice for sexual deviation, and treatment failures were attributed not to a deficient procedure but to a failure to arrange the correct temporal relationship between the deviant stimulus and the onset of the aversive stimulus. More recently, this enthusiasm has been tempered by the realization that electrical aversion will not reliably reduce deviant arousal and that the treatment of sexual deviation is more complex than the mere elimination of deviant arousal (Barlow, 1973; Marks, 1976; Barlow and Abel, 1976). Although aversion procedures are statistically more effective in reducing deviant arousal than group therapy, traditional psychotherapy, and no treatment, they are not necessarily *very* effective. With the exception of the findings of Feldman and MacCulloch (1965, 1971), the results of aversion therapy are far more impressive clinically (Barlow, 1973). This clinical reality has called into question the efficacy of aversion procedures in eliminating deviant arousal.

Deficiencies in Appropriate Arousal

The second major component of sexual functioning is the degree of arousal to appropriate sexual stimuli. Oftentimes clients in need of treatment for sexual deviation exhibit little or no arousal to heterosexual stimuli. Originally, both behavioral and psychoanalytic theorists concluded that fear of hetersexuality was critical in the development and maintenance of deviant sexual behavior (e.g., Wolpe, 1969; Rado, 1949). Although sexually deviant clients will sometimes exhibit fear of or avoidance to heterosexual behavior, there is no support for a casual relationship. In addition, the absence of heterosexual arousal need not be attributed soley to avoidance, but perhaps to the lack of typical learning experiences that are responsible for heterosexual arousal.

There are a number of techniques that have been employed to remedy a deficiency in heterosexual arousal. This area has been extensively reviewed by Barlow (1973) and is presented only briefly in this chapter.

Aversion Relief

Aversion relief involves pairing an appropriate stimulus with the termination of an aversive stimulus. In the treatment of sexual deviation, the presentation of a deviant stimulus is followed by the onset of electrical shock, the termination of which is paired with a heterosexual stimulus. In the first investigation to employ aversion relief, Thorpe, Schmidt, Brown, and Castell (1964) treated three homosexuals, one transvestite, and one fetish. Electrical shocks to deviant words projected on screen were terminated when a heterosexual word (e.g., intercourse) appeared. Self-report revealed some heterosexual responsiveness as a result of treatment. However, the lack of more objective measures of heterosexual arousal in this study and in other case studies (Gaupp, Stern, and Ratliff, 1971; Larson, 1970) makes it difficult to evaluate the results. McConaghy (1969) found no difference between electrical aversion with an aversion-relief component and chemical aversion with no attempt to increase heterosexual responsiveness. Subjects treated by Feldman and MacCulloch (1971) reported increased heterosexual interest, but the experimental design made it impossible to evaluate differences between the conditioning group and the traditional psychotherapy group. In addition, several investigators (Solyom and Miller, 1970; Abel, Levis, and Clancy, 1970) have showed aversion relief to have little effect on heterosexual responsiveness.

Aversion relief has never been investigated in the absence of aversion therapy, which makes it difficult to evaluate. There have been reports that heterosexual responsiveness increases without any attempt to accomplish this (Bancroft, 1970; Gelder and Marks, 1969; Barlow, Leitenberg, and Agras, 1969), which further obscures the aversion relief findings. Barlow (1973) has concluded that there is no evidence that aversion relief increases heterosexual responsiveness.

Systematic Desensitization

It has been advanced that fear of or aversion to heterosexual behavior is important in the genesis of sexual deviation (e.g., Wolpe, 1969). In a survey of homosexual subjects, Bieber, and coworkers (1963) reported that 70 of the 106 patients reported aversion to female genitalia. Ramsay and Van Velzen (1968) administered a questionnaire to homosexuals and found strong negative emotional feelings toward heterosexual practices. In the cases where "heterophobia" is present, systematic desensitization would be indicated to reduce the fear, but not necessarily to directly increase heterosexual arousal.

Fookes (1968) produced some increases in heterosexual behavior in 15 homosexuals, seven exhibitionists, and five tranvestites by pairing relaxing music with heterosexual slides subsequent to electrical-aversion therapy. A more recent study by Obler (1973) found a combination of systematic desensitization and assertion training more effective than psychoanalytically oriented group therapy or no treatment in 13 females and 8 males with "severe sexual disorders." Systematic desensitization combined with electrical aversion has been found effective in case studies involving the treatment of homosexuals (Levin, Hirsh, Sugar, and Kapche, 1968; Gray, 1970) and a fetishist (Cooper, 1963).

Bancroft (1970) made the only experimental comparison between systematic desensitization and electrical aversion in 30 homosexuals. Both treatments increased heterosexual arousal with no differences between groups at a 6-month follow-up. A host of case studies employed systematic desensitization as the sole intervention for sexual deviation. Kraft (1967a, 1967b, 1969a, 1969b) reported the successful use of systematic desensitization and suggests it may decrease homosexual behavior as well as increase heterosexual behavior. LoPiccolo (1971) and Huff (1970) reported increases in heterosexual responsiveness using systematic desensitization with homosexuals as did Wickramesekera (1968) with an exhibitionist. In a controversial case study, Kohlenberg (1974) used *in vivo* desensitization along with a Masters and Johnson type therapy approach in the treatment of a homosexual pedophile. The outcome was successful adjustment to a homosexual lifestyle with adults as partners. The clinical reports of success using systematic desensitization as a treatment of sexual deviation are encouraging enough to merit further investigation. Currently, however, there is little experimental evidence to support the notion that systematic desensitization directly increases heterosexual responsiveness (Barlow, 1973).

There are a group of techniques designed to increase heterosexual arousal by pairing heterosexual stimuli with elicited sexual arousal. These techniques vary in the temporal presentation of the sexual stimuli and in the method of initially eliciting sexual arousal. These procedures have been variously labeled as pairing, counter-conditioning, fading, masturbatory conditioning, orgasmic reconditioning, or classical conditioning.

These procedures have been generated from the notion that sexual arousal can be conditioned. Several studies have verified this hypothesis and have lent credence to the conditioning approaches. Rachman (1966) paired a picture of women's boots with slides of nude females in normal volunteers and found increases in penile circumference measures to just the boots. McConaghy (1970) produced penile circumference increases to geometric configurations paired with erotic slides, and both Lovibond (1963) and Wood and Obrist (1968) conditioned autonomic responses to nonsexual stimuli that were repeatedly paired with sexual arousal.

Orgasmic Reconditioning

Several authors have employed masturbation as a stimulus to produce sexual arousal. This procedure is labeled orgasmic reconditioning and involves masturbation to deviant imagery, with a heterosexual image being substituted just prior to ejaculation. The appropriate image is then gradually substituted at an earlier stage of the masturbatory sequence until it becomes its sole content. Case studies have demonstrated the usefulness of this technique for increasing heterosexual arousal in subjects seeking treatment for homosexuality (Thorpe, Schmidt, and Castell, 1963; Marquis, 1970; Annon, 1971; LoPiccolo, Stewart, and Watkins, 1972), sadomasochism (Davison, 1968; Mees, 1966; Marquis, 1970), voyeurism (Jackson, 1969), heterosexual pedophilia (Annon, 1971), vaginismus (Wilson, 1973), and several other deviations (Marshall, 1973).

In the only controlled attempt to evaluate orgasmic reconditioning, Conrad and Wincze (1976) provided four male homosexuals with therapy designed to increase heterosexual arousal. All subjects reported improved sexual adjustment, but physiological and behavioral measures of arousal did not change as a result of treatment. The disagreement between measures suggests that evidence amassed in the aforementioned case studies may have yielded false positives. However, generally positive results with orgasmic reconditioning are promising, and further investigation is necessary to fully evaluate its usefulness.

Fading, Pairing, and Exposure

Several procedures have involved the direct visual presentation of heterosexual stimuli in an effort to enhance heterosexual responsiveness. There is some evidence suggesting that high-intensity exposure to heterosexual stimuli may increase heterosexual responsiveness (Herman, Barlow, and Agras, 1971; Herman, 1971). Two homosexuals and one pedophiliac were intensively exposed to movies of a nude, seductive female in controlled, single-case designs. Exposure to the female film increased heterosexual arousal in all subjects and generalized to reports of fantasies and behavior. No other reports of this exposure technique have appeared in the literature, which makes its clinical usefulness difficult to evaluate.

In an attempt to change the stimulus control of sexual deviation, Barlow and Agras (1973) treated three homosexuals in a series of controlled, single-case studies. This fading procedure consisted of superimposing a slide of a nude female on a slide of a nude male, with an adjustable transformer used to alter the brightness of each. During treatment the female slide was faded in contingent upon the maintenance of 75% full erection as measured by a penile strain gauge. Throughout the graduated series of 20 steps, each subject was taken from the 100% male slide to the 100% female slide. There was a substantial increase in heterosexual arousal for all subjects.

In the treatment of a heterosexual pedophile, Beech, Watts, and Poole (1971) increased heterosexual arousal to mature females by pairing slides of young girls with slides of increasingly older females. Herman, Barlow, and Agras (1974) analyzed the pairing procedure in a series of single-subject controlled experiments. Three male homosexuals chose a slide or movie of a nude male as an unconditioned stimulus and a slide of a nude female as a conditioned stimulus. The experimental design demonstrated that classical conditioning pairing was more effective than backward pairing and was effective in increasing heterosexual arousal in two of the three subjects.

Deficiencies in Heterosocial Skills

The third component of sexual functioning that often accompanies deviant arousal (and may even generate sexual deviation) is a deficit in heterosocial skills. Very specific social skills are needed in a variety of heterosexual situations including meeting, dating, and relating socially and sexually to persons of the opposite sex (Barlow, Abel, Blanchard, Bristow, and Young, 1977). A deficiency in these skills would render a person incapable of maintaining a significant heterosexual relationship even in the presence of adequate arousal to heterosexual stimuli. Careful behavioral assessment reveals that sexual deviants (as well as many nondeviants) are often deficient in socio-sexual skills necessary to initiate and develop a heterosexual relationship. Past approaches to the treatment of sexual deviation have generally overlooked this component of sexual functioning. There are numerous reports of producing deviant arousal, increasing heterosexual arousal, and then having the subject unable to "act on" this new found arousal due to a lack of social skills (Barlow and Agras, 1973; Herman, Barlow, and Agras, 1971; Annon, 1971).

Improving Heterosocial Skills

Inability to relate socially and sexually in heterosexual situations may result from interpersonal anxiety or from a skills deficit, each requiring careful assessment.

Interpersonal anxiety involving interactions with the opposite sex occurs with some frequency (Martinson and Zerface, 1970) and has a reactive component as well as a conditioning component (Curran and Gilbert, 1975; Kanfer and Phillips, 1970). Systematic desensitization has been used to alleviate the conditioned anxiety, and a variety of techniques including assertion training, behavioral rehearsal, and social skills training have been used to decrease reactive anxiety. Stevenson and Wolpe (1960) increased heterosexual behavior and decreased deviant behavior in three subjects by teaching assertion skills. Edwards (1972) reported similar results with a pedophile. In conjunction with aversion therapy administered by a male therapist, Cautela and Wisocki (1969) employed a female therapist to desensitize heterophobia and to offer information regarding dating skills to homosexual patients. Case studies have shown increases in heterosexual responsiveness with the use of skills training (as part of a multifaceted program) in the treatment of male homosexuals (Ovessey, Gaylin, and Hendin, 1963; Hanson and Adesso, 1972) and a female homosexual (Blitch and Haynes, 1972). These findings argue for careful assessment of a patient's behavioral excesses and skill deficits, the absence of which precludes an educated choice of techniques in the treatment of sexual deviation.

Social skills may be taught in a variety of fashions. In a direct attempt to increase heterosocial skills in dating-anxious subjects, Curran and Gilbert (1975) trained subjects in listening skills, techniques to handle periods of silence, giving and receiving compliments, non-verbal methods of communication and so forth. Homework assignments, social reinforcement, videotape feedback, behavioral rehearsal, and assertion training were used, and subjects receiving social-skills training acquired these skills significantly more than control subjects or subjects receiving systematic desensitization. These results are consistent with those generated by studies teaching subjects assertion skills (McFall and Marston, 1970; McFall and Twentyman, 1973). Hersen and Bellack (1976) have developed a comprehensive program designed to train psychiatric patients in social skills (e.g., eye contact, fluency of speech, etc.). These authors have developed reliable assessment devices, and although their work was not completed on sexually deviant subjects, they have forwarded a technology with which to teach social skills (see Hersen and Eisler, 1976; and Hersen and Bellack, 1976, for a review of this area).

For those cases in which a deficit in heterosocial skills accompanies deviant sexual arousal, these procedures hold considerable promise. Unfortunately, a component analysis has yet to be completed on a program training sexually deviant subjects in heterosocial skills, hence making it impossible to determine the factors which might contribute to improvement. There is substantial evidence indicating that people can learn from viewing a model performing appropriate behaviors (cf. Bandura, 1969). Recent evidence indicates that modeling may be covert as well as overt, and it may be more beneficial to view a model who gradually accomplishes a target behavior than a model who is initially masterful (Kazdin, 1974a, 1974b).

Gender-Role Deviation

The fourth component of sexual functioning is gender role or gender identity. Gender-role deviation is a condition in which opposite sex-role behaviors are present and a preference for the opposite sex role exists. If the person consistently believes, thinks, and feels as if a person of the opposite sex, this mistaken gender identity is labeled transsexualism (Green and Money, 1969). This condition is characterized by cross-dressing, statements like "I am really a woman in a man's body," and a request for sex-reassignment surgery.

Stoller (1969) rejects the traditional dichotomous conceptualization of gender identity and suggests that gender identity lies on a continuum between completely male and completely female. Freund and coworkers (1974) administered a gender-role questionnaire to homosexual, transsexual, and heterosexual subjects, and found evidence supporting Stoller's position. It is important to note that gender role is a construct that has many components including physiological arousal, motor behavior, cognitions, verbal behavior, and so forth, and each of these components lies on a male-female continuum for a given client.

Stoller (1969) and Green (1974) identify the true transsexual as one in whom opposite sex-role behaviors were performed early in childhood (e.g., spontaneous cross-dressing) and in whom the request for sex-reassignment surgery is persistent. In addition to transsexualism there are several other diagnostic categories in which opposite sex role behaviors are present. A very effeminate homosexual or transvestite may be difficult to distinguish from a transsexual (Barlow, 1973).

Treatment of Gender-Role Deviation

In those people whose biological sex and gender identity are disparate, attempts have been made to alter the gender identity to be consistent with the biological genetic sex. Behavioral and psychoanalytic attempts to accomplish this have not been successful (Pauly, 1965; Gelder and Marks, 1969), and several authors have cautioned against the deleterious emotional effects of this practice (Money and Ehrhardt, 1972; Stoller, 1968). This has led to the conclusion that the biological—gender role disparity is best solved by allowing the established gender role to prevail and refitting the physical secondary sex characteristics to person's self-concept (Money and Ehrhardt, 1972; Stoller, 1968, 1969). To qualify for surgery in the reputable sex-change clinics, a patient must live completely in the opposite sex role for at least 1 year. Prior to the irreversible surgical procedures, reversable changes are undertaken that include hormone administration to facilitate secondary sex characteristic development as well as breast development (Green, 1974). Psychological counseling is also undertaken to insure a healthy adjustment to the new patterns. Subsequently, sex-reassignment surgery is completed. These procedures have been successful in coordinating the patient's physical characteristic with gender identity and appear to suffer from less psychological "fallout" than attempting to alter gender identity. These procedures are not without medical and emotional complications (Stoller, 1973; Green, 1974), and such a massive surgical and psychological procedure is not to be hastily undertaken.

A case study by Barlow, Reynolds, and Agras (1973) demonstrates a psychological rather than surgical approach to gender identity difficulties in the treatment of a 17-year-old transsexual male. A thorough behavioral assessment revealed that the patient was strongly aroused by transsexual fantasies, had no heterosexual arousal, was grossly deficient in social skills, and presented severe gender-role deviation.

The authors first altered gender-specific motor behaviors by modeling and videotape feedback. Masculine and feminine components of sitting, standing, and walking were treated in a multiple baseline design, and each behavior changed only when specifically treated. The patient reported that his new-found masculine behavior was rewarding since people did not stare at him as before, and the severe ridicule from his peers decreased substantially. There were no changes, however, in his arousal patterns or his social skills deficit. Social skills training was then instituted in order to teach the patient to interact with females and males in his environment. Behaviors such as eye contact, appropriate affect in social situations, content of conversation, and so forth were taught by behavioral rehearsal. Teaching the patient to lower his voice by instructing him to place his finger on his thyroid cartilage while speaking was also successful. Upon completion of this phase, the patient reported interacting quite capably in social situations.

Continuing assessment of arousal patterns revealed no heterosexual arousal and strong attraction to males. Heterosexual arousal was then increased in the patient by the fading technique described by Barlow and Agras (1973). A combination of covert sensitization and electrical aversion was employed to eliminate deviant arousal.

This case provides an illustrative example of systematic assessment and intervention into each of the four components of sexual deviation. Most encouraging is the favorable emotional adjustment by the subject as a result of the changes and the maintenance of these changes for over 4 years. Two subsequent replications lend further credence to the results.

However, enthusiasm regarding these results must be tempered by the fact that massive intervention (a total of 110 sessions) over a 1-year period was required in the initial case.

In an attempt to remedy gender-role deviation in young children and thus prevent later sexual problems, Green, Newman, and Stoller (1972) treated five very feminine boys (ages 2 to 7) and their parents. The basic components of this program are described by Green (1974, p. 246):

1) Developing a relationship of trust and affection between a male therapist and the feminine boy; 2) educating the child as to the impossibility of his changing sex; 3) stressing to the child the advantages of participating in some of the activities enjoyed by other boys, and promoting greater comfort in such activity; 4) educating the parents as to how they may be fostering sexual identity conflict in their child; 5) advising the parents of the need for them to consistently disapprove of very feminine behavior and to consistently encourage masculine behavior, if they desire change in their sons; and, 6) enhancing the fathers' or father substitutes' involvement in the feminine boy's life.

These results suggest that young boys would indeed develop more masculine gender behaviors. Although these are promising results, the lack of controls, the nonspecified nature of the interventions, and the absence of long-term data make it difficult to promote the widespread use of this approach.

In a well-controlled, single-subject analysis, Reckers and Lovaas (1974) treated deviant sex role behaviors in a 5-year-old male child manifesting "childhood cross-gender identity." The child exhibited behaviors typical of retrospective reports by adult transsexuals. The experimenters trained the child's mother to be his therapist both in the clinic and at home. With the use of social reinforcement and a token program, the mother reinforced masculine behaviors and extinguished feminine behaviors. A 3-year follow-up suggested normalization of the boy's sex-role behaviors. The results of Reckers and Lovaas (1974) and Green and coworkers (1972) are quite promising in terms of possible preventive intervention in the early stages of gender-identity conflict. However, even if it is possible to intervene successfully with feminine boys, it is not yet possible to determine which feminine boys are pretranssexuals, prehomosexuals, or preheterosexuals (Green, 1974; Lebovitz, 1972).

Any gender-role deviation must be taken into account when treating sexual deviation. The behavioral approach of Barlow and Agras (1973) is encouraging in light of past failures to effect such changes. Green and coworkers (1972) suggest that early enough intervention may prevent stabilized gender role difficulties, which have been very resistant to change historically. These results are further substantiated by the results of Reckers and Lovaas (1974). Nevertheless, from what little evidence exists, surgical alteration of physical appearance remains the most fruitful method of treating a disparity between gender role and physical characteristics.

In the treatment of sexual deviation, it is important to assess excesses or deficits in the four components of sexual deviation. There are a variety of methods designed to deal with difficulties in any one of the areas. Failure to recognize problems in any of the four areas will make therapeutic attempts to treat sexual deviation incomplete at best and at worst, harmful. The lack of consistently positive findings in past research programs may have resulted from concentration on only one aspect of sexual functioning. That is, improvement might occur to the degree that an investigator intentionally or unintentionally utilizes only subjects with difficulty in one particular area.

Therapeutic Process

A host of factors are involved in the treatment of sexual deviation. The clinical application of behavioral techniques entails much more than the mechanical presentation of a procedure. Client expectancy, therapist attitude, treatment setting, the influence of significant environmental persons, and other factors combine with technique administration to yield a final therapeutic product. These variables have been neglected in the early behavioral literature due to difficulties in definition and measurement along with an emphasis on technique development. More recently, these variables have come within the scope of behavioral quantification and hence are important to include in a chapter on the clinical treatment of sexual deviation.

This section of the chapter presents clinical guidelines concerning therapist and client variables as well as experimental evidence bearing upon the use of specific techniques. In some cases, this information is best imparted by the use of verbatim case material. Therefore, we present one specific case in detail and allude to others when appropriate. Since the approach to the treatment of sexual deviation is roughly similar across diagnostic categories (i.e., the conceptualization of the treatment of pedophilia is similar to that of exhibitionism, fetishism, etc.), the content of therapy varies only as a function of each individual's constellation of behaviors' and environmental circumstances. In presenting data from one particular case, we will illustrate our general intervention strategies for the treatment of sexual deviation.

Setting and Family Variables

Inpatient versus Outpatient Treatment. The setting can be an important variable in the treatment of sexual deviation. Often a decision must be made regarding inpatient versus outpatient treatment. In cases where the individual's behavior is a risk to society (e.g., an aggressive pedophile or rapist), inpatient hospitalization is clearly indicated. Determining whether a patient is a risk can be a difficult task however. Having experienced humiliating social or legal sanctions for the first time, most patients are certain they will "never do it again," and deviant arousal may actually be suppressed for several months after the incident. One such patient claimed "I am so frightened about being in jail and losing my family that I am sure that I won't do it again." In this case, the therapist pointed out the temporary suppression effect by stating "I can see that the behavior has produced these terrible feelings. Sometimes, however, these feelings are transient and the behavior will return. After all, it is something you have found quite pleasurable for a number of years." When in the presence of highly arousing sexual stimuli, many patients subsequently lose sight of the long-term aversive consequences of losing friends, jobs, and so forth and repeat the behavior. Patients with long-standing histories of deviant behavior should be cautioned against the false security of believing the arousal has vanished. This suppression is artificial and most often temporary. Therefore, some degree of caution must be exercised when evaluating the patient's self-report in order to determine the need for inpatient treatment.

Inpatient hospitalization allows for several environmental manipulations that aren't possible in outpatient settings. First, some control can be gained over the patient's exposure to arousing stimuli, thereby preventing highly reinforcing sexual contact during therapy. An important issue, however, is whether discouraging contact with sexual stimuli is desirable in treatment. Some behavioral programs, particularly those dealing with less "antisocial" behaviors (e.g., transvestism), use a shaping process in which the patient is gradually moved from deviant to appropriate behavior and exposure to deviant stimuli is an integral part of treatment. For example, in the treatment of exhibitionists, shame aversion involves actual genital exposure in front of a controlled audience (e.g., Wickramasekera, 1972). However, in the case of behavior that jeopardized the rights of others (e.g., pedophilia), contact with arousing stimuli must be discouraged—something that hospitalization can facilitate.

Second, more frequent treatment and assessment are possible in an inpatient setting. No experimental evidence has been put forth to indicate whether intensive inpatient treatment or a less-frequent outpatient treatment is most effective in sexual deviation. However, it is the authors' clinical impression that some patients profit from being removed from troubled environments and receiving intensive treatment. In addition, the hospital milieu may be beneficial when extraneous social and cognitive factors are impeding progress. An exhibitionist treated by the authors vehemently stated "I only exposed myself when my wife didn't love me. It is her fault. If she loved me I wouldn't have done it. There's nothing wrong with me." This patient was resistant to even attempting change until convinced by the ward staff and fellow patients that the problem was his and the impetus for change must come from him. In this case, the social context of inpatient treatment was very important and set the stage for direct modification of deviant behavior.

The physical location of treatment can also be important. For example, if covert sensitization is the treatment of choice to reduce arousal to deviant stimuli, then a sound-proof office is necessary. Distracting noises can hinder progress with any technique, particularly those involving imagery or relaxation. Privacy is required if explicit sexual material is being discussed or displayed. An example from one of the author's recent experiences at a university medical center highlights this issue. Simultaneous sessions were being conducted in adjoining rooms. In one room a biofeedback experiment was being conducted in which the patient was to relax completely in a very quiet atmosphere to decrease pain from headaches. In the next room covert sensitization was being used in a very loud tone of voice. Needless to say, the loud sexual statements did little for the other patient's headaches! Also, depending upon the sophistication of assessment and treatment, a laboratory setting will be necessary if physiological measurements are being taken (e.g., a penile plethysmograph) or if videotape equipment is utilized for social skills training.

The Role of Family and Friends. As with most behavior, sexual deviation does not occur in a social vacuum. Social factors may be responsible for the maintenance of deviant behavior, may be utilized in the modification of deviant behavior, or may be dramatically influenced by changes in the behavior. When treating sexual deviation, it is important to consider the involvement of significant family members or friends of the patient.

Social influence may act directly or indirectly in sexual deviation. Indirect support in the form of social reinforcement for constructive changes can be mobilized by enlisting the cooperation of significant others. At times this is difficult to elicit, particularly if the deviant behavior has occasioned embarrassing legal contingencies. However, treatment effects can be facilitated and maintained to a greater degree when important social influences are consonant with the influence of the therapist. In some instances, mutual pathology within a marriage can seriously hamper treatment efforts. The wife of a transvestite patient, for example, purchased female clothing for her husband, told her husband he was "cute" while cross-dressed, and would only conduct "serious" discussions at these times. In these cases, spouse involvement in therapy is quite important.

Resistance and hostility on the part of family members can be obstacles in the development of a treatment program. There are several reasons for this lack of cooperation. First, intense anger is often generated by the embarrassing social consequences of a family member being arrested. The coincident breakdown of trust and the threat of losing a partner may place an otherwise willing partner in a precarious situation. Frequently a spouse will feel somehow responsible for the deviant behavior and may feel "If only I loved him more" or "I should have seen it coming." Many feel as if they have failed at all attempts at suppressing the deviant behavior themselves. The wife of a transvestite begrudgingly agreed to be interviewed for "only one session." During the initial interview, the woman stated,

> I have tried everything. At first I felt I wasn't loving him enough, so I tried to be nice and supportive. When he complained of me being cold, I had sex with him more often. I felt that if he had sex with me he wouldn't have to dress up in public. But it didn't work. Next I tried to ignore the perverted behavior and to pretend it wasn't happening. That didn't work either. Finally, I'd had it. When he dressed, I screamed at him and threatened to leave. I would cry and be very upset. What good am I? No matter what I do he doesn't stop. It's going to ruin our marriage.

In this case, initial cooperation from the wife was elicited by acknowledging her distress, minimizing her role as a contributor to the problem, and reinforcing her motivation as evidenced by her previous attempts to help her husband. In response to her anger and frustration, the therapist replied:

> You seem to be feeling upset about your husband's embarrassing behavior. It puts you in a very difficult position. What seems to be even more distressing is the fact that you've tried to help him in so many ways, and nothing appears to be effective.

I am amazed by your willingness and desire to help your husband. Many wives in your situation would have given up and thrown in the towel long ago. This is a positive sign and could possibly improve your husband's progress.

As you know, your husband's behavior was occurring at a high frequency even before you met him. Therefore, you certainly can't be targeted as a contributing factor in the development of his problem. Most likely, the behavior would have continued regardless of who he married or what she did to help him. These high-frequency, powerfully reinforcing behaviors are very resistant to change.

I feel your involvement in the treatment program can be helpful for several reasons. First, I'm sure you are curious about the program your husband is about to begin. By involving yourself, you will know what the treatment procedures entail. Second, your mere presence may aid your husband because of this display of your commitment. Also, there are certain portions of the program in which you could be of great help.

Given adequate assessment of each component of sexual deviation, social and familial factors may become directly involved in therapy. For example, a deficiency in heterosocial skills may include primary or secondary impotence, in which case a couples sex-therapy approach is indicated (Masters and Johnson, 1970). We have treated a married man with a long history of high-frequency homosexual behavior. Despite his heterosexual marriage, he and his wife engaged in no mutual sexual activity. After treatment the patient was experiencing sexual arousal to his wife and was exhibiting less homosexual behavior. At this point, the wife requested treatment for being preorgasmic, and it became evident that her husband's changes were very distressing to her. Quite possibly the lack of sexual activity was one of the reasons she chose this man for marriage. Another example is that of a 14-year-old male referred by his parents for treatment of transvestism. Attempts to work with the boy proved nonproductive until a behavioral contract was established involving the entire family and concentrating on transvestite behavior as well as oppositional behavior. Therefore, the social context in which the deviant behavior occurs is important to assess and sometimes modify. Wholesale changes in a patient are likely to influence other concerned parties and may disrupt an otherwise stable pattern of interrelationships.

Therapist Variables

An issue rarely addressed when discussing sexual deviation is the importance of the therapist/client relationship, a subject not often confronted by behavior therapists (Wilson and Evans, 1977). Although there is a paucity of experimental evidence, comprehensive coverage of any treatment must deal with this issue. First and foremost, it is important to establish a warm and trusting relationship. Since therapeutic effectiveness is dependent upon the ability to elicit detailed information as part of a behavioral assessment, the absence of such a relationship makes it difficult for the patient to discuss intimate sexual matters. Many potentially important components of the therapist's ability to create a warm and trusting relationship are difficult to convey without audiovisual aids. Specifiable variables like tone of voice, nods of the head, posture, eye contact, and so forth have been discussed in detail by Wilson and Evans (1977).

The therapist's introductory statements to a patient with sexual problems can set the stage for appropriate interchange. Remaining nonjudgemental, reflecting the patient's feelings, and treating the target behavior matter of factly can facilitate meaningful interaction. In the initial session for a patient referred for the treatment of sadomasochistic behavior (bondage), introductory statements were as follows:

T: As you know, you were referred to me specifically because of your sexual problem. In our Sexual Disorders Clinic we deal with various sexual difficulties and very likely will be able to develop a treatment program to assist you.
Many people I see are very upset about their sexual behavior. Combined with the fact that many people are not accustomed to speaking frankly about sexual matters, some degree of discomfort is what I would expect.

C: I've had this problem for such a long time and I haven't been able to talk to anyone about it. Even my former wife—she would let me tie her up, but we never talked. No one realizes I have this problem. I don't know how to talk about it. I must be sick to do this. I don't know anyone else who does it.

T: You appear very distressed by the fact that you have a problem so serious and "strange" that you are the only person interested in bondage. Any difficulty you might have talking about the bondage problem is quite understandable, given that you've never spoken to anyone about it.

C: Do you think I'm weak? Maybe it's my parents' fault. I'll bet it's because they beat me up when I was little. If I could figure out why I do it, I could stop.

T: It will be very imporant for us to find out as much as we can about your sexual problem. As you know, it is a very complex matter, and our detailed assessment should give us the necessary information.

Most people with sexual problems are reluctant to let their problems become public knowledge. Therefore, problems like yours are more common than you think. Your confusion about your sexual behavior will diminish as we proceed. Before long, I'm confident that you will feel comfortable discussing your sexual behavior.

As you've told me, you've tried many ways to stop the behavior yourself. As a result, your feelings of skepticism about a treatment program are understandable. Many of our patients feel this way during the initial stages of the program.

Sexual attraction between the patient and therapist is another matter of concern. This can occur between the therapist and opposite-sexed patient or between the therapist and same-sexed patient when homosexual arousal is present.This is most often manifested in patient's becoming overly "casual" with the therapist and being overtly or covertly seductive or flirtatious. Occasionally a patient will verbalize this attraction and will express a desire to become more intimately involved. This may prevent therapeutic effectiveness and can often be directly confronted within the therapist/client relationship by an open and frank discussion. If sufficiently prohibitive, the patient should be referred to another therapist.

To date, there is no experimental evidence indicating the choice of either a male or female therapist for a particular pattern of deviant arousal. Cautela and Wisocki (1969) utilized a female therapist with male homosexuals in order to offer information regarding dating skills. It is difficult to determine whether this offsets the advantage of using a male therapist to provide an appropriate model. These are empirical questions and will hopefully be answered by future research.

The difficulty in communicating sexual information by most patients can be minimized by appropriate therapist attitudes. Sexual matters should be discussed in a forthright fashion, for hesitancy on the part of the therapist will damage the patient's confidence that the therapist can effectively deal with the sensitive situation. It is also our opinion that the terms chosen by the therapist can also be important. That is, some clients profit from discarding clinical labels like vagina and intercourse in favor of the more vernacular "cunt" or "fuck." This factor is especially important when employing covert techniques in which the vividness of a sexual scene can be enhanced by using terms that are meaningful to the particular patient.

Developing meaningful communication begins in the initial session. In our Sexual Disorders Clinic, the following interaction is typical of the therapist's effort to anticipate the patient's discomfort when discussing sexual matters and to model appropriate sexual discussion behaviors:

T: When a person is not accustomed to discussing sexual matters of such a personal nature, these initial assessment sessions are often uncomfortable. I expect you'll have similar feelings when you begin revealing information that you have never spoken to anyone about.

C: I saw a psychiatrist for 6 months after my last arrest. We spoke about my parents, my marriage, and my self-confidence. We never discussed the grim details of the sex acts. Why do we have to go into it?

T: In my evaluation, I want to develop a clear picture of you as a total person. That is, your social and sexual functioning are important as well as your thoughts, feelings, and images of yourself and your sexual behavior. Direct and detailed questioning concerning your sexual-arousal patterns is necessary to develop this picture. Your thoughts and feelings may be quite different from those of another person who engages in exactly the same behavior. We will also be discussing your parents, your marriage, and your self-confidence, but your sexual behavior is also important.

C: Well, I guess I'll have to talk about it if I want to get better. What kinds of questions are you going to ask?

T: I'll be asking about your sexual development from childhood on. I'll want to know of exactly what arouses you—it could be the other person, certain clothing, fantasies of past behavior, and so forth. We will discuss your images, thoughts, and fantasies that occur during any sexual behavior—especially masturbation. Also, the response of the other person and your feelings about that response will also be considered.

C: How will I know what to say and what you want to know?

T: I will ask direct and specific questions. If you have difficulty with a particular topic we may come back to it later. In some instances I'll let you know what we will be discussing in the next session. In this way, you will be able to devote time and thought to your answers.

Most clients are comfortable with the evaluation sessions being quite structured by the therapist. This sense of structure can relieve the client of the responsibility to decide which information is pertinent. As a general rule, it is helpful to progress from the least intimate information to discussion of specific sexual behavior. Initial discussion might focus on the client's courtship period (if married) and what attracted him to his future spouse. A gradual progression to more intimate topics is tolerable to most clients. In the case of the client who objects to or has difficulty with this structure, a more indirect approach during initial sessions is helpful. Introductory, nondirective statements like "Tell me about yourself" can allow the client to comfortably volunteer information. More direct questions can be introjected when appropriate.

Therapeutic discussion about whether to decrease deviant arousal is often couched in terms of legal and social contingencies. Indeed, the deviant behavior may be distressing only to the degree that it elicits punishment from the patient's environment. Pleasurable aspects of the deviant behavior may re-emerge as societal punishment becomes more remote. Sexual deviants often initiate therapy only to later resist change and express a desire to terminate treatment. This can be magnified when there is no readily available outlet if the deviant behavior is reduced (e.g., as when a pedophile is impotent in the presence of adult women).

There is evidence indicating that patients seeking treatment by their own choice profit from aversion therapy more than those driven by social and legal pressures (Freund, 1960; Feldman and MacCulloch, 1971; Bancroft, 1974) (see section on Prognostic Factors). Therefore, treatment of sexual deviation should be undertaken with discretion and should not proceed without a clear impression of the patient's desire to change. A homosexual might request a change in sexual orientation, but careful questioning may reveal intense familial pressure to eliminate the "abnormal" behavior. In such a case the patient may not desire change, and counseling would be aimed at helping the patient and his/her family accept the homosexual lifestyle. In order to elicit this type of information, a nonjudgmental stance by the therapist is facilitative. This is difficult for some therapists when emotional or physical violence is perpetrated by the deviant behavior—as in the case of a rapist or pedophile. Here, the task of the therapist is to clearly outline the realistic consequences involved in the deviant behavior. The decision to change is most meaningful if it emanates from the patient.

Careful questioning aimed at evaluating the patient's desire to change is illustrated in the following discussion with a homosexual pedophiliac:

T: When people enter our clinic for the treatment of sexual disorders, there are many reasons that motivate them. In fact, each person may have several reasons for seeking treatment. Could you explain some of the reasons you have decided to see me?

C: This is my third arrest for having sexual contact with young boys. So far, I've stayed out of jail, but if it happens again, they won't let me off. I'm afraid for my life if I go to prison.

T: You seem to be upset at the prospect of going to prison. I'm sure that this reason is foremost in your mind at this time. Are there other reasons?

C: My wife almost dies each time this happens. She has been a saint staying with me through all this. However, I don't think she can hold out much longer. I'm afraid she'll leave me if I do it again. Also, I hate to feel I upset her so much.

T: It must be very difficult for you to think of losing your wife. I'm sure she has gone through a lot, just as you have.

C: You know, another thing I hate about this is wondering who knows. Everytime I see a neighbor, go to the store, or go to church, I think people know and are talking about me. They probably think I'm a sex maniac.

T: Any other reasons which made you decide to enter treatment?

C: Well, I can't think of any.

T: What thoughts do you have about the impact this sexual behavior has on the boys with whom you're involved?

C: I really can't understand why other people think it would hurt them. I don't think it's done them any harm. I didn't initiate any of them. Each had done it before with someone else, so I can't be blamed. If those kids got the love they need at home, they wouldn't be coming to me. If it weren't for me, they'd never get any love.

T: This behavior seems quite pleasurable to you, and you appear to get good feelings that you've given the boys the love they really need. Do you feel the behavior can change if it is so enjoyable and rewarding to you?

C: I'm sure if these kids don't get it from me, they'll get it from someone else. I've got to change, or else I'll go to prison and lose my wife.

In this case, the client displayed the common perception that the victims profited from the deviant sexual behavior and that the victims actually initiated the behavior (see section on Prognostic Factors for a further discussion). Therefore, the client did not desire change because he felt the behavior was "wrong." The reasons for change were a well-founded fear of imprisonment, social ostracism, and marital conflict. Making these fears more salient and dispelling the client's myths about the effect on his victims can prepare the client for the therapeutic process.

CASE STUDY

In order to illustrate a comprehensive behavioral approach to the treatment of sexual deviation, a detailed case study is presented that includes verbatim material from each portion of the treatment program. This case is presented to demonstrate a conceptual approach to assessment and treatment. Each person exhibits idiosyncratic patterns of behavior, and changes in the treatment program must be specifically tailored to the individual. The authors utilize the same theoretical framework for each client, but interventions differ according to the presenting problems. Therefore, it is not suggested that the following case study offers a global treatment program for sexual deviation, but rather an approach that outlines a framework from which to develop a clinical regimen.

Adequate assessment is critical when formulating a treatment plan for sexual deviation. Material gathered from the assessment will determine which procedures are most appropriate. An inadequate assessment may overlook important aspects of sexual functioning and may lead to untoward therapeutic effects. For example, eliminating deviant arousal in a person lacking heterosexual arousal and the requisite heterosocial skills may lead to depression or other serious difficulties. Behavioral assessment has been discussed in detail elsewhere (Kanfer and Saslow, 1969; Tharp and Wetzel, 1969), and Barlow (1977) has outlined a behavioral approach to the assessment of sexual problems. This approach appears to be the most fruitful and yields information that directly relates to treatment.

Sexual History and Background Information

The patient was a 46-year-old, white, married middle-class male, father of three children, who was employed as a corporate executive. He was referred to the authors by his psychiatrist for the treatment of heterosexual pedophilia. Recent sexual contact between the patient and a 10-year-old girl had been reported to the police. The court had agreed to postpone proceedings awaiting the patient's release from the hospital.

The patient reported his first knowledge of sexual impulses at age 12, at which time he began masturbating to pictures of adult females. Sexual experience was very casual until marriage and involved light petting and kissing during the high school years. The patient was a virgin at the time of his marriage at age 23. During the first 2 years of his marriage, intercourse occurred three to four times per week and consisted of brief foreplay and intercourse in the missionary position. At this point the couple decided to have children, with intercourse becoming more frequent. Their attempts met with failure, and sex became a burden rather than a pleasure. They were informed by a physician that conception was highly unlikely due to a low sperm count for the patient. The frequency of intercourse then decreased and stabilized at two to three times per month until age 40.

Around age 40 the patient began having impotency problems. As a result, his wife stopped initiating sex to avoid pressuring her husband, and intercourse occurred at night or early morning when the patient would awaken with an erection. The impotency problem worsened since the onset at age 40, and as a result, intercourse occurred approximately once per month. The patient reported the desire to be more adequate sexually and to experiment with a variety of positions during intercourse. The range of sexual behavior remained very restricted throughout most of the marriage, although both partners enjoyed oral-genital contact.

The patient reported awareness of pedophilic arousal patterns around age 40. In retrospect, however, he reported engaging in semi-sexual behaviors with young girls prior to this time. A chronological history of pedophilic events is presented as follows:

1. At approximately age 30, the patient had playful but semi-sexual contact with a 10-year-old girl in a swimming pool. This consisted of touching the girl in a nongenital area and terminated upon the request of the child's mother.

2. At approximately the same time, the patient was in the presence of a 10-year-old neighbor girl and allowed his bathrobe to open "accidentally" so that his penis was exposed. The patient reported no visible reaction from the girl. He recalled masturbating to that particular image for several years after the incident.

3. At age 35, the patient had nongenital contact (hugging and kissing) with a 10-year-old friend of his daughter's. He reports feeling sexually aroused, and that this girl, like all the others, was "childishly flirtatious."

4. At age 38, when the patient and his family moved to a new state, the patient exposed himself to several young girls. The patient reports wearing shorts or swimming trunks that he could maneuver to have his penis exposed. According to the patient, there were no visible reactions from those girls or other people.

5. At age 38, the patient made a "pass" at a 14-year-old babysitter in which he attempted to kiss her and asked if she would have sex with him. Again, the patient reported "no reaction" from his victim. Later, the patient discovered that the babysitter had informed his daughter of the incident, but that she did not discuss the matter with others.

6. At age 42, the patient reported watching T.V. in a room alone with a

10-year-old daughter of a neighbor. He took her hand and placed it
on his penis. The girl withdrew, went away, and there were no reper-
cussions. He did not have an erection during this contact, but did report masturbating to the image at a later date.

7. At age 44, the patient had sexual contact with a 15-year-old female
friend of his daughter, who was staying overnight. During the night,
the patient entered the girl's room and stroked her breasts. She
awakened, did not give any visible reaction, but later reported the
incident to the patient's daughter. The daughter did not report the incident to anybody, and it did not become public.

8. The event preceding treatment involved a 10-year-old female neighbor. The girl was staying overnight at the patient's house at her parents' request. The patient entered the girl's room to "see if she was
sleeping well." He took the girl's hand and placed it on his penis.
After several minutes of this, he placed his penis near the girl's
mouth. The girl was "half awake" and "didn't realize what was happening." The patient reported being sexually aroused but did not
achieve a full erection. After 10 minutes of contact, the patient returned to his bedroom and had intercourse with his wife. At this
point, the girl began to cry and was escorted home. She explained
the incident to her parents, and the police arrived promptly. The local prosecutor decided to pursue the matter in the courtroom, and legal action was pending during hospitalization.

In summary, the patient exhibited a 15-year history of intense sexual
arousal to pedophilic images and fantasies and an 8-year history of actual
pedophilic contact. He had exposed himself to young girls approximately
ten times during this period and had engaged in genital contact on two occasions. In addition, the patient reported numerous "playful" situations
with young girls that he found sexually arousing.

During the assessment phase of treatment, the patient claimed that his
arousal to young girls was quite different from his arousal to adolescent
girls and that each pattern of arousal was elicited from specific cues.
When engaging in sexual contact with young girls, the patient would perceive a "childish flirtatiousness" and would attend primarily to the facial
features and buttocks of his victim. He reported an actual aversion to the
thought of intercourse with a young girl. For adolescent girls, however,
the patient would attend to developing breasts and pubic hair and would
become intensely aroused at the prospect of intercourse. Therefore, these
were treated as separate patterns of deviant arousal and were assessed accordingly.

Masturbation began at age 12 at the frequency of two times per month.
The patient masturbated to pictures of nude women and fantasies of hav-

ing intercourse with older women. He recalled having images of himself engaged with "*Playboy*-type females" in fellatio or intercourse and reported occasionally masturbating to images of women who were casual acquaintances. The patient never masturbated to images of his wife.

Twelve years prior to treatment, the patient began masturbating to images of young girls, which then became the sole content of his fantasies. These images consisted of sexual contact with one of the young girls he had known (approximately age 10). In such an image the patient would begin having "playful fatherly contact" with the girl (tossing the girl up and down in the air and catching her in his arms). The girl would then ask questions of the patient regarding sexual matters in the context of asking a father for knowledge. This would lead to the patient's touching the girl in nongenital areas. The patient would then envision the young girl stimulating his penis with her hand. If the fantasy progressed, the young girl would stimulate the patient's penis with her mouth. The patient was quick to report that there was never any contact with the girl's genitals. He stated that he would not enter the girl's vagina with his hand or his penis because he would be responsible for her loss of virginity.

The patient reported two extramarital sexual relationships that occurred approximately 2 years prior to treatment. The first incident occurred at a massage parlor, where a woman manually stimulated his penis to ejaculation. The other incident involved meeting a woman at a bar while on a business trip. The patient took the woman to a motel, but neither could perform sexually due to their state of intoxication.

The patient claimed that he had never experienced sexual arousal to his children, two daughters (ages 16 and 17) and a son (age 14), each of whom were adopted. In addition, the patient reported having one homosexual contact during his lifetime at age 13 when he and another boy stimulated each other's penis, but not to ejaculation.

At the time of treatment, the patient appeared to be functioning adequately in most areas of his life. He was a highly respected member of the community and his church, and belonged to several charitable organizations. He had received two college degrees and was successful in his position as a corporate executive. Both the patient and his wife reported a fulfilling social life, and both felt that child rearing had progressed satisfactorily.

Assessment Instruments and Devices

In addition to a detailed sexual history, it is more important to include systematic measures of sexual arousal.

Assessment devices have been developed for measuring an array of sexual behaviors, attitudes, beliefs, and orientation. A detailed description of the behavioral approach to sexual assessment is presented by Barlow (1977). Measures vary from behavioral ratings of motor behavior to physiological measures of penile erection or vaginal vasocongestion (Zuckerman, 1971; Hoon, Wincze, and Hoon, 1976). Prior to treatment, the therapist must decide which assessment devices to utilize. There are many factors to consider when choosing measures:

1. *Types of behavior to be assessed.* Certain behaviors are more appropriately measured with specific assessment devices. For example, if persistent deviant images are contributing to sexual arousal, it would be important for the patient to self-monitor the frequency of these thoughts. However, this type of measure might not yield information regarding actual arousal to deviant stimuli, and direct physiological or subjective assessment of sexual arousal would be indicated. The choice of measurement device must correspond to the behavior being evaluated.

2. *Empirical evidence for each measurement device.* Many different measurement devices have been reported in the literature, but very few have been subjected to psychometric evaluation. Thus it is necessary to judge the experimental evidence relevant to each device or instrument.

3. *Ease of administration.* The usefulness of a particular instrument must be weighed against the amount of time and effort necessary for administration. Sophisticated laboratory equipment sometimes requires an inordinate degree of therapist time. If the patient is to self-monitor any behaviors, then the instrument must be easily used and nonaversive.

4. *The cost of measurement.* Some measures require laboratory equipment that can cost thousands of dollars, whereas the cost of many other devices is negligible. The relative merits of different devices must be viewed in terms of cost.

5. *Client's belief that an instrument is a "real" measure of change.* Ongoing assessment serves an informative function and can give the patient an indication of measurable but not noticeable changes. Some patients will claim that "the numbers and graphs really don't mean anything." Therefore, measures that are meaningful to the patient may serve an important feedback function in therapy.

In the present case, a decision was made regarding the aspects of the patient's social and sexual functioning that were most important to evaluate. The patient stated that he wished to decrease deviant arousal so that he would not be inclined to molest young girls or adolescent girls. In addition, the patient's heterosexual arousal was important to measure. The patient reported that his arousal was dependent upon many situational factors, including setting, attributes of the young girl, and the presence of other people. Therefore, measurement of arousal and urges was important in a variety of situations, most of which did not occur in the presence of the therapist. These constraints necessitated instruments that were portable, quickly complete, and nonobtrusive. In addition, a decision was made to measure the patient's sexual and social interactions with both deviant and appropriate stimuli. Two measures were chosen for baseline, treatment, and follow-up phases of treatment. These measures were chosen because they measured relevant aspects of the patient's functioning and had been previously used in a variety of experimental investigations; they were easy to administer, could be self-administered, cost very little, and the patient expressed confidence that the measures would adequately reflect any changes during treatment. The measures are described in detail and offer an example of behavioral measurement possible in most therapeutic settings. One advantage of these particular measures is that they do not require equipment usually not available to private clinicians.

Card-Sort Measure

This measure was developed by Barlow, Leitenberg, and Agras (1969) and consists of having the patient rate arousal to scenes depicting relevant sexual and nonsexual interactions. The scenes are typed on individual index cards after they are generated by the patient and the therapist. The card sort measure has been used in a variety of experimental investigations (e.g., Brownell and Barlow, 1976), and although not specifically investigated, the card-sort measure appears to correlate with self-report of sexual thoughts and images (Barlow, Leitenberg, and Agras, 1969) and physiological measures of penile circumference (Barlow, 1977; Harbert et al., 1974).

In addition to measurement of deviant arousal, it is important to assess whether the intervention influences other social and sexual aspects of the patient's life. For example, the patient did not want to eliminate the pleasurable qualities of social interactions with young girls, and it was, therefore, necessary to measure the social aspects of the patient's functioning. For the patient, scenes were prepared to measure the patient's heterosexual arousal and his desire to interact socially with young girls, as well as deviant patterns of arousal.

Developing meaningful scenes for the card sort requires specific input from the client. A scene must be sufficiently detailed to allow the client to develop a clear image of the situation. Fantasies and images of sexual behaviors vary widely among people. The following dialog demonstrates specific questioning designed to elicit idiosyncratic components of arousal:

T: In developing the card-sort scenes, it will be important to provide enough detail so you can secure a vivid image of the scene. In this fashion, you are most likely to become aroused. The scenes may be actual behavior from the past, thoughts of potential partners, or masturbatory images. Can you give me several situations in which you would likely become sexually aroused by a young girl?

C: Sometimes I imagine them touching my penis.

T: Fine. What about locations and circumstances that might lead up to this?

C: Well, I usually imagine being with the girl in the house, or maybe swimming. I really get turned on when I see girls in bathing suits.

T: Let's use the swimming situation first. Where would you and the girl be and what would you be doing?

C: We'd be swimming. Probably in shallow water so we could both stand up. We would be having fun and playing in the water.

T: What would happen then?

C: The girl would become more friendly and maybe swim between my legs. Since nobody could see us, I would show her my penis.

T: If you were using this image to masturbate, how would it progress further?

C: I might rub myself against her as we both got turned on. That's as far as I'd imagine.

T: Good. We'll be using this as one of the scenes.

This is the manner in which the following scenes were developed:

Arousal to Sexual Interactions with Young Girls (ages 8 to 10)

Scene 1:   I am swimming at a lake with a young girl in shallow water. She swims underwater between my legs. I expose myself and hold her from behind and rub my penis against her legs.

Scene 2:   A young girl comes into the house to play with the dogs. I put my arms around her and pick her up. She puts her arms around me. I put her down and hold her hands against my penis.

Scene 3:   I am driving a car with a young girl sitting beside me. I put my arm around her and my hand under her clothes, rubbing her on the belly and buttocks.

Scene 4:   A young girl visits at the house. We are alone. I get an erection and rub against her. She asks if she can touch my penis. I say yes and ask if she wants to taste it also. She does.

Scene 5: I am in bed, alone in the house. A young girl comes in the bedroom. She climbs into bed with me. She cuddles against me and rubs my penis with her hands.

Arousal to Sexual Interactions with Adolescent Girls (ages 13 to 16)

Scene 1: I am taking the teenage babysitter home. She begins talking about her childhood sex history. We stop for fatherly talk. I make gentle advances, and we begin petting and she responds. We have intercourse.

Scene 2: An adolescent girl is at our house waiting for my daughter. We talk. I turn the conversation to the girl's sexual experience. She is not a virgin; we have intercourse.

Scene 3: I pick up a female hitchhiker when going on a solo camping/fishing trip. She spends the night with me. We have intercourse.

Scene 4: I am at a family reunion with a 14-year-old cousin. It becomes bedtime, so I drive her to the motel and put her to bed. I begin touching her breasts, and as she becomes excited she begins to stroke my penis.

Scene 5: I am on a camping trip with my daughter and a 15-year-old girl. After my daughter is asleep the girl is restless so we go for a walk together. When we are alone I begin to fondle her breasts and she begins to fondle my penis.

Arousal to Sexual Interactions with Wife

Scene 1: I am in a motel room with my wife. We put a wine bottle in the icebucket. We remove each others clothes and the bedspread and have intercourse.

Scene 2: I am in the pool at night with my wife at a small hotel. We swim and begin petting. We remove our swimming suits and continue petting, then grab, touch, and go to our room.

Scene 3: I am alone in the house with my wife, and it is dark outside. We go from the kitchen to the living room. We undress each other and have intercourse on the couch.

Scene 4: I am asleep in bed with my wife. I wake up with an erection. I wake my wife by stroking her breasts and cuddling. Then we move around and are stimulating each other with our mouths.

Scene 5: I am in the shower with my wife. I feel and hear the water. I am behind her and I am rubbing her breasts and vagina. She turns around and rubs my penis and I feel myself getting an erection. I can feel my penis between her legs.

Arousal to Nonsexual Interactions with Young Girls

Scene 1: I am a house guest at a house with a young girl present. The girl and I are alone in the house. She says she has a stiff neck and asks me to massage her neck and shoulders. I do.

Scene 2: A young girl is walking with me in a field at night. The grass is damp. She asks me to give her a piggy-back ride. I do.

Scene 3: A young girl is riding in a car with me. She is cold and asks if she can sit close to me with my arm around her. We ride that way.

Scene 4: A young girl is spending the night at our house. She asks me to tuck her into bed and kiss her goodnight. I do.

Scene 5: I am walking down the street at night with a young girl. She squeezes my hand either affectionately or for security.

Desire to Continue Appropriate Interactions with Young Girls

Scene 1: I am with a daughter of a friend at religious services. My friend has to leave and asks if his daughter can sit with me. We sit together.

Scene 2: A young girl is bicycling by the house, and the bicycle breaks. She comes to the door and asks me to help her. I go outside and fix the bicycle.

Scene 3: A young girl is a beginning skier. I help her get started, including holding her. She holds me.

Scene 4: A young girl falls while skiing and twists her knee. I splint her leg, take her off the hill via toboggan, and carry her into the first-aid room. She clings to me.

Scene 5: I am swimming with a young girl. She has difficulty, and I help her get into shallow water.

During a given session, the patient was presented the cards in random order, asked to secure a vivid image of the scene, and then to rate his level of arousal by placing the cards into one of five envelopes labeled zero to four: 0 no desire; 1 little desire; 2, a fair amount of desire; 3, much desire; and 4, very much desire. Separate scores for each category were obtained by totaling the arousal scores for the five cards within that category. A score of 20 indicated maximum arousal for a given category, and a score of zero indicated no arousal. For the category measuring desire to continue appropriate interactions with young girls, higher numbers indicated increased desire to engage in these interactions. The patient completed the card sort twice daily, once in the morning and once in the afternoon.

Report of Sexual Behavior and Fantasies

A behavioral record was the second measure employed. This scale was designed to assess frequency of appropriate and inappropriate sexual urges and fantasies. The record was divided into daily segments in which the patient could total the number of occurrences of each category of behavior for each day. The patient was asked to carry the record with him at all times and to record an urge or behavior immediately upon its occurrence. An urge or fantasy was defined as a sexual thought, image, or fantasy regardless of whether the patient was in the presence of an arousing object. The patient recorded any sexual urges to young girls (ages 8 to 10), adolescent girls, his wife, and the frequency of masturbation. In order to ensure that the patient was keeping the behavioral record appropriately, several examples were given of possible thoughts or images that he might have throughout the day. A discussion followed in which it was decided which behaviors, thoughts, and images would be included in the rating scale. For example, a sexual image of a young girl was to be recorded as one occurrence, regardless of duration.

T: It is very important for me to know the thoughts and images you have throughout the day. Previously, these urges may have been so fleeting that you weren't fully aware of their content or frequency. In order for you to become more aware of the urges and for me to better gauge your arousal in various situations, I would like you to complete a log of every fantasy, urge, or thought you have throughout the day.

C: How can I keep track of every thought? All I'll be doing is writing.

T: It would be useful to know all your thoughts, but it isn't practical, and there are many thoughts that a person likes to keep private. We are concerned about your specific sexual urges. After you have completed the log for several days, it will no longer be obtrusive and will provide us with useful information.

C: Should I write down each thought about little girls?

T: In the beginning, I'd like you to record the frequency of urges in several categories. It is not necessary to write out the content of each urge. Any urges of young girls are to be recorded. Since you are also interested in decreasing your arousal to adolescent girls, these images should also be recorded. Sexual thoughts of your wife will be another category in order to monitor any changes during or after treatment. In addition, I would like for you to record the frequency of masturbation and to make note of each masturbatory image.

C: What if a thought is quite long, and what if I think about two categories in the same thought?

T: I'm going to define a thought as any time a person of a given category enters your mind and physical contact is involved. If a thought begins, ends, and begins again—two thoughts are recorded. The length of a thought is not important. If you imagine an adolescent girl in the scene with a young girl, then you record a thought in each category.

Table 1 presents the Behavior Record of Sexual Urges.

Table 1. Behavioral Record of Sexual Urges

	Mon.	Tues.	Wed.	Thurs.	Fri.	Sat.	Sun.	Weekly Total
Date:								
Pedophilic urges (young girls)								
Hebephilic urges (adolescent girls)								
Heterosexual urges (wife)								
Frequency of masturbation								

Many investigators have physiologically evaluated sexual arousal in males with the use of a mechanical strain gauge that measures penile circumference (Barlow, Becker, Leitenberg, and Agras, 1970). At the present time, this measure appears to be the most reliable assessment of sexual arousal (Zuckerman, 1971) and may be less susceptible to demand characteristics than self-report measures. The authors routinely utilize the physiological measure in the treatment of sexual deviation, but malfunctioning equipment during the treatment of the patient presented in this chapter precluded its use. Correlations between subjective and physiological arousal have been consistently high (Barlow, 1977), and, therefore, it is likely that the measures used in this case study reflect actual changes in arousal patterns. However, the use of physiological measurement substantially enhances the validity of experimental findings.

The assessment phase of treatment consisted of combining information from the assessment instruments as well as from the sexual history and then conceptualizing the data into the four categories of sexual functioning. The following is a synthesis of the findings.

Deviant Arousal

The patient was highly aroused by exposure to and images of young girls and adolescent girls. The patient's high level of arousal combined with his subjective experience of the behavior being "out of control" necessitated inpatient treatment. The card sort was administered several times during the assessment phase and showed very high levels of arousal for both deviant patterns. The patient was also administered the Sexual Orientation Method (Feldman, MacCulloch, Mellor, and Pinschof, 1966), which was adapted for the measurement of pedophilic arousal and was chosen because of its prior experimental use and ease of administration. Very high arousal to young girls was clearly evident on this measure. In addition, the patient's masturbatory fantasies were exclusively pedophilic.

Heterosexual Arousal

The patient reported that he was highly aroused by sexual contact with his wife. Both the card-sort measure and the Sexual Orientation Method corroborated the patient's subjective report. The presence of heterosexual images in the patient's early masturbatory fantasies was favorable in light of the patient's goal to decrease pedophilic arousal and to improve sexual functioning with his wife. However, in the 12 years prior to treatment there had been no heterosexual content in his masturbatory fantasies, and the patient had never masturbated to images of his wife. In summary, it appeared that the patient was adequately aroused by actual contact with his wife, but deviant images were the sole content of the patient's masturbatory and fantasy behavior.

Heterosocial Skills

For the 6 years prior to treatment, the patient had been distressed by impotence. The patient and his wife were quite concerned about this and felt that the situation could not be remedied. Other than sexual dysfunction, there were no deficits in heterosocial or interpersonal skills. That is, the patient had the skills necessary to develop a meaningful heterosexual relationship. His marriage appeared stable, but in the event of its dissolution the patient had the skills necessary to develop a new meaningful heterosexual relationship.

Gender Role Deviation

A pretreatment behavioral measure of male and female sex-role motor behaviors while sitting, standing, and walking revealed a preponderance of male appropriate behaviors. There was no evidence of spontaneous

cross-dressing at an early age or the development of opposite sex-role behaviors. Assessment revealed no gender role deviation, either on self-
report or objective measures.

Preparing the Client

Adequately preparing the client can be the cornerstone of effective therapy. As Bandura (1974) has pointed out, behavior change is difficult to occasion without the knowledge, willingness, and cooperation of the client.
Cooperation of the patient is, in part, dependent upon the degree to which
the patient is convinced that change is necessary and that the therapist
will be able to bring about that change. These social influence processes
have been studied and variously labeled as subject expectancy, placebo
effects, demand characteristics, and so forth and have a demonstrated
effect on therapeutic outcome (Ullmann and Krasner, 1975). In addition,
therapy rationales vary in credibility, and this credibility itself influences
outcome (Borkovec, 1973; Steinmark and Borkovec, 1974).

Behavioral therapists have long been proponents of measurement and
assessment of behavior change. In clinical practice this often entails data
collection by the patient, or at least the patient's cooperation in the therapist's data collection procedures. The absence of this cooperation makes
it impossible to evaluate therapeutic outcome and to quantify behavior
changes. Therefore, it is important to impress upon the patient the importance of record keeping. The following is a rationale presented to the patient being discussed in this section:

T: One of the most important components of our therapy will be measurement. That is, we need an accurate impression of your behavior,
thoughts, and feelings, in order to evaluate our progress.

C: I know myself pretty well, so I'll be aware of when I change. Isn't
that what's important?

T: How you view your progress is terribly important. I have found
several measures that provide you with an easy method of recording
your thoughts and feelings about your progress. As you know, people often differ in how they view subjective changes. I may think
you're making progress and you may not—or vice versa. If we have
some measure of how the situation is changing, then we are less likely to disagree. Changes are sometimes difficult to see, which leads
some therapists and clients to become discouraged. Adequate measurement can avoid this discouragement by showing changes that are
often obscured by other factors.

C: I guess I can do it, but it doesn't make much sense. Are you testing
something on me? Is this research?

T: Your concerns are understandable. It has only been in recent years that therapists have tried to be scientific with their choice of procedures. Since it is novel to take measures, some people feel they are being experimented upon. Given the seriousness of your problem, I'm sure a proven program would give you confidence that your behaviors could change.

The procedures we are going to use have been proven effective in many experimental studies. Therefore, based upon research findings I am confident that the procedures are the best for your problem. This does not guarantee that the procedures will work for you. Much depends upon your committment and your willingness to help yourself.

The treatment is research in the sense that we will evaluate how well the procedures are working for you. Careful evaluation is the way in which we improve our therapy programs. I can offer you a proven program only because our predecessors have measured what they've done. If we measure your progress we will be able to improve our program for those needing it in the future. Also, we can improvise during the course of treatment if our measures indicate lack of change.

This type of preparation is necessary when introducing any portion of the treatment program. The credibility of an intervention may be damaged if the patient does not fully understand the purpose and rationale for a particular approach.

Therapeutic Intervention and Treatment Results

In order to evaluate the effects of treatment procedures, a single-subject multiple-baseline design was employed. In this design, multiple behaviors are measured throughout treatment, with interventions being successively applied to each behavior (Barlow and Hersen, 1973; Hersen and Barlow, 1976). In so doing, an attempt can be made to control for "history" effects and to determine the effects of treatment on patterns of behavior (Kazdin and Kopel, 1975). This design has been used to measure different behavioral components of a single deviation such as fetishism (Marks and Gelder, 1967) and, more recently, to measure multiple sexual deviations exhibited by an individual (Brownell and Barlow, 1976).

Subsequent to assessment of each component of sexual functioning, decisions must be made to determine appropriate treatment procedures. If a given patient exhibits deficits in heterosexual arousal or heterosocial skills in addition to deviant arousal, the order of interventions must be determined. That is, is it most prudent to eliminate deviant behaviors or to first improve appropriate functioning? There is some evidence suggesting that training in appropriate arousal and social skills should precede reduction of deviant arousal (Barlow and Abel, 1976; Bancroft, 1974). To decrease deviant functioning in the absence of appropriate sexual outlets is tantamount to leaving the client "sexless"—a condition that can be emotionally distressing (Barlow, 1972).

Orgasmic Reconditioning

With the present patient, assessment revealed deviant arousal, no gender-role deviation, appropriate heterosocial skills with the exception of secondary impotence, and adequate heterosexual arousal *in vivo* but not in fantasy. Although not yet experimentally investigated, it appears that the content of sexual fantasies and images (particularly during masturbation) may exert a pivotal influence on sexual functioning. At the time of treatment, the patient's masturbatory images and sexual urges were exclusively pedophilic. Therefore, the initial goal of therapy was to increase heterosexual arousal and fantasy and to provide appropriate future masturbatory images. In addition, it was felt that shifting masturbatory imagery in a more appropriate heterosexual direction might serve the dual purpose of increasing heterosexual arousal and decreasing deviant arousal. In some instances, deviant arousal has been decreased by increasing appropriate arousal (Davison, 1968; Barlow, 1973).

Orgasmic reconditioning was chosen to establish appropriate sexual urges and to develop heterosexual imagery for masturbation. As previously mentioned, orgasmic reconditioning involves systematic substitution of appropriate sexual images for deviant images during masturbation. The following is the rationale presented to the patient and the actual procedures involved in orgasmic reconditioning:

T: It is evident that you are highly aroused by the presence or images of young girls. It is particularly striking that during recent years you have been masturbating almost exclusively to images of young girls. It would be most beneficial if you could replace these images of young girls with more appropriate sexual images of, let's say, your wife.

C: I've felt so guilty about imagining girls when I'm having sex with my wife that I've tried to change my thoughts. The thoughts of the girls keep coming back. Of course, I can get more aroused by these images, but I still feel bad. It's like I don't really love my wife, but I know that I do love her.

T: Your sexual encounters with the young girls, both in fantasy and activity, have been very exciting. This novelty and excitement explain why the images of girls frequently enter your mind. In and of itself, this does not indicate that you don't love your wife. Rather it shows that you are highly aroused to young girls in addition to your wife.

C: What does masturbation have to do with my interest in my wife and girls?

T: Very often, sexual arousal to a particular object will be enhanced by repeated use of a particular fantasy during masturbation. After hundreds of times, the image becomes quite arousing, and the actual behavior seems even more pleasurable.

C: Do you want me to masturbate to thoughts of my wife? If so, I don't know if I can get an erection.

T: In essence, you will be masturbating to images of your wife. It is much more complicated than simply thinking of her while you stimulate yourself. The procedure is straightforward and will serve two purposes. First, since you have never masturbated to images of your wife, the ability to do so should enhance your arousal to her. In addition, by replacing the young-girl images, you will be decreasing the number of times you associate the pleasure of sexual arousal with an inappropriate object. This may reduce your arousal to young girls. We don't want to decrease your arousal to young girls without first putting something equally pleasurable in its place, hence the usefulness of enhancing arousal to your wife.

The procedure we will use is called orgasmic reconditioning. It means we will recondition the images you associate with arousal and orgasm. This technique has been used in numerous investigations and has been proven quite effective. Your ability to imagine sexual scenes so vividly will be of great assistance when using this procedure. I think the technique will work quite well for you.

C: I don't like the sound of this conditioning procedure. I've read about shock treatment being used for severe disturbances. Are you going to use shock on me?

T: Conditioning is used as a label when an event is associated repeatedly with a feeling. In this case, the event becomes positively or negatively valenced depending upon the outcome. For example, if a paperboy is delivering the morning Tribune and a ferocious dog bites his leg, unpleasant feelings develop. If this happens repeatedly, and the boy has no other experience with dogs, he will have an unpleasant association with dogs. These associations can be changed; hence the word reconditioning.

Shock treatment has been used in the past for a variety of problems. In some cases, it is the treatment of choice. However, for your problem, there are procedures that are more effective and certainly less painful than shock treatment.

C: So how can I change my masturbation thoughts if I've had them for so many years?

T: In essence, orgasmic reconditioning consists of gradually modifying the images you have during masturbation. At present you are easily aroused by sexual fantasies of young girls. We want to replace these with images of your wife. I would like you to achieve an erection by the images of young girls. Use the images you are accustomed to and make sure you are highly aroused. Just prior to ejaculation, secure an image of your wife in a sexual position. If you lose the erection, regain the image of the young girl until the erection returns. At the point of ejaculatory inevitability, switch to the image of your wife.

C: What is ejaculatory inevitability?

T: For all males, there is a period of time just before they ejaculate in which they know they can't avoid ejaculation. This period of time can range from 3 to 6 seconds and is called ejaculatory inevitability. It is at this point that you should bring in the images of your wife.
We want to completely replace the young girl images with images of your wife. The most effective way to accomplish this is by a process we call shaping. This refers to taking small and gradual steps towards your final goal with no step being undertaken until you are comfortable with the last. Therefore, if you can comfortable insert the image of your wife 3 seconds prior to ejaculation, try increasing the time span to 10 seconds. When you are able to comfortably accomplish this, further increase the time. I am merely training you in a skill. It is analogous to learning how to ride a bicycle. Initially it is quite difficult and progress might be painfully slow. With practice, however, it becomes almost second nature. The more you practice the more progress we will make.

Initial attempts at orgasmic reconditioning can be less than successful for some clients. Most often, there is difficulty in changing images, securing an appropriate image, or maintaining an erection. In these cases, the therapist can minimize feelings of failure by expecting these problems and by having a solution at his/her disposal. The present client did indeed experience some difficulty.

C: When I try to think of my wife the young girl images keep jumping back into my head. I try to keep them out but I can't. Then I get all mixed up and lose the erection. I don't know if I can do this.

T: There is no reason to be distressed. In fact, this gives us valuable information on how to proceed. It shows me that we took too big a step. That is, the switch from young girls to your wife was a little

hasty. Let's try taking it a little more gradually. Just before you ejaculate, try replacing *part* of the young girl image with something related to your wife. For example, you might envision the young girl with
your wife's breasts, her face, or her buttocks. As you can comfortably replace some aspects, add a few more of your wife's more mature attributes. Remember, if you have difficulty it merely means we
have taken too large a step.

The patient reported success with this approach after several trials, and
then proceeded until the images of his wife became the sole content of his
masturbatory fantasies.

An examination of Figure 1 reveals the baseline levels of all pertinent
arousal patterns as measured by the card sort. Arousal to sexual contact
with young girls, sexual contact with adolescent girls, and sexual interactions with young girls was also at a high level, but was below that of sexual interactions with the same girls. The desire to engage in appropriate fatherly interactions with young girls was also high. Figure 2 displays the
frequency of sexual urges for each arousal pattern. During baseline measurement, the patient reported very few heterosexual urges, many sexual
thoughts of adolescent girls, and a fairly high amount of pedophilic images.

During the orgasmic-reconditioning phase, arousal towards the wife increased slightly and then plateaued at nearly maximum levels. The patient
claimed that he was pleased with his increase in arousal and that he was
relieved to know he could masturbate to images of his wife. Coincident
with this increase in arousal was a substantial decline in arousal to sexual
and nonsexual interactions with young girls, and a slight decline in arousal
to sexual interactions with adolescent girls.

The orgasmic reconditioning was successful in training the patient to be
aroused in fantasy to an appropriate heterosexual stimulus (his wife). At
this point, the patient related that he had originally doubted the usefulness
of this procedure, but was reserving judgment until he tried it. "I felt that
it was an indirect method of treatment. After all, I came here because of
wanting sex with young girls, and you were telling me to masturbate to
pictures of my wife." This suggested that the rationale did not adequately
convince the client as to the importance of the procedure and that for future cases more care had to be taken to fully explain the reasons for such
decisions. The patient was quite surprised and very pleased with the results of orgasmic reconditioning. He remarked "This is the first time I
have masturbated to images of my wife. I am really looking forward to going to bed with her."

Although the patient's arousal to young girls decreased during orgasmic

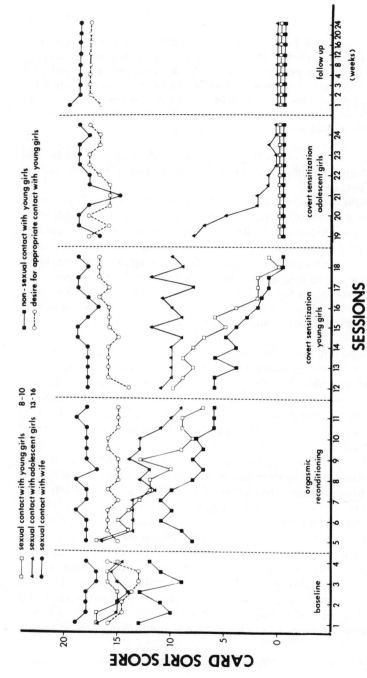

Figure 1. Card sort ratings of sexual arousal to appropriate and deviant stimuli. Ratings are averaged to yield a session score. Desire for appropriate contact with young girls reflects interest in social rather than sexual contact.

Legend:
- sexual contact with young girls   8-10
- sexual contact with adolescent girls   13-16
- sexual contact with wife
- non-sexual contact with young girls
- desire for appropriate contact with young girls

SESSIONS

CARD SORT SCORE

baseline   orgasmic reconditioning   covert sensitization young girls   covert sensitization adolescent girls   follow up

(weeks)

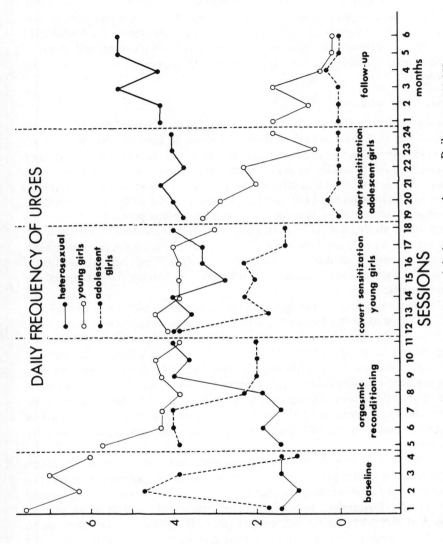

Figure 2. Daily frequency of appropriate and deviant sexual urges. Daily measures are averaged to yield a session score.

reconditioning, the measures revealed that the reduction was not complete. Indeed, the patient reported "I know my arousal has gone down, but I still don't feel as if I have control over my impulses. I am afraid if I get into an intimate situation with a young girl I will force myself on her." Therefore, the decision was made to directly intervene with the deviant arousal.

Covert Sensitization

Covert sensitization, in which aversive images are paired imaginally with deviant stimuli was chosen to directly reduce deviant arousal for several reasons. In reducing deviant arousal, electrical aversion has also been used. However, electrical aversion therapy requires sophisticated equipment that is not often available to the practitioner and is not amenable to self-administration between sessions. Covert sensitization has been demonstrated effective in several experimental investigations. In the only controlled study, covert sensitization was as effective as electrical aversion on a physiological measure of arousal and more effective on subjective measures (Callahan and Leitenberg, 1973). The patient's ability to vividly imagine sexual scenes was a further indication for the use of covert sensitization.

When employing aversion procedures, care must be taken to avoid several of the dangerous associated effects of punishment such as generalization to similar stimulus situations and stress in the presence of the punishing agent (Azrin and Holz, 1966). With the present client, a decrease in sexual arousal to young girls was desired, but not a decrease in arousal to appropriate sexual stimuli. Also, generalization of the aversion to nonsexual interactions with young girls was to be avoided. Therefore, ongoing assessment of these related areas of functioning was an integral part of therapy, and very specific stimulus conditions were paired with aversive images.

As previously mentioned, the patient reported that his arousal patterns toward prepubertal girls (ages 8 to 10) were topographically dissimilar to those toward adolescent girls (ages 13 to 16), the difference being arousal to "childly flirtatious" behavior in the young girls and to more mature physical attributes in the adolescent girls. Therefore, it was decided to pair the aversive scenes with the young girl images first, while continuing baseline measurement of arousal to adolescent girls.

The rationale for covert sensitization was given to the patient at this point. It was emphasized that he must obtain vivid images of both arousing and aversive scenes and that the effectiveness of the procedure would be greatly enhanced by self-administration of the procedure between sessions.

T: Your arousal to your wife is at a very high level. This is a good therapeutic indication of improvement. How do you feel about your progress at this point?

C: I am much more aroused to images of my wife, and I can't wait to get home to have sex with her. Maybe if we have more fun in bed I won't go after girls. But I can't be positive. When I think of young girls I still get very aroused.

T: You have mentioned a most important point. Our measures show a decrease in arousal to young girls, but not to the satisfaction of either of us. Therefore, I want to directly reduce the arousal to young girls with a technique called covert sensitization. This procedure involves having you imagine a sexual scene with young girls (similar to those you have been using to masturbate) and to pair an aversive image with that scene. This procedure has been successfully employed with many people with problems like yours, and should be quite successful in your case.

Covert sensitization is effective for two reasons. First, we want to develop an automatic aversion reaction to arousing situations with young girls by having the arousing image repeatedly paired with the aversive image. In so doing, you will not become aroused in "dangerous" situations. To accomplish this you will need to vividly imagine all the scenes I present. Second, the procedure is useful because you will be learning a skill that you can apply to situations in which you find yourself aroused. If you become aroused by young girls, you can imagine one of the aversive scenes and eliminate the arousal. It is a self-control procedure that you can use regardless of the situation you're in. Since you will be learning a skill, it is very important that you practice.

C: Are you saying that I can hold back from touching young girls even if I am around them and feel myself getting aroused?

T: I will be instructing you to plan your activities in order to avoid situations that are potentially dangerous. For example, it wouldn't be wise for you to volunteer your time for a troop of Campfire Girls.

The covert sensitization will make thoughts of sexual contact with girls very unpleasant. If you find yourself in the presence of girls you will very rarely feel any arousal. If you do, you will have learned a procedure to eliminate the arousal.

C: It sounds fine if it will work. I will sure be happy if I don't have to worry about this anymore. What do I do?

T: I will be presenting sexual scenes of young girls. I will want you to make yourself comfortable, close your eyes, and imagine the scene as if you are actually there. It is very important that you "live" the scene. You should feel, hear, and sense every part of the image. You should not see yourself in the scene, but should actually be there. We will develop some aversive scenes that are to be paired with arousing scenes. Don't forget that anything we do in the sessions can be done on your own between sessions.

In most of the original reports using covert sensitization (e.g., Cautela, 1967), aversive scenes consisted of images of physiological phenomenon such as feeling anxious, feeling nauseous, vomiting, and so forth. More recent reports (e.g., Harbert et al., 1974) have utilized scenes depicting environmental events that are at least partially realistic (e.g., being arrested, etc.). In our more current treatment cases (Brownell and Barlow, 1976), we have begun using more than one aversive image throughout the course of treatment because there is a tendency for patients to habituate to a particular aversive scene, thus decreasing its potency. In addition, by increasing the number of scenes there is a greater likelihood that the patient will find one particularly salient in the presence of the arousing object.

The patient was instructed to produce three different aversive images to be used during covert sensitization. At least two of the three scenes were to be realistic aversive consequences of his behavior if he were to be apprehended. The scenes were as follows:

Aversion Scene 1: Being caught by my daughter. Having her cry hysterically and scream "I hate you." I think of killing myself.

Aversion Scene 2: The young girl's mother catches me. She is terrified of what I have done to her daughter. She tells her priest, who informs the police. They arrest me and tell my family and my boss. I am forced to leave town.

Aversion Scene 3: Being caught by my daughter. She runs upstairs to tell my wife and my mother, who is visiting. They come downstairs and see me naked. I run out of the house and want to die.

Before each session the patient was asked to imagine each of the three scenes and to indicate the most aversive. That scene was then used for the session. The patient appeared to select each scene approximately the same number of times throughout treatment.

During each session, the patient was presented with the five pedophilic arousal scenes, each of which were paired with an aversive scene. Each presentation lasted approximately 3 to 5 minutes with a 5-minute intertrial interval. The interval between trials was necessary because the patient developed acute myotonia during presentation of the aversive scenes and required a period of relaxation. An example of a typical scene is as follows:

Sit back in the chair and get as relaxed as possible. Close your eyes and concentrate on what I'm saying. Imagine yourself in the playroom of your home. Notice the furniture . . . the walls . . . and the feelings of being in the room. The door opens and the 10-year-old girl walks in. As she comes toward you, you notice the color of her hair . . . the clothes she is wearing . . . and the way she is walking. She comes over and sits by you. She is being flirtatious and very cute. You touch her playfully and begin to get aroused. She is asking you questions about sex education, and you begin to touch her. You can feel your hands on her smooth skin . . . on her dress . . . and touching her hair.

As you become more and more aroused, you begin taking off her clothes. You can feel your fingers on her dress as you slip it off. You begin touching her arms . . . and her back. . . . Feeling your hands on her thighs and her buttocks. As you get more excited, you take her hand and place it on your penis. She begins rubbing your penis. You're noticing how good it feels. You are stroking her thighs and getting very aroused. As you both get more aroused she begins using her mouth on your penis. You can feel how warm and wet it is, and how very good it feels.

You hear a scream! As you turn around you see your daughter! She sees you there—naked and molesting that little girl. She begins to cry. She is sobbing hysterically. She falls to her knees and holds her head in her hands. She is saying "I hate you, I hate you!" You start to go over to hold her, but she is afraid of you and runs away. You start to panic and lose control. You want to kill yourself and end it all. You can see what you have done to yourself.

The aversive scenes were presented in great detail during early treatment sessions in order to elicit arousal and to facilitate the imagery process. As treatment progressed, the aversive scenes were introduced earlier into the arousing sequence. In this fashion, the aversive reaction was paired with behaviors early in the chain of sexual arousal.

During the presentation of the aversive scenes the patient would clutch the chair, tense his facial muscles, and writhe in his chair. He reported being physically exhausted after each session. Although more pronounced than usual, these signs are often indications of the ability of the patient to vividly imagine the aversive scene. By monitoring these signs throughout treatment, the therapist can evaluate the aversiveness of particular scenes as well as the patient's physiological response to covert sensitization. It is not uncommon for patients to cry, or to resist attending sessions due to the properties of the aversive scenes. This can usually be handled by relating to the patient the importance of decreasing his deviant arousal and by pointing out the realistic aversive consequences of continued deviant behavior.

Covert sensitization was effective in eliminating arousal to sexual interactions with young girls (see Figure 1). In addition, sexual arousal to nonsexual (fatherly) interactions with young girls declined to a near-zero level. The patient reported that he was no longer having sexual feelings about young girls and that this aspect of his deviant arousal was under control. "My image of contact with young girls has changed from sexual to social. I was walking the other day, and when I was done I realized I had seen several young girls and had not had any feelings about them whatsoever." During this time, arousal for his wife and the desire to continue appropriate interactions with young girls remained high. However, the arousal to adolescents remained at a level slightly below that of baseline. This indicated that the aversion-conditioning procedure was very specific in the arousal patterns it reduced. Examination of Figure 2 reveals similar findings on the behavioral rating scale. After an initial increase, the frequency of pedophilic thoughts declined to zero during covert sensitization.

At this point, it was decided to apply covert sensitization to the adolescent (hebephilic) response patterns. The procedure was identical to that used during the pedophilic phase with adolescent scenes substituted for pedophilic ones. Since the patient reported that the more mature physical attributes of the adolescent girls provoked different arousal patterns than did images of prepubertal females, the presence of mature breasts, pubic hair, and so forth, was important when presenting these sexual scenes.

During this phase of treatment, arousal to adolescent girls dropped to zero and was maintained at that level (see Figure 1). Arousal to sexual and social interactions with young girls stabilized at zero, and the desire to continue appropriate interactions with young girls and sexual contact with the wife remained high. The behavioral rating scale indicated that the frequency of pedophilic thoughts declined to zero. The number of sexual thoughts of the wife also continued to rise (see Figure 2).

Summary of Treatment Findings

The results from this case reveal several different findings. Each pattern of deviant arousal declined to zero only when specifically treated with covert sensitization. This suggests that the procedure, rather than nonspecific therapy factors, was responsible for the positive changes. The decrease in both patterns of deviant arousal, as well as the patient's report that the deviant images had acquired aversive properties, argues for the efficacy of the aversion procedures.

The choice of covert sensitization was undertaken cautiously, and with the hope that its effects would be very specific (Harbert et al., 1974). That is, the procedure would be contraindicated if the aversion to deviant sources of arousal were to generalize to more acceptable sources of arousal (contact with his wife). In addition, the aversion to sexual contact with young girls and adolescent girls should not generalize to appropriate social interactions with the same girls. The data clearly documented the specificity of the covert sensitization. At no time did the patient's sexual arousal to his wife decrease, and his desire to continue appropriate interactions with young girls remained very high. The patient reported that the aversive scenes only entered his mind when he thought of sexually explicit interactions with young girls.

T: I would like to discuss how you are feeling about the various sexual arousal patterns we have been discussing.

C: Most importantly, I am relieved that this burden has been lifted. I feel confident that I can safely be around young girls without the danger of becoming intimate.
Something happened today which might interest you. One of the other patients had several members of her family visit the unit. One of them was a 10-year-old girl. She was pretty, and as soon as I even noticed it I started feeling nauseous and tense. I couldn't have done anything to her even if the chance would have arisen. She came over and worked a puzzle with me, and I felt good. She liked me, and I didn't have any dangerous thoughts.

T: Very good. Your control over these urges can continue and can even increase when you practice as we've outlined. I would expect no recurrences of the urges. If by chance they do come back, you can use the procedure to eliminate them again.

C: I have also learned very much about communicating my feelings to others. I am going to talk more with my wife. It should help us out very much.

T: What do you anticipate happening in your sexual relationship with your wife?

C: I am very excited about how it will be. As you've told me, she may have trouble adjusting to my changes, and there's a chance I'll have trouble getting an erection. I am happy that you referred us back to our therapist at home to help deal with these problems.
As I think about it, I hope I'll be able to do a better job at work. I won't always be feeling guilty and frightened about having bad sexual thoughts. This program has helped me in several ways.

During each session, the patient was instructed to imagine each of the three possible aversive scenes and to select the most potent. Therefore, on any given day, the patient was able to select a scene that he found aversive. It is felt that this procedure increases the chance of finding a truly aversive image. With some patients, the authors have experimented with presenting the aversive scenes in a random fashion so the subject does not anticipate the scene and prematurely end the aversive sequence. Realistic aversive scenes (e.g., being apprehended by family, police, etc.) were used in this case study in lieu of the traditional aversive scenes (becoming violently ill, etc.) used in most early reports (e.g., Cautela, 1967). Many patients report that the realistic scenes are much more aversive and threatening than noxious bodily reactions, but no evidence yet exists as to their relative efficacy.

The patient reported that the formerly uncontrollable deviant behavior was under his control as a result of treatment. He was praised for self-administration of the procedure and was told that he had mastered a skill which he could utilize in difficult situations. The patient was instructed to self-administer the procedure daily for 2 weeks, weekly thereafter for 6 months, and as needed subsequently. Emphasis was placed on the fact that the procedure was an acquired skill that could be self-administered, since the patient had traveled more than 1000 miles to receive treatment from the authors and could not return for booster sessions.

Due to the fact that the patient had traveled so far for treatment, his wife was not available for direct involvement in the treatment program. Sexual contact between the patient and his wife was not possible during treatment, so it could not be determined whether the patient's impotency problems would remain. Even though arousal to his wife had increased and was quite high, there was no guarantee the impotency problem would disappear. Had the patient's wife been available, ongoing assessment and intervention would have been indicated. In the event of impotency, a program modeled after the Masters and Johnson (1970) approach would have been undertaken. The patient's local psychiatrist was notified and made aware of this situation.

In summary, the patient appeared to benefit greatly from treatment of his sexual deviations. A 6-month follow-up revealed no return of deviant arousal, either to young girls or adolescent girls. The patient, his wife, and his psychiatrist reported no recurrences of pedophilic behavior. The patient claimed his arousal towards his wife remained high as a result of the orgasmic reconditioning. Continuing therapy with their psychiatrist improved the couple's communication, and a condensed version of the Masters and Johnson (1970) program alleviated the impotency problem. The patient reported being pleased that he was able to interact socially with young girls with no feelings of sexual arousal. Approximately 2 months after treatment, legal charges for the patient's sexual offense were dropped.

SPECIAL CONSIDERATIONS

Numerous social, environmental, and physical factors influence the course of therapeutic intervention. Verbatim accounts of therapy sessions and data-based research articles often obscure the importance of these factors. Individuals seeking treatment for the same disorder may emerge from widely divergent environments and may exhibit strikingly different behavioral repetoires. Therapy is considerably more complex than the mere application of procedures. Traditionally, behavior therapists used the label "nonspecifics" to include social influence variables that were not directly measured or modified. Contrary to the implication that these variables are nonspecifiable, behavioral clinicians are suggesting that standard principles of assessment and modification are applicable to these variables (Wilson and Evans, 1977). Failure to evaluate the importance of these factors in each individual case precludes a comprehensive treatment program, and mitigates the chance of post-treatment adjustment on the part of the patient. An attempt is made to present the variables that are most influential in the treatment of sexual deviation.

Prognostic Factors

When treating patients with sexual difficulties, it is useful to know the factors that predict successful outcome: and, more importantly, which factors indicate the use of a particular intervention. There is an unfortunate lack of experimentally sound data from which to extract prognostic factors. However, some authors have addressed this issue and have advanced some tentative conclusions.

Previous Heterosexual Adjustment

Several attempts have been made to evaluate the importance of pretreatment heterosexual adjustment when dealing with sexual deviation (e.g., Bancroft, 1974). Some psychoanalytic therapists have suggested that pretreatment heterosexual behavior and heterosexual dream content are more favorable indicators of treatment success in homosexuals than exclusively homosexual arousal patterns (Bieber et al., 1962). Feldman and MacCulloch (1971), using behavioral approaches, have hypothesized that the total absence of heterosexual behavior is the best predictor of poor outcome in the treatment of homosexuals. Of their "improved" group, significantly more subjects had had previous heterosexual experience (secondary homosexuality) than had been exclusively homosexual (primary homosexuality). This finding is not surprising in light of the tendency to concentrate on only one of the aspects of sexual functioning. For example, decreasing deviant arousal by aversion procedures would not be expected to yield favorable outcome in individuals lacking arousal to appropriate stimuli. Therefore, successful outcome would be expected in those patients with a reasonable premorbid heterosexual adjustment. Utilizing an early behaviorial adage, the best predictor of future behavior may be past behavior (Mischel, 1968).

Bancroft (1974) has noted that the findings of Feldman and MacCulloch cannot be used to develop a theory of the etiology of sexual deviation, and that even though significantly more secondary homosexuals improved, this factor is not reliably predictive.

The Individual's Desire to Change

Recently, behavioral clinicians have argued that the goals of therapy are established by the individual whose behavior is to be altered (e.g., Bandura, 1969; O'Leary and Wilson, 1975). This issue is seriously complicated when intense legal and social pressures are influencing an individual. Courts often require psychotherapy for people convicted of sexual offenses. Upon becoming aware of deviant behavior, significant family members may apply massive social contingencies aimed at having the offender seek treatment. Patients often enter treatment to show the relevant public that they are attempting to change or even to prove to themselves that all possibilities for change have been exhausted. Obviously, the mere physical presence of a patient in therapy does not indicate a desire to change.

Motivation to change on the part of the patient is assumed to be a significant factor in therapy. Despite public opinion to the contrary, conditioning is not an automatic process and rarely occurs without the awareness and willingness of the subject (Bandura, 1974). Similarly, many behavioral programs fail when the goals of the client and therapist are discrepant, a phenomenon labeled "counter-control" (Davison, 1973). This suggests that a patient lacking a clear desire to change may profit very little from efforts to alter deviant behavior.

In an early study involving the treatment of homosexuals, Freund (1960) examined the results for 20 cases referred by courts or other social agencies. None of these subjects exhibited lasting improvement. Poor outcome was also noted in the seven patients under extreme pressure from relatives. In the Feldman and MacCulloch (1971) sample, 11 patients were referred by court order and seven others referred after a court appearance. Eight of these 18 improved, as contrasted with 17 of 25 of the remaining subjects (a statistically non-significant difference). Although the evidence is far from conclusive, many authors are suggesting that modification of deviant sexual behavior should not be undertaken as a result of court orders except in cases of extreme antisocial behavior (Bancroft, 1974). Parenthetically, the presence of legal action or extreme social pressure does not rule out a genuine desire to change, and conversely the apparent absence of these factors does not ensure motivation. The patient's motivation must be assessed independently of the other social forces. We generally refuse to treat court-referred sexual deviants unless the court rescinds the mandate for treatment and the patient enters treatment by his/her own choice.

Client Variables

Cognitive, behavioral, and environmental client variables interact with treatment techniques to yield a final therapeutic result. In treating sexual deviation, several of these variables exert an important influence on the course of therapy. Several of the most important factors are discussed in detail in order to present a comprehensive view of the social and cognitive context in which the sexual behavior takes place.

The Client's Moral View of Behavior

There is little question as to how society in general views sexually deviant behavior. That is, the behaviors that define pedophilia, exhibitionism, and so forth are considered morally and ethically reprehensible, which in turn motivates society to initiate legal and social action to prevent their occurrence. However, the patient does not always share the belief that his/her behavior is "wrong." Patients will often construct elaborate cognitive systems within which their behavior is justified. A heterosexual pedophile treated by the authors provides an example of this phenomenon. Prior to treatment the patient claimed "there was nothing wrong with my behavior. I was within the limits of normality." This patient maintained that he was giving his victims the "sex education necessary for healthy living." This belief was present even though the patient was well-educated and responsible, and was clearly aware of the difficulties that might ensue from his behavior.

It is also common for sexual deviants to feel that their victim was "asking for it" and that they were helpless participants in an act which was destined to occur. The previously mentioned pedophile claimed that "each girl was being childishly flirtatious and wanted to know more about sex." Within this cognitive framework, the victim was seen as "needing" the deviant behavior to occur, actively eliciting it from an ambivalent person and thereafter being grateful for its occurrence. This patient stated "I physically and emotionally cringe at the thought of doing harm to a young girl," and, therefore, felt that the behavior was acceptable only when the child was being flirtatious and somehow desirous of the behavior. Even in the fact of disastrous emotional consequences for the victim, these patients will often adhere to the notion that the victim "really wanted it."

Dispelling these cognitive misconceptions is important before embarking upon direct attempts to alter behavior. If the client believes he/she is somehow doing the victim a favor, the motivation for change may be minimal. Direct confrontation can be helpful in dealing with this difficulty. That is, most patients respond to repeated suggestions that irreparable emotional damage is often perpetrated by their actions and that there is little likelihood that the victim actually wanted the behavior to occur. With the development of a new cognitive framework, additional motivation may arise which may facilitate treatment.

False Suppression of Arousal

Another phenomenon that arises in the treatment of sexual deviation is the false sense of security accompanying temporary suppression of deviant arousal. After a very short time in treatment and often before treatment begins, patients will claim that they are "no longer interested" in the deviant behavior and that it is "completely under control." This notion is most often a result of embarrassing social or legal events that prompt statements like "how could I have done such a thing, I'll never do it again." It is at this point that some patients wish to terminate therapy, feeling that there is no longer a problem. The patient should be cautioned that in all probability, the suppression is temporary. The strength of the aversive events can fade with time, and the prepotent deviant arousal patterns may again be dominant.

To illustrate the therapist-client interaction regarding the false suppression of arousal, the following is an excerpt from a therapy session with an exhibitionist:

C: I don't really need to go through all these procedures we are talking about. I know my flashing happened many times, but it won't happen anymore. I don't want to lose my wife, my job, and everything.

T: You seem to be pretty confident that the behavior is under control.

C: Every time I think about the night I got arrested, I just about die. I would be stupid to do it again.

T: Thinking of the possible consequences appears to have made exposing yourself less desirable.

C: I've learned my lesson. I think that will be enough. I'll just use willpower.

T: Your feelings are understandable given how upset you and your family were about your arrest. Many of the patients I see have similar feelings. They are so overwhelmed by the aversive consequences of their actions that with complete certainty, they feel they can refrain forever. In one way, those bad feelings are useful. For a short time at least, they will allow you to avoid dangerous situations.

C: Are you saying that these feelings might wear off and I might go back to it?

T: Exposing yourself has been a very positive and rewarding experience for you for many years. During that time, you have expressed yourself hundreds of times, very often in high-risk situations. Even though you are frightened about the consequences, the behavior itself will remain highly reinforcing until a direct attempt is made to reduce it.

As they say, time heals all wounds—including wounds received when arrested. Most of our patients experience a decline in how they feel about an arrest or another aversive circumstance as time goes on. At this point, the behavior is likely to re-emerge.

C: Do you mean that it may be under control now, but later it will come back?

T: I can't guarantee that it will come back. For some people, an arrest is enough. However, your behavior is of such duration, frequency, and intensity that your willpower may be only temporary. If you deceive yourself now and avoid treatment, you may pay a steep price later.

C: To play it safe, I should probably go through treatment.

T: Right. This is a crucial time for you and I am confident that our program can help you.

Clinical Indications of Progress

An issue rarely dealt with in the behavioral literature is the presence of "soft" signs of improvement. That is, reliable and valid measurement devices are by definition accurate indices of therapeutic progress. However, there are also nondata-based indicators of progress that are rarely mentioned and can be useful for the clinician. Many of these factors have yet to be subjected to the rigors of experimental scrutiny, but in the absence of quantification, a clinical discussion of their importance could benefit the practitioner.

One such factor is the client's self-report of his/her ability to imagine both arousing and aversive scenes during covert sensitization. This can often change throughout treatment, and in our experience it has been highly correlated with successful outcome. That is, many of our patients have had increasing difficulty securing and maintaining the deviant images as treatment progressed. This must be assessed relative to the patient's ability to achieve the images early in treatment. This is most often seen when the patient self-administers covert sensitization. The patient may report shifting from a participant role to a spectator role in the arousing scenes. After several therapist-administered sessions of covert sensitization and numerous self-administered sessions, the patient presented earlier reported that "I am having a harder time becoming aroused by the sexual scenes of young girls. I am picturing having had an erection rather than actually having one." The patient was not informed beforehand that this might occur and volunteered the information spontaneously. Often, this will be an exciting breakthrough for the patient. Many will feel encouraged by this lack of arousal in situations that were previously stimulating.

A similar phenomenon may occur with the aversive image. Early in treatment the aversive scene does not enter the image until explicitly presented. As treatment progresses, some patients will report that the aversive scene is "jumping into the picture" prior to its presentation by the therapist. One patient began violently writhing in the chair during the arousing image. He stated that "The aversive scene came in and I couldn't get rid of it even though you were presenting the sexual image." This may generalize to self-administered covert sensitization in which the aversive image will enter the deviant scene prior to an effort by the patient to have this happen. In addition, patients sometimes report the presence of the aversive images in dreams. Although these indicators of progress have not been systematically evaluated, the authors have noted these phenomena in a striking number of successful patients.

Self-Administered Covert Sensitization

The authors also consider it useful to train patients in the self-administration of covert sensitization. This is a general treatment approach adopted by the authors and can be particularly useful in treating sexual deviation. Patients are instructed to practice the procedure several times each day, and in some instances a tape-recorded session is used by the patient until imagery techniques are mastered. In addition, each patient is trained to summon the aversive scene upon recognition of any deviant urge or impulse. This gives the patient a coping strategy with which to avoid the deviant behavior in any situation. This may also decrease dependency on the therapist and increase the likelihood of maintenance.

Anxiety and Loss of Pleasure

Several other factors can impede therapeutic progress and need to be evaluated prior to technique administration. Incapacitating anxiety sometimes arises in patients with sexual difficulties. This anxiety is most often a result of legal action or extreme social pressure applied by members of the immediate family or community. For many of our patients, court action has been pending during treatment. The potential loss of family, friends, and job, combined with the possibility of a jail sentence, can create intense anxiety. Such difficulty must be remedied before treatment can be productive. Systematic desensitization, flooding, thought stopping, anti-anxiety medication, or other anxiety-reduction techniques may be indicated in these cases. Most patients are under some degree of stress from related problems, and a comprehensive assessment should include evaluation of this factor.

Patients must also be prepared for the loss of pleasure to be experienced as a result of treatment. That is, deviant arousal is to be reduced in most cases, and the patient may be divested of massively rewarding experiences. Sexual arousal to deviant stimuli should not occur after treatment. This loss of pleasure can lead to feelings of depression, and the patient may doubt his/her ability to develop other meaningful sexual contacts. In these cases it is helpful to explain to the patient that the ability to initiate appropriate sexual contacts is a major focus of treatment and that he/she will not be "sexless."

CONCLUDING COMMENTS

One of the distinguishing characteristics of behavior therapy is the attempt to subject therapeutic techniques to the rigors of experimentation (O'Leary and Wilson, 1975). This emphasis on methodology and evaluation has generated an impressive body of knowledge that has been useful in the treatment of many disorders. More importantly, many clinicians are beginning to objectively determine the effectiveness of their procedures and are being guided by experimental evidence rather than subjective impression.

The use of single-subject experimental methodology (Hersen and Barlow, 1976) has significantly enhanced the researcher's ability to evaluate clinical techniques. This has been especially relevant in the treatment of disorders whose incidence do not permit experimentation with large and homogeneous groups of subjects (e.g., autism and obsessive-compulsive behaviors). In the treatment of sexual deviation, large groups of subjects exhibiting similar behavioral patterns have been difficult to assemble. Accordingly, many of the recent well-controlled investigations have utilized single-case designs.

Sexual functioning is a multifaceted phenomenon in which a particular individual may present excesses and deficits in a variety of areas. Barlow

(1974) has proposed four principal areas of concern when treating sexual disorders: heterosexual arousal, heterosocial skills, deviant arousal, and gender-role deviation. The absence of detailed assessment in each area increases the likelihood of therapeutic failure. In the treatment of transvestism, for example, a decrease in deviant arousal might lead to serious difficulties if the patient does not exhibit heterosexual arousal and is, therefore, not able to develop alternative sexual outlets. Indeed, the actual decrease in deviant arousal should be preceded by treatment of difficulties in the other three areas.

It is possible that various components of sexual behavior are functionally autonomous. For example, heterosexual arousal may not be influenced by changes in deviant arousal, and changes in gender-role deviation may not influence the degree to which a person is heterosocially skilled (Brownell and Barlow, 1976). However, an important caveat must be issued. There is little experimental evidence to suggest whether any consistent relationship exists between various components of sexual functioning. Further research may provide an answer to this important question, but presently each area requires individual assessment in order to develop a comprehensive treatment program.

Sexual deviation does not occur in a social vacuum. A constellation of environmental, interpersonal, and cognitive factors can profoundly influence outcome. Adequate assessment of these factors is necessary to develop a comprehensive treatment program. Deviant behavior is often overtly or covertly reinforced by family members, and intervention with significant others may be important. Extreme legal or familial pressure can temporarily boost a patient's motivation and may prompt some patients to become less than totally involved in treatment. The therapist patient relationship is also important, and the lack of credibility and warmth on the part of the therapist can inhibit disclosure and cooperation. The patient's cognitive view of his/her own behavior must also be evaluated prior to treatment. If the patient believes that the victims are actually profiting from the deviant acts, then cognitive restructuring of this notion is necessary. Assessment in each of these areas often reveals the need for intervention into problems only indirectly related to actual sexual behavior. Sexual behavior is very complex, and actual techniques are only a portion of the total treatment picture.

REFERENCES

Abel, G., Levis, D., and Clancy, J. Aversion therapy applied to taped sequences of deviant behavior in exhibitionism and other sexual deviation: A preliminary report. *Journal of Behavior Therapy and Experimental Psychiatry*, 1970, *1*, 59–60.

Annon, J. S. The extension of learning principles to the analysis and treatment of sexual problems. *Dissertation Abstracts International*, 1971, *32*(6-B), 3627.

Azrin, N.H., and Holz, W.C. Punishment, In W.K. Honig (Ed.), *Operant behavior: Areas of research and application*. New York: Appleton-Century-Crofts, 1966.

Bancroft, J. A comparative study of aversion and desensitization in the treatment of homosexuality. In L.E. Burns and J.L. Worsley (Eds.), *Behavior therapy in the 1970's*. Wright: Bristol, 1970.

Bancroft, J. *Deviant sexual behaviour: Modification and assessment*. Oxford: Clarendon 1974.

Bandura, A. *Principles of behavior modification*. New York: Holt, Rinehart, and Winston, 1969.

Bandura, A. Behavior therapy and the models of man. *American Psychologist*, 1974, *29*, 859–869.

Barlow, D.H. Aversive procedures. In W.S. Agras (Ed.), *Behavior modification: Principles and clinical applications*. Boston: Little Brown, 1972.

Barlow, D.H. Increasing heterosexual responsiveness in the treatment of sexual deviation. *Behavior Therapy*, 1973, *4*, 655–671.

Barlow, D.H. The treatment of sexual deviation: Towards a comprehensive behavioral approach. In K.S. Calhoun, H.E. Adams and K.M. Mitchell (Eds.), *Innovative treatment methods in psychopathology*. New York: Wiley, 1974.

Barlow, D.H. Assessment of sexual behavior. In R.A. Ciminero, K.S. Calhoun, and H.E. Adams (Eds.), *Handbook of behavioral assessment*. New York: Wiley, 1977.

Barlow, D.H., and Abel, G.G. Recent developments in assessment and treatment of sexual deviation. In W.E. Craighead, A.E. Kazdin, and M.J. Mahoney (Eds.). *Behavior modification: Principles, issues, and applications*. Boston: Houghton Mifflin, 1976.

Barlow, D.H., Abel, G.G., Blanchard, E.B., Bristow, A.R., and Young, L.D. A heterosocial skills behavior checklist for males. *Behavior Therapy*, 1977, *8*, 229-239.

Barlow, D.H., and Agras, W.S. Fading to increase heterosexual responsiveness in homosexuals. *Journal of Applied Behavior Analysis*, 1973, *6*, 355–366.

Barlow, D.H., Agras, W.S., Leitenberg, H., Callahan, E.J., and Moore, R.C. The contribution of therapeutic instructions to covert sensitization. *Behaviour Research and Therapy*, 1972, *10*, 411–415.

Barlow, D.H., Becker, R., Leitenberg, H., and Agras, W.S. A mechanical strain gauge for recording penile circumference change. *Journal of Applied Behavior Analysis*, 1970, *3*, 73–76.

Barlow, D.H., Leitenberg, H., and Agras, W.S. The experimental control of sexual deviation through manipulation of the noxious scenes in covert sensitization. *Journal of Abnormal Psychology*, 1969, *74*, 596–601.

Barlow, D.H., Reynolds, E.J., and Agras, W.S. Gender identity change in a transsexual. *Archives of General Psychiatry*, 1973, *28*, 569–576.

Beech, H.R., Watts, F., and Poole, A.D. Classical conditioning of sexual deviation: A preliminary note. *Behavior Therapy*, 1971, *2*, 400–402.

Bieber, B., Bieber, I., Dain, H.J., Dince, P.R., Drellich, M.G., Grand, H.G., Grundlach, R.H., Kremer, M.W., Wilbur, C.B., and Bieber, T.D. *Homosexuality*. New York: Basic, 1963.

Birk, L., Huddleston, W., Miller, E., and Cohler, B. Avoidance conditioning for homosexuality. *Archives of General Psychiatry*, 1971, *25*, 314–323.

Blitch, J.W., and Haynes, S.N. Multiple behavioral techniques in a case of female homosexuality. *Journal of Behavior Therapy and Experimental Psychiatry*, 1972, *3*, 319–322.

Bond, I.K., and Evans, D.R. Avoidance therapy: Its use in two cases of underwear fetishism. *Canadian Medical Association Journal*, 1967, *96*, 1160–1162.

Borkovec, T.D. The role of expectancy and physiological feedback in fear research: A review with special reference to subject characteristics. *Behavior Therapy*, 1973, *4*, 491–505.

Brownell, K., and Barlow, D.H. Measurement and treatment of two sexual deviations in one person. *Journal of Behavior Therapy and Experimental Psychiatry*, 1976, *7*, 349-355.

Callahan, E.A., and Leitenberg, H. Aversion therapy for sexual deviation: Contingent shock and covert sensitization. *Journal of Abnormal Psychology*, 1973, *81*, 60–73.

Cautela, J.R. Covert sensitization. *Psychological Reports*, 1967, *20*, 459–468.

Cautela, J.R., and Wisocki, P.A. The use of male and female therapists in the treatment of homosexual behavior. In R. Rubin and C. Franks (Eds.), *Advances in behavior therapy, 1968*. New York: Academic, 1969.

Colson, C.E. Olfactory aversion therapy for homosexual behavior. *Journal of Behavior Therapy and Experimental Psychiatry*, 1972, *3*, 1–3.

Conrad, S.R., and Wincze, J.P. Orgasmic reconditioning: A controlled study of its effects upon the sexual arousal and behavior of adult male homosexuals. *Behavior Therapy*, 1976, *7*, 155-166.

Cooper, A.A. A case of fetishism and impotence treated by behavior therapy. *British Journal of Psychiatry*, 1963, *109*, 649–652.

Curran, D., and Parr, D. Homosexuality: An analysis of 100 male cases seen in private practice. *British Medical Journal*, 1957, *1*, 797–801.

Curran, J.P., and Gilbert, F.S. A test of the relative effectiveness of a systematic desensitization program and interpersonal skills training with date anxious subjects. *Behavior Therapy*, 1975, *6*, 510–521.

Davison, G.C. Elimination of a sadistic fantasy by a client-controlled counterconditioning technique: A case study. *Journal of Abnormal Psychology*, 1968, *73*, 84–90.

Davison, G.C. Counter-control in behavior modification. In L.A. Hamerlynck, L.C. Handy, and E.J. Mash (Eds.), *Behavior change methodology, concepts, and practice.* Champaign, Ill: Research, 1973.

Davison, G.C. Homosexuality: The ethical challenge. Presidential address, Annual Convention of the Association for the Advancement of Behavior Therapy, Chicago, December 1974.

Davison, G.C., and Valins, S. Maintenance and self-attributed and drug attributed behavior change. *Journal of Personality and Social Psychology*, 1969, *11*, 25–33.

Edwards, N.B. Case conference: Assertive training in a case of homosexual pedophilia. *Journal of Behavior Therapy and Experimental Psychiatry*, 1972, *3*, 55–63.

Evans, D.R. An exploratory study into the treatment of exhibitionism by means of emotive imagery and aversive conditioning. *Canadian Psychologist*, 1967, *8*, 162.

Feldman, M.P., and MacCulloch, M.J. The application of anticipatory avoidance learning to the treatment of homosexuality. I. Theory, technique, and preliminary results. *Behaviour Research and Therapy*, 1965, *2*, 165–183.

Feldman, M.P., and MacCulloch, M.J. *Homosexual behavior: Therapy and assessment.* Oxford: Pergamon, 1971.

Feldman, M.P., MacCulloch, M.J., Mellor, V., and Pinschoff, J. The application of anticipatory avoidance learning to the treatment of homosexuality. III. The sexual orientation method. *Behaviour Research and Therapy*, 1966, *4*, 289–299.

Fookes, B.H. Some experiences in the use of aversive therapy in male homosexuality, exhibitionism, and fetishism-transvestism. *British Journal of Psychiatry*, 1968, *115*, 339–341.

Ford, C.S., and Beach, F.A. *Patterns of sexual behavior.* New York: Harper, 1951.

Freud, S. *New introductory lectures in psychoanalysis* (1932). New York: Norton, 1933.

Freund, K. Some problems in the treatment of homosexuality. In H. J. Eysenck (Ed.), *Behavior therapy and the neuroses.* Oxford: Pergamon, 1960.

Freund, L., Langevin, R., Cibiri, S., and Zajac, Y. Heterosexual aversion in homosexual males. *British Journal of Psychiatry*, 1973, *122*, 163–169.

Freund, K., Nagler, E., Langevin, R., Zajac, A., and Steiner, B. Measuring feminine gender identity in homosexual males. *Archives of Sexual Behavior*, 1974, *3*, 249–261.

Gagnon, J.H., and Davison, G.C. The enhancement of sexual responsiveness in behavior therapy. Paper presented at the American Psychological Association convention, New Orleans, September 1974.

Gaupp, L.A., Stern, R.M., and Ratliff, R.G. The use of aversion-relief procedures in the treatment of a case of voyeurism. *Behavior Therapy*, 1971, *1*, 585–588.

Gelder, M.G., and Marks, I.M. Aversion treatment in transvestism and transsexualism. In R. Green and J. Money (Eds.), *Transsexualism and sex reassignment*. Baltimore: Johns Hopkins U.P., 1969.

Gray, J.J. Case conference: Behavior therapy in a patient with homosexual fantasies and heterosexual anxieties. *Journal of Behavior Therapy and Experimental Psychiatry*, 1970, *1*, 225–232.

Green, R. *Sexual identity conflict in children and adults*. New York: Basic, 1974.

Green, R., and Money, J. *Transsexualism and sex reassignment*. Baltimore: Johns Hopkins U.P., 1969.

Green, R., Newman, L.E., and Stoller, R.J. Treatment of boyhood transsexualism. *Archives of General Psychiatry*, 1972, *26*, 213–217.

Hanson, R.W., and Adesso, V.J. A multiple behavioral approach to male homosexual behavior: A case study. *Journal of Behavior Therapy and Experimental Psychiatry*, 1972, *3*, 323–325.

Harbert, T.L., Barlow, D.H., Hersen, M., and Austin, J.B. Measurement and modification of incestuous behavior: A case study. *Psychological Reports*, 1974, *34*, 79–86.

Herman, S.H. An experimental analysis of two methods of increasing heterosexual arousal in homosexuals. Unpublished doctoral dissertation. University of Mississippi, 1971.

Herman, S.H., Barlow, D.H., and Agras, W.S. An experimental analysis of classical conditioning as a method of increasing heterosexual arousal in homosexuals. *Behavior Therapy*, 1974, *5*, 33–47.

Hersen, M., and Barlow, D.H. *Single case experimental designs: Strategies for studying behavior change*. New York: Pergamon, 1976.

Hersen, M., and Bellack, A.C. Social skills training for chronic psychotic patients: Rationale, research findings, and future directions. *Comprehensive Psychiatry*, 1976, *17*, 559-580.

Hersen, M., and Eisler, R.M. Social skills training. In W.E. Craighead, A.E. Kazdin, and M. J. Mahoney (Eds.), *Behavior Modification: Principles, Issues, and applications*. Boston: Houghton Mifflin, 1976.

Hoon, P., Wincze, J., and Hoon, E. Physiological assessment of sexual arousal in women. *Psychophysiology*, 1976, *13*, 196-204.

Hore, B.D., Nicolle, F.V., and Calnan, J.S. Male transsexualism in England: Sixteen cases with surgical intervention. *Archives of Sexual Behavior*, 1975, *4*, 81–88.

Huff, F. The desensitization of a homosexual. *Behaviour Research and Therapy*, 1970, *8*, 99–102.

Jackson, B. A case of voyeurism treated by counter-conditioning. *Behaviour Research and Therapy*, 1969, *7*, 133–137.

Kanfer, F.H., and Phillips, J.S. *Learning foundations of behavior therapy*. New York: Wiley, 1970.

Kazdin, A.E. Covert modeling, model similarity, and reduction of avoidance behavior. *Behavior Therapy*, 1974a, *5*, 325–340.

Kazdin, A.E. Effects of covert modeling and model reinforcement on assertive behavior. *Journal of Abnormal Psychology*, 1974b, *83*, 240–252.

Kazdin, A.E., and Kopel, S.A. On resolving ambiguities in the multiple-baseline design: Problems and recommendations. *Behavior Therapy*, 1975, *6*, 601–608.

Kinsey, A.C., Pomeroy, W.B., Martin, C.E., and Gebhard, P. *Sexual behavior in the human female*. Philadelphia: Saunders, 1953.

Kohlenberg, R.J. Treatment of a homosexual pedophiliac using in vivo desensitization: A case study. *Journal of Abnormal Psychology*, 1974, *83*, 192–195.

Kolvin, I. "Aversive imagery" treatment in adolescents. *Behaviour Research and Therapy*, 1967, *5*, 245–249.

Kraft, T. A case of homosexuality treated by systematic desensitization. *American Journal of Psychotherapy*, 1967a, *21*, 815–821.

Kraft, T. Behavior therapy and the treatment of sexual perversions. *Psychotherapy and Psychosomatics*, 1967b, *15*, 351–357.

Kraft, T. Desensitization and the treatment of sexual disorders. *The Journal of Sex Research*, 1969a, *5*, 130–134.

Kraft, T. Treatment for several perversion. *Behaviour Research and Therapy*, 1969b, *7*, 215.

Larson, D. An adaptation of the Feldman and MacCulloch approach to treatment of homosexuality by the application of anticipatory avoidance learning. *Behavior Research and Therapy*, 1970, *8*, 209–210.

Lebovitz, P. Feminine behavior in boys: Aspects of its outcome. *American Journal of Psychiatry*, 1972, *128*, 1283–1289.

Levin, S., Hirsch, I., Shugar, G., and Kapche, R. Treatment of homosexuality and heterosexual anxieties with avoidance conditioning and systematic desensitization: Data and case report. *Psychotherapy: Therory, Research, and Practice*, 1968, *5*, 160–168.

LoPiccolo, J. Case study: Systematic desensitization of homosexuality. *Behavior Therapy*, 1971, *1*, 394–399.

LoPiccolo, J., Steward, R., and Watkins, B. Treatment of erectile failure and ejaculatory imcompetence of homosexual etiology. *Journal of Behavior Therapy and Experimental Psychiatry*, 1972, *3*, 233–236.

Lovibond, S.H. Conceptual thinking, personality, and conditioning. *British Journal of Social Clinical Psychology*, 1963, *2*, 100–111.

Maletzky, B.M. "Assisted" covert sensitization: A preliminary report. *Behavior Therapy*, 1973, *6*, 117–119.

Marks, I. Management of sexual disorders. In H. Leitenberg (Ed.), *Handbook of behavior modification*. New York: Appleton Century Crofts, 1976.

Marks, I.M., and Gelder, M. G. Transvestism and fetishism: Clinical and psychological changes during faradic aversion. *British Journal of Psychiatry,* 1967, *113,* 711–729.

Marquis, J.N. Orgasmic reconditioning: Changing sexual object choice through controlling masturbatory fantasies. *Journal of Behavior Therapy and Experimental Psychiatry,* 1970, *1,* 263–271.

Marshall, W.C. The modification of sexual fantasies: A combined treatment approach to the reduction of deviant sexual behavior. *Behaviour Research and Therapy,* 1973, *11,* 557–564.

Martinson, W.D., and Zerface, J.P. Comparison of individual counseling in a social program with nondaters. *Journal of Counseling Psychology,* 1970, *17,* 36–40.

Masters, W., and Johnson, V. *Human sexual inadequacy.* Boston: Little Brown, 1970.

Max, L.W. Breaking up a homosexual fixation by the conditioned relaxation technique: A case study. *Psychological Bulletin,* 1935, *32,* 734. (Abstract)

McConaghy, N. Subjective and penile plethysmograph responses following aversion relief and apomorphine aversion therapy for homosexual impulses. *British Journal of Psychiatry,* 1969, *115,* 723–730.

McConaghy, N. Penile response conditioning and its relationship to aversion therapy in homosexuals. *Behavior Therapy,* 1970, *1,* 213–221.

McConaghy, N., and Barr, R.F. Classical, avoidance, and backward conditioning treatments of homosexuality. *British Journal of Psychiatry,* 1973, *122,* 151–162.

McFall, R., and Marston, A. An experimental investigation of behavior rehearsal in assertive training. *Journal of Abnormal Psychology,* 1970, *76,* 295–303.

McGuire, R., Carlisle, J., and Young, B. Sexual deviations as conditioned behavior: A hypothesis. *Behaviour Research and Therapy,* 1965, *2,* 185–190.

Mees, H.L. Sadistic fantasies modified by aversion conditioning and substitution: A case study. *Behaviour Research and Therapy,* 1966, *4,* 317–320.

Mischel, W. *Personality and assessment.* New York: McGraw Hill, 1968.

Money, J., and Erhardt, A.N. *Man and woman, boy and girl.* Baltimore: Johns Hopkins. U.P., 1973.

Obler, M. Systematic desensitization in sexual disorders. *Journal of Behavior Therapy and Experimental Psychiatry,* 1973, *4,* 93–101.

O'Leary, K.D., and Wilson, G.T. *Behavior therapy: Application and outcome.* Englewood Cliffs, N.J.: Prentice-Hall, 1975.

Oversey, L., Gaylin, W., and Hendin, H. Psychotherapy of male homosexuality. *Archives of General Psychiatry, 9,* 19–31.

Pauly, I. Male psychosexual inversion: transsexualism: a review of 100 cases. *Archives of General Psychiatry,* 1965, *13,* 172–181.

Rachman, S. Sexual fetishism: An experimental analogue. *The Psychological Record,* 1966, *16,* 293–296.

Rado, S. An adaptational view of sexual behavior. In P. Hoch and J. Zubin (Eds.), *Psychosexual development in health and disease.* New York: Grune and Stratton, 1949.

Ramsey, R.W., and Van Velzen, V. Behavior therapy for sexual perversions. *Behaviour Research and Therapy,* 1968, *6,* 17–19.

Reckers, G.A., and Lovaas, O.I. Behavioral treatment of deviant sex-role behaviors in a male child. *Journal of Applied Behavior Analysis,* 1974, *7,* 173–190.

Serber, M. Teaching the nonverbal components of assertive training. *Journal of Behavior Therapy and Experimental Psychiatry,* 1972, *3,* 179–183.

Silverstein, C. Book review of J. Bancroft, *Deviant sexual behaviour: Modification and assessment. Behavior Therapy,* 1975, *4,* 576–580.

Simon, W., and Gagnon, J. Psychosexual development. In J.H. Gagnon and W. Simon (Eds.), *The sexual scene.* New York: Transaction, 1970.

Solyom, L., and Miller, S.A differential conditioning procedure as the initial phase of behavior therapy of homosexuality. *Behaviour Research and Therapy,* 1965, *3,* 147–160.

Steinmark, S.W., and Borkovec, T.D. Active and placebo treatment effects on moderate insomnia under counterdemand and positive demand instructions. *Journal of Abnormal Psychology,* 1974, *83,* 157–163.

Stevenson, I., and Wolpe, J. Recovery from sexual deviations through overcoming nonsexual neurotic responses. *American Journal of Psychiatry,* 1960, *116,* 739–742.

Stoller, R.J. *Sex and gender.* New York: Science House, 1968.

Stoller, R.J. Parental influences in male transsexualism. In R. Green and J. Money (Eds.), *Transsexualism and sex reassignment.* Baltimore: Johns Hopkins U.P., 1969.

Stoller, R.J. Male transsexualism: Uneasiness. *American Journal of Psychiatry,* 1973, *130,* 536–539.

Thorpe, J.G., Schmidt, E., Brown, P.T., and Castell, D. Aversion-relief therapy: A new method for general application. *Behaviour Research and Therapy,* 1964, *2,* 71–82.

Thorpe, J., Schmidt, E., and Castell, D.A comparison of positive and negative (aversive) conditioning in the treatment of homosexuality. *Behaviour Research and Therapy,* 1963, *1,* 357–362.

Ullmann, L.P., and Krasner, L. *A psychological approach to abnormal behavior: Second edition.* Englewood Cliffs, N.J.: Prentice-Hall, 1975.

Wickramasekera, I. The application of learning theory to the treatment of a case of sexual exhibitionism. *Psychotherapy: Theory, Research, and Practice,* 1968, *5,* 108–112.

Wickramasekera, I. A technique for controlling a certain type of sexual exhibitionism. *Psychotherapy: Theory, Research, and Practice,* 1972, *9,* 207–210.

Wilson, G.T. Innovations in the modification of phobic disorders in two clinical cases. *Behavior Therapy,* 1973, *4,* 426–430.

Wilson G.T., and Davison, G.C. Behavior therapy and homosexuality: A critical perspective. *Behavior Therapy*, 1974, *5*, 16–28.

Wilson, G.T., and Evans, I.M. The therapist-client relationship in behavior therapy. In R.S. Gurman and A.M. Razin (Eds.), *The therapist's contribution to effective psychotherapy: An empirical approach.* New York: Pergamon, 1977.

Wolpe, S. *The practice of behavior therapy.* New York: Pergamon Press, 1973.

Wood, D., and Obrist, P. Minimal and maximal sensory intake and exercises as unconditioned stimuli in human heart-rate conditioning. *Journal of Experimental Psychology*, 1968, *76*, 254–262.

Woodward, M. The diagnosis and treatment of homosexual offenders. *British Journal of Delinquency*, 1958, *9*, 44–59.

Zuckerman, M. Physiological measures of sexual arousal in the human. *Psychological Bulletin*, 1971, *75*, 297–329.

CHAPTER 11

The Treatment of Stuttering

DAVID BURNS AND JOHN PAUL BRADY

Department of Psychiatry
University of Pennsylvania
Philadelphia, PA.

INTRODUCTION: THE NATURE OF STUTTERING

Many theories concerning the cause of stuttering have been proposed in this century (Webster, 1974), but the pathogenesis of this puzzling disorder remains to be revealed. While some investigators have proposed an organic basis for stuttering—emphasizing the possible role of genetic, physiologic, or biochemical factors—others have focused on the role of psychological factors such as stress and disturbed interpersonal relationships. Approaches to treatment have been characterized by a similar theoretical proliferation, and a variety of therapies have been proposed including the use of drugs, psychotherapy, and numerous speech-training methods. In his review, Webster (1974) has suggested that the field can be characterized by an overabundance of methodologies and hypotheses, many of which have been inadequately investigated. He has emphasized the need for well-controlled quantitative research to advance our understanding of this affliction.

In recent years there has been a growing consensus among behaviorally oriented clinicians that it is therapeutically and experimentally useful to view the disorder of stuttering in learning-theory terms. A behavioral analysis published elsewhere (Brady, 1968) may be summarized as follows. The disorder of stuttering consists of two components that continuously interact: (1) nonfluencies in speech generally recognized by the patient and his listeners as "stuttering," and (2) anxiety and tension in a variety of speaking situations. The anxiety and tension are largely in anticipation of stuttering, which, in fact, make stuttering all the more likely in that particular situation. Since the production of speech sounds is largely voluntary in nature, it is greatly influenced by operant (skeletal motor) conditioning. Since the anxiety and tension associated with speaking are largely involuntary in nature, they are viewed as the product of Pavlovian (autonomic) conditioning.

The behavioral approach requires that attention be focused on the antecedent events (or situations) that lead to stuttering in susceptible persons, and an examination of the consequences of the stuttering that tend to reinforce and maintain the behavior. For most patients, the dysfluencies occur only in social situations defined by the presence of one or more individuals who can hear and evaluate the stutterer's speech. For severe stutterers, the presence of any other individual may be a sufficient cause for difficulty; for others, periods of fluency may be interrupted by periods of dysfluency only in response to certain types of stimuli. Such stimuli may include members of the opposite sex, groups, telephones, authority figures, and so forth, as well as certain emotionally charged interactions (e.g., during angry encounters).

The probability and severity of stuttering in response to such stimuli depend on the amount of tension and anxiety experienced by the individual as the moment of *speaking* approaches. The tension, frustration, and embarrassment experienced when the stuttering actually occurs tend to confirm the stutterer's belief that such situations will in fact be difficult, leading to an intensification of the link between the external stimulus and the conditioned emotional responses. In other words, the stutterer's prediction that he will stutter in certain situations tends to be confirmed over and over again in his everyday experience, resulting in a fixed belief that he is indeed bound to fail whenever such situations are encountered. Thus the expectations and experiences interact in a self-confirming closed system. This self-generating aspect of stuttering is recognized by stutterers themselves as well as by therapists who work with them.

The repeated frustrations in efforts to *speak* are frequently interpreted by the stutterer as an inability to *relate* in various stressful situations. As a result, the negative beliefs about speech frequently evolve into negative beliefs about the self, such as "I am always bound to fail in relating to women. I am basically inferior. People in authority are bound to reject me. I will always make a fool of myself in groups," and so forth. Such irrational attitudes are maintained with a high degree of belief and are associated with ongoing negative affects such as anxiety and depression. Not only do such beliefs and emotions tend to propagate the dysfluent speech pattern, but they are also associated in varying degrees with socially maladaptive behavior patterns, including avoidance, passivity, and withdrawal. This withdrawal can in some cases take the form of giving up certain career aspirations, avoiding marriage, and with juvenile stutterers can sometimes lead to frankly antisocial behavior, including truancy, fighting, and problems with those in authority. These maladaptive patterns frequently result in negative feedback from others, which is interpreted by the stutterer as further confirmation of his beliefs about his own inadequacy. Thus the distorted beliefs about his own identity, image and worth become a part of the dysfluency syndrome.

In summary, the disorder called stuttering may be viewed as a system in which several components continually interact: an abnormal speech pattern (dysfluency), anxiety or tension in a variety of interpersonal interactions, and a series of beliefs or expectations that stuttering and interpersonal failure will in fact occur whenever certain stressful situations are encountered. In the treatment program described in the following, some procedures are directed to speech retraining. The aim is to help the patient develop a more fluent pattern of speaking. Other procedures such as systematic desensitization and cognitive restructuring are directed at reducing the anxiety generated in speaking situations, and at enabling the stutterer to develop a more realistic set of attitudes about himself and to acquire more appropriate social skills and behavior patterns. Finally, the use of psychopharmacologic agents with dopamine-blocking properties is discussed as an ancillary short-term treatment modality that in most patients can facilitate fluent speech.

THERAPEUTIC PROCESS

Therapeutic Setting

Environmental Variables

The treatment is usually administered on a one-to-one basis in an outpatient setting. Family members can be included in the therapy, especially during the first several weeks when therapy is focused primarily on the techniques of speech retraining. Such individuals are designated as "home coaches." Their job is to practice on a daily basis with the client and to provide feedback to the client about the correct use of the various speech-retraining methods introduced by the therapist.

Although the therapy is usually carried out in the office, it can be beneficial for the therapist to accompany the client outside of the office to practice speaking in a more public situation. This can include walking back and forth with the client in the hallway at the clinic, encouraging conversation in a crowded elevator, or chatting in a local snackbar where others will be sure to overhear the conversation. Although this procedure is stressful to the majority of clients, it does build considerable confidence, and the presence of the therapist is helpful in overcoming the anxiety inherent in the process of the generalization of fluent speech.

It can also be helpful to arrange group-therapy meetings to supplement the individual therapy, especially in the later stages of treatment and when considerable fluency has been achieved. This helps to overcome the fear of group situations that is almost universal among stutterers. In addition, this group allows for role-playing situations that various individuals find stressful. For example, a high school student had a great fear of having to give a talk in class. The therapy-group members arranged their chairs as in a class room and acted out the feared scene. The young man did well and spoke fluently in spite of considerable anxiety. This successful experience gave him the needed confidence to speak up more frequently when he was actually called on in school.

Therapist Attitudes

A traditional therapeutic relationship—in which a transference develops on the part of the client—is not encouraged. Rather, the therapist and client work as equal team members toward the resolution of the problem. Similarly, few if any interpretations are made of unconscious factors, motivations, or childhood experiences.

It is important that the therapist adopt a nonjudgmental attitude toward any uncooperativeness on the part of the client. Many clients have at least a mildly negative attitude toward treatment, which is based on years of frustration and failure. We find it most beneficial to adopt a patient and confident attitude. We try to expose the illogic in the client's negativism by encouraging him to evaluate actual evidence concerning his progress.

We have not found it necessary to utilize "therapeutic contracts" with patients who do not do their home practice regularly. In such a contract, the continuation of therapy is typically made contingent on a regular homework completion. Such contracts do not counteract the lack of confidence in the treatment that is the cause of the failure to cooperate. Such a contract may backfire and result in termination by the client.

Data Gathering

While the diagnosis of stuttering does not ordinarily present any difficulties, a thorough assessment of the extent of the disorder for each individual patient is quite important in designing an optimal therapeutic strategy. It is important to obtain a thorough history during the first meeting with the client, including the following information:

Reason for Referral for Treatment

Why is the client seeking help at this particular time? How did he or she hear about the clinic? Was he recently in treatment with another therapist? Did he desire treatment, or did someone such as a parent or spouse encourage the client to come? How does the client feel about treatment?

A significant percentage of patients referred to us perceive themselves as being "pushed" by someone else into treatment and frequently feel resentful. These are usually teenagers or preteenagers who are brought in by their parents. It is important to uncover this immediately so that the therapist can help the client deal with the resentment and prevent a premature termination.

For example, Fred was a 13-year-old boy whose parents saw an article about stuttering in a local paper. He was unusually quiet and sullen during the first session. The parents provided most of the history, which included years of unsuccessful speech therapy in special classes at school in which he often felt "singled out." Fred gave only brief, uninformative answers to questions, and when probed by the therapist he finally burst out with "I *don't like* speech therapy." When such a situation develops it is important to acknowledge the client's feelings and to emphasize that he or she may not have had a good experience with previous therapies that in truth didn't help much and did last a long time. The therapist pointed out that many clients find the current therapy different in three respects: (1) it actually works quite well for most clients. (2) it doesn't take years and years, and (3) it can be fun.

After explaining that the therapy can be fun, the therapist demonstrated this to Fred by introducing the concept of a "chip reinforcement" system which he felt Fred would like. The therapist took out a collection of poker chips from his desk and asked: (T, therapist; F, Fred; P, parents)

T: What kind of things do you like? Watching late movies on TV? Going to a '76er Basketball game?

F: I like tropical fish. I have a 55-gallon aquarium.

T: Is there a special fish you need?

F: I'd like to have a Discus fish, Angel Fish, Spotted Pim Cats, and 4-Lined Pim Cats.

T: (To parents) Would it be okay for your son to earn some of the fish as a part of the therapy?

P: Yes, that would be fine.

T: Okay, you get a Discus fish if you earn 100 chips. Now these white chips are worth one, these red chips are five, and these blue chips are worth ten. Now you need 100 chips.

F: So I can get the fish?

T: Right. Now you just earned five chips for listening to me and another five chips for talking. That's ten so far. (He hands a blue chip to Fred.)

F: I like this. How long will it take to earn 100 chips?

T: That was good. You talked some more so I'm giving you three more chips. You may earn 100 by the end of this session. Some clients earn hundreds every day. You can earn chips by practicing at home, by participating in therapy sessions, and so forth.

F: What all can I use the chips for?

T: That's up to you and your parents to work out. It will be like a store, and you can cash in your chips for all kinds of special privileges, fish and other rewards you want. Different rewards will cost different amounts of chips. And if you work hard, you can earn hundreds and maybe over a thousand chips.

F: I think I like this therapy a lot. Can I earn more time to play ice hockey with my Dad?

T: We can speak with him about that. It is a good idea and might be worth 500 chips. By the way you just earned a bonus of twenty chips for all the talking you're doing.

F: I want to keep talking some more.

T: Great—that's worth another chip. Now I want to get some more information about your history.

It is quite impressive how rapidly this method works in converting a negative attitude into a positive one and in enlisting support and cooperation in a potentially resentful young client. It is of course important that the reward system be worked out in collaboration with the parents so that it is within acceptable financial and behavioral limits.

History of the Problem

At what age did the stuttering begin? How has the problem developed through time? How does he perceive the attitudes of others, including parents and friends, toward his speech?

History of Treatments

At what ages did the client receive therapy? How long did each period of therapy last? What was the frequency of treatments? What was the type of treatment? Were any of these treatments beneficial, and did any approach actually make the problem worse?

A number of the clients referred to us have been previously treated with analytically oriented psychotherapy or with supportive therapy and have not experienced significant improvement in their speech. For example, Frank was a 44-year-old single attorney who had been treated for 10 years with 5 days a week psychoanalysis prior to referral to our clinic. He had contacted us about the speech-retraining program a year before he began treatment, but he had been strongly discouraged by his analyst, who told him that the speech retraining would be in conflict with the continuation of his analysis. Frank explained "The analyst feels that stuttering results from unconscious conflicts about aggression. . . . I was told that any fluency resulting from speech retraining would be artificial and a form of obsessive behavior. . . . I've been working on the analysis for years, but my speech hasn't improved significantly. I've been told I'll become fluent when the conflicts are resolved, but I've begun to doubt this." Frank naturally wanted to know about the nature of the psychotherapy he would be receiving at our clinic.

The therapist explained that "The first emphasis will be on speech retraining so as to develop fluent speech. In this way the program differs significantly from psychoanalysis, in which an attempt to manipulate speech may be viewed as counterproductive. In cognitive/behavioral therapy there is no interpretation of unconscious motivations or childhood experiences. Rather, the focus is on the here-and-now with the aim of finding specific solutions to emotional problems that impede the generalization of fluent speech. For you such problems include the fear of speaking before the judge and anxiety when speaking into the dictaphone. The cognitive therapy is based on the hypothesis that such emotional disturbances are not due to these *situations*, but to the *attitudes* you have when you are in these situations. The attitudes of stutterers are frequently maladaptive and involve distorted beliefs about the distressing experience. Therapeutic interventions are directed at correcting these distortions and developing a more appropriate set of attitudes which will facilitate fluent speech. As a result of this, there is frequently a rapid change in the emotional state leading to increased fluency and self-confidence. We call this attitude restructuring. Unlike psychoanalysis it is not time consuming, and we should make significant headway in the initial treatment contract of 20 therapy sessions."

Family History

Are there any relatives who had a speech disorder? Did this difficulty clear up spontaneously or persist into adulthood? It is important to inquire specifically about siblings, children, parents, grandparents, aunts, uncles, and cousins.

In our experience, approximately half of the clients referred to us do have a positive family history of a speech disorder. These data are consistent with the hypothesis that there may be a genetic component to the disorder, although further research will be needed to confirm this possibility and to clarify the mode of inheritance as well as the relative role of genetic and environmental influences. It is important to discuss any concerns the client has in this regard.

The fears of parents concerning their role in their children's dysfluency can at times be considerable. For example, a 38-year-old dysfluent woman with two fluent children, aged 6 and 8, expressed considerable guilt and depression resulting from her belief that one or more of the children would become dysfluent and that this would be her fault:

T: What gives you the idea that your children will stutter?

C: I've heard it is possibly a genetic disease and that the parent's tension can somehow make it worse. I'm very tense.

T: Let's look at each of these fears. First, you say it is a genetic disease. That may be partially correct. The final answer is not yet in. But what is known is that there are many stutterers who have fluent children, and conversely there are many stutterers whose parents did not stutter. So the genetic contribution is not an all-or-nothing phenomenon. At this time there is no evidence that either of your children has ever stuttered, and there is no evidence that this will occur.

C: But if it does occur it will be my fault.

T: What is the cause of stuttering?

C: I don't know. You said the cause was not yet known. That's probably correct.

T: If the cause is not known, we could not say that you are the cause. And if you are not the cause, how could it be your fault?

C: But I feel my tension will be the cause.

T: There is no proof of that. Many mothers are tense, and their children are fluent. You have been tense up until now, and your children are fluent. While we could not state with absolute certainty that your children will never develop dysfluency, it does seem quite unlikely considering their ages. If they did become dysfluent, we could discuss various approaches for early treatment. But since this problem does not now exist, there is no need to try to solve it. Why don't we try to solve problems that do exist—namely, your dysfluency and anxiety? The main problem with your tension is that it makes you uncomfortable and it probably does make *you* less fluent. It might be beneficial to work on this tension, but for your own benefit, as a part of your therapy. This will help to enhance your own self-esteem and alleviate any concerns about your adequacy as a mother.

Medical History

Is the client under treatment for any medical illness? Does the client take any medicines? Has the client at any time been treated by a psychiatrist or psychologist for any emotional difficulties? Does the client use drugs such as hallucinogens, amphetamines, and so forth? How much alcohol does the client drink? Does the client have any illness, including epilepsy, liver disease, or cardiac arrhythmia, that might preclude the use of a psychotropic agent (such as haloperidol) during the course of therapy?

Although there is no definitive evidence linking stuttering with any other specific psychiatric disorder, some stutterers will simultaneously suffer from other emotional difficulties including depression, schizophrenia, drug abuse, and so forth. The presence of such difficulties may interfere with speech retraining and should be taken into account by the therapist. Due to the limits of this chapter, the treatment of such combined disorders will not be discussed in any detail. However, in such cases therapy should be directed at both dysfluency as well as any other disabling emotional disorder.

Behavioral Analysis

The behavioral analysis consists of a determination of the types of situations in which speech is most difficult and a review of the ways that stuttering has interfered with the client's adjustment to life. The therapist can ask the client to develop a hierarchy of feared situations, ranking this from one (least difficult) to ten (most difficult). If more detailed information is desired, the client can be asked to fill out the Stutterer's Self-Rating of Reactions to Speech Situations, a form developed by Johnson and coworkers (1963). This inventory lists 40 common speaking situations and asks the stutterer to rate the severity of his stuttering in each one on a five-point scale ranging from "I don't stutter at all in this situation" (rated 1) to "I stutter severely in this situation" (rated 5).

Information about life adjustment can be obtained with questions such as "In what ways do you feel that stuttering has interfered with your life?" or "Is there anything about your life that might be different if you didn't have a speech problem?" and so forth. It is helpful to ask specifically about school, career, and interpersonal relationships including romance and marriage.

For Frank, the attorney discussed previously, a prominent behavioral impairment involved his career. Although highly qualified and a top graduate of a prestigious law school, Frank had the belief that his dysfluent speech made him only "half an attorney." He felt intensely inadequate when speaking to his boss and had avoided asking for a raise. He explained his situation:

F: "Well, as you know I am an attorney. At the present time I am looking around for a new job that would be more rewarding than the job that I have. For me to go looking for a new job is not a new thing since I have done this before, but it involves a lot of anxiety and a lot of self-doubts. You have to attempt to measure yourself up against all the other people who are in the market place looking for jobs.

My experience and my record are not too bad, and I would have gone a long way I think in the legal profession had it not been for this speech impediment that limited my ability to perform as a lawyer. Not only was speaking difficult, but I also lacked the self-confidence because I could not count on myself to come through in speaking situations in which a lawyer normally would have to perform. This had a bad effect when it came to getting a job because a lot of people were reluctant to hire me when they could hire a lawyer who not only had a good background but who also could speak fluently and, therefore, would be more useful. So, I had to attempt to find jobs in which I would be able to survive and make a living while I was working on my psychological problems, hoping that some day I would have the speech problem resolved and could then move on to things that were more in line with what I aspired to.

For a long time I was a magazine editor, after having lost a job at a law firm as a result of not being able to speak in speaking situations. Then I obtained a job in my present law firm. But I still feel reluctant to really go out and try to find a better job because my speech is not resolved. I don't really want to expose myself to potential employers more than necessary before I get the speech resolved because otherwise I would become more known as not being able to speak. I would rather have people know me as being a person that could speak.

T: After we have developed an acceptable level of fluency, we might want to work on your job situation. It might be that some assertiveness training and role playing would be helpful to you in either requesting a raise or in speaking to potential employers and in negotiating terms of a contract. We can work on these issues later on in therapy if you are interested. Once you have learned to *speak*, you might want to learn more about *speaking up*."

Frank's poor self-image and work difficulties illustrate the intimate relationship between speech dysfluency and social deficiencies. Frank expressed relief that the treatment would attempt not only to improve his speech but also to train him in needed behavioral skills.

Emotional Assessment

The therapist can elicit the maladaptive attitudes and feeling that have contributed to any behavioral difficulties. The therapist might inquire "In what way does stuttering prevent you from achieving this goal?" For example, Ted, a 32-year-old, self-employed single man with a mild stuttering problem was referred to our clinic after his father, a prominent attorney, had read about the speech-retraining program in a local newspaper. At the initial evaluation, Ted explained that he never married: "Being a stutterer, I felt I could never provide adequate financial security for a wife. I broke off two engagements because of this concern." He had dropped out of college after 2 years because of his belief that "A stutterer could never make it as an attorney. Since I can't become an attorney, what's the point of going to college?" Ted emphasized that the feelings that accompany such attitudes include loneliness, frustration, anxiety, guilt, and depression.

Maladaptive attitudes and feelings usually accompany the stressful experiences listed on the client's hierarchy of feared situations. Ted had great difficulty ordering food in restaurants, especially if he was on a date. He explained: "I feel tense and fearful, and I have the expectation that I will stutter and then be rejected. The waitress will be impatient, embarrassed, and uncomfortable. This will ruin the evening for the people I am with, and I will make a fool of myself."

The therapist administered the Beck Depression Inventory (Beck, 1967) to Ted. This is a 21-question multiple-choice self-rating test that can be administered briefly in the office. The test indicated that Ted was experiencing a mild chronic depressive reaction that was clinically significant. The therapist proposed that cognitive restructuring treatment might be directed toward depressive as well as anxiety reactions in the later phases of therapy when fluency was established. The methods of this cognitive therapy are illustrated subsequently.

Quantitative Analysis

A quantitative assessment of the severity of the stuttering is desirable because this provides an objective measure of the disorder at the beginning and at the end of treatment, allowing for a realistic evaluation of the success of the therapy. If assessments are repeated at weekly intervals, this will provide the patient with accurate feedback about the amount of improvement he has achieved. This is of considerable importance because of the tendency of many stutterers to overlook their improvement and to focus on any dysfluency as a sign of "total failure" in the treatment program. Even a 40% improvement early in treatment can be the beginning of an important trend that would probably be overlooked by many clients if not demonstrated by objective measures.

Another advantage of quantification is to allow the therapist to determine in the first session how much dysfluency the client is actually aware of. Some clients are aware of only a fraction of their actual verbal errors. It is a paradox that while clients often *overemphasize* the importance and significance of their difficulty they frequently *underestimate* the actual number of dysfluencies in their speech. Since successful treatment depends on the clients awareness of his dysfluencies, it is important to provide feedback that will facilitate the acquisition of self-monitoring skills.

The method we recommend involves obtaining a 3-minute tape recording of reading. The difficulty of the reading material should be geared to the client's educational level. The recording should be obtained toward the end of the first session after taking the history. This enables the client to become comfortable with the therapist and the office. Many clients are anxious at the first session, and any speech recording made in the first few minutes might lead to a false overestimation of the severity of the problem. After the recording, the therapist can ask the client if he feels that his speech during the recording was representative of the type of speech he has at other times.

During the recoding the therapist counts the number of dysfluencies, which are defined as a clear hesitation or block: the repetition of a syllable, word, or phrase: the prolongation of a sound: or the use of a "filler" ("ah," "er," "like," "you know," etc.) No effort was made to assign different "weights" to nonfluencies of different duration or severity. From these data, three parameters are obtained: (1) the total dysfluencies per 3 minutes; (2) the total words spoken (rate of speaking) and: (3) the percent dysfluency rate, defined as the ratio of total dysfluencies to total words spoken times 100%. The total words spoken can be quickly calculated from the total lines read times the number of words per line. The therapist can also note which sounds are especially difficult for the client and should observe what secondary phenomena are present, including tremors, lip puckering, and so forth.

The following is a transcript of the quantitative analysis of the speech of an American-born Asian premedical University student with a near-straight-A average with unusually severe dysfluency. He was instructed to read out loud from an easy adventure novel containing no difficult or unusual words. All dysfluencies are underlined, and blocks are indicated by parentheses:

Uhnay you and I *(10 second silence)* T.A.'s *Uhnay* Joseph *uhhhn (3 second silence) ssst und (10 second silence)* talk *uhhhhn (2 second silence) Naybimbee (3 second silence) uhnay* share *anaaa (14 second silence)* to a *aaaananaaa (4 second silence)* coalition and the government. (The first minute of recording is completed.) *Iuh Iuh Iuh neto und* a *anda* I *gets* along *ahnay* I will with *(13 second silence) aaaa* and I *benbe aa an a a a a a aaa (4 second silence) and assss* and *I* associated *and I associ* and I moved *uhawuhaw* and might avoid *undi undi* (The second minute of recording is completed.) *(10 second silence)* further *aaandI andI* bloodshed *aaaandi sssince (13 second silence)* you and I *(7 second silence) ta aaaandI andI comans enue aaandI* travels *sst (4 second silence) danort anda aaanouh soth (13 second silence) toaaaa* I deny the *aaaa* NPLA *aaaaaaaa (4 second silence)* outright. (End of 3 minute test.)

This individual's speech was quite difficult to understand and at times nearly incoherent. It is not difficult to empathize with the frustrations of this brilliant young man aspiring to a professional career with a heavy emphasis on verbal skills. The multiple silences were associated with facial grimacing as he attempted to force out the sounds. In addition to prolongations, distortions and repetitions of sounds, he uses numerous odd fillers such as "ahnay," "Iuh," and so forth. The total number of dysfluencies during this 3-minute period, including blocks, was 67. The total number of words read, not including repetitions or dysfluencies, was 37. Thus the dysfluency rate was unusually high, 181%. The reading rate was quite slow, only 13 words per minute.

After completing the recording it is helpful to ask the patient to estimate his total number of dysfluencies. When there is a significant discrepancy from the therapist's actual count, the tape can be replayed so as to enable the client to improve his ability to self-monitor his dysfluencies.

It is the goal of therapy to reduce the percent dysfluency rate, which best measures the severity of stuttering and takes into account both the number of dysfluencies as well as the rate of speaking. Some clients initially have a tendency to speak too rapidly, and a goal of therapy would be to reduce the percent dysfluency rate as well as the rate of speech. Other patients with prolonged blocks such as this premedical student may initially be able to speak only 10 or 20 words per minute. For such individuals, successful treatment will result in an increased rate of speech.

Preparing the Client

After assessing the severity of dysfluency, the therapist can ask how much improvement the client would require in order to consider the treatment successful and worthwhile. The majority of clients, because of previous frustrations in treatment, give low estimates, such as 40 to 60% improvement. In such cases, the therapist can explain that it is not unusual for the client to do at least that well—and often much better—in the course of treatment. However, an occasional client, such as an adolescent client named Jerry, will say "I will only be happy with 100%." In such a case, the therapist used the following strategy:

T: Then what would you conclude if you had a 90 or 95% improvement?

J: Well, that would be great.

T: But you told me you will only settle for 100%. If you achieve 95%, you will have failed to reach your goal.

J: But 95% would be a great improvement.

T: And how about 85 or 75%?

J: That would still help, but not as much as 95%.

T: Many clients do, in fact, reach 90 to 95% or even greater degrees of improvement. But if you say 'I'll only settle for 100%.' then you will be constantly upset, and this upset feeling will, itself, get in the way for further improvement. In point of fact, few people—if any—are *perfectly* fluent. Occasional mild dysfluencies are a part of normal speech. So if you aim for 100%, you will almost definitely fail, because nobody is perfectly fluent. But if you aim to do the best you can, you will have an excellent chance of reducing your dysfluency to the point that it is either not a problem, or is at least much less a problem than it has been.

It is helpful at this point to show the client a typical progress chart of a successfully treated client. In such a chart, the individual's dysfluency rate is plotted as a function of weeks in therapy.

Such a chart indicates several important features of the therapy. First, many clients experience an initial "honeymoon" effect, which is characterized by rapid improvement early in treatment. In fact, it is not unusual for mild-to-moderate stutterers to become almost completely fluent during their first therapy session. However, the maintenance of this fluency and its generalization into stressful situations outside of the office requires patience and ongoing hard work. This is referred to as the "marriage" period of therapy.

The therapist can also point out the oscillating nature of the improvement curve, with periods of improvement alternating with transient "set-backs." Such "set-backs" usually occur in the context of tension and stress. If the client is alerted to this at the start of treatment, this can help to minimize the feelings of discouragement and hopelessness and the urge to give up that typically arise at some point during therapy.

The therapist emphasizes to the client that the first stages of therapy will focus primarily on speech retraining so as to develop fluency. When issues about the use of these techniques in stressful situations arise, the client will be introduced to the use of cognitive and behavioral methods to restructure feelings and attitudes concerning the feared situations on the behavioral hierarchy. The therapist proposes that if the client finds that this works satisfactorily, he might also want to develop some new approaches to other problem areas in his life such as school, career, and interpersonal relations so as to overcome the behavioral impairments caused by his previous dysfluency.

The therapist explains to the client that he will function as a coach, whose job it is to suggest various exercises that the client is expected to perform on his own during daily practice sessions outside of therapy. We emphasize that the successful completion of the daily "homework assignments" is the major mechanism that results in changed speech as well as the development of a more appropriate and realistic self-image. The rationale for such daily practice is that the client has been practicing bad speech habits every waking hour for many years. Since speech retraining involves *learning* new speech habits, it is not unreasonable to spend some time every day to counterbalance the hours and hours of practicing bad speech habits in the past. The image of the therapist as coach is particularly helpful to young stutterers who have an interest in athletics. If they have some skill of special interest—like weight-lifting—the therapist can emphasize that progress in any athletic activity results from first learning the correct technique and then applying this technique patiently and persistently over a period of time. Defining the therapist as a coach seems particularly helpful in circumventing the fears and anxiety that many individuals experience during their first session and emphasizes collaboration and training as important components of the therapy.

Course of Therapeutic Intervention

The Pacing of Speech (Session 1)

The first therapy session can be scheduled immediately following the initial evaluation, resulting in two 1 hour, back-to-back sessions. This minimizes anxiety about the nature of the treatment process and allows the client ample time to become comfortable with the new therapist.

The treatment program is most likely to be successful if it includes not only the proper methodology for producing fluent speech in the office and at home, but also techniques for reducing the tension and anxiety that inhibit the generalization of fluent speech in a variety of situations which the client perceives as stressful and threatening. In order to achieve these goals, it is necessary that a strong sense of teamwork between therapist and client evolve.

We introduce the method by explaining to the client that one of the most intriguing phenomena in the puzzling disorder of stuttering is the marked increase in fluency that usually occurs when a stutterer paces his speech with an external stimulus. The effect is especially striking if the stimuli are rhythmic, as when a stutterer paces his speech with a metronome (Barber, 1940). We explain that it is not known why pacing speech with a metronome has this effect. From a series of experiments, however, it is clear that the effect is not due merely to slowing the rate of speech or providing a distraction (Brady, 1969). Further, it is not merely a matter of "suggestion" or a "placebo response," since the effect is very reliable and does not "adapt out" over time. Although the efforts to use metronomes for the treatment of stuttering date back more than a century (Colombat De L'Isere, 1831), the principle has been of limited use therapeutically, mainly because of poor carry-over of fluency from speaking with a metronome to speaking without one. We emphasize that the problems of carry-over appears to be solvable because of two technical developments: one electronic and the other behavioral. Miniaturized, electronic metronomes have been developed that can be worn unobtrusively by the patient on his body. This makes the metronome available to the stutterer in a great variety of speaking situations: in particular, in the situations he encounters in his daily life in the natural environment. Equally important is the development of a behavioral program for extending the use of the metronome into these various situations and then systematically withdrawing its use while allowing the patient to remain fluent.

The first step in the metronome-conditioned speech retraining (MCSR) program is to find conditions under which the patient can be highly fluent with the aid of a desk metronome. For a severe, chronic stutterer this may require being alone with the therapist and pacing one syllable of his speech to each beat of a loud metronome set as slow as 40 beats per minute, while using easy reading material as the source of words. A less severe stutterer might be able to begin with extemporaneous, conversational speech with the metronome set at 80 and pacing one word to each beat.

Conditions can almost always be found under which the patient speaks in an easy, relaxed, and fluent manner.

The therapist introduces the metronome after taking the complete history and explaining the theory of its use. He helps the patient by modeling the use of the metronome as follows:

T: Now you've heard about the theory. Let's try an experiment and see what your reaction is. This is a desk-top metronome. I'll set it at its slowest, 40 per minute. Now, —can—you—talk—like—this—pac—ing—one—syl—la—ble—to—each—beat?

C: (Fluently) Do—you—mean—like—this? I—think—I—can—talk—like—this.

T: Fine—was—that—dif—fi—cult—or—ea—sy?

C: (Fluently) It—seemed—ea—sy.

T: (Turning up speed slightly) Fine—now—let's—speed—it—up—to—fif—ty.

C: (Fluently) I—think—I—can—do—this—fine—al—so.—Yes—I—can—keep—up—at—this—speed.

T: Was—that—dif—fi—cult—or—ea—sy?

C: Ea—sy.

For the next several minutes the therapist continued to speed up the metronome. The client was able to speak fluently at a rate of 80 per minute. The therapist continued to speak with the metronome, along with the client.

T: Now, did you stutter during that time?

C: I don't recall that I did.

T: How long did it take you to become fluent?

C: Just a little while.

T: Yes, in fact less than a minute. What do you conclude?

C: I feel good.

T: Perhaps we can conclude that you have a good aptitude for this method, since it seems quite helpful for you. Yet you must realize that transferring this good initial result into an acceptable final product will require substantial time and effort, and considerable dedication on your part. Would that be worth it to you?

This demonstration that the client can speak with nearly 100% fluency with the aid of the desk metronome usually makes a significant impression on him. For many severe stutterers, this experience of almost 100% fluency when first exposed to the metronome is the only experience with non-stuttering speech they have had in many years and results in substantial immediate mood elevation and a sense of hope. This is the commencement of the "honeymoon period" referred to earlier. The client must be cautioned that the development of normal-sounding speech in a variety of situations without the help of a metronome will require considerable dedication and patience.

Following this demonstration, the patient is given an overview of the total treatment program: the manner in which the fluency he is now demonstrating will gradually be modified to successively approximate speech of normal rate and cadence as well as the way in which this fluency will be extended to situations in the natural environment. He is instructed to practice speaking with a desk metronome at home in the same manner before the next visit. Some of this may be done while the patient is alone, even though most patients are almost totally fluent in this situation. This low-stress situation allows the patient to practice the technique of pacing his speech under ideal conditions. Assuming that he can remain fluent while doing so, he is instructed also to practice pacing his speech with the metronome in the presence of one other person with whom his stuttering is usually minimal: his spouse, a parent, roommate, girl friend, and so forth. Patients are usually expected to practice at least ¾ of an hour daily.

Therapeutic Feedback. It is wise to reserve 10 minutes at the end of each therapy session to get information from the client about his reactions to the session. Positive as well as negative reactions should be elicited. The therapist can ask "Was there anything I said that might have been helpful to you, and is there anything I said that turned you off or irritated you, or left you feeling discouraged?" The rationale for this is to help establish rapport, since the sense of teamwork is crucial. If the patient does not see the therapist as an ally, it is unlikely he will be motivated to work hard on his treatment. Many stutterers not only have difficulty in speaking, but also in *assertiveness.* These feedback periods train the patient in the expression of feelings about the therapeutic process. If the patient's only response is that the session was "Okay" or "Fine," the therapist can ask "Can you honestly and realistically say there was anything at all that impressed you favorably today?" or "Was there anything about me or what I said that might have irritated you even to a slight, insignificant extent?"

In addition, it is helpful to encourage the client to ask questions about the material presented. For example, one client expressed the belief that he would be unlikely to do as well as others who have been treated with this method. The client explained that "I have been to six previous therapists, and none of them did me any good. So I think my speech problem must be unusually bad." In such a case, it is explained that a lack of success with numerous previous therapists is typical of patients referred for treatment and that this does not place the client in a "bad-prognosis" group. In most instances, the previous therapeutic failures have not been due to the refractory nature of the patient's speech difficulty, but rather to the lack of availability of adequate treatment methods.

The Shaping of Speech (Sessions 2 to 7)

Usually the shaping of speech of more usual rate and cadence begins with the second session. The rate is increased by gradually and systematically increasing the rate at which the metronome is beating and by beginning to pace longer units of speech to each of the metronome's beats. A patient who previously paced one syllable to each beat might begin to pace two-syllable words to one beat on some occasions; a patient who was previously pacing whole words to one beat might begin to pace small groups or sequences of words to one beat, and so forth. This gradual increase in the rate of speaking is also done during the home practice. More normal cadence and juncturing of speech can be accomplished by allowing some beats to be voluntary pauses, varying the number of syllables to each beat, and so forth. In addition, the patient begins to extend the situational dimension in his practice by varying the person who is present during his home practice and by having more than one person present at a time. This phase of treatment is completed when the patient is able to speak with the metronome at a rate within the normal range (100 to 160 words/minute) with no pronounced blocks in speech and a nonfluency rate that is no more than 20% of the nonfluency rate he exhibited before treatment without a metronome. During this phase of treatment many patients report that their speech in daily situations without the metronome is more fluent. However, failure of this to happen is not a cause for concern since this is still an early phase of the retraining program.

Lack of Motivation. One of the most common psychological difficulties during this early phase of therapy is the unwillingness of the client to follow through on his daily practice between therapy sessions. It is helpful for the client to fill out a mimeographed daily schedule on which he can record the actual minutes spent in practice, with whom he practiced, and what difficulties arose in that day. When there is evidence that such "homework" has not been completed, the therapist can explore the cognitions and attitudes of the client. A typical response would be "What's the use? It won't work." This is not unusual of the *hopelessness* often felt by such patients and typifies the expectations for failure that are often based on unsuccessful treatment in the past. Even more important, such attitudes often have generalization to other areas of the client's life, including problems with family, peers, and school or work achievement. It is, therefore, important to expose the *illogic* in the patient's belief.

Essentially, the client has usually trapped himself in a self-fulfilling prophecy that takes the form, "This practice is upsetting and will be a waste of time. Therefore, I won't bother with it this week." Then, a week later at the therapy session, he says to himself "See, I haven't improved this week, so I was right." He then is upset because he has "proven" that this therapy, like others in the past, will not be beneficial. Such patients are playing a "no-win game" that may also extend into many areas of their lives.

The therapist's strategy is to convert this into a "can't lose" situation in the following way. He can propose "Why don't we test out your prediction that the practice will not be beneficial? As an experiment, you could do the homework every day, and then we can study your dysfluency rate at the end of the week. If it turns out you improve, then you may want to continue with the practice until you have achieved your goal. If, as you suspect, you do not improve or actually become worse, this will be very valuable information for us. We can then revise the treatment strategy so as to come up with an approach that will be more beneficial for your particular problem." Such an approach avoids a direct confrontation or power struggle with the client and acknowledges the possibility that he *may be right* about the lack of value of the suggested homework. However, the issue is to be decided with a neutral test that is under the control of the client, and the therapist is willing to base his next approach on whatever the outcome of the trial might be.

The homework issue with younger clients who have been referred at the insistence of their parents is often of a different nature. Such individuals often do not dispute the potential value of the therapy or the importance of practice, but may not have acquired the patience and self-discipline necessary for daily homework sessions, and so the resistance takes another form.

For example, Dean was an 11-year-old son of an accountant who insisted that he just didn't have the time to practice. Sensing that an argument might alienate the client, the therapist responded "You may very well be right. Let's see how you spend your day." He then instructed Dean to fill out a daily activity schedule for the previous day, showing what he actually did on an hour-by-hour basis from the point of arising to the time he went to bed at night. Although the schedule wasn't really filled up, Dean insisted that he didn't have any real "free time." Rather than confronting him, the therapist "bought into" this belief and used a paradoxical technique in the following way:

T: I can see you have very little free time, as you said, but I also see that after dinner, from 6 PM to 7 PM, you like to play basketball with your neighbor. You might actually be better off not taking any of this time for speech practice. What are some of the advantages of playing basketball each night?

D: Well, it's *fun* to play basketball, and I'd like to be on the team next year.

T: I agree entirely. Those things are important. Now, what are the advantages of spending some time each day for speech practice?

D: Well, I might get better and stop stuttering so much.

T: What would that mean to you? Would you want that?

D: Of course I would.

T: Why? What's so great about becoming fluent?

D: Well, it's no fun being a stutterer.

T: So you're saying it would be important for you to practice and to become more fluent?

D: That's why I'm coming here.

T: So essentially you have to weigh the advantages of speech practice versus basketball practice. What seems more desirable: the fun of playing basketball every night or the fun of being fluent?

Dean acknowledged that if he absolutely had to choose he would pick fluency, but he insisted he didn't want to give up basketball. The therapist replied: "I wouldn't expect you to give up the whole hour of basketball, but maybe you could give up just a part. What amount of time do you think you *could* devote to speech practice as a way of getting started?" They were then able to develop an initial contract in which Dean agreed to practice for 15 minutes a day. Later in treatment, when Dean began to experience some improvement, he expressed more enthusiasm and interest, and it was possible to build up the total daily practice time in a gradual fashion until he achieved the full 45 minutes per day.

Contingency Management. Another problem with younger clients is that when a parent is the designated coach, the issue of daily practice sometimes becomes the battleground for numerous familial squabbles. In such situations, a contingency-management program can often provide the necessary motivation for successful treatment.

Jeff was a 14-year old black youth whose parents were divorced when he was five. He was brought to the clinic by his mother after she received a note from school that "his speech problems, deficiency of confidence, difficulty relating to peers, and lack of academic success may mean he will not be able to move on to the ninth grade. . . . He needs social and academic success. . . . His problem is not learning *material* but gaining confidence. . . . We recommend speech therapy that focuses on psychological factors as well."

At the initial evaluation, Jeff described five previous therapeutic failures, including speech clinics, family therapy, and individual therapy. He explained "These were horrible experiences. One counselor told me I was rude. He's stupid and I ignored him. . . . I don't want help from you or anybody else. Therapists ask too many stupid questions and I don't like to spend all my time traveling back and forth to the clinic."

His speech problem was severe, characterized by numerous prolonged blocks, grotesque facial grimacing, and arm flapping. After a 5-minute exposure to the desk metronome, he became almost completely fluent. He had such a high aptitude for the method that after a few minutes of metronome practice he was able to continue to speak in a rhythmic but natural way without the metronome for an additional 15 minutes, during which time he spoke with no dysfluencies on the telephone as well as to his mother. This high degree of immediate improvement during the evaluation session indicated that he could do unusually well in the speech-retraining program.

In spite of the dramatic initial response, there were great difficulties in getting Jeff and his mother to practice together on a daily basis. Although he was nearly completely fluent during therapy sessions, his speech at home and at school was unchanged and was disturbing to those around him. He expressed some positive feelings toward the clinician, but acknowledged anger and resentment toward his family, teachers, and peers and refused to use the method when he was not with the therapist. He said "Mom bugs me and pressures me. I hate it. . . . When I feel nagged I feel angry and I don't care what problems I have, and I don't care about this stupid speech thing. . . . I feel lousy and I talk lousy."

The mother explained "He's hyper and causes family tensions. He gets angry and walks out of every practice session." She attributed this to artificial beverages and margarine and insisted he couldn't use these at home.

During the first several months of therapy, there was little improvement except during therapy sessions, when he spoke consistently with 80 to 95% improvement in the absence of secondary phenomena such as grimacing. The one area of success in his life was a Saturday baseball league, where he was becoming the star of the team and appeared to be leading his team to a possible state championship. In order to overcome the resistance to treatment, a contingency management program was utilized. The mother was instructed that in order for Jeff to attend the Saturday baseball game, he would have to practice 30 minutes per day for 5 of the 7 days of the preceeding week. If he failed to practice, he would have to stay home. Aside from enforcing this contingency, the mother was instructed to be patient and not to pressure Jeff in any way. The therapist was not sure whether the method would be helpful or would backfire as a result of causing increased resentment, but he felt a dramatic change in strategy was necessary to break the ice.

The next therapy session Jeff and his mother reported a marked improvement in speech. Jeff explained "In all honesty, Mom threatened me, and this helped. I didn't want to have to give up the baseball. Then when I got to go this Saturday, after I practiced all week, it was like getting a chocolate bar for dessert when you eat your supper. . . . I really wasn't trying before. This week I learned that trying really helped. Then I knew I could do it, so I did."

One month later he had continued to improve, with generalization of the fluency at home and at school. He said to the therapist "When you didn't give up on me I began to think that maybe you weren't just after my mother's money. I realized you have plenty of other patients, but maybe you really wanted to stick with me. You don't really need me, but maybe you want to help me."

One month later there were favorable reports from school. His class standing was above average, and his peer relations had markedly improved. Jeff stated:

> Some kids seem to *like* me because they like kids they can talk to. . . Last year they wouldn't let me play basketball, but this year when they ask me to join the game I say "sure."
>
> When I stutter, I used to say "I'm a freak," and this therapy all seemed to be a waste of time. Now when I stutter I just say "It's time for more practice." Last year I bragged a lot and told kids how great I was, but it didn't work—I tried to make up for my speech that way. Now that I can talk I don't brag anymore.
>
> I'm not so bad at school work, and I'm not so great, either, but maybe I don't need to be.

The contingency-management program, and the therapist's refusal to accept defeat, seemed to be interpreted by Jeff as a sign of caring and apparently helped to undercut the emotional struggles that had become an intimate part of the speech program. The pairing of the desired behavior—practice—with a desired reward—baseball—also enabled Jeff to receive other rewards, such as friendship and an average level of achievement. This was associated with simultaneous cognitive changes, and he no longer saw himself as a "loser" who was bound to be rejected by others.

The Generalization of Fluency (Sessions 8 to 15)

At this juncture, the desk metronome is replaced by a miniaturized, electronic metronome in all treatment and practice situations. Sometimes the transfer to the miniaturized metronome is associated with partial relapse, that is, a decrease in metronome-aided fluency. This may be due to the unfamiliarity of the new sound, the fact that it is less loud, presented to one ear only, or other unrecognized factors. This is handled by reducing the rate of speaking and/or constricting the situational dimensions (kind and number of persons present while using the device) sufficiently to reestablish fluency. Then, as before, these are gradually and systematically extended at a rate determined by the patient's progress.

During this phase of treatment the patient reviews the hierarchy of feared speaking situations he encounters in his daily life, arranging them in an increasing order of anticipated speaking difficulty. The patient then begins to use his metronome in the first situation, that is, the situation associated with the least anticipatory anxiety and the least probability of severe stuttering.

The following is an excerpt from the eighth therapy session with Fred, the 13-year-old discussed previously who utilized the "chip reinforcement" system. In this session, the therapist introduced Fred to the concept of the hierarchy of feared situations.

T: It seems that you have mastered the method very well here in the office. Now I would like to work with you to help you learn to do this at other times. It will first be important for us to find out which speaking situations are easiest for you and which are the most difficult.

F: Some situations are easier than others.

T: Which ones are especially easy?

F: Talking to my friends. I talk to them all day and so I don't get tense.

T: Okay. Now suppose we rate these situations on a scale from 0 to

10. Zero would be the easiest of all, and ten would be the most difficult. How would you rate speaking to friends?

F: That would be a two.

T: Okay, I'll write all these down on a scale. What would be a hard
situation.

F: Talking to a teacher.

T: How would you rate that?

F: That would be a nine.

T: How about something somewhere in between?

F: Talking to my parents around the house would be a four.

The therapist continued with Fred in this way until a variety of situations were rated from 0 to 9. Fred, however, could not think of a 10.

T: Think of what would be the worst of all. We need a ten rating. How
about standing up in front of the class to talk?

F: No, that's only a five. That's not too difficult because a lot of my
friends are there.

T: How about when people are mad at you?

F: Oh yes, that's a ten. Like when my brother gets mad if I break his
model and he threatens to tell on me.

T: Good, now we have all the information. We can begin working on
the easiest situations first, and as you are successful we can go on to
those that are more difficult. Do you think you can begin to use the
method with your friends? They only rate two in difficulty.

F: I don't know.

T: Suppose I told you to keep track, and every time you use the method with a friend you get ten bonus chips. If you use it ten times in one
day that's a hundred chips.

F: A hundred?

T: Right—you could get that discus fish for your aquarium.

F: I think I might be able to.

(After Fred gained experience and self-confidence speaking fluently in
this category of situation he was ready to begin using the metronome in
the next, etc.)

Metronome-Conditioned Relaxation. Some patients who develop a high
degree of fluency in the therapist's office and other "low-stress" situa-

tions have special difficulty in carrying their improved speech into high-anxiety situations. These patients seem to require additional treatment focused on the anxiety side of the anxiety-dysfluency cycle described earlier. A technique well suited for this is the procedure, developed largely by Wolpe (1969), called systematic desensitization. This behavior technique is applicable to a wide variety of neurotic disorders, especially those in which the stimulus antecedents of the anxiety that mediates the neurotic responses can be identified. It has been applied with some success to stuttering by Browning (1967) and others.

Recently we have been combining speech retraining and systematic desensitization with a procedure known as metronome-conditioned relaxation (MCR) (Brady, 1973). Many patients have reported to us that the metronome tends to induce relaxation even when they are not actually speaking or pacing their words with this device, and this relaxation-inducing property probably contributes to the efficacy of the metronome. For these reasons we have tried to enhance the relaxing property of the metronome by having the patient associate the beats of the metronome with a deeply relaxed state. This is accomplished mainly by the use of a tape recording in which relaxation instructions, in the form of an abbreviated Jacobson progressive-relaxation procedure, are paired with a metronome set at 60 beats per minute. In the tape, the suggestions to "re-lax" and "let-go" (the muscles) are paced with the metronome. The patient listens to the 30-minute tape once daily while deeply relaxing in a comfortable couch or reclining chair. The notion is that when the patient subsequently wears his metronome in speaking situations during the day, the metronome's beats will function as conditioned stimuli and elicit (or at least facilitate) relaxation. When he has achieved a deeply relaxed state with the tape, he is instructed to imagine speaking in the various situations described in the hierarchy of feared speaking situations as described previously, beginning with a scene that provokes minimal anxiety (and stuttering). The expectation is that the patient's emotional tranquility will counter-condition the anxiety usually associated with this speaking situation. Then, progressing systematically up the hierarchy, the anxiety associated with the other scenes is also deconditioned.

Several modifications of the procedure are employed in the present treatment program. Rather than merely fantasize speaking in an imagined situation, the patient actually speaks out loud in a manner appropriate to the imagined scene. Although this interferes somewhat with the state of relaxation, much is gained by making the situation more realistic, and carryover to actual speaking occasions outside the therapist's office is facilitated. This conditioned-relaxation procedure complements the use of the metronome to pace speech. Preliminary clinical results with this combination of speech retraining and MCR are promising. However, careful research will be necessary to separate out the contribution of the two procedures to the improvement in stutterers seen in our program.

During this phase of treatment, it is not uncommon for the patient to experience unexpected difficulty in some situations from time to time. If this occurs it is essential for the patient to regain fluency in the situation as soon as possible by the same means he has used before, that is, by reverting to a slower rate of speech and, if necessary, to more strict pacing (one syllable or one word per beat). When he becomes more fluent and regains the feeling of "control" of his speech he may gradually return to more rapid speech and less strict pacing on a trial basis. This is an important principle and sometimes requires much coaching by the therapist. Often it is helpful for the patient to rehearse this procedure in the therapist's office by simulating outside speaking situations.

In the following session, the therapist introduced this to the patient by actually modeling the method:

T: You say that sometimes when you are nervous you will begin to stutter or get stuck on a particular sound?

C: Yes. Then I get even more nervous and the situation gets worse.

T: Do you remember the first session we had and how nervous you were?

C: I remember that.

T: And when you paced your speech ve—ry—slow—ly—like—this—you—be—came—flu—ent—im—med—i—ate—ly? (The therapist spoke slowly pacing his speech to an imaginary metronome.)

C: I remember that.

T: Now you can take advantage of the fact that the very slow single syllable pacing creates fluency even under stress. Whenever you become anxious and lose control then just slow—down—like—this (spoken very slowly) for a few words and then you can speed up to your normal rate (spoken more rapidly) after you have regained control. This is called the "slow-fast method." When you get good at it, it will become hardly noticeable to the listener. Now that I've demonstrated it, why don't you give it a try?

The therapist then coached the client until the method was mastered. The client was instructed to slow down suddenly to single-syllable pacing whenever the therapist raised his hand and then to resume a normal rate and cadence whenever the hand was lowered. The client later reported that this "slow-fast" method was quite helpful because it gave him the knowledge that he could re-establish control and fluency in virtually any speaking situation, even those which are normally quite stressful. The knowledge that he had something to fall back on gave his confidence a boost.

The time required for this phase of treatment varies a great deal from patient to patient. If other therapeutic procedures are not needed, sessions may now be spaced out at less frequent intervals. The goal is being able to speak in a relaxed, fluent manner in virtually all speaking situations. When difficulties in the generalization of fluency are encountered, the therapist can utilize both behavioral as well as cognitive techniques to help the client.

Cognitive Therapy. While the relaxation techniques are sufficient to help many clients in the process of generalization of fluent speech, others develop a substantial resistance to applying their speech techniques in a variety of situations. When the therapist senses that the client is experiencing substantial emotional problems the use of cognitive restructuring techniques can help refractory clients overcome their fears and inhibitions. It is important for the therapist to explore the cognitive basis for the resistance to speaking and to expose the irrational beliefs and maladaptive attitudes that result in the client's emotional discomfort. Sometimes these issues can be handled in a matter-of-fact way. For example, the client might state that "I'll look funny wearing that hearing aid." The therapist can point out that the majority of individuals can style their hair such that the metronome is not visible.

Other individuals will insist that their metronome-conditioned speech "might sound peculiar." However, with most stutterers, even before near perfect speech is obtained, the metronome-facilitated speech is much less abnormal sounding than their old dysfluent speech pattern. Even when this is demonstrated with the tape recorder, some patients are still extremely reluctant to give up their usual way of speaking with their friends. The following is a transcript of a session with a 22-year-old, single dental student named Phillip with a mild dysfluency that rapidly diminished early in treatment. He agreed that his new speech sounded "fluent and normal" but insisted that his friends would realize he was speaking "differently."

T: Of course they will notice you are speaking "differently." You will be stuttering less, for example. Why is that so bad?
P: They might find out I was in therapy.

T: So what would happen then? What is the worst that could happen?

P: In all honesty, Doctor, I think they might reject me.

T: You really believe you will be rejected because your speech is different and you are in therapy?

P: Yes, I really believe that might happen, and I couldn't stand that.

T: Who is your best friend?

P: Mike—he's in my class.

T: Suppose Mike rejected you tomorrow because he insisted your hands had turned green, and he believed you were a Martian monster? Just think about that—he comes up to you tomorrow, insists your hands are green, and refuses to have anything more to do with you.

P: (Laughing) Well, that wouldn't be quite so bad, because *I know my hands aren't green.* I'd think he needed to see a psychiatrist, and I wouldn't feel quite so rejected. I might even give him your phone number.

T: And why would you not feel rejected?

P: Because he wasn't rejecting me for a reason I agreed with.

T: Now suppose he rejected you because you were in speech therapy and were becoming more fluent. Just imagine he came up and said "Phil, as a stutterer you're a great guy, but if you continue to become fluent I'll reject you." Would you agree with his reason?

P: No. When you put it that way it sounds almost as irrational as saying I had green hands.

T: And is it logical to feel rejected because he has this irrational belief? Does that reflect in any way on you?

P: No, I suppose not, but I do believe that at least some of my friends will reject me if they find out I'm in speech therapy.

T: What percent, do you think?

P: Maybe 5 or 10% of them.

T: How many friends and acquaintances do you talk to every week?

P: At least 40 or 50—probably more with school.

T: That means that if you use your fluent speech this week, at least two to four people will reject you. Why don't you try it as an experiment, and find out? What evidence would you accept that people do not think you sound funny?

P: If they have no negative responses to me.

T: Record in your notebook all the conversations next week when you don't have any evidence of being rejected, as well as the number of times you are rejected. What do you think will happen?

P: It seems unlikely anyone will reject me for speaking fluently since they don't reject me when I stutter. The whole thing seems absurd.

T: It may and may not be. But if you get some data, then we can evaluate things objectively. If you actually do get rejected, which you say is unlikely, we can see if we can find a way to cope with that. Ultimately, rejection by your friends is something you can't control. All you can control is your speech and doing what you believe is best for you, and then you'll have to let the chips fall where they may. But at least you will not have to take the rejection as your own fault—it will be their problem for having the erroneous belief that only stutterers are desirable as friends. But right now we have no evidence the problem exists, and nonexistent problems by definition cannot be solved. In the meantime, we can work on some problems that you really do have.

In the next week his cousin came to visit him for several days. She was not aware of his speech therapy. As an experiment, he used the method constantly when he was around her. His fluency was markedly improved, and he received some positive comments from her about his speech which she said had spontaneously cleared up.

Like Phillip, many stutterers at this phase of therapy are unaware of the degree of fluency they have achieved, and their self-image is quite different from the image they actually project to other individuals. For example, a 30-year-old, married architect named John was particularly upset by his inability to make telephone calls due to severe anxiety and blocking. The therapist instructed him to make numerous calls during the therapy session, pacing his speech to the desk metronome. The metronome was situated a considerable distance from the phone so that the beats would not be audible to the individuals being called. After an hour of this practice, John found that he was able to make telephone calls with few dysfluencies. He was given a homework assignment to make telephone calls to department stores every day inquiring about merchandise, to record these on a cassette recorder, and to bring the tape to his next therapy session.

The next week the patient brought a recording of several calls. The therapist noted a high degree of fluency, with natural-sounding speech and only two barely noticeable dysfluencies in 10 minutes of recorded telephone speech. However, John insisted that his speech was "abnormal and unpleasant-sounding" and that he was a "total failure."

John's reaction to this performance is typical of the "defeatism" so often encountered in patients in therapy. Rather than feeling encouraged about his remarkable improvement, he focused on the few remaining dysfluencies and took those as a sign of defeat. He completely overlooked the fluency as if the dysfluencies were all that counted. This type of all-or-nothing thinking can cause significant obstacles in treatment if it is not corrected by the therapist.

In order to demonstrate the degree of distortion in the patient's self-perception, the therapist asked if John would mind if he gave the tape to the secretary in the adjoining office and asked her to guess the patient's probable diagnosis. John was convinced that she would quickly identify him as a stutterer, but agreed to allow the secretary to hear the tape.

A short time later in the session the secretary knocked on the door and entered looking embarrassed. She stated that she thought that the doctor must be pulling a joke on her as she assumed that it was his voice on the tape and not the voice of a patient at all. When the therapist assured her that the voice was indeed that of a patient, the secretary stated that the only other diagnosis would be that the patient had a compulsion to spend money excessively and spent his time ordering merchandise from department stores. John, who had not previously met the secretary, was amazed that he had not been identified as having a speech problem. He informed her that he was the patient and that the diagnosis was "stuttering." The secretary was surprised and stated that the person on the tape did not appear to be a stutterer. This feedback enabled John to develop a more realistic concept of the type of image he projected when speaking. The therapist suggested he view himself as a "former stutterer" rather than a "stutterer." This experience gave John the courage to use his retrained speech in a variety of threatening situations. As he began to perceive that he actually was fluent when using the method, his anxiety levels diminished, resulting in increased fluency and greater confidence.

One of the most difficult problems encountered in the generalization phase of therapy is the fear of speaking in groups. This type of difficulty is, of course, not limited to individuals who stutter. Public-speaking anxiety is experienced to some extent by most individuals. Such problems can be dealt with both by behavioral as well as cognitive techniques.

The cognitive method, as previously mentioned, is based on an exploration and evaluation of the images and beliefs that produce the panic attacks when speaking in the presence of groups of people. Initially, the therapist proposes as a hypothesis that it is not the actual group that produces the anxiety, but the individual's interpretations and beliefs concerning what might occur as a result of speaking in the group.

Ben is a 20-year-old engineering student who had an initial dysfluency rate of 17% when first referred for treatment. He responded rapidly and had achieved well over 95% improvement in the office, at home, and around friends after 14 treatments. He still avoided speaking in groups and had not attempted to speak or to use his method in any gathering involving more than one or two individuals.

T: What is it that upsets you about speaking before a group?

B: I'll make a fool of myself.

T: Now that's very interesting. How would you do that?

B: I'd stutter, then I'd become embarrassed, people would snicker, and they might call me a fool.

T: Suppose they did. Are they omnipotent? If they call you a fool, would you become a fool?

B: Perhaps not, but it certainly makes me feel foolish to stutter when speaking to a group.

T: But it makes you feel foolish because you say it *is* foolish. What evidence do you have that it really is foolish?

B: I don't follow you.

T: Just because you feel a certain way, that doesn't mean the beliefs that create the feelings are true. The belief that stuttering in a group is foolish may not be accurate. For example, in order to overcome your fear of groups, it will be necessary for you to speak in groups. Initially, you will probably have difficulty, but you must remember that initially you also stuttered here in the office, but with practice and effort, you got better.

B: But I couldn't stand to try and fail.

T: How can stuttering in a group make you a failure? Do you expect to be fluent at the very beginning?

B: I don't suppose I will.

T: Then it may be unrealistic to upset yourself with expectations of perfection at the start. You probably will stutter some at first, but that will be a *victory*, not a failure, because you had the courage to try, and with further efforts you will be bound to improve.

The therapist then proposed that Ben accompany him to a lecture on stuttering therapy to a group of speech pathologists at a local university. After the therapist introduced the theory methodology of the speech retraining program, Ben was to speak for 10 to 15 minutes about his experiences as a patient and then was to field questions from the audience. The therapist emphasized that he had no expectation that Ben would speak fluently, or even as well as he could speak in the office. He was instructed to concentrate on *how* he was speaking, and not on what he was talking about or on the reactions of the people in the audience.

We refer to this as the TIC-TOC technique. Because the client cannot control the reactions of others, thoughts about being rejected or laughed at are referred to as "Task-Interfering Cognitions," or "TICS." These TICS distract the stutterer from concentration on his or speech techniques. The therapeutic intervention involves replacing such TICS with TOCS, or "Task-Oriented Cognitions." An example of such a TOC would be "If I speak slowly when I have difficulty, I will quickly regain control." Using this approach, Ben did quite well in his presentation to the speech therapists. Although not perfectly fluent, he was much improved compared with his baseline prior to treatment. What was more important, the experience gave him the courage to express himself whenever he was in a group. He even began to seek out groups of people in order to practice. As a result of this, he achieved near-perfect fluency in all situations prior to completing his speech therapy.

Ben emphasized that it was helpful for the therapist to actually go with him into potentially difficult situations so as to provide on-the-spot coaching and feedback. For other patients we have also made use of such *in vivo* practice by scheduling sessions in local restaurants so the client can practice speaking to the waitress, the cashier, and so forth. It is important for the patient to predict how well he will do prior to the actual experience. Not infrequently, the patient does much better than expected. The therapist may then compare the actual to the predicted performance so as to challenge the patient's belief that he is always bound to fail.

To summarize, psychological difficulties during the phase of generalization of fluent speech include the intense anxiety experienced by many clients when exposed to certain feared situations, and this can frequently be reduced with the combination of metronome-conditioned relaxation and systematic desensitization. When the therapist encounters a significant resistance on the part of the client to attempt to generalize his fluency, it is important to expose the irrational beliefs that underly this resistance, including such statements as "If I stutter at all I'll be a total failure. If I'm not perfectly fluent I'll make a fool of myself," and so forth. Such maladaptive attitudes, or "TICS," result from a lifelong history of frustration and humiliation, and interfere with generalization by producing anxiety and distracting the client from the use of proper techniques. The aim of therapy is to learn to recognize and confront such "TICS" and to replace them with "TOCS," or "Task Oriented Cognitions." As a result of such restructuring, there is frequently a significant reduction in anxiety levels that allows the client to begin to speak more fluently in a number of situations previously avoided. This success then leads to greater confidence and fluency.

Weaning from the Metronome (Sessions 15 to 20)

In this phase the patient discontinues the use of the metronome. This is also done gradually and systematically, starting with the speaking situations in which the patient has the least amount of difficulty. During this phase many patients find it helpful to pace their speech to the beats of an "imaginary" metronome. If in any situation during this process the patient finds himself having appreciable difficulty, he must again immediately return to stricter pacing of his speech even though the metronome is not present. Only a few sentences may be required before control is regained. If he continues to have difficulty in this and related situations, he may need to return to the use of the actual metronome again. Thus the withdrawal of the metronome proceeds in a cautious, trial-and-error manner until the patient is not using a metronome at all.

For example, Mark, a junior high school teacher, mastered all speaking situations with the use of a miniaturized metronome after 5 months of therapy. Discontinuing the use of the device in speaking with his family and friends and speaking in the classroom was easily accomplished over a matter of weeks. However, talking with the principal of the school, an aggressive man with whom he had difficulties, presented problems as did speaking in faculty meetings with a large number of other teachers present.

Accordingly, he practiced these situations in the therapist's office. He would imagine himself talking with the principal (out loud) with the metronome ticking, then with the device turned off but still behind his ear, and finally with the silent device in his pocket. When he experienced any dysfluency in these simulated situations he would "imagine" the ticking of the metronome for pacing purposes to regain fluency. After practicing this situation and that of speaking at faculty meetings in the office for several sessions, his fluency improved in the corresponding real-life situations. Any time he experienced the slightest difficulty he would use this dysfluency as a discriminative stimulus to begin imagining the ticks of the metronome and pacing his speech with them. This allowed further progress in the systematic withdrawal of the device. This all worked well, and after two additional months he was not using the metronome at all. However, as the end of the school term approached he again experienced difficulty in these two stressful situations.

This was traditionally a period of increasing tension and anxiety because of the pressure of work at this time of the school year and was in the past accompanied by an exacerbation of his stuttering. Now it was accompanied by a return of some stuttering in the absence of the metronome. Accordingly, he went back to using the metronome part of the time and again relied on pacing his speech with an imaginative metronome to get him through the period. Now, 2 years after initially experimenting with discontinuing the device, the patient is virtually fluent in all situations at all times. However, he occasionally experiences some difficulty during periods of high tension (such as occur in his work in the school cycle) and will return to the device for at least a few days to regain control of his speech.

The end point of this phase of treatment is variable. Some patients succeed in withdrawing the use of the metronome in all situations. A second category of end result is being able to speak in most situations without a metronome but continuing to use the device in situations of high anxiety and tension. For one patient this may mean continuing to use the metronome only while delivering lectures or conducting seminars. For another the only situation requiring the metronome might be talking over the telephone. Among the patients we have studied in this category, the number of situations in which they require the metronome tends to diminish over time. It may be that eventually most of these patients also will not be using the metronome at all.

In the final phase of therapy, many clients begin to achieve significant personal growth along with increased fluency. However, in spite of significant success in speech therapy, some clients still have an "inferiority hangover" and the feeling that they are second-rate human beings. For example, following a completely fluent conversation with an associate, a client had an intense feeling of failure. She explained: "Although I realize that I did not stutter once, I seem to have the feeling that the word 'Stutterer' is branded on my forehead, and I expect people to reject me no matter how I sound." For such individuals, emotional maturation can be facilitated by cognitive techniques.

Mrs. Smith is a 32-year-old married, secretary who initially had a moderately severe speech problem that responded well to treatment. However, Mrs. Smith felt particularly tense and found it difficult to generalize her fluency in conversations with a particular individual to whom she felt inferior. This individual was an older woman named Joan, who was an executive secretary in the same firm where Mrs. Smith worked. This was dealt with using a technique known as *operationalization.*

T: Tell me, how is it that you conclude that you are inferior when you are around Joan?

C: I don't know, I just *feel* inferior.

T: If you *feel* inferior, does that mean that you *are* inferior?

C: That's right.

T: But that's circular reasoning. The *feeling* of inferiority confirms that you are inferior, but since you believe you are inferior when you are around her you *feel* inferior, and so forth.

C: Well you're right. But there are certain things that really do make me inferior.

T: Make a list of these for me.

C: Well, she is more intelligent than I am; she is more articulate; she is more involved in art, theatre, and social activities; and she is wealthy.

T: Let's evaluate these one by one. One way to measure intelligence is by IQ. What is your IQ and what is hers?

C: Well mine is around 125, but I don't know what hers is.

T: Well you are certainly well above average. But what evidence do you have that she is more intelligent?

C: Well, looking at it that way I have no definite evidence.

T: It might be of interest for you to get that information from her. You could tell her sometime that you found her quite intelligent and wondered just how high her IQ was. Now suppose you found out that in fact her IQ was 165. What would you conclude?

C: That I was inferior.

T: You could certainly conclude that you were less intelligent along the lines measured by IQ tests, including digit span, and so forth, but how would this make you inferior?

C: Less intelligent people are inferior.

T: Are you saying that people with IQs less than 165 are inferior human beings? What led you to conclude this? How realistic is it? How many people in the United States do you suppose have IQs below 165?

C: Probably millions of people.

T: Right, and you can include me in the group. Now is it true that millions of us are inferior?

C: (Laughing) No, I see what you mean. I don't suppose that millions of Americans with IQs under 165 are inferior. But there are other things that make me inferior to Joan.

T: Such as?

C: Well, she's more involved in theatre, sculpturing, and the arts.

T: So that may mean you are less artistic or less interested in art. But how can that make you inferior?

C: I don't follow.

T: Nor do I. You were arguing that her activities in art made you inferior, and I don't see how that can be, unless you are arguing that people who are not particularly artistic are inferior. But then you'd have to include me in the group of inferior people again.

C: I guess I don't mean that. But Joan is so involved in politics and civic activities. That's why I feel inferior. All I've done is raise my family.

T: She may be more politically involved than you are. But how does that make you inferior? It seems to me it makes you less political. Are less political individuals inferior?

C: Well, people are *supposed* to be involved in civic affairs.

T: Who made up that rule? I'm not involved in civic affairs. Does that make me inferior?

C: I suppose not.

T: Then do we have any real, concrete evidence that you are inferior?

C: Maybe not. But then why do I *feel* inferior?

T: Because you have been saying "I am inferior" and believing it. It is this *thought* that makes you feel inferior. But when you say you are inferior you are using arbitrary, inflammatory language to upset yourself. It *may* be that you have a lower IQ than Joan—we really don't have any evidence for that—and it may be that you are less oriented toward art and politics. But these things do not make you inferior. If you want to become more artistically involved, then enroll in an art class. But you would do that because you enjoyed it, not in order to become superior.

C: I've always wanted to get more involved in art, but I never felt I had the time.

T: If you have the time, it might be quite worthwhile for you. Now if you are truly not inferior to Joan, whom you seem to admire, then the question is—would there be anything to prevent you from getting to know her better?

In the therapy sessions, the strategy known as operationalization was particularly successful with Mrs. Smith. The therapist repeatedly urged Mrs. Smith to state *specifically* what quality she lacked that made her inferior. When she stated intelligence, he then urged her to *quantify* the parameter, in this case IQ, and pointed out that Mrs. Smith did not have any actual data to support her belief that she was less intelligent. The quantification also showed that it is quite illogical to assume that people above a certain cut-off point are superior, while the rest are inferior. Essentially Mrs. Smith was upsetting herself with all-or-nothing thinking. Thus the statement "I am inferior" was reduced to absurdity. When the irrational belief was dispelled, the feeling of inadequacy rapidly diminished with an increase in self-esteem and fluency.

ADJUNCTIVE TECHNIQUES

In addition to the basic treatment methods outlined in the previous section, certain other techniques can be quite fruitful for selected patients. For example, many stutterers are shy and retiring and have difficulties not only in speaking but also in expressing themselves effectively. Such individuals will frequently benefit from assertive training with the therapist.

Assertive Techniques

For example, Robert is a 28-year-old, single, unemployed musician living with his parents. Robert had a rapid response to treatment, and after several weeks of therapy he was able to speak with near-complete fluency with natural-sounding speech in most situations. However, at times he had the tendency to speed up, lose control, and become dysfluent. This was particularly pronounced when he was around his father, who was the owner of a construction company.

R: My Dad has a way of either ignoring me when I talk or interrupting me, so when I'm around him I get the feeling that if I talk fast, I might be able to get all the words out before he interrupts. When he interrupts, I either blow up at him and we have an argument, or else I leave the room feeling angry and upset.

T: Are there any other ways you might handle the situation?

R: I can't think of any. It is very frustrating to be around him, and then my habit of speeding up carries over into conversations with other people, especially when I am excited.

T: As you see it, when your father doesn't pay attention to you, your only options are to become angry or to leave?

R: That's what usually happens.

T: Tell me more about this.

Then as Robert began to explain more about his feelings, the therapist interrupted politely to ask if he could excuse himself for a moment to make sure the secretary was taking care of an important phone call. When the therapist returned, he politely apologized and asked Robert to continue. As Robert again began to speak, the therapist picked up some papers from his desk and began to study them, occasionally nodding his head saying "Mmmmm" or "Uh-huh." Robert flushed with irritation and began to speak in a rushed manner, with increased dysfluencies. The therapist then began interrupting him midway through each sentence with statements such as "What you're saying is quite interesting, and I hope you don't mind if I catch up on some paperwork while you talk."

Finally in exasperation, Robert asserted himself: "I'm paying for this therapy. I think you're being rude." The therapist answered: "You're quite right. Could you repeat that once again, quite loudly and slowly, using your speech technique?" At this point, Robert realized that the therapist had been playing a role so as to mimic his father and that there were actually numerous options available to him when responding to his father.

The therapist encouraged Robert to practice methods that he could use to assert himself when he felt his father was not being sufficiently attentive. This included a role reversal in which Robert would play the father and the therapist would play Robert. This allowed Robert to model and develop interpersonal skills more effective than passive withdrawal or aggressive outbursts. In addition, the therapist suggested that the criteria for success at home would not be whether he actually modified his father's behavior, but (1) that he simply tried a new, less upsetting, approach when speaking to his father and (2) that he would speak more slowly, using the speech technique, at such times.

To his surprise, Robert found that when speaking slowly and deliberately, he was not interrupted very often and that when he was interrupted he could handle the situation quite effectively simply by saying slowly "I think you are interrupting me, and I'd appreciate it if you wouldn't."

There are a number of excellent references on the subject of assertive training (Smith, 1975; Lazarus and Fay, 1975) that can be helpful to patients as well as therapists who wish to learn more about this modality.

Two other types of treatment that can be quite useful are the "Air-Flow Technique" and pharmacotherapy.

Air-Flow Technique

Some stutterers have the particular difficulty of speaking with excessive muscular tension in the mouth and throat, resulting in pronounced blocks with extreme difficulty initiating speech. For such individuals, the air-flow method can be an extremely valuable ancillary speech technique. The method was recently popularized by Schwartz (1976) and is based on (1) initiating speech only toward the end of an easy expiration of air, similar to a sigh; (2) stretching of the first syllable to make the first speech sound into a smooth-flowing movement that blends imperceptibly with the exhalation of air; and (3) speaking more slowly. This method has also been

called "easy onset." It differs from metronome-conditioned speech retraining in that the focus is on getting ready to speak rather than on the
method of speaking per se. Thus the "air flow method" is a "starter"
technique that can be especially helpful in overcoming blocks.

The treatment proceeds as follows: The client is first taught to exhale
air in a prolonged, audible sigh. While exhaling the client must remember
two important principles: the client must not pause at the peak of inspiration prior to letting the air out, and he must avoid *blowing* or *forcing* the
air out. Rather, the flow of air is passive. The breathing is to be done
slowly and through the mouth. It usually takes less than 5 minutes to
teach this breathing technique. The therapist must caution the client to
avoid breathing too rapidly, because hyperventilation will result in light-
headedness and discomfort. The breathing is to be calm and gentle, much
like the breathing taught in Eastern meditation exercises.

Once the client has mastered this, he is then taught to say one word
with each exhalation and to initiate speech only when the air has been 2/3
exhaled. This is because the vocal cords and articulators are most relaxed
during this phase of breathing, making dysfluent speech quite unlikely. It
takes considerable concentration and practice to avoid speaking earlier in
the exhalation. When the client begins to speak, he must elongate or
stretch the first syllable of the word, thus allowing the breath to blend imperceptibly with the sound. For example, if the word is "fireplace" he is
to say "f f i i r r r e–place."

The client then practices saying single words with this method—limiting himself to one word per exhale—until *perfect fluency* is achieved. This
frequently can be accomplished in a few minutes of training, but individuals with severe blocking and substantial anxiety may require several
weeks of daily practice before complete fluency for every kind of sound is
consistently achieved.

The next step is to say two or three words with each exhalation. Only
the first syllable of the first word need be stretched, but the other words
are to be said *slowly.*

Once this is mastered and perfect fluency has again been achieved, the
client may advance to more natural groupings of five to ten words with
each exhalation, and may read and carry on conversations using the method.

After normal conversations can be maintained with perfect fluency, the
final step is to shape the speech to sound entirely natural by using shorter
and shorter exhalations and by using a less pronounced stretching of the
first syllable of each utterance. However, whenever control is lost and
dysfluency appears, the technique must be used in a more exaggerated
fashion until control is reestablished.

The client must now begin to use the method on an ongoing daily basis. The therapist proposes that he give up his old way of speaking entirely, so that the "easy-onset" method can become second nature. We emphasize that although a high degree of fluency can often be quickly achieved with the method, many weeks to months of diligent daily practice are required before the air-flow techniques become the normal speech pattern.

For example, the attorney discussed earlier achieved virtual complete fluency in the office and at home with the air-flow method after about ten therapy sessions. In addition, he was successful in using the method to speak in a number of situations that were previously very difficult or impossible. For example, he could now order gasoline and say "Fill her up." He could order an "ice cream cone" in an ice cream store, and he could say "Fresca, please" at the snack bar in his office building. However, he only estimated his improvement at this point at about 80 to 85% because of unexpected situations in which he would forget to use the method, as discussed in the following excerpt from a therapy session:

T: You seem to be making progress in your efforts to use the air-flow method in a variety of situations. I have some individuals who do it very well in the office but who have a lot of internal resistance to using the method elsewhere. They say "I am going to sound funny" or they claim that they forget to use the method. We have to put a lot of energy into working through these difficulties and urging them to go out and give the method a try. You and I have not really talked about that in any detail yet, and I get the impression it is not so much of a problem for you. You have successfully used the method in many situations which were difficult for you in the past. Have you experienced any difficulties in extending the use of the method into any areas of your life?

F: Well as a matter of fact it is a problem and it has not been completely solved. When I'm not here in the office, when I'm faced with speaking situations which just pop up without a chance for me to really think about them in advance, I find myself forgetting to use the method. This results in some hesitation and a loss of fluency. It's never reached the level of severity that I experienced before. It's just a matter of—well, it's also a matter of faith I think. It's a matter of faith that has to be applied in a certain situation. The most difficult is when I'm outside of the doctor's office and I'm suddenly confronted with a speaking situation. My mind might be on a lot of things besides the air-flow technique. For example, I may think about what is to be said and how I'm going to approach the situation. I won't be thinking about the air-flow technique, and if I have a lot an anxiety as well, this is especially difficult. It's a funny thing, particularly if I happen to meet people whom I haven't seen for a long time.

This morning I met a man in the bank. He was working there as a teller. Last year he was a client of ours. I didn't realize that he was working in this particular bank, and this was a new job and he just happened to be there. In the past when I had spoken to him, I had to take down a lot of information about him. I was not fluent speaking to him then, and at that time I used to feel very embarrassed and very inadequate. I would wonder what clients would think of me in not being able to speak fluently. What kind of a lawyer am I? Well, suddenly this morning in the bank all of these same feelings came leaping into my mind when I met this man which was a complete surprise. I felt a lot of anxiety about speaking to him, and I felt myself using the little mental tricks that I had tried to use before and falling right back into the old pattern. The meeting that I had with him was very brief, and when it was all over, I felt kind of ridiculous that all of this had suddenly descended upon me and that I had forgotten about the airflow technique. I suddenly felt myself in a kind of flashback, as if I were in the same situation as in the past. Out of habit I would be thinking the same thoughts and relying on the same obsessive devices that I used to rely upon as if that was all I had going for me. Those earlier methods didn't have effectiveness at any time but nevertheless I used to cling to them out of anxiety like a talisman or magic charm. When I find myself in the same situation and when I feel the same anxiety the tendency is for me to have faith in hiding behind these little methods even though they don't work. You know, it's like if you learned a religion when you were a child and it has some kind of significance or magic to you and later on when you find yourself in a period of anxiety you might automatically tend to go back to the old religion.

T:　Aside from these occasional periods of anxiety, how effective has the method been for you?

F:　Well, I would say that I think it's a technique, it's a skill, it's a method, it's mechanical, and I don't know why the hell it wasn't developed or made known a long time ago because it's so darn simple that it's hard to believe that it really exists. However, in so far that it works, it only works as a mechanical kind of thing, and the mechanism of it has to be attended to and has to be respected. It does not work if it's used as a magical device because when I tend to think of it as a magical device I find that I'm not really paying attention to the mechanics of it. What it seems to be is a way of relaxing the vocal chords.

T:　If it is *mechanical* and not magical, then do you suppose you could go back to the bank on another occasion and speak to the teller again? This time you could plan ahead of time to use the air-flow method and see how it works out. We could do some role playing here. I'll be the teller, and you can be yourself making a deposit.

Such practice with repeated exposure to difficult situations is quite helpful in building confidence in the speech method. The most successful patients have emphasized the importance of persistence and determination during this phase of therapy. It is important that the client continue formal home practice sessions for at least 30 minutes per day during this phase of treatment.

As with the metronome technique, it is quite helpful for the client to have a home "coach"—a friend, parent, or spouse—who provides feedback during daily practice sessions. The coach does *not* provide feedback about dysfluencies, but focuses entirely on the *correct use of the method.* This is because the client is almost always fluent when using the method properly, and feedback about speech technique is less threatening and more meaningful than feedback about dysfluencies. We provide the home coach with forms (Table 1) for recording feedback for the client. Essentially a rating from zero to ten is provided concerning breathing technique, stretching of the first syllable, rate of speech, and word groupings. A zero means the client did not use the principle at all, and a ten means perfect application. The coach should attend several therapy sessions so as to understand the theory and technique as thoroughly as the client.

Pharmacotherapy of Stuttering

There are a number of reports in the literature that certain psychopharmacologic agents appear to have a beneficial effect in the treatment of

Table 1: Coaching Form [a]

Date	Length of Practice (Minutes)	Breathing Technique (1–10)	Stretching of First Syllable (0–10)	Rate of Speaking (0–10)	Grouping of Words (0–10)

[a] Explanation for Ratings: A zero is the lowest score and a ten is a perfect score. For a ten in breathing technique the client must not pause at the peak of inspiration. He must let the air flow out passively without blowing, and he must initiate speech only when the air is 2/3 exhaled. For a ten in stretching, the first syllable of the first word spoken after exhaling must be noticeably elongated. For a ten in the rate of speaking, he must speak slowly and deliberately. For a ten in grouping, only the agreed upon number of words may be spoken with each exhalation; initially there will be one word per breath, then two to three per breath, then five to eight, and eventually groupings of ten or more words.

stuttering. In a double-blind trial, Goldman (1966) reported that ten patients receiving thioridazine plus speech therapy improved significantly while a control group receiving placebo plus speech therapy failed to improve. In double-blind clinical evaluations of haloperidol versus placebo, several investigators (Wells and Malcolm, 1971; Swift et al., 1975; Rosenberger et al., 1976) confirmed that drug administration was associated with significant improvement, although Tapia (1969) reported only modest gains in an uncontrolled study with a group of young stutterers treated with haloperidol.

Because these reports are consistent with our clinical experience that low doses of haloperidol seem to have a beneficial antistuttering effect, we decided to investigate this further under double-blind conditions in our speech laboratory in conjunction with Dr. L. Kuruvilla, who was on sabbatical from the Christian Medical College in Vellore, South India. We selected twelve moderate-to-severe stutterers not currently in treatment to participate in the study.

On the first study day no drug was given, and 6 minutes of the client's speech was recorded (3 minutes of reading plus 3 minutes of spontaneous speech). On the subsequent days the clients received injections of either 0.5 mg haloperidol or saline in randomized order, and recorded speech was again obtained 45 minutes after the injections. Neither the client nor the individual recording the speech were aware of what agent was given on which day. In addition, a side-effects check list was completed by the client so as to record sedation, dry mouth, dizziness, and so forth.

The tape-recorded speech was analyzed, and the dysfluency rate was calculated by raters who were unaware of the order of drug administration (vide supra).

The data indicated that 10 of 12 clients were more fluent after haloperidol as compared with placebo or baseline conditions, and these findings were significant at the $p < 0.05$ level (Wilcoxon matched-pair signed-ranks test). The percent improvement varied in the haloperidol response between 17 to 54%. Side effects after this low dose of haloperidol were negligible.

In our clinical practice we administer 0.5 mg of haloperidol orally either once or twice daily for limited periods of time, usually four to eight weeks. This is given in conjunction with speech retraining and cognitive psychotherapy. We reserve the use of haloperidol for individuals who are having difficulty in their therapy, either in the development or generalization of fluency. While side effects on this low dose regimen are almost always absent, we could not rule out the possibility of the development of tardive dyskinesia if the drug were given chronically for many years

(Crane, 1968). This is why we administer the drug solely on a short-term basis, usually during a 2- to 3-month period. We emphasize increased intensity of practice during the withdrawal period to minimize the possibility of a relapse at this time. We do not give anticholinergic anti-Parkinsonian agents simultaneously because extrapyramidal side effects have not been observed in our patients at the dose levels we recommend.

We do not know the basis for haloperidol's antistuttering effects. While we cannot rule out the possibility that anxiety reduction causes the decrease in stuttering, Leanderson and Levi (1967) reported that diazepam—which has a pronounced antianxiety effect—did not have a marked effect on stuttering compared with placebo. In addition, the haloperidol did not produce pronounced sedation nor a slowing of speech, ruling out these mechanisms as responsible for the fluency.

It is of interest that both of the agents that have been reported to have antistuttering properties, including haloperidol and thioridazine, appear to have a specific effect in blocking dopamine receptors in the brain (Carlsson and Lindqvist, 1963; Nyback et al., 1968; Anden et al., 1968; Snyder, 1973). This raises the question of whether increased central dopaminergic activity may play a role in the pathogenesis of this disorder. Abnormalities of central dopaminergic systems have been implicated in several other disorders involving rhythmic locomotor control including Parkinsonism (Barbeau, 1974), tardive dyskinesia (Klawans, 1973), and Gilles de la Tourette syndrome (Shapiro et al., 1973). While the role of dopaminergic mechanisms in stuttering is at this time speculative, the possibility deserves investigation, and further studies by our group are in progress.

OVERVIEW: THE STUTTERING AND FLUENCY CYCLES

Although the phenomenon of stuttering is generally defined in terms of verbal dysfluencies, the disorder also involves in varying degrees the thoughts, emotions, and actions of the individual who is afflicted. Although no systematic personality differences have been observed in stutterers, there is widespread agreement that these individuals appear to be anxious, tense and withdrawn (Anderson, 1967; Gray and Karmen, 1967; Santostefano, 1960; Moleski and Tosi, in press). While it is not known whether high anxiety levels precede the onset of dysfluency in the child or occur as a result of the disorder, it is clear that the existence of the stuttering provides a fertile soil in which secondary difficulties are likely to develop. These difficulties include repeated frustrations and humiliation in interpersonal encounters with parents and peers, which in turn intensify the dysfluency.

We, therefore, find it useful to conceptualize the stuttering syndrome as a system with behavioral, cognitive and emotional components which continually interact in a self-perpetuating closed system (Figure 1). According to this model, the ongoing sense of failure when attempting to speak results in the development of a negative automatic belief system in which the stutterer views himself or herself as an inadequate, inferior human being. These beliefs result in ongoing anxiety in a variety of stressful situations, emotional tension that results in increased stuttering, and maladaptive behavior such as decreased assertiveness and interpersonal withdrawal. The increased dysfluency and the social isolation confirm the stutterer's negative belief system, and the vicious cycle is maintained.

The speech-retraining program is designed to intervene at the cognitive, emotional and behavioral levels using a variety of treatment methodologies (Table 2). The first phase of treatment is the development of fluency

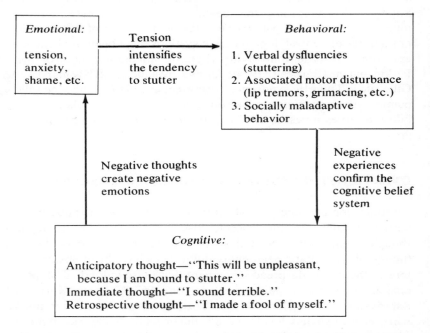

Figure 1. Stuttering cycle: The stutterer finds himself in a self-perpetuating cycle in which cognitive, emotional, and behavioral components continually interact in a closed system (see text).

Table 2: Synopsis of Treatment Methods Used in the Speech-Retraining Program

Target Symptoms	Specific Therapeutic Modalities
Stuttering (verbal dysfluency)	1. Metronome-conditioned speech retraining 2. Air-flow technique 3. Haloperidol
Lack of motivation	1. Contingency management
Embarrassment, anxiety, and tension in feared situations	1. Systematic desensitization 2. Metronome-conditioned relaxation
Negative thoughts: fear of rejection, self-blame, defeatist attitude, etc.	1. Cognitive restructuring
Passivity, social withdrawal, inability to express feelings	1. Assertive training

at the office and at home, thus disproving the stutterer's expectation that he is bound to speak in an abnormal manner. At the same time, the distortions involved in many of the client's beliefs are dealt with using cognitive-restructuring techniques. The client is shown that many of these beliefs are simply self-fulfilling prophecies, while others are based on logical errors such as "all-or-nothing" thinking. The purpose of therapy is to replace maladaptive attitudes, or "TICS" (Task Interfering Cognitions), with more appropriate ways of interpreting experiences, or "TOCS" (Task Oriented Cognitions). Behavioral techniques, such as systematic desensitization and assertive training, are also helpful in reducing the anxiety associated with feared situations and in teaching more appropriate and productive interpersonal skills.

As a result of such interventions, the stuttering cycle fades out and the fluency cycle emerges (Figure 2). The dysfluent behavior subsides and is increasingly replaced with fluency. Negative cognitions yield to a more appropriate and positive belief system. Emotionally, self-confidence and relaxation begin to develop in areas previously dominated by excessive anxiety. In the new fluency cycle, a more realistic self-image and expectations along with new social skills contribute to the mutually reinforcing growth system. The end point of therapy involves a reduction of dysfluen-

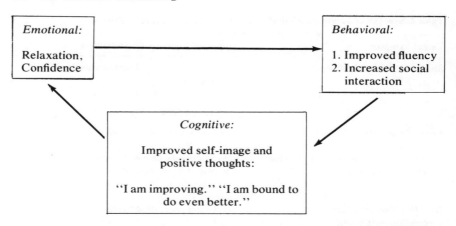

Figure 2.   Fluency cycle: The aim of treatment is to create a cycle in which increased fluency, positive attitudes, and increased relaxation interact in a mutually reinforcing system.

cy to the point that it no longer interferes to a significant extent with the client's life goals or sense of emotional well-being.

ACKNOWLEDGMENT

The research on which this article was based was supported in part by USPHS Grant No. 1 RO3 MH 27690-01. Dr. Burns was a Fellow of the Foundations' Fund for Research in Psychiatry at the time this manuscript was prepared.

REFERENCES

Anden, N. E., Butcher, S. G. Corrodi, P . et al. Receptor activity and turnover of dopamine and noradrenaline after neuroleptics. *European Journal of Pharmacology*, 1970, *11*, 303–314.

Anderson, E. G. *A comparison of emotional stability in stutterers and nonstutterers*. Unpublished doctoral dissertation, Wayne State University, 1967.

Barbeau, A. Drugs affecting movement disorders. *Annual Review of Pharmacology*, 1974, *14*, 91–113.

Barber, V. B. Studies in the psychology of stuttering-XVI: rhythm as a distraction in stuttering. *Journal of Speech Disorders*, 1940, *5*, 29–42.

Beck, A. T. *Depression: Causes and Treatment*. Philadelphia: University of Pennsylvania, 1967.

Brady, J. P. A behavioral approach to the treatment of stuttering. *American Journal of Psychiatry*, 1968, 125, 843–848.

Brady, J. P. Studies on the metronome effect on stuttering. *Behavior Research and Therapy*, 1969, 7, 197–204.

Brady, J. P. Metronome-conditioned relaxation: a new behavioral procedure. *British Journal of Psychiatry*, 1973, *122*, 729–730.

Browning, R. M. Behaviour therapy for stuttering in a schizophrenic child. *Behavior Research and Therapy*, 1967, *5*, 27–35.

Carlsson, A., and Lindqvist, M. Effect of chlorpromazine or haloperidol on formation of 3-methoxytyramine and normetanephrine in mouse brain. *Acta Pharmacology and Toxicology*, 1963, *20*, 140–144.

Colombat De L'Isère, M. *Du begaiement et de tous les autres vices de la parole traites par de nouvelles méthodes* (2nd ed.). Paris: Mansuet, 1831.

Crane, G. E. Tardive dyskinesias in patients treated with major neuroleptics: a review of the literature. *American Journal of Psychiatry*, 1968, *124* (Suppl.), 40–48.

Goldman, R. The use of Mellaril as an adjunct to the treatment of stuttering. *Proceedings of the IV World Congress of Psychiatry*, Excerpta Medical International Congress Series No. 150, 1966.

Gray, B., and Karmen, J. The relationship between nonverbal anxiety and stuttering adaptation. *Journal of Communication Disorders*, 1967, *1*, 141–151.

Johnson, W., Darley, F. L., and Spriesterbach, D. C. *Diagnostic methods in speech pathology*, New York: Harper & Row, 1963.

Klawans, H. L. The pharmacology of tardive dyskinesias. *American Journal of Psychiatry*, 1973, *130*, 82–86.

Lazarus, A., and Fay, A. *I can if I want to*. New York: Morrow, 1975.

Leanderson, R., and Levi, L. A new approach to the experimental study of stuttering and stress. *Acta Otolaryngology*, 1967, *224* (Suppl.), 311–316.

Moleski, R., and Tosi, D. J. Comparative psychotherapy: rational-emotive therapy vs. systematic desensitization in the treatment of stuttering. *Journal of Consulting and Clinical Psychology* (in press).

Nyback, H., Borzecki, Z., and Sedvall, G. Accumulation and disappearance of catecholamines formed from tyrosine-C in mouse brain: effect of some psychotropic drugs. *European Journal of Pharmacology*, 1968, *4*, 395–403.

Rosenberger, P. B., Wheelden, J. A., and Kalotkin, M. The effect of Haloperidol on stuttering. *American Journal of Psychiatry*, 1976, *133*, 331–334.

Santostefano, S. Anxiety and hostility in stuttering. *Journal of Speech and Hearing Research*, 1960, *3*, 337–347.

Schwarz, M. *Stuttering Solved*. Philadelphia: Lippincott, in press.

Shapiro, A. K., Shapiro, E., and Wayne, H. Treatment of Tourette's Syndrome with haloperidol, review of 34 cases. *Archives of General Psychiatry*, 1973, *28*, 92–97.

Smith, M. J. *When I say no, I feel guilty*. New York: Dial, 1975.

Snyder, S. H. Amphetamine psychosis: A "model" schizophrenia mediated by catecholamines. *American Journal of Psychiatry*, 1973, *130*, 61–67.

Swift, W. J., Swift, E. W., and Arellano, M. Haloperidol as a treatment for adult stuttering. *Comprehensive Psychiatry*, 1975, *16*, 61–67.

Tapia, F. Haldol in the treatment of children with tics and stutterers—and an incidental finding. *The Psychiatric Quarterly*, October, 1969.

Webster, R. L. A behavioral analysis of stuttering: treatment and theory. In K. S. Calhoun, H. E. Adams, and K. M. Mitchell (Eds.) *Innovative treatment methods in psychopathology*. New York: Wiley, 1974.

Wells, P. G. and Malcolm, M. T. Controlled trial of the treatment of 36 stutterers. *British Journal of Psychiatry*, 1971, *119*, 603–604.

Wolpe, J. *The practice of behavior therapy*. New York: Pergamon, 1969.

Author Index

723

Subject Index

continued from inside front cover